*Economics and Financial
Management for Nurses and
Nurse Leaders*

Susan J. Penner, MN, MPA, DrPH, RN, CNL, is part-time faculty at the School of Nursing and Health Professions, University of San Francisco (USF), where she teaches courses on health care economics and financial management, instructional design, informatics and epidemiology/evidence-based practice courses for the clinical nurse leader (CNL), and Health Systems Leadership programs. She has experience teaching in traditional BSN and MSN programs at California State University East Bay, Holy Names College in Oakland, and Samuel Merritt College in Oakland. She has experience teaching online BSN and MSN programs at the University of San Francisco and California State University at Fullerton. Dr. Penner earned her DrPH from the University of California, Berkeley, and her MN and MPA from Wichita State University. She has 16 peer-reviewed publications. In addition to publishing the first edition of *Introduction to Health Care Economics and Financial Management* (2004), Dr. Penner has contributed chapters to five textbooks, including *Financial and Business Management for the Doctor of Nursing Practice*, Springer Publishing Company, 2012.

Economics and Financial Management for Nurses and Nurse Leaders

Second Edition

Susan J. Penner, MN, MPA, DrPH, RN, CNL

SPRINGER PUBLISHING COMPANY
NEW YORK

Springer Publishing Company, LLC
11 West 42nd Street
New York, NY 10036
www.springerpub.com

Acquisitions Editor: Margaret Zuccarini
Production Editor: Joseph Stubenrauch
Composition: Newgen Imaging

ISBN: 978–0–8261–1049–7
e-book ISBN: 978–0–8261–1050–3

Instructor Supplementary Materials ISBN: 978-0-8261-6916-7
Student Supplementary Materials ISBN: 978-0-8261-6917-4

Student Materials are available from Springerpub.com/penner-student-supplements

Instructors Materials: Qualified instructors may request supplements by emailing textbook@springerpub.com

15 / 5 4

The author and the publisher of this Work have made every effort to use sources believed to be reliable to provide information that is accurate and compatible with the standards generally accepted at the time of publication. The author and publisher shall not be liable for any special, consequential, or exemplary damages resulting, in whole or in part, from the readers' use of, or reliance on, the information contained in this book. The publisher has no responsibility for the persistence or accuracy of URLs for external or third-party Internet websites referred to in this publication and does not guarantee that any content on such websites is, or will remain, accurate or appropriate.

Library of Congress Cataloging-in-Publication Data

Penner, Susan J., author.
 [Introduction to health care economics & financial management]
 Economics and financial management for nurses and nurse leaders / Susan J. Penner. — Second edition.
     p. ; cm.
 Revised edition of: Introduction to health care economics & financial management / Susan J. Penner. c2004.
 Includes bibliographical references and index.
 ISBN 978-0-8261-1049-7 — ISBN 978-0-8261-1050-3 (e-book)
 I. Title.
 [DNLM: 1. Economics, Nursing. 2. Delivery of Health Care—economics. 3. Financial Management—methods. 4. Nurse Administrators. WY 77]

 338.4'33621--dc23   2013000629

Printed in the United States of America by Bradford & Bigelow.

Contents

Reviewers

Kathryn Fenton Brown, RN, MSN, MBA, CPHQ
Director of Quality
Kaiser Foundation Hospital Redwood City
Redwood City, California

Theresa Dentoni, MSN, RN, CNL
Director Perioperative/Critical Care/Specialty Clinic/Emergency Department Nursing
San Francisco General Hospital and Trauma Center
San Francisco, California

Patricia L. Hubrig, RN, BS, CCM, LHRM
Regional Vice President
South Florida Healthcare Partners
Coral Springs, Florida

Courtney Keeler, MS, PhD
Assistant Professor
University of San Francisco
School of Nursing and Health Professions
San Francisco, California

Bridget Monohan, RN, MSN-CNL, PHN
Sigma Theta Tau International Honor Society
Washington Hospital
Fremont, California

Kate Nakfoor, EdD, MSIS, MBA, RN
Principal, Nak4Health Consulting
Adjunct Faculty, School of Nursing and Health Professions
University of San Francisco
San Francisco, California

Preface

*Money is the opposite of the weather. Nobody talks about it, but
everybody does something about it*—Rebecca Johnson

Nurses experience the effects of economics, finance, and budgeting with challenges such as budget cutbacks, cost control efforts, and complicated insurance guidelines. Nurses also make an impact on health care costs and revenues whenever they provide patient care or other health services. In any type of health care setting, inpatient or outpatient, private practice or nationwide health care system, monetary concerns influence day-to-day performance and the organization's long-term survival.

Factors such as new technologies and an aging population lead to rising health care costs and changes in health care financing. The passage of the Patient Protection and Affordable Care Act (PPACA) introduces new policies and approaches to extend health care to all Americans while managing health care costs. It is more important than ever for nurses to obtain an understanding of the fundamentals of health care economics, finance, and budgeting in order to make a business case for improving patient care.

Unfortunately, many nurses lack formal preparation in the basics of economics and financial management. For example, in a study of 86 American staff nurses, Caroselli (1996) found that only 26 of these nurses had obtained any general knowledge of budgeting or finance. Of the 26 nurses, only 4 reported they obtained this knowledge from a nursing instructor, and the largest number, 11, reported they were self-taught. Further, the economic awareness of these of 86 staff nurses was not shown to increase based on factors such as age, work experience, education, or even management experience.

Economics and Financial Management for Nurses and Nurse Leaders is designed to meet the learning needs of a broad range of nurses, from staff to nurse managers, from entry-level undergraduate students to master's-level clinical practitioners. These nurses will learn the fundamentals of economics, financing, and budgeting that affect their work setting and their delivery of health care. These nurses also will develop practical, hands-on skills in budgeting, financial analysis, and making a business case for improving patient care as they apply concepts from this textbook.

OVERVIEW

Economics and Financial Management for Nurses and Nurse Leaders is organized into four major sections. Part I includes Chapter 1: Economics of Health Care, Chapter 2: Health Insurance and Fee-for-Service Financing, and Chapter 3: Managed Care and Performance Measurement. These chapters provide an overview of the health care economics, context of health care, and financing in the United States. A discussion of the provisions of the PPACA updates information about health care insurance and financing mechanisms.

Part II includes Chapter 4: Measuring Nursing Care, Chapter 5: Reporting and Managing Budgets, Chapter 6: Budget Planning, and Chapter 7: Special Purpose, Capital, and Other Budgets. These chapters present indicators that are frequently reported in health care budgets, with strategies for controlling budget costs and techniques for budget preparation. The budgets that nurses most frequently review when working in acute care and outpatient settings are presented, particularly the operating budget.

Part III includes Chapter 8: Cost-Finding, Break-Even, and Charges; Chapter 9: CBA, CEA, CUA, and CER; Chapter 10: Writing a Business Plan; and Chapter 11: Health Program Grant Writing. These chapters help nurses demonstrate the financial benefits of nursing interventions and develop a business case or grant proposal for improving patient care.

Part IV includes Chapter 12: Financial Statements and the Nurse Entrepreneur, Chapter 13: Ethical Issues and International Health Care Systems, and Chapter 14: Health Policy and Future Trends. These chapters enable nurses to assess the organization's overall financial health, and to gain a broader understanding of other health care systems and anticipated changes in health care financing in the United States and around the world.

Economics and Financial Management for Nurses and Nurse Leaders is organized so that in Part I the student first gains an overall understanding of the dynamics of health care economics and financing. In Part II, the student is prepared to plan and control costs and to recognize the importance of revenues and profitability. Skills in developing and analyzing budgets provide a foundation for leadership, and for developing further proficiencies in financial management. Part III extends skills development by helping students create a financial analysis that supports a business case or grant proposal that will improve patient care. Part IV introduces more advanced topics, including understanding financial statements, entrepreneurship, international systems, and policy analysis that reinforce life-long and self-directed learning about economics, finance, and budgeting.

TEXTBOOK FEATURES

Important objectives and competencies from the AONE Nurse Executive Competencies; American Association of Critical-Care Nurses (AACN), Financial Management in Healthcare Organizations module; and the American Association of Colleges of Nursing, Clinical Nurse Leader (CNL) certification examination are addressed throughout the textbook. In addition, end-of-chapter exercises and ancillary instructor materials incorporate concepts drawn from Quality and Safety Education for Nurses (QSEN) competencies. **Instructor ancillary materials include: Excel data files, PowerPoint presentations, test questions, answer keys, glossary, sample syllabus, and teaching ideas and are available by contacting textbook@springerpub.com.**

The book uses practical case examples drawn from inpatient and outpatient health care settings to illustrate the application of content. This technique assists students in developing hands-on approaches in working with financial data and financial management concerns. Nurses will learn concepts and develop fundamental skills in using tools to help them understand the economic and financial forces driving today's health care system. Nurses will learn how to prepare budgets, business plans, and health program grant proposals with practical applications in their work settings.

A nursing course in economics and finance should facilitate the synthesis of information from across the curriculum and from experience working in the health professions. Students are encouraged to draw upon competencies gained from their education and experience, including:

- Evidence-based practice and research principles that help in developing valid and reliable support for making a business case

▨ Biostatistics and epidemiology concepts that enable the application and analysis of relevant data
▨ Nursing management, leadership, and health policy theories that provide a psychosocial and political context for understanding economic and financial strategies and for evaluating and implementing business plans and grant proposals
▨ Writing and critical-thinking skills to communicate and critically appraise approaches and ideas for evaluating budgets and other financial reports including business plans and grant proposals

Each chapter begins with a set of learning objectives and a list of key terms introduced and defined within the chapter and also included in the glossary at the end of the book. Tables, figures, and text boxes help illustrate concepts covered in the chapter. Electronic ancillary resources are provided to allow further exploration of topics. Exercises at the end of each chapter help students discuss, apply, and review knowledge. **Student ancillary materials include crossword puzzles/answer keys, Excel data files, PowerPoint presentations, and glossary that provide information and data from each chapter and are available from Springerpub.com/penner-student-supplements.** The Excel files also organize chapter terms and definitions so they can be converted to text files and uploaded to software such as the BlackBoard™ online course Glossary; Quizlet© online flash cards; or ArmoredPenguin.com word games. Selected terms and definitions are included in each chapter as crossword puzzles generated by ArmoredPenguin.com. The instructor ancillary materials provide access to test questions and PowerPoint slides as further aids in teaching and learning.

SUGGESTIONS FOR FACULTY

This textbook is designed for use either in a traditional in-class format or with online and distance-teaching and -learning technologies. The 14 chapters can be covered within traditional and accelerated curriculum schedules. As noted previously, a sample syllabus and suggested assignments are provided for faculty to help in developing this nursing course. The end-of-chapter exercises can be adapted for online discussions or in-class group work. The electronic ancillary resources and supplemental materials such as sample reports and Excel files give students additional information and data for problem solving, hands-on applications, and independent learning.

Content in Chapters 10 and 11 can provide the basis for student use in developing a business plan or a grant proposal as a course project and paper assignment. Such a course project emphasizes critical thinking and supports building skills in budgeting and financial analysis. The business plan or grant proposal may be assigned as individual or group work in traditional or distance-learning courses. The worksheets included in Chapters 10 and 11 provide guidelines and rubrics. Students will develop and refine writing skills and gain practice in providing an evidence base as they discuss the problem and intervention in their business plan or grant proposal.

SUGGESTIONS FOR STUDENTS AND PRACTITIONERS

Some readers might be concerned about the math required in learning and applying the concepts in this book. The book is designed for students who have mastered basic math skills. A nurse who is able to safely calculate medication dosages should be able to accurately develop a budget or calculate a simple financial ratio or analysis as presented in this book. If needed, there are many math review websites (www.mathforum.org) for further practice. The HelpingWithMath.com, Calculating Percentages website; the patrickjmt.com, Just Math Tutorials; and the Ask Dr. Math, Percentage of Increase website (www.mathforum.org) are all examples of online resources that students can access for basic math review. In addition, online resources are included in book chapters to enhance understanding of financial calculations and concepts.

Readers are encouraged to review examples within the chapters and to complete the end-of-chapter exercises to reinforce concepts. It is assumed that health care economics, finance, and budgeting are new to the reader. Nurses require practice to develop their clinical skills, and they require practice to develop skills in budgeting, financial analysis, and making a business case.

Nursing students represent the future of health care delivery and health care economics, finance, and budgeting. There are tremendous challenges facing health professionals and the institutions in which they work to provide access to high-quality care at a reasonable cost. The skills nurses and nursing students gain from this book and related assignments provide capabilities and insights to help meet these challenges.

REFERENCE

Caroselli, C. (1996). Economic awareness of nurses: Relationship to budgetary control. *Nursing Economics, 14*(5), 292–297.

Acknowledgments

This book would not have been possible without the support of my husband, Maurice Penner, and my editors, Margaret Zuccarini and Chris Teja. Thanks to all of the reviewers of this book for their hard work, commitment, and valuable feedback. My colleagues in the School of Nursing and Health Professions at the University of San Francisco provided opportunities and resources to expand my skills in teaching economics and finance concepts to nurses at several academic levels. I also want to thank my graduate student contributors and all my students over the years; their dedication and enthusiasm are inspiring.

Participating Graduate Students

Those who contributed the Appendices to Chapters 10 and 11, at the time of their contribution, were graduate students in the University of San Francisco School of Nursing & Health Professions, MSN Clinical Nurse Leader program.

Corinne Allen

Natalie Bower

Whitney Bralye

Yonatan (Ty) Breiter

Alexandra Carr

Seth Cloues

Samanthika De Alwis

Jasmine Erguiza

Gehrig Ertle

Emily Finzen

Caitlin Flanagan

Candace Fleming

Janet Giachello

Alex Guevarra

Angelica Holguin

Jennifer Ma

Madeira Macedo

Sara Moschetto

Christina Nardi

Cara Perlas

Alysia Porter

Lindsey Reardon

Deb Rosenberg

Heather Rothhammer

Jennifer Schmid

Asja Serdarevic

Hector Solano

Diane Trinh

Cassen Uphold

Paige Weisbrod

Chapter 1: Economics of Health Care

People want economy and they will pay any price to get it—Lee Iacocca

Learning Objectives

1. Explain at least three major characteristics of the U.S. health care competitive market.
2. Give examples of at least three economic concepts applied to health care.
3. Evaluate the impact of price on health care consumer behavior.
4. Summarize the history of health care economics and policy in the United States.

Key Terms

allocative efficiency
barriers to entry
competitive market
cost
cost shifting
demand
derived demand
economies of scale
economies of scope
efficiency
externalities
fixed costs
free-rider problem
income redistribution

inputs
market
market disequilibrium
market equilibrium
market failure
market power
monopoly
monopsony
natural monopoly
negative externalities
opportunity cost
outputs
pent-up demand
positive externalities

production efficiency
public goods
shortage
socialized medicine
substitutes
supply
surplus
technical efficiency
throughputs
trade-off
transparency
trusts
union
variable costs

"I went to nursing school, not business school. I don't need to learn about economics!" "It's wrong to think about making a profit when we have patients who need care!" "Why should I care about controlling costs? That's the nurse manager's problem!" "I'm already overwhelmed with providing patient care—leave things like supply and demand to the experts."

Many nurses and nursing students feel the same way about economics and requirements to learn economic principles. What many nurses don't realize is that they are active participants in the health care economics system, and in the even larger national and global economies. A basic introduction to fundamental concepts of health care economics is essential to understand how the U.S. health care system and health care organizations operate. This introduction links the patient care role of nurses with economic forces driven by costs, revenues, and profits.

HISTORICAL CONTEXT OF HEALTH CARE AND NURSING ECONOMICS

This chapter begins with a general overview of some important past events in health care and public policy, which will help nurses better understand the current economic issues and concerns in an historical context. Looking back is often a first step toward moving forward because many of our current health system problems and policies are shaped and influenced by past decisions. These examples show the development of health care in the context of economics and are not a comprehensive history. The timeline is largely limited to the history and culture of Western society, overlooking many developments and achievements in other world regions and cultures. Those interested in learning more about the history of health care should refer to resources provided at Health Care History 101 (Leonhardt, 2009).

Prehistoric times. Think back to what life was like and how health care was delivered in prehistoric times. The earliest health services would have occurred within the confines of one's family or tribe. Interpersonal help and support in times of injury, illness, or childbirth were the only care or health "coverage" available.

Circa 400 BCE. Modern civilization progresses with the emergence of cities in locations such as Babylon and Ancient Greece. Hippocrates and other physicians manage the care of the ill and injured, and establish fees for their services. A closer look at the emergence of medical care and health care markets in Ancient Greece is provided at the website Health, Economics, and Ancient Greek Medicine (http://historyoftheancientworld.com/2011/03/health-economics-and-ancient-greek-medicine/). Nursing care remains the work and responsibility of untrained family members and caregivers, who most likely provide care for free. At the same time, universal health care was instituted in Ancient India, and information is available in an online video, Universal Health Care in Ancient India (http://www.beaconbroadside.com/broadside/2010/03/video-bruce-rich-on-universal-health-care-in-ancient-india.html).

Circa 400 CE. During the Middle Ages, hospices are established, with religious orders providing nursing care to travelers, the poor, and the sick and dying. Although the care is compassionate and charitable, these providers are untrained, and health care is based largely on superstition. Hospices are places where patients come to die rather than to be healed. These early hospitals and nurses establish a tradition of providing free charity care rather than requiring reimbursement or wages. Wealthier individuals rely on care from physicians, whom they can afford to pay, and from family and private caregivers for nursing care in the home.

1600s. The English Poor Law of 1601 reinforces society's distinction between poor and vulnerable people who are thought to deserve or not deserve charity. The values reflected in the Poor Law influences U.S. welfare policy on into the 21st century. For example, undocumented immigrants are specifically denied health coverage benefits in the Patient Protection and Affordable Care Act of 2010 (PPACA, 2010).

1776. The American Revolution launches principles of self-governance and personal independence that become the bedrock of American culture. Events such as the Boston Tea Party and the Whiskey Rebellion further shape American cultural beliefs and attitudes about taxation rights and resistance. Americans continue to oppose taxation on into the 21st century, as evidenced by complaints about tax increases and calls for tax cuts at local, state, and national levels. This cultural context influences policies and politics of health care funding and programs.

1820 to 1910. Florence Nightingale is born of English parents in Florence, Italy in 1820 and dies in 1910. Nightingale not only transforms and professionalizes the training of nurses, but she is also influential in English health policy, an expert in health care data analysis, and one of the first nurses to write about financial management issues such as utilization and length of stay (Penner, 1987). Germ theory and concepts of personal hygiene and public sanitation begin to replace the largely superstitious beliefs that persisted in medicine up to this point (Diamond, 1997). Hospitals evolve as places where patients might expect to heal, with professional nursing education and care beginning to be recognized as essential to successful outcomes.

1854. The reformer Dorothea Dix successfully lobbies Congress to pass a bipartisan bill providing federal support to build asylums for the insane throughout the United States. President Franklin Pierce vetoes the bill, claiming that it is unconstitutional to involve the Federal government in public charity (Holt, Holt, Schlesinger, & Wilentz, 2010). This Presidential proclamation limits U.S. health care and social services policies, programs, and funding on into the 20th century.

1883. The first government-sponsored health insurance program is inaugurated in Germany with Otto von Bismarck's Health Insurance Act of 1883. German and other European health insurance programs begin by covering low-income workers and eventually cover all citizens. By the early 1900s, many European governments have established universal health coverage. The European approach differs from the "hands-off" approach to social welfare policies in the United States.

1901 to 1909. In the United States, President Theodore Roosevelt leads a successful charge against **trusts**, which are business agreements or practices that restrict free trade. Antitrust laws such as the Sherman Antitrust Act of 1890 are passed and enforced to protect consumers and promote open markets and competition. These antitrust laws focused on railroad and oil monopolies.

In the health care market, antitrust laws have led to unforeseen consequences. Antitrust laws limit efforts to develop innovations to improve clinical services integration and more standardized health care pricing. Thus, the antitrust movement of the early 1900s complicates the implementation of current health reform efforts to increase transparency and collaboration among providers (Burke, Cartwright-Smith, Pereira, & Rosenbaum, 2009).

1910. The Flexner Report, published in 1910 by the Carnegie Foundation, critiques the preparation of U.S. physicians. The Flexner Report leads to profound changes in U.S. medical education, influencing the education of nurses and other health professionals, as well. One implication is that increasing resources are required for the adequate preparation of the health care workforce. Health professionals who pay high costs for their training and education also have higher expectations for adequate pay and reimbursement. The strong emphasis on restricting medical practice also impedes the education, employment, and reimbursement of **mid-level providers (MLPs)** such as nurse practitioners and nurse midwives.

1920 to 1929. By the 1920s, U.S. hospitals feature enough sanitation, professional staff, and technology (such as x-rays) to become places where lives are saved and seriously ill or injured patients are fully rehabilitated. Hospitals not only become institutions of healing, but also settings for physicians and surgeons to learn and advance medical practice.

Staff and technology are costly and require adequate and reliable financial support. Physicians increasingly expect state-of-the-art facilities and equipment, as well as highly trained nurses and staff to carry out increasingly advanced procedures. It becomes increasingly important for hospitals to operate as businesses rather than charitable institutions. Although hospitals are still largely charitable, religious, or public institutions, hospital administration moves toward a business model to obtain adequate revenue to cover these costs.

1929 to 1939. The Great Depression results in large numbers of unemployed, destitute people who cannot afford to pay health care bills. In the United States, the Depression leads to the creation of nonprofit and for-profit health plans such as Blue Cross for hospitalization and Blue Shield for medical care. Prepaid plans also develop to cover large employee groups, introducing the innovation now known as managed care. The growth of private health insurance in the United States is stimulated by a number of stakeholders. Physicians and hospitals support health insurance because it assures that they will receive adequate reimbursement for their services. Patients and families trust that they can access affordable health care and that they are protected from financial ruin should a catastrophic health event occur. Insurers serve the community and profit from providing health coverage.

1939 to 1945. During World War II, the U.S. government provides tax exemptions for employer and employee health insurance premiums. The health insurance tax exemption is an incentive for home front factory workers when the war effort makes it impossible to raise worker wages. Enrollment in health insurance plans grows from 20.6 million in 1940 to 142.3 million in 1950 (Blumenthal, 2006).

1945. President Harry S. Truman proposes a national health program, including the creation of a voluntary health insurance program to be operated by the Federal government. In opposition, the American Medical Association coins the term **socialized medicine**, linking the national health insurance proposal to communism (Truman Library, 2011). Successful lobbying and the widespread adoption of private health insurance likely contribute to the defeat of Truman's government-sponsored health insurance proposal.

1965. Lyndon B. Johnson oversees the passage of Title XVIII, Medicare, and Title XIX, Medicaid, of the Social Security Act of 1965. In the 1960s, the highest poverty rates are among senior citizens, and only about half of the elderly in 1965 can afford health insurance. Medicare and Medicaid extend health coverage to nearly all elderly Americans as well as to eligible low-income children, adults, and people with disabilities (HCFR, 2005–2006).

1970 to 1979. National health expenditures soar as the fee-for-service provisions of Medicare, Medicaid, and most insurance plans pay full charges for hospitalization and medical care with little oversight. During the Carter Administration, concerns about rising health care costs lead to new legislation. The Health Maintenance Organization (HMO) Act of 1973 removes legal restrictions to establishing managed care plans. The HMO Act also requires employers to offer at least one HMO insurance option to employees. As a result, managed care spreads and improves efforts to review and control hospital and physician charges.

1980 to 1989. Concerns about health care costs increase, with employers increasingly worried about the effect of rising health premiums on profits and American global competitiveness. The Reagan Administration establishes the Medicare Prospective Payment System (PPS) to better control hospital utilization and costs for Medicare patients. The Consolidated Omnibus Budget Reconciliation Act of 1986 (COBRA) regulates continuation of health insurance after termination of employment. The Emergency Medical Treatment and Active Labor Act (EMTALA) is passed as part of the COBRA legislation, making emergency rooms the health care safety net for many Americans, including the uninsured.

1990 to 1999. The Clinton Administration enacts the Health Insurance Portability and Accountability Act of 1996 (HIPAA), which among other provisions helps protect consumer rights and privacy related to health insurance coverage. Clinton also signs the Balanced Budget Act of 1997, which establishes State Children's Health Insurance Program (SCHIP) to expand health insurance coverage for poor, uninsured American children. However, the Clinton Administration's effort to enact universal health coverage ends in failure. A detailed history of 20th century U.S. health insurance is available at the EH.net Health Insurance in the United States website (www.eh.net).

2000 to 2008. During the George W. Bush Administration, concerns about health costs continue, and there are over 43 million uninsured Americans. Policies encourage the development of high-deductible, consumer-driven health plans to make American citizens more aware of and responsible for the costs of health care. A soaring national deficit and the onset of a global economic recession raise even more concerns as Americans lose jobs and homes. The increased utilization of pharmaceuticals, medical devices, and other technologies pushes the cost of care higher.

For the first time in recorded history, chronic diseases such as cardiovascular disease and diabetes surpass communicable diseases as the leading cause of death (WHO, 2011). This change shifts health care needs and utilization on into the future, as aging populations require ongoing services and support. The importance of primary prevention is also underscored to reduce the prevalence of many chronic disorders.

2009 to the present. With partisan opposition and amid considerable controversy, the Patient Protection and Affordable Care Act of 2010 (PPACA) is enacted by the Obama Administration (PPACA, 2010). Health reform provides increased opportunities for professional nurses and nurse practitioners to expand their practice to the full extent of their role (IOM, 2011). The June 2012 U.S. Supreme Court ruling upheld the provisions of the PPACA, but allows states to opt out of the expansion of Medicaid to Americans with incomes less than 133% of the federal poverty level (Galewitz & Serafini, 2012). Continued increases in health care costs, along with a stagnant economy and government budget deficits, add to challenges for a U.S. health care model that controls costs while assuring access to high-quality care.

Figure 1.1 summarizes many of the historical events in health care economics as a visual timeline. Physicians have utilized a fee-for-service business model for many years. Over the last century or so, hospitals evolved from being charity institutions to a business model of billing for charges. By contrast, from prehistoric times, nurses worked largely within homes

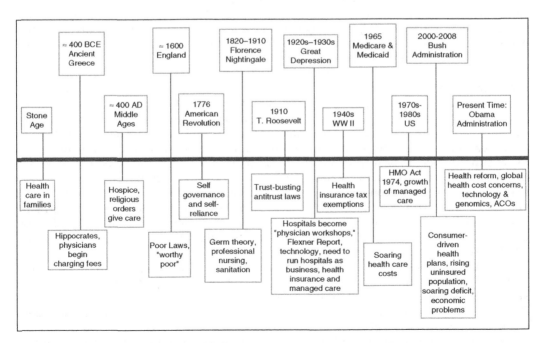

Figure 1.1 *Timeline for the History of Health Care and Nursing Economics*

Note: The timeline is not drawn to scale.

and later in hospitals as free or low-paid helpers, reaching professional status only since the late 1800s. Until relatively recently, nurses did not negotiate wages or advocate for wage increases. A review of literature on costing out nursing services finds little agreement on terms such as "direct nursing care" and "direct nursing costs" (Eckhart, 1993). Nurses lag far behind physicians and hospital administrators in linking financial principles to clinical practice.

This historical overview reinforces that improvements in life-saving technologies are offset by mounting costs and limits on resources. Public values about who should pay for and who should receive health care are often based on thinking passed down from earlier times. In the United States, partisan politics play an important role in setting or opposing health care policies. Nurses, with the exception of leaders such as Nightingale, have historically been at the forefront of patient care, not health care policy making or the design of health care systems. As the largest segment of the health care workforce, the potential for nurses to educate the public about health policy and to develop workable, cost-effective, and compassionate strategies for health care delivery is considerable. If nurses intend to meet future challenges by working to the full extent of their capability (IOM, 2011), they must understand the economic implications of health care and play a role in setting health care policy.

HEALTH CARE COSTS

Health care represents one of the largest industry segments in the United States, providing 14.3 million jobs in 2008, and encompassing nearly 596,000 settings for the delivery of health care services. The health care sector is expected to continue to grow, related to factors such as the aging population and the expansion of health coverage provisions in the ACA (BLS, 2010).

Nurses represent the largest sector of health professionals in the United States (IOM, 2011) with more than three million registered nurses (RNs). The United States has more nurses than any other country and is also a major importer of international nurses (Carnevale, Smith, Gulish, & Beach, 2012). Nursing employment and access to nursing care are influenced by the economics of the health care industry. Nurses also make an important impact on health care costs and cost savings.

America has the most costly health care system in the world, and costs are rising. U.S. health care expenditures increased from 5.2% to 17.6% of gross domestic product (GDP) from 1960 to 2009 (Centers for Medicare & Medicaid Services, Office of the Actuary, National Health Statistics Group; U.S. Department of Commerce, Bureau of Economic Analysis; U.S. Bureau of the Census, 2012). Expenditures for U.S. health care totaled $2.6 trillion in 2010. Health care costs are predicted to grow at a faster rate than the U.S. economy over the coming decade, to $4.6 trillion or 19.8% of the GDP by 2020 (Centers for Medicare & Medicaid Services, Office of the Actuary, 2012). In other words, by 2020, roughly one of every five dollars in the U.S. economy will be spent on health care. Figure 1.2 shows the actual and projected growth in U.S. health care costs from 1966 to 2018. These costs are borne by American consumers, employers, and taxpayers. Concerns about costs are intensified by the growing needs of an aging population and a society that expects advanced technologies and high-quality care.

Health care costs are not spread evenly across the American population. In 2009, only 1% of the American population accounted for 21.8% of total health care expenditures. These very high-cost patients averaged $90,061 per year for health care. In both 2008 and 2009, only 5% of the U.S. population accounted for nearly 50% of all health care expenditures, averaging $35,829 per high cost patient per year in 2008 (Cohen & Yu, 2012).

Health care financing in the United States is complicated and fragmented. A diverse and often uncoordinated mix of national, state, local, and private funders and providers are responsible for health care funding and services. In many cases, people in need of health care

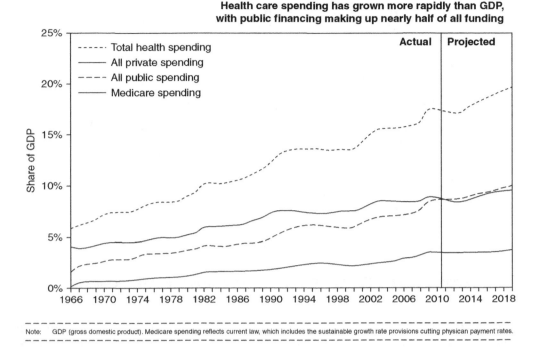

Figure 1.2 *National Health Expenditures, 1966 to 2018*

Source: Centers for Medicare & Medicaid Services, National Health Expenditures.

"fall through the cracks" of the health care system because they lack eligibility for services or advocacy to represent their needs. An illustration and explanation of the complex flow of U.S. personal health care expenditures is presented at the New York Times Economix: The Money Flow from Households to Health Care Providers blog post (Reinhardt, 2011).

More information on U.S. national health expenditures is available at the CMS National Health Expenditure Data website (www.cms.gov). The California HealthCare Foundation report, Health Care Costs 101: Slow But Steady (www.chcf.org), summarizes U.S. health expenditures from 1960 to 2010.

HEALTH CARE ECONOMIC CONCEPTS

This section presents some basic economic concepts relevant to health care. Some fundamental principles of economics are provided, with implications for health care and health care economics. These concepts will help provide a basis for understanding nurse employment and wages. It is important to remember that these are somewhat simplified and general examples. More detailed information about health care economics is available from textbooks such as Phelps (2009).

Efficiency

Figure 1.3 presents a diagram of the flow of resources and activities in health care systems. **Inputs** represent the resources and "raw materials" required for the production of products (goods or services). The activities, processes, or work applied to the inputs are known as

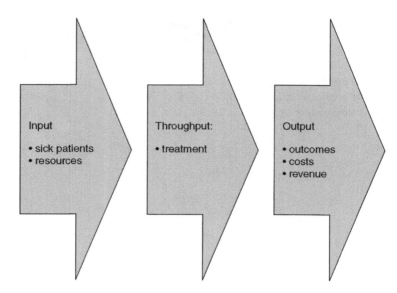

Figure 1.3 *Input-Throughput-Output Model With Inpatient Care Example*

throughputs. The goods, services, or other outcomes produced are known as **outputs**. For example, patients arrive at a hospital as inputs. They receive nursing care, such as intravenous (IV) therapy and wound dressings, as throughputs, and are discharged from the hospital in better health as outputs.

Maximizing the production or value of goods or services while minimizing the resources or costs required for production is called **efficiency**. Efficient production is economically beneficial. Concerns about efficiency in health care are related to problems of excessive costs, waste, and inadequate access to services. Policies and initiatives often aim to improve the efficiency of health care delivery. For example, the Patient Protection and Affordable Care Act Hospital Value-Based Purchasing Program is intended to link hospital payment to quality measures to improve the efficiency of patient care (PPACA, 2010).

Text Box 1.1 shows four types of efficiency. **Technical efficiency** represents the production of the maximum amount of outputs given the minimum amount of inputs, or maximizing outputs for a given set of inputs.

For example, inpatient hospital care to receive intravenous cancer infusion services requires an intensive and costly combination of inputs such as nursing services, dietary and housekeeping services, medical supplies such as bed linens and medications, equipment, and a patient room. If patients can instead receive the same infusion services in an outpatient clinic, the intensity of inputs is reduced and of a shorter duration, and the costs are lower. Many of the inputs, such as 24-hour nursing supervision, dietary services, some

Text Box 1.1 *Types of Efficiencies*

Technical efficiency: Producing the maximum amount of outputs (goods or services) compared with the inputs (resources) required for production.
Production efficiency: Minimizing the costs of producing outputs or maximizing the production of outputs at a given cost.
Allocative efficiency: Minimizing the amount or cost of inputs while maximizing the value or benefit of outputs, or producing outputs of maximum value or benefit for a given amount or cost of inputs.
Opportunity cost and trade-off: When one must give up all or part of a benefit or value in order to increase or acquire another benefit or value. The opportunity cost is the value of the trade-off.

medical supplies, and a patient room, are not required or are needed at a substantially reduced level. Technical efficiency is achieved because the same or greater level of outputs is possible with fewer inputs—the same number of patients can be served with fewer inputs, or more patients are served with the same amount of inputs.

Production efficiency minimizes the costs of producing outputs or maximizes the production of outputs at a given cost. Note that instead of focusing on the inputs or the actual resources required to produce outputs such as medications and supplies, the focus is on the monetary costs of those inputs. For example, if the outpatient clinic manager is able to negotiate a substantial discount on the cost of intravenous medication needles, tubing, and related supplies, the clinic is able to manage the same number of patients receiving infusion services at less cost, or more patients at the same cost, thus achieving production efficiency.

Allocative efficiency represents minimizing the amount or cost of inputs while maximizing the value or benefit of outputs, or producing outputs of maximum value or benefit for a given amount or cost of inputs. For example, the outpatient clinic might offer videos educating the patient about the cancer medications and other health topics to watch while in the waiting room or while receiving the intravenous medications. Follow-up assessments might be scheduled in coordination with medication administration. These inputs might be small or relatively low cost, but add substantially to the value of the outpatient visit, thus achieving allocative efficiency.

An **opportunity cost** is the cost related to a **trade-off**. A trade-off occurs when it is necessary to choose between one alternative and another and to weigh alternative costs in making decisions (Mankiw, 2011). In the outpatient clinic example, the opportunity cost is related to decisions to increase cancer infusion services compared with other clinic services. Increasing cancer infusion services will require a reduction in other services the clinic can provide. The value of this reduction in services (trade-off), such as the loss in reimbursement from the other clinic services, represents the opportunity cost.

Opportunity costs also apply to nonmonetary resources, such as time. For example, delays in appointments and long waiting lists cause at least some patients to delay care or seek care elsewhere. A person's time is of enough value to present as an opportunity cost. One way to estimate the opportunity cost of a person's time is to use the person's hourly wage or an estimated hourly wage as a measure of the time's value.

Competitive Markets

A **market** is a group of buyers and sellers of specified products, which may be goods or services (Mankiw, 2011). The U.S. and most other world economies support the formation of **competitive markets**, also referred to as free or open markets. According to economic theory, perfect competition ensures rational distribution of resources under conditions of economic exchange. In other words, competitive markets enable societies and nations to distribute resources efficiently.

Characteristics of competitive markets include the following:

▪ There are large numbers of both producers selling products and of consumers purchasing those products.
▪ Producers are free to enter or leave the market.
▪ The products offered by competing producers are similar and comparable.
▪ Neither a single consumer nor producer (or small group of consumers or producers) is able to influence the market price of the products (Mankiw, 2011).

One example is to imagine a perfectly competitive market for apples. There are many producers growing and selling apples and many consumers purchasing apples. Producers are free to choose to enter the market to grow and sell apples or leave the market and produce other products. Producers choose to enter the market if the price they obtain from growing apples covers their costs. Producers are even more interested in entering the market if the price covers their costs and allows for profit. Producers choose to leave the market if the price from growing apples is not enough to make the venture profitable.

The apples sold are similar and comparable enough that consumers can "shop around" to select apples at a price they are willing and able to pay. If the price for apples rises to a level that consumers cannot afford, consumers are able to choose other comparable products, such as peaches. In other words, consumers can choose whether or not to purchase apples.

Multiple producers ensure that no single producer or group of producers can control the price of the apples. Multiple consumers ensure that no single consumer or group of consumers can control the price of apples. The price of apples thus is expected to approach the amount that consumers are willing to pay and that is sufficiently profitable for producers.

This example is simplified, as there are various types of apples and consumer preferences may differ, with some consumers preferring one type of apple and some consumers preferring another. There may be other complicating factors as well, such as the growing season or shipping costs. However, the description of the market for apples shows that there are relationships between producers, consumers, and the price of products sold in competitive markets. In a perfectly competitive market, the interaction between producers and consumers leads to a price that allows for the rational distribution of apples.

Health Care Markets

Health care markets are not perfectly competitive, although in many cases economic theory can be applied to health care markets. The simplified market for apples provides a basis for applications to the health care market. This section discusses how producers, consumers, products, and price in health care markets can differ from the competitive market.

Producers. Producers of health care are often referred to as providers. In many cases, health care providers cannot freely enter health care markets because they face **barriers to entry,** or restrictions to entering markets. For example, many health care professionals such as nurses cannot legally practice without extensive training, credentialing, and licensure, which pose barriers to entry. Hospitals and other health care settings often require extensive regulation and accreditation requirements to operate, which serve as barriers to entry. Barriers to entry restrict competition and reduce the consumer's choice of providers. The rationale for restricting competition is to ensure quality and integrity in health care goods and services.

Barriers to entry limit the number of health care providers and may lead to shortages. Other factors contributing to shortages of health care providers include low wages or reimbursement and rural locations, or both. The Health Resources and Services Administration (HRSA) enables searching by primary medical care, dental services, or mental health services to identify Health Professional Shortage Areas (HPSAs) in the HPSA by State and County website (http://hpsafind.hrsa.gov/).

Shortages of health care providers limit consumer choice and increase costs. Health care consumers often cannot simply choose not to receive services that may be necessary for comfort or well-being, or to sustain life. Satisfactory substitutes are not available for many health services. Shortages of health care providers also increase costs, as consumers must travel longer distances or wait for longer periods of time to obtain needed services. For example, if a patient requires a total hip replacement and orthopedic services are not readily available, the patient must either travel and possibly delay care until treatment can be scheduled or suffer pain and disability.

Consumers. There may be large numbers of consumers wanting to enter the health care market who are unable or unwilling to pay the high costs. As out-of-pocket (personal) costs for health care increase, the demand for health care decreases. For example, the use of prescription drugs among the elderly tends to increase as the out-of-pocket costs decrease

(Polinski, Kilabuk, Schneeweiss, Brennan, & Shrank, 2010). In a 2011 survey, nearly half of the respondents reported that they delay health care because of cost concerns (PwC, 2011). Uninsured Americans frequently delay or forgo health care because they are unwilling or unable to pay the out-of-pocket costs or have difficulties finding a provider (Bailey, 2012).

Health care consumers often differ from the consumer in a perfectly competitive market. As already mentioned, health care consumers may put themselves at risk of suffering or premature death if they forego health services, and they often cannot choose satisfactory substitutes for services that are not affordable. Health care consumers are often ill and unable to make fully informed decisions about health care products and services. For example, a person who is unconscious cannot choose his or her ambulance service or hospital. Even when able to make informed decisions, health care consumers must often rely on the recommendations of the physician or other provider. Concerns related to informed decisions are discussed in more detail in Chapter 2.

Products. The goods and services produced in health care markets are often not similar or comparable. For example, a person who needs a total hip replacement requires total hip replacement surgery. As previously mentioned, many health care products are essential to health and comfort, and possibly life saving. Even if products are comparable, the consumer cannot "shop around" if seriously ill or unconscious. Health care providers are often the source of health care products by providing health care services. As a result, shortages of health care providers result in a shortage of the supply of services.

Price. Provider and product shortages can increase the price or cost in health care markets because consumers cannot choose other satisfactory substitutes. Government payers establish nonnegotiable reimbursement rates in health care markets and generally will not pay a higher price. Health insurance complicates the impact of price, as it makes the consumer less sensitive to health care costs. Chapter 2 discusses issues related to price and insurance in more detail.

Another factor that causes health care prices to differ from competitive market prices is the lack of **transparency,** or information that is available about pricing. One reason for transparency problems is that health care often involves multiple providers submitting bills, such as a surgeon, an anesthesiologist, and a hospital for a patient having surgery. Another reason prices are not transparent is that there are differences in the structure of health insurance plans, such as different out-of-pocket rates. Providers also often find it difficult to predict an individual's health care costs in advance. For example, one patient might have serious complications that greatly increase the overall costs of a procedure that is usually relatively low cost (GAO, 2011).

U.S. hospital charges (prices) often vary widely. A survey of 19 U.S. hospitals revealed that the price quoted for a full knee replacement surgery ranged from about \$33,000 to \$101,000 (GAO, 2011). In 2008, Medicare expenditures per beneficiary were only \$6,971 in Portland, Oregon, compared with \$15,571 in Miami, Florida, adjusting for age, sex, race, and price (Skinner, Gottlieb, & Carmichael, 2011). More discussion of the lack of hospital price transparency is provided in Chapter 8. The lack of health care price transparency prevents consumers from making informed choices about the costs of health services.

Supply and Demand in Health Care Markets

The quantity of health care services supplied should ideally meet the quantity of health services that consumers demand. This section presents some concepts to show how supply, demand, and price interact in theoretical competitive markets compared with health care markets.

Supply represents the quantity of a product that producers are able and willing to produce and sell at a given price over a specific time period. In competitive markets, changes in price result in changes in the quantity of products supplied. Increases in price lead to increases in the quantity supplied, as shown in Figure 1.4. This relationship between the quantity supplied and the price was described earlier in this section, with apple growers entering the market if the price of apples is profitable. In a competitive market, as the price of apples increases, so does the quantity of apples supplied.

Supply may change based on changes in other factors, such as the costs of production. If the cost of growing apples rises considerably, then the supply of apples will drop, unless consumers are willing to pay a higher price that covers those added costs. For example, if the price of land increases, it may cost apple producers more to enter the market, so the supply of apples may decrease. The biz/ed Interactive Supply and Demand Part 2 website (www.bized.co.uk) provides interactive graphics to show the effects of price and other factors on the quantity of products supplied.

Health care markets also must cover costs of production for goods and services that are produced. However, as explained in Chapter 8, the price or charge applied to health services may be discounted by the insurance payer, or a government payer may reimburse at less than the price charged. As a result, the relationship of price to supply is not always as clear in health care markets as in purely competitive markets.

Some health providers such as hospitals engage in **cost shifting** to cover costs of production when the price or reimbursement is not adequate. Cost shifting occurs when a producer increases the price of a good or service to cover the costs of an unprofitable good or service. For example, a diagnostic procedure might cost a hospital $500 to perform. Medicaid might only reimburse $100 for the procedure. The hospital might set its charges higher than $500 so that private insurers cover the losses incurred from procedures reimbursed by Medicaid. Cost shifting is a strategy used in health care that is not typical in most other competitive markets.

Demand refers to the quantity of a product for which consumers are able and willing to pay at a given price over a specified time period. In competitive markets, changes in price result in changes in the quantity of products demanded. The demand curve in Figure 1.4 shows that as the price falls, the quantity of a product demanded increases. For example, if the price of apples goes up, the quantity of apples demanded by consumers goes down.

Factors other than price may change demand for products, including income. Consumers with higher incomes are not as sensitive to increases in price, so they may continue

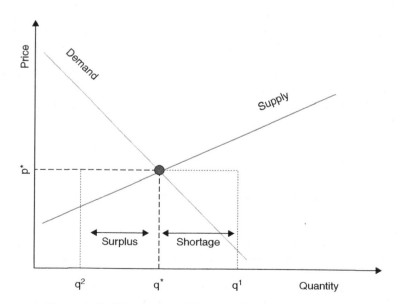

Figure 1.4 *Shortage and Surplus Related to Quantity Supplied, Quantity Demanded, and Price*

purchasing the same quantity of apples even if the price rises. The biz/ed Interactive Supply and Demand Part 1 website (www.bized.co.uk) provides interactive graphics to show the effects of price and other factors on the quantity of products demanded.

Health care differs from most competitive markets in that payment for many products is covered by health insurance. Insurance has the same effect as income, making the consumer less sensitive to price. Health care also differs because consumers often cannot "shop around" for the best price. Consumers may not be able to learn the price of health care products or may not know how much health care they will need to consume.

In addition, satisfactory **substitutes** for health care consumption are often not available. In terms of the quantity demanded, an example of substitutes is the consumer choosing to buy peaches when the price of apples rises, thus reducing the quantity of apples demanded. In other words, the price of one (substitute) product reduces the demand for another comparable product (Mankiw, 2011). In some situations, satisfactory substitutes exist in health care, such as substituting some less costly generic drugs for higher cost brand-name drugs. In many other situations, satisfactory substitutes do not exist, thus restricting perfect competition.

Because of these factors, the demand for health care services may remain unchanged or even increase as health care costs and prices increase. One example is the relatively high utilization of health care services by elderly Americans with limited incomes. Medicare coverage enables these beneficiaries to demand high-cost health care services.

Market equilibrium and disequilibrium. Under competitive market conditions, the push and pull on price between producers and consumers leads to **market equilibrium**. The price reaches a level satisfactory to both the buyer and the seller, and the quantity supplied equals the quantity demanded. Figure 1.4 shows the market equilibrium at the point where the supply and demand curves cross. The equilibrium price is noted as p^* and the equilibrium quantity supplied is noted as q^*. However, **market disequilibrium,** or an imbalance between the quantity of a product supplied and the quantity demanded, is a common occurrence.

Shortage. When the market price for a product falls to a level lower than the equilibrium price, a condition of disequilibrium occurs, resulting in excess demand known as a **shortage**. A shortage might also occur when consumers demand a higher quantity of a product than is supplied. Figure 1.4 shows that the quantity demanded rises from q^* to q^1, resulting in a shortage. An increase in the price will increase the quantity supplied and decrease the quantity demanded, bringing the market back to equilibrium.

A recent concern in health care is the increasing number of drug shortages. In 2010, the U.S. Food and Drug Administration (FDA) reported 178 incidents of drug shortages, and this problem is expected to grow. Most of these shortages occur among generic drugs that are important for anesthesiology and cancer treatment (PwC, 2011). Generic drugs are typically sold at a lower price than brand-name drugs, which may reduce incentives to maintain their supply. To learn more about drug shortages, see the U.S. Food and Drug Administration website, Frequently Asked Questions About Drug Shortages (http://www.fda.gov/Drugs/DrugSafety/DrugShortages/ucm050796.htm).

Another example of higher demand leading to disequilibrium in health care markets is **pent-up demand**. One example of pent-up demand in health care markets occurs when consumers defer health care, usually for financial reasons. These people then utilize health care as soon as health coverage becomes available. Thus, large numbers of uninsured persons may cause substantial increases in health care utilization and costs at the time that they become eligible for health coverage (Damler, 2009).

Surplus. When the market price for a product rises to a level higher than the equilibrium price, a condition of disequilibrium occurs, resulting in excess supply known as a **surplus**. A surplus might also occur when consumers demand a lower quantity of a product than is supplied. Figure 1.4 shows that the quantity demanded drops from q^* to q^2, resulting in a surplus. A drop in the price will decrease the quantity supplied and increase the quantity demanded, bringing the market back to equilibrium.

For example, an economic downturn results in many people losing their jobs and health insurance. Fewer of these people and their families seek hospitalization for elective procedures, resulting in a surplus of hospital beds and nurses. Hospitals schedule fewer nurses and may close some nursing units in response to the lower demand. This brings the hospital market closer to equilibrium, as the quantity of hospital services drops in response to the drop in the quantity demanded. The biz/ed Interactive Supply and Demand Part 3 website (www.bized. co.uk) provides interactive graphics to show the effect demand on surpluses and shortages.

Market Failure

When markets are unable to allocate resources efficiently, the result is **market failure.** An example of market failure is **market power,** which occurs when a single buyer or seller (or a few buyers or sellers) can control market prices, so price and quantity supplied are not brought into equilibrium (Mankiw, 2011). Consumers often think of market power as unfair. From an economist's perspective, the problem with market power is that the control over price leads to inefficiencies. Supply and demand are not in balance, so the market is in disequilibrium and resources are not allocated efficiently.

Monopoly. A **monopoly** occurs when a single producer has the market power to charge a price that exceeds the equilibrium price, leading to market failure (Mankiw, 2011). For example, the Federal Trade Commission (FTC) and the State of Minnesota recently took action against a pharmaceutical company that was thought to have a monopoly over the only two drugs used to treat congenital heart disease for approximately 30,000 babies each year in the United States. The company's market power allowed it to impose a 1300% price increase when it acquired the patent for one of the two drugs, leading to the investigation (FTC, 2011).

Not all monopolies are undesirable. A **natural monopoly** occurs when one producer can supply a product more efficiently or at a lower cost than if two or more producers enter the market. A water purification plant is an example of a natural monopoly, as it typically has no competitors. Most communities only have one water purification plant, which is an efficient way to provide the community's water supply. Governments may run or regulate natural monopolies, which helps ensure adequate supply and protects consumers from excessive prices (Mankiw, 2011).

Monopsony. A market with one buyer or one small group of buyers is known as a **monopsony,** another form of market failure (Mankiw, 2011). One example is that hospitals might exert monopsony power in the nursing labor market. For instance, a single hospital (purchaser) employing the majority of nurses in a local health care market might be able to control the wage (price) level for nurses (producers of health care). The hospital's market power might push nurse wages below the level of a competitive market, thus creating inefficiencies.

One way that nurses and other workers address monopsony power over wages is to form a **union.** A union consists of a group of workers attempting to influence market power in a labor market by bargaining with the employers (Mankiw, 2011). However, unionization may push wages higher than market equilibrium, which is also inefficient.

Job mobility, which is common in the nursing profession, is another way of reducing monopsony power in nursing labor markets (Hirsch & Schumacher, 2005). The hospital monopsony might lead to a nursing shortage if nurses migrate to other hospitals that pay higher wages. The hospital may need to increase wages to attract nurses and end the shortage.

Other Health Care Economic Concepts

This section reviews some additional concepts related to health care economics. An understanding of these concepts helps nurses better understand economic forces and relationships in this chapter and throughout the textbook.

Costs. The resources or inputs required to produce goods or services are known as **costs.** Costs and types of costs are discussed throughout this textbook. One type of cost is a **fixed**

cost, or a cost that does not change with adjustments in the level of production over a specified time period. For example, a hospital's physical plant, such as the buildings and new construction, remain fixed over a fiscal year, regardless of the number of patients admitted. **Variable costs** vary with the level of production. For example, the supplies needed to provide patient care will vary depending on the number of patients admitted to the hospital.

Economies of scale. **Economies of scale** are achieved by increasing the efficiency of production. Economies of scale occur when the fixed costs of production can be spread across a large number of products and the variable costs decrease. For example, a medical device manufacturer may be able to invest in equipment (fixed cost). The manufacturer is able to increase production as needed to fill orders for the medical device. The variable cost of materials needed to produce the devices will decrease because the manufacturer is able to purchase larger amounts of materials at a lower price. Because of the reduction in production costs, the manufacturer can charge a lower price for the medical devices while making a profit and attract more consumers to purchase the devices.

Economies of scale often occur in a natural monopoly. An enterprise such as a water purification plant has high fixed costs and low variable costs. The costs of constructing the plant (fixed costs) can be spread across all consumers who pay for a water supply, and the low variable costs have relatively little impact on the price of the water. The economies of scale, therefore, enable the water purification plant to serve a community at a reasonable price.

Economies of scope. In situations where the costs of production decline when two or more goods or services are produced together, the producer achieves **economies of scope**. Hospitals, for example, typically combine nursing care, emergency services, laboratory and radiology procedures, surgery, and other related services in one facility. This is more efficient than sending the patient to one facility for a radiology exam, another facility for surgery, and so on.

Externalities. Production and consumption of some goods and services may create **externalities**. Externalities represent costs of production that are not borne by the producer. Externalities also represent costs of consumption that are not paid for by the consumer. **Positive externalities** are benefits to a third party that result from production or consumption. For example, widespread immunization often results in "herd immunity," or protection from the disease of persons who were not immunized.

Negative externalities or risks and problems borne by third parties from production or consumption may raise serious concerns. A factory may release lead, which is ingested by young children. However, these children and their families often bear the costs of lead exposure, rather than the factory owner. Tobacco consumption not only creates health risks for the consumer, but also for those exposed to environmental tobacco smoke, yet the tobacco consumer is not expected to pay for the health risks to those exposed individuals.

Government and Competitive Markets

The government may become closely involved in the operations of competitive markets. For example, government defines and enforces rights, including property rights, and maintains law and order so that markets can effectively function. The commonly accepted medium of exchange, money, is established by government, which is essential as a measure of price and cost. As nearly half of all health care in the United States is funded by federal, state, or local agencies, it is important to consider the role of government in the health care market.

Nonprofit and government providers. In most industries, firms operate as for-profit entities. In health care, there is a mix of for-profit, nonprofit, and government institutions with various financing mechanisms. Nonprofit hospitals and public hospitals often provide less profitable services, such as Level 1 trauma units (Harrison & McLane, 2005). Nonprofit institutions are allowed tax exemptions in return for services provided to the community, but nonprofits must still earn a profit in order to survive and grow. Government institutions are funded by tax dollars and must operate efficiently in order to maximize scarce resources. As a result, the health care industry must balance ethical values with the need to generate profits.

Public goods. One approach to market failure is government's production of **public goods,** or goods that are collectively consumed and relatively inexhaustible and nonexclusive. Safe drinking water and sewage systems are examples of public goods, which are not profitable to produce in a competitive market, yet are of considerable value to society. In some cases, the provision of public goods may be influenced by market conditions. For example, a remote, rural area may require government support to provide a community hospital as a public good. In urban areas, market competition may support the provision of hospital services.

If a government provides a public good, the public often has free access to the good. People may be able to use the public good without paying, for example, the use of public highways by persons who do not pay taxes to support that highway. In some cases, eligibility is required to use the public good. For example, all school-age children are eligible to attend public schools.

The quantity of a public good that consumers demand depends on its value. For example, a community may support the maintenance of high-quality schools that reflect the value placed on public education. The production of a public good depends on the society's willingness to pay, typically through the imposition of fees and taxes. It is assumed that the residents of communities who value public education are willing to pay taxes to support this public good.

Free-rider problem. One potential concern about the provision of public goods is the **free-rider problem,** or when shortages of a product occur because consumers have access to the product but are not required to pay for the product. An example is allowing persons to obtain care at a free clinic who are able to afford clinic services. The use of clinic services by these free riders may increase waiting times and make it more difficult for others to get care at the clinic. Eligibility criteria help to limit the free-rider problem. Imposing taxes and user fees requires consumers who benefit from public goods to contribute to support those public goods.

Income redistribution. Governments may mandate **income redistribution**, transferring income from one group to another based on established criteria. For example, persons below an established poverty line may be able to obtain welfare assistance, paid for by taxing wealthier citizens. Concerns about free riders lead to eligibility requirements and limitations to these benefits.

Regulation. Other government functions include regulating producers to protect consumer safety, such as requiring that all motor vehicles are equipped with seat belts. Regulations may also be developed to reduce or control negative externalities, such as factory emission of air or water pollutants. These regulations often pose trade-offs between consumer or environmental interests and market efficiency. As a result, producers may oppose government regulation.

Taxation. In order to pay the costs of public goods, the enforcement of regulations, income distribution, and other functions, government must levy taxes. Producers often see taxes as inhibiting the competitive market and therefore oppose taxation. Taxes are also politically unpopular with many Americans. American culture strongly supports individualism and the rights of business to be competitive and profitable. These factors influence the economics and financing of health care in the United States.

Values, culture, and politics. Ethical values affecting health care policies and financing are not limited to questions about profitability. Political and ethical controversies regarding issues including reproductive health care and end-of-life planning affect decisions about resources and access to services. In some cases, states have the power to limit eligibility or funding for services, causing geographic variation in government programs such as Medicaid. In other cases, individuals require modification of services related to their religious or cultural beliefs. These ongoing political and cultural concerns influence government interventions in health care.

ECONOMICS AND THE NURSING WORKFORCE

Nurses are participants in the health care economy. Nursing costs are frequently the largest source of labor costs for hospitals, and, in many hospitals, nursing is the largest part of the total budget (Douglas, 2010). As employees in health care agencies and institutions, nurses make up a labor market that is influenced by economic forces. This section provides some examples linking economic concepts to the nursing workforce.

Wages and labor supply. Note that, in labor markets, employees are the suppliers of services, and wages represent the price of those services. As a result, wages influence the supply of labor in labor markets. For example, in the nursing labor market, nurses are the suppliers, and wages represent the price of nursing care. As a result, increasing nurse wages would be expected to increase the supply of nurses. In many cases, employers are not able or willing to increase wages, so nursing shortages may occur.

Costs and labor supply. In labor markets, the costs of education and training may decrease the supply of labor. Opportunity costs include the time required for education and training, as well as waiting lists if there are shortages in the availability of educational or training programs. If resources such as scholarships or paid internships are available, the costs of education and training are reduced. Reasons for the shortage of doctorally prepared nurses include the high financial and opportunity costs for graduate nursing education. In addition, the market may change over the time student nurses receive their education. New graduate nurses who began their education during a nursing shortage may enter a market that is now experiencing a nursing surplus.

Alternative labor markets. Alternative labor markets increase the overall demand for the workers in those labor markets. Hospitals are traditionally the largest employers of nurses. However, if changes in health care require that more patients require follow-up care in the home, the demand for home health nurses will increase. Increasing home health wages closer to the level of hospital wages will likely attract some hospital nurses to home health agencies, as both hospitals and home health agencies compete for the supply of nurses. The demand from the alternative labor market, home health, will increase the overall demand for nurses.

Productivity and labor demand. Increasing worker productivity expands output while reducing the inputs required, thus increasing production efficiency. If increasing productivity results in the satisfactory care of more patients per nurse, then fewer nurses are required and the demand for nurses will decrease. The labor-intensive nature of inpatient settings may increase the demand for nurses in acute care, even though the numbers of inpatients may remain the same or decrease.

Substitutes and labor demand. As in other markets, in the labor market satisfactory substitutes may reduce the demand for nurses. If nurse assistants are as productive as RNs, the nurse assistants are less costly and may be used as substitutes for RNs. The demand for RNs may therefore decrease compared with nurse assistants. MLPs such as nurse practitioners may serve as "physician extenders," substituting for the primary care physician. In some health care settings, resources such as equipment might be substituted for labor. For example, telemonitoring technologies may enable more patients to remain in their homes, with fewer nurses needed to manage these patients in the hospital.

Note that barriers to entry often reduce the use of substitutes in health care settings. Regulations regarding professional scope of practice and quality concerns may reduce the amount of substitution of one health care worker for another. However, in settings such as long-term care, nurse assistants may be employed in higher numbers than RNs. In rural or other underserved areas, nurse practitioners may provide primary care that is not available from primary care physicians.

Derived demand for labor. The labor market for nurses is based on **derived demand,** or the quantity of labor or other products demanded for the sake of an ultimate output. As much as patients may like their nurses, the actual reason patients demand hospital care is to protect and improve their health and well-being. Nurses are needed (demanded) to provide hospital care. If the demand for hospital care decreases, demand for acute care nurses will likely decrease accordingly.

Nursing shortages and surpluses. Remember that increasing nursing wages and decreasing nurse education and training costs are ways to increase the nursing supply and address nursing shortages. Nursing surpluses result when the quantity of labor supplied is greater than the quantity demanded. Job mobility helps address nursing surpluses, because while one local area may be oversupplied with nurses, other communities may suffer nursing shortages and have ample employment opportunities available. The continued aging of the U.S. population and increased use of labor-intensive health care technologies makes it likely that nursing shortages will be more of a problem in future years than nursing surpluses.

Profitability and reimbursement. Increasing reimbursement and profitability increases the quantity of labor demanded. As the reimbursement for health care increases, more resources are available to employers to expand programs and staffing, so the demand for nurses may increase. If reimbursement decreases, health care programs and staffing may contract, thus reducing the demand for nurses. However, quality concerns and regulations such as nurse-to-patient ratio laws limit the extent to which many health care employers can reduce their demand for nurses.

Events. The state of the overall U.S. economy affects trends in the nursing workforce. During economic downturns such as the recession that began in December 2007, more nurses seek employment, so that in some areas of the country there is a nursing surplus. Many part-time nurses find full-time work when overall national unemployment is high, to help their families during times of economic difficulty. When the overall rate of unemployment in the Unites States falls, nurses are more likely to leave the workforce, increasing the likelihood of nursing shortages. Researchers predict that as the U.S. economy improves over the next few years, and as nurses in the Baby Boomer cohort retire, the country will face a shortage of RNs (Staiger, Auerbach, & Buerhaus, 2012).

Other planned and unplanned events increase or decrease the quantity supplied or demanded in nursing labor markets. Laws requiring mandatory nurse-to-patient ratios increase the demand for hospital nurses. Changes in immigration requirements for foreign nurses, making it easier to find jobs in the United States, increase the supply of nurses. The aging nursing workforce is anticipated to decrease the supply of nurses and contribute to a potential nursing shortage over the years to come. The shortage of nursing faculty also contributes to potential nursing shortages as the faculty shortage limits the enrollment of nursing students.

CONCLUSION

This chapter introduces the topic of health economics by reviewing the historical context of financing health care and nursing services. Principles of economics and competitive markets are applied to the health care market. It is important to remember that health care markets are often not purely competitive, and that many factors other than economic forces influence health care economics and financing. This historical and economic context provides implications for nurse employment and wages. These concepts also provide background for understanding the principles of insurance and managed care, presented in Chapters 2 and 3.

Discussion and Exercises

1. List events in your work setting (or a health care setting of interest) that shift the quantities demanded and supplied of the goods or services produced. What is the impact on consumers (patients and families)?

2. Try drawing supply and demand curves for what you believe is the labor market for nursing in your local area. Is the market in a competitive equilibrium—for example, are wages in balance with the quantity of health workers supplied and demanded, so neither shortages nor surpluses are a problem? If there is market failure, what would you propose to return the market to competitive equilibrium?

3. What do you believe are the most important reasons for cost increases in health care? Compare and contrast your ideas about health care costs with other students, using evidence (statistics and literature) to support your views.

REFERENCES

Bailey, K. (2012, June). *Dying for coverage: The deadly consequences of being uninsured.* Washington, DC: Families USA. Retrieved from www.familiesusa.org

Blumenthal, D. (2006). Employer-sponsored health insurance in the United States–Origins and implications. *The New England Journal of Medicine, 355,* 82–88. Retrieved from http://www.nejm.org

Burke, T., Cartwright-Smith, L., Pereira, E., & Rosenbaum, S. (2009, July). Health System Reform and Antitrust Law: The antitrust aspects of health information sharing by public and private health insurers. *BNA's Health Law Reporter, 18*(29), 1–18. The Bureau of National Affairs, Inc. Retrieved from http://www.bna.com

Carnevale, A. P., Smith, N., Gulish, A., & Beach, B. H. (2012, June 21). *Healthcare. Georgetown University Center on Education and the Workforce.* Retrieved from http://cew.georgetown.edu/healthcare/

Centers for Medicare & Medicaid Services, Office of the Actuary (CMS). (2012, March 1). *National health expenditure projections 2010–2020.* Retrieved from https://www.cms.gov/NationalHealthExpendData/03_NationalHealthAccountsProjected.asp

Centers for Medicare & Medicaid Services, Office of the Actuary, National Health Statistics Group (CMS); U.S. Department of Commerce, Bureau of Economic Analysis; & U.S. Bureau of the Census. (2012, March 10). *Table 1: National health expenditures aggregate, per capita amounts, percent distribution, and average annual percent growth: Selected calendar years 1960–2009.* Retrieved from https://www.cms.gov/Research-Statistics-Data-and-Systems/Statistics-Trends-and-Reports/NationalHealthExpendData/NationalHealthAccountsHistorical.html

Cohen, S. & Yu, W. (2012, January). *The Concentration and persistence in the level of health expenditures over time: Estimates for the U.S. population, 2008–2009.* Statistical Brief #354. Rockville, MD: Agency for Healthcare Research and Quality. Retrieved from http://www.meps.ahrq.gov/mepsweb/data_files/publications/st354/stat354.pdf

Damler, R. (2009, August). *Experience under the Healthy Indiana Plan: The short-term cost challenges of expanding coverage to the uninsured. Milliman Health Reform Briefing Paper.* Indianapolis, IN: Milliman. Retrieved from http://www.milliman.com

Diamond, J. M. (1997). *Guns, germs, and steel: The fates of human societies.* New York, NY: W.W. Norton.

Douglas, K. (2010, July–August). Taking action to close the nurse-finance gap: Learning from success. *Nursing Economics, 28*(4), 270–272.

Eckhart, J. G. (1993, March–April). Costing out nursing services: Examining the research. *Nursing Economics, 11*(2), 91–98.

Federal Trade Commission (FTC). (2011, April). *The FTC in 2011. Federal Trade Commission Annual Report, April 2011*. Washington, DC: FTC. Retrieved from http://ftc.gov/os/2011/04/2011ChairmansReport.pdf

Galewitz, P., & Serafini, M. W. (2012, June 28). *Ruling puts pressure on states to act. KHN Kaiser Health News Judging the Health Law. Henry J. Kaiser Family Foundation*. Retrieved from http://www.kaiserhealthnews.org/Stories/2012/June/28/pressure-on-states-to-act-after-supreme-court-ruling.aspx

Harrison, J. P., & McLane, C. G. (2005, September–October). The Importance of level 1 trauma services in U.S. hospitals. *Nursing Economics, 23*(5), 223–232.

Health Care Financing Review (HCFR). (2005–2006, Winter). Key milestones in Medicare and Medicaid history, selected years: 1965–2003. *Health Care Financing Review, 27*(2), 1–3.

Hirsch, B. T., & Schumacher, E. J. (2005). Classic or new monopsony? Searching for evidence in nursing labor markets. *Journal of Health Economics, 24*(5), 969–989.

Holt, M. F., Holt, M. F., Schlesinger, A. M., & Wilentz, S. (2010). *Franklin Pierce*. Macmillan.

Institute of Medicine (IOM). (2011). *The future of nursing: Leading change, advancing health.* Committee on the Robert Wood Johnson Foundation Initiative on the Future of Nursing, at the Institute of Medicine. Washington, DC: The National Academies Press. Retrieved from http://www.nap.edu/catalog/12956.html

Leonhardt, D. (2009). Health Care History 101. Retrieved at http://economix.blogs.nytimes.com/2009/11/05/health-care-history-101

Mankiw, N. G. (2011). *Principles of economics* (6th ed.). Mason, OH: South-Western College Publications.

Patient Protection and Affordable Care Act (PPACA), Pub. L. No. 111–148, §2702, 124 Stat. 119, 318–319 (2010). Retrieved from http://housedocs.house.gov/energycommerce/ppacacon.pdf

Penner, S. J. (1987, May). The remarkable Miss Nightingale. *The Kansas Nurse, 62*, cover and p. 11.

Phelps, C. (2009). *Health economics*. New York, NY: Pearson-Addison Wesley.

Polinski, J., Kilabuk, E., Schneeweiss, S., Brennan, T., & Shrank, W. (2010). Changes in drug use and out-of-pocket costs associated with Medicare Part D implementation: A systematic review. *Journal of The American Geriatrics Society, 58*(9), 1764–1779.

PwC Health Research Institute (PwC). (2011, November). *Top health industry issues of 2012: Connecting in uncertainty*. New York, NY: PricewaterhouseCoopers LLP. Retrieved at http://www.pwc.com/us/en/health-industries/publications/top-health-industry-issues-of-2012.jhtml

Reinhardt, U. E. (2011). The Money Flow from Households to Health Care Providers. Retrieved at http://economix.blogs.nytimes.com/2011/09/30/the-money-flow-from-households-to-health-care-providers

Skinner, J. S., Gottlieb, D. J., & Carmichael, D. (2011, June 21). *A new series of medicare expenditure measures by hospital referral region: 2003–2008. A report of the Dartmouth Atlas Project, The Dartmouth Institute for Health Policy & Clinical Practice*. Hanover, NH: The Dartmouth Institute for Health Policy & Clinical Practice.

Staiger, D. O., Auerbach, D. I., & Buerhaus, P. I. (2012, March 22). Registered nurse labor supply and the recession—Are we in a bubble? *The New England Journal of Medicine, 366*, 1463–1465. Retrieved from http://www.nejm.org

Truman Library. (2011, December 12). *This Day in Truman History—November 19, 1945—President Truman's Proposed Health Program. The Harry S. Truman Library and Museum website, administered by The U.S. National Archives and Records Administration*. Retrieved at http://www.trumanlibrary.org/anniversaries/healthprogram.htm

US Bureau of Labor Statistics (BLS). (2010, February 2). *Career guide to industries, 2010–11 edition: Healthcare*. Retrieved at http://www.bls.gov/oco/cg/cgs035.htm

U.S. Government Accountability Office (GAO). (2011, September). *Health care price transparency: Meaningful price information is difficult for consumers to obtain prior to receiving care. Report to Congressional Requesters*. GAO-11–791. Washington, DC: GAO. Retrieved from http://www.gao.gov

World Health Organization (WHO). (2011). *Global status report on non-communicable diseases 2010*. Geneva, Switzerland: WHO Press.

CROSSWORD: *Chapter 1—Economics*

Across

1 The quantity of a product for which consumers are able and willing to pay at a given price over a specified time period.

3 Resources and raw materials needed for production.

6 Resource or expense required as input to produce goods or services.

8 Making information available, such as health care pricing.

11 When one party has control over production, thus controlling price.

12 A group of workers attempting to influence market power in a labor market by bargaining with the employers.

14 A group of buyers and sellers of products such as goods and services.

15 Excess supply resulting from the market price for a product rising to a level higher than the equilibrium price.

16 A product that is similar to and reduces demand for another product.

Down

2 Costs of production not borne by the producer, or costs of consumption not paid for by the consumer.

4 Maximizing the production or value of goods or services while minimizing the resources or costs required for production.

5 When one party has control over consumption of a product, thus controlling price.

7 The quantity of a product that producers are able and willing to produce and sell at a given price over a specific time period.

8 Activities, processes, or work applied to inputs in order to achieve outputs.

9 Excess demand resulting from the market price for a product falling to a level lower than the equilibrium price.

10 Business agreements or practices that restrict free trade and are often illegal.

13 Goods, services, or other outcomes produced from inputs and throughputs.

Chapter 2: Health Insurance and Fee-for-Service Financing

There are worse things in life than death. Have you ever spent an evening with an insurance salesman?—Woody Allen

Learning Objectives

1. Analyze at least two problems related to the high number of uninsured Americans in the United States.
2. Explain at least one reason why the passage of Medicare and Medicaid led to increased health costs.
3. Point out at least two ways that financial incentives can make consumers either more or less aware of health care costs.
4. Compare the cost concerns of health care providers to the cost concerns of health insurance plans.

Key Terms

actuarial

adverse selection

advertising

agent

align incentives

allowable costs

area wage index (AWI)

asymmetric information

bad debt

benefits management

capital

case mix index (CMI)

charge-based reimbursement

coinsurance

community rating

conflict of interest

consumer-driven health plans (CDHPs)

copayment

cost-based reimbursement

cost-sharing

cost-shifting

deductible

defensive medicine

discounted charge

disproportionate share hospitals (DSHs)

dual eligibles

entitlement

experience rating

fee-for-service (FFS)

flexible spending account (FSA)

health reimbursement arrangement (HRA)

health savings account (HSA)

high-deductible health plans (HDHPs)

Hospital Insurance (HI)

hospital-acquired conditions (HACs)

incentives

information problems

Medicare Advantage (MA)

Medicare Advantage prescription drug plans (MA-PDPs)

Medicare Part A

Medicare Part B

Medicare Part C

Medicare Part D

Medicare severity diagnosis-related groups (MS-DRGs)

Medigap insurance

moral hazard

negotiated charges

outlier

per diem

preexisting condition clause

prescription drug plan (PDP)

principal

prospective payment

reimbursement

retrospective payment

risk

risk pooling

Supplementary Medical Insurance (SMI)

supplier-induced demand

third-party payers

volume-based

Nurses care for patients who may be insured or uninsured. Some of these patients or their families may seek advice about health insurance choices or coverage from their nurse. Americans face growing concerns about health care coverage, including how to pay for health care, both as individuals and as a nation. A basic understanding of the principles of health insurance and health care financing is therefore important for nurses. This chapter builds on the concepts presented in Chapter 1. This chapter is also linked to Chapter 3, which discusses managed care and other alternatives to traditional ways that U.S. health care has been reimbursed over the years.

HEALTH CARE COVERAGE AND THE UNINSURED

In 2010, an estimated 49% of Americans had employer-sponsored health insurance. An estimated 5% of Americans were covered by private nongroup insurance, 12% by Medicare, and 17% by Medicaid and other government programs. An estimated 16% of the population was uninsured in 2010, representing 49.9 million Americans without health insurance. By comparison, in 2001, a little over 38 million Americans (13.5%) were uninsured (DeNavas-Walt, Proctor, & Smith, 2011).

Only about 792,000 of the uninsured in 2010 were elderly. Most of the uninsured in 2010, 41.1 million, were under age 65. Nearly one in five Americans under age 65 (18.5%) were uninsured in 2010 (DeNavas-Walt et al., 2011). A quarter of Americans aged 19 to 64 experienced a gap in their health coverage in 2011, and 69% of these persons were without coverage for a year or longer (Collins, Robertson, Garber, & Doty, 2012). Concerns about the lack of health insurance are serious and growing throughout the United States.

The lack of health insurance has implications for health and mortality. In 2006, near-elderly Americans (ages 55–64) were less likely to have health insurance, but more likely to have at least one chronic health condition compared to younger adults (Vistnes, Cooper, Bernard, & Banthin, 2009). In addition, the expansion of insurance programs such as Medicaid is found to reduce mortality rates and improve self-report health ratings of "excellent" or "very good" health (Sommers, Baicker, & Epstein, 2012).

Another study of the near-elderly estimated that there were 3.5 million uninsured persons aged 55 to 64 in 2002. The researchers predicted that for the years 2003 to 2010, more than 105,000 excess deaths (over 13,000 deaths a year) would be attributed to the lack of health insurance among these near-elderly Americans. This would make the lack of insurance coverage the third leading cause of death for persons aged 55 to 64, only surpassed by heart disease and cancer. The near-elderly age group is expected to double to 61.9 million, or nearly one in five Americans, by 2015, so the lack of insurance in this age group has considerable health impact (McWilliams, Zaslavsky, Meara, & Ayanian, 2004).

Concerns about the health impact of being uninsured are not limited to the near-elderly. In 2000, an estimated 18,000 Americans between the ages of 25 and 64 died because they lacked health coverage. A similar study found that, in 2010, an estimated 26,100 Americans age 25 to 64 died prematurely from the lack of health insurance, a rate of three Americans every hour. The uninsured often cannot find a source of primary care other than emergency rooms, and are more likely to delay or forgo preventive care such as mammograms than insured populations. Cancer patients without insurance are five times more likely to delay cancer care because of costs than insured patients (Bailey, 2012).

The lack of health insurance is not just a problem of the poor. In 2009, nearly one in three (32%) Americans aged 18 to 64 with family incomes two to three times the poverty level did not have health insurance for part of the preceding year. More than one in five (21%) Americans aged 18 to 64 with family incomes three to four times the poverty level went without health insurance for part of the preceding year in 2009. Increasing numbers of Americans at middle income levels are uninsured, and delay or forgo needed medical care as a result (Fox & Richards, 2010).

People who are uninsured face financial as well as medical health risks. In 2010, three out of five uninsured adults (60%) under the age of 65 reported problems with medical bills or medical debt (Bailey, 2012). In the first half of 2011, one in three persons in the United States were in a family that reported their medical bills as a financial burden (Cohen, Gindi, & Kirzinger, 2012). More than one in 10 of the nation's elderly (10.3%) reported medical bill problems in 2010 (Sommers & Cunningham, 2011).

Middle income uninsured persons may not qualify for charity care, and would be better off financially as well as medically from health insurance coverage (Penner, Penner, Verkade, & Brooks, 2002). The Association of Credit and Collection Professionals provides more statistics on medical debt, medical costs, insurance coverage, and related topics at the Health Care Collection Statistics website (www.acainternational.org).

Government policies to address the problems of the uninsured may lead to inefficiencies and higher costs of care. For example, the Emergency Medical Treatment & Labor Act (EMTALA) was enacted as part of the Consolidated Omnibus Budget Reconciliation Act of 1986 (COBRA) legislation. EMTALA requires that patients coming to hospital emergency rooms receive evaluation and treatment until stable or appropriately transferred. One consequence is that EMTALA makes emergency rooms the safety net health provider for many Americans, including the growing number of uninsured. Access to less costly preventive services provided in an outpatient medical center could reduce the over-use of costly emergency room services for primary care. More information about EMTALA is available at the CMS.gov Emergency Medical Treatment & Labor Act website (www.cms.gov).

FLOW OF HEALTH CARE FUNDING, 2010

Figure 2.1 features pie charts that explain the sources of health care dollars for 2010. Nearly three-fourths of U.S. health care funding is from public or private insurance plans. Private insurance accounts for a third (33%) of health care funding. Government sources account for over 42% of health care funding, including government insurance programs, public health activities, and publicly funded third-party programs. Most of the government sources come from Medicare, Medicaid, and other government insurance programs that account for 39% of health care funding. Nearly one in eight health care dollars (12%) comes from personal out-of-pocket payments.

Figure 2.2 features pie charts that explain how health care dollars were spent in 2010. Nearly a third of health care spending (31%) goes to hospital services. One in five dollars spent on health care (20%) is for physician and clinic services. Spending on prescription drugs accounts for one in 10 (10%) dollars of health expenditures. These charts reinforce the importance of private and public insurance programs as sources of funding for hospital, physician, and other health care services.

HEALTH INSURANCE HISTORY AND COSTS

As reviewed in Chapter 1, before the late 19th century, health care was largely provided by one's family, within one's immediate social setting, and later, in Europe and the United States, through charitable religious groups. During the Industrial Revolution, donations from factory owners or workers provided money for ill or injured workers and their dependents. In some industries, "sickness funds" were created, and some factory and other industrial owners began hiring "company doctors." Throughout the late 1800s and early 1900s, national health plans were established throughout most industrialized European countries.

In the United States, the government at all levels (federal, state, and local) played a much smaller role in financing and insuring health care than in many other industrialized nations. It was not until the economic upheaval of the Great Depression during the 1930s that health insurance began to gain popularity. One early plan was the nonprofit enterprise, Blue Cross, which began providing group health insurance plans for hospitalization. By covering groups such as employees of large companies instead of individuals, hospitalization plans could spread health care costs across a population of predominantly healthy consumers paying the plan's premiums.

Hospitals benefited from hospitalization insurance plans such as Blue Cross, because rather than their historical reliance on charity from religious groups and donors, hospital operators could now bill for services. The 1930s represented the beginning of the use of many technologies such as improved sanitation, surgical techniques, and diagnostic equipment. Hospitalization insurance helped hospitals fund these new technologies, attract physicians, and establish a reputation as a place to be treated and cured.

Other health insurance plans, such as Blue Shield, arose to provide coverage for physician care. Although physicians historically charged fees for their services, this greater certainty of payment greatly enhanced the financial status of physicians. The establishment of medical societies increased the political power of physicians compared to other health care professionals. Political power also enabled physicians to maintain fee-based payment systems and to successfully oppose alternative financing strategies such as prepaid health plans.

Tax exemptions for employers and employees enacted during World War II stimulated the growth of employer-sponsored health insurance in the United States. The Social Security

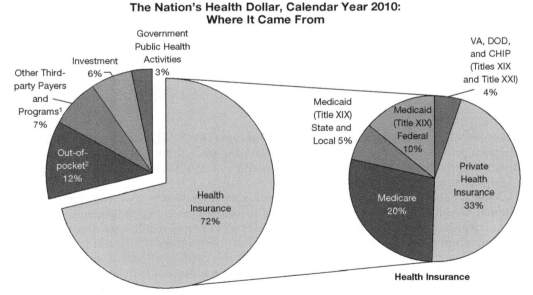

The Nation's Health Dollar, Calendar Year 2010: Where It Came From

[1] Includes worksite health care, other private revenues, Indian Health Service, workers' compensation, general assistance, maternal and child health, vocational rehabilitation, Substance Abuse and Mental Health Services Administration, school health, and other federal and state local programs.
[2] Includes co-payments, deductibles, and any amounts not covered by health insurance.
Note: Sum of pieces may not equal 100% due to rounding.

Figure 2.1 *Sources of U.S. Health Care Financing, 2010*

Source: CMS.gov. Retrieved July 2, 2012 at http://www.cms.gov/Research-Statistics-Data-and-Systems/Statistics-Trends-and-Reports/ NationalHealthExpendData/Downloads/PieChartSourcesExpenditures2010.pdf

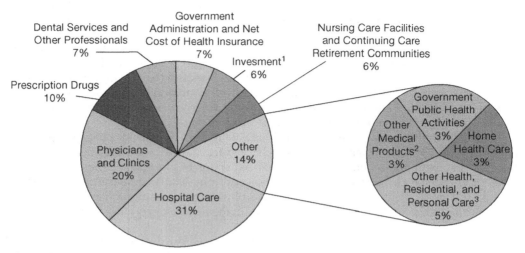

The Nation's Health Dollar ($2.6 Trillion), Calender Year 2010: Where It Went

[1] Includes research (2%) and structures and equipment (4%).

[2] Includes durable (1%) and non-durable (2%) goods.

[3] Includes expenditures for residential care facilities, ambulance providers, medical care delivered in non-traditional settings (such as community centers, senior citizens centers, schools, and military fields stations), and expenditures for Home and Community Waiver programs under Medicaid.

Note: Sum of pieces may not equal 100% due to rounding.

Figure 2.2 *U.S. Health Expenditures, 2010*

Source: CMS.gov. Retrieved July 2, 2012 at http://www.cms.gov/Research-Statistics-Data-and-Systems/Statistics-Trends-and-Reports/NationalHealthExpendData/Downloads/PieChartSourcesExpenditures2010.pdf

Acts of 1965 that established and financed the Medicare (Title XVIII) and Medicaid (Title XIX) programs provide coverage for elderly Americans and poor American families. The lack of sufficient utilization and cost controls in these private and public health plans led to rapidly soaring increases in health care costs.

Table 2.1 shows national health expenditures for each decade year from 1960 to 2010. National health expenditures include all health consumption expenditures and investments. Health consumption expenditures include all personal health care spending, government administration and net cost of private health insurance (PHI), and public health activities. Personal health expenditures represent the costs of all goods and services to prevent or treat disease in a particular person, such as hospital care and physician services. Investment represents the costs of research, construction, and **capital** equipment purchases. Price inflation estimates are incorporated in these data (Centers for Medicare & Medicaid Services, 2010).

From 1960 to 2010, per capita health care spending increased from US $147 to US $8402 (Table 2.1). Health care expenditures also grew at a higher rate than the overall U.S. economy (GDP) in each of these decade years except 2010. National health expenditures as a percentage of the GDP rose from 5.2% in 1960 to 17.9% in 2010. It is clear that health care costs pose financial concerns to the nation and nation's economy, as well as to individual Americans. More details about U.S. national health expenditures are available at the CMS National Health Expenditure Data website (www.cms.gov).

Table 2.1 *National Health Expenditures Summary and GDP: 1960–2010*

	1960	1970	1980	1990	2000	2010
Levels in billions						
National health expenditure	27	75	256	724	1377	2594
Health consumption expenditure	25	67	236	676	1290	2445
Personal health care	23	63	217	617	1165	2186
Admin and net cost of PHI*	1	3	12	39	81	176
Public health	0	1	6	20	43	82
Investment	3	8	20	49	88	149
Per capita amounts						
National health expenditure	147	356	1110	2854	4878	8402
Health consumption expenditure	133	319	1023	2662	4568	7919
Personal health care	125	300	943	2430	4128	7082
Admin and net cost of PHI*	6	12	52	153	288	570
Public health	2	6	28	79	152	267
Investment	14	37	87	192	310	483
Annual % change						
U.S. population		1.2	1.0	1.2	1.0	0.8
Gross domestic product (GDP)		5.5	8.8	5.8	6.4	4.2
National health expenditure		13	15.4	11.9	7.0	3.9
Health consumption expenditure		13.5	15.2	11.9	7.4	4.0
Personal health care		13.6	16	11.8	6.9	3.7
Admin and net cost of PHI*		9.1	0	13.8	15.1	7.2
Public health		15.5	19.9	12.5	5.5	8.2
Investment		9.5	18.2	10.7	2.4	1.9
U.S. population in millions	186	210	230	254	282	309
GDP in billions	526	1038	2788	5801	9952	14,527
National health exp. share of GDP	5.2	7.2	9.2	12.5	13.8	17.9

*private health insurance.

Source: Centers for Medicare & Medicaid Services, Office of the Actuary, National Health Statistics Group; U.S. Department of Commerce, Bureau of Economic Analysis; U.S. Bureau of the Census.

PRIVATE INSURANCE AND COST CONCERNS

As shown in Figure 2.1, nearly half of all health insurance in the United States is provided by private insurance. In 2011, employer-sponsored plans covered 150 million people in the United States, over 90% of the private insurance market. Employer-sponsored retiree health benefits are also an important supplement to Medicare for many Americans over age 65 (Haviland, Marquis, McDevitt, & Sood, 2012; Kaiser Family Foundation and Health Research & Educational Trust [KFF], 2011). However, employers find it increasingly difficult to manage rising health costs, putting employer-sponsored health insurance at risk (Galvin & Delbanco, 2006).

Rising health costs borne by employer-sponsored health plans are in part related to rising health costs in government insurance programs. One way that Medicare and Medicaid control costs is to limit their reimbursement rates. As a result, for most years between 1990 and 2010, hospital reimbursement fell below the cost of patient care. For example, in 2010, the Medicare payment-to-cost ratio for U.S. community hospitals was 92.4%, or 7.6% below costs. The 2010 Medicaid payment-to-cost ratio for U.S. community hospitals was 92.8%, or 7.2% below costs (American Hospital Association [AHA], 2012).

The strategy of controlling costs by limiting Medicare and Medicaid hospital reimbursement results in **cost-shifting**, or passing the costs from one party to another. While Medicare and Medicaid payment-to-cost ratios are frequently below the cost of patient care, private payer payment-to-cost ratios consistently exceed the hospital's costs. For example, in 2010, the private payer payment-to-cost ratio was 133.5%, or 33.5% greater than the hospital's costs. In addition, when the payment-to-cost ratios for Medicare and Medicaid rise to 100% (full payment of costs) or greater, the private payer ratios decline (AHA, 2012). Private payers, including employer-sponsored health plans, increase their premiums to cover these added costs passed on by hospitals and other providers. Health coverage therefore becomes less affordable both for U.S. employers and their employees.

Additional reasons for rising health costs affecting private insurance are discussed in following sections of this chapter. Insurance coverage can lead consumers and providers to become insensitive to the costs of health care. The way that payers design payment systems and insurance plans can influence consumers and providers to be more or less cost-aware.

HEALTHY OR UNHEALTHY?

Throughout this chapter individuals or populations are referred to as "healthy" or "unhealthy." Unhealthy individuals or populations include people who currently suffer from health problems, or who are at greater risk for health problems or higher health costs. Unhealthy individuals or populations may be identified by:

- demographic variables, such as persons over age 65
- epidemiological findings and measures of health status, such as immunization rates
- health risks and health behaviors, such as family history of diabetes

Other individuals or populations may be considered healthy. The determination of health is often relative. Measures of health status for one population may be compared to another population to distinguish between populations that are healthy or unhealthy. An example of health status measures for counties in the United States is available at the County Health Rankings website (www.countyhealthrankings.org).

Many believe that healthy people require less health insurance coverage than unhealthy people, or that healthy people can manage with no insurance coverage at all. However, nurses know that there is a probability that healthy persons can become unhealthy, and can suddenly face high health costs. An injury or onset of a previously asymptomatic disorder can shift apparently healthy people into the unhealthy category. In addition, people need access to appropriate preventive care. For example, an otherwise healthy child requires immunizations from communicable diseases that could result in serious illness, disability, and possibly death.

In purely competitive markets, consumers are able to make rational choices based on complete information. However, as discussed in Chapter 1, the health care market is not purely competitive. The risks any individual faces for health problems that could be serious and costly limits the ability of consumers to rationally choose to forgo health care coverage. Discussions in this chapter may refer to the needs or behaviors of healthy or unhealthy individuals or populations. However, affordable health coverage is assumed to be needed by all individuals, regardless of their current health status.

REIMBURSEMENT MECHANISMS

This discussion of reimbursement mechanisms or payment strategies in health care largely focuses on hospital reimbursement. Hospital care often presents the highest costs to payers, compared to physicians, other outpatient care, or other sources of health care costs (Figure 2.2). Chapter 3 discusses physician reimbursement related to managed care strategies. Chapter 12 discusses reimbursement and revenue management for small practices.

Charges, costs, and reimbursement. The terms charges, costs, and reimbursement are often used in discussing health care financing. The **charge**, also referred to as the list or published price, represents the full price before any reductions are applied. A provider may charge $1000 for a given procedure. **Costs** represent the expenses incurred by the provider in producing the good or service. The procedure may cost the provider $700 to perform.

Reimbursement, or payment made for a good or service, is the actual amount the provider receives from the payer. In health care settings, the reimbursement for the procedure varies based on the payer and on criteria payers may establish for payment. Reimbursement for the procedure might be as high as the full $1000 charge. Other payers might reimburse less than the charge but more than costs, at some amount between $700 and $1000. Some payers reimburse at levels less than the cost to providers. The reimbursement may fall to $0 if the charge is denied by an insurance plan or if the consumer has no insurance and is unable to pay the charge. Charges, costs, and reimbursement are therefore often quite different amounts in health care financing.

Third-party payers. The source of most health care reimbursement is from **third-party payers**, entities that pay on behalf of another party, such as a health plan paying costs for a plan member's care. Government third-party payers include the Medicare and Medicaid programs. Major sources of nongovernmental third-party reimbursement include private commercial health insurance and managed care plans. Reimbursement for managed care plans is explained in Chapter 3.

There are benefits to all parties involved in third-party transactions in health care insurance markets. Consumers benefit from lower insurance premiums because the risk of high costs from a catastrophic health event are spread (pooled) across a large group, rather than borne by the individual. Providers are assured that their claims will be paid. In addition, providers have a greater volume of utilization because consumers have insurance coverage, so third-party transactions are profitable for providers. Insurers gain from third-party transactions because private insurance enterprises are profitable. Government insurers benefit because citizens value government insurance services.

Self-pay. Reimbursement for persons who do not have insurance coverage is known as self-pay, also referred to as private pay. Many individuals who do not have health insurance are not able to pay their medical bills, or to pay their bills in full. These unpaid bills may go to collection agencies, hurting the patient's credit rating and in some cases leading to bankruptcy (Sommers & Cunningham, 2011).

Uninsured patients are often unable to negotiate discounts to charges. Therefore, uninsured patients may be charged more for health care than insured patients, because health plans frequently negotiate discounts with providers (Bailey, 2012). Concerns about hospital pricing fairness for self-pay patients have led some states to enact fair pricing laws. Details about California's fair pricing law are available at the Hospital Fair Pricing Policies website (www.oshpd.ca.gov).

The Patient Protection and Affordable Care Act (PPACA) contains provisions enacted in March 2012 for nonprofit hospitals to charge patients who are eligible for financial assistance a price comparable to charges made to insured patients. The PPACA also requires nonprofit hospitals to establish policies for financial assistance and for charges made for emergency care. In addition, these hospitals must determine whether patients are eligible for financial assistance before engaging in aggressive collection actions such as lawsuits or liens on homes (Patient Protection and Affordable Care Act [PPACA], 2010).

Retrospective Payment and Fee-for-Service Financing

Retrospective payment is reimbursement paid to the provider after health care services are provided. This reimbursement strategy is probably the oldest payment method in health care, based on the historical practice of physicians charging fees for care provided to their patients. One approach to retrospective payment is **charge-based reimbursement**, in which the provider bills the payer for the full charges of the good or service. The charge-based reimbursement system is similar to many other purchases made by consumers, such as for clothing or groceries.

A similar approach is **cost-based reimbursement**, in which the payer agrees to pay **allowable costs**, or costs directly related to providing an acceptable standard of health services. Medicare used the cost-based reimbursement payment approach for hospitals until the early 1980s, when the prospective payment system was introduced.

Charge-based reimbursement and cost-based reimbursement payment mechanisms led to spiraling health costs providers billed payers with no negotiation or review. An increasingly common reimbursement approach that attempts to better control costs is **negotiated charges,** in which the payer negotiates a reduced rate that is less than the charge, or an enhanced level of care for the rate reimbursed to the provider. Many private health plans, including managed care plans, reimburse using negotiated charges.

A **discounted charge** differs from a negotiated charge because it is a nonnegotiated flat fee reimbursed by the payer that is less than the provider's full charge. Government-sponsored health plans often use discounted charges for reimbursement. Medicaid reimbursement is an example of discounting. Another example of discounted charges is Medicare reimbursement.

Fee-for-Service Reimbursement System

Fee-for-service (FFS) reimbursement is a term used for retrospective payment of all allowable costs meeting accepted standards of care. Providers bill payers using an itemized list of charges, and are reimbursed based on the volume of patients or services. Physicians are typically reimbursed based on their charges (which are often negotiated or discounted) or on some predetermined fee schedule such as the Resource-Based Relative Value Scale (RBRVS). Hospitals are typically reimbursed based on charges, **per diem** (a set amount of reimbursement per patient day), or per case (Cleverley & Cameron, 2002).

The FFS reimbursement system is based on the assumption that both the insured consumers and the providers billing insurance will be prudent users of health care services. However, the FFS system makes consumers insensitive to the costs of health care, because the assumption is that the insurer will pay any claims that are submitted, so the consumer can demand services that might be medically unnecessary. FFS health plans also allow consumers to freely choose providers, including more costly specialists, without determining the necessity of specialist care.

FFS can make providers insensitive to costs as well. FFS is a **volume-based** payment system, in which reimbursement is tied to utilization or the number of patients or patient services provided. More patient visits or procedures lead to greater reimbursement for physicians and other outpatient providers. The same is true for hospital readmissions and for patient length of stay, because hospitals receive more reimbursement for generating more volume in FFS systems.

Hospitals also have high fixed costs that do not change in proportion to changes in utilization. As a result, under FFS systems, if hospitals reduce their volume, they lose reimbursement, but do not reduce their costs proportionately. Miller (2012) points out that under FFS, a 20% reduction in hospital volume results in close to a 20% reduction in hospital revenue, but only a 7% reduction in costs.

FFS systems encourage cost-shifting. Unlike other markets, in the health care market there are many consumers who receive goods and services, but cannot or do not pay for them. Many uninsured and self-pay patients only pay part of their medical bills, or do not pay them at all. In traditional FFS systems, providers increase their charges so that insurance reimbursement covers these unpaid bills. The cost is thus shifted to the insurance plan, and to insured consumers who must pay higher premiums because their health plan is covering these added costs.

Another problem is that FFS may encourage providers to increase the intensity of services. Insurance plans with FFS systems typically pay claims only when there is a diagnosis provided. As a result, this reimbursement approach may discourage the use of preventive services when there are no symptoms of health problems. Better coverage is provided for more intensive services such as hospitalization, rather than efforts to improve wellness. Under FFS, physicians may be rewarded for hospitalizing patients, and hospitals may be rewarded for keeping patients hospitalized as long as is reasonably possible (Shi & Singh, 2008). In addition, under FFS, provider claims often do not undergo review unless there is reason to suspect fraud. Costs are thus largely uncontrolled under traditional FFS insurance plans.

It is important for nurses to understand how the FFS reimbursement system works. For many years, the FFS system has dominated U.S. health care financing. Physicians and medical societies have used their political power to block other financing mechanisms such as prepaid health plans. Medicare and Medicaid were enacted with strong provisions requiring FFS reimbursement. It was not until health care costs rose rapidly in the 1970s that alternative financing strategies such as managed care plans were implemented.

FFS is also supported by many consumers of health care services. Consumers value the ability to freely choose their providers without restriction. Consumers also want to be able to access health care without waiting for prior authorization for services, such as elective surgeries. FFS is a financing system with which many consumers are familiar and comfortable using. Many consumers fear losing the providers they have chosen, and fear that restrictions implemented in financing systems such as managed care will lead to poorer quality care. As a result, FFS has strong public as well as provider support, despite widespread concerns about health care costs.

It is important to note that the traditional charge-based or cost-based FFS reimbursement systems have been largely replaced with other payment mechanisms that attempt to better control costs. Health plans increasingly establish per diem rates based on a patient's diagnosis, or negotiate discounted hospital rates. Health plans may limit or refuse payment for excessive length of stay or preventable complications. Provider claims undergo rigorous review and reimbursement may be denied if services are not supported as medically necessary. Alternative payment systems, including managed care, discussed in Chapter 3, and prospective payment, discussed in the next section, apply strategies to reduce overutilization of services and better control costs.

Prospective Payment

Prospective payment uses fixed reimbursement rates that are established prior to the provision of services, based on standard expectation of average length of stay and costs based on diagnostic categories, the amount of nursing care required, and other factors. If providers cannot manage the patient's care within the prospective payment rates, they face financial loss. Prospective payment is the reimbursement approach used by the Centers for Medicare and Medicaid Services (CMS) and some private insurance companies to reduce the growth in health care costs that can result from the fee-for-service reimbursement system.

Medicare prospective payment originated in 1983 to address problems with cost-based hospital reimbursement. Prospective payment systems now extend to skilled nursing care facilities and home health care. The following discussion describes prospective payment financing for acute care hospitals. Updated explanations of payment systems for other providers reimbursed by CMS, including home health, skilled nursing care, and physicians, is available at the MedPAC Payment Basics website (www.medpac.gov).

Diagnosis-related groups. Medicare established the Inpatient Prospective Payment System (IPPS) in 1983 using diagnosis-related groups (DRGs). The DRGs group medical conditions or surgeries according to the reason for hospital admission, procedures provided, and patient complications or comorbidities that occur during the hospital stay. This approach of grouping patients with similar medical or surgical conditions that are expected to consume similar amounts of hospital resources continues, with some changes implemented in 2008.

In 2008, the Centers for Medicare and Medicaid Services (CMS) transitioned from DRGs to **Medicare severity diagnosis-related groups (MS-DRGs)**. As was the case with DRGs, each of the 745 MS-DRGs are assigned a weight based on the relative cost, across all participating hospitals, for treating cases classified within that MS-DRG. The hospital is reimbursed a predetermined payment for each Medicare case.

One important difference between DRGs and MS-DRGs is that, as of October 1, 2008, secondary diagnoses identified as preventable **hospital-acquired conditions (HACs)** might not be reimbursed if the condition is not present upon hospital admission. CMS implemented further refinements to the HAC provisions in 2009, and in 2010 included financial penalties for selected preventable 30-day hospital readmissions (Hackbarth, 2008).

Case mix index. The MS-DRG relative weights are summed and divided by the number of patients to assign a **case mix index (CMI)** to each hospital each year. A CMI of 1.0 indicates the hospital's relative costs are average. A higher CMI indicates a greater complexity of patient care and a greater amount of resources required for patient care (Beaty, 2005). CMS makes higher payments to some qualifying rural and urban hospitals based on their case mix. Hospital CMIs are available at the CMS.gov Case Mix Index website (www.cms.gov).

Base IPPS payments. CMS establishes a base or standardized payment amount for each patient discharge that represents the costs that efficient hospitals would be expected to incur in providing inpatient services. The base payment is separated into operating and capital payments. Operating payments are intended to cover day-to-day expenses such as the costs of labor and supplies. Capital payments cover long-term or fixed expenses such as rent and equipment. For 2012, the operating payment is $5210 and the capital payment is $421. Adjustments are then applied the operating and capital payments (MedPac, 2011).

Area wage index. CMS adjusts the operating base payment using the **area wage index (AWI)**. The AWI adjusts for differences in wage rates across geographic areas of the United States, and is updated each year (MedPac, 2011). An AWI greater than 1.0 indicates higher than average cost of living and salaries, and an AWI less than 1.0 indicates a lower than average cost of living and salaries. More details about the AWI, and files with the AWI for U.S. hospitals, are available at the CMS.gov Wage Index website (www.cms.gov).

Figure 2.3 shows how the operating base payment is adjusted depending on whether the AWI is less than or equal to 1.0 or whether the AWI is greater than 1.0. The full amount of the operating base payment is not adjusted for AWI, because factors other than area wage differences account for hospital operating costs. Additional payments are made to hospitals using some types of new technologies for patient treatment. A portion of a hospital's **bad debt** or uncollected bills from Medicare recipients is also reimbursed by CMS. The operating base payment is further adjusted using the MS-DRG relative weight, as shown in Figure 2.3 (MedPac, 2011).

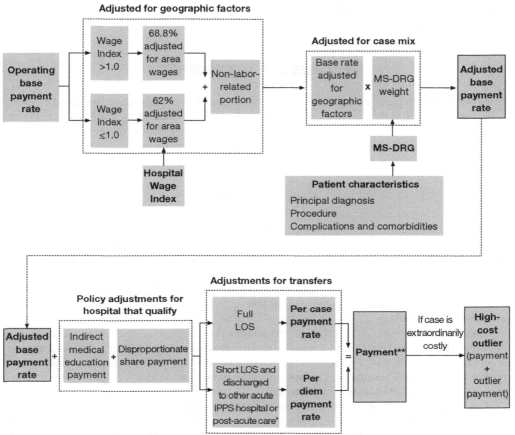

Figure 2.3 *Medicare Acute Inpatient Prospective Payment System Flow Chart, 2011*

Source: MedPac. (2011). Hospital acute inpatient services payment system (*payment*basics) http://www.medpac.gov/payment_basics.cfm

Medical education and disproportionate share payments. Figure 2.3 shows that qualifying hospitals have further adjustments to their payment rates. Some of the costs of medical education are added as an adjustment to the operating payment rate for teaching hospitals. **Disproportionate share hospitals (DSHs)** that serve a higher proportion of low-income patients receive adjustments to increase their operating and capital payment rates. Payment rates are reduced for certain cases that are transferred, and rates are increased for unusually costly **outlier** cases. The resulting rate is assumed to cover the costs of high quality care provided by reasonably efficient hospitals (MedPac, 2011).

One problem with the IPPS is that higher payments for some MS-DRGs compared to others may lead to financial incentives for hospitals to increase the volume of more profitable diagnoses. The incentives for more profitable diagnoses increase the potential for fraud, thus requiring careful oversight of claims by health plans. For example, one hospital came under investigation for performing more profitable open-heart surgeries rather than medically managing patients with heart disease (Dafny, 2003). Fraud is a problem for private health plans as well as government insurance programs such as Medicare. Chapter 13 discusses health care fraud in more detail.

PRINCIPLES OF HEALTH INSURANCE

Principles of health insurance are based on concepts such as information, the predictability of risk, and ways that the insurers may control the costs generated by consumers and providers of health care. Health care plan design may influence the utilization of health care goods and services. This section provides an overview of some fundamental health insurance principles useful to nurses.

Information Problems

In a perfectly competitive market, the buyer and seller possess the same information about the product, the product's price, and any substitute products. In health care settings, consumers, providers, and insurers frequently experience **information problems**. An information problem occurs when consumers, providers, or insurers do not possess enough information to make a rational economic choice. For example, in some situations neither a patient, provider, nor an insurance plan are able to predict the clinical course and costs of a patient's health problem.

Asymmetric information. Health care consumers, providers, and insurers more frequently encounter the related problem of **asymmetric information**. Asymmetric information problems occur when one party possesses knowledge needed for rational decision making that another party lacks. This unequal balance of information can lead to one party possessing a financial advantage over the other parties.

Health care consumers often experience asymmetric information, and are usually not expected to possess as much information as providers to make rational choices. Most patients are unable to adequately diagnose and treat their health problems, or they would not need to seek health care in the first place. The patient is the **principal** lacking the knowledge needed for health care. The principal delegates decision-making authority to the **agent**, or provider who is assumed to possess the necessary knowledge to treat or manage the health problem. In addition, the agent is expected to act in the best interests of the principal. The consumer also assumes that, as an insurance beneficiary, adequate access to health care and the costs of health care are covered by the insurance plan, and may not know about exceptions or exclusions to coverage.

Health care providers may experience problems with asymmetric information. Patients may fail to share important information such as the use of illicit drugs or other health risks. Thus, in some situations patients may possess knowledge needed by the provider.

Insurers also encounter asymmetric information problems. Consumers might know they have a medical condition such as diabetes, but not share this information when joining a health plan. This may encourage consumers to delay purchasing health insurance until they experience or anticipate the need for medical services. Insurers also encounter asymmetric information problems from providers. In the past, under many FFS plans, insurers did not routinely review a provider's claims or charges before authorizing payment. Providers therefore had incentives to bill for care that may not have been medically necessary.

Risk and actuarial estimates. A fundamental principle of insurance markets is that neither the consumer nor the insurer can predict, on an individual basis, when an event that requires insurance reimbursement will occur. For example, when people purchase home or auto insurance, the assumption is that neither they nor their insurer can predict whether or when a fire, theft, or accident may occur. Insurance plans estimate the **risk** or probability of catastrophic events and their associated costs, also known as **actuarial** estimates. The term actuarial is applied to the use of statistical methods to estimate risk for insured populations. Statistics used in preparing actuarial estimates for health plans include the population's age and sex mix, past health care utilization rates, and the past costs for health care.

Asymmetric information problems are important to consider in understanding principles of health insurance compared to other insurance markets. Actuarial estimates based on the best available information are essential for the health plan to establish premiums that consumers pay for their insurance. Unlike home or auto insurance, consumers may be aware of their past and current health problems or health risks. Some consumers may even plan for health expenditures, such as childbearing.

If consumers do not disclose information about their health problems, the population's risks, utilization, and costs may be higher than estimated by the health plan. If providers are reimbursed for unnecessary care, utilization and costs are also likely to increase more than the actuarial estimates. The health plan must either raise its premiums to cover these additional costs, find a way to control costs, or go out of business.

Risk pooling. Spreading the risk and costs of a catastrophic event such as serious health problems across a specified population is known as **risk pooling**. In general, larger risk pools reduce the probability that any one individual will experience a high-cost catastrophic health event. If the risk pool is drawn from the general population, actuarial estimates should be able to predict the risk of health problems and health care costs. The spread of risk and costs helps to reduce individual insurance premiums, making health plans more competitive, and increasing insurance coverage.

Experience rating. Health plans rate risk pools in order to establish premiums. **Experience rating** is a method used by many traditional indemnity health insurance plans, in which premiums are based on the utilization or claims history of the group, rather than on the characteristics of the community's population as a whole. As a result, a plan year in which a group experiences an unusual number of high-cost claims may result in higher premiums the following year. States may regulate health plans so that premium increases are not excessive, especially for small employers.

Community rating. **Community rating** is a method in which premiums are based on the characteristics of an entire population, not the insured group. In many cases, community ratings are adjusted for age and sex. Younger populations are typically healthier populations, so a health plan for young adults would likely charge lower premiums than for an older group, such as retirees. Over much of the life span, women generate higher health costs than men, so community-rated premiums might also be sex-adjusted.

In some cases, premiums established using community rating might also be adjusted by industry, so that employee groups working in industries with documented health risks that predict increased utilization might be charged higher premiums. States may require community ratings for small employer groups so they have lower and more stable premiums than with experience rating. More information about experience and community rating is available at the What Is A Health Insurance Community Rating? website (www. livestrong.com).

Adverse selection. The over-selection of a health plan based on its coverage of persons likely to have high health care costs is known as **adverse selection**. Adverse selection is related to the asymmetric information problem. When consumers are more knowledgeable about their health status than the insurer, adverse selection may result, because consumers anticipate high health costs that require coverage. Adverse selection may also occur when high-risk pools, such as elderly populations, are established for health care coverage. Adverse selection creates problems both for the insurer and for consumers.

Adverse selection creates financial problems for health plans. For example, a health plan with competitive premiums in the health insurance market attracts a greater proportion of persons at health risk than would be expected in the overall risk pool. As higher premiums drive away lower-risk members and attract more high-risk, high-cost members, the health plan's costs increase at a greater rate than competing health plans. The health plan must raise its premiums, causing healthier plan members who are unable or unwilling to pay these higher premiums to choose a cheaper plan or to become uninsured.

Even when premiums increase, the health plan may continue to attract high-risk individuals. Insurance premiums are likely far less than the self-pay costs of care for these high-risk plan members. Premiums therefore continue to rise as more lower-risk members leave the plan and a higher proportion of higher-cost members participate in the plan.

Adverse selection reduces access to health insurance, thus creating problems for consumers. Healthier individuals cannot afford the higher premiums and may forgo health insurance coverage. Attempts by the health plan to reduce coverage of high-risk individuals may result in these less healthy individuals losing insurance coverage, as well.

Earlier in this chapter a discussion of healthy compared to unhealthy populations concluded that health coverage is beneficial regardless of health status. An additional reason to support coverage for the healthy as well as the unhealthy is that the participation of healthy members in health plan risk pools helps control the costs of premiums. The problem of adverse selection is reduced when healthy individuals or populations join health plans. Health coverage thus not only provides coverage for catastrophic or chronic health problems and for preventive care, but is more financially beneficial when the risk pool includes the healthy as well as the unhealthy.

Preexisting condition. One way health plans attempt to address adverse selection is by implementing a **preexisting condition clause**. The clause requires the consumer to disclose any illnesses or conditions to the health insurance plan upon enrollment. The health plan may limit coverage accordingly, often excluding (dropping) the enrollee from the plan. This practice protects the plan from the consequences of asymmetric information and adverse selection. Preexisting condition clauses prevent unhealthy people from joining health plans based on asymmetric information. However, preexisting condition exclusions also restrict people who require health services from obtaining health coverage, thus intensifying health care access problems.

As of January 1, 2014 the PPACA (2010) will prohibit health plans from denying coverage because of pre-existing conditions. In the individual and small group market, health plans will not be permitted to charge higher rates based on health status. Until 2014, the Pre-Existing Condition Insurance Plan (PCIP) program will provide coverage for uninsured individuals with preexisting conditions.

Moral hazard. As mentioned in Chapter 1, health insurance has a similar effect on health care demand as income. Health plan members can, at least in theory, afford all the health care they require, and are therefore insensitive to health care prices or costs. In FFS financing systems, providers have incentives to increase prices as well as utilization if their claims and charges are paid without restrictions or review. This insensitivity to costs affects incentives and the behavior of health care consumers and providers.

Higher utilization of goods or services by a health plan member or provider is known as **moral hazard**. Unlike adverse selection, the member is not at higher risk for health care utilization and costs. The problem of moral hazard is that because costs are covered by insurance, the member or provider utilizes more health care goods or services than are necessary. For example, a person with vision coverage might purchase new glasses more frequently than necessary because the costs are covered by the plan.

Moral hazard is also a problem when providers are insensitive to costs and recommend more health goods and services than are necessary. Providers have a dual role related to patients. The provider serves as an agent who presumably manages care in the best interests of the patient. The provider is also a producer of health services, billing and profiting from reimbursement.

The provider's roles as agent and producer creates a potential for **conflict of interest**, an ethical discord between two or more desired but opposing circumstances. For example, a provider serving as an agent advises a patient to schedule an office visit that reassures the patient but that is not medically necessary. The provider, in the role of producer, bills the insurer for the office visit. The provider therefore profits from recommending medically unnecessary care.

Moral hazard and conflict of interest contribute to the practice of **defensive medicine**. Defensive medicine is when a provider orders excessive diagnostic tests and procedures in order to protect against possible malpractice suits, even though these tests and procedures are medically unnecessary (Shi & Singh, 2008). If the health plan reimburses for these tests and procedures, the provider profits from providing this unnecessary care.

Supplier-induced demand. Moral hazard, asymmetric information, and conflict of interest may lead to **supplier-induced demand**, in which agents use their knowledge and authority over the principal to increase demand. For example, a provider might continue to recommend patient visits for treatment such as massage, that patients like to receive, and that may be fully covered by insurance, for far longer than clinical standards might determine are medically necessary.

Moral hazard and supplier-induced demand therefore contribute to rising health costs. The goods and services provided are not medically necessary, so while consumers may in some cases enjoy the added consumption, the added costs do not enhance health care quality. In some situations, this "over-care" may reduce health care quality. For example, patients who remain in the hospital more days than necessary may suffer hospital-acquired conditions that would be avoided if they were discharged when appropriate.

Advertising. A growing phenomenon related to moral hazard is **advertising**, or mass media communication purchased by a sponsor, such as a pharmaceutical company, to persuade a target audience. Advertising differs from supplier-induced demand in that the agent-principal relationship does not exist. Rather, the advertising message primarily focuses on persuasion rather than information, and is prepared on behalf of the sponsor. Advertisements for prescription medicine are frequently seen on television, billboards, the Internet, and in popular magazines and newspapers. A similar phenomenon is the increasing consumer use of the Internet for health information, who then approach their physician with requests for interventions publicized on the Internet.

Advertising increases demand for the health care products promoted by the sponsor. Advertising stimulates moral hazard both among consumers and providers. Direct-to-consumer advertising encourages patients to ask their physician for interventions that might not be entirely necessary or that might be provided by less costly alternatives. Product promotions directed to providers encourages the recommendation or adoption of products that may not be necessary or cost-effective compared to competing products.

Aligning Incentives

One strategy insurers employ to reduce health care costs is the use of rewards or reinforcements, often referred to as **incentives**, to influence both consumer and provider behavior. The payer may use incentives to improve health care access and quality as well as to control costs and utilization. Probably the most powerful and commonly used incentive is money. Financial incentives include cost-sharing requirements, savings, reimbursement modifications, and the denial of reimbursement.

Another important incentive for consumers and providers is choice. Many consumers want free choice in the selection of their physician, hospital, and other providers. Providers want to be able to choose the types and amount of services they think are best. Controlling choice reduces utilization and costs, as consumers and providers can only select services based on requirements of medical necessity, and are limited to providers who contract with the health plan.

Time is an incentive, as well. Chapter 1 discusses opportunity costs, and points out that time, as when consumers must wait for services, is a nonmonetary opportunity cost. Consumers often want to be able to schedule services without delay, and providers want prompt reimbursement. Strategies such as review mechanisms that require delays in scheduling serve as incentives to reduce utilization, because some consumers will forgo care if it is delayed.

Increasingly, health plans attempt to **align incentives** or strategically apply incentives to influence the behavior of consumers and providers. An example of a misaligned incentive is volume-based reimbursement for hospitals. Reimbursement based on the number of patients, patient days, and procedures rewards hospitals for admitting and treating as many patients as possible. Volume-based reimbursement therefore may reward hospitals for preventable readmissions and preventable complications, in other words, for poorer quality care.

The purpose of aligning incentives is to reward consumers and providers for utilizing health care goods and services prudently and appropriately. A further goal of aligning incentives is to encourage providers to improve quality while controlling costs. Penalties, often the denial of payment, may be applied to consumers or providers if they over-utilize services or generate excessive costs that are not medically necessary. A number of strategies to align incentives are used by managed care plans, and are discussed in Chapter 3.

The IPPS established by CMS is an example of aligning incentives in a health plan that is based on FFS reimbursement. Prospective payment attempts to reduce moral hazard and supplier-induced demand that can occur in volume-based reimbursement systems. The IPPS rewards hospitals for providing appropriate, efficient inpatient care. Financial penalties for excessive hospital costs, preventable complications, and preventable hospital readmissions are implemented to better control hospital costs and improve patient care quality.

Cost-Sharing Strategies

As discussed earlier in the chapter, when consumers and providers are insensitive to costs, they may over-utilize or over-prescribe health services. Several strategies payers use to align incentives involve **cost-sharing**, requiring consumers and providers to assume some of the costs of covered services. **Cost-sharing** aligns incentives by making consumers and providers more aware of costs. It is assumed that consumers and providers are more likely to limit utilization to medically necessary goods and services if they must share the costs of health care.

Deductibles. Health plans may require members to pay a **deductible**, a minimum threshold payment members make before a plan begins to cover health care costs. For example, there may be a $500 annual deductible for prescription medications. After the beneficiary pays the first $500, the insurance plan covers the remainder of the prescription medication costs for the plan year.

Coinsurance and copayment. Payer cost-sharing strategies include **coinsurance** and **copayment**. Coinsurance is a percentage of a given health care cost that the insurer requires the plan member to pay. Copayment is a specified dollar amount of a given health care cost required of the plan member. For example, health plans may require members to pay a 20% coinsurance for the inpatient hospital bed rate after the fifth inpatient day. If the bed rate is $1000 per day, the patient must pay $200 of that amount. Health plans might require members to pay a $20 copayment for every visit to a primary care physician's office. The health plan covers the remainder of the office visit costs. Deductibles, coinsurance, and copayments make consumers more sensitive to the cost of health care services, thereby reducing unnecessary utilization and reducing costs.

Caps. Another cost-sharing strategy is for health plans to establish caps, or specified limits to coverage. Caps are most frequently set on either an annual or a lifetime basis. For example, a dental plan may set an annual cap of $1500. Beyond that limit, any additional dental expenses must be paid by the health plan member until the following plan year. A lifetime cap might be a $100,000 or 90-day limit on inpatient psychiatric care.

One implication of the use of annual or lifetime caps is the role of **benefits management** as part of case management for patients with costly or long-term disorders. Benefits management involves continual monitoring of a member's benefit status for patients with frequent hospitalizations or other high-cost care. Another important function in benefits management is conserving the benefit whenever possible. One example of conserving the benefit is replacing high-cost psychiatric inpatient care with outpatient day programs whenever appropriate, or referring the patient to public sector programs as needed. The benefits manager is also responsible for alerting the employer and the health plan of the need for extension of benefits, and for educating plans and employers. Health plans may hire or contract with benefit or case managers and assign them to high-cost or potentially high-cost cases.

High-deductible and consumer-driven health plans. In recent years, **high-deductible health plans (HDHPs)** have become more widespread as a health plan innovation to provide health coverage at a lower cost. HDHPs require a $1000 minimum deductible for single coverage or $2000 deductible for family coverage. **Consumer-driven health plans (CDHPs)** provide an account, usually a **health savings account (HSA)** or a **health reimbursement arrangement (HRA),** in combination with the HDHP (Fronstin, 2012).

An HSA is a pretax or tax-deductible account. Employers or employees can make contributions to an HSA. An HRA is similar to an HSA, but is managed under somewhat different tax provisions than the HSA, and only the employer can contribute to the HRA. Both HSAs and HRAs allow plan members to withdraw funds from the account to pay for specified medical expenses, including deductibles and copayments required by the HDHP. Any unspent money can be carried over into the next year.

HDHPs and CDHPs provide incentives for employees to be more cost-aware and prudent about health care spending. In addition, high-deductible plans are believed to encourage members to take more responsibility for their health and to engage in activities that promote wellness, such as tobacco cessation programs. CDHPs grew from 4% of all employer-sponsored health plans in 2006 to 13% in 2010. CDHPs are seen as an effective strategy for aligning consumer incentives to help reduce health care costs (Haviland et al., 2012).

There are some concerns about HDHPs and CDHPs. One problem is that members may delay or forgo preventive or recommended care in order to save money. For example, spending on cancer and diabetes prevention services was found to be less for families in CDHPs compared to traditional insurance plans. Another problem is the potential for adverse selection, as healthier employees opt for the lower-cost CDHPs, leaving a greater proportion of less healthy members in the traditional employer-sponsored health plans. However, more than 50% of all large employers in the United States offered a CDHP option in 2011, and more employers are expected to offer these high-deductible plans in the future (Haviland et al., 2012).

Flexible spending account. A health savings option that can supplement health insurance is the **flexible spending account (FSA)**. FSAs are a benefit provided by some employers, usually large employers. Employees are able to open accounts using pretax earnings, up to a designated limit such as $1500 per year. The account must be spent over the following year or rolled back to the FSA. The employee may draw from the account for reimbursement for approved medical and dependent care expenses. For example, an employee may use the account to pay for new glasses when vision benefits are not provided in a health plan, or for dependent child care services. FSAs are not health plans and do not provide comprehensive health coverage. However, the tax advantages of FSAs make this an affordable option to cover out-of-pocket costs that employees and their families expect to pay over the coming year.

Nurses are often employed in hospitals and health systems that offer CDHPs and FSAs. When hired or when health plan enrollment is available, nurses are encouraged to learn about the best options for employee and family coverage. One suggestion is to contact the employer's Human Resources Department for information. The Plan for Your Health – FSA, HSA, HRA: What Does It All Mean? website provides a comparison of the features of these savings options (www.planforyourhealth.com).

GOVERNMENT HEALTH INSURANCE PROGRAMS

As shown in Figure 2.1, more than half of all health insurance in the United States is provided by Medicare, Medicaid, and other federal, state, and local government programs. This section provides an overview of the major federally funded programs that provide health insurance for elderly, poor, and other eligible Americans. A discussion of the PPACA enacted in 2010 is provided.

Medicare

President Johnson's War on Poverty initiatives in the 1960s expanded the government role in health care. The Social Security Acts of 1965 established and finance the Medicare (Title XVIII) and Medicaid (Title XIX) programs that provide coverage for elderly Americans and poor American families. Medicare is a federal health insurance program for persons over age 65. Persons under age 65 may also be covered if they have permanent disabilities and are recipients of Social Security Disability Insurance. Persons under age 65 with end-stage renal disease or amyotrophic lateral sclerosis are also eligible for Medicare (Kaiser Family Foundation [KFF], 2010).

There are four Medicare programs: Parts A, B, C, and D. **Medicare Part A**, the **Hospital Insurance (HI)** program, provides hospital, skilled nursing facility, home health, and hospice care coverage. Long-term care and custodial care are not covered. Most Medicare beneficiaries do not pay premiums for Part A, as payments were made as payroll deductions while the beneficiary or spouse were working. Table 2.2 shows that, in 2010, 8.3 million beneficiaries used Part A benefits at a cost of $176.2 billion.

Medicare Part B is the **Supplementary Medical Insurance (SMI)** program. Part B helps cover outpatient care, physician services, and some other medical expenses such as

Table 2.2 Medicare Fee-for-Service (FFS) Persons Served and Payments by Type of Service, Calendar Year 2010

Service	Persons Served (in millions)	Program Payments (in billions)
Part A	8.3	$176.2
Inpatient hospital	7.5	$128.7
Skilled nursing facility	1.8	$27.3
Home health agency	1.7	$7.3
Hospice	1.2	$13.0
Part B	31.9	$154.9
Physician	31.4	$95.1
Outpatient	23.7	$47.6
Home health agency	1.9	$12.2
Total (Parts A and/or B)	**32.9**	**$331.1**

Source: CMS/Office of Information Products and Data Analytics, June 25, 2012.
Retrieved from https://www.cms.gov/Research-Statistics-Data-and-Systems/Statistics-Trends-and-Reports/CMS-Fast-Facts/index.html

home health and preventive services. Most beneficiaries pay premiums for Part B (KFF, 2010). Table 2.2 shows that, in 2010, 31.9 million beneficiaries used Part B benefits at a cost of $154.9 billion. Medicare Parts A and B use FFS reimbursement to make payments to physicians, hospitals, and other health providers.

Medicare Part C, the **Medicare Advantage (MA)** program, pays for the same benefits as Parts A, B, and D. However, Part C allows enrollment in private plans such as health maintenance organizations (HMOs), preferred provider organizations (PPOs), or private FFS plans as an alternative to Medicare FFS coverage. Most Part C beneficiaries are enrolled in HMOs or PPOs. Although the majority of Medicare enrollees are in the traditional FFS program, enrollment in Part C is growing, increasing from 5.3 million in 2003 to 11.5 million in April 2010 (KFF, 2010).

In 2006, **Medicare Part D** was established to provide outpatient prescription drug coverage for beneficiaries of the traditional FFS program as a **prescription drug plan (PDP)**. Part C beneficiaries may enroll in **Medicare Advantage prescription drug plans (MA-PDPs)**. Beneficiaries pay premiums for Part D, as well as cost-sharing payments for prescriptions. Some limited-income beneficiaries may be eligible for financial assistance for premiums and cost-sharing payments. The PPACA will change the Part D premium structure and is phasing in coverage for the Part D coverage gap (KFF, 2010).

Another insurance product for Medicare beneficiaries is known as **Medigap insurance**. Medigap insurance is offered by private health plans to cover services not covered by Medicare Parts A or B. Federal and state laws regulate the design of Medigap insurance policies. More information about Medigap plans is available in the CMS Medigap (Medicare Supplement Health Insurance) website (www.cms.gov).

Insurance Information for Seniors

The American elderly and some younger persons with disabilities receive comprehensive benefits under Medicare. However, the choices and trade-offs in selecting among traditional FFS Medicare plans, Medicare Advantage, Part D, and Medigap policies can be confusing for Medicare beneficiaries and their families. Nurses should be aware of provisions in the Older Americans Act (2006) that establish programs for Medicare information.

The Older Americans Act (2006) requires that each state provides a Medicare information, counseling, and assistance program. The program is free, run by trained volunteers who meet face-to-face with the client to assist with Medicare plan enrollment decisions, and is available at local senior centers. California's program is the Health Insurance Counseling and Advocacy Program (HICAP; www.cahealthadvocates.org/hicap/). Programs in other states may be contacted by calling the local Area Agency on Aging (listed in the telephone book) or by searching for health insurance information for seniors on the Internet. Nurses can refer patients and caregivers to this resource if they have questions about Medicare or Medicare enrollment.

Medicaid

Medicaid is a health insurance program for poor Americans, jointly funded by the federal and state governments, with the federal government matching Medicaid spending made by the states. The federal government currently funds about 66% of the costs of Medicaid. The Medicaid program was originally limited to persons receiving welfare assistance. Many states have expanded Medicaid coverage to ensure insurance coverage for populations such as pregnant women, or to develop demonstration models for low-income populations. In 2008, about 70% of Medicaid enrollees were provided some or all of their services through managed care contracts (Kaiser Commission on Medicaid and the Uninsured [KCMU], 2010). Medicaid provides coverage to more people than any other U.S. government or private insurance program. Table 2.3 projects that 56.6 million Americans on average were enrolled in Medicaid in 2012.

Table 2.3 *CMS Program Enrollment (Populations) in Millions, 2010–2012*

Populations[1] (millions)			
Medicare (average monthly)	CY 2010	CY 2011	FY 2012[2]
Parts A and/or B	47.7	48.8	50.2
Aged	39.6	40.5	41.5
Disabled	8.0	8.4	8.7
Fee-for-service (FFS) enrollment	35.9	36.5	37.7
Prepaid enrollment	11.8	12.4	12.5
Medicare advantage (MA) enrollment	11.3	11.9	12.0
Part D (MA Part D+prescription drug plan)	28.0	29.5	31.9
Medicaid (average monthly)[2]	FY 2010	FY 2011	FY 2012
Total	53.5	55.6	56.6
Aged	4.7	4.8	5.0
Blind/disabled	9.5	9.7	9.8
Children	26.3	27.4	27.9
Adults	12.1	12.6	12.9
Children's health insurance program (average monthly)	5.4	5.6	5.9

Notes: [1]May not add due to rounding. [2]Projected estimates.

Source: CMS/Office of Information Products and Data Analytics/Office of the Actuary, June 25, 2012. Retrieved from https://www.cms.gov/Research-Statistics-Data-and-Systems/Statistics-Trends-and-Reports/CMS-Fast-Facts/index.html

Medicaid provides insurance coverage to many Americans who cannot afford health insurance, or who cannot obtain health insurance because of chronic conditions or disabilities. During economic downturns, Medicaid eligibility increases as people lose their jobs and private health insurance. Medicaid enrollment is estimated to increase by one million recipients for every one percent increase in the unemployment rate. However, as the income guidelines vary from state to state, a number of low-income Americans, particularly adults, are not eligible for Medicaid and go without health insurance (KCMU, 2010).

Medicaid is an important funding source for long-term care and nursing homes. Close to 70% of nursing home residents are Medicaid recipients, and Medicaid funds more than 40% of nursing home and long-term care services. Medicaid is also an important source of funding for hospitals and community health centers (KCMU, 2010).

Children's Health Insurance Program (CHIP)

The Children's Health Insurance Program (CHIP), originally called the State Children's Health Insurance Program, was established as part of the Balanced Budget Act of 1997. The purpose of CHIP is to reduce the number of children lacking health insurance. Like the Medicaid program, CHIP is implemented as a partnership between the Federal government and the states. CHIP represents the largest expansion of children's health coverage since Medicaid was established.

CHIP provides health care coverage to low-income children who reside in families that may not qualify for Medicaid coverage. Some states have expanded CHIP to cover the child's entire family. One concern is that over 70% of uninsured children who are eligible for CHIP remain unenrolled. Families' lack of awareness of CHIP and burdensome requirements for enrollment and renewal create difficulties for program implementation. The federal government, in an effort to ensure health coverage for all needy children, pays bonuses to states that exceed CHIP enrollment targets (KCMU, 2010).

Table 2.3 shows the average monthly enrollment for 2010 to 2012 in the Medicare, Medicaid, and CHIP programs. The aging population and longer life spans are major factors in the Medicare enrollment increases. The continuing economic downturn and unemployment are factors related to increased enrollment in Medicaid and CHIP. Information about the FFS provider payment process for Medicaid is available at the Medicaid and CHIP Payment and Access Commission (MACPAC) website (www.macpac.gov).

Dual Eligibles

Medicaid provides some additional assistance to qualifying low-income Medicare beneficiaries, known as **dual eligibles**. Close to one in six Medicare beneficiaries are dual eligibles. Most dual eligibles receive Medicaid coverage for long-term care services. Dual eligibles may also receive coverage for expenses such as Medicare premiums, deductibles, and Part D plans (KCMU, 2010).

Persons who are dual eligibles are poorer and have more health problems compared to other Medicare beneficiaries. The overall health costs of dual eligibles are higher than many other Medicare or Medicaid recipients. In 2008, dual eligibles accounted for only 15% of Medicaid enrollment, but accounted for 39% of Medicaid expenditures and 31% of Medicare expenditures. Most of the spending on dual eligibles in 2008 (69%) was for long-term care (Young, Garfield, Musumeci, Clemans-Cope, & Lawton, 2010). A video tutorial explaining more about dual eligibles is available at KaiserEDU.org.

Medicare and Medicaid Sustainability and Expansion

In addition to Social Security, Medicare and Medicaid are designated as **entitlement** programs. People meeting the eligibility criteria for entitlement programs have a federal right to the program's benefits. As a result, a state cannot establish waiting lists or limit enrollment for persons meeting Medicaid eligibility criteria in that state. The entitlement status of these programs set them apart from other programs such as CHIP, which are able to limit enrollment (KCMU, 2010). In addition, entitlement programs do not have requirements for annual renewals by Congress.

The growing numbers of elderly, longer life spans, and rising health care costs are some of the reasons for increasing Medicare costs. In recent years, concerns have been raised about the sustainability and future solvency of the Medicare Part A Trust Fund. The continued economic downturn and job losses increase enrollment and costs to both the federal government and states for Medicaid. Concerns about the federal deficit and state budget problems lead to ongoing debate about the sustainability of Medicare and the need to reduce the growth in costs for both Medicare and Medicaid. Some states are reducing efforts to enroll children in CHIP as a way to save costs (KCMU, 2010; KFF, 2010).

The Supreme Court ruling that upheld the PPACA also allows states to opt out of PPACA provisions to expand Medicaid coverage. The PPACA provides that Medicaid is expanded to cover all Americans under 133% of the federal poverty level. The federal government will cover all the costs of new Medicaid enrollees under this expansion beginning in 2014, and 90% of costs after 2019. If states opt out of Medicaid expansion, many poor Americans will continue to lack insurance coverage, even with health reform (Galewitz & Serafini, 2012).

Health Coverage for the Military and Veterans

The Department of Defense funds TRICARE, which offers managed care health coverage for 9.7 million active duty military and retirees, as well as their families. Persons serving in the Army, Navy, Air Force, Marine Corps, Coast Guard, Public Health Service, and National Oceanic and Atmospheric Administration are included in TRICARE plans. Some National Reserve and Guard members are also eligible for TRICARE (KaiserEDU.org, 2012).

TRICARE for Life (TFL) is a program for military retirees, their families, and their survivors who are beneficiaries of Medicare Part B. If Medicare and TFL cover the same services, Medicare is the first payer and TFL pays any remaining costs. Unlike TRICARE, TFL is an entitlement program (KaiserEDU.org, 2012).

The Veterans Administration (VA) is part of the U.S. Department of Veterans Affairs. The VA provides health coverage and health services for veterans and their families. CHAMP/VA provides health care in the VA system for eligible family members of disabled or deceased disabled veterans. Over 9.5 million veterans over age 65 are enrolled in both Medicare and the VA. These beneficiaries must choose whether Medicare or the VA will pay for services when they access care.

The VA is the largest integrated health care system in the United States, with more than five million inpatients and outpatients. However, an estimated one in eight veterans under age 65 are uninsured and unable to receive VA benefits. The lack of insurance coverage is related to problems such as eligibility for benefits or lack of geographic access to VA services.

Table 2.4 summarizes 2010 national health expenditures from all sources of health insurance. Private health insurance generates the largest expenditures, at $848.7 billion. Medicare and Medicaid are the second and third leading sources of health expenditures, at $524.6 billion and $401.4 billion, respectively. As health expenditures threaten to increase and represent a greater percentage of the GDP, concerns and debates about the future funding of government programs, including entitlement programs, will likely only intensify.

The Indian Health Service (IHS) originated in 1787 based on constitutional and treaty agreements. At a 2011 cost of approximately $4.3 billion, the IHS is operated by the U.S. Department of Health and Human Services (HHS). The IHS provides preventive and medical services to about 2 million of the nation's estimated 3.4 million American Indians and

Table 2.4 *National Health Expenditures, 2010*

Total national health expenditures	$2593.6
% of GDP	17.9%
Per capita	$8402.3
Private health insurance	$848.7
Medicare	$524.6
Medicaid (Title XIX)	$401.4
CHIP (Title XIX & XXI)	$11.7
Department of Defense	$38.4
Department of Veterans Affairs	$46.0
Total health insurance expenditures	**$1870.8**

Note: Dollars in billions except for per capita.

Source: CMS/Office of the Actuary. Retrieved from https://www.cms.gov/Research-Statistics-Data-and-Systems/Statistics-Trends-and-Reports/CMS-Fast-Facts/index.html

Alaska Natives. Most IHS services are delivered to Indians living on or near reservations or native villages, but some programs are available in urban areas (IHS, 2012).

Indians and Alaska Natives experience more health disparities compared to other Americans. For example, Indian life expectancy is 72.6 years, more than five years less than the 77.8 years life expectancy for the U.S. general population (IHS, 2012). Many Indians and Alaska Natives also live in poverty, and would likely lack health coverage and access to health services if IHS programs were not available.

THE PATIENT PROTECTION AND AFFORDABLE CARE ACT OF 2010

Because the overall purpose of the PPACA is "quality, affordable health care for all Americans" (2010, p. 1), many of the PPACA provisions increase the regulation of private health insurance plans. The PPACA will be fully implemented in 2015, with a series of provisions that have begun to be phased in since the enactment of this law in 2010. This section summarizes some of the regulations that have already affected private health plans, and that will affect private health plans as the PPACA continues its implementation. New regulations and programs that apply to government-sponsored health programs are also discussed.

2010. One of the first provisions implemented following the enactment of the PPACA is to mandate continued coverage of children under their parents' policies until their 26th birthday. Eligible small businesses and nonprofit organizations are able to obtain health insurance tax credits, and financial assistance is made available to employer plans to help ensure health coverage for persons age 55 to 65. All new health plans must cover specified preventive screening services for adults without charging a deductible, coinsurance, or copayment.

A number of additional provisions implemented in 2010 provide additional consumer protections for private health insurance. Health plans may not cancel coverage except in specified cases such as deliberate misrepresentation. Consumers have rights to appeal health plan decisions and to seek outside review of denials and cancellations of coverage. Lifetime and annual coverage limits are eliminated or restricted. Children may not be denied health coverage based on preexisting conditions. Health plans that make excessive or unjustified premium increases will face penalties.

PPACA provisions implemented in 2010 that affect government-sponsored insurance include federal matching funds to allow states to expand Medicaid funding to more low-income individuals and families. A one-time cash rebate was provided to Medicare beneficiaries who experienced gaps in their Part D prescription drug coverage. A health plan for persons with preexisting conditions is established to be operated by states, or by HHS if states choose not to participate.

2011. Depending on the type of plan, private health plans must spend at least 80% to 85% of their premium revenues on health care and quality improvement, or pay their members a rebate. PPACA provisions that affect government-sponsored insurance include funding to help states establish private insurance consumer assistance programs. Prescription drug discounts begin for Medicare Part D beneficiaries. Medicare benefits allow specified preventive care without requirements to pay a deductible, coinsurance, or copayment. Medicare Advantage rates are addressed to reduce the amount of overpayment to private insurance plans. Funding is made available for community-based Medicaid programs to keep people in their homes and out of nursing homes. Programs and funding are created to develop innovations that will reduce the costs of Medicare, Medicaid, and CHIP, and to protect the sustainability of Medicare.

PPACA in the Future

By 2014, the PPACA will establish insurance exchanges in all the states, and allow Medicaid expansion for persons up to 133% of the federal poverty level. Tax credits will be provided to make health insurance more affordable for small businesses and middle-income Americans. Health plans will be prohibited from requiring annual limits on coverage and preexisting condition exclusions. A timeline of the PPACA and its development, a glossary of terms and definitions used in the PPACA, and information for consumers who want to learn more about PPACA provisions are available at the HealthCare.gov website.

Although the Supreme Court upheld the PPACA in June 2012, the law faces considerable criticism and political opposition. Cost concerns and the impact of a stagnant economy raise more difficulties for full implementation of the PPACA. For example, the Community Living Assistance Services and Supports (CLASS) Act was enacted as part of the PPACA. The CLASS Act was intended to establish a voluntary program to help Americans fund long-term care. As discussed in A Report on the Actuarial, Marketing, and Legal Analyses of the CLASS Program (www.aspe.hhs.gov) prepared by HHS, the CLASS Act will not be implemented at this time, as its feasibility is uncertain.

CONCLUSION

This chapter discusses the importance of private and government-sponsored health insurance in the United States, as well as serious problems related to the growing numbers of Americans who lack health coverage. Principles of health insurance are discussed to help nurses understand how financial incentives influence health care and economic behavior. Government health insurance programs are described, and a review of the recent PPACA is presented. Americans will continue to debate about approaches to offer and fund health insurance, given concerns about costs, quality, and access.

Discussion and Exercises

1. Request health plan information from the Human Resource department in your work setting. Evaluate the types of plans offered in terms of benefits, and any coinsurance, copayments, deductibles, or caps. Compare and discuss the health plans in terms of adverse selection, moral hazard, cost control, cost-sharing, and access.
2. Discuss the organization and financing of your health care work setting. To what extent are there mechanisms imposed by managed care? To what extent is the setting financed by FFS mechanisms? Does a particular payer dominate, such as Medicare? How does the organization and financing of your setting affect costs, quality, and access?
3. Download and review a Medicare payment system for home health, skilled nursing care, physicians, or other provider from the MedPAC Payment Basics website (www.medpac. gov). Compare the payment system with the Medicare hospital payment system discussed in this chapter. Discuss whether this payment strategy is satisfactory in controlling costs while adequately reimbursing the provider.

REFERENCES

American Hospital Association. (2012). *TrendWatch chartbook 2011*. Trends in Hospital Financing (Chapter 4). Chicago, IL: Author. Retrieved from http://www.aha.org/research/reports/tw/chartbook/ch4.shtml.

Bailey, K. (2012). *Dying for coverage: The deadly consequences of being uninsured*. Washington, DC: Families USA. Retrieved from www.familiesusa.org.

Beaty, L. (2005). A primer for understanding diagnosis-related groups and inpatient hospital reimbursement with nursing implications. *Critical Care Nursing Quarterly, 28,* 360–369.

Centers for Medicare & Medicaid Services. (2010). *National health expenditure accounts: Methodology paper.* Definitions, sources, and methods. CMS.gov. Retrieved July 1, 2012 from http://www.cms.gov/Research-Statistics-Data-and-Systems/Statistics-Trends-and-Reports/NationalHealthExpendData/NationalHealthAccountsHistorical.html

Cleverley, W. O., & Cameron, A. E. (2002). *Essentials of health care finance* (5th ed.). Gaithersburg, MD: Aspen.

Cohen, R. A., Gindi, R. M., & Kirzinger, W. K. (2012). *Burden of medical care cost: Early release of estimates from the National Health Interview Survey, January–June 2011.* National Center for Health Statistics. Retrieved from http://www.cdc.gov/nchs/nhis/releases.htm

Collins, S. R., Robertson, R., Garber, T., & Doty, M. M. (2012). *Gaps in health insurance: Why so many Americans experience breaks in coverage and how the Affordable Care Act will help. Findings from the Commonwealth Fund Health Insurance Tracking Survey of U.S. Adults, 2011.* The Commonwealth Fund. Retrieved from http://www.commonwealthfund.org/~/media/Files/Publications/Issue%20Brief/2012/Apr/1594_collins_gaps_in_hlt_ins_tracking_brief_v2.pdf

Dafny, L. S. (2003). *How do hospitals respond to price changes? NBER Working Paper No. 9972.* Cambridge, MA: National Bureau of Economic Research. Retrieved from http://www.nber.org/papers/w9972. HospitalsPriceChanges-3.pdf

DeNavas-Walt, C., Proctor, B. D., & Smith, J. C. (2011). *Income, poverty, and health insurance coverage in the United States: 2010.* P60–239. United States Census Bureau. Issued September 2011. Washington, DC: U.S. Government Printing Office. Retrieved from http://www.census.gov/prod/2011pubs/p60–239.pdf

Fox, J. B., & Richards, C. L. (2010). Vital signs: Health insurance coverage and health care utilization – United States, 2006–2009 and January–March 2010. *MMWR Morbidity and Mortality Weekly Report, 59*: 1448–1454. U.S. Department of Health and Human Services Centers for Disease Control and Prevention. Retrieved from http://www.cdc.gov/mmwr

Fronstin, P. (2012). *Health savings accounts and health reimbursement arrangements: Assets, account balances, and rollovers, 2006–2011.* Issue Brief No. 367. Washington, DC: Employee Benefit Research Institute. Retrieved from http://www.ebri.org/pdf/briefspdf/EBRI_IB_01–2012_No367_HlthAccnts.pdf

Galewitz, P., & Serafini, M. W. (2012). *Ruling puts pressure on states to act. KHN Kaiser Health News Judging The Health Law.* Henry J. Kaiser Family Foundation. Retrieved from http://www.kaiserhealthnews.org/Stories/2012/June/28/pressure-on-states-to-act-after-supreme-court-ruling.aspx

Galvin, R. S., & Delbanco, S. (2006). Between a rock and a hard place: Understanding the employer mind-set. *Health Affairs, 25,* 1548–1555. http://www.healthaffairs.org

Hackbarth, G. M. (2008). *MedPAC IPPS Comment Letter. File Code CMS-1390-P.* Washington, DC: Medicare Payment Advisory Commission (MedPAC). Retrieved from http://www.medpac.gov/documents/06102008_IPPS_comment_JS.pdf

Haviland, A. M., Marquis, S., McDevitt, R. D., & Sood, N. (2012). Growth of consumer-directed health plans to one-half of all employer-sponsored insurance could save $57 billion annually. *Health Affairs, 31,*1009–1015. http://www.healthaffairs.org

Indian Health Service (IHS). (January 2012). *Indian Health Service: A quick look. IHS Fact Sheets.* Retrieved at http://www.ihs.gov/PublicAffairs/IHSBrochure/QuickLook.asp

Kaiser Commission on Medicaid and the Uninsured. (2010). *Medicaid a primer: Key information on our nation's health coverage program for low-income people.* Publication Number: 7334-04. Menlo Park, CA: Henry J. Kaiser Family Foundation. Retrieved from http://www.kff.org/medicaid/upload/7334–04.pdf

KaiserEDU.org. (July 7, 2012). *Military and Veterans' Health Care. Background Brief.* Retrieved July 7, 2012, from http://www.kaiseredu.org/Issue-Modules/Military-and-Veterans-Health-Care/Background-Brief.aspx

Kaiser Family Foundation. (2010). *Medicare a primer 2010.* Report #7615–03. Menlo Park, CA: Henry J. Kaiser Family Foundation. Retrieved from http://www.kff.org/medicare/upload/7615–03.pdf

Kaiser Family Foundation and Health Research & Educational Trust. (2011). *2011 Kaiser/ HRET employer health benefits survey (EHBS).* Menlo Park, CA: Henry J. Kaiser Family Foundation. Retrieved from http://ehbs.kff.org/pdf/2011/8225.pdf

McWilliams, M. J., Zaslavsky, A. M., Meara, E., & Ayanian, J. Z. (2004). Health insurance coverage & mortality among the near-elderly. *Health Affairs, 23,* 223–233.

MedPAC. (2011). *Hospital acute inpatient services payment system: Payment basics.* Washington, DC: MedPAC. Retrieved from www.medpac.gov

Miller, H. D. (2012). *Creating Win-Win Strategies for Successful Payment & Delivery Reform. Presented at San Francisco Premier Seminar.* Health Care Reform: Show Me the Money. University of San Francisco. Retrieved from www.paymentreform.org

Patient Protection and Affordable Care Act. (2010). Pub. L. No. 111–148, §2702, 124 Stat. 119, 318–319. Retrieved from http://housedocs.house.gov/energycommerce/ppacacon.pdf

Penner, M., Penner, S., Verkade, S., & Brooks, J. (2002). Physician office access for the uninsured: An observational study. *Research in the Sociology of Healthcare: Social Inequalities, Health and Health Care Delivery, 20,* 219–234.

S. 3570–109th Congress: Older Americans Act Amendments of 2006. (2006). In *GovTrack. us (database of federal legislation).* Retrieved from http://www.govtrack.us/congress/bills/109/s3570

Shi, L., & Singh, D. A. (2008). *Delivering health care in America: A systems approach.* Burlington, MA: Jones & Bartlett.

Sommers, A., & Cunningham, P. J. (2011). *Medical bill problems steady for U.S. families, 2007– 2010. Tracking Report No. 28.* Washington, DC: Center for Studying Health System Change. Retrieved from www.hschange.org

Sommers, B. D., Baicker, K., & Epstein, A. M. (2012). *Mortality and access to care among adults after state Medicaid expansions.* New England, Journal of Medicine Online First. Retrieved from http://www.nejm.org/doi/full/10.1056/NEJMsa1202099

Vistnes, J., Cooper, P., Bernard, D., & Banthin, J. (2009). *Near-elderly adults, ages 55–64: Health insurance coverage, cost and access.* Rockville, MD: Agency for Health Care Policy and Research. Retrieved from http://www.ahrq.gov/data/meps/mepsneareld/

Young, K., Garfield, R., Musumeci, M., Clemans-Cope, L., & Lawton, E. (2012). *Medicaid's role for dual eligible beneficiaries. Kaiser Commission on Medicaid and the Uninsured (KCMU).* Menlo Park, CA: Henry J. Kaiser Family Foundation. Retrieved from http://www.kff.org/medicaid/upload/7846–03.pdf

CROSSWORD: *Chapter 2—Insurance*

Across

1 A percentage of a given health care cost that the insurer requires the plan member to pay.

3 Mass media communication purchased by a sponsor to persuade an audience.

6 Health plan that requires a minimum $1000 deductible for single coverage or $2000 deductible for family coverage (abbreviation).

9 Health plan with high deductibles thought to encourage consumer wellness (abbreviation).

14 Retrospective payment of all allowable costs meeting accepted standards of care (abbreviation).

15 Measure of overall acuity among Medicare patients in hospitals (abbreviation).

16 A government benefit that people have a right to receive as long as they are eligible.

17 A reward or encouragement, often financial, that influences behavior.

18 Adjustment factor for differences in wage rates across geographic areas of the United States (abbreviation).

20 A pre-tax or tax-deductible health care account to which only the employer may contribute (abbreviation).

21 A pre-tax account used for expenses not covered by health insurance (abbreviation).

Down

2 The actual payment for health care services that may be less than the charges.

4 Hospital caring for a higher proportion of low-income patients than other hospitals (abbreviation).

5 Probability of an adverse event.

7 A required payment made by a consumer before the health plan begins to cover costs.

8 Unusually costly and frequently long-term case, usually in acute care settings.

10 A party lacking knowledge who delegates authority to an agent.

11 Long-term expenditures, such as construction and equipment purchases.

12 A party in authority acting on behalf of a principal.

13 Having to do with insurance risks.

19 A pre-tax or tax-deductible health care account in which an employer or employee can make contributions (abbreviation).

20 Preventable conditions as specified by Medicare for which hospitals may not be reimbursed (abbreviation).

Chapter 3: Managed Care and Performance Measurement

Givers have to set limits because takers rarely do—Irma Kurtz

Learning Objectives

1. Point out at least two major differences between managed care reimbursement and fee-for-service reimbursement.
2. Give at least two examples of how managed care review mechanisms reduce health care costs.
3. Explain at least three utilization or financial measures for providers working in managed care settings or under managed care contracts.
4. Compare at least two distinct characteristics of managed care organizations and accountable care organizations.

Key Terms

accountable care organization (ACO)

administrative loss ratio (ALR)

admission rate

average length of stay (ALOS)

brand-name medication

bundled

capitation

capitation revenue

carve-in

carve-out

claims review

concurrent review

drilling down

exporting risk

formulary

gainsharing

gatekeeping

generic medication

group model

health maintenance organization (HMO)

horizontal integration

hospitalization rate

incurred but not reported (IBNR)

independent practice association (IPA)

managed care organization (MCO)

medical home

medical loss ratio (MLR)

member months

mid-level provider (MLP)

profit & loss statement
(net P&L)

over-care

overhead

paid charges

PMPM

PMPY

point-of-service (POS)

preauthorization

preferred provider
organization (PPO)

primary care

primary care physicians
(PCPs)

prospective review

prudent layperson's
standard

referral percentage

referral rate

retrospective review

risk sharing

shared risk

shared savings

small tests of change

specialty care

staff model

stop-loss insurance

under-care

utilization review

value-based purchasing

vertical integration

visit

Chapter 1 discusses nationwide concerns about rising health care costs. Chapter 2 discusses limitations of **fee-for-service (FFS)** reimbursement systems, and the problems in aligning health insurance incentives to ensure access while controlling costs. Health reform initiatives, including the Patient Protection and Affordable Care Act of 2010 (PPACA), are leading providers and payers to explore alternatives to the traditional FFS systems. It is likely that managed care and other reimbursement systems will increase in importance and replace FFS models in many settings. Nurses need to understand how managed care and other alternative reimbursement systems are structured and how they affect quality, efficiency, and patient outcomes.

This chapter discusses how managed care systems operate compared to the fee-for-service model. Strategies implemented by **accountable care organizations (ACOs)** are described as new financing models. Approaches used in managed care and ACO systems are intended to **align incentives** or reinforce and reward improving quality and access while controlling costs. A case example of an immunization program illustrates the application of indicators for performance measurement in managed care or other health systems.

One of the settings introduced in this chapter is the Millway University Nurse-Managed Health Center (MNC), operated by Millway University's School of Nursing in Bigtown Hospital. MNC employed one nurse practitioner (NP) and generated $108,000 in annual revenue in 2011, with 850 patient visits over the year. Most of MNC's start-up funding was from grants, with a small contract in 2011 from Welby ACO. MNC expanded its operations in 2012, adding more NPs and patient care contracts. MNC and the Pediatric Services of PTMG provide examples for explaining managed care concepts and performance measures.

Welby ACO is a joint venture aligning the Welby HMO with Bigtown Hospital and community providers such as Pine Tree Medical Group (PTMG) and MNC. PTMG is a group of **primary care physicians (PCPs)**, often the first point of patient contact for diagnosis, treatment, and prevention. The PCPs organized their group practice into an **independent practice association (IPA)** in which the physicians own the practice but contract with the Welby ACO for members and reimbursement. To expand their primary health services, PTMG also contracts with **mid-level providers (MLPs)** such as the nurse practitioners who are providers at MNC.

HISTORIC FOUNDATIONS OF MANAGED CARE

Prepaid medical plans began about the same time that commercial health insurance developed in the United States, just before and during the Great Depression of the 1930s. In 1929, Dr. Ross and Dr. Loos started the Ross-Loos prepaid group practice plan in California. Instead of charging fees, the practice received monthly payments to cover all medical and hospital services for municipal workers in the Los Angeles area. Dr. Ross and Dr. Loos were expelled from their local medical society because of opposition from the local medical community. Other early prepaid health plans met with similar opposition and sanctions from state and local medical societies.

In 1933, Dr. Sidney R. Garfield established a prepaid plan for construction workers in the Mojave Desert. Henry Kaiser then employed Dr. Garfield to create a prepaid group practice plan for construction workers at the Grand Coulee Dam. During World War II, the Kaiser health plan covered shipyard workers on the West Coast. Unlike most of the early prepaid health plans, Dr. Garfield's plan grew into what is now called Kaiser Permanente (Kaiser Permanente Newsroom, 2002). The term **health maintenance organization (HMO)** originated to represent a **managed care organization (MCO)**, or a managed care plan that provides health care to persons enrolled in a prepaid plan.

Managed care plans continued to face prohibitive state and local regulations that protected the interests of physicians and hospitals favoring fee-for-service reimbursement. By the early 1970s, the largely uncontrolled costs of public and commercial fee-for-service health plans led to increasing support for more cost-effective approaches. The growth of managed care was stimulated by the HMO Act of 1973 (Public Law 93–222), which removed legal restrictions to HMOs. By 1986, nearly all states passed regulations for licensing HMOs.

The 1980s saw rapid growth of HMOs to reduce health care costs. Employers realized that rising health care costs made many American industries less competitive and less profitable. There was also more public awareness and concern about the potential dangers of unnecessary health care, such as hospital-acquired infections. HMOs and MCOs became increasingly popular among employers as a way to better control their health plan costs.

HMOs and other MCOs expanded from 9.1 million enrollees in 1980 to 33.0 million in 1990 and 81.3 million enrollees in 1999 (US Census Bureau, 2002). The 1990s were a time of intensive MCO competition, mergers and acquisitions, and new forms of managed care. New models of health care delivery emerged. **Vertical integration** of health care delivery combined and coordinated various levels of services, such as hospitals acquiring and operating community-based clinics and home health services. **Horizontal integration** increased the market share of health care enterprises across the same level of services, such as a health care system acquiring hospitals nationwide.

Government programs such as Medicare, Medicaid, and CHAMPUS (health coverage for military retirees and dependents) began contracting with HMOs and developing managed care plans in the public sector. States used funding approaches, such as disproportionate share hospital (DSH) payments, and policy initiatives, such as Medicaid waivers, to encourage managed care plans for Medicaid recipients (Bataille, Anderson, & Penner, 1995).

Over the last decade, managed care growth leveled off, although managed care continues to be an important strategy for controlling costs (Managed Care On-Line, 2011). Medicare and Medicaid continue to develop managed care approaches to cut the growth in costs. More developments are discussed in the section on ACOs.

PRINCIPLES OF MANAGED CARE

The principles of managed care were developed to address and correct problems with fee-for-service health coverage, such as third-party transaction problems, supplier-induced demand, and moral hazard, as discussed in Chapter 2. Managed care strategies based on these principles align incentives so that patients, providers, and payers benefit from improving quality and access while controlling costs.

Provider Contracting

HMOs commonly contract with physicians using the **staff model** or the **group model**. In staff-model HMOs, physicians are employees and are paid a salary. In group-model HMOs, the HMO contracts with a physician group practice. Physicians may be employees or partners in the group practice. The group model is the arrangement between PTMG and Welby HMO.

Capitation and Financial Risk

One principle underlying managed care plans is that of prepayment for the care of populations, or **capitation**. Capitation realigns incentives to resolve problems with third-party transactions between the patient and the provider. Fee-for-service systems reward providers based on the volume and intensity of services. For example, under a fee-for-service system, Bigtown Hospital is fully reimbursed for inpatient admissions, even when the hospitalization is a preventable readmission. By contrast, capitation rewards providers for promoting population wellness and for only providing medically necessary services. PTMG physicians, for example, must report and monitor their utilization of costly procedures and verify that these services are medically necessary. PTMG must also show improvements in population health, such as raising vaccination rates to target levels.

Rather than the insurance plan paying the provider's charges following the provision of health care goods and services, managed care plans estimate and negotiate a capitation contract for a specified period, with reimbursement for the coverage of a specified number of members paid in advance. The capitation rate is adjusted by members' age and sex, so the capitation rate for the Pine Tree Medical Group pediatricians is somewhat lower than that for the PTMG physicians treating adult and elderly members.

The capitation finance model is a method of **risk sharing** or **exporting risk** for the costs of care from the payer to the provider. The managed care provider shares financial risk because, in capitation contracts, providers may keep any surplus funds if they are able to provide care under the capitation budget amount. If providers cannot control costs and their costs exceed the capitation budget, they are not reimbursed for these excess costs. Risk sharing aligns incentives to make providers more sensitive to health care costs than in fee-for-service systems.

Risk sharing leads to penalties for providers who provide more procedures and other services than are medically necessary, because providers share the costs of their decisions. Capitation therefore addresses problems with third-party transactions such as moral hazard and supplier-induced demand, discussed in Chapter 2. Providers in capitated systems are rewarded if they are careful to only recommend medically necessary services and face financial penalties if they recommend medically unnecessary services.

The physicians at PTMG must keep the costs of care at or under the capitated amount or the practice will lose money. PTMG risks financial penalties related to **over-care,** or the provision of medically unnecessary services, which occurs when providers are not sensitive to costs. PTMG physicians must also monitor the utilization and costs of specialist care and hospitalizations, as they share the risk of specialist costs and 50% of the risk of hospitalization costs.

Concerns that the PTMG physicians may have shifted from over-care to **under-care** (failing or refusing to provide adequate and medically necessary care) are addressed by using hospital readmission rates, emergency room visits, and other performance and outcome measures as indicators for quality and access. The financial incentives of risk-sharing in capitation encourage the PTMG physicians to keep the plan members healthy by providing better preventive and chronic illness care. Physicians might schedule more office visits if the added outpatient care helps keep a patient from requiring more costly hospitalization.

One problem with assuming financial risk is that providers may face unanticipated and uncontrollable financial losses from **outliers,** or unusually high-cost patient episodes or diagnoses. **Stop-loss insurance** coverage protects providers or managed care organizations from unusually costly cases or from overall financial losses that exceed a given percentage of the total capitation contract. It is important for physician practices such as PTMG to purchase stop-loss insurance, as a small group practice could become bankrupt if unable to manage the high costs of outlier cases.

Gatekeeping

Gatekeeping is a requirement that access to specialists or other specified services must be authorized by a PCP or other designated provider. For example, a patient covered by the Welby HMO who presents with a rash must first see a PCP to either diagnose and treat the rash, or authorize a referral to a dermatologist. If the patient insists on seeing a dermatologist without authorization, the dermatologist's claim will likely be denied by Welby HMO and the patient will have to pay the full costs of specialist care.

Gatekeeping uses financial incentives to limit the consumer's choice of more expensive specialists for care that can be provided at the same level of quality by a less costly PCP or

MLP. This strategy reduces moral hazard (consumer overuse of unneeded services) and increases the consumer's sensitivity to costs. Consumers who prefer greater choice of providers must pay higher deductibles, copayments or premiums, or must go outside the plan altogether and incur out-of-pocket expenses for the costs of care.

Emergency care is exempted from gatekeeping requirements under the PPACA. The standard for an emergency medical condition is based on the existing **prudent layperson's standard** (Patient Protection and Affordable Care Act [PPACA], 2010). If an acute condition with severe symptoms arises such that a prudent layperson with average knowledge of health and medicine would believe the patient requires medical attention, the condition is considered an emergency. More information about the prudent layperson's standard is available at the CMS.gov Emergency Medical Treatment & Labor Act website (www.cms.gov). A discussion of the Emergency Medical Treatment & Labor Act (EMTALA) is in Chapter 2.

Gatekeeping may lead to under-care for disorders such as severe mental illness. Delaying appropriate diagnosis and treatment may result in poor patient outcomes. Managed care models to address problems with gatekeeping and improve appropriate access to specialist care developed in the 1990s. One model is the managed care **carve-in**, where a specialist MCO operates within a medical MCO. For example, Woodside Oncology Care is a managed care carve-in that is part of Welby HMO. Patients covered by Welby HMO can obtain cancer screenings at Woodside and can self-refer if they have concerns about possible signs or symptoms of cancer. PTMG PCPs are encouraged to refer patients to Woodside for screening and for follow-up of suspicious findings.

Another model for addressing gatekeeping concerns is the managed care **carve-out**, where a specialist MCO operates independently and contracts with an MCO or health plan. MindFree Behavioral Health is a carve-out that contracts with Welby HMO. Patients covered by Welby can self-refer to MindFree for psychological or addictive disorders, with no requirements to discuss these problems with their PCP. Both the carve-in and the carve-out models use managed care strategies to control specialist costs, so procedures and hospitalizations are closely monitored.

Carve-ins and carve-outs often lead to more timely diagnosis and treatment and more comprehensive follow-up care of some disorders, so that overall costs of care may be better managed than with PCP gatekeeping. However, carve-in and carve-out models do not work well unless there is close communication between the specialists and the PCPs, so that the patient receives continuity of care. Communication among all physicians involved in the patient's care is particularly important for ensuring preventive and chronic care coordination.

Provider Reimbursement Mechanisms

Capitation is one approach to align incentives in a managed care system, but a mix of reimbursement mechanisms is often used in health care settings. For example, MCOs or managed care plans may reimburse physicians based on a flat rate, such as a negotiated, contracted capitation amount (as with PTMG). Some managed care plans might base physician reimbursement on a fee schedule, such as the one devised for Medicare reimbursement.

Hospitals may be reimbursed by MCOs or managed care plans under a fee schedule or an established per diem rate. Some managed care plans might base hospital reimbursement on a patient's diagnosis and procedures, such as Medicare's prospective payment system, discussed in Chapter 2. When the MCO or managed care plan and the hospital do not have a contract, reimbursement may be based on the hospital's full charges. New and innovative reimbursement approaches are developing as part of the national movement to develop ACOs (Centers for Medicare & Medicaid Services [CMS], 2011). Updated explanations of the Medicare payment systems for physicians, hospitals, and other providers are available at the MedPAC Payment Basics website (www.medpac.gov).

Review Mechanisms

Unlike the traditional fee-for-service reimbursement systems that often pay provider charges with little oversight, managed care plans apply various review mechanisms to reduce unnecessary costs. **Prospective review** (or **preauthorization**) involves reviewing a provider's plan for care prior to the intervention, and authorizing whether or not the plan will pay the costs. For example, many HMOs require prospective review for elective surgeries, reviewing the patient's history and the treatment plan to ensure that the surgery is medically necessary.

Concurrent review (or **utilization review**) occurs during hospitalization when the reviewer evaluates the medical record and determines whether continued hospitalization is medically necessary for each additional day of hospitalization. **Retrospective review** (or **claims review**) occurs after health care is provided and the claim for reimbursement is filed. The claim and other documentation are reviewed to determine whether the intervention was medically necessary and may be authorized for payment.

Review mechanisms are intended to align incentives to reduce procedures and hospitalizations that are medically unnecessary. Providers must demonstrate a rationale for treatment and document their treatment plan and patient outcomes. However, these review mechanisms lead to disputes between providers and the health plan around patient care decisions. Review mechanisms also generate added work for providers as well as considerable administrative costs for both providers and the managed care plan. The appeals process that frequently follows the denial of claims adds to the administrative costs of review mechanisms.

Problems With Managed Care

Probably the most serious problem with managed care is the concern about under-care, since providers and health plans have strong financial incentives to reduce patient visits, hospitalizations, and procedures. Concerns about under-care have largely been addressed over the years. Many states have enacted patient protection laws and regulations. Some states such as California, Minnesota, and New Jersey have established an office or department of managed care to improve consumer protection. The National Committee for Quality Assurance (NCQA) requires MCOs to report quality indicators and to address concerns about under-care as part of their accreditation requirements. The NCQA uses the Healthcare Effectiveness Data and Information Set (HEDIS) for quality reporting by HMOs and other health plans.

Another problem with managed care is the backlash that occurred in the 1990s. Despite the expansion of MCOs in the 1990s, increased physician resistance to managed care limited the negotiation of HMO contracts in many communities. Consumers and some employers also became resistant to participating in managed care plans, leading to a "retreat" from managed care enrollment (Gabel et al., 2001). This backlash was related to concerns about under-care because of reports that necessary care was sometimes denied by managed care plans. Closer regulation of managed care plans and requirements for quality monitoring and reporting are approaches that have addressed under-care.

One response to managed care backlash was the development of the **preferred provider organization (PPO)**, in which the managed care plan contracts for services with independent providers at a discounted rate. The PPO option offers more generous coverage if the member selects from these preferred providers, even without gatekeeper authorization, than if they choose providers outside the plan. A second strategy is the **point-of-service (POS)** plan, a variation of the PPO, in which the plan covers services from providers within the plan more generously than services from providers outside the plan.

A related problem that emerged in the 1990s is that despite the proliferation of managed care and mechanisms to control health costs, national health expenditures continued to increase as a percentage of the GDP, from 7.2% in 1970 to 17.9% in 2010 (Centers for Medicare & Medicaid Services, Office of the Actuary, National Health Statistics Group, U.S. Department of Commerce, Bureau of Economic Analysis; U.S. Bureau of the Census, 2012). This problem was partly related to strategies allowing more consumer choice, such as PPOs, which were not as effective in controlling costs as plans requiring gatekeeping. However, rising hospital and pharmaceutical costs were major factors that reduced the effectiveness of managed care plans in controlling health care costs (Shi & Singh, 2008).

By the early 2000s, the thinking arose that the locus of responsibility for health costs needed to be focused on the patient, stimulating the popularity of consumer-driven high-deductible health plans (CMS, 2011). In 2011, 55% of covered employees were enrolled in PPOs, followed by HMOs (17%), high-deductible health plans (17%), POS plans (10%), and one percent in conventional plans (The Kaiser Family Foundation and Health Research & Educational Trust, 2011).

ACOs COMPARED TO MCOs

Although managed care approaches have helped align some incentives to reduce costs, new ways of financing health care are currently being explored. One problem with managed care is that hospital incentives are often not aligned with risk-bearing physicians and managed care plans. As explained in Chapter 2, hospitals have high fixed costs and strong incentives to maintain a high volume of inpatient care. On the other hand, risk-bearing physicians and managed care plans have strong incentives to keep members healthy and out of the hospital, as this saves the physicians and health plan money. The accountable care organization (ACO) is an attempt to better align hospital, physician, and health plan incentives.

In 2012, the U.S. Department of Health and Human Services began to establish ACOs for Medicare beneficiaries. Private insurers, hospitals, and physicians began establishing ACOs for other patient populations. Section 3022 of the PPACA of 2010 allows ACOs to establish partnerships and networks that include payers, patients, and providers such as hospitals, physician groups, subacute care facilities, and home health agencies that follow the patient across the entire continuum of a disease episode (Holmes, 2011; PPACA, 2010).

ACOs share the same goals as MCOs of controlling costs while ensuring access and high quality patient care. However, reimbursement for care is on a per-episode, **bundled** basis, including all care provided from disease onset to recovery, rather than a predetermined capitation rate (CMS, 2011). For example, patient care provided for a total hip replacement would extend from hospitalization and surgery through skilled nursing care and rehabilitation, on through home health care and transition to the home setting.

Another feature of ACOs is agreements between providers and payers known as **shared savings, shared risk, or gainsharing**. When providers such as physicians and hospitals work together to reduce health care costs, a negotiated portion of the savings is returned to the providers as an incentive. For example, the Welby ACO is able to reduce costs for total hip replacements. The insurer returns a portion of these savings to Welby ACO, which is divided between Bigtown Hospital and the orthopedic surgeons participating in the ACO. Chapter 7 presents an example of budgeting bundled payments.

A key provision of ACOs is **value-based purchasing**, which directly links payment to quality of care. ACOs must demonstrate application of evidence-based practice, care coordination, reporting quality indicators, and quality improvement efforts. In addition, ACOs must develop processes ensuring patient engagement and patient-centered care (CMS, 2011). For example, patients in ACOs must be empowered to engage in shared decision-making about treatment options. Health care information must be provided at a level the patient can understand.

The emphasis on care coordination throughout a patient episode, payment based on disease episodes, evidence-based care, and patient engagement set ACOs apart from MCOs. In addition, ACOs are prohibited from gatekeeping. One goal of the ACO is to create a patient-centered **medical home**, a collaboration between patients and their primary care and other health care providers to offer culturally sensitive, comprehensive health care (CMS, 2011).

ACOs are thought to remedy many of the problems that occur in managed care. Potential under-care is addressed by ensuring open access and a well-coordinated vertical system of care from hospital to community. Potential over-care is addressed by implementing strategies such as bundled payment for episodes of care that aligns all the providers. Requirements that ACOs submit detailed reports of quality indicators with plans for quality improvement reduce both under-care and over-care concerns. The emphasis on evidence-based practice and on quality improvement supports the adoption of best practices. Patient-centered care that requires patient engagement promotes culturally sensitive approaches and improved health literacy (CMS, 2011). Although ACOs differ from MCOs in some important ways, both require substantial changes in provider incentives, thinking, and practice compared to fee-for-service systems.

One of Welby ACO's first initiatives is developing a bundled payment strategy for patients with heart failure. Bigtown Hospital's 30-day readmission rate for these patients is 34% compared to the overall national rate of 24.6 % (Yale New Haven Health System Corporation Center for Outcomes Research and Evaluation, 2010). The protocol for patients with heart failure admitted to Bigtown Hospital now includes extensive in-hospital patient and family education. The PTMG cardiologist works closely with the hospitalist, utilizing best practices based on current evidence. Once a heart failure patient is discharged, MNC works with PTMG cardiologists to provide telephone follow-up and support. A local home health agency, HomeNurse Home Health, contracts with Welby ACO, so hospital patients who are at high risk for readmissions receive up to three home visits for assessment, education, and monitoring. The 30-day heart failure readmission rate dropped to 30% within 6 months of initiation, with the bundled payment shared by Bigtown Hospital, PTMG, HomeNurse Home Health and MNC.

PRIMARY CARE UTILIZATION AND FINANCIAL MEASURES

It is important for managed care providers to continually monitor utilization and financial data. Utilization and financial indicators are explained using examples based on reporting for PTMG Pediatric Services. Figure 3.1 summarizes the managed care indicators discussed in this section, with their calculation and suggestions for interpretation.

Outpatient visits. An outpatient **visit** occurs any time that a physician or MLP has direct contact with a patient to provide outpatient services (Bureau of Primary Health Care [BPHC], 2011). Reimbursement policies and regulations may require that specific guidelines are met to allow billing for the patient visit (BPHC, 2011). Outpatient services funded by grants or capitation contracts generally do not involve billing the patient or insurer on a per-visit basis.

Member months. It is important for health care providers in managed care settings to know the size of the population they cover. Staffing and other resources must be adequate to serve the population, as the population size is the basis for many cost and revenue indicators. A common population measure is **member months**, or the total of all coverage months for each health plan enrollee over the plan year. Member months may also be averaged by dividing the total number of member months by the months in a specified time period. Member months may be annualized by multiplying the average member months by 12 months in a year. Table 3.1 presents a recent profit and loss statement from PTMG's Pediatric Services, showing an increase in the number of covered lives in the Welby HMO contract, from 120,000 in the first quarter of 2011 to 125,000 in the first quarter of 2012.

Indicator	Calculation	Interpretation
Utilization and Financial Performance		
Member months	Sum or average of enrollees for specified number of months	Total or average of covered lives.
Per member per month (PMPM)	Cost, revenue, or utilization measure ÷ Member months	Ratio of cost, revenue, or utilization to the total or average of covered lives for performance evaluation.
Per member per year (PMPY)	Cost, revenue, or utilization measure ÷ Member months over a year	Annual ratio of cost, revenue, or utilization to the total or average of covered lives for performance evaluation. Could use average member months x 12 to annualize member months.
Capitation revenue	Total revenue − Non-capitation revenue	Amount of an organization or program's revenue from capitation contracts, compared to other revenue sources. May convert to percent.
Medical Loss Ratio (MLR)	Total medical expenses ÷ Total revenue	Also called Medical Expense Ratio, inverse of ALR. Proportion of medical expenses to total costs, showing how much the organization invests in medical services.
Administrative Loss Ratio (ALR)	Total administrative expenses ÷ Total revenue	Also called Administrative Expense Ratio, inverse of MLR. Proportion of administrative expenses to total costs, showing how much money goes to administration and profits.
Outpatient Utilization and Costs		
Outpatient visits	Total or average of billable patient visits	Patient visits that qualify for billing or capitation reimbursement. May track visits by PCP, specialist, or MLP.
PCP referral rate	Specialist visits referred by PCP ÷ PCP visits x 1000	Indicator of overall utilization of specialty services by PCPs.
PCP referral percentage	Specialist visits referred by PCP ÷ PCP visits x 100	Indicator applied to specialist utilization by individual PCPs.
Specialist referral visits	Total or average of visits per patient referral	Measure of cost and utilization of specialist referrals. May also measure PCP and MLP visits per patient.
Mid-level practitioner (MLP) visits	Total or average of patient visits per MLP	Mid-level practitioners include nurse practitioners, nurse midwives, physician assistants, and any other non-physician providers authorized to manage and bill for a patient visit.
Cost per visit	Total or average cost per outpatient visit	Measure of provider's financial performance and utilization of services.
Other provider costs per visit	Total or average of other office visit costs per visit	May include lab tests or supplies used during a patient visit. May track costs by PCP, specialist, or MLP.
Inpatient Utilization and Costs		
Admission rate	Inpatient admissions ÷ Member months x 1000	Inpatient utilization for covered lives.
PCP admission rate	Inpatient admissions ÷ Patient visits x 1000	These are inpatient admissions for members referred to the hospital by the PCP. Inpatient utilization per PCP. May also calculate for specialist physicians.

Figure 3.1 *Managed Care Indicators*   *(continued)*

Hospitalization rate	Inpatient days ÷ Member months x 1000	Overall inpatient utilization for all covered lives.
Average cost per inpatient admission	Total inpatient charges ÷ Total admissions	May calculate overall or per PCP or specialist physician as a financial performance measure.

Note: Measures used in these calculations must be over the same time period.

Figure 3.1 *Managed Care Indicators*   *(continued)*

Per member per month (PMPM). Financial indicators in managed care settings often report revenue, expenses, or utilization as a ratio of plan membership. One commonly used indicator is **PMPM**, in which the revenue, cost, or utilization measure is divided by the number of plan enrollees for over a monthly time period. If more than 1 month of data is involved, PMPM is calculated by dividing the revenue, cost, or utilization value for a specified time period by the same time period's member months. For example, Table 3.1 shows the 23,500 pediatric PCP visits for the first quarter 2012 are divided by the member months of 125,000 for a 0.19 PMPM utilization indicator.

Per member per year (PMPY). **PMPY** represents a measure of revenue, expenses, or utilization for each health plan enrollee per year. The PMPY may be annualized by multiplying the average PMPM by 12 (months in a year). The average PMPM utilization of 0.023 specialist visits in Table 3.1 is annualized and reported as 0.28 for the first quarter of 2012.

Primary and specialist care visits. **Primary care** services include diagnosis, treatment, maintenance, and prevention services from PCPs or MLPs. **Specialty care** services include practices such as dermatology, orthopedics, and psychiatry that may be referred from PCPs or MLPs, particularly when gatekeeping is required. Other outpatient visit costs include authorized expenses for services such as laboratory, radiology, and pharmacy. As shown in Table 3.1, both primary and specialty care visits have increased from the first quarter of 2011 to the first quarter of 2012, with a greater cost increase for specialists compared to PCPs.

Referral rate and percentage. As PTMG must pay the costs for specialist referrals, it is important to monitor the **referral rate,** or the number of patient visits with specialists referred by the PCPs divided by all PCP visits and converted to a rate, as shown in Figure 3.1. When reviewing specialist utilization by individual providers, a **referral percentage** may be calculated, which is the number of patient visits with specialists referred by the PCP divided by all of the PCP's visits times 100 (Kongstvedt, 2007). The PTMG's pediatric population is more healthy than average, so specialist utilization is relatively low.

Admission and hospitalization rate. Hospitalizations are costly and require even more oversight and management than the use of specialty services. The **admission rate** is the number of admissions divided by member months for the same time period times 1000. The **hospitalization rate** is the number of inpatient days divided by member months for the same period times 1000. Both the admission and hospitalization rates indicate overall hospital utilization for plan members covered by PTMG. Additional information is obtained by estimating the average length of stay by dividing the number of inpatient days by the number of hospital admissions, discussed in Chapter 4. Improvements in primary wellness care, such as improving asthma care for PTMG patients, should help reduce admissions and inpatient days, which might be a reason for the decrease in these indicators from the first quarter of 2011 to the first quarter of 2012.

Average cost per admission. The average cost per admission allows estimation of the monetary value of inpatient care, calculated by dividing total hospital costs by the number of admissions. One can estimate the financial savings possible from reducing preventable hospital readmissions by reviewing the average costs per admission. Although costs are

Table 3.1 *Pine Tree Medical Group, Pediatric Services, Profit and Loss Statement, 1st Quarter 2011–2012*

Indicators	1st Qtr. 2011	1st Qtr. 2012	% change
Total member months	120,000	125,000	4.2%
Outpatient utilization			
Total PCP visit	23,000	23,500	2.2%
PMPM	0.19	0.19	−1.9%
PMPY	2.30	2.26	−1.9%
PCP cost per visit	$100	$100	0.0%
Other PCP cost per visit	$50	$55	10.0%
Total specialist encounters	2800	3000	7.1%
PCP referral rate	0.12	0.13	4.9%
PMPM	0.023	0.024	2.9%
PMPY	0.28	0.29	2.9%
Specialist cost per encounter	$150	$160	6.7%
Other specialist cost per encounter	$100	$110	10.0%
Inpatient utilization			
Total inpatient days	800	750	−6.3%
Hospitalization rate	6.7	6.0	−10.0%
Admissions	230	220	−4.3%
Admission rate	1.9	1.8	−8.2%
Average cost per inpatient admission	$2800	$3000	7.1%
Financial performance			
Total capitation revenue	$5,000,000	$5,210,000	4.2%
PMPM	$42	$42	0.0%
PMPY	$500	$500	0.0%
Paid Charges and IBNR	$4,472,000	$4,782,500	6.9%
PCP charges	$3,450,000	$3,642,500	5.6%
Specialist charges	$700,000	$810,000	15.7%
50% Risk inpatient charges	$322,000	$330,000	2.5%
Estimated charges IBNR	$770,000	$1,105,000	43.5%
Estimated % charges IBNR	17.2%	23.1%	34.2%
Administrative costs	$250,000	$250,000	0.0%
Medical loss ratio	89.4%	91.8%	2.6%
Administrative loss ratio	10.6%	8.2%	−22.3%
Total expenses	$4,722,000	$5,032,500	6.6%
Net P&L	$ 278,000	$ 177,500	−36.2%

rising, on average, the costs per pediatric admission are relatively low compared to adult and elderly admissions. Reasons for lower costs include fewer procedures, a lower rate of chronic illness, and fewer multi-system health problems for pediatric patients. However, one lengthy and costly admission to a neonatal intensive care unit (NICU) can impact on hospitalization costs for the PTMG pediatricians.

Capitation revenue and paid charges. Table 3.1 shows that the **capitation revenue,** or amount of authorized capitation reimbursement, allocated to PTMG Pediatric Services in the first quarter of 2013 was $5,210,000, which increased by 4.2% in 2012 to match the negotiated increase in member months. The **paid charges,** or the charges authorized by the capitation plan and used as a measure of costs, are largely generated by PTMG Pediatric Services to reimburse for PCP visits and other PCP costs, amounting to $4,782,500 in the first quarter of 2011. The Pine Tree Medical Group assumes 50% of the risk of inpatient hospitalization, so the inpatient paid charges are 50% of the total inpatient paid charges, with Welby HMO at risk for the 50% remaining.

Incurred but not reported. In health care, considerable time might elapse for a bill to be processed and reimbursed. Patients might be hospitalized or see a specialist during one reporting period, but the IPA might not receive the bill until the following reporting period. It is important for providers with capitation revenue to carefully estimate the **incurred but not reported (IBNR)** or unreported expenses for which the IPA or MCO will be liable, to ensure an adequate reserve of funds to pay those expenses. The amount and percentage of estimated IBNR expenses for PTMG Pediatric services increased substantially between the first quarter of 2011 and the first quarter of 2012. One reason is that Welby ACO is developing new financial oversight systems for bundled payments, so the billing process is somewhat slower than the previous year.

Administrative costs. Costs are generated for the provision of direct goods and services, such as nursing care, physician consultations, and pharmaceuticals. Administrative costs are the indirect costs of running a program or service, also referred to as **overhead**. The administrative costs for Pediatric Services at PTMG are estimated as the salaries for the clerical staff who manage the office. Other settings might include rent, utilities, stop-loss insurance, and other support services as part of overhead. Physician practices might also pay the MCO a fee for managing administrative requirements.

Medical loss and administrative loss ratio. The **medical loss ratio (MLR)** represents the portion of a health plan's expenses allocated to clinical services compared to total revenue. Table 3.1 shows that the MLR for Pediatric Services at PTMG is the total paid charges and IBNR divided by capitation revenue, reported as 91.8% in the first quarter of 2012. The **administrative loss ratio (ALR)** represents the portion of a health plan's expenses allocated to administrative costs and profit compared to total revenue. The ALR is also the inverse of the MLR, so the MLR plus the ALR must equal 100%. The ALR for the first quarter of 2012 is therefore 8.2 % (100%–91.8%). The MLR and the ALR serve as indicators that adequate resources are provided for clinical services compared to administration and profit.

The PPACA establishes more stringent rules and guidelines for setting MLRs than in the past, with minimum MLR ratios in the neighborhood of 80% to 85% (Yin, 2010). This regulation helps ensure that managed care plans and other health insurance plans adequately fund health care services and reasonably control their profits.

Total expenses and net P&L. All expense sources added together result in total expenses. In Table 3.1, total expenses represent paid charges and IBNR plus administrative costs. In order to determine whether the Pediatric Services at PTMG operates at a financial profit or loss, total expenses are subtracted from the total capitation revenue to calculate the **profit and loss statement (P&L).** Note that the pediatric PCPs report increasing expenses and decreasing profitability from the first quarter of 2011 to the first quarter of 2012. It would be important to review whether there were any unusually high-cost cases during this time period that may have reached the need for stop-loss coverage. Only one very high-cost case could have an impact on the expenses of a relatively small group practice such as PTMG Pediatric Services.

PERFORMANCE MEASURES FOR INPATIENT AND AMBULATORY CARE

Although Table 3.1 provides an overall view of utilization and financial indicators for Pediatric Services at PTMG, it is also important to closely track individual provider performance in managed care settings. Some providers may provide better quality of care, some providers may provide less costly care, and some providers may maintain high quality as well as cost savings. Good performance tracking links costs to the quality of care. This section presents an example of **drilling down** the aggregate data in Table 3.1 to analyze individual provider performance in greater detail. This example focuses on the performance of the three pulmonary specialists that PTMG pediatricians, used for referrals and is reported in Table 3.2.

Most of the pulmonary specialty care PTMG pediatric patients require is for diagnoses of asthma, bronchitis, or pneumonia. Pulmonary specialists A, B, and C receive 350 referrals over the first quarter 2012, with 1200 total patient visits. Average charges are reported as $140 specialist charges per visit and $80 other charges per visit, shown in Table 3.2. However, when reviewing the individual indicators for each specialist, differences in performance become apparent.

Average visits per referral. Table 3.2 provides information on the number of patients or referrals to each pulmonary specialist. By dividing the total number of visits by the total referrals, the average visits per referral is calculated. This indicator reports the intensity of specialist utilization per referral, with Dr. C close to average, Dr. A below average, and Dr. B above average. Not only does Dr. B schedule more visits for referrals than the other specialists in this report, but Dr. B's charges and other costs are substantially higher. The total costs for Dr. B account for a greater proportion of overall ambulatory specialist care than the other pulmonologists evaluated in this report.

Hospital utilization and average length of stay (ALOS). One of the goals of Welby ACO and PTMG pediatricians is to reduce preventable hospital utilization. Hospital admissions and inpatient days are therefore reported in Table 3.2, as well as **average length of stay (ALOS)**. ALOS is estimated by dividing the total inpatient days by the number of admissions. Although Dr. A reports the lowest specialist charges, Dr. A's inpatient days, ALOS, and costs per admission are the highest. Dr. A may have problems with patient under-care in the specialist office setting, which might result in poor outcomes and longer, more costly inpatient care. In contrast, Dr. C developed a pediatric asthma management protocol in 2011 that appears to reduce hospitalizations, length of stay, and hospital costs in the first quarter of 2012. This asthma management protocol requires further examination, as PTMG pediatricians may want to discuss this protocol as a recommendation for the other specialists in their panel

Readmissions and readmission rate. Readmission to the hospital following a specified time after discharge (usually 7, 15, or 30 days) is a performance measure that shows the effectiveness of hospital and transitional care. As part of the ACA 2010 provisions, the Centers for Medicare and Medicaid Services (CMS) will reduce payments to hospitals with high readmission rates for conditions such as heart failure and pneumonia (Silow-Carroll, Edwards, & Lashbrook, 2011). Table 3.2 reports that Dr. A has 12 hospital readmissions 15 days following discharge, and a 15-day readmission rate of nearly 22% for the first quarter of 2012, reinforcing concerns about under-care of patients when they transition from the hospital to home. Further drilling down for patient admission and 15-day readmission diagnosis would provide more information about reasons for these readmissions and whether the readmissions might be preventable.

Emergency room visits and costs. The managed care utilization, financial, and performance indicators presented in this section might be used in other health care settings, as

Table 3.2 *Pulmonary Specialist Performance Report, PTMG Pediatric Services,*
1st Quarter 2012

Performance Indicator	Dr. A	Dr. B	Dr. C	Total or Average
Number of referrals (patients)	120	80	150	350
Total encounters	200	500	500	1200
Avg. encounters/referral	1.7	6.3	3.3	3.4
Specialist cost per encounter	$100	$200	$120	$140
Other specialist cost per encounter	$50	$125	$65	$80
Total specialist charges	$30,000	$162,500	$92,500	$285,000
Specialist inpatient utilization				
Total admissions (including readmissions)	55	50	25	130
Total inpatient days	175	125	50	350
ALOS	3.2	2.5	2.0	2.7
15-day readmissions	12	6	2	20
15-day readmission rate	21.8%	12.0%	8.0%	15.4%
Cost per admission	$2800	$2500	$2200	$2500
Total inpatient costs	$154,000	$125,000	$55,000	$334,000
50% risk inpatient costs	$77,000	$62,500	$27,500	$167,000

well. These are not all of the indicators that might be used in managed care settings; sources such as the NCQA have more information about measurement and data. For example, both PCPs and specialists might report emergency room (ER) utilization not only by provider but for the presenting diagnosis. Dr. C's office tracks and follows up on their pediatric patients when they visit the Bigtown Hospital ER for asthma attacks.

Formulary, generic, and brand-name drugs. PTMG reports the prescribing and costs of medications that are or are not in the **formulary**, or approved prescribing list. MCOs or other health plans often establish formularies to manage the cost and utilization of pharmaceuticals, and may charge patients all or part of the cost of nonformulary prescriptions. **Generic medications** are equivalent to chemically similar **brand-name medications** for which a drug company retains the patent. Generic medications cost less than their brand-name counterparts, so generic medications are often listed in formularies. Brand-name medications may or may not be included in the formulary if a generic substitute is available. Managed care plans thus have the potential to encourage providers to make cost-effective choices among formulary and generic medications. (Penner, Penner, & Keck, 2004).

COMPARING AND TRENDING INDICATORS

The indicators discussed in this chapter as well as other indicators can be compared and followed over time. Comparison to other departments (such as the financial performance of PTMG Adult Services to PTMG Pediatric Services) or settings (PTMG compared to Group

MD, another local IPA) helps in evaluation compared to other similar work units. Indicators may also be compared to benchmarks such as aggregate averages or industry standards. Comparison of current to past indicators allows for trending that identifies improvement or decline over time. Indicators can also be used for baseline and outcomes measure in evaluating small quality improvement projects, also known as **small tests of change** (Institute for Healthcare Improvement, 2011).

Small Test of Change

The pediatricians at PTMG are concerned that the vaccination rates for their preschool and preteen members have fallen over recent years. The state has not strongly enforced requirements for proof of vaccinations for students in elementary schools. A survey indicates that many parents are busy and find it difficult to schedule appointments, are concerned about the cost of vaccines, or don't understand the importance of immunization. In 2011, an outbreak of pertussis sent over a dozen young children to the Bigtown Emergency Room. Several of these patients required hospitalization, and one of these children died of complications. The PTMG pediatricians keep childhood vaccines available and document educating and immunizing during patient visits, with an estimated 95% vaccination rate for patients seen in their office. The concern is child health plan members who do not regularly visit the pediatrician, as the community vaccination rate for Bigtown children has dropped to about 70%.

The goal of PTMG's pediatricians is to raise vaccination rates to 95% for all preschool and elementary school-aged children in the Bigtown community. The strategy is for PTMG to work with nurses at MNC to improve community outreach and access over the coming year. Pediatric nursing faculty and a pediatric NP organize an evening as well as a weekend drop-in clinic at the MNC so parents don't have to wait for an appointment to bring their children. MNC nurses also staff vaccination stations at local sports events, community centers, and schools. PTMG provides the needed vaccines, supplies, and equipment. MNC utilizes volunteer student nurses to assist the NPs.

Indicators used for baseline and outcome measures in evaluating this small test of change include the completed vaccination rate for the preschool and school-age target group, which improved from about 70% to 93% from 2011 to 2012. Other indicators include the number of vaccination visits, the cost per visit, and the total costs for this initiative. ER visits and hospitalization for pertussis and other vaccine-preventable diseases are additional indicators to help PTMG pediatricians know if this small test of change is effective. The increase in vaccinations and drop in preventable ER and hospital utilization is convincing. In addition, the nurse-run program is far less costly than treating children stricken with these preventable diseases. The PTMG pediatricians decide to contract with MNC in 2012 for immunization outreach services.

CONCLUSION

Managed care strategies are developed to counter the high and growing costs of fee-for-service systems and to reduce incentives related to third-party transactions, moral hazard, and supplier-induced demand. New strategies such as bundled payment approaches are evolving as the United States faces increasing pressures to improve health care quality while controlling costs.

This chapter provides examples of reporting managed care performance indicators in health care settings. A list of some commonly used health insurance terms and definitions are available at the California Department of Managed Care Useful Terms website (www.dmhc.ca.gov). More discussion of performance indicators relevant to health care utilization and nursing care is presented in Chapter 4.

Discussion and Exercises

1. Your neighbor asks for advice in choosing a health insurance plan. Give at least two examples of information sources you could share that might be helpful in this situation.

2. You're a medical-surgical staff nurse, and you notice fewer patients admitted over the last year for elective surgery, since your hospital became an ACO. Discuss the factors that might lead to fewer elective surgery admissions, related to strategies such as shared savings.

3. Stage a debate arguing the value of enrolling patients in medical homes.

REFERENCES

Bataille, G., Anderson, K., & Penner, S. (1995). A public-private sector venture in managed mental health: Solano County's experience. *Administration and Policy in Mental Health, 22,* 327–344.

Bureau of Primary Health Care. (2011). *User's manual: Uniform data system* (16th ed.). Health Resources and Services Administration (HRSA). OMB Control Number 0195–0193 Expiration date 01/31/2014. Retrieved from http://bphc.hrsa.gov/healthcenterdata statistics/reporting/2011manual.pdf

Centers for Medicare & Medicaid Services. (2011). *Program; Medicare Shared Savings Program: Accountable Care Organizations Final Rule.* 42 CFR Part 425 [CMS-1345-F] RIN 0938-AQ22. Department of Health and Human Services. Retrieved from http://www.gpo.gov/fdsys/browse/collection.action?collectionCode=FR&browsePath=2011%2F11%2F11–02\%2F4%2 FCenters+for+Medicare+%26amp%3B+Medicaid+Services&isCollapsed=false&leafLevel Browse=false&isDocumentResults=true&ycord=164

Centers for Medicare & Medicaid Services, Office of the Actuary, National Health Statistics Group, U.S. Department of Commerce, Bureau of Economic Analysis; and U.S. Bureau of the Census. (2012). Table 1 *National health expenditures aggregate, per capita amounts, percent distribution, and average annual percent change: Selected calendar years 1960–2010.* Retrieved from https://www.cms.gov/Research-Statistics-Data-and-Systems/Statistics-Trends-and-Reports/NationalHealthExpendData/downloads//tables.pdf

Gabel, J., Levitt, L., Pickreign, J., Whitmore, H., Holve, E., Rowland, D.,... & Hawkins, S. (2001). Job-based health insurance In 2001: Inflation hits double digits, managed care retreats. *Health Affairs, 20,* 180–186. Retrieved from http://www.healthaffairs.org/

Holmes, A. (2011). Executive Extra. CNO and the ACO: An alphabet soup of healthcare reform. *Nursing Management Issue, 42,* 46–48.

Institute for Healthcare Improvement. (2011). *Science of improvement: Testing changes.* Retrieved from: http://www.ihi.org/knowledge/Pages/HowtoImprove/Scienceof ImprovementTestingChanges.aspx

Kaiser Permanente Newsroom. (2002). History. Retrieved from http://www.kaiserpermanente.org/newsroom/history.html

Kongstvedt, P. R. (2007). *Essentials of managed health care* (5th ed.). Burlington, MA: Jones & Bartlett.

Managed Care On-Line (MCOL). (2011). *Fact sheet: Managed care national statistics, 2010.* Retrieved from http://www.mcareol.com/factshts/factnati.htm

Patient Protection and Affordable Care Act. (2010). Pub. L. No. 111–148, §2702, 124 Stat. 119, 318–319. Retrieved from http://housedocs.house.gov/energycommerce/ppacacon.pdf

Penner, M., Penner, S. J., & Keck, W. (2004). Chapter 5: The Formulary, Physician, and Pharmacist: Managing and Delivering Outpatient Drug Benefits. Jennie (Ed.). *Research in the Sociology of Health Care: Chronic Care, Health Care Systems and Services Integration, 22,* 81–97.

Shi, L., & Singh, D. A. (2008). *Delivering health care in America: a systems approach*. Burlington, MA: Jones & Bartlett.

Silow-Carroll, S., Edwards, J. N., & Lashbrook, A. (2011). *Reducing hospital readmissions: Lessons from top-performing hospitals. Synthesis Report*. The Commonwealth Fund pub. 1473 vol. 5. Health Management Associates.

The Kaiser Family Foundation and Health Research & Educational Trust. (2011). *Employer health benefits 2011 annual survey*. Menlo Park, CA: Henry J. Kaiser Family Foundation and Chicago, IL: Health Research & Educational Trust.

US Census Bureau. (2002). HMO enrollment, selected years, 1980–2001. Statistical Abstract of the United States: 2002. Retrieved from http://www.census.gov/statab/www/

Yale New Haven Health System Corporation Center for Outcomes Research and Evaluation. (2010). *Medicare hospital quality chartbook 2010:Performance report on outcomes measures for acute myocardial infarction, heart failure, and pneumonia*. Centers for Medicare & Medicaid Services (CMS).

Yin, S. (2010). *New Affordable Care Act rules give consumers better value for insurance premiums*. HHS Press Office. Retrieved from http://www.fiercehealthcare.com/press-releases/new-affordable-care-act-rules-give-consumers-better-value-insurance-premium-0

CROSSWORD: *Chapter 3—Managed Care*

Across

4 Reimbursement by pre-paying for the care of a specified population over a specified time period, used in managed care contracts.

6 Health professional who enables the expansion of primary care services, such as a nurse practitioner (abbreviation).

8 A managed care organization or plan that provides health care to persons enrolled in a pre-paid plan (abbreviation).

9 The portion of a health plan's expenses allocated to clinical services compared to total revenue (abbreviation).

10 New model of health care financing and delivery featuring shared savings strategies for all providers for an episode of patient care (abbreviation).

12 A managed care indicator in which the revenue, cost, or utilization measure is divided by the number of plan enrollees for a monthly time period (abbreviation).

13 An outpatient contact with a physician, MLP, or other health care professional that meets criteria for billing and reimbursement.

15 ACO incentive in which a negotiated portion of the savings is returned to the providers as an incentive, also called shared risk or shared savings.

18 Reimbursement system that includes payment for all care provided from disease onset to recovery.

Down

1 Physician in general or pediatric practice who is often the first point of patient contact for diagnosis, treatment, and prevention (abbreviation).

2 Managed care requirement that access to specialists or other specified services must be authorized by a PCP or other designated provider.

3 Approved prescribing list for pharmaceuticals.

5 Expenses that are not yet reported for a specific time period, but that the MCO or other organization will be responsible to pay (abbreviation).

6 A managed care plan that provides health care to persons enrolled in a pre-paid plan (abbreviation).

7 A managed care plan that covers services from providers within the plan more generously than services from providers outside the plan (abbreviation).

10 Total inpatient days divided by the number of admissions to determine, on average, how long patients are hospitalized (abbreviation).

11 Indirect, administrative and support expenses such as rent and clerical services.

12 A managed care indicator in which the revenue, cost, or utilization measure is divided by the number of plan enrollees over a year (abbreviation).

14 A managed care plan offering more generous coverage if members select the preferred providers rather than providers outside the plan (abbreviation).

16 A physician group practice model where the physicians own the practice but contract with an MCO for members and reimbursement (abbreviation).

17 The portion of a health plan's expenses allocated to administrative costs and profit compared to total revenue (abbreviation).

Chapter 4: Measuring Nursing Care

A hospital bed is a parked taxi with the meter running—Groucho Marx

Learning Objectives

1. Explain the importance of measuring all values included in an indicator over the same time period.
2. Calculate at least three indicators that measure nursing performance.
3. Differentiate between capacity, utilization, performance, and financial indicators used in settings where nurses provide care.
4. Justify the measurement of HPPD related to patient acuity levels.

Key Terms

absenteeism	discharge	indicators
acuity	financial indicator	indirect hours
admission	fiscal year	indirect staffing
agency nurse	fixed capacity	job position
available beds	fixed FTE	licensed beds
average daily census (ADC)	flexible FTE	metrics
	FTE coverage factor	microsystem
bed turnaround time	full-time equivalent (FTE)	net revenue
bed turns	global budgeting	nonoperating expense
capacity	gross revenue	nonpersonnel expenses
census	hours per patient day (HPPD)	nonproductive hours
contractual allowance		nonproductive percent
direct care hours	hours per unit of service (HPUOS)	nurse to patient (N/P) ratio
direct staffing		

nursing hours per patient day (NHPPD)

observation

occupancy rate

operating expense

out-of-pocket

overtime

patient day

patient flow

payer mix

per diem nurse

performance

permanent staffing

personnel expenses

potential patient days

productive hours

productive nursing hours per patient day (PNHPPD)

referral

revenue

salary

self-pay

self-referral

skill mix

staffed beds

staffing capacity

staffing indicators

structural capacity

travel nurse

unit of service (UOS)

utilization

variable capacity

variable staffing

volume

wage

Nurses may work in health care for years, yet never think about how nursing care is measured. Many nurses do not understand how their work affects health care costs, or how nurses contribute to health care revenues. Nurses are an important part of the health care economy, and changes in health care financing impact on nurses and nursing care. It is therefore important for nurses to understand concepts and definitions used in measuring and valuing nursing care.

In 2008, hospitals employed 62.2% of nurses (Health Resources and Services Administration, 2010). Nursing costs often represent the largest part of hospital labor budgets, and in some hospitals the largest part of the total budget (Douglas, 2010). Nurses work in other 24-hour inpatient settings such as skilled nursing facilities (SNFs) and nursing homes. Nursing support is often essential in outpatient settings such as medical offices, clinics, and other ambulatory health care centers, as well as in home health, public health, and other community-based agencies. There are many ways to measure nursing care across these settings.

This chapter discusses the use of **indicators**, also known as **metrics** or measures, that signify a specific condition or a specified level or value. Most nurses are familiar with clinical indicators such as normal and abnormal blood pressure values. The indicators discussed in this chapter serve a similar purpose, alerting the nurse about problems or progress that affect the financial health of the organization. The indicators presented in this chapter are often seen in performance and financial reports such as clinic or nursing unit budgets.

RULES AND CONVENTIONS FOR REPORTING INDICATORS

There are some rules (practices common to all settings) and conventions (practices followed in one's individual setting) that are important to consider when reporting indicators. It is also important to be aware of these rules and conventions when reading reports that present indicators. One purpose of these rules and conventions is to ensure accuracy, so that the report can be trusted as a basis for decision-making. Another reason for rules and conventions is to provide a clear and consistent approach that makes it easier to understand and interpret the indicators. Table 4.1, an activity report for the Millway University Nurse-Managed Health Center (MNC), provides examples for indicator reporting rules and conventions used throughout this textbook.

Consistent Time Period

Reports should follow the rule to clearly indicate the time period represented by the indicators used in reporting. The **fiscal year,** or annual reporting period, may follow the calendar or run from July 1 to June 30, or another designated 12-month cycle. Most inpatient and outpatient settings use standard calendar months for monthly reporting. Some inpatient settings organize monthly reports using 13 "months" of 28 days, based on two pay periods per 28-day "month." Regardless of how the time periods are defined, all indicators in the report must be measured over the same interval.

Examples provided assume that the indicators used in calculations and reporting are all measured over the same time period. It is recommended that the time period over which indicators are reported is included in the report title, as shown in the title of Table 4.1. All of the indicators reported for MNC for 2011 were collected in 2011, and are compared to the indicators collected and reported for 2012.

Indicators in calculations use the same time period. A related rule is that all indicators used in calculations are based on the same time period. For example, Table 4.1 reports a cost per patient visit of $112 for 2011. This indicator is calculated by dividing the total program costs of $95,300 for 2011 by the 850 total visits for 2011. The 2012 cost per visit of

Table 4.1 *Millway University Nurse-Managed Health Center Activity Report, 2011 to 2012*

Description	2011	2012
Capacity		
Examination rooms	1	3
NPs on staff	1	3
Total NP visits per day	4.0	18.0
Total NP visits per year	850	3943
Utilization (referrals)		
Total ACO referrals	160	984
Self-pay drop-in referrals	105	230
Total referrals	265	1214
Performance		
Total ACO visits	640	3332
ACO visits per referral	4.0	3.4
Self-pay drop-in visits	210	611
Self-pay visits per referral	2.0	2.7
Total visits	850	3943
Financial		
Personnel expense NPs	$70,000	$210,000
Benefits @ 30%	$21,000	$63,000
Clinic Manager 0.5 FTE	$0	$30,000
Clerical 0.8 FTE × 2	$0	$40,000
Total personnel expense	**$91,000**	**$343,000**
Nonpersonnel (supplies)	$4300	$19,500
Other nonpersonnel expenses	$0	$58,648
Total program expenses	$95,300	$412,500
Cost per patient visit	$112	$105
Welby ACO contract revenue	$35,000	$330,000
Grant revenue	$50,000	$50,000
Private collections	$3000	$6000
Donations	$20,000	$18,000
Total revenue	$108,000	$404,000
Revenue per patient visit	$127	$102
Net profit or loss (P&L)	$12,700	−$8500
Profit or loss per patient visit	$14.94	−$2.55

$105, and all other indicators that are calculated in this chapter and textbook, use the same time period for indicators used in their calculation.

Use raw data for calculations. It is best to follow the rule to use raw data that has not been rounded or already calculated for further calculations. Many reports and data analysis programs such as spreadsheets allow for rounding raw data to make it easier to report, or more meaningful to interpret. For example, Table 4.1 could report the actual self-pay visits per referral in 2012 as 2.656522, but rounding the value to 2.7 visits per referral is easier to report and understand. If calculations are based on the rounded amount rather than the raw data, error is introduced into the results that reduce accuracy. It is therefore best to use the original source data for further reporting and calculating. Spreadsheet software makes it easy to format data rounded to a readable value, and to save the exact value for further calculations. Calculations based on rounded data should be considered estimates, not exact results.

Rounding conventions. It is advisable to learn and follow conventions for rounding numbers in reports using indicators. When dollar figures are reported, the convention followed in this textbook is to report cents for amounts of $100 or less, and to round higher amounts to the nearest dollar. For example, Table 4.1 reports the net profit for MNC in 2011 as $12,700, but reports $14.94 as the profit per patient visit.

Percents, rates, and ratios. Indicators may be measured and reported in absolute amounts, or converted to rates or percentages. For example, hospital readmissions may be reported as the number of readmissions over a specified time period, defined as a readmission rate. Converting numbers to rates or percentages makes it possible to compare indicators across time or between settings.

Benchmarks. An indicator is often compared to a **benchmark**, or value that represents performance targeted to an internal or industry standard. Benchmarks vary across settings and indicators. Frequently performance is benchmarked (compared) to past performance, as shown in Table 4.1, comparing MNC's performance from 2011 to 2012. National benchmarks may be available, as for Medicare inpatient 30-day readmission rates for congestive heart failure. Frequently the benchmark represents average performance, such as the average hours per patient day (HPPD) of nursing care established as the target for nursing care on East Wing. Benchmarks enable the reader of a report to evaluate performance based on the indicators.

Learn and follow your setting's reporting conventions. Settings and institutions might establish practices for determining the time period for reports or for rounding indicators that differ from this textbook. Indicators might be defined or calculated in somewhat different ways across various settings. For example, a commonly used calculation of average length of stay (ALOS) is dividing patient days by discharges for the same time period. Some settings might instead divide patient days by admissions to calculate the ALOS. This chapter focuses on the most commonly recognized practices, definitions, and calculations for reporting health care indicators. However, when reviewing or preparing reports, make sure to learn the definitions and calculation methods used in the health care setting. It is also recommended to learn the commonly used performance benchmarks in your health care setting.

CATEGORIES OF INDICATORS

Commonly used indictors for measuring nursing care are organized into several categories in this chapter. **Capacity** indicators measure the extent to which a health care setting can meet consumer demand. **Utilization** indicators measure the extent of consumer demand for services in a health care setting. **Performance** indicators measure how well the health care setting's capacity operates in managing utilization. **Financial** indicators may be attached to capacity, utilization, or performance indicators to measure the associated monetary values. Figure 4.1 presents examples of indicators within each of these categories.

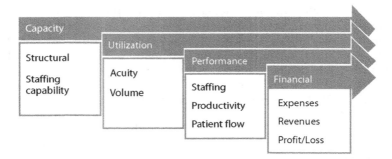

Figure 4.1 *Categories and Examples of Indicators for Measuring Nursing Care*

This chapter focuses on the categories of capacity, utilization, performance, and financial indicators because they represent the most commonly used indicators for measuring nursing care. Each of these indicators are explained, then their applications are discussed related to the ambulatory setting of MNC, and the inpatient nursing unit of East Wing at Bigtown Hospital. Hospital-wide indicators are presented in Chapter 12.

Capacity Indicators

Capacity indicators measure the extent to which a health care setting is able to meet consumer demand. The capacity of a health care setting is a starting point for measuring health care services. There are always limits to capacity, so strategies such as scheduling admissions are required to control utilization. In addition, health care settings cannot be expected to function at full capacity all of the time. Unexpected events such as delays and emergencies require health care systems to operate at some level less than full capacity. In other words, efficiency requires that utilization must be somewhat less than capacity. For example, a nursing unit staffed for 20 patient beds has a capacity of no more than 20 inpatients at any point in time. The daily census of that nursing unit is expected to average fewer than 20 patients per day because of delays in patient discharges, staff shortages, or other unexpected events.

Fixed and variable capacity. In many situations, the capacity of a health care setting is **fixed**, or will not increase or decrease at least over the course of a fiscal year. A hospital may equip only two operating rooms, so it cannot exceed the capacity of those operating rooms. In other situations, capacity may be **variable,** or adjusted based on utilization (volume). On days when few surgeries are scheduled, fewer nurses may be scheduled to attend the operating rooms; when there is a higher volume of surgeries, more nurses may be scheduled.

Structural Capacity

The **structural capacity** of a health care setting refers to the capability for providing services allowed by the facility's layout. Structural capacity is usually fixed. Settings in which procedures are performed (such as operating rooms) might measure capacity based on the rooms equipped for those procedures. Indicators may include the number of rooms available per day and the number of days per week that the procedure room is available. Structural capacity is important because it establishes physical limits on the number of patients who can be managed at any point in time.

Inpatient beds. Settings for inpatient care frequently measure capacity as the number of inpatient beds. An inpatient facility may have a specified number of **licensed beds** approved by regulatory agencies. Licensed beds represent fixed capacity. The facility might only equip and staff some of these licensed beds for patient care, which are referred to as **staffed beds** or **available beds.**

Potential patient days. An inpatient setting's **potential patient days** represent the maximum possible utilization over a specific time period given the bed capacity. Potential patient days are calculated by multiplying the number of staffed beds by the number of days in the time period. In other words, if a nursing unit has 20 staffed beds, the potential patient days are 600 for a 30-day month (20 × 30).

Staffing Capacity

The **staffing capacity** of a health care setting refers to the maximum number of patients health care providers can manage at any point in time. The staffing capacity of outpatient settings is often measured by the number of patient visits that can be managed by the outpatient providers, who might be physicians or **mid-level providers (MLPs),** such as nurse practitioners (NPs), nurse midwives, or physician assistants (Washington State Department of Social and Health Services, 2010). Although the number of patients seen by outpatient providers may vary, national benchmarks estimate 4400 patient visits per family practice physician per year, and 2500 patient visits per NP per year (Chicago Health & Health Systems Project, 2012).

Nurse to Patient Ratio (N/P ratio). In addition to available beds or rooms, the staffing for health care services is essential in measuring capacity. The **nurse to patient ratio**, also referred to as the nurse-patient ratio, or **N/P ratio,** represents the maximum number of patients assigned per nurse per shift. For example, if there are three nurses working a shift in a nursing unit with 20 beds, and the N/P ratio is 1:4, the nurses cannot be assigned more than four patients per unit, and the staffing capacity of the nursing unit is only 12 patients for that shift. Many inpatient settings have N/P ratio policies, and some states, such as California, have enacted N/P ratio regulatory mandates, based on required HPPD for patients at specified acuity levels.

Even when specific staffing ratios are not required, staffing is an important factor in capacity. For example, a hospital provides two operating rooms, then there must be sufficient staffing of surgeons, nurses, and other support staff to carry out procedures or the operating rooms cannot be utilized. In outpatient settings, providers are able to manage a specified number of patient visits per day. Pushing staff beyond their capacity increases the risk of medical errors and staff burnout, as well as violations of standards and regulations.

Utilization Indicators

Utilization indicators measure the extent of consumer demand for services in a health care setting. Patient utilization provides the basis for planning and managing health care services, given the capacity available. Utilization is variable. For example, the number of patients with respiratory disorders often increases in winter months, and decreases in summer months.

Patient Acuity

Most inpatient staff nurses realize that it is not just the number of patients that affect their workload on the nursing unit. The **acuity,** or severity of patient illness, influences the intensity of nursing care needed as well as the level of utilization of other health care services. Outpatient settings, other than home health, typically do not report acuity measures, although the trend to transition more seriously ill patients to the home and community may require more focus on outpatient acuity measures in the future (Jennings, 2008). In home health settings, acuity may be measured using indicators such as the number of nursing problems the patient presents (Harris, 2010). Inpatients require more nursing staff, more hours of nursing care, and more resources as their acuity level increases. Two inpatient acuity indicators are the case mix index (CMI) and the hours per patient day (HPPD).

Case mix index. The **case mix index (CMI)** is a measure of the intensity of care related to acuity, which is usually reported at the hospital level. The CMI represents the average **Medicare severity diagnosis-related group (MS-DRG)** relative weight. MS-DRGs are established by Medicare for hospital reimbursement classification, and are used by some private insurance plans, as well. The CMI is calculated by summing the MS-DRG weights for all Medicare discharges and dividing by the number of Medicare discharges. A CMI of 1.0 represents a national average. A CMI greater than 1.0 indicates the hospital serves patients requiring a higher than average intensity of care. One purpose of the CMI is to adjust Medicare reimbursement so hospitals treating more seriously ill patients receive an added proportion of resources (Centers for Medicare and Medicaid Services, 2005). A CMI can also be calculated for nursing units using the Medicare relative weights for discharges from that unit.

Hours per patient day. The **hours per patient day (HPPD)** indicates the amount of direct nursing care time an inpatient requires per day. In hospitals, patient classification systems (PCSs) are often used to estimate the HPPD based on the patient acuity. A PCS often links patient acuity as determined by case mix or other acuity measures to HPPD, and predicts the staffing and scheduling needs (Fasoli & Haddock, 2011).

Less acute settings, such as SNFs and nursing homes, may use a regulation or standard HPPD for all inpatients. A patient in an intensive care unit may require 24 HPPD, the maximum possible daily hours of care. HPPD requirements have a direct impact on nurse staffing, so this indicator is reviewed later in this chapter when performance indicators are discussed, related to direct care hours.

Patient Volume

The number of patient visits, procedures, or inpatients is a utilization measure often referred to as **volume** or **units of service (UOS)**. In outpatient settings, utilization may be measured as **referrals,** or the number of individuals directed to the setting for care. In some situations, the patient is referred by another health care provider. For example, many managed care plans require that a primary care provider determine whether or not a patient is referred to a specialist. In other situations, the patient selects a provider, which is known as **self-referral**. Outpatient utilization is also commonly measured as patient visits, discussed in Chapter 3.

Admissions. Patients are counted as **admissions** when they transfer from home or another facility to an inpatient facility. Admissions are a measure of inpatient utilization. Admissions to the nursing unit include transfers from home and other facilities as well as patients transferred from other departments within the facility. **Observation** patients who require close monitoring but who usually occupy an inpatient bed for less than 48 hours are also counted as admissions. Infants born in a hospital delivery room are typically not counted as admissions.

Daily census and average daily census. Nurses who provide inpatient care have probably heard of the daily **census** count of all inpatient beds that are occupied at a specific time. Most hospitals record the census at midnight, when patient activity is assumed to be low. The midnight census is used for billing reimbursement purposes as well as in measuring utilization (Green, 2004). The **average daily census (ADC)** is calculated as the patient days (sum of the daily census for a time period) divided by the number of days in that time period. For example, for a 30-day month, if the daily census totals 540 patient days, the ADC is 18.0 (540/30).

Patient days. The count of 24-hour days that patients occupy an inpatient setting is referred to as the number of **patient days**. The daily census is used to determine patient days. Patient days are such an important measure of inpatient services that many other indicators, such as HPPD, incorporate the patient day in their calculation.

Occupancy rate and average occupancy rate. The **occupancy rate**, also known as percent occupancy, measures how closely the utilization of a 24-hour nursing unit approaches its full capacity. To calculate a daily occupancy rate, the daily census is divided by the number of staffed beds and reported as a percent. For example, if the census on a nursing unit is 17 and there are 20 staffed beds, then the occupancy rate is 85% (17/20). To calculate the average occupancy rate over a longer time period, the actual patient days are divided by the potential patient days. If over a month the potential patient days are 600 and the actual patient days are 540, there is a 90% average occupancy rate for that month (540/600). The average occupancy rate can also be estimated by dividing the ADC by the number of staffed beds. If the ADC is 18 and there are 20 staffed beds, the average occupancy rate is 90% (18/20).

Performance Indicators

Performance indicators tell the reviewer how efficiently capacity is managed to meet the demands of utilization. As explained in Chapter 1, resources for health care are costly, so efficiency in meeting consumer demand is essential for all health care settings. This section therefore discusses a number of performance indicators related to staffing, staff productivity, patient flow through the health care setting, and patient outcomes.

Staffing Indicators

Health care is labor-intensive, requiring the expertise and efforts of nurses and other health care providers to assess and manage consumer health care. In outpatient and community-based settings, staffing is often relatively simple and similar to work settings in industries other than health care. For example, a nurse-managed health center might employ three full-time nurse practitioners who are scheduled to work 40 hours a week, less vacation or other approved leave time.

Inpatient care staffing is more complex and costly than in outpatient settings. Inpatient care must be provided 24 hours a day, seven days a week. Staff scheduling requires assigning multiple shifts and coverage for weekends and holidays. **Staffing indicators** measure the workload and labor needed for providing health care services, and are typically reported in more detail for inpatient staffing compared to outpatient staffing. Inpatient staffing and scheduling typically occur at the **microsystem** level, which is often the nursing unit or a work setting such as the Emergency Department.

Job positions. In many industries, employees work a standard full-time **job position** or defined occupation within the employing organization. Job positions may define the staffing in many outpatient and community-based settings in which nurses work. An earlier example describes three NPs who each have a job position working 40 hours a week at a nurse-managed health center. Many employees assigned to job positions are paid based on an annual **salary**, or compensation that does not change regardless of the number of hours worked over the year. Job positions are relatively simple to measure and report, representing a count of the number of employees working in a given setting.

Full-time equivalents. A standard measure for hourly employment is the **full-time equivalent** (**FTE**), indicating a full-time employee working eight hours a day, five days a week, for 52 weeks a year, for a total of 2080 hours per year. A job position might be filled by an employee working 1.0 FTE. However, an employee assigned to an FTE is likely to earn an hourly **wage**, or compensation based on the number of hours worked. FTEs also allow hiring and compensation for employees working part-time, or less than 1.0 FTE. For example, an employee working 20 hours a week represents 0.5 FTE. The FTE also allows the measurement of overtime or other hourly rates.

Fixed FTEs. **Fixed FTEs** resemble job positions, and are also referred to as **permanent staffing** or **indirect staffing**. Fixed FTEs are often reported by inpatient settings to represent staff hours scheduled regardless of patient volume. For example, many hospital nursing units require a nurse manager and a unit clerk, whether the census is high or low. These employees are often reported as fixed FTEs.

Flexible FTEs. **Flexible FTEs**, also called **variable staffing** or **direct staffing**, represent staffing based on actual or projected patient volume (Kirk, 1981). In other words, as the census increases, more staff nurse hours are required than if the census drops. Flexible FTEs allow employees to be assigned to work more or fewer hours per week so that the staffing capacity corresponds to volume. The number of patients, patient acuity, HPPD of care needed, and standards for N/P ratios are factors in determining the flexible FTEs required. To ensure high-quality patient care, and to manage the costs of RN staffing, the use of flexible staff nurse FTEs must be closely monitored.

Hourly shifts. FTEs are calculated based on the hours worked per shift, as well as the number of shifts worked per pay period. Shifts must be spread over the 2-week pay period, as labor laws and regulations apply if employees work more than 40 hours in a week. Table 4.2 shows how shift hours and FTEs are calculated for a 2-week pay period. These calculations demonstrate the applications of FTEs for estimating scheduling based on various shift schedules.

The examples of FTEs used in reports throughout this chapter assume inpatient nurses work 8-hour shifts. A full-time (1.0 FTE) nurse working 8-hour shifts will work 10 shifts, or 80 hours per pay period. Each shift therefore counts as 0.1 FTE, as shown in Table 4.2, so if a nurse only works five shifts per pay period the nurse is staffed at 0.5 FTE.

Table 4.2 *Calculations for Shift Hours and FTEs Over a 2-Week (14-Day) Pay Period*

Data and Calculations	Shift Schedules		
Hours worked per shift	8	10	12
Shifts worked for 1.0 FTE per pay period[a]	10	8	6
Hours per shift × days per pay period	8 × 10	10 × 8	12 × 6
Hours worked per pay period[b]	80	80	72
Hours worked per pay period ÷ 80 hours for 1.0 FTE per pay period	80 ÷ 80	80 ÷ 80	72 ÷ 80
FTE	1.0	1.0	0.9
Hours worked per shift ÷ hours worked per pay period	8 ÷ 80	10 ÷ 80	12 ÷ 72
FTE per shift	0.1	0.125	0.17
Days in pay period ÷ shifts for 1.0 FTE in pay period	14 ÷ 10	14 ÷ 8	14 ÷ 6
7-Day week FTE coverage factor for one shift	1.4	1.75	2.3
Coverage factor for shift × shifts in 24 hours	1.4 × 3	1.8 × 3	2.3 × 2
7-day WEEK 24-hour coverage factor	4.2	5.25	4.7

Notes: [a]Must spread shifts over 14-day pay period or factor overtime and labor law restrictions.

[b]12-hour schedules may be adjusted to reach 80 hours per pay period, or 1.0 FTE.

Nurse scheduling may differ from the standard 8-hour shift. Some settings schedule nurses to work 10-hour shifts. Full-time (1.0 FTE) nurses working 10-hour shifts must work 8 days per pay period. Each shift is estimated as 0.125 FTE (10 hours each shift divided by 80 hours per pay period), as shown in Table 4.2.

Inpatient settings increasingly schedule nurses to work 12-hour shifts. Nurses working 12-hour shifts are scheduled to work three shifts a week, or 72 hours over a 2-week pay period (12 hours per shift times 6 days per pay period). Table 4.2 shows that 72 hours per pay period equals 0.9 FTE (72 hours per pay period divided by 80 hours per pay period for 1.0 FTE). One 12-hour shift is estimated as 1.7 FTE (12 hours per shift divided by 72 hours per pay period). In some settings, nurses working 12-hour shifts receive full-time employee benefits, but the 12-hour staffing is budgeted at 0.9 FTE. In other settings, adjustments are made to 12-hour scheduling so that nurses working 12-hour shifts work an additional 8 hours per pay period for 1.0 FTE.

FTE coverage factor. Table 4.2 shows calculations for an **FTE coverage factor** for adjusting inpatient FTEs. Inpatient settings must schedule staff seven days a week, based on their hourly schedules. For example, inpatient settings where nurses work 8-hour shifts require 1.0 FTE to cover the 10 weekdays in the pay period. An additional 0.4 FTE is required to cover the four weekend days in the pay period. The 7-day weekly FTE coverage factor is therefore 1.4 for staff working 8-hour shifts. To calculate 7-day and 24-hour FTE coverage, the coverage factor is multiplied by the number of shifts. As a result, 4.2 FTE (1.4 FTE per shift times three 8-hour shifts in 24 hours) are required each week for 8-hour shift nursing coverage.

A 7-day and 24-hour coverage factor is estimated for nurses working three 10-hour shifts, shown in Table 4.2. However, some settings such as procedure rooms may only schedule nurses for one 10-hour shift every 24-hour day, and staff only for weekdays. The coverage factor would need to be adjusted to fit the scheduling in the specific work setting. One way to estimate 10-hour coverage is to remember that each 10-hour shift accounts for 0.125 FTE. The number of 10-hour shifts required are multiplied by 0.125 FTE to determine the number of 10-hour FTEs needed.

Table 4.2 shows the 7-day and 24-hour coverage factors for nurses working 12-hour shifts. Only two 12-hour shifts are scheduled per 24-hour day. The 7-day coverage factor of 2.3 FTE is therefore multiplied by two, estimating 4.7 FTE (due to rounding error) for 7-day and 24-hour nursing coverage. These staffing estimates may vary based on the staffing and scheduling systems used in health care settings. However, these calculations show the basic relationships between shifts and FTEs.

Skill mix. An inpatient nursing unit's **skill mix** measures the proportion of RNs compared to other nursing staff, such as licensed practical nurses (LPNs) nurse assistants. For example, if three RNs and one LPN are scheduled for a shift, the skill mix is 75% RNs and 25% LPNs. There are financial considerations in determining the skill mix, as RNs are more costly to employ than other nursing staff, such as LPNs and nurse assistants. However, standards and regulations around scope of practice and quality of patient care must also play a role in determining the staffing skill mix (American Nurses Association, 1999; Clarke & Donaldson, 2008; Institute of Medicine [IOM], 2004). It is assumed in these examples that only RNs are staffed, so the skill mix need not be calculated.

Productivity Indicators

Productivity indicators measure the efficiency of staff that are assigned to provide patient care. While staffing indicators measure how many staff and staff hours are scheduled, productivity indicators measure how well these staff perform.

Outpatient visits. In outpatient settings, such as clinics, productivity is often measured using patient visits. Productivity may be calculated as the average number of visits a provider manages over a specified time period, such as an hour, day, month, or year. The number of visits per referral is another productivity measure for ambulatory care, measuring the number of visits that individual patients make to a provider during an episode of care. Assuming the patient concern is successfully resolved, fewer visits required per referral indicates a higher level of performance. Chapter 3 discusses some additional performance measures for outpatient care, including the number of referrals that primary care providers make to specialists.

Productive hours. The time that employees are paid to carry out their work assignments are known as **productive hours**. Productive hours can be measured in outpatient settings. However, because of the importance and costs of staffing and scheduling, much of the discussion of productive hours focuses on inpatient settings.

Direct care hours. Most of inpatient staff nurses' productive hours represent **direct care hours**, also referred to as **nursing hours per patient day (NHPPD)** or **productive nursing hours per patient day (PNHPPD)**. In some settings, the terms "direct care hours" and "productive hours" are used interchangeably, because most staff nursing work involves direct patient care. Direct care hours are scheduled based on the estimated or required HPPD. The first step in measuring direct care hours over a 24-hour period is to determine the HPPD needed for each day. Direct care hours are then estimated by multiplying the number of staff each shift by the hours in the shift. The total direct care hours for a patient day should be the same or a little more than the HPPD. If direct care hours are less than the HPPD, the unit is under-staffed.

Hours per unit of service (HPUOS). In settings that do not provide or measure inpatient hours, direct care hours are referred to as **hours per unit of service (HPUOS).** For example, an outpatient setting reports direct care per patient visit. A setting that provides procedures, such as the OR, reports direct care per procedure.

Indirect hours. Some productive hours represent **indirect hours,** such as staff education, orientation, meetings, or other work activities that do not involve direct patient care. Staff nurses' indirect hours are measured in some settings, as direct care staff may need to be scheduled to cover the indirect hours. Other settings measure all hours worked as direct care or productive hours.

Nonproductive hours and nonproductive percent. Paid hours such as sick leave, holidays, and vacations are considered **nonproductive hours,** as these hours do not contribute direct or indirect services to the employer. In some settings, break and lunch time may be carefully monitored to guard against the abuse of nonproductive work time. Sick leave is often monitored because **absenteeism**, excessive use of sick leave, is costly and reduces staff productivity (Kirk, 1981).

The paid **nonproductive percent** is the proportion of all paid hours that are nonproductive. Penner and Spencer (2012) estimate that vacations, holidays, sick leave, and other sources of paid nonproductive time total about 350 hours per year, for an estimated 17% of nonproductive hours to total paid hours. Nonproductive hours for any additional required training, such as to meet regulatory requirements, can push the paid nonproductive percent into the range of 20% to 25% of all paid hours.

Nonproductive hours are measured and monitored because of their high cost. Employees using approved nonproductive time are paid a full wage for the hours they are absent. Staff or agency nurses who replace employees using nonproductive time are also paid a full wage or fee. The replacement staff or agency nurses may also be somewhat less productive than the employee using nonproductive time, related to factors such as less experience on the nursing unit. Nonproductive hours may therefore cost up to twice or more the expense while reducing overall productivity. Total paid hours are the sum of productive and nonproductive paid hours, excluding overtime and nurse agency hours.

Overtime. Employees working more than 8 hours per day (without prior agreement to work 10-hour or 12-hour shifts at regular pay) or more than 40 hours per week are eligible for **overtime** pay. Overtime hours are costly, typically 50% more than and up to double the base wage. In many inpatient settings, overtime is closely monitored and requires approval.

In some situations, such as an unexpectedly high census, overtime may be the only alternative for staffing needs. In other situations, nurses might not be working efficiently, and overtime indicates productivity concerns. Total paid hours and total overtime hours provide an overall measure of employee staff nurse productivity.

Agency nurse hours. Paid time worked by RNs who are not employees represent **agency nurse** hours. Agency nurses, also referred to as **per diem nurses,** are provided by temporary nurse staffing firms to fill shifts when enough employed nursing staff are not available. Some agency nurses fill vacant positions for weeks or months at a time, and may be referred to as **travel nurses**. Agency nurse hours are not counted in calculating staff FTEs, as these nurses are not health care facility employees. The use of agency nurses is usually closely monitored in acute care settings, because agency nurse use is an additional cost to nursing units beyond the employee paid hours. In addition, reliance on agency nurses may impact on the quality of patient care, so there must be a satisfactory mix of agency nurses and experienced nursing staff (IOM, 2004; Page, 2008). Agency hours reflect on productivity because problems such as absenteeism or approved nonproductive time, such as vacations, increases the need for agency nurses to fill in for employed staff.

Patient Flow Indicators

Some performance measures are indicators of **patient flow,** or the efficient and timely patient transfer to the appropriate level of care. Patient flow indicators are typically applied to inpatient settings, although outpatient settings might use indicators such as waiting times for patients to be seen by a provider. Admitting or transferring patients to the unit and discharging or transferring patients off the unit without excessive delay are examples of good patient flow. Poor patient flow reduces capacity, because patients who no longer require inpatient care occupy beds needed by patients waiting to be admitted. Delays in admission and transfer also can lead to complications and handoff errors.

Length of stay (LOS) and outliers. Patient length of stay is determined by counting the total number of patient days for each individual inpatient. LOS is often determined by adding the number of times a specific patient is counted in the midnight census. In some situations, such as cases of severe trauma or serious complications, patients may experience a far greater LOS than average. Patients with unusually long LOS are often referred to as **outliers**. These patients are more costly and may require intensive discharge planning for appropriate transfer from the nursing unit. As explained in Chapter 2, Medicare may provide some additional reimbursement for outlier cases. However, the high costs of outlier cases can impact on a hospital's budget.

Average length of stay (ALOS). The **average length of stay (ALOS),** or average number of days that a patient occupies an inpatient bed, is an indicator of the throughput time for acute care. The ALOS reflects on nursing performance because efficient nursing care that reduces errors and complications likely reduces the days the patient must be hospitalized. ALOS is calculated by dividing the total patient days by the number of discharges over a specified time period. For 2011, the ALOS for East Wing is 6000 patient days divided by 1200 discharges, or 5.0 days, compared to the 2011 national benchmark ALOS of 4.6 days (Thomson Reuters, 2011).

Length of stay varies from one diagnosis to another, and is influenced by many factors, including the quality of nursing care. Nurses must perform well by implementing treatment plans and preventing complications so the patient's length of stay is within MS-DRG and benchmark values. Appropriate length of stay improves patient flow because beds are not occupied with patients with preventable complications or who should be discharged.

Discharges. A patient **discharge** represents a patient's release home or to another facility. Deaths are also usually counted as discharges. Discharges are discussed as a performance indicator because nurses are crucial in carrying out discharge orders in a timely manner. Discharges are also a patient flow indicator because an occupied bed must be made available before another patient can be admitted to that bed. Discharge teaching and planning, and attention to discharging patients early in the day are strategies that facilitate efficient discharge practices.

Bed turns. **Bed turns** measure throughput by showing the number of times an inpatient bed is used for an admission or observation (Institute for Healthcare Improvement, March 20, 2011). Admissions and observations are divided by the number of staffed beds to calculate bed turns. In 2011 there are 1200 admissions divided by 20 staffed beds, for 60.0 bed turns.

Bed turnaround time. The **bed turnaround time** measures the time from discharge until an inpatient bed is ready for an admission (Institute for Healthcare Improvement, March 22, 2011). Delays in contacting housekeeping to prepare a vacated room for a new admission increases turnaround time and reduces patient flow. Efficient bed turnaround improves patient flow because patients can be admitted more quickly from the emergency room or other settings. Timely bed turnaround therefore prevents backlogs of patients waiting in other departments of the hospital. Bed turns and bed turnaround depend on nurses discharging patients and notifying appropriate departments, such as housekeeping, in a timely manner. Bed turns and bed turnaround time therefore measure nursing performance.

Financial Indicators

Financial indicators are related to all of the previously discussed indicators of capacity, utilization, and performance. Nurses increasingly realize the importance of financial performance in their work settings. This section presents some general concepts about financial indicators, then applies financial indicators to ways that nursing care is measured.

Expense Indicators

The costs for resources used in producing goods or services are known as expenses. Even if nurses do not review a budget, they are often directed by nurse managers to be mindful of expenses. Nursing care, from the nursing FTEs needed for direct care hours to the use of medical supplies, generates expenses. In many settings, nurse managers monitor excessive expenses, such as abuse of nonproductive time and waste of medical supplies. Therefore, expense indicators are useful in measuring nursing care.

In health care settings, some expenses are **fixed,** or do not change with patient volume. For example, the rent and utility expenses for a nursing unit is fixed. The expenses in many outpatient settings may be largely fixed. Inpatient settings often report **variable** expenses that change with patient volume. The expenses for staffing and supplies are typically lower when the inpatient census is low, and increase when the census is high. However, inpatient settings such as hospitals have high fixed compared to variable expenses, because building, equipping, and required minimal staffing costs are often higher than variable costs.

Expenses that enable the setting to achieve its primary purpose in providing health care services, whether fixed or variable, are known as **operating expenses**. Fixed operating expenses include items such as rent and equipment maintenance. Wages and salaries for fixed staff, such as the nurse manager, are another fixed operating expense. Variable operating expenses include items such as medical supplies used in patient care. Staff overtime is another variable operating expense.

Expenses for goods or services not related to the organization's primary purpose in providing health care services are known as **nonoperating expenses**. For example, fixed and variable expenses generated by a hospital gift shop represent nonoperating expenses.

Expenses are also classified by the source of expense. **Personnel expenses** represent labor costs such as employee salaries, wages, and overtime. **Nonpersonnel expenses** include costs such as medical supplies and equipment maintenance. Personnel and nonpersonnel expenses are added together for total expenses. Chapter 5 discusses sources of expenses in health care settings in more detail.

Revenue Indicators

Income from reimbursement or payment provided for goods and services is known as **revenue**. Unlike expenses, in most health care settings, staff nurses and their managers cannot control the amount of revenue generated. Nurses are therefore less likely to learn about the revenues generated in their workplace. However, it is important to realize that nurses in outpatient settings and inpatient nursing units help generate revenues by their contributions to patient care. Revenue indicators are used to measure nursing care, for example, inpatient revenue per nursing FTE.

Health care reimbursement comes from a variety of government and private insurers, as well as **self-pay** or **out-of-pocket** payments made directly from consumers. As a result, revenues may be measured and classified by the revenue source (Medicare, Medicaid, commercial insurance, and self-pay). The sources of reimbursement that contribute to a health care setting's revenue are known as the **payer mix**. Most health care revenues are variable, because health care reimbursement is typically based on volume, with payments per patient visit, procedure, or inpatient day. Revenues from all sources added together is reported as total revenues.

Chapter 3 discusses capitation and other financing strategies that attempt to separate reimbursement from patient volume, so that revenues are fixed over the fiscal year. A financing strategy such as capitation that prepays total revenues as a fixed payment is sometimes referred to as **global budgeting**.

Gross revenue. Revenue is classified and reported based on how it is calculated. The full charges assigned by the health care provider are reported as **gross revenue**. Gross revenue less any deductions or discounts is reported as **net revenue**. The difference between gross and net revenue is often considerable, depending on the **contractual allowance** or difference between the amount the insurer pays compared to the charges. For example, Medicare and Medicaid reimburse using nonnegotiable rates that are often far less than the charges. Private insurers often negotiate discounts to charges. **Bad debt**, or unpaid bills, are also deducted from gross revenue in calculating net revenue. When funding comes from grants or from global budgets such as capitation contracts, gross and net revenue are the same.

Profit or Loss

Total expenses are subtracted from total revenues to determine the extent of profit (revenues are greater than expenses) or loss (revenues are less than expenses). The measure of profit or loss is an important indicator of the financial health of the institution. More discussion of financial health measures and their interpretation is provided in Chapter 12.

The following sections present case examples applying capacity, utilization, performance, and financial indicators to measuring nursing care. One example is the MNC nurse-managed health center, using indicators for measuring nursing care in an outpatient setting. The other example is East Wing medical-surgical nursing unit, with indicators measuring inpatient nursing care.

MEASURING NURSING CARE IN A NURSE-MANAGED HEALTH CENTER

Table 4.1 presents an activity report for 2011 and 2012, the first and second years of operation for MNC. Many of the outpatient capacity, utilization, performance, and financial indicators discussed earlier in this chapter are included in this report. A discussion of Table 4.1 provides examples for application of these measures of outpatient nursing care.

Outpatient capacity. The first section of Table 4.1 presents indicators for outpatient capacity. MNC's structural capacity increased from 2011 to 2012, with the increase in examination rooms. Staffing capacity also increased, from one to three NPs. In addition, staffing capacity increased from a workload of four patient visits to six patient visits per NP per day from 2011 to 2012, because the NPs were relieved of administrative duties beginning in 2012. The capacity, or maximum number of visits, considered feasible for MNC to manage therefore increased from 896 in 2011 to 4032 in 2012.

Outpatient utilization. Table 4.1 measures outpatient utilization using referrals, or patients who are directed or assigned to MNC for care. The referrals from Welby ACO contracts make up the largest number of referrals. Some patients also self-refer to MNC as drop-in patients to the nurse-managed health center. The numbers of both ACO and self-referred patients increase from 2011 to 2012.

Outpatient performance. Table 4.1 measures NP performance by counting the number of visits that are made by patients referred to MNC. Note that the total visits made by patients from the ACO contract and by self-pay patients are somewhat less than the NP capacity. For example, in 2011 it was estimated as having the capacity to manage 896 visits, but only 850 visits actually occurred. These figures reinforce the principle that health professionals and health settings typically operate at a level somewhat less than full capacity, given the likelihood of delays or other unplanned events that reduce capacity. The number of visits per referral dropped from four visits per ACO referral in 2011 to 3.4 visits per ACO referral in 2012, indicating improved performance assuming the patient concern is resolved. The visits per referral for self-pay patients remain unchanged over this time.

One indicator not reported in Table 4.1 is the average wait time for patients who visit MNC. The MNC manager is considering ways to measure this indicator, given the variety of disease management, employee wellness, immunization, and drop-in services this nurse-managed center provides. Wait time is a useful measure for patient access and patient satisfaction, and staff may be requested to collect this information in the future.

Outpatient expenses. The personnel expenses for MNC in Table 4.1 increase substantially from the start-up year in 2011 to 2012. In 2011, there was only one MNC employee, an NP who managed both clinical services and the health center's administration. In 2012, two additional NPs are hired, as well as a half-time nurse manager and two part-time clerical staff. The manager and clerical staff assume all administrative duties so the NPs can focus on clinical services. Personnel expenses more than triple from $91,000 in 2011 to $343,000 in 2012.

Nonpersonnel expenses also increase substantially for MNC, as shown in Table 4.1. More medical supplies are required as the number of patient visits increases from 2011 to 2012. Other nonpersonnel expenses include the purchase of furnishings and equipment for the examination rooms. Despite the increased expenses, the increase in patient visits causes the cost per patient visit to decrease from $112 in 2011 to $105 in 2012.

Outpatient revenues. MNC negotiates expanded contracts with Welby ACO for services such as disease management and employee wellness, so the ACO contract revenues increase substantially from 2011 to 2012 (Table 4.1). This expansion enables MNC to add staff and equipment to the health center. The grant funding is from a three-year, $150,000 grant, allocated as $50,000 of funding per year from 2011 to 2013. Private collections increase from 2011 to 2012, related to the increase in self-pay drop-in patients who are billed for services. Cash donations make up the remainder of MNC's total revenues, which reach $108,000 in 2011 and $404,000 in 2012. Although the revenue increase is substantial, the revenue per patient visit drops from $127 in 2011 to $102 in 2012.

Outpatient P&L. Although volume and revenues increased substantially in 2012, the health center reports a profit of $12,700 in 2011, compared to a loss of $8500 in 2012, as shown in Table 4.1. The profit per patient visit is $19.84 in 2011, dropping to a loss of $2.55 per patient visit in 2012. The net profit in 2011 is enough to cover the net loss in 2012. However, the MNC manager must carefully monitor utilization, performance, and financial indicators to improve financial outcomes in 2013. Continued financial losses will put the nurse-managed health center at risk of going out of business. This activity report therefore serves to alert the manager and staff about the need to think about ways to improve utilization and performance within MNC's capacity so that financial outcomes allow the MNC to survive and grow.

MEASURING NURSING CARE IN AN INPATIENT NURSING UNIT

Patient care, staffing, and scheduling are more complex for inpatient compared to outpatient settings. This section therefore presents several reports showing applications of inpatient nursing care indicators from the East Wing medical-surgical nursing unit. Actual reports may not present information according to the categories of capacity, utilization, performance, and financial indicators. However, these categories are useful to consider in thinking about applying and interpreting these indicators when measuring nursing care. These tables include reminders about the indicator calculations that are reported.

Daily Inpatient Capacity, Utilization, and Staffing

Table 4.3 presents a daily activity report for East Wing's capacity, utilization, and staffing. Capacity measures include the total staffed beds and the daily census, as well as the unit occupancy at the time the census is recorded. Acuity is measured as the target of 8.0 HPPD. The total HPPD for all 17 patients is 136 hours for this daily report.

Daily staffing for the report in Table 4.3 is scheduled so that the direct hours scheduled match the 136 HPPD requirements based on patient acuity. If direct hours are less than the

Table 4.3 *East Wing Medical-Surgical Unit, Daily Capacity, Utilization, and Staffing Report, Monday, June 11, 2012*

Indicator	Calculation	June 11, 2012
Staffed beds	Total beds staffed and available for patient occupancy	20
Census	Census not counting admissions, discharges, or transfers	17
Occupancy	Beds occupied at census ÷ total staffed beds	85.0%
HPPD	Target hours of care per patient day	8.0
Total HPPD	Total hours of care for all patients on the unit	136.0
Staffing 7–3	Number of staff scheduled for day shift	7
Direct hours 7–3	Direct hours = number of staff × 8 hours in shift	56.0
Staffing 3–11	Number of staff scheduled for 3–11 shift	6
Direct hours 3–11	Direct hours = number of staff × 8 hours in shift	48.0
Staffing 11–7	Number of staff scheduled for 11–7 shift	4
Direct hours 11–7	Direct hours = number of staff × 8 hours in shift	32.0
Total staff	Total staff for 24-hour period	17
Total FTEs	Daily FTEs = direct care hours ÷ hours in shift	17.0
Total direct care hours	Total direct hours for 24-hour period	136.0

HPPD, the unit is under-staffed. Staff are distributed so there are more staff scheduled during the busier day and evening shifts, and fewer staff during the night shift. There are 17 staff assigned to cover all three shifts in this daily report, and as all of them are expected to work full 8-hour shifts, the daily FTE is also 17.0 (136 direct hours divided by 8 hours per shift).

Monthly Inpatient Performance and Expense

Table 4.4 presents a monthly report on nurse performance and nursing unit expenses for the East Wing medical-surgical unit. The first section of this report summarizes information on the days in the time period, staffed beds, HPPD, patient days, and FTEs for June 2012. This information provides an overview for evaluating nurse performance and reviewing expenses.

Note that FTEs for the monthly report in Table 4.4 are calculated differently than for the daily staffing report in Table 4.3. The monthly report uses total paid productive and nonproductive hours instead of direct care hours, because over the course of a month, staff are expected to use sick leave or other nonproductive time. The total paid hours are divided by 160 hours, which are the two pay periods in the month. Weekend coverage during the month requires that the FTEs are multiplied by the 1.4 FTE coverage factor. The result is that 41.1 FTEs are required to cover all paid productive and nonproductive hours for June 2012.

The next section of Table 4.4 reports nurse performance for June 2012. The required direct care hours, based on 8.0 HPPD acuity, is calculated for the month at 3840 hours. The total direct hours actually worked plus 96.0 hours of overtime add to 3848 paid productive hours, a little more than the HPPD requirement. Total productive and nonproductive hours are added to determine the 4698 total paid hours. Nonproductive hours are about 18% of total paid hours, a little more than the 17% nonproductive hours that Penner and Spencer estimate (2012). An additional 16.0 hours are reported for agency nurses during the month. It is possible that increased nonproductive time such as sick leave resulted in the use of overtime and agency nurses to cover direct care needs.

The ALOS reported in Table 4.4 is slightly higher than the overall national average of 4.61 days (Thomson Reuters, 2012). As the reported ALOS of 4.8 days is close to the national average, it appears that patient flow is satisfactory on the East Wing medical-surgical unit. On average, each patient bed in East Wing had five turns over June 2012, or had five admissions during the month.

The final section of Table 4.4 reports expenses for East Wing over June 2012. The direct care and nonproductive wage estimates are based on an average hourly wage of $32 an hour, less than the national average of $35 an hour (The KPMG Healthcare & Pharmaceutical Institute, 2011). Overtime wages are estimated at "time-and-a-half," so overtime hours are multiplied by $48 an hour. The agency nurse hourly fee is estimated at $70 per hour. Employee benefits such as health insurance are excluded from this report, as are wages and salaries for fixed employees such as the nurse manager and the unit clerk. The focus of this report is on direct care variable staff nurse performance and expenses.

Total personnel costs nearly reach $153,000 for the month. Overtime wages on East Wing are 3% of total personnel costs ($4608 divided by $152,992, not shown in Table 4.4), a little over the national benchmark of 2% (Bateman, 2012). Nonpersonnel expenses in Table 4.4 include medical supplies and other expenses, such as equipment maintenance and travel. Personnel and nonpersonnel expenses are added to report a total expense of $187,992 for June 2012. By far, the largest proportion of East Wing's expense is for personnel costs. Expenses are $392 PPD and $4573 per FTE for the month.

Annual Revenue

Table 4.5 shows a revenue report for the East Wing medical-surgical nursing unit for 2012. The first section of this report summarizes indicators for capacity, utilization, and staffing

Table 4.4 *East Wing Medical-Surgical Unit Monthly Performance and Expense Report, June 2012*

Indicator	Reporting or Calculation	June 2012
Days in time period	Days in the month	30
Staffed beds	Beds staffed and available for patient occupancy	20
Hours per patient day (HPPD)	Acuity requires 8 HPPD	8
Patient days	Sum of census count for time period	480
Full-time equivalents (FTEs)	(Total paid hours ÷ 160 hours) × 1.4 coverage factor	41.1
Performance		
Direct care hours target	HPPD × days in a month	3840
Scheduled direct care hours	Total direct hours excluding overtime	3752
Overtime hours	Total hours of paid overtime	96.0
Total paid productive hours	Total direct hours and total paid overtime hours	3848
Total paid nonproductive hours	Total paid hours other than direct care	850
Paid nonproductive %	Nonproductive hours ÷ total paid hours	18.1%
Total paid hours	All paid hours for direct care staff	4698
Agency nurse hours	Total agency nurse hours	16.0
Average length of stay (ALOS)	Total patient days ÷ discharges	4.8
Discharges	Discharges + deaths + transfers off the unit	100
Bed turns	Discharges ÷ staffed beds	5.0
Expenses		
Scheduled direct care wages	Hourly wage × hours	$120,064
Overtime wages	Time-and-a-half wage = hourly wage × 1.5	$4608
Nonproductive wages	Hourly wage × hours	$27,200
Total hourly wages	Excludes agency nurses	$151,872
Agency nurse expense	Agency nurse hour × hourly expense	$1120
Total personnel expenses	Total hourly wages + agency costs	$152,992
Supplies		**$15,000**
Other nonpersonnel expenses		$20,000
Total nonpersonnel expenses		$35,000
Total expenses	Personnel expenses + nonpersonnel expenses	$187,992
Expenses PPD	Total expenses ÷ patient days	$392
Expenses per FTE	Total expenses ÷ FTEs	$4573

for 2012. The gross and net revenue figures are the estimates that show how revenues are reported for inpatient settings.

Total gross revenue in Table 4.5 is estimated as all hospital charges for all the patient days in 2012. Net revenues are presented for Medicare, Medicaid, and commercial insurance. The net revenue from each source is added for the total net revenue. Note that the total net revenue is substantially less than the gross revenue. The flat fees paid by Medicare and Medicaid, commercial insurance deductions, and bad debt deductions from revenue considerably reduce gross revenue.

The total expenses for East Wing are estimated at $2,927,880, as shown in Table 4.5. This amount is subtracted from the total net revenue to report the annual profit of $362,770 for 2012. The profit PPD is $60.07 and the profit per FTE is $8456. Medical services are not as profitable as surgical services, so other nursing units and departments might show a higher amount of profit than East Wing.

The report in Table 4.5 compares gross and net revenue estimates. However, most nursing unit budgets only report gross revenues. Net revenues are usually estimated on a hospital-wide basis, not at the nursing unit level.

CONCLUSION

This chapter reviews and discusses commonly used indicators that measure nursing care and the financial value of nursing care. Nurses can think about these indicators in terms of their setting's capacity, utilization, staff performance, and financial outcomes. Chapter 5 applies many of these indicators to budgets prepared in settings where nurses deliver care.

Table 4.5 *East Wing Medical-Surgical Unit, Annual Revenue Report, 2012*

Measure or Indicator	Reporting or Calculation	2012
Days in time period	Days in calendar year	366
Staffed or available beds	Equipped and staffed for occupancy	20
Patient days	Sum of census count for time period	6039
Full-time equivalents (FTEs)	(Total paid hours ÷ 2080 hours) × 1.4 coverage factor	42.9
Total gross revenue	Total charges for patient care	$5,435,100
Medicare net revenue	Charges to Medicare less deductions	$934,290
Medicaid net revenue	Charges to Medicaid less deductions	$407,630
Commercial insurance net revenue	Charges to commercial insurance less deductions	$1,948,730
Total net revenue	Total gross revenue less deductions	$3,290,650
Net revenue PPD	Net revenue ÷ patient days	$545
Net revenue per FTE	Net revenue ÷ FTEs	$76,705
Total expenses	Personnel expenses + nonpersonnel expenses	$2,927,880
Net profit or loss	Net revenues–total expenses	$362,770
Profit or loss PPD	Profit or loss ÷ patient days	$60.07
Profit or loss per FTE	Profit or loss ÷ FTEs	$8456

Discussion and Exercises

1. Discuss and, if possible, review nursing reports, indicators, or benchmarks used in your work setting or clinical assignments. How is nursing care measured? Is this information shared with nursing staff?
2. Give at least two examples of capacity, utilization, performance, and financial indicators that are used in your work setting or clinical assignments. Discuss advantages and disadvantages of sharing this information with nursing staff.
3. Review Table 4.6. Change the number of patients and/or the HPPD, recalculate the number of nurses needed per 24-hour day, and estimate the number of nurses you would schedule each shift. If your results show a fraction, such as 11.25 nurses needed per day, should you round the number of nurses down to 11, or up to 12? See the Exercise 3 worksheet in the Chapter 4 Excel file (provided in the supplementary electronic material) for rounding advice.

   Note that:
   Total HPPD = number of patients × HPPD for each patient.
   Nurses per day = Total HPPD ÷ Hours per shift.

4. Review Table 4.7, also in the Exercise 4 worksheet in the Chapter 4 Excel file (provided in the supplementary electronic material). Change the number of patients and/or the HPPD, recalculate the number of nurses needed per 24-hour day, and estimate the number of nurses you would need for the entire 7-day week. How do these numbers change if nurses work 12-hour shifts?

Table 4.6 *Nurse Staffing for a 24-Hour Period, 8-Hour Shifts*

Patients	15
HPPD	8
Total HPPD	120
Hours per shift	8
Nurses needed per day	15.0
7–3 shift	6
3–11 shift	5
11–7 shift	4

Table 4.7 *Nurse Staffing for 7-Day, 24-Hour Coverage, 8-Hour Shifts*

Patients	15
HPPD	8
Total HPPD	120
Hours per shift	8
Nurses needed per day	15.0
24-hour 7-day coverage factor for 8-hour shifts	1.4
Nurses needed per week	21.0

REFERENCES

American Nurses Association. (1999). *Principles for nurse staffing with annotated bibliography.* Retrieved from http://www.nursingworld.org/DocumentVault/NurseStaffing/PrincipleswithBibliography.aspx

Bateman, N. (2012). *The business of nurse management: A toolkit for success.* New York, NY: Springer Publishing Company.

Centers for Medicare and Medicaid Services. (September 8, 2005). *Details for case mix index.* Department of Health and Human Services, Center for Medicare and Medicaid Services. Retrieved from http://www.cms.gov/AcuteInpatientPPS/FFD/itemdetail. asp?filterType=none&filterByDID=-99&sortByDID=2&sortOrder=ascending&itemID=C MS022523&intNumPerPage=10

Chicago Health & Health Systems Project. (March 29, 2012). *Special notes. Community health profiles: Primary care capacity.* Retrieved March 29, 2012 from http://www.cchsd.org/tn_ notes.html

Clarke, S. P., & Donaldson, N. E. (March, 2008). Nurse staffing and patient care quality and safety (Chapter 25). In R. G. Hughes (Ed.). *Patient safety and quality: An evidence-based handbook for nurses* (AHRQ Publication No. 08–0043). Rockville, MD: Agency for Healthcare Research and Quality. Retrieved from http://www.ahrq.gov/qual/nurseshdbk

Douglas, K. (2010). Ratios—if it were only that easy. *Nursing Economic\$, 28*(2), 119–125.

Fasoli, D., & Haddock, K. (2011). Results of an integrative review of patient classification systems. *Annual Review of Nursing Research, (28)* 295–316.

Green, L. V. (2004). Capacity planning and management in hospitals. In M. L. Brandeau, F. Sainfort, & W. Pierskalla (Eds.). *Operations research and health care: A handbook of methods and applications.* Norwell, MA: Kluwer Academic Publishers.

Harris, M. (2010). *Handbook of home health care administration* (5th ed.). Sudbury, MA: Jones & Bartlett.

Health Resources and Services Administration. (March, 2010). *The registered nurse population: Initial findings from the 2008 national sample survey of registered nurses.* U.S. Department of Health and Human Services Health Resources and Services Administration. Retrieved from http://datawarehouse.hrsa.gov/nursingsurvey.aspx

Institute for Healthcare Improvement. (March 22, 2011). *Glossary of frequently used financial terms.* Retrieved from http://www.ihi.org/knowledge/Knowledge Center Assets/Tools-GlossaryofFrequentlyUsedFinancialTerms_91f0184f-6607–4644-bf5a-b3f7cf8093e6/ GlossaryofFrequentlyUsedFinancialTerms.doc

Institute for Healthcare Improvement. (March 20, 2011). *Patient flow tools.* Retrieved March 20, 2011 from http://www.ihi.org/IHI/Topics/Flow/PatientFlow/EmergingContent

Institute of Medicine (IOM). (2004). *Keeping patients safe: Transforming the work environment of nurses.* Washington, DC: The National Academies Press.

Jennings, B. M. (March, 2008). Patient acuity (Chapter 23). In R. G. Hughes (Ed.). *Patient safety and quality: An evidence-based handbook for nurses.* (Prepared with support from the Robert Wood Johnson Foundation). AHRQ Publication No. 08–0043. Rockville, MD: Agency for Healthcare Research and Quality. Retrieved from http://www.ahrq.gov/ qual/nurseshdbk

Kirk, R. (1981). *Nursing management tools.* Boston, MA: Little, Brown and Company.

Page, A. E. (March, 2008). Temporary, agency, and other contingent workers (Chapter 27). In R. G. Hughes (Ed.). *Patient safety and quality: An evidence-based handbook for nurses.* (Prepared with support from the Robert Wood Johnson Foundation). AHRQ Publication No. 08–0043. Rockville, MD: Agency for Healthcare Research and Quality. Retrieved from http://www.ahrq.gov/qual/nurseshdbk

Penner, S. J., & Spencer, M. D. (2012). Acute care utilization, staffing and financial indicators (Chapter 4). In K. T. Waxman (Ed.). *Financial & Business management for the doctor of nursing practice.* New York, NY: Springer Publishing Company.

The KPMG Healthcare & Pharmaceutical Institute. (April, 2011). KPMG's 2011 U.S. hospital nursing labor costs study. www.kpmghealthcarepharmainstitute.com

Thomson Reuters. (March 28, 2011). *100 top hospitals: Study overview and research findings* 18th ed.). Retrieved from http://www.100tophospitals.com/top-national-hospitals

Thomson Reuters. (April 16, 2012). *100 top hospitals: Study overview and research findings* 19th ed.). Retrieved from http://www.100tophospitals.com/top-national-hospitals

Washington State Department of Social and Health Services. (May 9, 2010). *Department/MPA federally qualified health centers billing instructions.* Washington State Department of Social and Health Services, Health and Recovery Services Administration. Retrieved May 9, 2010 from http://hrsa.dshs.wa.gov/Download/Resources_Available.html

CROSSWORD: *Chapter 4—Measuring Nursing Care*

Across

5 The amount of time an inpatient requires of direct nursing care per day (abbreviation).

6 A value that represents performance targeted to an internal or industry standard.

8 Another term for utilization (abbreviation).

10 Patients who require close monitoring but who usually occupy an inpatient bed for less than 48 hours.

12 Income from reimbursement or payment provided for goods and services.

14 Employee compensation that does not change regardless of the number of hours worked over the year.

16 A standard measure for hourly employment, indicating a full-time employee working 2080 hours per year (abbreviation).

17 A specified work unit, such as an inpatient nursing unit or an Emergency Department.

22 The extent of consumer demand for services in a health care setting, measured by indicators such as patient days.

23 Productive hours of inpatient staff nurses providing patient care (abbreviation).

25 Measures that signify a specific condition or a specified level or value, also called indicators.

Down

1 A measure of direct care hours for settings that perform procedures (abbreviation).

2 Excessive use of employee sick leave.

3 Level of patient illness or case complexity.

4 Another term for utilization.

7 An individual directed to a health care setting for health care services.

9 The extent to which a health care setting can meet consumer demand.

10 Work hours exceeding 40 hours per week.

11 Measures that signify a specific condition or a specified level or value, also called metrics.

13 Employee compensation based on the number of hours worked.

15 How efficiently a setting's capacity operates in managing production or utilization.

18 The number of inpatients on a nursing unit at any point in time, often measured at midnight.

19 Patients transferring from home or another facility to an inpatient facility, used as a measure of inpatient utilization.

20 The release of a patient to home or another facility, usually includes death.

21 Another term for NHPPD.

24 Average number of patients in a nursing unit, calculated as the patient days divided by the number of days in a time period (abbreviation).

Chapter 5: Reporting and Managing Budgets

A budget is just a method of worrying before you spend money, as well as afterward—Unknown

Learning Objectives

1. Explain at least three reasons why an operating budget is important in nursing care settings.
2. Differentiate between the management functions of budget monitoring, investigation, and control.
3. Specify the important features of an operating expense budget.
4. Compare applications of fixed and flexible budgeting in nursing care settings.

Key Terms

adjustment authority	lag time	statistics budget
balance the budget	line item	step-fixed
budget justification	line-item flexibility	trend
control	monitoring	trend line
cyclical	operating budget	unfavorable budget variance
depreciation	percent variance	
favorable budget variance	performance target	variance
investigation	seasonal	year to date (YTD)

All too often, nurses hear that "we can't approve more staff, new equipment, or other requests because of the budget." Nurses therefore think of budgets in terms of cutbacks and limits, rather than choices and possibilities. Budgets are tools nurses can use to assess and improve the financial health of inpatient and outpatient settings. Even if a staff nurse does not review or manage a budget, understanding budget principles helps in understanding how nursing care is financed. This chapter builds on the review of nursing care indicators discussed in Chapter 4. The focus of this chapter is on the budgets nurses are most likely to encounter.

Budgets have three important functions: reporting, managing, and planning. These functions are essential to ensure the best use of resources in providing health care services. The functions of reporting, managing, and planning are also related to each other. Figure 5.1 illustrates a budget's three functions and their relationships. Reviewing the budget report enables the nurse to better manage available resources. The plan for the next year's performance determines the budget that will guide activities over the future year.

Reporting. Budgets provide a report or description of activities and resources used in health care settings. **Operating budgets**, which are used in the day-to-day management of health settings, are the focus of this chapter. Operating budgets describe the amount and sources of **volume**, also known as **units of service (UOS),** or the number of patient days, patient visits, or services, such as procedures. Operating budgets also describe the amount and sources of **expenses**, also referred to as the costs incurred in the process of producing goods and services. Another financial activity that operating budgets describe is the amount and sources of **revenue**, or income derived from the reimbursement provided or the price paid for goods and services. Some operating budgets focus on volume, others on expenses or revenue, and some operating budgets report on all these performance areas. For example, a nursing unit operating budget might report how many patients occupy the unit's beds, the costs of nursing care provided, and the revenues generated over a time period.

Throughout this chapter, the term "budget" refers to an operating budget report, unless otherwise specified. The following section explains budget reporting in more detail. Budget reports are presented throughout this chapter as examples of ways budgets describe activities and resource use.

Managing. Budgets are an important tool in managing health care resources. Three important activities in managing a budget are **monitoring, investigation,** and **control** (Figure 5.1). Monitoring involves carefully reviewing the budget report to identify any budget concerns, by comparing the budgeted amount to actual performance. Investigation examines events, processes, or staff performance that might be reasons for budget concerns, and determines whether the budget concern can be controlled. Budget control applies management strategies to address and resolve the budget concern that was identified in monitoring. For example,

Figure 5.1 *Functions of Health Care Budgets*

a clinic manager monitors the budget and sees that the amount spent for supplies is more than the amount budgeted for the month. The manager investigates and finds that supplies are being wasted because staff is not familiar with a new clinical procedure. The manager controls the budget concern by providing additional training and supervision to the staff, so the waste no longer occurs and the supplies budget returns to normal. Budget management is discussed in more detail later in this chapter.

Planning. Budgets not only report and aid in management, but serve as plans to guide and predict activities and resources in health care settings. For example, a nurse-managed clinic might negotiate an expanded contract with a physician group practice for wellness care. The predicted increase in patient UOS leads to planning and budgeting to hire more nurse practitioners (NPs) for the coming year. The increased revenue from the contract is projected to cover the NP salaries. Budget planning is discussed in more detail in Chapter 6.

REPORTING OPERATING BUDGETS

Budget reports that nurses are most likely to review are based on the operating budget. The purpose of the operating budget is to establish targets and report actual performance on the day-to-day operations of a setting, such as a clinic or nursing unit. Operating budgets are prepared for the **fiscal year,** or 12-month time period for the organization's budget and other financial reporting. Budgets are often reported on a monthly and quarterly schedule. Capacity, utilization, performance, and financial indicators are estimated and reported in operating budgets. A budget report includes the budgeted amounts (plan) and the actual amounts (performance) for a time period.

Some concepts and definitions related to the layout and development of operating budgets are provided before reviewing examples from Millway University Nurse-Managed Health Center (MNC) and the East Wing medical-surgical inpatient unit at Bigtown Hospital. Operating budgets in other health care settings, such as long-term care (LTC) facilities and home health agencies, follow similar principles as the examples from MNC and East Wing. Hospital-wide budget indicators are presented and discussed in Chapter 12.

Budget Report Layout

The organization of budget reports may vary from one health care setting to another, but some basic concepts apply. Budget reports present UOS, expense, and revenue information over a specified time period. Although budget layouts might include chart or graph formats, the usual layout is a table with information presented in the title, rows, and columns. It may be helpful to review the rules and conventions commonly used in reporting indicators, presented in Chapter 4, as these rules and conventions apply to budget reporting. It is also helpful to review printouts of budgets with a calculator at hand, or, if possible, to review budgets as spreadsheets. In this way, the calculations used in the budget report can be identified and better understood. Readers can link to the Springer Publishing website to download budget reports featured in this chapter (Tables 5.1 and 5.2).

Title and identification. The title of a budget report provides important information to the reader. A title should identify the budget report's location, such as the clinic or hospital unit, the purpose or type of budget, and the specific time period of the report. The reader should be able to understand the context of the budget report from reading the title. For example, a reader might expect different nurse staffing levels from an outpatient clinic budget report compared to a budget report from an intensive care unit.

Time period. The time period for the budget must be clearly specified in reporting. It is important to know if the budget report is current rather than reflecting past performance. As with reporting any set of indicators, all the information in a budget should be reported

Table 5.1 *Millway University Nurse-Managed Health Center (MNC) Variance Report, 2nd Quarter 2012*

Item	2nd Quarter 2012			YTD 2012		
	Budget	Actual	Variance	Budget	Actual	Variance
NPs on staff	3	3	—	3	3	—
Total visits	980	997	17	1960	1987	27
Revenue						
Welby ACO revenue	$112,500	$112,500	$0	$225,000	$225,000	$0
Grant funding	$12,500	$12,500	$0	$25,000	$25,000	$0
Private collections	$3750	$3102	($648)	$7500	$6431	($1069)
Donations	$5000	$5489	$489	$10,000	$8789	($1211)
Total Revenue	**$133,750**	**$133,591**	**($159)**	**$267,500**	**$265,220**	**($2280)**
Expenses						
Cost per patient visit	$128	$134	($5.99)	$128	$136	($8.07)
Personnel expense NPs	$52,500	$52,500	$0	$105,000	$105,000	$0
Benefits @ 30%	$15,750	$15,750	$0	$31,500	$31,500	$0
Clinic Manager 0.5 FTE	$7500	$7500	$0	$15,000	$15,000	$0
Clerical 0.8 FTE × 2	$10,000	$10,000	$0	$20,000	$20,000	$0
Total personnel expense	$85,750	$85,750	$0	$171,500	$171,500	$0
Medical supplies	$25,000	$33,563	($8563)	$50,000	$70,217	($20,217)
Nonmedical supplies	$1500	$1417	$83	$3000	$2874	$126
Depreciation	$1000	$974	$26	$2000	$1949	$51
Capital expenses	$10,000	$9743	$257	$20,000	$19,486	$515
Overhead	$2500	$2500	$0	$5000	$5000	$0
Total nonpersonnel expense	$40,000	$48,197	($8197)	$80,000	$99,525	($19,525)
Total health center expense	**$125,750**	**$133,947**	**($8197)**	**$251,500**	**$271,025**	**($19,525)**
Net Profit or Loss (P&L)	$8000	($356)	—	$16,000	($5805)	—

Note: Values in parentheses refer to loss.

for the same time period. Budgets are often reported annually, quarterly, and monthly. Weekly or even daily reporting might be provided, particularly for variable and high-cost items such as nurse staffing or nurse overtime expenses.

In many settings, there is **lag time,** or a delay, in reporting actual budget figures related to the time required for collecting and tabulating the data. For example, a budget report issued in March 2012 might include actual budget data from January 2012, but the figures for February 2012 might not be available. This delay leads to a one-month lag in reporting.

Budgets often report **year-to-date (YTD)** totals of financial performance measures from the beginning of the budget year to the current time period. For example, a budget report for

Table 5.2 *East Wing Medical-Surgical Unit, Variance Report, July 2012*

Item	July 2012				July 2011
	Budget	Actual	Variance	Variance %	Actual
Days in time period	31	31	—	—	31
Staffed beds	20	20	—	—	20
Patient days	527	498	(29.0)	−5.5%	415
Total RN FTEs	45.1	50.1	(5.0)	−11.1%	36.7
Revenue					
Gross patient revenue	$460,450	$441,932	($18,518)	−4.0%	$417,883
Personnel expense					
Total salaries and wages	$171,920	$192,845	($20,925)	−12.2%	$141,552
Benefits	$51,576	$52,797	($1221)	−2.4%	$42,466
Total personnel expenses	$223,496	$245,642	($22,146)	−9.9%	$184,018
Overtime wages %	2.0%	6.1%	--	--	3.2%
Personnel costs PPD	$424	$493	($69)	−16.3%	$327
Personnel costs per FTE	$4960	$4908	$52	1.1%	$3697
Nonpersonnel expense					
Medical supplies	$23,700	$23,498	$202	0.9%	$21,839
Depreciation	$10,000	$10,000	$0	0.0%	$10,000
Other nonpersonnel	$3500	$2899	$601	17.2%	$2734
Total nonpersonnel	$37,200	$36,397	$803	2.2%	$34,573
Total expenses	**$260,696**	**$282,039**	**($21,343)**	**−8.2%**	**$218,591**

Note: Values in parentheses refer to loss.

the first quarter of 2012 for a budget year beginning January 1, 2012 might total the budgeted and actual amounts from January through March to show the overall performance for the year so far. The 2011 first quarter YTD performance might be included to allow comparison between the current year and the prior year's performance. It is desirable for actual performance to roughly equal budget targets by the end of the fiscal year, so the budget is balanced. YTD comparisons allow the nurse to determine how closely the budget is balanced as the fiscal year progresses.

Line items. The specific types of items in each row (line) of the budget are known as **line items**. Line items represent measures of volume, expense, or revenue, organized into categories or sections of the budget. Codes are frequently used to identify individual line items as well as groups of line items. For example, an individual code might designate a particular type of dressing that is part of medical supplies, or a group code might be used to designate all the medical supplies. Line item codes might be defined in the budget report, or the reader may need to refer to the institution's budget codebook to find the definition of budget codes. High-cost and highly variable line items such as nurse staffing and nurse overtime are more likely to be reported individually rather than grouped together.

Sections or categories. Related sets of line items are grouped together in sections or categories of the budget. Typical sections of a health care budget include UOS or utilization measures, revenues, personnel expenses, and nonpersonnel expenses. Budgets might report some or all of these categories, depending on the purpose of the budget report. For example, nursing unit budgets often report UOS and expenses, and omit reporting revenues.

Sub-totals, totals, and other calculations. Most budgets include sub-totals or totals of each budget section or category. For example, staff wages, benefits, overtime, and other related personnel expenses are frequently sub-totaled as total personnel expenses. All the line items for nonpersonnel expenses are sub-totaled as nonpersonnel expenses. These sub-totals are then added together to report the major budget category of total expenses. An estimated **profit and loss (P&L) statement** is calculated by subtracting total expenses from total revenues. A line might report an indicator such as total expenses per patient day (total expenses divided by patient days). Many of the financial indicators calculated and presented in Chapter 4 are included in budget reports.

Fixed, Step-Fixed, and Flexible Budgeting

The resources required to provide patient care may or may not change based on the UOS (patient days, patient visits, or procedures). Budget reporting differs depending on the extent that volume affects expenses or revenues.

Fixed budget. Budgets or budget line items for direct care services that do not change over time when the volume statistics change are known as **fixed**. For example, an operating room may have a full-time nurse manager and a capacity of 60 procedures a day. The manager is budgeted whether the operating room completes five or 50 procedures that day. A clinic with a capacity of 25 patient encounters may employ two administrative staff, who are budgeted whether the clinic schedules 10 or 20 patient encounters. Other examples of fixed expenses are nonpersonnel line items, such as equipment maintenance costs. Note that fixed budgets must reflect the setting's capacity limits.

Fixed budgets are typically reported for expenses, not revenues. In most health care reimbursement systems in the United States, revenues are based on UOS, so are variable. Chapter 2 discusses the reliance of many hospitals on volume-based (variable or flexible) fee-for-service (FFS) reimbursement strategies.

In managed care organizations, providers are often reimbursed using risk-sharing capitation models. A fixed amount of reimbursement is negotiated for a specific population over a specified time period, so in capitated reimbursement systems, revenues are fixed. The capitation revenue is prepaid, and the providers have the responsibility to efficiently manage expenses within that amount of revenue.

Step-fixed budget. Budgets or budget items that are **step-fixed** remain fixed until changes in volume require a change in capacity. For example, a nurse practitioner in a clinic might be expected to manage up to 800 patient encounters per year. If the budgeted encounters exceed 800, another nurse practitioner is added to the staff to increase the clinic's capacity and meet the needs for patient care. The step-fixed budget is discussed in more detail in Chapter 6.

Flexible budget. Budgets or budget items are **flexible** or **variable** when they are budgeted based on the UOS. Note that in fee-for-service financing models, health care revenues are variable, as reimbursement is based on each procedure provided or patient served. Flexible budgeting is also important in budgeting inpatient service expenses when the UOSs are variable. For example, in many hospital nursing units, more nurses are scheduled when the patient census is high, and fewer nurses scheduled when the census drops. Flexible budgets are more difficult to prepare and review than fixed budgets, but are essential when changes in volume lead to changes in expenses and revenues.

MANAGING OPERATING BUDGETS

Nurses new to budgets and budgeting may wonder, "What do I look for when I look at a budget?" It is important to think of the operating budget not only as a report, but as a management tool. Linking the management steps of monitoring, investigation, and control help guide the nurse in obtaining meaningful information and effective results from budget reports.

Budget Monitoring

Budgets are tools for evaluating and improving performance. Budget figures represent **performance targets**, or indicators that specify whether a performance standard is reached in actual practice. Budget monitoring involves the ongoing critical review of the budget focused on identifying performance problems that require investigation. Undesired, unexpected, or unusual performance is identified by budget monitoring, allowing for investigation of the source of performance problems. The actual performance is compared to a budgeted target, to past performance, or to performance YTD. The amount or percent of variance is used to consider whether further analysis is necessary.

As shown in Table 5.1 and all other budget tables in this chapter, the first column of the budget report usually describes the line item or indicator. The next two columns generally report budget and actual measures for the budget report's current time period. Comparing the budgeted to actual performance is a basic and essential step in budget monitoring. The reviewer is able to determine whether actual performance measures are lower, higher, or the same as the budget targets.

Budget targets. In some cases, specific budget targets are established in operating budgets, using internal or external benchmarks. For example, East Wing applies an internal benchmark to budget 8.0 HPPD of nursing care based on average patient acuity levels and nurse staffing policies, as shown in Table 5.2. Other settings may budget HPPD differently. For example, California has a nurse/patient ratio law that specifies nurse staffing requirements and thus requires meeting minimum HPPD levels in acute care settings (California Nurses Association and National Nurses Organizing Committee, 2009).

East Wing applies an external national benchmark to budget 2% of labor expenses as overtime expense (Bateman, 2012). Other settings may develop internal benchmarks that differ from the national benchmark, based on their patient and staffing needs. The application of internal or external benchmarks to budgets enables comparison of performance with organizational or industry standards.

Budget YTD. The columns for budgeted and actual measures are often followed by columns reporting YTD budgeted and actual figures, as shown in Table 5.1. The reviewer can therefore compare performance for the current time period to performance over the fiscal year. The YTD report helps the reviewer determine whether annual budget targets are likely to be met. In some settings, it is important to spend the entire budget by the end of the fiscal year, or the budget surplus is withheld and the next year's budget may be reduced.

Prior year. Budget reports can compare current to past performance. Budget reports often include a column with the actual performance reported for the prior year, as shown in Table 5.2. Comparing current with prior year performance is helpful in identifying **cyclical** or **seasonal** budget patterns. For example, a medical nursing unit may have higher patient volume and higher expenses in winter months related to increased rates of respiratory disorders. The December 2012 performance may therefore be over budget, but similar to December 2011 performance. Patient volume and nursing unit expenses may drop in the summer, so the July 2012 and July 2011 performance may be under budget.

Trends. In some cases, budget reports might present actual performance for each month of the fiscal year to date. Comparing current to past performance helps the budget reviewer

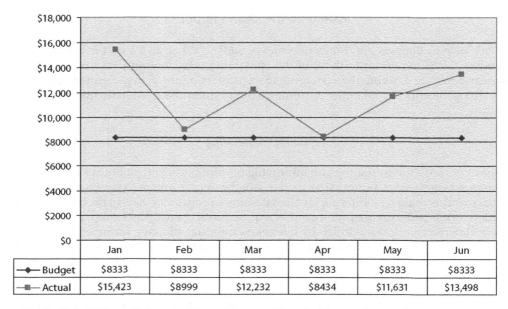

	Jan	Feb	Mar	Apr	May	Jun
—◆—Budget	$8333	$8333	$8333	$8333	$8333	$8333
—■—Actual	$15,423	$8999	$12,232	$8434	$11,631	$13,498

Figure 5.2 *Millway University Nurse-Managed Health Center (MNC) Medical Supplies Variance, January to June 2012*

identify **trends** or patterns in performance. For example, overtime expenses might increase month after month, alerting the reviewer that this trend is a possible budget concern. It is helpful to graph this information as a **trend line** so the reviewer has a visual representation of the performance trend over the fiscal year. Figure 5.2 shows monthly budget reporting graphed as a trend line.

Budget variance. Following the budgeted and actual figures, budgets often report the **variance,** or difference, between the budgeted target and actual performance. The budget variance calculation is done by finding the difference between budgeted values and actual performance. **Favorable budget variance** is a desirable difference between budgeted and actual amounts. Actual expenses that are similar or less than budgeted indicate a favorable variance. Revenues that are similar or greater than budgeted also show a favorable variance. **Unfavorable budget variance** is an undesirable difference between budgeted and actual values, as when revenues are less than budgeted or expenses are higher than budgeted.

Variance for volume or revenue is calculated by subtracting the budgeted value from the actual performance (variance = actual – budget). For example, if a nurse-managed clinic budgets $100,000 in revenue and is reimbursed $110,000, the variance is $10,000 ($110,000–$100,000). Subtracting the budgeted value from the actual performance results in a positive number for favorable volume or revenue variance, interpreted as a gain. When actual performance is less than budgeted, the negative number for unfavorable volume or revenue variance is interpreted as a loss.

Variance for expense is calculated by subtracting the actual performance from the budgeted value (variance = budget – actual). For example, if a nurse-managed clinic budgets $10,000 for supplies and actually spends $9000, the variance is $1000 ($10,000–$9000). Expenses that are less than budgeted are interpreted as a gain or favorable variance. Expenses greater than budgeted are interpreted as a loss or unfavorable variance.

Percent variance. In some budget reports, such as Table 5.2, the **percent variance,** or percent difference, between budgeted and actual measures is calculated in a column following the amount of variance. The percent variance is the proportional difference between the budgeted and actual values, calculated as the variance divided by the budgeted value and reported as a percent. For example, if a nursing unit budgets $100 for an item and spends $90 for that item, the expense budget variance is $10 ($100–$90) and the percent variance is 10% ($10 ÷ $100). The item is 10% under budget. If the item was 10% over budget, it would be reported as –10% or (10%).

The percent variance helps the reviewer understand the magnitude of the variance, not just the amount. Percents can also be compared across settings, so one nursing unit reporting a 25% increase in the monthly medical supplies budget might be compared to a similar nursing unit reporting a 20% increase. If not reported, the percent variance can be calculated using the budgeted and actual values.

Averages per unit. The actual and budget figures are converted to averages and included in some budget reports, allowing the reader to compare total with averages per unit. Inpatient settings often use patient days. For example, personnel expenses might be reported as nursing expenses PPD. Revenues might also be reported PPD. Outpatient settings might use patient visits as the unit for averaging expenses or revenues. Reporting and comparing budget figures to averages shows the impact of budget performance on the costs and revenues for the UOS.

Budget Investigation

Budget investigation identifies the source or sources of a budget performance problem, and determines whether the problem and its related budget variance can be controlled. The focus is therefore on unfavorable variances. Nurses are also more likely to focus on unfavorable expense variances, as these are usually more controllable than revenue variances.

The greater the amount or percent of unfavorable variance, the more likely that budget investigation is required. In practice, there is nearly always some variance between budgeted and actual performance. It is therefore important to determine the extent of budget variance that is not only unfavorable, but of enough concern to require investigation.

A budget such as the MNC statistics budget in Table 5.1 reports many variances. The nurse must use strategies and guidelines to help pinpoint the variances that most require further investigation. These strategies and guidelines differ among health care settings, and there is no single rule or set of rules to apply in all situations when budget variances are reported. Text Box 5.1 lists some reasons for investigating budget variance that are discussed in this section.

Possible error. A first step in reviewing budget variances that appear unusual or excessive is to recheck the reported values and calculations for possible data entry or computational errors. A misplaced decimal point or other data entry error can considerably affect a budget value. Checking data sources and calculations when unfavorable variances are reported, particularly when these variances appear unusual, may save considerable frustration.

Variance amount. In some settings there are administrative policies that establish a threshold for the investigation of line items budgets. For example, if the unfavorable variance for supplies exceeds a threshold of $500 in a month, investigation might be required. If the entire monthly expense budget is over budget by $1000, then investigation might be required. Policy may require budget investigation if a net loss is reported, in other words, if total expenses exceed total revenues.

Magnitude of variance. Thresholds might also be established for the percent of unfavorable variance. A general rule is that the percent variance should not exceed 10% to 20% of the budget (Issel, 2009). A percent variance threshold might be developed from analyzing the percent variance from past reports.

Variance pattern. Variance frequency is important in determining a pattern. A continuing upward trend in unfavorable variance is an indication that budget investigation may be required. A general rule is that three data points indicate a trend. For example, if a monthly budget reports an increasing unfavorable variance over a quarterly period, the budget item may require investigation.

The longer the duration of an unfavorable variance, the more likely it requires budget investigation. Some settings establish policies that require the investigation of unfavorable budget variances if they exceed a specified amount over a specified time period, such as $1000 per month over 3 months.

Another approach is to determine whether the unfavorable variance would be considered excessive if it continued for the remainder of the fiscal year. For example, a monthly budget reports a line item that is $1000 over budget in June. This line item would be $7000 over budget for the fiscal year, assuming the fiscal year ends in December. If a $7000 unfavorable variance for the item would cause concern, the variance should be investigated based on the monthly June report.

Unusual variance. Unexpected or unusual variances may require budget investigation. For example, if a percent variance represents a 9% increase over the budget, when previous reports have never shown more than a 5% increase in this line item, the variance is unusual and should probably be investigated. An example of an unexpected variance that should be investigated is if the unfavorable variance for variable expenses, such as staffing, increases at the same time that the volume decreases. Variable expenses should follow the same pattern as volume.

Unbudgeted expenses are unusual and require attention. Most facilities have policies requiring approval for purchases to prevent staff from generating unbudgeted expenses. However, unplanned events sometimes occur that lead to unbudgeted expenses that must be investigated. For example, equipment in a nurse-managed clinic might be damaged by flooding and require replacement during the fiscal year.

Text Box 5.1 *Reasons to Investigate Budget Variance*

- Identify data entry or calculation error
- Amount of unfavorable variance
  - Policies, guidelines, or thresholds
  - Net loss: total expenses exceed total revenues
- Percent unfavorable variance
- Pattern of unfavorable variance
  - Continual increase (trend) in unfavorable variance
  - Duration of unfavorable variance
  - Impact if unfavorable variance continues the entire fiscal year
- Unexpected or unusual variance
  - Unbudgeted expense
  - Variable expense increases when volume decreases
- Determine if variance is controllable
  - Expense variance: prices or wages, efficiency
  - Revenue variance: reimbursement, charges, collections
- Personal knowledge and experience

Controllable Variance

Budget investigation not only helps identify the source of the unfavorable variance, but determines whether the variance is controllable. Expenses are often considered to be more controllable than revenues. Nurses generally cannot control unfavorable revenue variance related to reimbursement changes or difficulties with revenue collections. Nurses also are frequently unable to increase patient volume to improve revenues and reimbursement.

However, nurses can control unfavorable revenue variances from missed charges by exercising more accountability in submitting all appropriate charges. In addition, nurses can make sure to accurately document patient status and the nursing care provided, so that patient care is appropriately reimbursed. Nursing care that decreases preventable complications and readmissions helps control reductions in reimbursement related to quality initiatives. Nurses therefore do have some impact on revenues and reimbursement.

Expense variances are often more controllable than revenue variances, but not always. For example, if a vendor raises the price for medical supplies, the nursing unit might need to continue purchasing supplies from this vendor (uncontrollable). In other situations, a new vendor could be selected who charges a lower price (controllable). If overtime hours are higher than budgeted, the unfavorable variance might be related to an unexpectedly high census from an influenza epidemic (uncontrollable) or from inefficiencies among nursing staff that need closer supervision (controllable). Unfavorable variances in fixed expenses, such as increases in rent, are often not as controllable as flexible expenses, such as wasted supplies.

Knowledge and experience. Over time, nurses apply what they know about their work setting and the operating budget to monitor and decide when to investigate unfavorable variances. Nurses might develop budget monitoring guidelines or apply a combination of the guidelines that have been discussed. Knowledge of the health care setting and the UOS, expenses, and revenues the setting generates is essential. For example, overtime hours and expenses are closely monitored on most inpatient units. Revenue might be more closely monitored in nurse-managed clinics.

Investigating Unfavorable Variance

Once an unfavorable variance is identified that requires investigation, the nurse must try to find the source of the unfavorable variance. One of the first steps in investigation is to **drill down** to obtain budget variance information in more detail. For example, the overtime hours and expenses show an unfavorable variance in a monthly report, requiring investigation. The nurse should request more detailed budget reports that indicate overtime hours on a daily and per-shift basis to obtain clearer information about when overtime occurs. This detail enables the nurse to understand when and why overtime variance is unfavorable for the month. If the medical supplies monthly report requires investigation, drilling down includes reviewing budget reports that list each type of medical supplies to determine what items contribute to the unfavorable variance.

Budget investigation then shifts from the numbers in the budget report to the activities and events in the health care setting. For example, if specific types of medical supplies cause the unfavorable variance, the nurse might investigate the following:

- Vendor contracts to determine if the price or shipping costs for these supplies have increased
- Security to determine if these supplies are being stolen or "borrowed"
- Possible sources of waste, such as procedure packages containing supplies that are discarded
- Changes in policies or procedures requiring increase in the use of these supplies

Budget Control

After investigating unfavorable variances, the nurse applies management and leadership strategies to address controllable variance. For example, more intensive staff supervision and training might reduce excessive overtime hours. Advance planning for seasonal and cyclical events might reduce staffing expenses. Quality improvement initiatives such as reducing unnecessary medical errors might reduce costs as well as improve revenues (Cady, 2011). The nurse or nurse manager must work as part of a team with other managers and with staff to control unfavorable variances, making leadership skills essential (Penner, 2004).

Following the implementation of budget control measures, mechanisms for ongoing feedback are essential. Monitoring and reinvestigation are important to confirm that the budget control measures are successful. The nurse may need to continue to drill down budget reports for detailed updates on the progress in controlling the unfavorable budget variance. It is helpful to develop good working relationships with financial officers who can help provide more detailed reports and other information useful in drilling down budget reports.

Budget Balancing

In many settings, nurses must struggle to control expenses while coping with various unexpected and uncontrollable cost increases. When budget variances become excessive and require investigation, the nurse manager may need to **balance the budget**. Budget balancing is a budget control strategy in which the manager adjusts the budget itself to compensate for actual performance. In other words, the budget is revised so that it better reflects actual expenditures that differ greatly from the original budget estimates. Budget balancing approaches require adherence to financial policies and executive approval, in order to guard against potential financial mismanagement. However, these approaches may be necessary in some situations of unusual budget overruns.

Line item flexibility. One way to balance a budget is **line-item flexibility**, or management authority to transfer funds in one line item to another line item. The line items must be within the same category of personnel or nonpersonnel expenses. For example, the nurse manager at MNC finds that the health center must purchase a new type of medical supplies that are not in the current year's budget. The manager transfers budget funds from medical supplies budget lines that are under budget to cover the expense for the new type of supplies. Most settings have policies the manager must follow in exercising line item flexibility, including requirements for administrative approval and limits on the types of transfers allowed.

Budget adjustment authority. Budgets may be balanced using **adjustment authority**, when the manager revises the budget over the remaining fiscal year to adjust for the excessive unfavorable variance. One strategy for budget adjustment is to cancel nonessential purchases. For example, a nurse-managed health center might cancel funding for conferences to adjust for budget overruns in nonpersonnel expenses.

Another strategy for budget adjustment authority is to obtain administrative approval to revise the budget mid-year. The East Wing medical-surgical unit might experience a considerable increase in UOS, requiring hiring an additional unbudgeted RN and **full-time equivalent (FTE)** during the course of the fiscal year. The nurse manager revises the FTE budget for the remainder of the fiscal year to include the increased staff. Budget adjustment authority thus enables the nurse manager to balance the budget for the remaining fiscal year.

Budget Justification

When a nurse manager presents a business case for an unusual or excessive budget variance, it is referred to as **budget justification**. This presentation is usually in the form of a budget justification report that is submitted for administrative review. Policy may require budget justification reports any time a budget item requires investigation. Budget balancing, including line item transfers and budget adjustments, also often require a budget justification report. Budget justification reports are usually relatively brief, frequently written as a memo of one to five pages.

Sections of a budget justification report include a clear description of the line item or items that are the focus of investigation and control. The report should be specific regarding whether the line item is revenue or an expense. If an expense item, the report should indicate whether the unfavorable variance is a personnel or nonpersonnel expense, and whether this is a fixed or flexible expense.

Budget justification reports provide information based on budget monitoring. The budget target, actual performance, variance amount, and percent variance are reported. If a pattern of unfavorable variance is identified, such as a trend, it is described. The potential fiscal year impact on revenue or expenses are identified.

The budget justification report then presents the results of the budget investigation. The source or sources of the unfavorable variance are described. An explanation of whether the source or sources of the unfavorable variance are controllable is provided.

If the unfavorable variance is controllable, the manager's approaches to control the budget are explained in the budget justification report. The report also indicates whether these approaches have been successful. The manager's plan for ongoing management of this line item is described, as well as feedback mechanisms such as more detailed budget reports for this item.

The budget justification report includes a copy of the budget report, presenting the items and variances requiring attention. If the mid-year budget must be revised, the revised budget is included, with notes to the budget explaining changes or adjustments. The report is submitted to the appropriate administrative staff, which may include the facility's chief executive officer (CEO), chief financial officer (CFO), and the nursing services executive. Further communication may be required before administrative approval is granted. A sample budget justification report is provided at the end of the chapter (Exhibit 5.1).

HEALTH CENTER AND INPATIENT UNIT BUDGETS

Although a complete operating budget reports UOS, expenses, and revenues, nurses are likely to see operating budget information reported in a number of ways. Some budget reports focus on UOS. Many budget reports summarize the UOS and provide more detail on personnel (nurse staffing) expenses. An operating expense budget includes volume, personnel, and nonpersonnel expenses, but omits revenue reporting. Operating revenues are the sole focus of some budget reports. The variance reports in this chapter are based on budget reports used in health care settings, and include volume, expenses, and revenues.

Statistics Budget

The **statistics budget** presents an estimate or forecast of the UOS over a specified time period. The statistics budget provides a basis for the estimates used in the operating budget. Other types of budgets may also base estimates on the statistics budget, as explained in Chapter 7. A statistics budget is essential in health settings such as hospitals, where a change in the UOS changes the amount of revenue and expense. Because indicators from the statistics budget are so frequently included in operating budgets, the statistics budget is discussed in this chapter as an operating budget report.

Patient volume statistics can be used and interpreted in many ways. As discussed in Chapter 4, indicators such as patient referrals, admissions, patient days, and occupancy rate are all measures of utilization. The number of surgical or other procedures is another utilization measure. Patient utilization reflects access to health care. For example, the volume of hospital admissions for elective surgeries may drop if a community experiences high unemployment and many residents lose health insurance coverage. Utilization may also reflect **market share,** or the consumer demand compared to competitors. For example, a nurse-managed health center featuring a convenient location and drop-in scheduling may attract more patient referrals than other outpatient facilities.

The statistics budget can reflect predictable changes in utilization that are often seasonal or cyclical. For example, outpatient visits and hospital admissions for respiratory illnesses frequently increase in winter months, when rates of influenza and pneumonia are typically higher. Changes in reimbursement or regulations may be shown in the statistics budget. For example, hospitals that are successful in reducing preventable readmissions related to recent quality initiatives are likely to report a reduction in utilization. Outpatient facilities managing these patients' care in the community may report an increase in patient utilization. Other changes or unusual events, such as new technologies that reduce hospital admissions and patient length of stay, may be reflected in the statistics budget report.

Personnel Expense Budget

Labor costs are often the largest part of health care budgets. Expenses for nursing personnel often make up the largest part of hospital budgets, and in some hospitals the largest part of the total budget (Douglas, 2010). Nurse managers are likely to focus considerable attention to the personnel expenses reported in the operating budget, whether the setting is inpatient or outpatient.

Chapter 4 discusses a number of indicators that might be included in personnel expense budget reports. Inpatient care settings frequently base nursing personnel staffing and budgets on patient acuity, measured as hours per patient day (HPPD). The direct hours needed to cover the HPPD and the paid nonproductive hours are combined and budgeted as nursing full-time equivalents (FTEs). Wages, salaries, and benefits paid for these hours reflect the nursing personnel expenses. Other inpatient nursing costs such as orientation and recruiting (Penner & Spencer, 2012) must be budgeted, but these expenses are often not reported at the nursing unit level.

Outpatient and other health care settings determine FTEs based on the UOS (patient visits or procedures). Budgeting in outpatient settings is usually less complex than inpatient settings. Nurses are not scheduled to work 24-hour or 7-day per week shifts in most outpatient settings except for emergency departments. Staffing for outpatient settings is often fixed, not flexible, so nursing expenses are less likely to change from day to day. However, nursing costs are often a substantial source of expense, so the personnel budget requires monitoring in outpatient settings, as well. This chapter focuses largely on inpatient nursing expenses, but many of these concepts and approaches can be applied to outpatient health care settings.

Some sources of unfavorable variances are difficult to identify without knowing the activities that take place on the nursing unit. For example, inpatients that are at risk for falls might require a "sitter," or nurse assistant who provides one-to-one care. In some situations, staff might be "pulled" or assigned to other units for all or part of their shifts. For example, East Wing might budget the paid hours for their staff that are pulled to work in North Wing. The nurse needs to know the context of the nursing unit in order to understand and accurately interpret the personnel budget.

The inpatient nursing personnel budget is often a complex and very detailed report to review. It is therefore helpful to think of some general areas to focus attention when a nurse monitors personnel expenses. Some areas to consider when reviewing the budget include flexible direct care, overtime and agency nurse utilization, nonproductive paid leave, and the nursing skill mix.

Flexible direct care. Personnel expense budgets report patient acuity and utilization statistics such as HPPD and patient days. Actual performance should indicate that the requirement for HPPD is met over the time period. If direct care hours exceed the required HPPD, the acuity might be greater than budgeted, or the nurses might not be working as efficiently as budgeted. Flexible budgets are based on UOS, so if the patient days increase over a time period, the variable staff hours and expenses are expected to increase accordingly. If the volume drops, variable staff hours and expenses should decrease accordingly.

Overtime and agency nurses. Overtime and agency nurses are expensive. The hours and expenses for overtime and agency nurses is monitored closely in most inpatient nursing units. Benchmarks or budget targets are often established for overtime and agency nurse utilization.

Nonproductive leave. The nonproductive hours, percent of nonproductive hours, and paid nonproductive expenses require close monitoring in most inpatient settings. Nonproductive hours not only are paid to the employee, but generally require paying another employee or agency nurse for staff coverage. Unplanned paid nonproductive leave is often more costly than if planned. For example, if a nurse is absent for a few days and the absence is planned, other nursing staff might be scheduled at the standard hourly wage. If the absence is unplanned, coverage may require more expensive overtime or agency nurse hours.

Skill mix. Wages for RNs are usually higher than for licensed practical nurses (LPNs) and unlicensed staff such as nurse assistants. Many settings therefore schedule a mix of skill levels to provide inpatient care to maximize productivity and control costs. Although the ideal skill mix has not been conclusively determined, it is essential to adjust the skill mix to ensure patient safety and quality of care (Clarke & Donaldson, 2008; Institute of Medicine, 2004).

Nonpersonnel Expense Budget

Some commonly reported categories of the nonpersonnel budget are discussed in this section. While usually not as complex or costly as the personnel expense budget, the nonpersonnel budget requires monitoring. Inpatient and outpatient settings must budget items such as medical supplies. Other nonpersonnel items include nonmedical supplies such as forms, equipment maintenance, and costs for staff training. Depreciation, overhead, and capital expenses are explained, as these items are often included in nonpersonnel expense budgets.

Medical Supplies Expense Budget

In many hospitals, the cost of medical supplies is the second largest part of the total budget. In 2010, the cost of medical supplies represented 31% of a hospital's expense per patient case (Know, 2010). Medical supplies costs are also growing rapidly, related to new technologies and shipping costs. The medical supplies budget therefore requires careful management. In addition, staff education may be needed, as staff often do not understand the impact medical supplies have on the budget. A few sources of unfavorable medical supplies expense variance are presented here.

Shrinkage. Shrinkage refers to supplies that are removed from the setting without authorization. One example of shrinkage is theft. Another example of shrinkage is sending supplies home with patients without charging for the supplies. "Borrowing" supplies for use in other units causes shrinkage. Hoarding medical supplies also results in shrinkage (Bateman, 2012).

Waste. Damaging or contaminating medical supplies so they cannot be used for patient care is an example of waste. Waste also occurs if supplies are improperly managed, so that they exceed their expiration date for use. The disposal of unused items, such as from a patient isolation room or from a procedure package, is another example of waste. Supplies are wasted when staff must repeat a procedure, such as making multiple attempts to start an IV.

Excessive expenditures. The lack of policies and procedures for managing vendors and vendor contracts may result in excessive expenditures, as the lowest possible price for the medical supplies is not negotiated. The lack of standardization therefore increases the cost of medical supplies. In addition, when supplies are not standardized, multiple brands and types of similar supplies are kept available, increasing the cost of storing and managing the supplies (Bateman, 2012). It is essential to work as a team with physicians and other staff to establish an inventory of standardized supplies that allow for high-quality care at the most reasonable cost.

Missed charges. When nurses fail to charge for supplies, the supply costs are not reimbursed and must be borne by the health care facility (Bateman, 2012). Missing charges therefore not only represents an expense, but a loss in revenue in the inpatient or outpatient setting. If procedures for making appropriate charges are difficult or cumbersome, charges are likely to be missed. Staff may not realize what items are included in the patient care expenses, and what items should be charged to patients. Nurses need to understand what items should be charged, how to charge supply items, and the importance of making appropriate charges for supplies.

Depreciation

Some nonpersonnel budgets include a line for **depreciation** expenses, which estimates and allocates the cost of a capital asset over its useful life. For example, a telemetry unit with high-cost capital equipment such as bedside monitors might budget for depreciation, spreading the costs of purchasing the monitors over the years the monitors are in use. Depreciation is not controllable, but is also not likely to vary throughout the fiscal year, so is not a source of unfavorable variance. More information about depreciation is presented in Chapter 12.

Overhead

Some nonpersonnel budgets include **overhead** expenses, also referred to as indirect or administrative costs. Examples of indirect expenses included as overhead are housekeeping, security, rent, and utilities. Overhead might be budgeted using cost-finding approaches to estimate and allocate indirect expenses for settings such as nursing units, as explained in Chapter 8. For example, the laundry department might charge the nursing unit for excessive use of linens, so the overhead expense might result in an unfavorable variance requiring control.

In many settings, overhead is budgeted as a proportion of the overall operating expense budget. For example, 10% of a nursing unit's expense budget might be added as a nonpersonnel budget item to cover overhead expenses. Overhead might be budgeted as a fixed dollar amount. For example, the MNC is charged $10,000 in overhead expenses per year by Bigtown Hospital, where the MNC is located. If budgeted as a proportion of overall expenses or as a fixed amount, the overhead expense does not vary over the fiscal year, so is not a source of unfavorable variance.

Operating Revenue Budget

Operating revenues are often not as controllable as operating expenses. Negotiating reimbursement rates and developing procedures for recovering payment are generally administrative responsibilities that do not directly involve nurses. Nurses can affect revenues by making appropriate charges for medical supplies or other services.

Nurses can affect revenues related to nurse productivity and patient flow. Efficient and productive inpatient nursing care can reduce excessive patient LOS that may increase costs to the facility and make beds unavailable to patients needing admission. More efficient management of patient admissions, discharges, and transfers can reduce revenue potentially lost to diversion or the inability of a hospital or hospital unit to admit patients because it is full. Outpatient and other settings may be able to schedule more patient visits or procedures if nurses are efficient and productive. However, nurses and nurse managers are generally held more accountable for operating expenses rather than operating revenues.

Gross revenue. The operating revenue budget for inpatient nursing units often presents a line for **gross revenue**, or the total amount charged for goods or services before any discounts are applied. Gross revenue varies according to volume, because there are typically charges applied to every patient visit, procedure, hospital day, or other UOS. In addition, charges or missed charges for supplies and services affect gross revenue.

Net revenue and contractual allowance. **Net revenue** is gross revenue less any reductions to the full charges, such as negotiated discounts or payment of a predetermined fee by insurers such as Medicare. The actual amount that insurers reimburse, compared to the health setting's charges, is known as the contractual allowance. Unpaid bills, known as **bad debt,** are deducted from gross revenue in determining net revenue. Charity care for persons unable to pay might also be deducted from gross revenue. Nursing units often report gross revenue rather than net revenue, because net revenue is more difficult to estimate and allocate to individual nursing units than the charges (gross revenue) generated.

Payer mix. The **payer mix** represents the various sources of reimbursement and reimbursement rates, such as Medicare, Medicaid, self-pay, and private insurance plans. Insurers often reimburse at a rate less than the health provider's charges, so understanding the payer mix helps in understanding actual reimbursement for the health care setting. Outpatient settings frequently collect more out-of-pocket and self-pay revenue compared to inpatient settings, with greater risk of bad debt and charity care. Publicly funded settings such as county hospitals receive less private insurance reimbursement than private hospitals, and serve more patients who are uninsured. The payer mix is therefore an overall indicator for net revenue.

OPERATING BUDGET CASE EXAMPLES

The following sections present case examples using variance reports from budgets in health care settings. The case examples from the MNC outpatient center and the East Wing inpatient unit include tables and figures to report and illustrate variance analysis used in budget reporting and management.

Nurse-Managed Health Center Budget

Table 5.1 presents a budget variance report for the Millway University Nurse-Managed Health Center (MNC) for the second quarter of 2012. The unfavorable variances are reported as negative values in parentheses, to help guide the reader in identifying potential budget problems for possible investigation. Variances are not calculated for the number of NPs, which remains fixed over the fiscal year. Variances are also not calculated for the P&L statement, but a negative value indicates a loss, which is an unfavorable profit report. The YTD figures allow the reader to compare the health center's budget performance so far for the fiscal year.

Health center budget reporting and monitoring. The revenue variances for the second quarter and 2012 YTD show that the ACO revenue and grant funding are being received as negotiated or awarded (Table 5.1). A fund-raising event was held during the second quarter, resulting in donations somewhat greater than budgeted. However, overall for the YTD, private collections from self-pay patients and donations are less than budgeted.

The personnel expense budget is balanced for the second quarter and 2012 YTD, as shown in Table 5.1. However, the nonpersonnel budget reports negative variances for medical supplies and for nonpersonnel expenses overall. The negative variance for medical supplies also affects the total expense budget. The negative variance for expenses is much greater than the negative variance for revenues for both the second quarter and for 2012 YTD. The MNC nurse manager will investigate the unfavorable variance for medical supplies.

Health center budget investigation and control. The MNC nurse manager decides to drill down and obtain a graph of the medical supplies monthly budget variance for 2012 YTD. Figure 5.2 presents the graph of medical supplies variance, showing actual performance over budget (negative variance) as any point greater than the budget target of $8333. The nurse manager had not been concerned about the negative variance for January 2012, assuming that supplies were being stocked at the start of the year, and that the following budget variances would be favorable. The drop in medical supplies expenses in February appeared to support the assumption that the expenses would continue to decrease. However, it is clear that medical supplies expenses are substantially greater than budgeted for most months YTD, and there appears to be a trend of increasing expenses for the second quarter of 2012.

The MNC nurse manager meets with the NPs to investigate the concerns about the medical supplies variance. It becomes apparent that the NPs are requesting supplies based on their individual preferences and that multiple vendors are involved in purchasing supplies. As a result, prices for similar items are highly variable. The NPs are unaware of the cost impact of the supplies they request, or of the impact the supplies budget makes on the overall budget and profitability of MNC.

The unfavorable variance for MNC medical supplies is determined to be controllable. The MNC nurse manager implements several strategies to control the medical supplies budget. One strategy is to collaborate with Bigtown Hospital, where MNC is located, to purchase medical supplies within the hospital's purchasing system. This approach allows MNC to obtain standardized supplies that can be purchased at negotiated discounts.

Another control strategy is to establish policies and procedures for any requests NPs make for medical supplies. The NPs are now required to submit supplies requests to the nurse manager for review and approval. The nurse manager also shares the medical supplies budget with the NPs at their weekly health center meetings, providing feedback to the NPs on budget performance. The NPs are developing a greater awareness of the impact of their practice on the health center budget.

The nurse manager also investigates the negative variances for private collections and donations that reduce revenue for the second quarter and 2012 YTD. One finding is that NPs are not comfortable asking patients to reimburse for their care. The nurse manager believes that private collections might be better controlled by improving collection procedures. However, donations are likely not controllable.

Procedures are developed at MNC to improve self-pay revenue control. The administrative staff will request payment from self-pay patients upon arrival for appointments. This procedure is expected to improve the private collections rate, although patients who cannot pay will not be turned away. The nurse manager will continue to monitor the revenue budget to determine if the collections procedure is effective.

Inpatient Unit Budget

Table 5.2 presents a monthly variance report for the East Wing medical surgical unit for July 2012. Variances and percent variances are not reported for days in the time period and staffed beds, which are fixed and not expected to change. Variances and percent variances are also not calculated for the percent of overtime expenses, which can be compared without variances. Actual performance in July 2011 is included in this variance report for comparison to past performance.

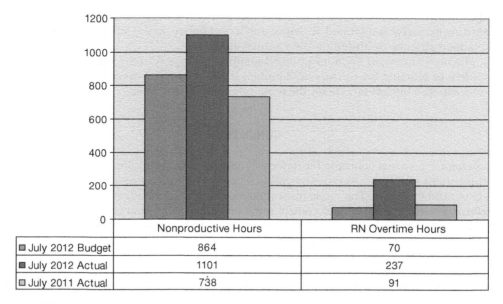

	Nonproductive Hours	RN Overtime Hours
July 2012 Budget	864	70
July 2012 Actual	1101	237
July 2011 Actual	738	91

Figure 5.3 *East Wing Medical-Surgical Unit, Nonproductive and Overtime Hours Variance, July 2012*

Inpatient unit reporting and monitoring. The nurse manager plans to investigate the first two variances. Although patient days are 5.5% under budget, RN FTEs are 11.1% over budget. This is an unusual variance, as FTEs would be expected to decrease if patient days decrease. In addition, the FTE budget variance exceeds the 10% variance threshold, so policy requires investigation.

The gross revenue also shows an unfavorable variance, 4% below budget. However, this drop in revenue is approximately consistent with the drop in patient days. Patient days are closely related to gross revenue, because gross revenue on East Wing largely consists of daily patient room charges. The nurse manager therefore does not see a need to investigate concerns about gross revenue.

The nonpersonnel budget shows favorable variances. It is clear that the personnel budget presents the most concerns for July 2012. Salaries and wages are 12.2% over budget, which reinforces the indication of overstaffing for the month shown by the unfavorable FTE variance. In addition, the percent of overtime pay to total personnel expenses is more than three times greater than budgeted. This budget requires investigation for unfavorable personnel expense variance.

Inpatient unit budget investigation and control. One way the nurse manager investigates is to drill down with more information about personnel hours. Figure 5.3 shows one of the reports, prepared as a bar chart, showing the variance for RN nonproductive hours and overtime hours. This chart reinforces the excess in overtime hours. The chart also indicates that paid nonproductive hours are much higher than both the budgeted and July 2011 hours and are a source of the unfavorable personnel expense variance.

The nurse manager meets with charge nurses to learn more about the problems with personnel expenses for July 2012. During the month, there was an increase in unplanned personal leave. These unplanned absences led to scheduling problems and the use of more overtime hours to cover staffing. The unfavorable variance is determined to be largely controllable.

The East Wing nurse manager works with the charge nurses and to improve control of personnel expenses. The manager and the charge nurses will supervise unplanned absences and overtime hours more closely for the remainder of the fiscal year. Policies are reviewed regarding excessive unplanned absences, and a new policy is developed that links excessive unplanned absences to the employee's annual evaluation.

The nurse manager submits a budget justification report to the Bigtown Hospital Vice President of Nursing for the July 2012 budget (Exhibit 5.1). The overall goal is to meet personnel expense budget targets for the remainder of the fiscal year.

CONCLUSION

This chapter presents concepts for reporting and managing nursing budgets in outpatient and inpatient settings. Variance analysis is a helpful tool in monitoring operating volume, revenue, and expenses. The nurse must then look beyond the budget to processes and staff performance to investigate and control unfavorable budget variances. Budget justification may be necessary to explain budget problems to administrators, and to communicate how these problems will be addressed.

Exhibit 5.1 *East Wing Personnel Expense Budget Justification Report, August 15, 2012*

MEMORANDUM

To: [name], Vice President of Nursing, Bigtown Hospital
From: [name], Nurse Manager, East Wing Medical-Surgical Unit
Date: August 15, 2012
Subject: Budget Justification for Personnel Variance, July 2012

BUDGET LINE ITEM(S) REQUIRING JUSTIFICATION

The East Wing Variance Report for July 2012 shows unfavorable variances for RN FTEs and personnel expenses that required investigation and control. The unfavorable variance for gross revenue is not addressed in this report, as the drop in gross revenue is concurrent with the drop in patient days for July 2012.

MONITORING AND IMPACT

Personnel expense items requiring investigation and control:

- RN FTEs are 5.0 FTEs and 11.1% over budget, although volume is 29 patient days and 5.5% less than budgeted.
- Total salaries and wages are $20,925 and 12.2% over budget.
- The percent of overtime expenses compared to all personnel expenses is 6.1%, or more than three times the budget target.
- The impact on total expenses for July 2012 is $21,343 and 8.2% over budget.

Up until July 2012, the RN FTEs and personnel expenses have been within budget, with no indication of upward trends. Comparison to July 2011 performance shows that July 2011 volume was lower than budgeted, but personnel FTEs and expenses also decreased so the unit performed within budget.

The impact of these unfavorable personnel expenses budget variances is serious, especially if they continue through the end of the fiscal year in December 2012.

Investigation Results

East Wing charge nurses reported an increase in unplanned personal leave during July 2012. These unplanned absences led to nurse scheduling problems and the use of more overtime hours to cover staffing. Overtime coverage was not well managed for the month.

This unfavorable variance is determined to be controllable.

Control Steps

The nurse manager and the charge nurses for East Wing are alerted to closely supervise unplanned absences and overtime hours for the remainder of the fiscal year.

The East Wing nurse manager is working closely with the Human Resources Department and other managers and directors to develop a new policy for unplanned absences. Excessive unplanned absences will be linked to the employee's annual evaluation. East Wing will implement this policy in September 2012.

The nurse manager and charge nurses will review daily scheduling reports and determine the effectiveness of these control steps in bringing the personnel expenses within budget. This daily feedback will provide early warning for problems with unplanned absences and excessive use of overtime.

Discussion and Exercises

1. Think of a program or project, such as a small test of change to improve the quality of nursing care in your work setting or clinical assignment. Discuss what line items you might include in a budget for this program or project. Include personnel and nonpersonnel line items.
2. Discuss at least three indicators you might use in monitoring a budget for an inpatient or outpatient nursing care setting. How will these indicators help you identify favorable or unfavorable variances?
3. Your budget monitoring helped you detect an unfavorable budget variance. Identify at least three events, processes, or observations of staff performance that would help you investigate the source of the variance. How will you determine if the variance is controllable?
4. Assume the unfavorable budget variance you investigated is controllable. Discuss at least two management strategies that will help bring the budget back in control.

REFERENCES

Bateman, N. (2012). *The Business of nurse management: A toolkit for success.* New York, NY: Springer Publishing Company.

Cady, R. F. (2011). Accountable care organizations: What the nurse executive needs to know. *JONA's Healthcare Law, Ethics, & Regulation, 13*(2), 55–60.

California Nurses Association and National Nurses Organizing Committee (. (2009). *The ratio solution.* Retrieved from www.CalNurses.org www.NNOC.net

Clarke, S. P., & Donaldson, N. E. (2008). Nurse staffing and patient care quality and safety (Chapter 25). In R. G. Hughes (Ed.). Patient safety and quality: An evidence-based handbook for nurses. AHRQ Publication No. 08–0043. Rockville, MD: Agency for Healthcare Research and Quality. Retrieved from http://www.ahrq.gov/qual/nurseshdbk

Douglas, K. (2010). Taking action to close the nurse-finance gap: Learning from success. *Nursing Economics, 28,* 270–272.

Institute of Medicine). (2004). *Keeping patients safe: Transforming the work environment of nurses.* Washington, DC: The National Academies Press.

Issel, L. M. (2009). Health program planning and evaluation: A practical, systematic approach for community health (2nd ed.). Sudbury, MA: Jones & Bartlett Publishers.

Know, W. P. C. (2010). *Reducing healthcare costs through supply chain management.* Arizona State University, W.P. Carey School of Business. Retrieved from http://knowledge.wpcarey.asu.edu/article.cfm?articleid=1871

Penner, S. J. (October 2004). *Controlling budget variance. Nursing Homes Long Term Care Management, 53,* 86, 88.

Penner, S. J., & Spencer, M. D. (2012).Acute care utilization, staffing and financial indicators (Chapter 4). In K. T. Waxman (Ed.), *Financial & business management for the doctor of nursing practice.* New York, NY: Springer Publishing Company.

CROSSWORD: *Chapter 5—Budget Managment*

Across

3 The difference between the budgeted target and actual performance.

5 Estimating and allocating the cost of a capital asset over its useful life.

6 When values rise or fall in a repeating pattern, such as more respiratory disease occurring in the winter, also known as seasonal.

8 When values rise or fall in a repeating pattern, such as more respiratory disease occurring in the winter, also known as cyclical.

9 A performance pattern, such as a budget expense item increasing month after month.

Down

1 Identifying the source or sources of a budget variance, and determining whether the variance can be controlled.

2 Ongoing critical review of the budget focused on identifying performance problems that require investigation.

4 Putting management strategies in place to address and prevent unfavorable budget variances.

7 A total of financial performance measures from the beginning of the budget year to the current time period (abbreviation).

Chapter 6: Budget Planning

*Never base your budget requests on realistic assumptions, as this could lead
to a decrease in your funding*—Scott Adams

Learning Objectives

1. Explain how budgets serve as plans.
2. Justify the nurse's role in budget planning for nursing care settings.
3. Give at least two examples of applications of budget forecasting for budget planning in nursing care settings.
4. Point out at least two steps in estimating staff nurse costs for an inpatient or an outpatient health care setting.

Key Terms

accountability

adjusted FTE

annual spend
down

annualizing

budget cycle

group purchasing
organization (GPO)

incremental budgeting

influence

prospective forecasting

qualitative

quantitative

retrospective forecasting

strategic planning

supply chain management

what-if scenario

zero-base budgeting (ZBB)

Budgets are plans, and planning is an important activity in budgeting. The budget management techniques discussed in Chapter 5 help the nurse to understand how well the budget plan is followed. This chapter presents methods for incorporating plans for the future into the operating budget over the next fiscal year. Budget planning anticipates change that will affect financial performance from year to year. Budget planning involves making predictions for next year's volume, revenue, and expenses. Budget planning is also a way to introduce and reinforce budget control, by setting financial performance targets that require reporting and efficient management.

This chapter focuses on planning the operating budget, which is used in the day-to-day management of health care settings. The operating budget typically projects financial performance over the short-term, time periods of a year or less. Examples for planning the operating budget include scenarios based on Millway University Nurse-Managed Health Center (MNC) and the East Wing medical-surgical inpatient unit at Bigtown Hospital. Budget preparation is important for other types of budgets, as well, such as for launching a new program or service. Chapter 7 discusses budget preparation for special projects and other types of budgets.

BUDGET PLANNING AND THE NURSE'S ROLE

Nurses assume various roles related to budget planning and management. One important role is **influence**, or the extent of impact the nurse's input exerts on the budget. Another important role is **accountability**, or the extent of responsibility the nurse is given to manage the budget. Figure 6.1 shows how these roles in budgeting are related and how they vary.

Nurses who have high influence and high accountability for their budgets are typically in positions of top leadership in the organization. Vice presidents of nursing, department or agency directors, or nurses who run their own businesses are examples. Persons with high influence over the health care budget, but low direct accountability include nonclinical and non-nursing leaders such as the CFO and other top administrators. These administrators often make budget decisions that nurses and nurse managers must implement.

Unfortunately, for many years, most nurses have had low influence on the budgets in their work settings. In some settings, nurse managers have relatively high influence on their budgets, with the authority to make budget requests and changes based on their nursing units' changing needs. In other settings, nurse managers have limited influence on the budget, but have high accountability for keeping the nursing unit or outpatient center within budget.

Staff nurses usually have little influence on budgets in their work settings. One example of an exception to this rule is the Magnet® hospital, where nurses are more empowered to collaborate with administration (American Nurses Credentialing Center, 2012). Nurses may believe they also have little budget accountability. However, the Institute of Medicine and other policy makers increasingly realize that nurses are essential in delivering high-quality, cost-effective health care (Institute of Medicine, 2011). It is important for

Influence	Accountability	
	High	**Low**
High	High influence and high accountability	High influence and low accountability
Low	Low influence and high accountability	Low influence and low accountability

Figure 6.1 *Roles in Health Care Budget Influence and Accountability*

all nurses to understand their impact on health care costs. Learning about budgeting and budget planning is a first step toward increasing the nurse's accountability for the budget. Accountability for the work setting's budget is important in expanding the nurse's role and influence in budgeting decisions.

STRATEGIC PLANNING AND BUDGET LINKAGE

Operating budgets establish financial plans for nursing microsystems such as inpatient nursing units and outpatient health centers. Operating budget preparation is also related to the institution's **strategic planning** process, which determines organizational goals for the future. Strategic planning often extends over the long-term, or more than one fiscal year (refer to Chapter 7 for more discussion of strategic planning). The operating budget is a way to establish and evaluate measurable objectives over the short-term for achieving these strategic organizational goals over the long-term. The operating budget reflects the institution's priorities for day-to-day resource use in moving toward its overall goals.

For example, a nurse-managed health center may develop a goal based on strategic planning to expand from three to five nurse practitioners (NPs) over the next two years. As this goal is achieved, the operating budget reflects the increase in staff, patient visits, revenues, and expenses associated with the health center's planned growth. Strategic planning may lead a hospital to set a goal to establish a cardiovascular center of excellence within the next three years. Resources might be transferred from nursing units with low census to the expanding telemetry unit, reflected in the operating budgets for those inpatient units.

The operating budget is also linked to other budgets that are reported and managed within the facility or institution. The basis for the operating budget is the **statistics budget**, an estimate of the units of service (UOS) for the setting, such as patients or procedures, discussed in Chapter 5. The **capital budget** focuses on long-term purchases and investments guided by strategic planning initiatives, compared to the operating budget, which focuses on short-term (annual) financial performance. The **cash flow budget** estimates the inflow and outflow of revenues and expenses that support the operating budget. Other budgets, such as special purpose budgets and service line budgets, plan for new initiatives or special populations based on strategic planning.

Capital budget planning is discussed in Chapter 7 in the context of strategic planning. Chapter 7 also discusses the cash flow, special purpose, and service line budgets in more detail, including approaches in planning these budgets. This chapter focuses on the methods for planning the operating budget, and the statistics budget that is the basis of the operating budget.

BUDGET FORECASTING

A key activity in preparing an operating budget is projecting the budget values for the next fiscal year. This section discusses some commonly used methods for making budget projections. Health care budgets are often complex, and in large institutions such as hospitals, the financial officers are frequently responsible for budget projections. However, nurses may become involved in budget planning and preparation, and will find these methods useful in developing budgets.

Benchmarks and Budget Targets

One of the simplest ways to develop budget projections is to use benchmarks or budget targets as the budgeted value. One example is using the national benchmark of 2% of labor expenses as the budget for overtime expenses (Bateman, 2012). An internally developed budget target might also be applied, such as reducing medical supplies expenses by 5% over the coming year, reflected in the budget target.

Retrospective Forecasting

Budget planners often use past performance as a guide for budget projections, a method known as **retrospective forecasting**. Retrospective forecasting methods use past event data to predict future values. Budgets are frequently developed based on various forms of retrospective forecasting. The assumption is that the best available predictor of future performance is past performance. Retrospective forecasts are generally **quantitative**, relying on numerical data. Retrospective forecasts can be supplemented with **qualitative** data that do not rely on numerical data. Qualitative data include an organization's history, policies, and politics, as well as the nurse's experience.

Incremental budgeting. A simple and frequently used approach to budget preparation is **incremental budgeting**, in which the current year's budget is used as the base for the next year's budget, making additions, reductions, or keeping the base the same. These incremental changes to the budget usually depend on administrative guidelines communicated during the budget preparation phase of the budget cycle. Administrative guidelines might require either a given dollar amount or a percent of incremental change for the new budget. For example, Bigtown Hospital might assume inflation and wage increases over the next fiscal year to support an incremental budget increase of 5% for all nursing unit operating expense budgets.

The advantage of incremental budgeting is that it is simple to understand and implement. Incremental budget decisions are largely centralized and controlled at the top administrative levels, although in some settings department directors or other staff responsible for budgets may provide input. One problem with incremental budgeting is that there is a tendency to increase the budget year by year, without always fully analyzing the actual need for an increase. For example, a 5% increase in East Wing's 2013 operating budget might be greater than actually required. Incremental budgeting may therefore be inefficient.

Incremental reductions (budget cuts) may also occur without a complete analysis of their need or consequences. For example, Bigtown Hospital administrators might require a 5% cut in the operating expense budgets of all departments and nursing units. The actual budget requirements may vary from one department to another, so an incremental budget reduction might be excessive for one department, while other departments could manage with a greater than 5% budget reduction. Because incremental budgeting relies on administrative guidelines, there may be little analysis or justification of budget items by the managers or staff who are most familiar with the nursing unit facing the budget cuts. Incremental budgeting does not account for the resources a nursing unit may require to operate efficiently and profitably. Other approaches discussed in this chapter that involve more analysis of the budget and the impact of budgeting decisions help overcome the limitations of incremental budgeting.

Annual spend down. Another of the more common approaches to retrospective forecasting is the **annual spend down,** or "use it or lose it" method. Managers are expected to spend their entire budget by the end of the fiscal year, or the amount not spent is cut from the next year's budget. For example, if a nurse manager has $100,000 budgeted for a line item over a year and only spends $90,000 that year, the next year's budget for that line item is reduced to $90,000.

The spend down method rewards managers who meet annual budget targets without going over or under budget. Grant funders use the spend down method to motivate grant writers to estimate as well as spend their budgets as accurately as possible. However, in many settings, managers are compelled to spend down the entire budget by the end of the year, whether this is the most efficient use of resources or not, so that they avoid budget cuts.

If the setting uses flexible budgeting, a spend down approach may either be inappropriate or complicated to apply, as expenses are expected to drop if volume drops. Spend down incentives may penalize managers who find innovative ways to reduce expenses without reducing quality.

Prior budget performance overall. Many operating budgets in health care settings use the prior year's overall performance as a guide for budget projections. Variance analysis and budget justification reports identify areas of uncontrollable variance that require adjustment to the next year's budget. For example, if price increases result in an uncontrollable increase in the expenses for medical supplies, the next year's budget may be adjusted to increase the amount budgeted for medical supplies.

In some situations, variance analysis indicates that an unfavorable variance is controllable. Rather than adjusting the budget over the next year, a controllable unfavorable variance is often addressed as a performance problem. For example, if an unfavorable overtime expense variance is determined to be controllable, the next year's budget likely will not increase the amount budgeted for overtime expenses. Instead, the manager is expected to develop strategies to improve the control of overtime expenses and to meet the overtime expense budget target over the next year.

Annualizing unbudgeted expenses. Unexpected events during the fiscal year might result in unbudgeted expenditures. As a result, earlier time periods in the annual budget might not reflect performance later in the year. One method to adjust for unbudgeted events in budget planning is **annualizing**. The monthly annualized amount is multiplied by the remaining months in the fiscal year to estimate a revised budget. The monthly annualized amount is multiplied by 12 to predict the amount required for the next year's annual budget.

For example, assume that East Wing medical-surgical unit experiences a surge in volume mid-year 2012. Beginning in September 2012, East Wing staffs an additional five beds for a total of 25 staffed beds (Table 6.1). The nurse salaries and wages are budgeted based on 20 staffed beds. However, the increase in UOS results in actual nurse salaries and wages of $161,536 in September and $158,464 in October. The increase in UOS is expected to continue, so the performance for September and October 2012 is annualized to budget an average $160,000 for nurse salaries and wages for November and December 2012 ($320,000 ÷ 2). This annualized estimate is used to estimate the annual nurse salaries and wages budget of $1,920,000 for 2013 ($160,000 × 12).

Table 6.1 *East Wing Medical-Surgical Unit, Annualized Budget and What-if Scenario for Increasing Bed Capacity, September to December 2012*

Item	Sept 2012		Oct 2012		Sept and Oct 2012	Annualized Nov 2012	Annualized Dec 2012
	Budget	Actual	Budget	Actual	Actual	Budget	Budget
Days in time period	30	30	31	31	61	30	31
Staffed beds	20	25	20	25	25	25	25
Patient days	510	631	520	619	1250	625	625
Occupancy	85.0%	84.1%	83.9%	79.9%	82.0%	83.3%	80.6%
Total RN FTEs	35.7	44.2	36.4	43.3	43.8	43.8	43.8
Total RN salaries and wages	$130,560	$161,536	$133,120	$158,464	$320,000	$160,000	$160,000

Trending. A **trend line** is a line created by a mathematical equation that estimates or predicts the movement of an economic variable over time. Budget data from prior years is used to create the trend line, which predicts the budget value in the future. The trend line provides a visual representation of the trend, making the trend data easier to present and understand.

Trend lines can be created using spreadsheet programs that calculate the trend line as part of a line graph. In many institutions, financial officers create graphs of historical budget performance with trend lines. Information on creating a trend line in Excel is available at the MrExcel.com Add a Trendline to a Chart website (http://www.mrexcel.com/tip067.shtml).

When creating a trend line, a general rule of thumb is to use at least as many data points (years or other specified time periods of budget data) as one plans to predict into the future (Millett, 2011). For example, Figure 6.2 presents a trend line to predict the total nursing costs for the East Wing medical-surgical nursing unit for 2013. The trend line predicts that the total nursing costs for 2013 will be similar to 2012 performance, a little over $2.5 million.

Prospective Forecasting

Another forecasting method is **prospective forecasting**, based on the assumption that current information enables the prediction of future events. Prospective forecasts are often related to knowledge of new or changed policies and regulations that will affect financial performance in the future. Some institutions have research departments that compile and analyze legislative reports, updates from health plans, and other information that helps forecast revenues and expenses for the next fiscal year. For example, the Patient Protection and Affordable Care Act of 2010 will impose financial penalties for hospitals with high readmission rates, and selected 30-day readmission rates for Medicare patients are reported to the public (Michigan Medicare/Medicaid Assistance Program, 2010). These regulations and initiatives likely result in hospitals providing more resources to reduce preventable readmissions and to consider the impact on hospital revenues.

Expert opinion. Related to the use of information is the application of expert opinion to prospective budget forecasting. For example, nurse managers and administrators may meet

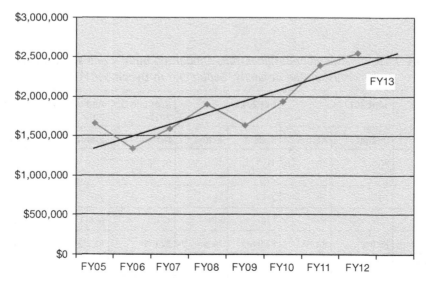

Figure 6.2 *East Wing Medical-Surgical Unit, Trend Line Forecast for 2013 Total Nursing Costs*

to discuss changes they anticipate over the next year that may impact on operating budgets as part of a strategic planning process. The expertise and experience of these leaders may be incorporated in projections of patient volume, revenue, and expenses. The results of expert opinion analysis often result in a range of predicted outcomes. Scenarios for patient volume might be rated as a specified range, to allow for differences among the experts who offer their opinions. For example, a strategic planning session might result in ranges of the highest to lowest predicted level of patient volume, or the most likely to least likely level of patient volume.

What-if scenarios. Another prospective forecasting approach is using **what-if scenarios** to analyze the possible impact of a change in revenues or expenses. Computer spreadsheets are well-suited to making "what-if" calculations. Calculating various "what-if" estimates allows for the review of potential alternative outcomes. This approach enables predictions of the impact of budget decisions for the next fiscal year.

The earlier example using Table 6.1 can be viewed as a what-if scenario. Before deciding to expand East Wing's capacity from 20 to 25 beds, the nurse manager can enter budget estimates to see what impact the expansion will have on patient days, nurse FTEs, and nurse salaries and wages. The nurse manager also wants to be sure that the change in capacity from 20 to 25 beds maintains an occupancy rate close to 85% for most days of the year. It is clear that expanding East Wing's capacity affects not only the 2012 budget, but will require increases in the 2013 budget. The nurse manager and Bigtown Hospital administration are thus better informed about the future impact of decisions that affect East Wing's operating budget.

New line items. Prospective budgeting includes budgeting for new line items. In some situations, the new line items are the result of unexpected expenses over the fiscal year. For example, the NPs at MNC may find that a number of their disease management patients require wound care management. MNC incurs expenses for medical supplies for these patients that were not anticipated in the 2012 budget. The additional time NPs need to manage these patients strains MNC capacity.

In many cases, special projects or new initiatives are planned that require additional line items in the next year's budget. For example, the MNC nurse manager writes a business plan to establish an outpatient wound care clinic in 2013. This new initiative requires budget projections for anticipated reimbursement and expenses for a wound care nurse, an examination room, and the necessary equipment and supplies. Chapters 7 and 10 discuss budgeting for special projects and business plans in more detail. Chapter 11 presents details of budgeting for health program grant proposals. Sustainability of these special projects requires including these new line items in the next year's operating budget, when the plan or proposal funding ends.

Inflation factor. Budget projections often include adjusting for predicted inflation. The same method may be used to estimate the impact of increases in salaries and wages over the next fiscal year. For example, based on the annualized estimates in Table 6.1, the 2013 nurse salaries and wages budget is estimated at $1,920,000. However, a salary and wage increase of 3% is planned for 2013. The 2013 salaries and wages budget is therefore adjusted for the projected increase, resulting in a budget estimate of $1,977,600 ($1,920,000 × 1.03).

Zero-based budgeting. Preparing a continuing budget as if it was intended for a new program or service is known as **zero-base budgeting (ZBB)**. ZBB is a prospective approach intended to improve the accuracy and control of the budgeting process, thus reducing waste and improving efficiency. In contrast to incremental budgeting, which automatically applies budget increases or cuts, ZBB requires detailed analysis of every line item as it is added to the budget.

Although zero-base budgeting increases efficiency and can improve financial performance, this approach also has limitations. The ZBB process is complex, requiring considerable time and effort, and is burdensome to require of all operating budgets each year. A better approach is to require zero-base budgets for selected programs or line items. For example, the MNC nurse manager believes that the $6,000 annual budget for nonmedical supplies is excessive and should be reduced for 2013. A ZBB approach requires that the nurse manager start with a budget of $0, and identify and evaluate each line item as it is added to the budget. This process is time-consuming, but assures that the 2013 budgeting for nonmedical supplies is accurate and cost-effective.

Step-fixed budgeting. When budget projections indicate changes that require a change in capacity, **step-fixed** budgeting is a useful approach. For example, the MNC NPs are able to manage about 1300 patient visits per year, or about 3900 total visits for the health center. The NPs are functioning close to their maximum capacity over 2012. If MNC assumes any additional contracts for patient visits, the health center must hire at least one more NP. As the workload increases beyond 1300 additional patient visits, another NP must be hired. In other words, three NPs are sufficient to cover 3900 patient visits, four NPs are needed to cover up to patient visits up to 5200 patient visits, and five NPs are required to cover up to 6500 patient visits. If these visits require the use of an examination room, then step-fixed budgeting may be used to budget an examination room for each additional NP.

More information about forecasting is provided at the Budgeting and Forecasting Process website (www.budgetingforecastingprocess.com). The eHow Money website for Budget Forecast Techniques (www.ehow.com) discusses incremental budgeting and ZBB. Readers interested in qualitative forecasting should review the website Qualitative Forecasting Methods and Techniques (www.accounting-financial-tax.com).

Forecasting Error

The future is always somewhat unpredictable, so the forecasting methods that have been presented must allow for error. One way to measure and understand error is to compare the forecasted to actual data at the end of the forecasted time period. For example, if in 2012 the MNC nurse manager projects 5000 patient visits for 2013, the predicted UOS can be compared to the actual 2013 UOS after the end of the 2013 fiscal year.

A forecast's accuracy is expected to decrease as the time frame for prediction increases. In other words, a forecast made in 2012 for 2013 is likely more accurate than a forecast made in 2012 for 2020. One implication is that nurses interpret forecasts using methods such as trend lines conservatively, and raise questions about long-term forecasts. It is also recommended to report any known error or possible sources of error when providing a forecast. For example, if the amount estimated for inflation is uncertain and based on one's best guess, this uncertainty should be reported when the budget figures that are adjusted for inflation are reported.

Another approach to address possible forecast error is to report a range of predictions rather than a single specific number. For example, the nurse managers of several medical-surgical units might be asked to predict the percent of change in patient volume for the next fiscal year. In addition, each nurse manager could be requested to provide both a high and low estimate. The high estimates and the low averages could each be averaged, resulting in an overall range of average high and low estimates from the nurse managers. Reporting a range of estimates helps account for forecasting error, as there are many factors that influence patient volume.

A combination of retrospective and prospective methods is often advisable in forecasting. It is also advisable to apply a combination of qualitative and quantitative methods when making forecasts. For example, in forecasting UOS, it is possible to review historical data and create a trend line (a quantitative, retrospective approach). The trend line prediction can then be compared to the predictions made by experienced managers and administrators (a qualitative, prospective approach). Further forecast refinement is possible by analyzing anticipated change in the coming fiscal year, such as employment rates that could affect the numbers of persons who are insured and thus more likely to access health care. Rapidly changing situations or forecasting error might lead to widely differing forecasts from each of these approaches. On the other hand, similar forecasts based on various approaches help reinforce the likely accuracy of these predictions.

Combinations of forecasting approaches help in considering all possible internal and external sources of change. Internal sources of change include the various factors in the work setting or institution that might affect the forecast. For example, if a hospital is expanding its cardiovascular services and programs, it is reasonable to predict that more nurses might need to be hired to staff these services and programs.

External sources of change include new laws, regulations, and findings from medical research that might affect the forecast. For example, in 2012 the Centers for Medicare & Medicaid Services (CMS) changed a number of regulatory requirements for hospitals. One change is that Advanced Practice Registered Nurses (APRNs) and other nonphysician practitioners may be appointed to the hospital's medical staff and function at their full scope of practice. These and other changes in CMS regulations should reduce costs to hospitals (Centers for Medicare & Medicaid Services, 2012). Strategic planning and hospital budgets will likely to be influenced by these new regulations.

PLANNING THE OPERATING BUDGET

Planning the operating budget requires projections for volume (patient days, visits, or procedures), revenue, and expenses (personnel and nonpersonnel). As mentioned earlier, these projections are based on various forecasting methods, and are often linked to strategic planning throughout the facility. Budget planning is therefore a complex process requiring teamwork and accurate information. A worksheet that may be helpful as a guide for operating budget planning can be found in Appendix 6A.

The Budget Cycle and Calendar

Although budgeting is a continuous managerial activity, most organizations establish a **budget cycle**, including a schedule for budget preparation, negotiation, approval, and implementation. As with other budgeting aspects, organizations differ in their policies for establishing the budget cycle. In many settings, a calendar for assignments such as budget reports, proposals, final budgets, and budget justification is distributed. Text Box 6.1 summarizes the elements of a typical budget cycle.

Following strategic plan development, department directors (ideally with staff assistance) prepare and submit departmental and other work unit budget proposals. These proposals include budgets for new programs, substantial changes in programs, or extensive capital improvements. Department directors or nurse managers also prepare the operating and capital budgets for continuing programs and services. After these budgets are submitted, there is a schedule of review, negotiation, and approval or denial of the budgets by upper level administration. Budgets may be required to be revised and resubmitted for final approval.

Text Box 6.1 *Elements of the Budget Cycle*

- Calendar with schedule and assignments for budget preparation
- Communication of the organization's assumptions, priorities, goals, objectives, and performance targets for the next budget year as part of the strategic plan
- Preparation of budget proposals, followed by the operating and capital budgets, then the cash budget
- Budget negotiation, revision, and final approval
- Preparation, presentation, and approval of the master budget
- Distribution of the next budget year budget worksheets and guidelines to begin budget implementation, monitoring, and control
- Evaluation of performance over the completed budget year

Statistics Budget Planning

The statistics budget is a projection of UOS that represents utilization of health services. The statistics budget is prepared before planning the operating budget, because health care revenues and expenses are usually based on volume. The volume statistics are also linked to a setting's capacity, or the maximum UOS that can be managed in a health care setting. Performance targets must be set at some point below capacity, because factors such as unexpected delays prevent health care settings from operating at full capacity for an extensive time period. Therefore, budget projections are often based on performance targets set at levels somewhat below capacity.

Table 6.2 presents the 2013 projected operating budget for MNC. The budget presents actual past budget performance data for 2011 and 2012. As budget indicators are discussed, examples of approaches to budget planning and projection are presented. The first items show the actual 2011 and 2012 statistics and the 2013 budgeted statistics.

The number of examination rooms and of NPs on staff are indicators of actual and budgeted capacity. The NP capacity is based on performance targets of four visits per day per NP for 2011 and six visits per day per NP for 2012 and 2013. The increase in capacity is because the MNC now has administrative support so the NPs can focus all of their time on clinical activities. The visits per day are multiplied by the 224 days each NP is budgeted to work. Actual performance is reported as actual visits per day and the total visits from ACO contracts and self-pay visits.

A line is reported for NP productivity, or the proportion of actual visits to NP capacity. The performance target is for the NPs to work at 95% of capacity overall, the level at which the NPs are believed to function most efficiently. The 2013 budget therefore projects 3830 patient visits, or 95% of the 4032 capacity. The nurse manager and NPs at MNC decide to maintain their current contracts with Welby ACO for disease management and wellness care. A contract for immunization of Bigtown school children is changed so that MNC will provide about 300 visits rather than the 500 visits contracted in 2012. The NPs will focus more on immunizing preschoolers entering the school system in 2013, compared to older children. Some continued increase in self-pay visits is anticipated for 2013.

Table 6.3 presents the 2013 projected operating budget for the East Wing medical-surgical unit. The actual performance for 2011 and 2012 is displayed, with budget projections for 2013. The statistics indicate that East Wing will increase its capacity from 20 to 25 staffed beds over the next year. Strategic planning led to the reorganization of medical-surgical units at Bigtown Hospital. The reorganization resulted in the closure of one medical-surgical nursing unit (North Wing) and the allocation of additional beds to East Wing. The 2013 budgeted patient days of 7756 reflect a performance target of 85% occupancy, a level at which East Wing is believed to operate most efficiently. These projections are based on strategic planning decisions and expert opinion, as well as historical information and trends for patient days.

Revenue Budget Planning

Operating revenue projections are based on the statistics budget and on anticipated reimbursement for the coming fiscal year. MNC negotiates the same reimbursement for 2013 as for 2012 (Table 6.2). Although MNC will manage about 200 fewer immunization visits over 2013, the continued reimbursement of $450,000 adjusts for inflation. Grant funding continues at $50,000 and additional revenue is anticipated from private collections from self-pay patients and from donations. Revenue is budgeted at $138 per patient visit, reflecting a per-unit increase.

Gross revenue for East Wing medical-surgical unit is estimated at $6,522,120 for 2013. The gross revenue reflects the charges for services on East Wing, not the actual

Table 6.2 *Millway University Nurse-Managed Health Center (MNC) Operating Budget Projection for 2013*

Item	2011	2012	2013
	Actual	Actual	Budget
Statistics			
Examination rooms	1	3	3
NPs on staff	1	3	3
Total NP visits per day	3.8	17.6	18
Total NP visits per year (capacity)	896	4032	4032
Total ACO visits	640	3332	3100
Self-pay drop-in visits	210	611	730
Total visits	**850**	**3943**	**3830**
NP productivity	94.9%	97.8%	95.0%
Revenue			
Welby ACO contract revenue	$35,000	$450,000	$450,000
Grant revenue	$50,000	$50,000	$50,000
Private collections	$3000	$8530	$10,000
Donations	$20,000	$18,000	$20,000
Total revenue	**$108,000**	**$526,530**	**$530,000**
Revenue per patient visit	$127	$134	$138
Expenses			
Personnel expense NPs	$70,000	$210,000	$216,300
Benefits @ 30%	$21,000	$63,000	$64,890
Clinic Manager 0.5 FTE	$0	$30,000	$30,900
Clerical 0.8 FTE × 2	$0	$40,000	$41,200
Total personnel expense	$91,000	$343,000	$353,290
Medical supplies	$4300	$127,930	$95,760
Nonmedical supplies	$0	$5780	$2000
Depreciation	$0	$3897	$0
Capital expenses	$0	$38,971	$10,000
Overhead	$0	$10,000	$10,000
Total nonpersonnel expense	$4300	$186,578	$117,760
Total health center expense	**$95,300**	**$529,578**	**$471,050**
Cost per patient visit	$112	$134	$123
Net profit or loss (P&L)	$12,700	-$3048	$58,950
Profit or loss per patient visit	$14.94	-$0.77	$15.39

Table 6.3 *East Wing Medical-Surgical Unit, Operating Budget Projection for 2013*

Item	2011	2012	2013
	Actual	Actual	Budget
Days in time period	365	366	365
Statistics			
Staffed beds	20	20	25
Patient days	6000	5750	7756
Discharges	1200	1100	1686
Total gross revenue	$5,289,839	$5,435,100	$6,522,120
Staffing			
Direct care hours PPD (actual HPPD)	7.5	8.2	8.0
Total direct care (productive) hours	44,700	47,300	62,050
Paid nonproductive hours	10,040	11,660	10,549
Total paid hours	54,740	58,960	72,599
RN overtime hours	5000	4800	1452
Total RN paid hours including overtime	59,740	63,760	74,050
Total RN FTEs	40.2	42.9	49.8
Agency nurse hours	1000	1100	1000
Personnel expenses			
Average RN hourly wage	$32.00	$32.00	$33.00
Total hourly wages	$1,751,680	$1,886,720	$2,395,751
Total fixed staff (manager and clerical)	$150,000	$150,000	$154,500
Total benefits	$356,565	$381,885	$478,172
Total RN wages and benefits	$2,258,245	$2,418,605	$3,028,422
Overtime expenses	$240,000	$230,400	$71,873
Agency nurse expenses @ $70/hour	$70,000	$77,000	$70,000
Total personnel expenses	$2,568,245	$2,726,005	$3,170,295
Nonpersonnel expenses			
Medical supplies	$240,000	$230,000	$275,347
Nonmedical supplies	$1832	$2187	$2000
Other nonpersonnel expense	$479	$531	$500
Total nonpersonnel expenses	$242,311	$232,718	$277,847
Total expenses	$2,810,556	$2,958,723	$3,448,142

reimbursement (net revenue) that is received by Bigtown Hospital. Bigtown Hospital administrators use a combination of retrospective and prospective approaches to estimate revenue and reimbursement for 2013. Retrospective approaches include historical data and trend lines of revenue and reimbursement for prior years. Prospective approaches include a review of new Medicare, Medicaid, and commercial insurance regulations and policies for reimbursement, and expert opinion regarding local employment and the anticipated **payer mix,** or type of health insurance coverage, expected for patients over the coming year.

Operating Expense Budget Planning

The operating expense budget is the budget most likely to be reported to nurses and nurse managers. Ideally, nurses and nurse managers provide input for the development of the next year's operating expense budget. Performance targets are frequently used to budget expenses, in order to motivate cost control and efficiency.

Personnel Budget Planning

An important first step in planning the personnel budget is to estimate staffing needs over the coming fiscal year. Staffing for MNC is simple, as three NPs are required to deliver services, with support from a part-time nurse manager and two part-time clerical assistants (Table 6.2). If MNC had negotiated any additional contracts or expanded any of its services, a step-fixed budgeting method would be applied to add an additional NP for every additional increment of 1300 patient visits.

The staffing for the East Wing medical-surgical unit is more complex than staffing for MNC. The nurse workload or direct care hours are estimated based on the performance target of 8 hours of direct nursing care per patient day, requiring one RN scheduled for an 8-hour shift for every three patients (Table 6.3). The 8 direct care hours are multiplied by the projected 7756 patient days to determine the total number of direct care hours budgeted for 2013.

The next step is to determine the paid nonproductive hours that staff are likely to use over the next year. The East Wing nurse manager uses a performance target to budget the 2013 nonproductive hours, establishing the budget at 17% of nonproductive hours to total paid hours. The 17% target accounts for holidays, vacations, sick leave, and other paid nonproductive time (Penner & Spencer, 2012). The performance target for overtime hours is established using the national benchmark of 2% of total paid hours (Bateman, 2012).

The next step is to determine the number of FTEs required for staffing over the coming fiscal year. The budgeted **full-time equivalent (FTE)** represents an **adjusted FTE** that accounts for direct care, nonproductive time, and overtime hours, as well as coverage 7 days per week. The adjusted FTEs are reported as total RN FTEs, and are calculated for 8-hour shifts by dividing the total paid hours including overtime by 2080 hours in an annual FTE, and multiplying that result by 1.4 to include staffing for weekends. Note that increasing the bed capacity and patient days for East Wing has increased the staff FTEs by nearly 7.0 FTEs from 2012 to 2013.

Agency nurse hours are budgeted for 2013 using an incremental budgeting approach. The administration issued a policy that the performance target for medical-surgical unit agency nurse hours may be budgeted at no more than 1000 hours. Nurse managers are expected to better control the use of agency nurse hours over the coming year.

The next step in preparing an inpatient personnel budget is to convert the projected staff hours to dollar figures. For simplicity, it is assumed that the staff are entirely RNs. A **skill mix** including other staff such as licensed practical nurses (LPNs) and nurse assistants requires estimating expenses based on various wage levels. Wages are an overall average $32 per hour for East Wing RNs in 2011 and 2012. Note that this is also a simplification, as in actual health care settings wage estimates are often more detailed and complex based on factors such as seniority and education. Shift and weekend differentials are also omitted from this example. The $32 per hour wage is multiplied by 1.03 and rounded to the nearest dollar ($33), to estimate a 3% wage increase for Bigtown Hospital employees in 2013. A 3% increase is also applied to the salaries for East Wing's fixed staff.

Benefits are estimated at 25% of total wages and salaries (excluding overtime) for 75% of the fixed and RN staff who are projected to be eligible for employee benefits. Overtime wages are calculated as 50% higher than the average base pay, or $49.50 per hour for 2013. The agency nurse expenses are estimated based on the performance target for agency nurse hours, at the estimated fee of $70 per hour. All these staffing expenses are added together for the $3,170,295 total personnel expenses budgeted for East Wing for the 2013 fiscal year.

Nonpersonnel Budget Planning

Nonpersonnel budgets are typically planned according to the type of nonpersonnel expense. The nonpersonnel budget is usually lower than the personnel budget. However, approaches such as zero-based budgeting and performance targets are often applied to nonpersonnel budgets to improve cost control and reduce waste.

Medical supplies and supply chain management. The cost of medical supplies is second only to the cost of labor in many hospitals and health care settings, and medical supplies represent one of the fastest growing sources of health care costs (Know, 2010). **Supply chain management** involves supervising the policies and procedures for ordering and purchasing products used in patient care (Bateman, 2012). Supply chain management is a strategy that helps nurse managers to better control the cost of medical supplies.

Medical supplies budget planning often incorporates supply chain management approaches. For example, the NPs at MNC were ordering their preferred brands of medical supplies, which resulted in the medical supplies budget increasing far more than budgeted in 2012. The MNC nurse manager now requires a process for requesting medical supplies that standardizes the brands of supplies ordered. NPs now work as a team to select the supplies they will share in the practice. The MNC is also able to contract for medical supplies using Bigtown Hospital's **group purchasing organization (GPO)**. A GPO negotiates prices with vendors on behalf of member hospitals so that purchasing contracts are more favorable for medical supplies and capital equipment. This arrangement enables MNC to obtain medical supplies for 2013 at a lower cost than in 2012.

The MNC nurse manager establishes a performance target for 2013 medical supplies expenses. In 2012, medical supplies for the MNC averaged $32.44 per patient visit. The performance target for 2013 is $25 per patient visit for medical supplies. Better supply chain management and closer supervision of the medical supplies budget are anticipated to allow the MNC to reduce its medical supplies costs for the coming year.

The East Wing medical-surgical unit must budget $100,000 more than in 2012 for the 2013 medical supplies budget. The increase in patient days is expected to increase the amount of medical supplies East Wing will utilize in the coming year. Another reason for the budget increase is that the prices for some medical supplies will rise over the coming year. Medical supplies expenses are therefore expected to increase from $40 PPD in 2012 to $42.55 PPD in 2013.

Nonmedical supplies. Nonmedical supplies include items that are not used in direct patient care, such as forms and office supplies. Supply chain management approaches can be applied to requesting and purchasing nonmedical supplies, so that items are standardized and purchased at the best possible price.

The MNC manager uses zero-based budgeting to prepare the 2013 budget for nonmedical supplies. The NPs are surveyed regarding their needs for educational brochures and other nonmedical supplies, and the clerical staff provide input regarding the use of forms and office supplies. Items not determined to be necessary are dropped from the budget. Approval is required for any requests for nonmedical supplies that are not already budgeted. Purchasing is now managed through Bigtown Hospital's GPO. The budget for nonmedical supplies for MNC is reduced to $2000 for 2013.

East Wing medical-surgical unit's 2013 budget for nonmedical supplies is also $2000 for 2013. The nonmedical supplies budget for this nursing unit has remained stable over the last two years. Price increases for nonmedical supplies are not anticipated, and even though East Wing is expanding by five patient beds, the use of nonmedical supplies is not expected to increase.

Capital expenses. Capital expenses are for equipment and other expenditures such as remodeling that represent investments for more than one fiscal year. As discussed in Chapter 7, capital budgets are usually prepared separately from operating budgets. However, the capital expenses might be included as a line in the operating expense budget, as the financing for capital improvements is based on operating revenues. MNC spent nearly $40,000 in capital expenses in 2012 to equip examination rooms for the staff NPs. In 2013, MNC budgets $10,000 in capital expenses to equip an additional examination room for use by students and instructors as part of their clinical education.

The East Wing medical-surgical unit does not budget for capital expenses in 2013. The nursing unit is able to equip the additional beds that are staffed for 2013 without incurring any capital expenses. Any needed equipment will be transferred from another medical-surgical unit. Capital expenses are therefore not included in the East Wing operating expense budget for 2013.

Depreciation. Some operating expense budgets include a line for **depreciation** expenses, reporting the estimation and allocation of a capital asset cost over its useful life. The MNC manager estimates depreciation as 10% of the capital expense for 10 years. However, although depreciation is reported as an actual expense, it is not budgeted. The capital expenditure was made when the capital item was purchased. The MNC budget for 2013 therefore does not include an amount for depreciation. The MNC manager will report an estimated $4897 of depreciation as actual expense over 2013 (10% of the $38, 971 capital expenditure for 2012 plus 10% of the $10,000 capital expenditure for 2013).

Capital expenditures for the East Wing medical-surgical unit have been limited over the last few years. The amount of depreciation is estimated at $2000 per year, reported as an actual expense, but not budgeted.

Overhead. Some nonpersonnel budgets include **overhead** expenses, representing indirect expenses such as rent, housekeeping, and other support services. Bigtown Hospital charges the MNC $10,000 per year to cover overhead expenses. However, nursing units at Bigtown Hospital are not charged overhead, so this item does not appear on East Wing's 2013 budget. Whether there is a charge for overhead or not, the indirect costs of running a clinic, nursing unit, or other health care setting are real and important to maintaining the organization and its services. Overhead expenses are often allocated based on formulas (such as a percent of the operating expense budget) as a way of distributing the expense. Overhead expenses are usually fixed, so do not vary with volume.

Other nonpersonnel expense. Other categories of nonpersonnel expenses may appear in an operating expense budget. MNC does not budget for other nonpersonnel expenses. The nurse manager of East Wing medical-surgical unit budgets $500 per year to send a staff nurse to an educational conference. The amount allowed for other nonpersonnel expenses is limited by Bigtown Hospital policy, so the nurse manager cannot negotiate an increase in this budget item.

CLOSING A PROGRAM

In some situations, a product, service, or program that is found to be unprofitable or no longer fit with the department or organization objectives. In such a case, it may be necessary to discontinue the program. For example, changes in patient utilization requires Bigtown Hospital to reorganize its medical-surgical nursing units. The decision is to close a medical-surgical unit (North Wing) and to expand East Wing medical-surgical unit by five patient beds.

Typically, the major concern in closing a program is not the budget adjustment, but human resources management. If the employees working in the unit that is closed are retained, they require reassignment to other departments or work, and possibly retraining. If employees are to be released, they require termination benefits and possibly job counseling and other services. Budget planning must therefore include these requirements in decisions around making the closure.

The expansion of the East Wing medical-surgical unit will require approximately 7.0 additional FTEs of nursing staff. This staffing need will be met by transferring staff nurses from North Wing to East Wing. Several of the North Wing staff have decided to retire or to reduce their employment to part-time. The remaining staff can be transferred to other departments or nursing units in Bigtown Hospital.

Another issue in closing a program is the use of the space made available. The space in North Wing will be used as a skilled nursing facility (SNF) for patients who require sub-acute care and rehabilitation before they can be discharged to their home or long-term care facility. Several of the North Wing staff will be retrained and will remain on the unit to operate the SNF. The skill mix will include a higher proportion of LPNs and nurse assistants, as the acuity of these patients is lower than for medical-surgical patients.

CONCLUSION

This chapter reviews concepts and methods for planning the operating budget for inpatient nursing units and outpatient health centers. The importance of budget targets, teamwork, and accurate information is emphasized in making realistic budget projections and in controlling costs over the next fiscal year.

Discussion and Exercises

1. Think of a program or project, such as a small test of change to improve the quality of nursing care in your work setting or clinical assignment. Prepare a budget projected over the next two years for this program or project, including personnel and nonpersonnel expenses. Use the worksheet in Appendix 6A as a guide for budget preparation. Include revenue projections if the program or project generates revenue. Discuss your assumptions and rationale for the amounts estimated in the budget.
2. Review Tables 6.2 or 6.3. Assume that the nurses working in MNC or in East Wing have a 5% raise for the following budget year. Calculate the change in personnel expenses and the impact on total expenses, and for MNC the impact on profits. Discuss other changes that might affect the MNC or East Wing budgets.
3. Make an appointment with a nurse manager, administrator, or health officer of a health program or facility. Arrange an interview, asking about the most important budget concerns and budget planning issues in that setting. Discuss what you learned from people who manage and plan health care budgets.

REFERENCES

American Nurses Credentialing Center. (2012). *ANCC magnet recognition center.*® Retrieved May 6, 2012 from http://www.nursecredentialing.org/Magnet.aspx

Bateman, N. (2012). *The business of nurse management: A toolkit for success.* New York, NY: Springer Publishing Company.

Centers for Medicare & Medicaid Services. (2012). *Medicare and medicaid programs; reform of hospital and critical access hospital conditions of participation.* Final Rule. 42 CFR Parts 482 and 485 [CMS-3244-F] RIN 0938-AQ89 Department of Health and Human Services (HHS). Retrieved from http://www.ofr.gov/inspection.aspx?AspxAutoDetectCookieSupport=1

Institute of Medicine. (2011). *The future of nursing: Leading change, advancing health.* Committee on the Robert Wood Johnson Foundation Initiative on the Future of Nursing, at the Institute of Medicine. Washington, DC: The National Academies Press. Retrieved from http://www.nap.edu/catalog/12956.html

Know, W. P. C. (2010). Reducing healthcare costs through supply chain management. Arizona State University, W.P. Carey School of Business. Retrieved from http://knowledge.wpcarey.asu.edu/article.cfm?articleid=1871

Michigan Medicare/Medicaid Assistance Program. (2010). *Affordable Care Act update: Implementing Medicare cost savings.* Retrieved September 21, 2010 from http://www.mmapinc.org/pdfs/ACA-Update-Implementing-Medicare-Costs-Savings.pdf

Millett, S. M. (2011) . *Managing the future: A guide to forecasting and strategic planning in the 21st century.* Devon, UK: Triarchy Press.

Penner, S. J. & Spencer, M. D. (2012). Chapter 4: Acute care utilization, staffing and financial indicators. In K. T. Waxman (Ed.), *Financial & Business Management for the Doctor of Nursing Practice* (pp. 57–75). New York, NY: Springer Publishing Company.

CROSSWORD: *Chapter 6—Budget Planning*

Across

2 Impact from the input a person provides in a situation.

3 An organization that negotiates prices with vendors on behalf of member hospitals (abbreviation).

4 A method of budget adjustment by calculating an average monthly budget value and multiplying the value by 12 to estimate the budget for a year.

6 Using or relying on numerical data.

7 Using or relying on non-numerical data.

Down

1 Extent of responsibility for managing a situation.

5 A budgeting approach that requires a detailed analysis of every line item as it is added to the budget (abbreviation).

APPENDIX 6A: WORKSHEET FOR ANNUAL OPERATING
BUDGET PREPARATION, PROJECTED FOR TWO YEARS

	Year One	Year Two
Volume or UOS		
Personnel expenses		
Total personnel expense		
Nonpersonnel expenses		
Estimated capital expenses		
Estimated depreciation		
Estimated overhead		
Total nonpersonnel expense		
Total expense		
Revenues by revenue source		
Total gross revenue		
P&L		

Chapter 7: Special Purpose, Capital, and Other Budgets

A penny saved is a penny earned—Benjamin Franklin

Learning Objectives

1. Explain at least three steps in preparing a special purpose budget.
2. Differentiate between a product line budget and an evidence-informed case rate.
3. Develop a measurable objective linked to a health care program's goal.
4. Demonstrate the application of a SWOT or priority matrix in strategic planning.

Key Terms

assumption
capital budget
cash flow budget
cash flows from operating
    activities
cash inflows
cash outflows from operating
    activities
direct costs
ending cash balance
evidence-informed case rate
    (ECR)
financial threshold
goal

indirect costs
lagged value
master budget
mission statement
net increase or decrease in cash
nonservice revenue
objective
operating leverage
priority
priority matrix
product line budget
receivables
service line budget
service revenue

SMART objective
solvent
special purpose budget
starting cash balance
start-up costs
strategic plan
SWOT matrix
total cash inflows
total cash on hand
total cash outflows
uncollectibles
values
vision
working capital

Nurses are more likely to review and be held accountable for the operating budget. However, nurses should know that there are other types of budgets used in health care settings. Each type of budget serves a purpose in reporting, monitoring and control, and planning for revenue and expenses. In some cases, nurses may have an opportunity to review these budgets. In other situations, nurses may become involved in preparing these budgets.

Nurses should therefore understand the purpose and preparation of the budgets presented in the following sections. These budgets include the special purpose budget, the product line budget, and the evidence-informed case rate (ECR). The capital and cash flow budgets are additional important budgets discussed in this chapter.

SPECIAL PURPOSE BUDGET

The **special purpose budget** is prepared for any purpose that has not been otherwise budgeted. Special purpose budgets are often developed for new projects or products developed during the fiscal year. Budgets prepared for business plans proposing new ventures or substantial changes in existing programs are examples of special purpose budgets. A health program grant proposal budget might also be considered a special purpose budget.

Preparing the Special Purpose Budget

It can seem overwhelming, especially for beginners, to prepare a special purpose budget for a new program or service. However, many projects that can improve health care are relatively simple to plan and budget. The example used in this chapter is a budget developed for telephone follow-up for recently discharged patients with congestive heart failure (CHF), shown in Table 7.1. Many nurses have opportunities to be involved in budgeting for these small but important projects. More complex projects such as building construction or establishing a new business are beyond the scope of this discussion, as they require extensive planning and the application of more advanced financial models.

Identify required resources. The first step in creating a special purpose budget is to carefully think through all the resources required to implement the project from one to three fiscal years. Staff, supplies, equipment, and overhead are categories of resources to consider. For example, a telephone follow-up program requires resources such as nurse staffing, supplies such as patient education materials, equipment such as telephones and computers, and overhead such as office space and administrative support. These resources should be identified at the beginning of the budget section of a business plan or health program grant proposal.

Review the project's goals, objectives, and activities to make sure that all required resources are included. Examples of special purpose budgets are presented in Chapters 10 and 11, related to writing business plans and health program grant proposals. These examples demonstrate the preparation of special purpose budgets in the context of the goals, objectives, and activities proposed for projects that benefit the health care setting and the community (Figure 7.1).

Identify available resources. The next item to identify and discuss in the budget section of a business plan or health program grant proposal is the required resources that are already available. These resources include personnel (staff) and nonpersonnel items (supplies and equipment) that are available for the project. Financial officers appreciate knowing that existing resources are fully utilized. Grant funders appreciate knowing that **in-kind contributions** from the sponsoring agency are made available for the proposed project, and that other resources might be provided from other community agencies. A review of available

Table 7.1 *Bigtown Hospital, Special Purpose Budget for CHF Nurse Follow-Up Project, 2013–2014*

Items	2013 (Start-up)		2014	
	Annual cost ($)	Monthly cost ($)	Annual cost ($)	Monthly cost ($)
Personnel expenses				
Salary @ 1.0 FTE	80,000	6667	80,000	6667
Benefits @ 30% salary	24,000	2000	24,000	2000
Total personnel expenses	104,000	8667	104,000	8667
Nonpersonnel expenses				
Office supplies	500	42	500	42
Patient education materials	1000	83	1000	83
Equipment maintenance	3000	250	3000	250
Telemonitoring equipment	100,000	8333	0	0
Total nonpersonnel expenses	104,500	8708	4500	375
Expenses – overhead	208,500	17,375	108,500	9042
Overhead @ 5% of budget	10,425	869	5425	452
Total expenses	**218,925**	**18,244**	**113,925**	**9494**

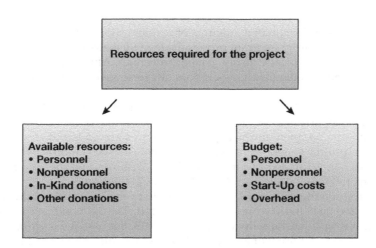

Figure 7.1 *Required, Available, and Budgeted Resources for Special Projects*

resources lets the financial officer or funder know that these items do not need to be budgeted or funded. For example, the office space, office furniture, telephone, and computer for the telephone follow-up project are already available at Bigtown Hospital. These items therefore do not require budgeting.

Budget for unavailable resources. After identifying required resources and determining which of these resources are already available, the next step is to create a budget for the remaining resources required for the project. In health care settings, labor is typically the highest cost budget item, reported in the personnel expenses section of the project budget. Staff salaries or wages are estimated for the personnel budget, often based on the **full-time equivalents (FTEs)** required. Employee benefits, as applicable, should also be estimated and included in the personnel budget, often amounting to about 30% of salaries and wages. The budget in Table 7.1 assigns 1.0 FTE to the telephone follow-up project.

Nonpersonnel expenses include supplies and equipment that must be budgeted. Supplies are items required for day-to-day operations and direct patient care. Examples in Table 7.1 include office supplies, patient education materials, and the supplies and services required to maintain the telemonitoring equipment. The telephone follow-up project requires few supplies, but other projects such as cancer screening programs may need to budget for many kinds of supplies.

Equipment and other fixed costs are frequently budgeted in the capital budget, discussed in more detail later in this chapter. Expenses for equipment and other fixed costs in a special purpose budget are often referred to as **start-up costs**, or one-time expenses that enable the project to be implemented. Start-up costs for the telephone follow-up project include telemonitoring equipment to enable the nurses to assess patient vital signs. The equipment is budgeted for 2013, the start-up year, at $100,000 (Table 7.1).

Staffing, supplies, and equipment represent **direct costs** that are required for direct patient care. Overhead represents **indirect costs** that support the project. Office space, clerical support, and phone and computer maintenance are examples of indirect costs that might apply to the telephone follow-up project. Overhead expenses might be borne by the facility as a type of in-kind donation. In other settings, it might be required to budget a percent of the project budget to account for overhead expenses. Table 7.1 shows that 5% of the project budget is added to the budget to cover overhead.

Identify revenue sources and estimate profit or loss. If the project is expected to generate revenues, the sources and estimated amounts of revenue should be included in the special purpose budget. Health program grant proposals do not usually include revenue estimates, as grant-funded projects typically do not generate revenues. Although the telephone follow-up project is expected to generate savings, it does not generate revenues, so revenues are not included in Table 7.1.

The special project budget is usually presented in a table that includes sections for personnel expenses, nonpersonnel expenses, start-up costs, and overhead. The budget categories are each sub-totaled, then all the expense categories are added to report the project's total costs. If the project generates revenues, the total costs are subtracted from the total revenues to report an estimated profit or loss. Table 7.1 shows that the 2013 total expenses for the telephone follow-up project are $218,925, or $18,244 per month.

A special project budget reporting a loss in the first year of operation may show a profit for the second year, once the start-up costs are covered. The 2014 budget for the telephone follow-up project drops substantially compared to 2013, because the start-up costs of purchasing telemonitoring equipment are not included in the 2014 budget. Table 7.1 shows the 2014 project expenses decreases to $113,925 annually and $9494 per month.

Explain and justify budget estimates. A final step in special purpose budget preparation is to explain and justify the budget estimates to the financial officer or grant funder. The explanation and justification might be included in notes attached to the budget or explained in the budget section of the business plan or health program grant proposal.

It is essential to critically review the budget items and cost and revenue estimates. The budget will likely require some revision and adjustment before submitting the business plan or health program grant proposal. Questions to ask in critically reviewing the special purpose budget include:

- Are any items missing from the budget?
- Are there any items that could be removed from the budget?
- Are there any items that could be reduced in cost?
- Is this budget feasible to fund?
- Are the revenue estimates realistic?
- Is any change expected in budget items, such as salary or price increases?

The budget discussion should include a brief rationale for budget estimates. High-cost staffing or equipment should be clearly justified. For example, the draft budget for the telephone follow-up project staffed the project with several cardiovascular clinical nurse specialists. A careful review of the budget indicated that the staffing costs raised concerns. Consultation with the health care team and review of the evidence indicated that staffing the project with one experienced registered nurse (RN) would be sufficient, with oversight and clinical updates provided by in-house cardiovascular clinical nurse specialists. The advantages and savings from budgeting telemonitoring equipment for high-risk CHF patients are discussed as part of the budget justification for start-up expenses.

PRODUCT LINE BUDGET

The **product line budget,** also referred to as the **service line budget,** focuses on a clinical specialty or on selected groups of patients with the same or very similar diagnoses. Product line budgets are useful when the care of a selected patient group can be standardized, so that benchmarks can be applied to the costs of care and length of stay. It is also helpful to prepare a product line budget when a nursing unit or hospital provides a substantial proportion of services to a selected patient group, with implications for potential profit or loss from these services. Table 7.2 presents a product line budget for total hip replacement without complications for Bigtown Hospital.

Preparing the Product Line Budget

The product line budget is organized to report expenses and revenues for one or more categories of specialty care, procedures, or patient cases. Information from all departments involved in generating expenses and revenues related to the selected case category is needed in preparing a product line budget. For example, the information in the product line budget shown in Table 7.2 requires input from surgeons, Nursing Services, and the outpatient (OT) and physical therapy (PT) departments.

Case definition and patient volume. The product line budget in Table 7.2 identifies that the focus is on the total hip replacement (arthroplasty) without complications. There are 500 cases of this procedure at Bigtown Hospital for 2012, representing the volume.

Expenses based on case treatment protocols. The hip replacement product line budget in Table 7.2 is organized according to the clinical pathway developed at Bigtown Hospital. Therefore, the first line budgets the cost of preoperative services, including patient admission, assessment, and medication. The services are budgeted based on length of stay or the amount of time for service utilization. For example, it is estimated that patients require about 2.5 hours for admission and preoperative care, so the utilization is reported as 0.1, or

Table 7.2 *Bigtown Hospital, Product Line Budget, Total Hip Replacement Without Complications (DRG 470), 2012*

Item	Utilization (days)	Per case ($)	Annual volume 500 cases
Pre-op	0.1	1500	750,000
OR and PACU	0.2	11,400	5,700,000
Nursing unit	3.7	20,000	10,000,000
Occupational therapy	0.08	1500	750,000
Physical therapy	0.17	2500	1,250,000
Discharge planning	0.04	100	50,000
Total days or expenses	**4.0**	**37,000**	**18,500,000**
Medicare reimbursement	–	**35,000**	**17,500,000**
P&L	–	2000	1,000,000

Notes: Assumes LOS 4 days, no serious clinical pathway variance or complications.
OT, PT, and discharge planning time billed but not added to LOS.

about one-tenth of a day (2.5 hours divided by 24 hours). The estimated cost of preoperative care is $1500 per case, or $750,000 for the 500 cases completed at Bigtown Hospital in 2012.

The next step of the treatment protocol is the surgical procedure, requiring about 5 hours of the first day of admission. All of the procedure's costs, including the surgeon fees and postanesthesia care (PACU), are included per case for 2012, as shown in Table 7.2. Medical-surgical nursing unit services are estimated as 3.7 days with a cost of $20,000 per case, or $10,000,000 for 2012. The preoperative, procedure, and nursing unit utilization total the budgeted LOS of 4.0 days.

Expenses for occupational therapy, physical therapy, and discharge planning are also budgeted to indicate the amount of time that services are utilized. However, the time budgeted for these services only apply to costs of care, not to the patient's LOS. Occupational therapy includes assessment and activities of daily living (ADL) training, budgeted at ½ hour per day. Physical therapy includes assessment, bed exercises, and gait training for 1 hour per day. Discharge planning typically occurs on the day of discharge for ½ hour. Table 7.2 shows that the costs for these services are added to the other expenses for a total of $37,000 per case, or $18,500,000 for 2012.

Estimate reimbursement and profit or loss. Most of the hip replacement reimbursement comes from Medicare, as most patients undergoing hip replacement at Bigtown Hospital are elders. Table 7.2 therefore reports Medicare reimbursement estimated at $35,000 per case, or $17,500,000 per year. Bigtown Hospital reports an estimated $2000 loss for each case, amounting to an estimated loss of about $1,000,000 in 2012 for total hip replacements.

ECR

An **ECR** is a budget based on an episode of care, including inpatient and outpatient services (de Brantes & Camillus, 2007). The ECR is useful for accountable care organizations (ACOs) to develop bundled payments for providers across the care episode (The Brookings Institution, 2012). The ECR resembles a product line budget as it focuses on categories of

Table 7.3 *Welby ACO, ECR, Total Hip Replacement Without Complications (DRG 470), 2013*

Item	Utilization (days)	Per case	Annual volume 500 cases
Physician fees		$1400	$700,000
Pre-op, OR, and PACU	0.3	$10,000	–
Nursing	1.7	$10,000	–
OT	0.08	$1500	–
PT	0.17	$2500	–
Discharge planning	0.08	$500	–
Rehab unit	2.0	$6600	–
Hospital costs		$31,100	$15,550,000
Total	**4.0**	**$32,500**	**$16,250,000**
Medicare reimbursement	–	**$35,000**	**$17,500,000**
Total savings	–	$2500	$1,250,000
Shared savings	Percent	Per case	500 cases
Physician shared savings	24%	$600	$300,000
Hospital shared savings	26%	$650	$325,000
Medicare shared savings	50%	$1250	$625,000

Notes: Assumes LOS 4 days, no serious clinical pathway variance or complications.
OT, PT, and discharge planning time billed but not added to LOS.

specialty care, procedures, or patient cases. The budget sections estimate costs generated by providers, including the hospital, surgeons, and any outpatient services such as home health. Shared savings or risk may then be allocated to providers according to their ACO contracts. Table 7.3 presents a budget that transforms the Bigtown Hospital 2012 product line budget for total hip replacements into an ECR for 2013 that represents Bigtown Hospital's participation in Welby ACO.

Preparing the ECR

The ECR in Table 7.3 is organized based on services from providers over an episode of patient care, rather than the progression of a clinical pathway. Some goals involved in the preparation of the ECR include reducing costs for total hip replacements while maintaining or improving quality, and developing a plan for sharing provider savings or risk. The first budget line reports the $1400 surgeon (physician) fee for the procedure. Table 7.2 included the surgeon fee as part of the OR and PACU costs, but for shared savings and risk it is important that all provider charges and fees are clearly indicated.

The following section of Table 7.3 reports the expenses for Bigtown Hospital. The preoperative, OR, and PACU expenses are $2900 less than in Table 7.2. One reason is that the $1400 surgeon fee is removed from the OR and PACU expense. In addition, the surgeons decided to better negotiate and control the costs of medical devices used in total hip replacements, thus reducing OR costs by $1500.

To reduce nursing costs, the plan for 2013 is for patients to spend two days in the medical-surgical nursing unit. Patients are then transferred to a less costly rehabilitation unit for the remaining two days of care (Table 7.3). The same amount of OT and PT services are provided as in 2012. In order to improve the patients' transition to the home and reduce preventable readmissions, the intensity of discharge planning is increased. The discharge planner will visit patients daily for assessment, education, and to ensure that equipment and other follow-up care is arranged. This increases the expense for discharge planning compared with the product line budget in Table 7.2.

It is expected that Bigtown Hospital will save $2500 per hip replacement case by reducing costs for medical devices and utilizing the rehabilitation unit. Total costs per case are estimated at $32,500, with the same Medicare rate of $35,000. The annual savings are estimated at $1,250,000 for 2013, as shown in Table 7.3. This represents a considerable financial improvement compared with the $1,000,000 loss reported for this product line in 2012.

Important concepts for providers contracting with ACOs are requirements for **shared savings** and **shared risk** (Miller, 2012). Table 7.3 shows an example of provider shared savings. The ACO contracts with the payer (in this case Medicare) to share 50% of the total savings, $1250 of the total $2500. The surgeons and hospital negotiate an agreement to share the remaining $1250 in savings. As a result, the surgeon receives an additional $600 for contributing to the total savings, and the hospital receives the remaining $650. Shared savings strategies are intended to reward providers as well as payers when the providers work together to reduce health care costs (Miller, 2012). Bigtown Hospital plans to maintain these savings throughout 2013, so the total savings for 500 cases per year are reported for the providers and payer.

Table 7.4 presents an example of shared risk. In this scenario, the surgeon and hospital contribute to a $3500 excess in costs, with a $1000 loss in Medicare reimbursement. Surgeons negotiate up to 10% of their fee in this shared risk arrangement. In this case, the surgeon loses 10% of the fee, or $160, and the hospital assumes the remaining risk or loss of $840. In the past, Bigtown Hospital has assumed all of the risk for excessive care costs, so this arrangement provides greater incentives for surgeons to be more attentive to costs and quality of care. Future ECRs and shared savings arrangements will include OP providers such as home health nursing and rehabilitation services for patients with total hip replacements.

The arrangements for shared savings and shared risk presented in Tables 7.3 and 7.4 are just examples of possible strategies for providers to work together to reduce health costs in ACO settings. The Patient Protection and Affordable Care Act of 2010 encourage ACOs to experiment with payment approaches that reduce costs, improve quality, and

Table 7.4 *Welby ACO, Case Example of Shared Risk for Total Hip Replacement Without Complications (DRG 470), 2013*

Item	ECR	Actual
Physician fees	$1400	$1600
Hospital costs	$31,100	$34,400
Total expenses	**$32,500**	**$36,000**
Medicare reimbursement	**$35,000**	**$35,000**
Total savings	$2500	($1000)
Physician share savings or risk	$600	($160)
Hospital share savings or risk	$650	($840)

adequately reimburse health care providers (Patient Protection and Affordable Care Act, 2010; Reid, 2012).

CAPITAL BUDGET

The **capital budget** is a budget for long-term investments that are often high cost. Capital budgets may focus on items as large and complex as the construction of a new building, with millions of dollars of expense and decades of useful life. Smaller capital budgets are prepared for maintenance and repair costs, or the purchase of equipment. For example, the Millway University Nurse-Managed Health Center (MNC) must purchase examination tables to equip additional examination rooms.

Nurses may become involved in the capital budget process in several ways. A nurse manager might ask nurses for their input on equipment or other capital purchases. Nurses might be involved in writing business plans or grant proposals (Chapters 10 and 11) that require capital equipment budgeting as start-up costs. Nurses might also work in a nurse-managed clinic or other OP setting where they have opportunities to participate in decisions around capital equipment purchases. Nurses need to learn about capital budgeting and be prepared to work with teams to obtain required capital items.

An item's cost does not determine its inclusion in the capital budget, but rather its useful life, which is assumed to be more than a year. Capital budgets are often reported separately from operating budgets. Reporting is separate because only a portion of a capital asset expense (useful life) is used by one year, and only a portion of the revenues generated by a capital asset is received by one year.

Smaller capital expenses in departments or nursing units may be summarized and entered as a line in operating and cash flow budgets or financial reports. For example, the total capital expenses in Table 7.5 are reported in the MNC profit and loss statements found in Chapters 3 and 4, and in the MNC budgets reported in Chapters 5 and 6. Nurses may be able to participate in planning for smaller capital budgets in their work units, such as the purchase of new equipment.

In practice, even if an item is used for more than a year, many health care settings do not include low-cost equipment in the capital budget. Frequently, policies are established with a dollar value specified as the limit, or **financial threshold,** for equipment that is required to be budgeted as a capital expense. For example, Bigtown Hospital's policy is that departments may include patient care equipment in the operating budget if the expenses do not exceed a total of $2500 per year. As a result, when East Wing replaced several wheelchairs at a cost of $500 each, the $2000 expenditure was included in the annual operating budget for 2012 as a nonpersonnel expense.

Table 7.5 *Millway University Nurse-Managed Health Center Capital Budget, 2013*

Item or project	Unit cost ($)	No. of units	Total expense ($)	Monthly ($)
Examination tables	1500	3	4500	375
Examination room equipment	650	3	1950	163
Adult scales	1000	1	1000	83
Pediatric scales	1000	3	3000	250
Examination room furniture	750	3	2250	188
Computers and peripherals	4550	6	27,300	2275
Total capital expenses	–	–	**40,000**	**3333**

Capital Budget Decision Making

It is important to be aware that there are many factors involved in decisions around the budgeting of high-cost, long-term expenditures. Individuals and groups in organizations have varying amounts of power and influence that they may use to serve their own interests and goals. Politics is therefore an important factor in capital budgeting, particularly when proposed expenditures are high and there are few resources. Planning strategies can be applied so that individuals and groups are compelled to work together to achieve long-term organizational goals and objectives.

One way to reduce the impact of political forces in capital budgeting is to establish policies for setting priorities and making decisions. Many organizations establish a capital budget calendar for submission of capital budget requests, with time allocated for budget planning, administrative review, and approval or rejection of the budget. The organization might also establish a capital budget committee of executives, department managers, and purchasing directors. The capital budget committee can evaluate capital budget requests, including requests for new technologies (Bateman, 2012).

Policies might require department managers to develop long-term plans for costly equipment replacement so that capital budget requests are anticipated several years in advance. Advance planning allows ample time to coordinate the needs of various departments with the capital funding that is available from year to year.

Risk and operating leverage. Capital budgets for high-cost items or projects require careful planning and review because these expenditures represent fixed, or "sunk," costs. These costs must be covered by the organization whether the project itself succeeds or fails. High fixed costs compared to variable costs increases an organization's use of **operating leverage**, or financial risk related to volume and reimbursement.

For example, a hospital may spend several million dollars renovating and re-equipping a telemetry nursing unit. If the telemetry unit census is lower than projected, reimbursement will likely be lower than projected, as well. Lower volume and reimbursement makes it more difficult for the hospital to cover the costs of the renovation and increases the hospital's financial risk. Therefore, hospital executives must critically review the business case for renovating the telemetry unit before making a decision to approve this high expenditure.

Preparing the Capital Budget

Capital budgets present expense estimates for high-cost and long-term items such as equipment, major maintenance and repair, renovation, and construction. Capital budgets usually require written justification and are reviewed and approved by the organization's top administrators. Chapters 8 and 9 provide financial analysis techniques that are useful in determining the profitability or benefits of capital expenditures. Chapter 10 discusses making a business case and writing a business plan to request, support, and justify capital and other new project expenditures. An essential step in preparing a budget for large capital expenditures is strategic planning.

Strategic Planning

Capital budgets develop to obtain or replace relatively small items of equipment may not require extensive planning. However, larger capital expenditures are frequently linked to the institution's **strategic planning** process for achieving organizational goals in the future. It is also advisable to use strategic planning approaches to evaluate smaller capital budgets, particularly within smaller organizations, such as nurse-managed clinics that have limited financial resources. Strategic planning is a strategy for building consensus and teamwork in the budgeting process.

Strategic planning is the basis for developing many of the budgets in a health care facility, including the operating, capital, and cash flow budgets. The **strategic plan** is a report that presents a plan for organizational financial management and performance for several fiscal years into the future. The organization's executive leadership generally prepare the strategic plan with input from department directors, clinicians, managers, and financial officers. In some cases, nurses may have opportunities to provide input for strategic planning. This section discusses the strategic plan, the strategic planning process, and some commonly used tools to evaluate capital budget decisions.

Environmental assessment. The strategic plan often begins by reporting an intensive internal and external environmental assessment of actual and potential situations or changes that may be favorable or unfavorable to the institution. The anticipation and analysis of strengths, weaknesses, opportunities, and threats over future fiscal years enables the organizational leadership to take a proactive approach to manage and profit from these situations.

Mission, vision, and values. Based on the environmental assessment and analysis, the strategic plan then presents the **mission statement** and **vision** for what the organization is desired or expected to look like in the projected fiscal years, based on the organization's **values**. An organization's mission statement communicates its overall purpose. The mission of a teaching hospital is focused on medical and health professional education in addition to providing health care services. An organization's vision describes where the organization wants to be or what the organization plans to accomplish.

A hospital's vision may be to expand and enhance its reputation for cardiovascular care over the next 3 years. An organization's values incorporate the ethics and beliefs reflected in the organization and the individuals who work in the organization. A nurse-managed clinic providing outreach to uninsured homeless populations reflects values supporting health care services regardless of the patient's ability to pay.

Assumptions and priorities. Assumptions and priorities are developed based on the environmental analyses, mission statement, vision, and values. **Assumptions** represent expectations or beliefs about the internal or external environment that influence administrative and financial decision making (Satinsky, 2007). For example, hospital administrators likely assume that concerns about preventable readmissions will increasingly lead to financial penalties.

Priorities are organizational activities or issues that are believed to be the most important for profitability or survival. A nurse-managed clinic director might decide that it is a priority to hire another nurse practitioner (NP) rather than develop a program to provide dental care. Setting priorities is one way to manage the trade-offs that result from the opportunity costs of alternative decisions, as discussed in Chapter 1.

Goals. Broad statements regarding what the organization intends to accomplish in the future are known as **goals**. The goals developed in a strategic planning process may be short-term or achievable in the next fiscal year. For example, East Wing's capital budget for several wheelchairs facilitates patient transportation and achieves a short-term goal. Many organizational strategic planning goals are long-term, often established for 3 to 5 years into the future. An example of a long-term goal is for a hospital to establish a cardiovascular center of excellence within the next 3 years.

Objectives and performance targets. The tasks that must be accomplished over the long- or short-term to achieve a goal are known as **objectives**. Objectives should be **SMART**: specific, measurable, achievable, relevant, and time-bound (Centers for Disease Control and Prevention [CDC], 2011). Specific objectives clearly describe the objective's target and activity. Measurable objectives can be evaluated using indicators to show the extent to which the objective was achieved. Objectives are achievable when it is feasible to meet the objective. Objectives are relevant when they are designed to have an impact in achieving the overall goal. Time-bound objectives include a specific time frame for achievement. A guide for writing SMART objectives is available at the Centers for Disease Control and Prevention (CDC) evaluation guide Writing SMART Objectives website (www.cdc.gov).

For example, a hospital with the goal of establishing a center of excellence for cardiovascular care might develop short-term objectives such as hiring three cardiovascular Clinical Nurse Specialists (CNSs) over the next fiscal year. Long-term objectives might include increasing the hospital's market share of open-heart surgeries from 30% to 60% over the next 5 years. These objectives are specific, measurable, and have a time frame for achievement. The planning team agrees that both of these objectives are also achievable and realistic.

Performance targets are the measurable indicators used to evaluate the achievement of objectives. Performance targets are contained within measurable objectives. Hiring the three cardiovascular CNSs and increasing open-heart surgery market share to 60% are examples of performance targets.

Proposals for new programs and for existing program expansion or reduction are presented in the strategic plan, based on the environmental assessment and other elements discussed in this section. Plans for major investments and projections of operating revenues and expenses are included. These plans, projections, and associated budgets are usually summarized to indicate overall estimates of volume, revenue, expenses, and profitability, and are reported in more detail when implemented and reviewed over a fiscal year. This section of the strategic plan is based on the assumptions, priorities, goals, objectives, and performance targets that were developed out of the environmental analysis, mission statement, and vision. The purpose of the proposals, plans, projections, and their associated budgets is to enable the organization to achieve its mission and vision within the environment anticipated over the next fiscal years.

The development of the organization's mission, vision and values, making assumptions and setting priorities, and the establishment of goals and objectives for strategic planning are often roles reserved for the top executive leaders. However, strategic planning may be more effective if the leadership ensures that all departments are included in the process, and if health professionals across the organization have some input in decision making (Porter-O'Grady, 2009). Smaller organizations such as nurse-managed health centers can bring together staff from all levels to develop strategic planning initiatives. Encouraging input and shared decision making help staff become engaged in organizational initiatives and motivated to achieve organizational goals.

Strategic Planning Tools

A number of tools and approaches are available to assist nurses with strategic planning. Many of these tools are helpful to use when developing and reviewing capital budgets. Two commonly used tools are discussed in the following sections. Additional resources for strategic planning are presented in Text Box 7.1.

SWOT matrix. Figure 7.2 presents the **SWOT matrix**. The SWOT matrix is a tool that helps in identifying and analyzing the strengths, weaknesses, opportunities, and threats related to a decision, project, or capital expenditure. Strengths represent internal factors that are positive or beneficial. Opportunities are external positive or beneficial factors. Weaknesses are internal negative or harmful factors, while threats are external negative or

Text Box 7.1 *Resources for Strategic Planning*

Encyclopedia for Business, 2nd ed. Strategic Planning Tools. http://www.referenceforbusiness.com/management/Sc-Str/Strategic-Planning-Tools.html

US Department of Health and Human Services. Strategic Plan and Priorities 2010–2015. http://www.hhs.gov/secretary/about/priorities/priorities.html

World Bank. Strategic Planning: A Ten-Step Guide. http://siteresources.worldbank.org/INTAFRREGTOPTEIA/Resources/mosaica_10_steps.pdf

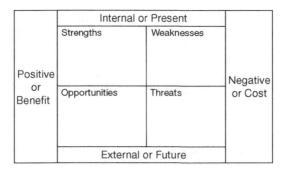

Figure 7.2 *Project or Capital Purchase SWOT Matrix*

Source: Adapted from http://rapidbi.com/swotanalysis

harmful factors (RapidBI, 2012). All of these factors are analyzed related to the issue of concern, in this example, the capital expenditure.

Even when capital expenditures are relatively small, a SWOT matrix can be helpful to determine needs and set priorities. When capital expenditures are large, such as for renovating a telemetry unit, the need to establish priorities is greater, as the organization must weigh the costs of the telemetry unit renovation compared to other competing requests for capital funding. For example, one health care team may advocate for the renovated telemetry unit, and another team may urge the expansion of operating rooms and surgical services. In addition, the higher the capital expenditure, the greater the financial risk. A tool such as a SWOT matrix can help both teams decide which project should have priority for funding, and help in weighing the risks of funding the project compared to benefits.

The capital budget in Table 7.5 may be evaluated using a simple SWOT analysis. Strengths include the fact that the MNC successfully began operation in 2011, and opportunities include negotiated contracts with physicians and the hospital that are part of Welby ACO that will enable MNC's ongoing operation and growth. One weakness is that MNC must obtain this equipment soon to be able to continue operations, so there is not enough time to seek donations or to conduct fund-raising. A threat is that if MNC's services are disrupted by lack of adequate equipment, the health center risks losing the ACO contracts and possibly going out of business. This review convinces the MNC leadership that the $40,000 for new medical equipment is justified for the 2012 capital budget.

Priority matrix. Another approach in justifying a capital budget is using a **priority matrix** that helps identify a project's level of priority or capital expenditure. The priority matrix in Figure 7.3 is a simple grid incorporating the need or importance, in this case for a capital expenditure, with the feasibility of making the expenditure. The priority matrix may be applied to MNC's proposed 2012 capital budget of $40,000 to purchase new medical equipment. MNC's continued operations depend on replacing its medical equipment, and there are funds in the 2012 budget so this expenditure is feasible. The plan to make the capital expenditure is therefore identified as a high priority. By contrast, some MNC staff suggested converting one examination room to a dental clinic. However, there is currently no reimbursement or other funding to support establishing and staffing a dental clinic. The plan for a dental clinic at MNC is therefore currently identified as low priority and is deferred for 2012.

The MNC capital budget for 2012 in Table 7.5 reports the items required to equip the clinic, along with expenditure estimates presented annually and monthly. For some items, such as the examination tables, four items are requested to equip each of the four examination rooms. The adult scales will be shared in a common area, so only one item is requested. The total capital expenditure is estimated as $40,000, or $3333 per month.

Priorities	Feasibility	
Need or Importance	**High**	**Low**
High	Highest Priority	High need, low feasibility
Low	Low need, high feasibility	Lowest Priority

Figure 7.3 *Project or Capital Purchase Prioritization Matrix*

Purchasing Capital Items

Once the capital budget is approved, nurses should work with their administrators or materials management staff in developing purchasing plans. The administrator or materials management staff is responsible for obtaining pricing information, negotiating the price and maintenance plans with vendors, overseeing the installation, and providing any other needed coordination or management. Group purchasing organizations (GPOs), discussed in Chapter 6, are often used to obtain capital equipment at the best possible price (Bateman, 2012).

CASH FLOW BUDGET

The **cash flow budget** or cash budget estimates the flow of money in and out of the business. Budgeting cash helps in anticipating whether there may be a substantial cash shortfall (negative cash balance) or surplus (positive cash balance). One important purpose of the cash flow budget is to ensure that the organization or business is **solvent**, able to pay its bills and meet its liabilities. Another reason for the cash flow budget is to estimate the extent of surplus funding available for investing, purchasing equipment, or expanding operations.

Cash flow budgets are usually not reported at department or unit levels within a hospital facility. It is therefore likely that most nurses will never review their institution's cash flow budget. However, nurses should understand the importance of adequate cash flow to the overall fiscal health of the business. Acute care nursing units contribute to the cash inflows (revenues) and outflows (expenses) incorporated in the cash flow budget. Nurses working in smaller settings such as medical offices or nurse-managed clinics may be far more aware of cash flow and cash flow difficulties. Smaller settings must carefully manage their **working capital** (cash and other liquid assets, such as savings accounts) or they may be forced out of business if unable to meet their financial obligations. The Millway Nurse Managed Health Center (MNC) quarterly report presented in Table 7.6 provides an example of a cash flow budget.

When cash shortfalls occur, one strategy is to borrow money to cover the shortfalls, but this approach has limits. Lending institutions may refuse services to businesses that try to rely on loans to meet their day-to-day expenditures. At the same time, labor laws require that employers pay all salaries and wages on schedule. Suppliers and other creditors also expect bills to be paid when they come due. It is quite possible for a profitable venture to go bankrupt because it cannot borrow the money to pay salaries and bills over a period of cash shortfalls. Therefore, estimating and budgeting cash flow is important to ensure salaries and bills will be paid on schedule, and to protect the business from bankruptcy.

Cash surpluses must be planned for and managed as well. It is poor financial management to hold onto surplus cash and allow it to sit idle, rather than drawing investment interest or contributing to operations. A cash flow budget enables decisions to be made

Table 7.6 *Millway Nurse-Managed Health Center Cash Flow Budget, 1st Quarter 2012*

Item	January		February		March	
	Budget	Actual	Budget	Actual	Budget	Actual
Beginning Cash Balance	$0	$0	$1000	$1000	$1000	
Cash inflows from operating activities						
Grant funding	$8333	$8333	$8333	$8333	$8333	
Disease mgt. service ACO contract	$29,167	$29,167	$29,167	$29,167	$29,167	
Well care service ACO contract	$20,833	$20,833	$20,833	$20,833	$20,833	
Private pay collections	$83	$20	$83	$60	$83	
Allowance for write-offs	($28)	$0	($28)	$0	($28)	
Total service revenue	$58,389	$58,353	$58,389	$58,393	$58,389	
Donations	$1667	$1500	$1667	$1000	$1667	
Investment income	$0	$0	$0	$0	$7.85	
Total nonservice revenue	$1667	$1500	$1667	$1000	$1675	
Total cash Inflows	$60,056	$59,853	$60,056	$59,393	$60,063	
Total cash on hand	$60,056	$59,853	$61,056	$60,393	$61,063	
Cash outflows from operating activities						
Personnel expense NPs	$29,250	$29,250	$29,250	$29,250	$29,250	
Clinic Manager 0.5 FTE	$4167	$4167	$4167	$4167	$4167	
Clerical 0.8 FTE x 3	$5000	$5000	$5000	$5000	$5000	
Total personnel expenses	$38,417	$38,417	$38,417	$38,417	$38,417	
Nonpersonnel expenses (supplies)	$7500	$6000	$7500	$8000	$7500	
Overhead	$5000	$5000	$5000	$5000	$5000	
Total nonpersonnel expenses	$12,500	$11,000	$12,500	$13,000	$12,500	
Capital expenses	$5000	$5000	$5000	$5000	$5000	
Total cash outflows	$55,917	$54,417	$55,917	$56,417	$55,917	
Ending cash balance	**$4139**	**$5437**	**$4139**	**$2977**	**$4147**	
Net increase or decrease in cash	$4139	$5437	$3139	$3977	$3147	
Investments or borrowings	$3139	$4437	$2139	$2977	$2147	

Note: Values in parentheses refer to loss.

about when and how much to invest or spend any surplus cash. In some settings, periods of surplus cash flow may be used to replenish inventory and supplies. Programs and services might be expanded based on a budgeted cash surplus.

Considerable time may pass before health care providers are reimbursed for their services. Laws and regulations also restrict providers from requiring patients to make advance payments. Self-pay patients may delay or default on their payments. Delays occur from third-party payers, such as lengthy utilization review procedures or denials of payment. Appeal processes require considerable time and effort from providers. Even after filing appeals, reimbursement may be reduced or denied.

The anticipated delay in payment makes the preparation of the cash flow budget somewhat different than for other budgets. Most budgets rely on current estimates, but cash flow budgets also incorporate **lagged values**, budget figures that reflect prior financial activities for specified periods of time. These lagged values enable estimates of when revenues are actually received as cash inflow. Table 7.6 uses lagged values for private pay collections, anticipating that about a third of these patients will delay or default on paying the amount charged for their appointment.

Given that delay is anticipated in the receipt of various revenues, the budgeted cash inflow is typically less than the budgeted operating net revenue. Some patients or insurers do not pay their bills in full within the 90-day period, and some do not pay their bills at all. These **uncollectibles** result in cash flow budget estimates that are less than the operating net revenue estimates.

Private pay collections are only a small portion of the revenues received by MNC. The estimated $28 per month allowance to write off uncollectible charges is a small amount deducted from the total revenues (Table 7.6). The MNC cash flow budget is discussed in more detail in relation to concepts relevant to understanding and managing cash in health care settings.

Cash Inflows

Cash flow budgets are usually prepared on a monthly basis for the entire year. The first three months of 2012 are reported in a quarterly report for MNC. The cash flow budget typically begins with the **starting cash balance**, or the amount of cash on hand at the beginning of the cash flow budget month. MNC was established in 2011, with a modest amount of grant funding and heavy reliance on donations from Bigtown Hospital and volunteer support from the Millway University School of Nursing. The report in Table 7.6 therefore reports a cash balance of zero, but revenues generated from ACO contracts enables MNC to budget a monthly cash balance of $1000. This provides for at least a small cash reserve on hand from month to month.

The next lines of the cash flow budget in Table 7.6 are expected sources of **cash inflows** (revenues), also referred to as **cash flows from operating activities**. Larger and more complex organizations such as hospitals that bill and await payment for most of their services refer to these revenue sources as **receivables**. The first section reporting cash inflows focuses on **service revenues** or operating revenues generated from providing direct care services to MNC patients.

Most of MNC's 2012 service revenues are from a $100,000 per year grant and annual contracts with Welby ACO for disease management ($350,000) and wellness care ($250,000). The grant funding and ACO revenues are spread across 12 months, so MNC budgets and receives cash flow from each of these sources on a reliable basis. Private pay collections began in 2012, comprising only a small amount of revenues and with allowances for delay and default of payment. All these revenue sources, less the estimated $28 write-off allowance, total a budget of $58,389 per month and actual cash inflow of $58,353 for January 2012, as shown in Table 7.6.

The next set of cash inflows reports **nonservice revenue,** or revenue received for goods or services other than direct care. MNC conducted a pledge drive for cash donations to help support their services, with $20,000 in pledged donations for 2012 or $1667 per month (Table 7.6). Actual donations may differ from the pledged amounts in the budget. Another source of nonservice revenue is investment income. As MNC is a small health care organization, the only source of investment income is a savings account that was opened in January

2012 and that begins to earn interest in March 2012. Larger health care institutions establish financial reserve policies and maintain cash reserves large enough to cover salaries and other operating expenses for a month or more.

The service and nonservice revenues are added together to report the **total cash inflows**, which amount to $60,056 in January, as shown in Table 7.6. The beginning cash balance is then added to the total cash inflows to report **total cash on hand**. In this example, as MNC reports a zero cash balance, the January amount for total cash on hand is $60,056, which equals the total cash inflow for that time period.

Cash Outflows

Budgeted monthly **cash outflows from operating activities** (operating expenses) are then entered. Personnel expenses (including all salaries and benefits) total $38,417 for January 2012 in Table 7.6. Note that as salaries must be paid when due, the budgeted and actual personnel expenses are equal for MNC, unless there are changes in staffing. Nonpersonnel operating expenses consist of supplies budgeted at $7500 per month, with overhead budgeted at $5000 per month. The actual nonpersonnel expenses are somewhat lower for January 2012 because fewer supplies were purchased that month than anticipated.

Capital expenses represent cash outflows for nonoperating activities. MNC purchased additional medical equipment for examination and treatment rooms used by the additional NPs hired in 2012. These expenses are budgeted at $5000 per month. All cash outflow sources, including personnel, nonpersonnel, and capital expenses, are added together to report **total cash outflows**. The total cash outflows for January 2012 are budgeted as $55,917, with the actual amount reported as $54,417.

Ending Cash Balance

The final section of Table 7.6 begins with the **ending cash balance**, calculated by subtracting the total cash outflows from the total cash inflows, which is budgeted at $4139 in January 2012. The ending cash balance plus the beginning cash balance results in the **net increase or decrease in cash**. As the beginning cash balance for January 2012 is zero, the ending cash balance matches the net increase or decrease in cash for that time period, with the actual amount reported as $5437. The MNC manager invests $4437 of this surplus in a savings account, as shown in the line for investments and borrowings. The remaining $1000 surplus is held in reserve as the beginning cash balance for February 2012. If the ending cash balance is negative, it might be necessary to secure a short-term bank loan or draw from the beginning cash balance and savings to cover the next month's expenses.

Preparing the Cash Flow Budget

It is important to carefully track cash flow to ensure that obligations such as payment of salaries and bills are met, and to maintain the day-to-day financial health of the facility. The preparation of the cash flow budget is more complicated than preparing operating expense and capital budgets. Unlike the operating or capital budget, unless the setting is very small, nurses will probably not be involved in providing input for preparing the cash flow budget.

Considerations in preparing the cash flow budget include anticipating the amount of revenue likely to be received over specified time periods from each revenue source. Uncollectible revenues must also be estimated, as well as any nonservice revenues such as investment income. These estimates are spread over 12 months, with operating and capital expenses included from the operating and capital budgets.

Overall Purposes of Budgets and Budgeting				
Reporting Monitoring and Controlling Planning				
Day to Day	**Operating Budget:** Expenses Revenues Profit or Loss	**Other Budgets:** Special Purpose or Project Budget Product-Line or Service-Line Budget Evidence-Informed Case Rate	**Capital Budget:** Equipment Renovation New Construction	**Long Term**
Statistics Budget: Volume or Utilization **Cash Flow Budget:** Cash Inflows and Outflows				
Underlying Foundation of Volume and Cash Flow				

Figure 7.4 *Health Care Budgets Relationships and Linkage*

BUDGET RELATIONSHIPS AND LINKAGE

Figure 7.4 illustrates relationships and linkages of all the budgets discussed in Chapters 5, 6, and 7. The overall purposes of these budgets include timely reporting, ongoing monitoring and budget control, and the support of planning for future resource needs and benchmarks. The operating budget focuses on short-term, day-to-day operations in settings such as acute care nursing units. Other budgets such as the special purpose budget, the service-line budget, and the ECR focus on specific projects, populations, or provider contributions and payments. The capital budget focuses on long-term investments for items such as equipment that may be guided by strategic planning initiatives. Underlying all of these budgets are the statistics budget and the cash flow budget. The statistics budget estimates the units of service (UOS) for the setting such as patients or procedures. The cash flow budget estimates the inflow and outflow of revenues and expenses that support the short-term and long-term operations.

After all of the budgets are prepared, submitted, negotiated, revised, and approved, budget worksheets and guidelines are distributed to implement the budget for the next fiscal year. In addition, many organizations develop a **master budget**, a budget report that combines the organization's strategic plan, long-range budget, operating budget(s), capital budget(s), cash flow budget(s), and budget proposals into one document to present the financial plan over the long term linked to planning for the next fiscal year.

CONCLUSION

This chapter reviews a number of budgets that nurses might review or prepare in addition to the operating budget. The special purpose budget will be revisited in Chapters 10 and 11 as part of a business plan or health program grant proposal. Changes in health care financing and delivery may require more attention to product line budgets and ECRs for developing bundled payments with shared savings and risk for the providers. The capital budget requires justification for large, long-term expenditures. Although few nurses may ever see the facility's cash flow budget, it serves to ensure adequate financing to meet payroll and other financial obligations that occur as part of a health care setting's day-to-day operations. These budgets, along with the statistics and operating budgets discussed in Chapters 5 and 6, are related and linked to the short-term and long-term operations of health care settings.

Discussion and Excercises

1. Think of some equipment in your work setting or clinical assignment that you believe should be obtained or replaced. Prepare a capital budget, estimating the cost of the equipment.
2. Use a SWOT or priority matrix to evaluate the capital budget you prepared in exercise 1. Discuss ways you might convince administrative leaders and the health care team of the importance of this capital budget decision, based on the results of the matrix.
3. Review the operating budget you prepared for Chapter 6 Discussion and Exercises 1. Revise the budget discussion to include what resources are required for the project, what resources are already available for the project, and what resources are needed for the project. Make sure the budget estimates expenses for all of the resources that are needed. Discuss the in-kind contributions that your work setting or clinical assignment could make to your project.
4. Think of a project that might generate revenues, such as increasing patient beds or patient visits in your work setting or clinical assignments. List some examples of cash inflows and outflows for this project.

REFERENCES

Bateman, N. (2012). *The Business of nurse management: A toolkit for success.* New York, NY: Springer Publishing Company.

Centers for Disease Control and Prevention (CDC). (September 2, 2011). Writing SMART Objectives. Retrieved at http://www.cdc.gov/dhdsp/programs/nhdsp_program/evaluation_guides/smart_objectives.htm

de Brantes, F., & Camillus, J. A. (2007). *Evidence-informed case rates: A new health care payment model.* The Commonwealth Fund. Retrieved from http://www.cmwf.org

Miller, H. D. (2012). Creating Win-Win Strategies for Successful Payment & Delivery Reform. Presented at San Francisco Premier Seminar. Health Care Reform: Show Me the Money. University of San Francisco. www.paymentreform.org

Patient Protection and Affordable Care Act. (2010). Pub. L. No. 111–148, §2702, 124 Stat. 119, 318–319. Retrieved from http://housedocs.house.gov/energycommerce/ppacacon.pdf

Porter-O'Grady, T. (2009). *Interdisciplinary shared governance: Integrating practice, transforming healthcare* (2nd ed.). Sudbury, MA: Jones & Bartlett.

RapidBI. (2012). *SWOT analysis made simple – History, definition, tools, templates & worksheets. How to do a SWOT analysis. Overview SWOT Matrix.* Retrieved from http://rapidbi.com/swotanalysis

Reid, T. R. (2012). US Health Care: The Good News. PBS television documentary. Accessed at http://www.pbs.org/programs/us-health-care-good-news/

Satinsky, M. A. (2007). *Medical Practice Management in the 21st Century: The Handbook.* London, UK: Radcliffe Publishing.

The Brookings Institution. (2012). Implementing bundled payment: A case study of Crozer-Keystone Health System. Engelberg Center for Health Care Reform at Brookings. www.brookings.edu/healthreform

CROSSWORD: *Chapter 7—Capital and Other Budgets*

Across

3 Strengths, weaknesses, opportunities, and threats (abbreviation).

4 A budget based on an episode of care, often used in ACOs to develop bundled payments (abbreviation).

6 A specified task that must be accomplished to achieve a goal, and preferably SMART.

8 Organizational activities or issues that are believed to be of the most importance for profitability or survival.

9 A brief statement that incorporates the ethics and beliefs reflected in the organization.

10 A broad statement regarding what the organization or program intends to accomplish.

11 Expectations or beliefs about the internal or external environment that influence administrative and financial decision-making.

Down

1 Bills not paid in full, or not paid at all.

2 An individual or business that is able to pay its bills and meet its liabilities.

5 Revenue sources for organizations such as hospitals that bill and await payment for most of their services.

7 A brief description of where an organization wants to be or what the organization plans to accomplish.

Chapter 8: Cost-Finding, Break-Even, and Charges

Money often costs too much—Ralph Waldo Emerson

Learning Objectives

1. Differentiate between direct costs and indirect costs relevant to nursing care settings.
2. Explain how to incorporate volume in calculating total variable costs.
3. Give at least two examples of projects where a break-even analysis might be useful.
4. Describe and critique at least two methods for setting prices in health care settings.

Key Terms

activity-based costing (ABC)
break-even analysis
charge
charge description master (CDM)
chargemaster
contribution margin (CM)
cost allocation
cost centers
cost driver
cost pool
cost-pool method
cost-finding
cost-plus pricing
cost-to-charge ratio (CCR)
cost-volume-profit (CVP) analysis
customer-focused pricing

direct distribution
fixed costs per unit (FCU)
Healthcare Common Procedure Coding System (HCPCS)
market share pricing
nonrevenue cost center
Omaha System
Outcome and Assessment Information Set (OASIS)
overhead rate
penetration pricing
Physicians' Current Procedural Terminology (CPT®)
profit center
profit-focused pricing
profit margin
reciprocal distribution

relative value unit (RVU)
Resource-Based Relative Value Scale (RBRVS)
revenue cost center
revenue per unit (RU)
skimming
step-down distribution
support services
target return pricing
total costs (TCs)
total costs per unit (TCU)
total fixed costs (TFCs)
total revenue (TR)
total variable costs (TVC)
unit contribution margin (UCM)
value-based pricing
variable costs per unit (VCU)

Nurses may realize that costs are generated in their workplace, but not fully understand the sources of these costs. Nurses may not appreciate the relationship of costs to prices and profits. This chapter begins with a discussion of how costs are identified and shared in health care settings. Methods of relating costs to units of service (UOS) and revenue are then presented. An overview of pricing and coding is provided. In this time of cost concerns, nurses must think about costs and the impact nursing makes on health care costs.

COST-FINDING

Identifying all cost sources and amounts involved in producing a UOS is known as **cost-finding**. Cost-finding is important in health care settings for a number of reasons. Costs estimated in budgets and other financial reports are more accurate when costs are identified using systematic methods. Better cost identification results in more accurate pricing so that inpatient and outpatient charges reasonably cover the costs of services.

Cost-finding captures all the costs of producing goods and services, including costs that might not be obvious. For example, nurses may overlook the fact that their work unit generates costs for the Dietary, Housekeeping, and Laundry Departments in the hospital. Costs of nurse staffing may be underestimated and require cost-finding to identify sources of costs such as recruiting, hiring, and orienting (Penner & Spencer, in press). Nurses and nurse managers need to recognize all of the sources of costs to be fully accountable for expenses generated in their work units.

Cost-finding provides better information for cost management. Cost-finding leads to better cost control in all departments and work units of a health care facility. It is clearer to see how departments or work units contribute to overall financial performance by using cost-finding methods. For example, the physical therapy and occupational therapy departments likely make important contributions in hospital rehabilitation nursing units. Cost-finding results provide information for further financial reporting, such as budget planning. Finally, cost-finding may be required for Medicare and other regulatory compliance.

After reviewing terms and definitions needed in understanding cost-finding and cost allocation, various cost allocation methods are discussed. Cost allocation methods are often complex, therefore a few simple but commonly used methods are presented to provide an overall view of the steps and concepts involved.

Terms and Definitions for Cost-Finding

A few terms require review and definition to begin learning about how costs are identified and assigned in health care work units. **Direct costs** include all costs related to the UOS. Examples of direct costs include nurse staffing and medical supplies. Direct costs are usually apparent to nurses, as these costs are closely related to patient care.

Costs that are not directly related to the UOS are known as **indirect costs**. Indirect costs are sometimes referred to as overhead or administrative costs, as explained in Chapters 5 and 6. Examples of indirect costs include administration and housekeeping. Indirect costs might be specified in a line item as an amount or a rate. For example, laundry services might be budgeted as an indirect cost of $2000 per year. Administrative overhead might be budgeted as 5% of the total direct care budget. Cost-finding identifies total direct and indirect costs of a service unit. Figure 8.1 illustrates cost-finding for a UOS.

Work units that generate and report operating expenses are known as **cost centers**. A **nonrevenue cost center** is a cost center that generates expenses but not revenues and typically provides indirect services. Hospital housekeeping departments are

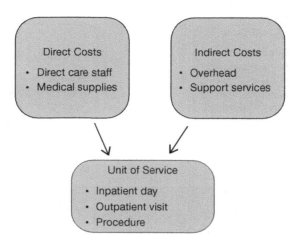

Figure 8.1 *Cost-Finding for the UOS*

an example of nonrevenue cost centers. A **revenue cost center** or **profit center** is a cost center that generates both expenses and revenues and typically provides direct services. Inpatient nursing units are an example of profit centers. In many settings, the term cost center applies to both nonrevenue and profit centers. Nursing units have been referred to as cost centers for many years, which overlooks the nursing unit's role in generating hospital revenues. This chapter refers to nursing units that generate revenue as profit centers.

Determining the total direct and indirect costs attributed to cost centers is known as **cost allocation**. Costs are allocated from one work unit or department to another. For example, nursing units generate costs for the hospital's Laundry Department. The Laundry Department determines the amount of cost generated and allocates or assigns those costs to the nursing units. Cost-finding methods are used to estimate these indirect costs, as well as the direct costs generated by the nursing units in providing direct patient care. Figure 8.2 illustrates how the **total costs (TCs)** of East Wing medical-surgical nursing unit include direct costs and indirect costs allocated as overhead and from other support services in Bigtown Hospital.

Costs grouped or selected for allocation to other cost centers are known as a **cost pool**. For example, all of the costs of a hospital's Housekeeping Department might be totaled as a cost pool, then these costs are allocated to other work units that make use of housekeeping services. Nonrevenue cost centers or cost pools that contribute costs to profit centers are frequently referred to as **support services**.

A **cost driver** is a measure or specification for cost allocations from a cost pool. Cost drivers must be measurable in relevant units. The housekeeping cost driver for a nurse-managed health center might be the health center's square feet of area. Whenever possible, cost drivers should allow for cost control by the cost center. For example, the Laundry Department cost driver for a nursing unit might be pounds of laundry used. The staff nurses can be encouraged to make efficient use of linens to better control laundry costs, which reduces the pounds of laundry used on the nursing unit.

The cost driver should also be reasonably "fair," or related to the actual amount of indirect resource used by the cost center. For example, outpatient units likely use less laundry services than inpatient units. It would be fairer to therefore allocate laundry costs based on laundry services utilization, such as pounds of laundry used in each setting, rather than allocating laundry costs equally across inpatient and outpatient units.

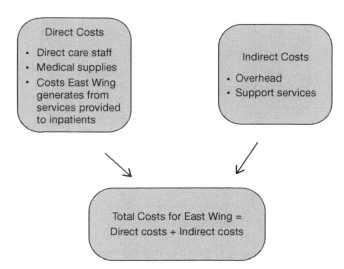

Figure 8.2 *Cost Allocation for East Wing Medical-Surgical Nursing Unit*

Activity-Based Costing

Activity-based costing (ABC) is a cost allocation method that focuses on the indirect and direct costs of specific activities performed within cost centers. The costs of these specific activities are used as the cost drivers for cost allocation. For example, the hospital laboratory might use ABC to allocate more costs to a cost driver for laboratory tests that require more labor and materials and are thus more costly to perform. Using a cost driver based on an overall average of laboratory test costs would not capture these costs adequately. ABC is a more complex approach to cost-finding, but is useful when costs of some activities provided as services to other cost centers are much higher or lower than others. More information about ABC is available at the Management Accounting Concepts and Techniques website: (http://classes.bus.oregonstate.edu/fall-07/ba321/Caplan/BA%20321%20Winter%202007%20table%20of%20contents.htm).

Direct Distribution Costing Approaches

The **direct distribution** method allocates indirect costs from support services to profit centers. Direct distribution is a widely used method of cost allocation. One of the simplest approaches to direct distribution is the **overhead rate** method of cost allocation. In this method, the costs for all support services are first totaled, then the indirect cost per UOS is calculated. This rate is then applied to each work unit that generates the UOS. For example, suppose Bigtown Hospital has support services including housekeeping, laundry, dietary, security, and maintenance, and the annual costs for all these support services total $1,000,000. The UOS for Bigtown hospital is patient days, and there is an annual total of 80,000 patient days. The overhead rate is therefore $12.50 ($1,000,000/80,000). The overhead rate allocation to East Wing, which generates 6000 patient days in a year, is $75,000 ($12.50 × 6000).

An average overhead rate is applicable to cost pools such as maintenance and general administration, for which the amount of resource use would not be expected to differ across revenue cost centers. However, other types of resource use may differ substantially among revenue cost centers and their service units. The **cost-pool method** of direct distribution is an approach to cost allocation that attempts to overcome the limitations of the overhead rate method. Rather than averaging support services cost pools over all service units, cost drivers are developed that reflect the estimated resource use by the respective revenue cost centers.

For example, the cost-pool method might allocate some support services such as maintenance and administration based on a UOS of patient days or patient visits. However, the Emergency Department might require more use of security services than other nursing units, so the cost driver for security might be 10% higher than for other nursing units. Inpatient nursing units likely require more dietary services than the emergency department, so the cost driver for dietary services might be 20% greater for inpatient nursing units compared with the Emergency Department. The cost pool method therefore attempts to allocate costs more fairly, based on actual resource use of support services by the cost center.

Reciprocal Distribution Costing

The **reciprocal distribution** method allocates costs for support services to all cost centers, not just to revenue cost centers. This is not only a more complex process than the direct method, but is also more accurate, as it takes all sources of costs into account, rather than only focusing on costs generated by revenue cost centers. The preparation of a reciprocal distribution cost report requires mathematical calculations beyond the scope of this text. Finance departments would prepare such reports.

Step-Down Distribution Method

The **step-down distribution** method, mandated by Medicare for cost reports, addresses the limitations of direct distribution methods and the complexity of reciprocal distribution methods. Costs are allocated among support services as well as profit centers. When all the costs from a cost center are allocated, the cost center is removed from further cost allocation procedures. Cost centers are entered into the allocation process in sequential order. This method improves cost allocation accuracy by assigning costs generated from one support service to another, such as the dietary department's use of housekeeping, yet is simpler to calculate than the more complex reciprocal distribution method. This is one of the most common cost allocation methods because of its use in Medicare cost reports.

Table 8.1 presents a simplified example of a step-down distribution method cost allocation worksheet for Bigtown Hospital, with total 2013 operating expenses of $200 million. It is assumed that there are only two profit centers in this example, Outpatient Services and Inpatient Services. The support centers include Property and Plant Operations, Administration, Security, Maintenance, Laundry, and Dietary departments.

The first line of the step-down cost allocation worksheet reports TCs for each cost center calculated as direct costs plus indirect costs (Table 8.1). The second line of the worksheet reports direct costs for each cost center, which represents each cost center's operating expenses. The direct costs and TCs for Property and Plant Operations are the same because no costs are allocated to that department.

Costs are first allocated from the Property and Plant Operations cost pool, with 5%, or $1,034,650, in property and plant operations expenses allocated to Administration, and 15%, or $1,488,510, to Security (Table 8.1). Cost allocations continue for each cost center down the second column of the worksheet, until all of the Property and Plant Operations expenses are allocated to the other support services and profit centers. The allocation amounts are entered as negative numbers (reported in parentheses), because these costs are transferred from the cost pool until the TCs after step-down distribution reaches $0. The percent of the cost pool that is allocated varies depending on the estimated resource use of each cost center.

The next cost pool reporting step-down cost allocation is Administration (Table 8.1). TCs for Administration represent $3,367,000 in direct costs plus $1,034,650 of indirect costs allocated from Property and Plant Operations. The allocations continue for the remaining cost centers down the third column of the worksheet, until all of the Administration expenses are allocated. Each of the support services allocates their expenses in order.

Table 8.1 *Bigtown Hospital, Step-Down Distribution Cost Allocation Worksheet, 2013*

Cost Allocations	Support Services						Profit Centers		Total Costs
	Property and Plant Operations	Administration	Security	Maintenance	Laundry	Dietary	Outpatient Services	Inpatient Services	
Total costs	$20,693,000	$4,401,650	$4,304,560	$7,170,716	$7,128,703	$5,003,068	$29,185,058	$170,814,942	$200,000,000
Direct costs	$20,693,000	$3,367,000	$2,724,000	$3,201,000	$3,135,000	$2,048,000	$21,734,000	$143,098,000	—
Direct cost PPD	—	—	—	—	—	—	$241	$1590	—
Property and plant operations	—	—	—	—	—	—	—	—	—
% property and plant operations	—	—	—	—	—	—	—	—	—
Administration	($1,034,650)	$1,034,650	—	—	—	—	—	—	—
% administration	5%	—	—	—	—	—	—	—	—
Security	($1,448,510)	($132,050)	$1,580,560	—	—	—	—	—	—
% security	7%	3%	—	—	—	—	—	—	—
Maintenance	($3,103,950)	($220,083)	($645,684)	$3,969,716	—	—	—	—	—
% maintenance	15%	5%	15%	20%	—	—	—	—	—
Laundry	($3,103,950)	($660,248)	($86,091)	($143,414)	$3,993,703	—	—	—	—
% laundry	15%	15%	2%	2%	—	—	—	—	—

Note: Values in parentheses refer to loss.

Cost Allocations	Support Services						Profit Centers		Total Costs
	Property and Plant Operations	Administration	Security	Maintenance	Laundry	Dietary	Outpatient Services	Inpatient Services	
Dietary	($1,448,510)	($308,116)	($129,137)	$0	($1,069,305)	$2,955,068	—	—	—
% dietary	7%	7%	3%	0%	15%	—	—	—	—
Outpatient services	($3,103,950)	($660,248)	($2,152,280)	($215,121)	($1,069,305)	($250,153)	$7,451,058	—	—
% outpatient services	15%	15%	50%	3%	15%	5%	—	—	—
Outpatient services PPD	—	—	—	—	—	—	$83	—	—
Inpatient services	($7,449,480)	($2,420,908)	($1,291,368)	($6,812,181)	($4,990,092)	($4,752,914)		$27,716,942	—
% inpatient services	36%	55%	30%	95%	70%	95%		—	—
Inpatient services PPD	—	—	—	—	—	—	—	$308	—
Total step-down costs	$0	$0	$0	$0	$0	$0	$29,185,058	$170,814,942	$200,000,000
Total % allocated	100%	100%	100%	100%	100%	100%	0%	0%	—
Total costs PPD	—	—	—	—	—	—	$324	$1,898	—

Notes: 90,000 patient days are reported for 2013. Outpatient visits adjusted for patient days. Values in parentheses refer to loss.

The remaining cost centers are Outpatient Services and Inpatient Services, as shown in Table 8.1. In this example, Outpatient Services does not allocate any of its costs to Inpatient Services. A total of $7,451,058 indirect costs are allocated to Outpatient Services, and a total of $27,716,942 are allocated to Inpatient Services. In other words, it is estimated that Outpatient Services utilizes approximately $7.5 million in support services, and Inpatient Services utilizes approximately $27.7 million in support services in 2013.

Direct, indirect, and total costs per patient day (PPD) are also reported for Outpatient and Inpatient Services (Table 8.1). These estimates are calculated by dividing the direct, indirect, and total costs by 90,000 adjusted patient days for 2013. It is therefore possible to determine the "true" cost of inpatient and outpatient care at Bigtown, including not only the costs of nursing care but also incorporating all relevant support services. Although this is a simplified example, it illustrates the principles of cost allocation and indicates the complexity of these reports.

In reviewing Table 8.1, it is important to note that the sequence in which cost centers are entered into cost allocation affects their indirect and total costs. The rationale used in selecting the sequence in this example was based on the assumption that all cost centers should share property and plant operation expenses such as utilities and the lease, remaining cost centers share all administrative costs, and most of the cost centers share security costs. Next, the costs for support services such as maintenance, laundry, and dietary were allocated based on the assumption that their services largely support the profit centers. It is also assumed that Outpatient Services does not provide any support services to Inpatient Services. Assumptions are also made regarding the percent of allocation to each cost center. If different assumptions were made, the order of entry into the step-down distribution and the allocations would differ from this example, which would change these departments' TCs.

The sequence of entry in step-down distribution might also omit or overlook some actual costs. For example, Administration might generate housekeeping or maintenance costs that are not allocated in the example shown in Table 8.1. It is important to carefully consider the cost center sequencing in step-down distribution as well as the cost drivers employed to allocate costs. It is also important to realize that decisions about the design of the step-down distribution have implications for costs attributed to work units and might be somewhat controversial among department heads and nurse managers.

More information about direct distribution, reciprocal, and step-down methods of cost allocation is available at the Management and Accounting website (www.maaw.info). Examples of UOS, staffing indicators, budget items, and cost allocations for actual hospital cost centers are available at the Washington State Department of Health Center for Health Statistics Hospital Data website (www.doh.wa.gov).

BREAK-EVEN ANALYSIS

How do managers determine how many goods or services they must deliver, and how much they must charge to cover their costs and generate profits? This section discusses the concept of **break-even analysis**, determining the UOS required to cover the costs of business, then make a profit, related to costs and revenue associated with the UOS.

Break-even analysis has many uses. Current performance can be evaluated by using break-even analysis to determine whether a program or service is profitable. Break-even analysis informs strategic planning and the preparation of operating, capital, and other budgets. The UOS required to break-even can be compared with the forecasted UOS to predict whether a program will be profitable. Decisions such as whether to purchase new equipment or expand a program can be supported by break-even analysis, as well as decisions to terminate or downsize programs. Break-even analysis demonstrates the impact of changes in UOS, costs, or revenues on profitability. Moreover, break-even analysis is a way to evaluate management and productivity by demonstrating the impact of cost control on profitability.

The fundamental principle of break-even analysis is that profits change with changes that occur in volume, costs, and revenue. It is therefore important to review relevant terms and definitions and to understand the relationships between volume, costs, and revenue. This section then discusses the calculation of break-even and break-even with profit. Further concepts related to break-even analysis are then presented.

Volume or UOS

Volume is discussed throughout this textbook; an overview of volume concepts is presented in Chapter 4. Volume is also referred to as utilization, UOS, or the quantity of a service unit (Q). In this chapter, the terms UOS or volume are used in reference to the quantity of inpatient days, outpatient visits, or health care procedures. In some situations, volume estimates are required for the break-even analysis. In other situations, break-even analysis is used to estimate volume. When volume estimates are required for break-even analysis, they should be as accurate as possible. In this ever-changing health care climate, accurate volume estimations may be difficult to obtain. The limitations of a volume estimate or sources of possible error in volume estimates should be reported when presenting a break-even analysis.

Costs

Costs represent the resources used in producing goods and services. One way to identify costs is to refer to the operating expense budget. Cost-finding methods are discussed earlier in this chapter as another approach to identifying all of the costs of a UOS. Costs should be estimated as accurately as possible.

In calculating a break-even analysis, it is necessary to examine costs in more detail. The nurse must identify and estimate **fixed costs**. Fixed costs are costs one assumes will not vary (at least over the fiscal year), regardless of changes in volume. For example, the costs of fixed staff and capital equipment represent direct fixed costs or fixed costs related directly to the provision of health services. If indirect costs (overhead) are allocated as a specified amount or percent of the annual budget, then the indirect fixed costs are added to the direct fixed costs to estimate the **total fixed costs (TFCs)**. The cost-finding methods discussed earlier in the chapter help in determining the indirect fixed costs. The TFCs do not change relative to volume.

TFCs can also be calculated on a per-unit basis, known as **fixed costs per unit (FCU)**. FCU is calculated by dividing the TFCs by the UOS. Figure 8.3 summarizes the calculation and interpretation of TFCs, FCU, and other terms used in break-even analysis. The relationship of each of these items to increases in volume is also presented in Figure 8.3. Note that the relationship of each of these terms works in the reverse. For example, if the UOS decreases, the FCU is expected to increase.

The FCU are related to a concept from Chapter 1, economies of scale. Fixed costs can be spread over an increasing number of UOSs, until production capacity is reached, thus increasing the efficiency of production. In addition, FCU may represent indirect costs or overhead, handling fees, markups, or surcharges. For example, a hospital pharmacy may allocate its overhead costs required for storing or processing pharmaceuticals as fixed costs.

Total variable costs (TVCs) are directly tied to changes in volume, as TVCs vary based on volume. Variable nursing staff and medical supplies are examples of variable costs. Variable costs usually represent direct costs. Indirect costs are usually not incorporated into

Term	Calculation	Does the value change with changes in volume?	Interpretation
UOS or volume	Estimated or predicted service units	–	UOS might be estimated using break-even or required in the break-even calculation
Total fixed costs (TFC)	Direct costs + Indirect costs	No	Direct costs might be identified in the operating expense budget. Indirect costs might be identified using cost-finding and cost allocation approaches
Fixed costs per unit (FCU)	TFC ÷ UOS	FCU decreases as UOS increases	Decrease in FCU reflects economies of scale; FCU also may represent indirect costs or overhead, handling fees, mark-up, or surcharge
Total variable costs (TVC)	VCU x UOS	TVC increases as UOS increases	Variable costs usually represent only direct costs, not indirect costs
Variable costs per unit (VCU)	Estimated based on variable resource use	No	Usually VCU are estimated, then used to estimate TVC
Total costs (TC)	TFC + (VCU x UOS)	TC increases as UOS increases	The calculation shows the relationship between TFC, VCU, and UOS in estimating TC
Total costs per unit (TCU)	TC ÷ UOS	TCU decreases as UOS increases	Decrease in TCU reflects economies of scale related to FCU
Price or revenue per unit (RU)	Estimated or established	No	The RU is usually estimated or established, then used to estimate TR
Total revenue (TR)	RU x UOS	TR increases as UOS increases	RU usually used to estimate TR based on UOS

Figure 8.3 *Terms, Calculations, and Relationships to Volume for Break-Even Analysis*

the estimation of TVCs. TVCs are often estimated by first estimating the **variable costs per unit (VCU),** or the variable cost associated with each UOS. The VCU is then multiplied by the UOS to estimate TVCs (Figure 8.3).

TFCs plus TVCs add to TCs. Figure 8.3 presents an expanded formula that incorporates TFCs, VCU, and UOS in calculating TCs. **Total costs per unit (TCU)** are calculated by dividing TCs by UOS. Note that while TCs increase as the UOS increase, TCU decrease as the UOSs increase. The cost side of the break-even analysis is now complete.

Revenue

Revenue is the income derived from the reimbursement for providing goods or services. Revenue is based on the price or **revenue per unit (RU)**. In health care, prices are often referred to as charges and may not be fully reimbursed by insurers or other payers. Payers such as Medicare and Medicaid pay a predetermined, established amount that is generally lower than the charges. Other payers such as commercial insurance plans might pay all or nearly all of the charges. The RU is multiplied by the UOS to estimate **total revenue (TR)**. Note that while the RU does not change with changes in volume, TR increases as the UOS increases (Figure 8.3). The elements necessary to calculate break-even (volume, costs, and revenue) are now defined and related to each other.

Purpose	Calculation	Interpretation
Break-even without profit	TFC + (VCU x UOS) = RU x UOS	TC = TR or total costs must be covered by revenue
Break-even with profit target	RU x UOS = TFC + (VCU x UOS) + P	TR = TC + P or revenue must cover total costs and profit
Profit margin	P% = P ÷ TR	Estimate or establish a profit target
Break-even volume without profit	UOS = TFC ÷ (RU − VCU)	Estimate volume required to break even
Break-even volume with profit target	UOS = (TFC + P) ÷ (RU − VCU)	Profit is added to TFC to incorporate the profit target
Break-even price without profit	RU = TC ÷ UOS	RU = TCU or revenues must cover the costs for each UOS to break even
Break-even price with profit target	RU = (TC + P) ÷ UOS	Profit is added to TC to incorporate the profit target
Contribution margin	CM = TR - TVC	Estimates the amount available to cover fixed costs and generate a profit
Profit	P = CM - TFC	Profit is total revenue less fixed and variable costs
Unit contribution margin	UCM = RU - VCU	UCM also known as indirect costs or overhead, handling fee, mark-up, or surcharge representing the FCU
Cost-to-charge ratio	CCR = Operating expenses ÷ charges	For work units or UOS, assume operating expenses are all associated direct expenses, and charges are all associated gross revenues

Figure 8.4 *Methods for Break-Even, Contribution Margin, and Work Unit Cost-to-Charge Ratio*

Break-Even Analysis Without Profit

The fundamental principle of break-even analysis is that revenues and costs change with changes in volume. "Breaking-even" means that the revenue from selling goods or services equals the expenses of producing those goods or services, so that costs are covered by revenues. The break-even analysis principle is expressed as TC = TR. Figure 8.4 shows the expanded formula for break-even without profit.

Table 8.2 presents an example of break-even analysis without a profit target, showing the impact on revenues as the volume changes. If the foot care clinic has 550 patient visits during 2013, TCs are estimated at $42,500 ($15,000 + [$50 × 550]). The total revenue for 550 patient visits is only $41,250 ($75 × 550), resulting in a loss of $1250.

If the volume reaches 600 patient visits to the foot care clinic over 2013, the program will break-even. The break-even amount is $0, meaning that the TCs equal the total revenues, so the revenue generated covers the program costs. If the volume of patient visits for 2013 is greater than 600, any visits over that amount generate a profit. Table 8.2 shows that if patient visits reach 650 for 2013, the care clinic will generate $1250 in profit.

Figure 8.5 shows a graph of the break-even analysis. The point where the lines for total revenue and TCs cross is the break-even point. The break-even point also represents market equilibrium, or the point at which volume, price, and costs are in balance (refer to Chapter 1). Below the break-even point, costs exceed revenue so the program

Table 8.2 *Bigtown Hospital, Nurse-Managed Foot Care Clinic, Break-Even Analysis Without Profit Target, 2013*

UOS	Total Fixed Costs	Fixed Costs per Unit	Total Variable Costs	Variable Costs per Unit	Total Costs	Total Costs per Unit	Price (Revenue per Unit)	Total Revenue	Break-Even	Contribution Margin
550	$15,000	$27	$27,500	$50	$42,500	$77	$75	$41,250	($1250)	$13,750
600	$15,000	$25	$30,000	$50	$45,000	$75	$75	$45,000	$0	$15,000
650	$15,000	$23	$32,500	$50	$47,500	$73	$75	$48,750	$1250	$16,250

Note: Value in parenthesis refers to loss.

Table 8.3 *Bigtown Hospital, Nurse-Managed Foot Care Clinic, Break-Even Analysis With a Profit Target, 2013*

UOS	Total Fixed Costs	Fixed Costs per Unit	Total Variable Costs	Variable Costs per Unit	Total Costs	Total Costs per Unit	Price (Revenue per Unit)	Profit Target	Total Revenue	Break-Even	Contribution Margin
600	$15,000	$25	$30,000	$50	$45,000	$75	$75	$2500	$45,000	($2500)	$15,000
650	$15,000	$23	$32,500	$50	$47,500	$73	$75	$2500	$48,750	($1250)	$16,250
700	$15,000	$21	$35,000	$50	$50,000	$71	$75	$2500	$52,500	$0	$17,500

Note: Values in parentheses refer to loss.

operates at a loss. Above the break-even point, revenue is greater than costs, so the program generates profits.

Break-Even Analysis With a Profit Target

Profit is an additional factor to consider in break-even analysis. Some financial experts refer to break-even analysis as **cost-volume-profit (CVP) analysis**, emphasizing the importance of generating enough volume to make a profit as well as cover costs. It is not only necessary that for-profit enterprises generate profit, but nonprofit enterprises must also generate profit to be able to grow and maintain the quality of their goods and services. Break-even analysis with profit is therefore applicable to many health care programs and services.

The principle of calculating break-even with profit is that the revenues generated must cover both costs and a predetermined profit target. The break-even formula with a profit target, as shown in Figure 8.2, therefore, becomes TR = TC + P. An amount of profit (P) might be established or estimated based on a target **profit margin** (P/TR expressed as a percent). The profit margin is an indicator of the amount of revenue that is retained as profit.

Table 8.3 presents a break-even analysis for the Bigtown Hospital foot care clinic, using a profit target of $2500 for 2013. In order to break-even, the foot care clinic must generate 700 patient visits over the year and obtain revenues of $52,500 to cover the $50,000 in TCs plus the $2500 profit target. This profit target is close to a 5% profit margin ($2500/$52,500), so that for every $1 the foot care clinic generates, approximately $0.05 profit is generated.

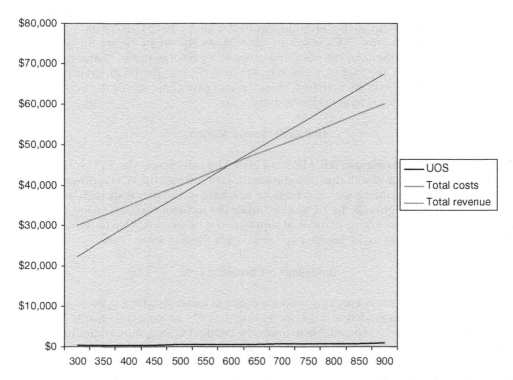

Figure 8.5 *Bigtown Hospital Foot Care Clinic, Break-Even Point Without Profit, 2013*

Break-Even Analysis for Estimating Volume or Price

The example of break-even analysis without profit illustrates the importance of volume related to costs and revenue. It is often helpful to use a break-even equation that estimates the UOS required to generate enough revenue to cover the costs of a service or program. Figure 8.4 shows that by dividing TFCs by the price less variable costs, a break-even volume is estimated. Using the figures from Table 8.2, the UOS required for the foot care clinic to break-even without profit is 600 patient visits ($15,000/[$75 – $50]).

When a profit target is set, the amount of profit is added to TFCs when calculating the UOS required to break-even. Using the figures from Table 8.3, the UOS required for the foot care clinic to break-even with the $2500 profit target is 700 patient visits. The UOS are calculated by adding the $15,000 in fixed costs to the $2500 profit target, and dividing that amount by $25 ($75 – $50 VCU).

Break-even analysis can be used to estimate the price to be set for goods or services. The break-even price is reached when the RU covers the TCU. Table 8.2 shows that RU = TCU at $75, at the break-even point of 600 foot care visits. It is therefore possible to estimate a break-even price by dividing TCs by the UOS (RU = TC/UOS). To calculate a break-even price with a profit target, the profit target is added to TCs (RU = [TC + P]/UOS). Using the figures in Table 8.3, the $75 price equals the $75 TCU plus profit ([$50,000 + $2500]/700).

Contribution Margin

The **contribution margin (CM)** represents the dollar amount available from revenues to first cover fixed costs (including overhead), then contribute to profits. A CM is useful to calculate for programs and services that require a large capital investment. Variable costs will not accrue if a program does not generate volume. However, even if a program does not generate volume, its fixed costs (capital investments) must be repaid. Calculating a CM enables the nurse to estimate the revenue required to cover those fixed costs.

Total revenues minus TVCs result in the CM, as shown in Figure 8.4. When TFCs are subtracted from the CM, the resulting amount represents profit. Using figures from Table 8.2, the CM for the foot care clinic equals the TFCs at the break-even point of 600 patient visits. Table 8.3 shows that the CM for the foot care clinic equals the $15,000 in fixed costs plus the $2500 profit target at break-even.

Unit Contribution Margin

The **unit contribution margin (UCM)** is calculated by subtracting the VCU from the price, as shown in Figure 8.4. Recall that in some health care settings the FCU represents indirect costs or overhead, handling fees, markups, or surcharges. Departments such as Pharmacy or Central Supply might use the UCM to estimate the indirect costs of storing, processing, or managing pharmaceuticals or medical supplies. The UCM could also be used to estimate markups or surcharges to the product's price to cover these indirect costs.

Guidelines for Breaking Even

Guidelines to remember in breaking even are easier to understand using the examples from Tables 8.2 and 8.3. One guideline is that increasing the UOS increases revenue and profitability. In some situations, it is profitable to lower the product's price, thus attracting more customers and increasing volume. However, it is also important to realize that volume cannot exceed capacity, and health care work units typically operate more efficiently if somewhat under capacity. Thus, there are limits to increasing profitability by increasing volume.

Another guideline is that an increase in price or reimbursement reduces the volume needed to break-even. For example, if the reimbursement rate for foot care increases to $100 per visit, the volume needed to break-even decreases. It is important to realize that a price increase might reduce demand below the break-even point. Insurance coverage makes customers less sensitive to price and price increases (as discussed in Chapter 1). When nurses submit all appropriate charges for supplies and procedures and document care to enable reimbursement (as discussed in Chapter 5), they improve the work unit's profitability by increasing revenue.

A guideline with implications for nurse managers is that reducing fixed and variable costs reduces the break-even volume required. Cost reductions improve profitability. It is therefore important to manage the operating budget and to control unfavorable budget variances whenever possible (as discussed in Chapter 5). Improving productivity and efficiency reduces variable costs and increases profitability. It is also important to carefully plan operating budgets and high-cost capital expenditures (as discussed in Chapters 6 and 7). If costs can be reduced, then drops in volume or revenue are less likely to reduce profitability. If the overall costs of providing a good or service exceed the revenues, there may be problems with efficiency or productivity.

Complicating Factors in Breaking Even

There are many factors that complicate the break-even calculation. This text does not cover these complicating factors in detail, but a few are briefly discussed. These complicating factors include:

- *Taxes.* Taxes increase TCs. An overall tax rate represents a fixed cost. A tax applied to each UOS sold either increases the variable costs or the price the customer must pay.
- *Product mix.* If multiple goods or services are produced with various combinations of costs, volume, and prices, the break-even analysis becomes more complex.
- *Payer mix.* In health care, there are often multiple payers, including government programs, commercial insurance, and self-pay, each reimbursing at somewhat different rates and making revenue estimates more complicated.
- *Case mix.* Patients may request or require different combinations of goods or services. For example, one patient on the unit may have cancer and require extensive care for weeks, whereas another patient may have asthma, require minimal care, and only stay in the hospital for a few hours for observation.
- *Volume forecasting.* It may be difficult to accurately predict utilization one or more years into the future.
- *Changes in reimbursement and costs.* Government and commercial insurers may increase or reduce their reimbursement. Prices for capital investments and supplies may increase or decrease, as well as salaries, wages, and benefits.
- *New financing mechanisms.* One example of a new financing mechanism is the bundled payment **accountable care organizations (ACOs)** use to reimburse providers for an entire episode of patient care, from hospitalization to services such as home health care. Determining the break-even and profitability of services is more complex when calculated across multiple inpatient and outpatient providers and settings.

Preparing break-even analyses in these more complex scenarios is beyond the scope of this text. These more complicated break-even analyses would require assistance from the financial officers in the health care setting. However, one further scenario, capitation financing, is worth discussing in light of the concepts covered in examining the break-even analysis.

Break-Even Analysis in Capitation

Think about the fundamental principle of capitation financing, which represents a fixed payment, per health plan enrollee, paid to the provider or provider system for a defined set of services over a specified period of time. Given that, under capitation, the total revenue is fixed by the payer, think about what the break-even point would be. Under capitation, the health care provider will break even when the TCs for covering the health plan enrollee population equals the total fixed capitation payment. The provider generates a profit if able to keep the health plan costs below the amount of the capitation payment and loses money if costs exceed the capitation payment.

PRICES AND PRICING

Nurses typically have little input regarding the charges set in their health care settings. However, this is a time of increasing **transparency,** or information that is available regarding health care prices. An understanding of some basic pricing concepts helps nurses understand health care charges and price setting.

Charges and the Charge Description Master

In health care, the **charge** represents the full price assigned to a good or service, before discounts or other reductions, also called **contractual allowances**, are applied. **Gross revenue** represents the full charges before contractual allowances. Payment for health care goods and services, particularly from government or private insurers, is known as **reimbursement** or **net revenue**. For most hospitals, net revenue averages only about 30% to 50% of gross revenue (IHI, 2011). However, gross revenue is usually reported in nursing unit budgets, because it is less variable than net revenue. Net revenue is typically reported for the institution as a whole and on a per-case basis.

A hospital **charge description master (CDM),** also known as a **chargemaster,** is a comprehensive list of the prices of all goods and services for which a separate charge exists. The CDM is used to generate a patient's bill, which is submitted to the payer for reimbursement. For many years, CDMs were proprietary. CDMs were not available to the public or even to nurses and nurse managers employed by the hospital. In California, state law now mandates that hospitals file their CDMs annually with the Office of Statewide Planning and Development (OSHPD), beginning in 2005. The Patient Protection and Affordable Care Act of 2010 requires that all U.S. hospitals make an updated list of their standard charges available to the public each year (PPACA, 2010).

One health economist refers to hospital pricing as "chaos behind a veil of secrecy," because hospital pricing practices are not transparent or standardized (Reinhardt, 2006, p. 57). Health system researchers find considerable regional variation in health care charges and spending across the United States, without any clear rationale to explain these differences. The Dartmouth Atlas of Health Care project (http://www.dartmouthatlas.org/) is a resource for further information about the regional variation of hospital charges. A resource useful to consumers who want to compare health care prices is the Healthcare Blue Book website (www.healthcarebluebook.com). The following section discusses some approaches that hospitals and other health care providers likely use in establishing charges.

PRICING METHODS

There are a number of approaches that can be used in setting prices. The methods discussed here reflect how hospitals and other health care providers might set prices in the health care market. Although hospital price lists are more available to the public, the strategies that underlie the establishment of charges remain secret. It is therefore difficult to explain why any particular hospital charge is set at a given amount. Nevertheless, this discussion should help nurses better understand some basic concepts of pricing methods.

Profit-focused pricing. **Profit-focused pricing** uses the desired level of profit as a basis for setting prices. One approach is **cost-plus pricing,** or setting the price at the cost of production cost plus a profit margin. A similar approach is **target return pricing,** or setting the price to achieve a targeted return on investment. The Bigtown Hospital foot care clinic example, shown in Table 8.3, demonstrates the usefulness of break-even analysis in profit-focused pricing. Profit-focused pricing methods are relatively simple to apply. However, these methods do not take consumer demand, price sensitivity, or market conditions into account (Nugent, 2004).

Customer-focused pricing. Setting the price based on the value the customer attributes to the product or service is known as **customer-focused** or **value-based pricing**. Customer-focused pricing is closely linked to elasticity of demand or the consumer's sensitivity to prices, which is discussed in Chapter 1. It is important to know the customer and the customer's needs to apply customer-focused pricing.

Customer-focused pricing can generate high profits (Nugent, 2004). For example, a provider could set a high price for products or services for which there is an inelastic demand, such as a life-saving cancer treatment. The demand is inelastic, as the customer needs the treatment to survive, and if equally effective and less costly treatments are not available, the customer is willing to pay the added cost. If able to choose equally effective, less costly treatments, the customer becomes more price sensitive and less likely to choose the higher priced treatment.

Customer-focused pricing can be quite profitable. However, this approach may be difficult to justify to the public (Nugent, 2004). Setting an excessively high price for health care goods and services when the demand is inelastic is sometimes referred to as **skimming** and is considered to be an ethically questionable practice. Public concern about skimming may also lead to fair pricing regulation, such as regulations for health plan and hospital pricing in the Patient Protection and Affordable Care Act of 2010 (PPACA, 2010).

Market-focused pricing. **Penetration** or **market share pricing** is an approach when the customer has a more elastic demand for health care goods or services and is more price sensitive. The provider lowers the product price, expecting the costs of production to decrease with the increase in volume. The lower price makes the health care provider more competitive in the market (Nugent, 2004). This approach is related to the concept of economies of scale discussed in Chapter 1.

A similar approach in market-focused pricing is to provide special offers or discounts to the customer (Nugent, 2004). For example, free glaucoma screenings might attract more patients to self-refer to an ophthalmologist's practice. Another example is to bundle or combine charges so that consumers can compare the costs of common procedures among health providers, such as the cost of delivering a baby. Discounts are also frequently negotiated between hospitals and commercial insurance plans. Market-focused pricing works best in situations where the customer is able and willing to "shop around" for health care at the best price.

Concepts in Establishing Hospital Charges

The information presented in this chapter on cost-finding, break-even analysis, and pricing methods can be applied in thinking about concepts in establishing or updating hospital charges. Many of these concepts also apply to other health care settings, such as nurse-managed health centers. If nurses are going to become more involved in pricing decisions, it is important to understand these basic concepts.

One essential element in establishing prices is to have accurate information about volume, costs, and revenue. Cost-finding and budget planning are important first steps in pricing. It is also important to involve clinical managers and clinicians, including nurse managers and nurses, as sources of input for pricing decisions (HFMA, 2004). Accurate information leads to estimating a break-even point that ensures profitability.

Another concept in pricing decisions is **cost-shifting,** or increasing the price of a good or service to cover the costs of an unprofitable good or service. Government payers such as Medicare and Medicaid often reimburse at a rate that is below the hospital's costs, so hospitals frequently set prices for commercial insurance payers at a more profitable rate to cover those costs. Nurses must become more aware of the more and less profitable Medicare severity diagnosis-related groups (MS-DRGs), diagnoses, and services in their facility.

It is also important to keep the hospital CDM current, accurate, and compliant with Center for Medicare & Medicaid Services (CMS) provisions. Accurate information about charges combined with accurate cost information enables the health care team to focus on the **cost-to-charge ratio (CCR)** at the UOS or program level. The CCR is usually calculated at the level of overall hospital costs and charges. However, the CCR estimated at the UOS or program level helps in determining the percentage to discount charges and provides a conservative estimate of costs (SFDPH, 2009).

A simplified method of calculating the CCR for a UOS or program is to divide the operating expenses associated with the procedure or unit by the charges or gross patient revenue, as shown in Figure 8.4. The operating expenses represent the direct costs of the UOS or program. A higher CCR indicates a closer relationship between costs and charges (SFDPH, 2009).

For example, using figures from Table 8.2, assume that $10,000 of the foot care clinic (a program) are indirect expenses. Also, assume that total revenues represent charges or gross patient revenue. To calculate the CCR for the foot care clinic, subtract $10,000 from TCs for each level of volume and divide that amount by the total revenue. The CCR is 77.8% at a volume of 600 patient visits a year ($35,000/$45,000).

CLASSIFICATION AND CODING SYSTEMS

Charges for services and procedures are generally classified and coded using standardized systems. A few of the more commonly used systems are briefly discussed here, with some resources included for further exploration.

As discussed in Chapter 2, in the 1980s, the prospective payment system of Medicare hospital reimbursement established diagnosis-related groups, revised in 2008 as MS-DRGs. The MS-DRGs are based on major diagnostic category (MDC) classifications of illness and standardized expected length of inpatient care. Besides their utility in prospective payment systems (which are now extended beyond acute care to home health and long-term care settings), MDCs and MS-DRGs enable the identification of average patient resource consumption by diagnosis. More information about MS-DRGs in hospital settings is available at the CMS Acute Inpatient PPS website (www.cms.gov).

The diagnostic categories for a patient's principal admitting diagnosis were originally based on the International Classification of Diseases, 9th Revision, Clinical Modification (ICD-9-CM). Health care providers are currently required to upgrade to the ICD-10. The U.S. Department of Health and Human Services (HHS) recently proposed extending the deadline for ICD-10 compliance to October 1, 2014. More information about the transition to ICD-10 is available at the CMS ICD-10 website (www.cms.gov).

CPT® and HCPCS Codes

The **Physicians' Current Procedural Terminology (CPT®)** is a coding system the American Medical Association (AMA) developed to identify specific medical services and procedures and classify outpatient services and costs. Inpatient cost centers may also use CPT® codes to group costs, as in radiology departments or other work units performing procedures that fit the coding system. More information about the development and use of CPT® codes is available at the About CPT® website (www.ama-assn.org).

The **Healthcare Common Procedure Coding System (HCPCS)** is a coding system CMS developed that incorporates and expands CPT® codes to classify services and products not included in the CPT® codes. HCPCS codes are also developed to reduce the use of "miscellaneous or nonclassified" codes for programs, products, and services. More information about HCPCS codes is available at the HCPCS General Information website (www.cms.gov).

Resource-Based Relative Value Scale and Relative Value Units

The Medicare **Resource-Based Relative Value Scale (RBRVS)** was developed in 1992 to quantify physician services for reimbursement purposes. The cost assigned to each **Relative Value Unit (RVU)** developed under the RBRVS corresponds to a CPT® or HCPCS code and includes three components. Approximately 55% of the cost assigned to the RVU is the value of the physician's work. The second component of the RVU, approximately 42% of the cost of the physician services, is the practice expense. Malpractice liability insurance expense is the third component assigned as the remaining portion of the RVU.

The approach in developing RVUs is similar to the ABC approach in that the specific service (activity) is analyzed for its direct and indirect resource use. This is also referred to as a weighted procedure, because the various RVU components are assigned different amounts. The type of procedure (medical or surgical), type of setting (facility representing inpatient and nonfacility representing outpatient), and level of malpractice risk are weighted and combined differently for each RVU. More information about RVUs is available at the Medical Group Management Association (MGMA) Relative Value Unit website (www.mgma.com).

Coding Systems for Nursing Care

The **Omaha System** is a clinical data-sharing coding system that combines information for problem classification, the intervention plan, and outcomes rating. Nurses and other health professionals use the Omaha System in settings across the continuum of care, including home health, public health, and hospital facilities. More information about this coding system that is increasingly used in clinical information systems is available at the Omaha System website (www.omahasystem.org).

Home health agencies (HHAs) require the **Outcome and Assessment Information Set (OASIS)** for Medicare compliance and reimbursement. CMS developed OASIS as a set of data items for the assessment and outcomes evaluation of adult home health clients. Data items address areas such as health status, functional status, the support system, and client sociodemographics. More information about this coding system for HHAs is available at the OASIS website (www.cms.gov).

CONCLUSION

This chapter gives nurses an overview of cost-finding and methods for allocating costs across departments and work units. The calculation and application of break-even analysis and the CM are presented as techniques to determine the impact of volume on costs and profits. Concepts relevant to setting prices and charges are explained, as well as some commonly used codes for classifying resources used by nurses and other health care providers.

Discussion and Exercises

1. Make a list of all the support services (such as housekeeping, security, and dietary services) required in your work setting or clinical assignment. Estimate the annual costs of each of these support services. Compare your estimates with the estimates made by your classmates and discuss.
2. Think about a health care program or project that generates revenues. What are the estimated TFCs for the program or project? The estimated variable costs per UOS? The estimated revenue (or price) per UOS? Discuss any questions or difficulties encountered in estimating fixed costs, variable costs, and revenue.
3. Using the information from exercise #2, prepare a break-even analysis to estimate the UOS needed to break-even. Include a profit target and revise the break-even analysis to estimate the UOS needed to break-even and reach your profit target. Do you think that there would be adequate demand (enough UOS) for your program or project to be profitable?

REFERENCES

Healthcare Financial Management Association (HFMA). (June 2004). *Strategic price setting: Ensuring your financial viability through price modeling.* Washington, DC: HFMA.

Institute for Healthcare Improvement (IHI). (March 22, 2011). *Glossary of frequently used financial terms.* Cambridge, MA: IHI.

Nugent, M. (2004, December). The price is right: for optimal price setting, you'll need a strategic focus that adjusts for recent industry trends. *Healthcare Financial Management, 58*(12), 56–63.

Patient Protection and Affordable Care Act (PPACA), Pub. L. No. 111–148, §2702, 124 Stat. 119, 318–319 (2010). Retrieved from http://housedocs.house.gov/energycommerce/ppacacon.pdf

Penner, S. J. & Spencer, M .D. (in press). Acute care utilization, staffing and financial indicators. In K. T. Waxman (Ed.), *Financial & business management for the doctor of nursing practice.* New York, NY: Springer Publishing Company.

Reinhardt, U. E. (2006). The pricing of U.S. hospital services: Chaos behind a veil of secrecy. *Health Affairs, 25*(1), 57–69.

San Francisco Department of Public Health (SFDPH) (2009, January). *Fiscal Year 2007 San Francisco Hospital Charity Care Report Summary.* Prepared by the San Francisco Department of Public Health Office of Policy and Planning. Presented to the San Francisco Health Commission January 2009. San Francisco, CA: San Francisco Department of Public Health Office of Policy and Planning. Retrieved from http://www.sfdph.org/dph/files/reports/PolPlanRpts.asp

CROSSWORD: *Chapter 8—Cost-Finding, Break-Even, and Charges*

Across

2 All direct fixed costs plus all indirect fixed costs associated with a given level of volume (abbreviation).

4 The fixed costs associated with each UOS, calculated by dividing TFC by the volume (abbreviation).

6 A cost allocation method that focuses on the indirect and direct costs of specific activities (abbreviation).

8 The dollar amount available from revenues to first cover fixed costs (including overhead), then contribute to profits (abbreviation).

9 All costs associated with a given level of volume that change based on changes in volume (abbreviation).

10 Setting an excessively high price for health care goods and services when the demand is inelastic.

11 The CM per UOS, which may reflect overhead, handling fees, mark-ups, or surcharges, calculated as price less VCU (abbreviation).

13 A coding system that quantifies physician services for reimbursement purposes (abbreviation).

14 The full price assigned to a good or service, before discounts or other reductions.

16 The amount of reimbursement for each UOS, also called the price (abbreviation).

Down

1 The variable cost associated with each UOS (abbreviation).

2 The total costs associated with each UOS, calculated by dividing TC by the volume (abbreviation).

3 A coding system CMS developed to classify services and products not included in the CPT® codes (abbreviation).

5 A hospital's comprehensive list of the prices of all goods and services for which a separate charge exists.

7 A coding system CMS developed to assess and evaluate outcomes for adult home health clients (abbreviation).

8 A hospital's comprehensive list of the prices of all goods and services for which a separate charge exists (abbreviation).

9 Total fixed costs plus total variable costs (abbreviation).

12 The revenue associated with a given level of volume at a given price or amount of reimbursement (abbreviation).

14 Dividing hospital costs by hospital charges (gross revenues) to determine the relationship of costs to charges (abbreviation).

15 Cost assignment that includes the three components of physician work value, practice expense, and malpractice liability insurance expense (abbreviation).

Chapter 9: CBA, CEA, CUA, and CER

Not everything that can be counted counts, and not everything that counts can be counted—Albert Einstein

Learning Objectives

1. Compare and contrast the application of CBA, CEA, and CUA in the financial analysis of health care programs and services.
2. Demonstrate the procedures for conducting a cost-benefit analysis.
3. Demonstrate the procedures for conducting a cost effectiveness analysis.
4. Critique assumptions about light-green dollars compared to dark-green dollars for projects that improve nursing care quality.

Key Terms

benefit-cost ratio (B/C ratio)
benefits
comparative effectiveness research (CER)
compounded
cost per unit of effectiveness (CE)
cost-benefit analysis (CBA)
cost-effectiveness analysis (CEA)
cost-utility analysis (CUA)

dark-green dollars
default
discounting
discount rate
effectiveness per unit of cost (EC)
evidence-based practice (EBP)
human capital
intangibles
light-green dollars
net benefits

net contribution
objective function
present value
primary benefits
program evaluation
quality-adjusted life year (QALY)
Rule of Seventy
secondary benefits
tangibles
willingness to pay

Chapter 5 presents budgeting and Chapter 8 discusses the use of break-even analysis in understanding financial performance and making financial decisions. This chapter presents three more financial analysis techniques that nurses might review or prepare to evaluate health care programs and services. **Cost-benefit analysis (CBA)** is a method of evaluating the benefits relative to the costs of a program or service. **Cost-effectiveness analysis (CEA)** is a method of evaluating and comparing the benefits and costs among two or more alternative programs or services. **Cost-utility analysis (CUA)** is a method of evaluating the benefits to quality of life relative to the costs of a program or service. CBA, CEA, and CUA are financial analyses that nurses might include to support a funding request in a business plan (see Chapter 10).

An additional approach is included in this chapter related to the evaluation of the benefits of clinical programs and services. **Comparative effectiveness research (CER)** relies on new and existing research comparing treatments, tests, procedures, or services in order to guide clinicians and consumers to make the best decisions about health care. This chapter first discusses basic concepts of CBA, CEA, and CUA, and ends with an overview of CER.

CBA

CBA has several applications that are useful to nurses. CBA is a technique that can help guide decision-making by determining the benefits achieved by a specific intervention. CBA helps identify the optimal size for projects or programs, and can provide a framework for program evaluation or the financial analysis in a business plan, as discussed in Chapter 10.

CBA requires that resources and benefits can be expressed as **tangibles**, measures that either are or can be converted to dollar amounts. For example, a nurse case management program for pregnant, diabetic women would measure the costs of the nurse case management services. These costs are compared to the program's benefits, such as the reduction in hospital days related to complications. The findings from the case management program CBA analysis is used in making decisions about the program's value, and to propose expanding the program to serve more women.

CBA is less useful when the analysis involves **intangibles**, measures that cannot be quantified as monetary units. For example, pregnant diabetic women might experience reduced fear and worry because they are monitored by the nurse case managers. Unless a way is found to quantify the dollar value of patient fear and worry, these intangibles cannot be included in the CBA.

The usefulness of CBA is also limited when **externalities**, events beyond the control of the program or service, increase risk or uncertainty about outcomes. Risk represents a calculated or estimated probability of an external event or outcome. For example, if some of the women in the case management program do not have a means of transportation, it might reduce their probability of participating in the program by 50 percent. If the nurse case managers cannot provide transportation for these women, this externality limits program participation and reduces the program's benefits.

Uncertainty represents a completely unknown probability of an external event or outcome. **Evidence-based practice (EBP)**, or the application of research evidence to improve health care interventions, is one way of reducing uncertainty. The use of accepted guidelines, procedures, and pathways in the nurse case management program reduces uncertainty about the outcomes for pregnant diabetic women. Reducing uncertainty more clearly establishes that the program costs result in tangible benefits.

CBA Procedures

The first step in conducting a CBA is to identify the **objective function**, or what the program or service is intended to achieve. The objective function or functions must be tangible and measurable. For example, the nurse case management program for pregnant and diabetic women is expected to reduce complications related to pregnancy and diabetes. The complications rate for the case-managed pregnant women is an example of a measure of an objective function.

Costs

Costs are resources required in producing the objective function of health care goods or services. Costs must be measurable, and in monetary units or in a form that can be converted to monetary units. For example, intangible costs, such as discomfort, must be possible to quantify and convert to dollars to be entered in the analysis. Opportunity costs are the dollar value of an alternative benefit that could result during the same time period or with the same amount of resources as invested in the current activity. For example, if it is possible to convert the value of the time a client spends waiting for health care services, wait time may be entered into the CBA as an opportunity cost.

Costs may be **direct costs**, or resources used as inputs in the production of an objective function. For example, the wages and benefits paid for nursing services in the nurse case management program are direct costs. **Indirect costs** are resources used that are not direct inputs in the production of an objective function. Expenses paid for the staff of the nurse case management program to attend conferences is an example of an indirect cost. Chapter 8 discusses direct and indirect costs in more detail.

When nurses prepare a CBA, one suggestion is to base the program costs or services on the operating expense budget. The operating expense budget for the nurse case management program should already include the direct and indirect costs required for providing services that address the objective function of reducing maternal complications among diabetic women. Chapter 6 discusses the preparation of the operating expense budget.

If the CBA is prepared to analyze the value of a capital expenditure, the nurse may measure costs using the capital budget. Chapter 7 discusses the preparation of a capital budget. Chapter 8 discusses approaches to cost-finding to more accurately allocate and include all direct and indirect costs in a budget or financial analysis.

Benefits

Benefits are the outputs or contributions produced by the objective function, including cost savings achieved by the intervention. Benefits, like costs, must either be in monetary units or in a form that can be converted to monetary units. For example, a reduction in hospital days achieved by reducing complications of pregnancy and diabetes with nurse case management results in a tangible cost savings that can be measured using inpatient hospital charges. Intangible benefits, such as patient satisfaction with the monitoring provided by the nurse case management program, must be quantified and converted to monetary units before they are entered into the analysis.

Benefits may be classified as **primary benefits**, which result directly from the objective function. For example, the reduction in hospital costs for the pregnant, diabetic women is a primary benefit of the nurse case management program. Primary benefits are most frequently entered into a CBA.

Secondary benefits represent indirect contributions that result from the objective function. For example, improved school performance of the children born to the participants of the nurse case management program is a secondary benefit. It is often difficult to obtain or include tangible measures of secondary benefits when calculating CBA. For example, the impact on school performance of the program participants' children occurs years after the participants complete the program. This extends the time required for the analyses and makes data collection difficult. In addition, many factors might impact on these children's school performance, making it difficult to verify that prenatal care actually contributed to school performance.

Net Benefits

Once the objective function(s), costs, and benefits are identified, and the costs and benefits converted to monetary units, **net benefits** (also referred to as **net contribution**) calculation is required. The dollar value of total costs are subtracted from the dollar value of total benefits to determine the net benefits. If benefits exceed costs, the intervention generates more benefits than costs, and may be recommended or supported on that basis. If costs exceed benefits, the intervention generates more costs than benefits, and may be considered too costly or inefficient to recommend or support.

For example, the nurse case management program reports that its annual cost, including direct and indirect costs, is $250,000 over the year, with benefits over the same year of $375,000. The benefits represent reductions in hospital and physician visit costs by reducing the rate of diabetes and pregnancy complications among the clients. Net benefits are calculated as $125,000 ($375,000–$250,000). In other words, the nurse case management program generated $125,000 in net benefits (cost savings) over the year of operation, demonstrating the program's value.

Another calculation used in CBA is the **benefit-cost ratio (B/C ratio)**, calculated by dividing the total benefits by the total costs. This calculation allows for comparisons across similar interventions. Interventions with B/C ratios greater than one generate more benefits than costs. If the B/C ratio is less than one, the costs exceed benefits. A B/C ratio of 2.0 means that for every $1 of cost, the intervention generates $2 in benefits. By contrast, a B/C ratio of 0.5 indicates that for every $1 of cost, the intervention only generates $0.50 in benefits.

For example, the nurse case management program generates $250,000 in costs and $375,000 in benefits over the same year. The B/C ratio is 1.5 ($375,000 ÷ $250,000). In other words, the nurse case management program generates $1.50 in benefits for every $1.00 in cost. This is another way to show that the program demonstrates value in reducing the costs of maternal complications. The program can also be compared to other similar programs using the B/C ratio.

Figure 9.1 summarizes terms and calculations for performing a CBA. A sample CBA presented in Appendix 9A presents both the net benefits and the B/C ratios for an adult asthma education program evaluation.

"Light-Green" and "Dark-Green" Dollars

One recent controversy in health care is the debate about light-green dollars that represent theoretical or potential savings, and dark-green dollars that can actually be tracked in budgets and other financial reports (Martin, Neumann, Mountford, Bisognano, & Nolan, 2009). For example, assume the nurse case manager program for pregnant diabetic women is funded by Welby ACO. The nurse case managers may justify the program based on savings from reducing hospital LOS related to maternal complications. If these savings can be clearly documented and associated with the nurse case management program outcomes, they will be interpreted as "dark-green dollars" and Welby ACO is more likely to continue funding the program. If it is not possible to clearly associate the nurse case management program outcomes with hospital savings, the CBA results may be perceived as "light-green dollars."

It is often more difficult to justify programs on the basis of "light-green dollars." Many administrators prefer to support programs and projects that generate revenues, which translate into "dark-green dollars." On the other hand, nurses should make a business case for programs and projects that can save money and improve patient care, whether

Item	Calculation	Interpretation
Costs	Total program or service costs	Estimate direct and indirect costs for each program or service compared in a CEA. Operating expense budget(s) useful in estimating costs.
Cost-benefit analysis (CBA):		
Benefits	Total program or service savings or contributions	Tangible primary and secondary benefits.
Net benefit	Total benefits - Total costs	Positive net benefits indicate program or service value or success. Estimates dollar amount of program savings or contribution after costs are covered.
Benefit-cost (B/C) ratio	Total benefits ÷ Total costs	Shows that for every $1 spent by program or service there is $x benefit. Enables comparison of CBA across various programs.
Cost-effectiveness analysis (CEA):		
Cost per unit of effectiveness	$CE = C \div E$	Want to minimize cost, find least expensive program or service that achieves the objective function.
Effectiveness per unit of cost	$EC = E \div C$	Want to maximize effectiveness, find the program or service that most effectively achieves the objective function for the amount of dollars spent.

Figure 9.1 *Terms and Calculations for CBA and CEA*

they generate light- or dark-green dollars. Advocacy for improving the quality of care, the patient's quality of life, the health of the community, and cost-effective services is an important part of the nurse's role. Nurses demonstrate leadership when they apply their knowledge to improve care and to point out potential short-term and long-term savings from improving care.

Improved financial reporting mechanisms and transparency in sharing information can help nurses overcome the "light-green" versus the "dark-green" dollars problem. Nurses must show a clear evidence base for their interventions, and learn how to accurately measure and report costs and benefits. Networking and open communication with health care administrators is an important step in demonstrating program or project value. More discussion on "light-green" and "dark-green" dollars is presented at the Healthcare Financial Management Association (HFMA) Finding the "Dark Green" Savings website (www.hfma.org).

Discounting, Discount Rate, and Present Value

Discounting, or converting the future value of a monetary unit to its present value, is discussed briefly and only in general terms in this text. Readers are expected to learn how to prepare simple, short-term CBAs for which discounting is not needed. Discounting is not included in the sample CBA.

Discounting enables the calculation and analysis of costs and benefits for specified numbers of years into the future. Discounting is required when very costly, long-term projects such as major renovation or construction are the objective function. Discount rate calculation is usually not required for smaller, short-term projects of only one year. Most program and quality improvement projects that nurses develop do not require discounting.

The **discount rate** is the interest rate used in the discounting calculation. Theoretically, the discount rate is determined by the rate at which people or institutions are willing to give up current consumption for future consumption by establishing savings. The discount rate also reflects the rate at which a borrower pays for funds, which depends to a large extent on the amount of risk, which may be real or perceived by the lender. The greater the risk of **default** (failure to repay the loan), the higher the interest rate charged to the borrower. The longer the life of the project, the higher the interest rate, as long-term projects requiring long-term debt are considered to carry more risk than short-term projects carrying short-term debt.

Discounting is calculated by finding the **present value** or monetary value of an investment and its discount (interest) rate for a specified number of years into the future. Present value calculation requires estimates of the interest rate (discount rate), time period of the investment, and future value of the investment. It is assumed that the interest is **compounded**, in other words, the interest earned in each time period earns interest in future time periods. If the cost of the investment equals or exceeds the present value, then the project may not be worth the investment. If the cost of the investment is less than the present value, the project is likely to be profitable.

For example, if the managers of XYZ Health Corporation evaluate a business plan to borrow money to build a new long-term care facility, they will determine the interest rate and the time period of the loan. Assume for this example there is an 11% interest rate and a 20-year loan. They will then estimate the present value of each of the annual cash inflows for the long-term care facility over the time period of the loan. Assume for this example that the long-term care facility is built in 2 years, so operates and generates cash flow for 18 years of the loan. The sum of the present values for the cash inflows from year 3 (when the long-term care facility begins generating revenue) through year 20 (the last year of the loan) is $6,200,000.

If the business plan proposes an investment of $6,200,000, the XYZ Health Corporation managers may reject the plan and put the money in what they feel might be a better, more profitable investment. If the proposed investment exceeds the present value of $6,200,000, the managers will almost certainly reject the proposal as unprofitable. However, if the business plan proposes an investment less than the present value of $6,200,000, for example, showing that the long-term care facility can be built with a current investment of only $5,500,000, then the managers are likely to see this as a profitable investment and accept the plan.

Table 9.1 shows the impact of various discount rates applied over selected time periods given a future value of $100. Note that as the discount rate increases, the present value of the investment decreases. For example, a $78.35 investment is required over 5 years for a $100 future value at a 5% discount rate, but only $49.72 is required when the discount rate increases to 15% for the same time period and future value. In addition, as the time period increases, the present value of the investment decreases. For example, a $78.35 investment is required over 5 years for a $100 future value at a 5% discount rate, but only $37.69 is required when the time period increases to 20 years.

A rule of thumb used in estimating financial returns is the **Rule of Seventy**, that an investment earning 7.2% interest compounded annually is estimated to double every 10 years. Table 9.1 shows that the Rule of Seventy also works in reverse. In other words, at a discount rate of 7.2%, the present value (investment) is about half the future value in 10 years. The present value of $49.89, located at the intersection of a 7.2% discount rate and a 10-year time period, is about half the future value of $100.

It is important to remember that the discount rate is closely related to the time frame of the intervention and analysis. For example, if benefits are analyzed over 10 years, a 10% discount rate reduces all long-term benefits to zero. One suggestion is to calculate net benefits using the best available discount rate, then re-calculate net benefits without including a discount rate to see the impact a discount rate makes on the long-term estimates. If discounting makes a substantial impact on the net benefits, then discounting should be included in

Table 9.1 *Effect of Discount Rates Over Specified Time Periods for Future Value of $100*

Year	5%	7.2%	10%	12.5%	15%
5	(78.35)	(70.64)	(62.09)	(55.49)	(49.72)
10	(61.39)	(49.89)	(38.55)	(30.79)	(24.72)
15	(48.10)	(35.24)	(23.94)	(17.09)	(12.29)
20	(37.69)	(24.89)	(14.86)	(9.48)	(6.11)

the CBA. More information on discounting is available at the Discount Rate Determination website (http://www.academicearth.org/lectures/discount-rate-information-healthcare).

CEA

CEA is useful in comparing alternatives among various programs and services, in order to determine the least costly means to obtain the desired benefit. Unlike CBA, CEA does not compare benefits to costs, but assumes a benefit is produced by an objective function, whether the benefit is tangible or intangible. Therefore, CEA is useful when benefits cannot be converted to dollar values.

For example, a public health department assumes that prenatal care for women with high-risk pregnancies is a desired benefit. The health department might then compare a nurse case management prenatal program with other prenatal programs, to determine the program that provides prenatal care for high-risk pregnant women at the lowest cost. The health department would then be expected to choose the least costly program that achieves the objective function of prenatal care for funding and support.

Although benefits need not be quantified for a CEA, it is essential to quantify and convert all costs into monetary units so the interventions may be compared to find the least costly alternative. Both direct and indirect costs are included, as in performing a CBA. If the project is long-term, discounting may also be applied to the total costs of each program. The operating expense budget for each program or service is a suggested source of information on total costs for CEAs that nurses might prepare. If comparing alternative choices for equipment or other capital expenditures, capital budgets for the alternatives are suggested sources for costs to enter in the CEA.

Effectiveness can be estimated for a CEA using objective function measures of achievement. For example, the effectiveness of a nurse case management program for high-risk women might be the number of healthy deliveries without maternal or infant complications. Figure 9.1 shows two approaches to a CEA that can be calculated using costs and effectiveness measures.

The first approach to a CEA is to calculate the **cost per unit of effectiveness (CE)**, shown in Figure 9.1. The total program cost for each program compared in a CEA is divided by the appropriate unit of effectiveness. In the prenatal program example, the program costs are divided by the number of healthy deliveries. Programs that minimize the CE demonstrate the greatest value, as they achieve the objective function at the lowest cost (Matthews, 2004).

A second approach to a CEA is to calculate the **effectiveness per unit of cost (EC)**. The appropriate unit of effectiveness is divided by the cost for each program, as shown in Figure 9.1. In the prenatal program example, the number of healthy deliveries are divided by the program costs. Programs that maximize the EC demonstrate the greatest value, as they achieve the highest level of achieving the objective function per dollar spent (Matthews, 2004).

Nurses might compare programs with the same or similar costs using CEA. For example, there are three prenatal programs in the community, and each of them cost about $250,000 over a given year, as shown in Table 9.2. Program A can ensure 50 healthy deliveries; Program B, 75 healthy deliveries; and Program C, 100 healthy deliveries. Program C demonstrates the highest value, with the lowest CE ratio (least cost per healthy delivery) and the highest EC ratio (more healthy deliveries per dollar spent). It makes the most sense to select Program C for funding.

In many situations, nurses must compare programs reporting different costs using CEA. This scenario presents three prenatal programs that all ensure 100 healthy deliveries for their high-risk clients. Program A costs $250,000, Program B costs $375,000, and Program C costs $500,000, as shown in Table 9.3. In this scenario, Program A demonstrates the highest value, with the lowest CE ratio and the highest EC ratio. It makes the most sense to select Program A for funding.

A sample CEA is featured in Appendix 9B, which compares alternative interventions for postsurgical pain reduction. More information about CEA is available at the Focus on CEA at the AHRQ website (www.ahrq.gov).

CUA

In some cases, it is important to consider the valuation of human life and quality of life in comparing costs to benefits. Financial analyses that include quality of life measures are often referred to as CUA.

Table 9.2 *Cost-Effectiveness Analysis (CEA) With the Same Program Costs*

Values	Alternatives		
	A	B	C
Cost	$250,000	$250,000	$250,000
Total healthy deliveries	50	75	100
CE ratio (cost per healthy delivery)	$5000	$3333	$2500
EC ratio (healthy deliveries given the cost)	0.0002	0.0003	0.0004

Source: Adapted from Matthews, November 3, 2004.

Table 9.3 *Cost-Effectiveness Analysis (CEA) With the Same Program Outcomes*

Values	Alternatives		
	A	B	C
Cost	$250,000	$375,000	$500,000
Total healthy deliveries	100	100	100
CE ratio (cost per healthy delivery)	$2500	$3750	$5000
EC ratio (healthy deliveries given the cost)	0.0004	0.0003	0.0002

Source: Adapted from Matthews, November 3, 2004.

One method of valuing human life is the **human capital** approach, in which the present value of a person's future earnings are estimated. This approach is commonly applied in assessing legal damages for death or disability. The human capital approach may also be applied in estimating the overall loss in national output from morbidity and mortality (such as the human capital costs of HIV infection), or the production gains for saving and extending life (such as the human capital benefits of influenza immunizations).

Another approach in valuing human life is estimating the **willingness to pay** for risk or safety. For example, wage differentials may be established based on the amount of occupational risk in work settings such as foundries or construction sites. This approach is also utilized in determining the amount consumers are willing to pay for safety devices such as bicycle helmets or smoke detectors. More information is available at an American Public Health Association website, featuring a 1982 article, The Economic Value of Life: Linking Theory to Practice (www.ajph.aphapublications.org).

QALY

The calculation of **quality-adjusted life years (QALYs)** enables nurses to assess the proportion of the state of health an individual experiences over a year. QALY is a method to assign dollar values to life and the benefits of health care, by weighting each remaining year of life by the expected quality of life measure for that year. A CUA might then compare the treatment costs to the benefits as valued by the QALY calculation. A CUA might also compare costs per QALY among different treatments to find the treatment with the lowest cost per QALY (McCabe, 2009).

QALYs are calculated using quality of life measures from standardized instruments such as the 15-D Health-Related Quality of Life Index. For example, an adult with emphysema might have a 15-D score of 0.75 (out of a maximum score of 1.0, which represents optimal health) for a given year. Multiplying the score by 1 year results in a QALY of 0.75. In other words, the individual lost 0.25 QALY because of the emphysema.

The person with emphysema might be expected to live for 10 years, experiencing a 15-D score of 0.75 for 5 years (designated as weight$_a$), and a 15-D score of 0.5 for the remaining 5 years of life (designated as weight$_b$). The QALY calculation for these 10 years of life is as follows:

QALY = (QALY weight$_a$ × years of life) + (QALY weight$_b$ × years of life)
6.25 QALY = (0.75 × 5) + (0.5 × 5)

In other words, the person with emphysema experiences 6.25 QALYs from the 10 remaining years of life.

Text Box 9.1 summarizes some of the fundamental applications and differences between CBA and CEA. The sample CUA in Appendix 9C estimates a dollar value based on the QALY scores and productivity measures. More information about CBA, CEA, and CUA is available at the National Institutes of Health (NIH) Cost Analysis Methods for health technology assessment website (www.nlm.nih.gov).

Program Evaluation

Program evaluation is the application of analytic methods to determine whether a program is needed, utilizes its resources effectively, operates as planned, and meets its objectives. When applied to health care settings, program evaluation helps identify strengths and problem areas, justify a program's continued existence, and support program expansion. In applying CBA to program evaluation, the first step is to identify measurable program objectives and expected outcomes. The direct and indirect costs for resources used to meet

Text Box 9.1 *Comparison of CBA, CEA, and CUA*

CBA	CEA	CUA
Both benefits and costs are evaluated	Costs are evaluated, but benefits are assumed to be of value	The focus is the costs per QALY
Must quantify and convert both costs and benefits to monetary units	Costs must be in monetary units, but benefits may be intangible	Costs are in monetary units; QALYs measure life and health that can be compared across individuals
Compare the costs of a project, program, or process to its benefits	Compare the costs of two or more alternative projects, programs, or processes, assuming the same benefits	Compare the costs of alternatives that feature different health outcomes or benefits

the program objectives are calculated, as well as the dollar value of the benefits from the outcomes. Costs are then subtracted from the benefits (or vice versa) to determine if the program's benefits equal or exceed its costs. A B/C ratio is also calculated to determine the value of benefits generated per dollar of costs.

In applying CEA to program evaluation, the total program costs under evaluation may be compared to the total costs of other programs providing similar benefits, to decide if the program under evaluation keeps its costs at or under that of the comparison programs. Program evaluation using CUA would link the total costs of the program under evaluation to the quality of life outcomes, using QALYs or other related measures. The CBA, CEA, or CUA may be the primary method of evaluating the program, or one of multiple methods used in combination for program evaluation. More information and resources for program evaluation are available from the Centers for Disease Control and Prevention (CDC) website, A Framework for Program Evaluation (www.cdc.gov).

Limitations of CBA, CEA, and CUA

It is important to understand that CBA, CEA, and CUA have limitations. The analyses are only as accurate and complete as the data used in the calculations. It may not be possible to measure all of the relevant costs and benefits or to convert all relevant measures to dollars. As a result, some relevant costs and benefits may be overlooked.

It is also important to remember that health care decisions are not solely based on generating savings or profits. For example, a CBA alone is likely insufficient in conducting a program evaluation. Other ways of determining program value, such as its fit with the organizational mission, reputation, and community support, are important considerations.

CUAs rely on QALY estimates, which might not be reliable or relevant for application in the CUA. There may also be conflicting ideas about how to approach the valuing of human life and disability. More discussion of possible QALY limitations in CUAs is available from the online article, CUA: Use QALYs Only With Great Caution (www.cmaj.ca).

CER

In recent years, increasing emphasis and attention has been focused on EBP. CER incorporates new and existing research to generate evidence useful for nursing practice and clinical guidelines.

CER does not necessarily involve cost or other financial analysis. However, CER is included as an approach in this chapter, because the value of clinical interventions must be based on the research evidence. Neither the least costly nor the most costly intervention is certain to result in the best clinical outcomes. Health professionals must use expert judgment and evidence to guide clinical decisions. Nurses must therefore not only weigh the costs of programs and services, but make sure that their interventions are supported by the evidence as informed by CER. More information about CER is available at the Agency for Health Research and Quality website (www.effectivehealthcare.ahrq.gov), What Is Comparative Effectiveness Research? The health economist Uwe Reinhardt also discusses CER in a blog post, 'Cost-Effectiveness Analysis' and U.S. Health Care (Reinhardt, 2009).

CONCLUSION

This chapter presents concepts in developing a CBA, CEA, or CUA for health care programs or services. Discounting is discussed so nurses are aware of the financial implications of very high-cost and long-term projects. CER is discussed to remind nurses that sound research evidence may be a more important basis for clinical guidelines than costs or financial benefits.

Discussion and Exercises

1. Think about a health care program or project that would improve care or save money in your work setting or clinical assignment. Using the budget planning worksheet in Chapter 6 (Appendix 6A), prepare a budget that represents the costs of your program or project.
2. Refer to your health care program or project from exercise #1. List all the possible benefits of this program or projects, tangible and intangible. Add up the dollar value of all the tangible benefits. Prepare a CBA and report whether the benefits or savings are greater than the costs.
3. Think about equipment purchases for your work setting or clinical assignment. How might you conduct a simple CEA, comparing prices and performance for several brands of equipment? What might be effectiveness measures?

REFERENCES

Martin, L. A., Neumann, C. W., Mountford, J., Bisognano, M., & Nolan, T. W. (2009). *Increasing efficiency and enhancing value in health care: Ways to achieve savings in operating costs per year.* IHI Innovation Series white paper. Cambridge, Massachusetts: Institute for Healthcare Improvement. Retrieved from www.IHI.org

Matthews, H. S. (2004). *Courses: Civil systems investment planning and pricing (12–706) and economic analysis of private and public projects (73–359).* Lecture 18-11/3/2004. PowerPoint presentation. Pittsburgh, PA: Civil & Environmental Engineering, Carnegie Mellon University. Retrieved June 2, 2012 from http://www.slidefinder.net/c/cost_effectiveness_analysis_cea_scott/lec18-cea-04/7513244

McCabe, C. (2009). *What is cost-utility analysis?* NPR09-1099. Hayward Medical Communications. Supported by Sanofi-Aventis. http://www.whatisseries.co.uk/whatis

Reinhardt, U. E. (2009). "Cost-Effectiveness Analysis" and Health Care. Retrieved from http://economix.blogs.nytimes.com/2009/03/13/cost-effectiveness-analysis-and-us-health-care

CROSSWORD: *Chapter 9—CBA, CEA, CUA, and CER*

Across

1   The total program cost for each program compared in a CEA is divided by the appropriate unit of effectiveness (abbreviation).
3   A method of evaluating and comparing the benefits and costs among two or more alternative programs or services (abbreviation).
4   The application of research evidence to improve health care interventions (abbreviation).
5   A method of evaluating the benefits to quality of life relative to the costs of a program or service (abbreviation).
8   Measures that cannot be converted to dollar amounts.
9   A method that assigns dollar values to human life by weighting each remaining year of life by the expected quality of life measure for that year (abbreviation).
12 The outputs or contributions produced by the objective function, including cost savings achieved by the intervention.

Down

1   The interest earned in each time period earns interest in future time periods.
2   Failure to repay a loan.
4   The appropriate unit of effectiveness is divided by the cost for each program compared in a CEA (abbreviation).
6   Converting the future value of a monetary unit to its present value.
7   Measures that either are or can be converted to dollar amounts.
10 A method of evaluating the benefits relative to the costs of a program or service (abbreviation).
11 A method for guiding health care decisions based on new and existing research comparing treatments or procedures (abbreviation).

APPENDIX 9A: A COST-BENEFIT ANALYSIS EVALUATING ADULT OUTPATIENT ASTHMA EDUCATION FEBRUARY 8, 2013

Patient Education Committee of the Healthy Ways Clinic and the Healthy Ways Hospital Financial Office

Asthma is an inflammatory disorder of an individual's airway that is chronic and may persist into adulthood. Symptoms include coughing, wheezing, chest tightness, and hypersensitivity to substances such as pollen or perfume. This breathing disorder may result in death; patient education is a way to help adults control their asthma and reduce risk as well as acute care costs. Studies have shown that asthma education helps adults reduce their symptoms and use of emergency care, and improves compliance with treatment.

This is a CBA evaluating FY 2012 Healthy Ways Clinic's Adult Asthma Education Program (AAEP), conducted by the Patient Education Committee of the Healthy Ways Clinic in collaboration with the Healthy Ways Hospital Financial Office. The asthma education classes are a disease management effort that began operation in January 2, 2012, as a series of year-round, weekly classes for adult outpatient asthmatics that last for 2 hours per class. Participants attend a class session scheduled from 5:30 p.m. to 7:30 p.m. every Tuesday, except holidays.

The classes are conducted by certified respiratory therapists employed by Healthy Ways Clinic, under the supervision of an RN Coordinator. All instructors are trained in asthma management and patient education techniques; only one instructor is scheduled per class. Class size is limited to no more than 10 patients, who may bring a family member or companion. Teaching approaches include lectures to the group, one-on-one personalized instruction, small group work, and peer support.

AAEP Costs

The FY 2012 budget for the AAEP is $10,500 (note that the actual budget was only $10,341 because variable costs were lower than projected). The Healthy Ways Hospital Medical Services (25%), Allergy Services (25%), and the Emergency Care Departments (25%) share funding for the adult asthma classes; the remaining 25% of funding is from Healthy Ways Clinic. All of these departments, particularly Emergency Care, are impacted by adult patients in acute asthmatic distress; this analysis demonstrates that each of these departments generated benefits (cost savings) over FY 2012 from their $2625 contribution to the AAEP.

Fixed costs for the adult asthma classes include staff time for the instructors, program coordinator, and clerical support. Other fixed costs include instructor training, instructor materials, and refreshments served each class session. Variable costs consist of educational materials provided to each patient attending the class. Indirect costs (overhead expenses) are excluded, as Healthy Ways Clinic is open during the times the classes are scheduled, so any additional housekeeping, security, or other indirect costs are assumed to be negligible. Table 9A.1 presents a detailed breakdown of the adult asthma education expense budget (the program does not generate revenues).

AAEP Participation

Table 9A.2 provides summary information about class attendance at the AAEP over FY 2012. Healthy Ways Clinic physicians, including family practitioners and allergy specialists, were

Table 9A.1 *Healthy Ways Clinic, Budget for Adult Asthma Classes, FY 2012*

Item	Cost per class	Cost per attendee	Annual cost
Fixed costs			
RN coordinator@ $30/hr for 1 hr/wk	$30	$6	$1530
RT@ $20/hr for 3 hrs/wk	$60	$12	$3060
Clerical@ $12/hr for 3 hrs/wk	$36	$7	$1836
Trainer training	$29	$6	$1500
Trainer materials	$6	$1	$325
Snacks & beverages	$15	$3	$765
Variable costs			
Patient education materials	$26	$5	$1325
Total	$203	$40	$10,341

Table 9A.2 *Summary Information for AAEP Participation, FY 2012*

	First 6 months FY 2012	FY 2012
Attendance	119	261
Average attendance/class	4.6	5.1
Number of classes	26	51

requested to refer symptomatic adult asthma patients to the AAEP for classes beginning January 2, 2012. Average class attendance is about 4 to 5 participants, improving somewhat over the second half of FY 2012. Over the first half of FY 2012, 119 patients attended the asthma management course, with a total of 261 attendees for FY 2012. Data were not available on the number of patients referred by Healthy Ways Clinic physicians, so it was not possible to report enrollment rates.

AAEP Benefits

The benefits of the asthma classes are measured in several ways, some of which are converted to dollar values, as shown in Table 9A.3. Tangible benefits that can be converted to dollar values include reductions in physician visits, ER visits, and hospital days related to asthma symptoms or complications. Data were collected from a review of patient medical records for 25 randomly sampled AAEP participants who attended an asthma management class between January 2 and June 26, 2012. A 6-month retrospective chart review from the date the participant attended the asthma management class provided the baseline data. A 6-month prospective chart review from the date the participant attended the asthma management class provided the AAEP completion data.

Table 9A.3 *Cost Savings Estimates for AAEP, FY 2012[a]*

Item	Baseline	Completion	Sample study savings	Sample study savings per class	Sample study savings per attendee	Estimated annual savings
MD visits	46	28	18	0.69	0.72	187.9
MD costs @ $85/visit	$3910	$2380	$1530	$58.85	$61.20	$15,973
ER visits	7	3	4	0.15	0.16	41.8
ER costs @ $320/visit	$2240	$960	$1280	$49	$51	$13,363
Hospital days	6	4	2	0.08	0.08	20.9
Hospital costs @ $1200/day	$7200	$4800	$2400	$92.31	$96	$25,056
Total medical costs	$13,350	$8140	$5210	$200	$208	$54,392

Note: [a] Annualized based on data from a 6-month retrospective and prospective review of medical records between January 2 and June 26, 2012.

As shown in Table 9A.3, physician visits are estimated at $85 per visit, ER visits at $320 per visit, and hospitalization at $1200 per hospital day. Over the first 6 months of FY 2012, the 25 randomly sampled participants in the AAEP experienced a reduction in physician visits for asthma symptoms or complications from 46 to 28 visits, with an estimated $1530 reduction in physician visit costs for the 25 study participants. ER visits were reduced from seven to three visits, with an estimated $1280 reduction in ER costs for the 25 study participants. Hospital days were reduced from 6 to 4 days, with a $2400 reduction in hospital costs for the 25 study participants.

The sample study medical cost savings per class are estimated by dividing the total sample study savings by 26 (the most conservative estimate for 6 months of weekly classes). On average, each asthma management class is estimated to save $58.85 in physician visit costs, $49.25 in ER visit costs, and $92.31 in hospital costs. Sample study attendee medical cost savings are estimated by dividing the overall cost savings by 25 (the number of attendees in the study). Each person attending the AAEP class is estimated to save $61.20 in physician visits, $51.20 in ER visits, and $96.00 in hospitalization costs.

The sample study medical cost savings were annualized for all participants over FY 2012 by multiplying the estimated per-attendee savings by 261 total attendees. On an annual basis, the AAEP generated an estimated $15,973 in physician visits, $13,363 in ER visits, and $25,056 in hospital costs. The total savings in medical costs generated by the AAEP are estimated at $54,392 (Table 9A.3).

Intangible benefits (not included in the analysis) include increased patient satisfaction and an enhanced reputation for both Healthy Ways Clinic and Healthy Ways Hospital. Patients also report that they can better manage their families, job responsibilities, and other aspects of their lives now that their asthma is under control. Physicians report satisfaction with increased patient compliance and fewer emergency calls.

Net Benefits and B/C Ratios

Table 9A.4 presents the results of the CBA of the AEPP for FY 2012, annualizing the 6-month data over the entire year. Results are estimated per class session, per attendee, and for FY 2012. Results are presented that omit the QALY savings in productive hours from calculations, and that include the QALY savings.

As shown in Table 9A.4, the FY 2012 cost of the AAEP is $10,341 (in line with the budget of $10,500). The cost per class session is calculated by dividing the annual cost by 51 weekly

Table 9A.4 *Cost-Benefit Analysis, AAEP, FY 2012[a]*

Item	Estimated per class	Estimated per attendee	Estimated annual
Program costs	$202.76	$39.62	$10,341.00
Program benefits (savings)	$200.38	$208.40	$54,392.40
CBA:			
Total program net benefits	($2.38)	$168.78	$44,051.40
B/C ratio	0.99	5.3	5.3

Note: [a] Annualized based on data from a 6-month retrospective and prospective review of medical records between January 2 and June 26, 2012.

sessions per year, amounting to $203. The estimated cost per attendee is calculated by dividing the annual cost by the 261 participants, amounting to $40. Program benefits, as shown in Table 9A.4, are first calculated by focusing on the savings in medical costs (MD visits, ER visits, and hospital days), as presented in Table 9A.3. Medical cost savings total $200 per class, $208 per attendee, and $54,392 over FY 2012.

Table 9A.4 then presents the net benefits and the B/C ratios. Net benefits are calculated by subtracting the total costs from the total benefits. For FY 2012 the total net benefits for the AAEP total $44,051. The costs and benefits are then converted to B/C ratios by dividing the medical cost savings by the program costs. The medical cost B/C ratio for FY 2012 is estimated at 5.3 ($54,392 ÷ $10,341). In other words, for every dollar of cost, the AAEP generates $5.30 in medical care savings. These data support the benefits of the AAEP and its continued funding for FY 2013.

One consideration is the opportunity cost of funding the AAEP rather than other health promotion efforts. A review of the literature indicates that the amount of savings for medical costs and QALY productivity is as great or greater for asthma control as for other health promotion efforts such as reduction of dietary fat, exercise programs, or cancer screening.

Additional Evaluation Issues

Several evaluation issues and concerns should be discussed that could not be entered into the CBA calculations. The AAEP was budgeted to accommodate at least 30 more participants than attended over FY 2012. Recommendations are to explore ways to improve the publicity of AAEP throughout the community, to consider weekend classes (Saturday morning or afternoon) for patients reluctant to attend evening classes, and to provide child care for participants. It is also suggested that the RN coordinator explore ways to improve collaboration with clinic and hospital physicians to refer symptomatic patients and follow up on referrals to ensure that patients attend an asthma management class.

Another recommendation is to employ an instructor who is bilingual in Spanish, to better serve potential participants who experience language barriers. There is also a need for a home visit nurse to conduct environmental assessments in patients' homes, so that they are better able to identify and control asthma triggers.

A final recommendation is to budget for annual evaluation costs, which was not done for FY 2012. The evaluation costs for FY 2012 were considered to be "overhead," but given the time required for the 6-month chart reviews, the Patient Education Committee and Financial Office recommend budgeting for these costs in the AAEP budget. Ongoing evaluation is considered essential in assessing the costs and benefits of AAEP, and budgeting these costs gives a more accurate picture of program costs.

A potential opportunity to explore over FY 2013 is a proposed program for children and adolescents, to be conducted in and with the cooperation of the local public school district. A team consisting of Patient Education Committee members and the Financial Office is exploring the possibility of grant funding for this expansion of the asthma education program.

In summary, the AAEP demonstrated benefits exceeding its costs over FY 2012, and has the potential for further improvement and expansion over FY 2013.

APPENDIX 9B: A CEA FOR PROPOSED ALTERNATIVE INTERVENTIONS TO POSTPROCEDURE SURGICAL PAIN REDUCTION DECEMBER 3, 2012

Orthopedic Department, Patient Education Department, Pain Clinic, and Financial Office of Bigtown Hospital

This document presents a CEA of alternative interventions to help Bigtown Hospital patients reduce or control pain following selected surgical procedures. The CEA was used to help the Surgical Pain Intervention Committee (SPI Committee), made up of representatives from the Orthopedic Department, Patient Education Department, Pain Clinic, and Financial Office of Bigtown Hospital, determine which intervention to recommend for funding and support for FY 2013.

The three interventions compared in this CEA are based on complementary and alternative health care approaches to pain reduction and management. Guided imagery is a mental process involving a sensory quality (not just visual, but aural, tactile, olfactory, and kinesthetic perceptions) that is used therapeutically. Hypnosis is achieved via a qualified hypnotist (certified hypnotherapist) who assists the patient to enter into an altered state of consciousness. Biofeedback is a therapeutic method using monitoring instruments to feed back to patients physiological data that normally would not reach their conscious awareness, such as skin temperature. By watching the biofeedback monitoring instrument, patients learn to adjust their mental processes to control bodily processes.

The objective of all these interventions is to help patients reduce and control postsurgical pain. An in-depth review of the literature and research on guided imagery, hypnosis, and biofeedback indicate that each of these approaches are effective in pain reduction and pain management, including pain experienced in the recovery from surgical procedures. Each of these alternative interventions is considered safe and of low risk to postsurgical patients.

Intangible benefits (benefits that cannot be easily quantified or put in dollar amounts) that the SPI Committee assumes from the interventions (guided imagery, hypnosis, and biofeedback) include increased patient satisfaction and better patient compliance. The SPI Committee also assumes each of the interventions would provide a number of benefits that could be measured and put into dollar terms, including reduced postoperative length of stay, reduced complications, fewer visits to the physician for problems with pain, reduced re-hospitalizations, reduced skilled or home health care use, and decreased pain medication use.

These tangible benefits are not quantified for the purposes of the CEA used for the proposal. The reduction of patient postprocedure pain using a low-risk alternative intervention is an objective the SPI Committee departments support. However, once a pain reduction and management intervention is implemented from the alternatives of guided imagery, hypnosis, and biofeedback, a 1-year evaluation will be conducted using CBA methods requiring the quantification and conversion to dollar amounts of as many costs and benefits as possible. A group of physicians from the Pain Clinic will conduct the evaluation to determine the outcomes of the selected intervention.

Intervention Costs

Tables 9B.1, 9B.2, and 9B.3 present per-patient and annual costs for the surgical pain interventions of guided imagery, hypnosis, and biofeedback, respectively. Fixed costs include hourly wages for staff implementing the intervention, staff education, and equipment. Annual fixed costs for staff are estimated by multiplying the estimated hourly wage by the number of hours expected each week, then multiplying by 50 weeks for the year (this excludes holiday schedules for the Surgery Department). Nonpersonnel fixed costs are provided using the best estimates available. Overhead costs (such as housekeeping and administration) are excluded, as they are assumed to be negligible for all of the interventions.

Fixed costs per patient are calculated in Tables 9B.1, 9B.2, and 9B.3 by dividing the annual costs by 197 patients estimated to receive selected surgical procedures for FY 2013.

Table 9B.1 *Patient and Annual Cost Estimates for Guided Imagery, 2013*

Item	Cost per patient ($)	Annual cost ($)
Fixed costs		
Psychology consultant @ $110/hour for 2 hours/week	55.84	11,000
Surgery PA coordinator @ $35/hour for 3 hours/week	26.65	5250
Clerical @ $12/hour for 3 hours/week	9.14	1800
Trainer training for surgery PA	3.81	750
Variable costs (patient "toolkit" package)		
Video cassette tape	4.00	860
CD	5.50	1183
Audio cassette tape	3.00	645
Workbook	7.00	1505
Packaging and mailing	7.15	1537
Total	122.08	24,530

Table 9B.2 *Patient and Annual Cost Estimates for Hypnosis, 2013*

Item	Cost per patient ($)	Annual cost ($)
Fixed costs		
Psychologist @ $110/hour for 12 hours/week	335.03	66,000
Clerical @ $12/hour for 5 hours/week	15.23	3000
Variable costs		
Informational brochure	1.00	215
Total	351.25	69,215

Table 9B.3 *Patient and Annual Cost Estimates for Biofeedback, 2013*

Item	Cost per patient ($)	Annual cost ($)
Fixed costs		
Psychology consultant @ $110/hour for 2 hours/week	55.84	11,000
Surgery PA coordinator @ $35/hour for 8 hours/week	71.07	14,000
Clerical @ $12/hour for 3 hours/week	9.14	1800
Trainer training for surgery PA	7.61	1500
2 video monitors with VCR, portable cart, and skin sensors	27.92	5500
Variable costs		
Video cassette tape	5.00	1075
Written information packet	6.00	1290
Total	182.57	36,165

These three procedures, spinal fusion, total hip replacement, and auto hema stem cell transplant, are selected for the application of the pain reduction and control intervention over FY 2013. After evaluating the intervention for FY 2013, a decision will be made about continuing and expanding this project to other surgical patients.

Per patient variable costs in Tables 9B.1, 9B.2, and 9B.3 are estimated using the best available estimates for educational materials. The guided imagery materials are to be mailed to patients in advance of their procedure, so packaging and mailing costs are included. The other two interventions, hypnosis and biofeedback, are implemented during the patient's hospital recovery. Annual variable costs are calculated by multiplying the per-patient variable costs by 215. Although the estimated number of patients are 197, this provides a somewhat more conservative cost estimate and allows for replacement of lost materials or mailings.

Table 9B.1 presents the cost estimates associated with the use of guided imagery. The Surgery PA coordinator will identify patients scheduled for the selected procedures; ensure that the educational items are sent to each patient; and will contact each patient by telephone to be sure the educational materials are received, that the patient is able to view and use these materials, and answer any questions. The Surgery PA coordinator will work in consultation with a staff psychologist. The costs of the guided imagery intervention are estimated as $122.08 per patient, and $24,530 for FY 2013.

Table 9B.2 presents the cost estimates associated with the use of hypnosis. A staff psychologist certified in hypnotherapy will perform the hypnosis, a one-day postprocedure for patients recovering from the selected procedures. Patients will require at least two hypnosis sessions, so staff costs are considerable, although equipment and variable costs are minimal. The hypnosis intervention costs are estimated as $351.25 per patient, and $69,215 for FY 2013.

Table 9B.3 presents the cost estimates associated with the use of biofeedback. As in the case of guided imagery, the Surgical PA coordinator will implement biofeedback in consultation with a staff psychologist. More time is required of the Surgical PA than for guided imagery, as at least one visit must be made to each patient while in the hospital to teach the patient how to use the biofeedback monitoring equipment. Equipment costs are highest for biofeedback, as a special video monitor must be purchased that can provide feedback to patients regarding their skin temperature, and special carts must be purchased so the video

Table 9B.4 Cost-Effectiveness of Interventions, 2013

Approaches	Cost per patient ($)	Annual cost ($)	Guided imagery vs. other intervention per patient ($)	Guided imagery vs. other intervention annual ($)
Guided imagery	122.08	24,530	–	–
Hypnosis	351.25	69,215	229.17	44,685
Biofeedback	182.57	36,165	60.49	11,635

Table 9B.5 Selected Surgical Procedure Costs and Additional Costs per Intervention, 2013

Procedure types and data			Percent increase cost per procedure			Annual added cost per procedure type		
Procedure	No. of procedures	Procedure cost ($)	Guided imagery (%)	Hypnosis (%)	Biofeed-back (%)	Guided imagery ($)	Hypnosis ($)	Biofeed-back ($)
Spinal fusion	111	6705	1.8	5.2	2.7	13,551	8989	20,266
Total hip Replacement	83	6492	1.9	5.4	2.8	10,133	29,154	15,154
Auto hema stem cell transplant	3	75,308	0.2	0.5	0.2	366	1054	548
Total	197							

monitors may be moved to the patient's bedside. The costs of the biofeedback intervention are estimated as $182.57 per patient, and $36,165 for FY 2013.

CEA of Pain Reduction and Control Interventions

The comparison of per-patient and annual costs show that guided imagery is the most cost-effective intervention for postsurgical pain reduction. As shown in Table 9B.4, on a per-patient basis, guided imagery is $229.17 less than hypnosis, and $60.49 less than biofeedback. For FY 2013, guided imagery is $44,685 less than hypnosis and $11,635 less than biofeedback.

Table 9B.5 presents the costs of the three surgical procedures selected to test the pain reduction and control intervention over FY 2013. The three procedures are spinal fusion, total hip replacement, and auto hema stem cell transplant. Of the three procedures, spinal fusion is most frequently performed in the Bigtown Hospital Surgical Department, with 111 procedures estimated for FY 2013 at an average cost per procedure of $6705. Total hip replacements are expected to number 83 over FY 2013, at an average cost of $6492 for auto hema stem cell transplant. The least frequent and most expensive procedure, auto hema stem cell transplant, is expected to be performed only three times, at an average cost per procedure of $75,308.

The addition of guided imagery to the surgical cost "package" would increase spinal fusion procedures by only 1.8%, total hip replacement procedures by only 1.9%, and auto hema stem cell transplants by only 0.2%. Note that as hypnosis and biofeedback are more

Table 9B.6 *Shared Departmental Costs for Interventions, 2013*[a]

Intervention costs			Shared departmental costs		
Approaches	Cost per patient ($)	Annual cost ($)	Pain clinic ($)	Orthopedic surgery ($)	Patient education ($)
Guided imagery	122.08	24,530	8177	8177	8177
Hypnosis	351.25	69,215	23,072	23,072	23,072
Biofeedback	182.57	36,165	12,055	12,055	12,055

Note: [a]Pain Clinic funds 25%, Orthopedic Surgery funds 50%, Patient Education funds 25%.

costly, they each would increase the costs of these procedures more than the use of guided imagery. Table 9B.5 also shows that the annual added costs for each of the selected surgical procedures would be low for guided imagery.

Funding and Cost-Sharing

One difficulty in designing this pain reduction and control program based on alternative and complementary interventions is funding. Many insurers and government payers will not cover the costs of guided imagery, hypnosis, or biofeedback except for very limited, selected conditions. As a result, it is proposed that the SPI Committee departments select the most cost-effective intervention, guided imagery, and implement that intervention for the three selected procedures of spinal fusion, total hip replacement, and auto hema stem cell transplant over FY 2013. Guided imagery will then be evaluated using CBA to determine if the benefits of providing this intervention are greater than the costs to fund the program.

It is further proposed that three Bigtown Hospital departments share the FY 2013 costs for providing guided imagery, as shown in Table 9B.6. If the Pain Clinic, Orthopedic Surgery Department, and Patient Education Department share costs equally, each department will only need to provide $8177 over FY 2013.

In conclusion, after comparing three alternative and complementary interventions for postsurgical pain reduction and control, guided imagery was found to be the most cost-effective. The SPI Committee recommends implementation of guided imagery for FY 2013, with funding shared equally between the Bigtown Hospital Pain Clinic, Orthopedic Surgery Department, and Patient Education Department. A program evaluation utilizing CBA is recommended to begin early in FY 2013 to evaluate the costs and benefits of using guided imagery as an intervention.

APPENDIX 9C: A CUA EVALUATING ADULT OUTPATIENT ASTHMA EDUCATION
FEBRUARY 8, 2013

Bigtown Clinic Patient Education Committee and the
Bigtown Hospital Financial Office

Asthma is an inflammatory disorder of an individual's airway that is chronic and may persist into adulthood. Symptoms include coughing, wheezing, chest tightness, and hypersensitivity to substances such as pollen or perfume. This breathing disorder may result in death; patient education is a way to help adults control their asthma and reduce risk as well as acute care costs. Studies have shown that asthma education helps adults reduce their symptoms and emergency care use as well as improves compliance with treatment.

This is a CUA evaluating FY 2012 Bigtown Clinic's Adult Asthma Education Program (AAEP), conducted by the Patient Education Committee of the Bigtown Clinic in collaboration with the Bigtown Hospital Financial Office. The asthma education classes are a disease management effort that began operation January 2, 2012, as a series of year-round, weekly classes for adult outpatient asthmatics that last 2 hours per class. Participants attend a class session scheduled from 5:30 p.m. to 7:30 p.m. every Tuesday except holidays.

The classes are conducted by certified respiratory therapists employed by Bigtown Clinic, under the supervision of an RN Coordinator. All instructors are trained in asthma management and patient education techniques; only one instructor is scheduled per class. Class size is limited to no more than 10 patients, who may bring a family member or companion. Teaching approaches include lectures to the group, one-on-one personalized instruction, small group work, and peer support. Each participant is also assessed using physiological measures, a review of medication compliance, and a standardized health survey to obtain a baseline Quality-Adjusted Life Year (QALY) score during the class session attended.

AAEP Costs

The FY 2012 budget for the AAEP is $10,500 (note that the actual budget was only $10,341 because variable costs were lower than projected). The Bigtown Hospital Medical Services (25%), Allergy Services (25%), and Emergency Care Departments (25%) share funding for the asthma classes; the remaining 25% of funding is from Bigtown Clinic. All of these departments, particularly Emergency Care, are impacted by adult patients in acute asthmatic distress; this analysis demonstrates that each of these departments generated benefits (cost savings) over FY 2012 from their $2625 contribution to the AAEP.

Fixed costs for the adult asthma classes include staff time for the instructors, program coordinator, and clerical support. Other fixed costs include instructor training, instructor materials, and refreshments served each class session. Variable costs consist of educational materials provided to each patient attending the class. Indirect costs (overhead expenses) are excluded, as Bigtown Clinic is open during the times the classes are scheduled, so any additional housekeeping, security, or other indirect costs are assumed to be negligible. Table 9C.1 presents a detailed breakdown of the adult asthma education expense budget (the program does not generate revenues).

Table 9C.1 *Bigtown Clinic, Budget for Adult Asthma Classes, FY 2012*

Item	Cost per class ($)	Cost per attendee ($)	Annual cost ($)
Fixed costs			
RN coordinator@ $30/hour for 1 hour/week	30	6	1530
RT @ $20/hour for 3 hours/week	60	12	3060
Clerical @ $12/hour for 3 hours/week	36	7	1836
Trainer training	29	6	1500
Trainer materials	6	1	325
Snacks & beverages	15	3	765
Variable costs			
Patient education materials	26	5	1325
Total	203	40	10,341

AAEP Participation

Table 9C.2 provides summary information about class attendance at the AAEP over FY 2012. Bigtown Clinic physicians, including family practitioners and allergy specialists, were requested to refer symptomatic adult asthma patients to the AAEP for classes beginning January 2, 2012. Average class attendance is about 4–5 participants, improving somewhat over the second half of FY 2012. Over the first half of FY 2012, 119 patients attended the asthma management course, with a total of 261 attendees for FY 2012. Data were not available on the number of patients referred by Bigtown Clinic physicians, so it was not possible to report enrollment rates.

AAEP Benefits

The benefits of the asthma classes are measured in several ways, some of which are converted to dollar values, as shown in Table 9C.3. Tangible benefits that can be converted to dollar values include reductions in physician visits, ER visits, and hospital days related to asthma symptoms or complications. Data were collected from a review of patient medical records for 25 randomly sampled AAEP participants who attended an asthma management class between January 2 and June 26, 2012. A 6-month retrospective chart review from the date the participant attended asthma management class provided the baseline data. A 6-month prospective chart review from the date the participant attended the asthma management class provided the AAEP completion data.

As shown in Table 9C.3, physician visits are estimated at $85 per visit, ER visits at $320 per visit, and hospitalization at $1200 per hospital day. Over the first 6 months of FY 2012, the 25 randomly sampled participants in the AAEP experienced a reduction in physician visits for asthma symptoms or complications from 46 to 28 visits, with an estimated $1530 reduction in physician visit costs for the 25 study participants. ER visits were reduced from seven to three visits, with an estimated $1280 reduction in ER costs for the 25 study participants. Hospital days were reduced from 6 to 4 days, with a $2400 reduction in hospital costs for the 25 study participants.

The sample study medical cost savings per class were estimated by dividing the total sample study savings by 26 (the most conservative estimate for 6 months of weekly classes). On average, each asthma management class is estimated to save $58.85 in physician visit costs, $49.25 in ER visit costs, and $92.31 in hospital costs. Sample study attendee medical cost savings were estimated by dividing the overall cost savings by 25 (the number of attendees in the study). Each person attending the AAEP class is estimated to save $61.20 in physician visits, $51.20 in ER visits, and $96.00 in hospitalization costs.

The sample study medical cost savings were annualized for all participants over FY 2012 by multiplying the estimated per-attendee savings by 261 total attendees. On an annual basis, the AAEP generated an estimated $15,973 in physician visits, $13,363 in ER

Table 9C.2 Summary Information for AAEP Participation, FY 2012

	First 6 months FY 2012	FY 2012
Attendance	119	261
Average attendance/class	4.6	5.1
Number of classes	26	51

Table 9C.3 *Cost Savings Estimates for AAEP, FY 2012*[a]

	Baseline ($)	Completion ($)	Sample study savings ($)	Sample study savings per class ($)	Sample study savings per attendee ($)	Estimated annual savings ($)
MD visits	46	28	18	0.69	0.72	187.9
MD costs @ $85/visit	$3910	$2380	$1530	$58.85	$61.20	$15,973
ER visits	7	3	4	0.15	0.16	41.8
ER costs @ $320/visit	$2240	$960	$1280	$49.23	$51.20	$13,363
Hospital days	6	4	2	0.08	0.08	20.9
Hospital costs @ $1200/day	$7200	$4800	$2400	$92.31	$96.00	$25,056
Total medical costs	$13,350	$8140	$5210	$200	$208	$54,392
Average QALY scores	0.83	0.87	0.04			
QALY productive hours	45,464	47,611	2146	82.55	85.8	22,406
QALY costs @ $5/hour	$227,322	$238,053	$10,731	$412.73	$429.24	$112,032
Total	$240,672	$246,193	$15,941	$613.12	$637.64	$166,424

Note: [a]Annualized based on data from a 6-month retrospective and prospective review of medical records and quality of life survey for a random sample of 25 attendees between January 2 and June 26, 2012.

visits, and $25,056 in hospital costs. The total savings in medical costs generated by the AAEP were estimated at $54,392.

The 15-D Health-Related Quality of Life Index was used to survey participants during the asthma management class. The AAEP 25 participants who were randomly sampled for a study of medical costs were also contacted by telephone 6 months after attending the asthma management class for a follow-up Quality of Life survey. Baseline and completion data focused on symptoms and functioning related to asthma were analyzed for the 25 participants who completed the AAEP course the first 6 months of FY 2012. These data are used to calculate QALY scores, then converted to dollar values by assuming that individuals average 12 productive hours per day, with each productive hour valued at $5 as a conservative average.

Given that there are 8760 hours in a year (365 × 24), if half of those hours are productive, they total 4380 hours. As the retrospective and prospective chart reviews for these participants were limited to 6 months, the productive hours for the baseline and completion are 2190 hours. A person with a QALY score of 0.75 would report a 25% loss in productivity, or only 1642.5 (2190 × 0.75) productive hours over the 6-month period. This represents a loss of 547.5 productive hours (2190–1642.5). At a value of $5 per hour, the dollar loss due to asthma symptoms is $2737.50 (547.5 × $5).

Table 9C.3 presents summary data for the QALY scores and value of productive hours from baseline to completion for the 25 sample participants attending an AAEP class the first half of FY 2012. QALY scores improved for these attendees from 0.83 to 0.87. Overall, the participants showed a 2146-hour increase in productive hours, related to better management and control of asthma symptoms. When valued at $5 per hour and annualized, the total savings are estimated at $112,032.

Intangible benefits (not included in the analysis) include increased patient satisfaction and an enhanced reputation for both Bigtown Clinic and Bigtown Hospital. Patients also report they can better manage their families, job responsibilities, and other aspects of their lives now that their asthma is under control. Physicians report satisfaction with increased patient compliance and fewer emergency calls.

Net Benefits and B/C Ratios

Table 9C.4 presents the results of the AEPP CUA for FY 2012, annualizing the 6-month data over the entire year. Results are estimated per class session, per attendee, and for FY 2012. Results are presented that omit the QALY savings in productive hours from calculations, and that include the QALY savings.

As shown in Table 9C.4, the FY 2012 AAEP cost is $10,341 (in line with the budget of $10,500). The cost per class session is calculated by dividing the annual cost by 51 weekly sessions per year, amounting to $203. The estimated cost per attendee is estimated by dividing the annual cost by the 261 participants, amounting to $40. Program benefits, as shown in Table 9C.4, are first calculated by focusing on the savings in medical costs (MD visits, ER visits, and hospital days), as presented in Table 9C.3. Medical cost savings total $200 per class, $208 per attendee, and $54,392 over FY 2012.

The QALY cost savings in Table 9C.4 are calculated based on the baseline and completion QALY scores from surveys of the 25 study participants, valued at $5 per productive hour saved. The annual QALY savings is estimated by multiplying the per-attendee savings estimated in the study of 25 participants by the total 261 participants. QALY cost savings are estimated at $413 per class, $429 per attendee, and $112,032 over FY 2012.

Table 9C.4 then presents the net benefits and the B/C ratios. Net benefits are calculated by subtracting the total costs from the total benefits. For FY 2012, the total net benefits omitting the QALY savings (focused only on medical cost savings) related to the AAEP total $44,051. The total net benefits including QALY savings amount to $156,083.

Table 9C.4 CUA, AAEP, FY 2012[a]

	Estimated per class ($)	Estimated per attendee ($)	Estimated annual ($)
Program costs	203	40	10,341
Medical cost savings	200	208	54,392
QALY cost savings	413	429	112,032
Total benefits	613	638	166,424
CUA			
Medical savings net benefits	(2)	169	44,051
Total program net benefits	410	598	156,083
Medical costs B/C ratio	1.0	5.3	5.3
Total program benefits B/C ratio	3.0	16.1	16.1

Note: [a]Annualized based on data from a 6-month retrospective and prospective review of medical records and quality of life survey for random sample of 25 attendees between January 2 and June 26, 2012.

The costs and benefits are then converted to B/C ratios by dividing the medical cost savings and total cost savings by the program costs. The medical cost B/C ratio for FY 2012 is estimated at 5.3 ($54,392÷ $10,341). In other words, for every dollar of cost, the AAEP generates $5.30 in medical care savings. The total program B/C ratio is 16.1 ($156,083 ÷ $10,341), indicating that for every dollar of cost, the AAEP generates $16.10 in benefits overall. These data support the benefits of the AAEP and its continued funding for FY 2013 (Table 9C.4).

One consideration is the opportunity cost of funding the AAEP rather than other health promotion efforts. A review of the literature indicates that the amount of savings for medical costs and QALY productivity is as great or greater for asthma control as for other health promotion efforts such as reduction of dietary fat, exercise programs, or cancer screening.

Additional Evaluation Issues

Several evaluation issues and concerns should be discussed that could not be entered into the CUA calculations. The AAEP was budgeted to accommodate at least 30 more participants than attended over FY 2012. Recommendations are to explore ways to improve the publicity of AAEP throughout the community, to consider weekend classes (Saturday morning or afternoon) for patients reluctant to attend evening classes, and to provide child care for participants. It is also suggested that the RN coordinator explore ways to improve collaboration with clinic and hospital physicians to refer symptomatic patients and follow up on referrals to ensure that patients attend an asthma management class.

Another recommendation is to employ an instructor who is bilingual in Spanish, to better serve potential participants who experience language barriers. There is also a need for a home visit nurse to conduct environmental assessments in patients' homes, so that they are better able to identify and control asthma triggers.

A final recommendation is to budget for annual evaluation costs, which was not done for FY 2012. The evaluation costs for FY 2012 were considered to be "overhead," but given the time required for the 6-month chart reviews and 15-D Health-Related Quality of Life Index surveys to provide QALY scores, the Patient Education Committee and Financial Office recommend budgeting for these costs in the AAEP budget. Ongoing evaluation is considered essential in assessing the costs and benefits of AAEP, and budgeting these costs gives a more accurate picture of program costs.

A potential opportunity to explore over FY 2013 is a proposed program for children and adolescents, to be conducted in and with the cooperation of the local public school district. A team consisting of Patient Education Committee members and the Financial Office is exploring the possibility of grant funding for this expansion of the asthma education program.

In summary, the AAEP demonstrated benefits exceeding its costs over FY 2012, and has the potential for further improvement and expansion over FY 2013.

Chapter 10: Writing a Business Plan

If opportunity doesn't knock, build a door—Milton Berle

Learning Objectives

1. Describe the components included in most business plans and their purpose.
2. Explain why a special purpose budget is an essential component of a business plan.
3. Identify at least two types of financial analysis useful in developing a business plan.
4. Justify the nurse's role in developing business plans in health care settings.

Key Terms

business case   Gantt chart   market share
entrepreneur   intrapreneur   principal proponent

This chapter helps nurses synthesize skills and concepts in budgeting and financial analysis reviewed throughout the textbook. Business plans enable nurses to make a **business case** that convinces the reader to provide funding and other resources to support the project, program, or other request made in the business plan. Business plans can support expanding programs or recommend starting a new business or venture. In addition, business plans can analyze the impact of staff cuts, program downsizing, or financial risk. Chapter 11 explains concepts in writing a grant proposal as another approach to obtain resources for projects or programs.

WRITING SKILLS FOR BUSINESS PLANS

Appendix 10A.1 provides a business plan feasibility checklist, discussed later in the chapter. The sample business plans found in Appendices 10A.2 through 10A.5 are guides for suggested formatting, content, and length. Note that the sample business plans are also academic papers submitted for course credit. As a result, the authors followed APA guidelines for citing and referencing all outside sources. Business plans prepared in work settings might not require citations and references. However, it is essential to be able to locate one's sources of financial data and other supporting evidence if the CEO, vice president for nursing, or other reviewers have questions. As a result, it is important to keep a file of all sources used in the business plan if citations and references are not included.

The design, formatting, level of detail required, and length of business plans differ across various health care settings, so it is important to learn the formal and informal guidelines and the accepted procedures in one's work setting. It is also important to consider the business plan's proposed size and scope. The scope might be as small as requesting an additional wound dressing cart for the nursing unit, or as large as building an additional wing for the medical center. In some settings or for some purposes, a one-page memo may suffice as a business plan. In other settings or situations, business plans may require many pages of text and extensive data tables and analyses.

The business plan represents the writer's credibility and expertise, and thus requires careful proof-reading for accuracy, clarity, organization, and grammar. Statements and figures must be accurate, with sources provided so the reader can verify assertions. It is essential to carefully check the numbers and calculations used in the plan, and to present calculations so they are clear to the reader.

Nurses should also avoid jargon, explain acronyms, and define terms as needed. Remember that the CEO, administrator, bank officer, or other potential funder may not be familiar with clinical problems or terminology, and must be able to understand the case made for financing what the plan requests. A business plan with grammatical errors and misspelled words reflects a lack of attention that leads to rejection. For all of these reasons, it is important to critically read and re-read drafts of the plan. The business plan should be carefully proofread and revised before it is submitted.

The business plan should have a logical flow and organization, with headings and sub-headings if the document is longer than a few pages. Points made throughout the business plan should logically build upon and link to one another. For example, the business plan's budget should make sense based on the project or program that is recommended.

A brief, one- to two-page executive summary of the business plan is important to include at the beginning of the business plan. In many settings, more than one person will review the business plan. Some administrators might only read the executive summary. It is therefore important to include an executive summary of the business plan that clearly, accurately, and succinctly summarizes the key points. The executive summary should include an overview of the total budget requested in the business plan. If the project in the business plan will generate revenues, the revenue and profit estimates should be included in the executive summary.

Nurse Roles in Writing Business Plans

Nurses may write business plans as **entrepreneurs**, starting or managing their own business enterprise. The idea to establish the Millway University Nurse-Managed Health Center (MNC) could be written as a business plan. An example of a business plan to start a nurse-run clinic is available at the Kansas State Nurses Association website (www.ksnurses.com). The Healthcare Entrepreneur Blog provides a guide for writing a medical practice business plan, as well as other resources (Quatre, 2008). Chapter 12 provides advice for nurse entrepreneurs who consider starting their own businesses.

Nurses frequently have opportunities to write business plans as **intrapreneurs**, or employees developing the business plan to improve the quality of care and profitability in their work setting. Nurses or nurse managers may write business plans as **principal proponents**, when their staff and setting benefit directly from the plan's approval. For example, the business plan for cleaning privacy curtains in Appendix 10A.2 reduces the potential for nocosomial infections on the South Wing nursing unit.

Nurses or nurse managers sometimes prepare business plans in supportive roles for other health professionals in their setting. For example, the nurse manager of Bigtown Hospital's operating rooms might write a business plan to obtain state-of-the-art surgical equipment for a group of surgeons practicing at Bigtown Hospital.

Whether nurses are principal proponents or serve in a supportive role, business plans are typically prepared by teams, not individuals. Nurses must often seek input from other disciplines and departments, and must establish an effective group process. For example, the business plan for cleaning privacy curtains in Appendix 10A.2 requires input from the Housekeeping Department, as housekeeping staff are the personnel who will implement the curtain cleaning.

Business plans often propose a new product or service. For example, Appendix 10A.3 presents a business plan to establish a new outpatient asthma teaching clinic in a public hospital. Business plans may also propose the expansion of an existing program or service. The expansion of East Wing medical-surgical unit discussed in Chapter 6 could be written as a business plan.

BUSINESS PLAN SECTIONS

Business plans are often developed in steps and include specific sections. The first step in developing a business plan, and the first section in most business plans, is problem or need identification, followed by product definition or describing the service or product to be developed. A market analysis follows, then budget estimates, any additional financial analysis, and a conclusion that includes a feasibility statement. Appendix 10A.1 provides a checklist for including all the sections in the business plan.

The business plan worksheet in Appendix 10A.1 provides reminders to consider the feasibility of each section of the business plan. These checkpoints indicate whether the business plan development should continue if the problem, product and market analysis, budget, or financial analysis indicate that the business plan is not cost-effective or profitable (Penner, Spring 2004). Evaluating feasibility as an ongoing part of writing the business plan helps ensure that the business plan is cost-effective and will not waste resources. Text Box 10.1 lists the sections of a business plan, with reminders to check feasibility throughout the process of writing the business plan.

Text Box 10.1 *Business Plan Components and Process*

---

1. Problem or need identification
   ✓ Continue or end here. If continued:
2. Product definition
3. Market analysis
   ✓ Continue or end here. If continued:
4. Budget estimates
   ✓ Continue, revise, or end here. If continued:
5. Additional financial analysis
   ✓ Continue, revise, or end here. If continued:
6. Timeline
7. Conclusion and feasibility statement
   ✓ Accept, reject, or revise the business plan.

Problem Identification

The first step in preparing a business plan is to identify the problem or need to be addressed. This is also the first section of the business plan, as readers considering funding a venture must first be convinced as to why the business plan is necessary. Examples of problems identified across inpatient, outpatient, and other health care settings that might lead to business plans can be downloaded from the Joint Commission website, Most Challenging Requirements for 2011 (www.jointcommission.org).

For example, the business plan in Appendix 10A.2 identifies the threat of nocosomial infection transmission via patient privacy curtains. The business plan in Appendix 10A.3 identifies the problem of excessive preventable pediatric asthma admissions to a children's hospital emergency room. The business plan in Appendix 10A.4 describes the under-utilization of a cardiac catheterization lab, and the business plan in Appendix 10A.5 addresses the problem of preventable antibiotic-associated diarrhea.

Nurses can often identify many problems in health care settings. However, it is important to carefully consider the extent to which a problem or need is a priority, either for the entrepreneur or the intrapreneur. Chapter 7 reviews the use of a SWOT analysis and a priority matrix in making capital expenditure decisions. SWOT analysis and a priority matrix are tools that are also useful in determining whether a problem is important and feasible enough to address in a business plan. The following questions are often useful to ask:

- *Is this a problem that can be solved by a new program or other intervention?* For example, are there methods to reduce colonization of infectious microbes on privacy curtains?
- *What is the political context of the problem?* For example, is it likely that the Bay General Hospital administration will support cost-effective measures to reduce potential nocosomial infections?
- *How well does the business plan fit with the organizational mission, values, and goals?* The better the fit, the more likely the business plan will receive attention and support. For example, does the plan to disinfect privacy curtains fit with the Bay General Hospital's mission to provide compassionate, high-quality care?
- *Where does this problem rank compared to other departmental and organizational priorities?* Even for a relatively small request, considerable time and effort may be spent in preparing and reviewing a business plan. Be sure to use time and resources to best advantage, focusing on the most important issues. For example, how important is the problem of nocosomial infections at Bay General Hospital?

Product Definition

Nurses sometimes find it difficult to clearly describe the product, program, service, or other intervention that is proposed. It is important to describe the specific product clearly so the reader knows exactly what is planned. Does the unit require a piece of equipment, added staffing, or more space? Is new construction or remodeling required?

It is often useful to propose or compare alternative ways in which the product could be provided. One alternative often used for comparison is to do nothing (Waxman, 2008), which may either be stated or implied in the business plan. The business plan to clean privacy curtains in Appendix 10A.2 explains that one alternative is to do nothing. Another alternative is to only disinfect the privacy curtains when there is a nocosomial outbreak on the nursing unit. The recommended alternative is to clean the privacy curtains as part of the routine patient room cleaning on patient discharge.

The use of alternative scenarios frequently leads to a CBA or CEA in which the costs and feasibility of alternatives are compared in the business plan. In the sample business plan in Appendix 10A.2, the costs and benefits of routinely cleaning the privacy curtains is compared to the costs of doing nothing.

Market Analysis

A market analysis is an important section of a business plan. However, a market analysis is new to many nurses and nurse managers, who have little or no experience evaluating the business environment. A market analysis identifies the estimated market share, clients and client mix, payers and payer mix, the strengths and weaknesses of actual and potential competitors, and the demand for a product or service. Further, the market analysis discusses anticipated change in any or all of these environmental factors, and considers any other trends that might affect the product or service.

Market share is the estimated percentage of the entire market for a provider- or organization-managed product or service. For example, if 20% of all patients requiring total hip replacement in a market area are admitted to Bigtown Hospital, then Bigtown Hospital has 20% of the market share. The estimated market share allows for comparison among competitors. It is important to consider whether the product or service proposed in the business plan is something for which there is already considerable competition. Is this a new product or service that is not offered in the market area, or is the business plan attempting to increase the organization's competitive position?

The business plan should clearly identify the clients and client mix for the proposed product or service. Who is likely to demand or utilize this product or service? What demographic characteristics are clients likely to share, including age, income, employment status, gender, and ethnicity? These demographic characteristics are likely to influence the anticipated payers and payer mix—for example, older persons are likely covered by Medicare, employed populations may have private health insurance, and poorer or chronically ill persons may be covered by Medicaid.

In addition to estimating the current and potential market share, it is necessary to examine the strengths and weaknesses of actual and potential competitors for the proposed product or service. Do other providers have a reputation for delivering this product or service? Is there adequate access for clients who demand this product or service? How would the proposed price or fee compare with that of competitors? Is it possible to market the product or service to large purchasers, such as employee groups, unions, or government programs? The demand for the product or service must be addressed—are clients or purchasers interested? What is the volume—the number of clients, units, or services—estimated for the coming year?

Regulatory Requirements and Quality Initiatives as Market Analysis

Another approach to market analysis is to consider the importance and impact of quality or regulatory initiatives to the organization. Nurses can frequently use regulatory requirements or quality initiatives as the basis for a market analysis. Increasing concerns about the quality of service delivery lead to increasing requirements that must be met, and initiatives that must be implemented.

For example, the business plan in Appendix 10A.2 points out that California now requires hospitals to report their MRSA and *C. difficile* infection rates. Bay General Hospital reports a higher rate for these infections than other local hospitals, indicating a quality concern that should be addressed. Although routinely disinfecting curtains is unlikely to increase market share or customer demand, this business plan recommendation supports Bay General Hospital's quality initiatives in reducing nocosomial infections.

After identifying the problem or need, defining the product, and reviewing the market analysis, the business plan team should check the business plan's feasibility at this point of development. It should be clear that the problem is important, and that the program or other project proposed in the business plan clearly addresses the problem. In addition, the market analysis should support how the business plan improves the organization's competitiveness or regulatory compliance. Further business planning may end at this stage if the problem is not considered to be important, the program that is proposed does not adequately solve the problem, or if the market analysis does not show how the organization might improve its competitive edge or better meet regulatory requirements.

Budget Estimates

The next step is to develop a special purpose budget, including operating and start-up costs associated with the proposed project. If the program or service will generate revenues, a revenue budget is also required, as well as a **pro forma profit and loss (P&L) statement**. The budget estimates should be as accurate and complete as possible. For example, the business plan in Appendix 10A.2 must largely budget for the curtain cleaning solution and sprayers to deliver the solution. Chapter 7 discusses the preparation of a special purpose budget for a business plan.

At this step, the decision to continue, end, or revise the business plan requires evaluating the budget. In some cases, it might be possible to reduce the estimated expenses. For example, one alternative for cleaning privacy curtains might be purchasing disposable curtains and replacing the curtains each time the patient room is cleaned on patient discharge. The use of a cleaning solution applied to the curtains when the room is cleaned is likely less costly and more feasible to budget.

If revenues are generated, it is important to review the pro forma P&L statement to determine if the project is profitable. If revenues exceed costs, the project generates profits and business planning is likely to continue. If costs exceed revenues, particularly in fiscal years following start-up, business planning is likely to be dropped or the business plan revised.

One reason to estimate a special purpose budget over 2 years rather than 1 year is that the start-up costs for the project's first year might be relatively high. Costs might drop considerably over the second and third year of operation. A project generating revenues that is unprofitable in the start-up year might therefore become profitable over the second year of operation.

Financial Analysis

Following the development of a special purpose budget, it is useful to conduct a financial analysis that builds on the budget estimates and provides further support for carrying out the business plan (or, in some cases, helps determine that the plan is not feasible). Break-even analysis, cost-benefit analysis (CBA), and cost-effectiveness analysis (CEA) are examples of financial analyses that may be used.

Chapter 8 discusses the preparation of a break-even analysis for business plan projects that generate revenue and profits. Chapter 9 discusses the preparation of a CBA or cost-effectiveness analysis (CEA) for business plan projects that generate savings. For example, the business plan in Appendix 10A.2 presents a CBA to support the benefits compared to the costs of routinely cleaning privacy curtains to reduce nocosomial infection risks.

Chapter 9 discusses the debate about **"light-green" dollars** that represent projected savings compared to **"dark-green" dollars** that represent actual financial outcomes. Administrators are likely to evaluate business plans for projects that generate revenues and profits more favorably, as they generate "dark-green" dollars. A break-even analysis helps verify the profitability of a revenue-generating project and reinforce that "dark-green" dollars will impact the organization's bottom line.

A CBA or CEA may support savings projections or "light-green" dollars. In many situations, quality improvement initiatives proposed in a business plan can be supported as improving care or meeting regulatory requirements. These quality improvement initiatives usually generate savings, or "light-green" dollars, not revenue, or "dark-green" dollars. Nurses should not limit their business plans to projects that generate revenue and profit when they have good ideas for cost-effective interventions that reduce costs and improve the quality of care.

For example, the business plan in Appendix 10A.2 potentially reduces the spread of infectious disease in the Progressive Care Unit at Bay General Hospital. The cost of curtain cleaning is minimal, and the potential savings are considerable by comparison. In addition, the business plan improves quality and regulatory compliance by improving patient room sanitation. This project is therefore likely to be funded, even though it generates "light-green" dollars and does not contribute revenues.

The financial analysis is another feasibility checkpoint. If the savings or profitability of the proposed project are not sufficient, the business plan might either require some rethinking or be rejected at this stage. If the savings or revenues exceed the costs (expense budget), the business plan is more likely to be seen as feasible and to be funded.

Timeline

It is important to develop a specific and realistic timeline to implement the project described in the business plan. Very large projects, such as new construction, may require more than one fiscal year for completion, but smaller programs or services are generally completed within a fiscal year. In some cases it is useful to estimate alternative best-case, worst-case, and most-likely scenarios for the timeline, to allow planning for unexpected events.

One way to create a timeline is to use a **Gantt chart**, a type of bar chart that enables the visualization of a project's schedule. The project start and finish dates for phases or elements of the project are indicated in the chart. Gantt charts can be helpful to use as the timeline for a business plan, as they are easy to create and interpret. The website Create a Gantt Chart in Excel (http://office.microsoft.com/en-us/excel-help/create-a-gantt-chart-in-excel-HA001034605.aspx) is helpful in preparing a Gantt chart for a business plan.

Conclusion and Feasibility Statement

As with most reports, the final section briefly summarizes and wraps up the business plan, concluding with a statement regarding the business plan's overall feasibility. There is an inherent bias and motivation, of course, to try to make one's proposed product or service as attractive as possible, and to overlook facts and figures that point to the unprofitability and infeasibility of the project. It is important to remember that it may well be far more valuable to the organization's financial health to re-think or reject a business plan, should the evidence indicate the project is infeasible. On the other hand, if the project is clearly feasible, the conclusion should be as convincing as possible, as it is the last impression made on the reader.

CONCLUSION

This chapter describes a business plan's components and demonstrates how to use skills in budgeting and financial analysis in developing a business plan. Text Box 10.1 summarizes the components and process used in developing a business plan. Another resource is the National Nursing Centers Consortium (NNCC) website (www.nncc.us). Chapter 11 focuses on the development of a health program grant proposal, another method to obtain resources for projects that improve quality and access to care.

Discussion and Exercises

1. Download and read the article by Cryer, Shannon, Van Amsterdam, and Leff (2012) in the References. Discuss how this idea could be developed as a business plan. What information from the article might be included in the various sections of the business plan?
2. Using information from exercises in Chapter 6 or Chapter 9, create an outline for a business plan based on your idea for a health care program or project. The program or project improves care and saves money, but does not generate revenue.
3. Using information from exercises in Chapters 6 or 8, create an outline for a business plan based on your idea for a health care program or project. The program or project not only improves care, but generates revenues.
4. Watch this video on The Elevator Pitch (http://www.bplans.com/business_planning_resources/videos/the_elevator_pitch) or use other sources to learn how to create an elevator speech. Present an elevator speech on your business plan idea that improves care and either saves money or generates revenue. Have fun!

REFERENCES

Cryer, L., Shannon, S. B., Van Amsterdam, M., & Leff, B. (2012). Costs for 'hospital at home' patients were 19 percent lower, with equal or better outcomes compared to similar inpatients. *Health Affairs, 31,* 1237–1243. Retrieved from http://www.healthaffairs.org/

Penner, S. J. (2004). Business plan feasibility checkpoints. *Society for Professionals in Healthcare Newsletter, 9,* 1–2, 5. Retrieved from http://sphealthcare.org/NewsletterPDF/Spring_2004.pdf

Quatre, T. (2008). A guide to writing a medical business plan. Retrieved at http://www.vantageclinicalsolutions.com/blog/2008/05/03/a-guide-to-writing-a-medical-practice-business-plan-marketing-plan-market-analysis-and-financial-projections/

Waxman, K. T. (2008). *A practical guide to finance & budgeting skills for nurse managers* (2nd ed.). Marblehead, MA: HC Pro.

CROSSWORD: *Chapters 10 and 11—Plans and Proposals**

Across

4 The name of a chart that helps the reader visualize a timeline.

5 A document that describes the contributions collaborating agencies will provide to the proposed program (abbreviation).

6 A type of money that represents funding for special project grants.

8 A type of money that represents grant funding that may or may not be available from year to year.

9 A grant application also referred to as an RFP (abbreviation).

11 An employee working within an organization to improve production and profitability.

Down

1 A person starting or managing their own business enterprise.

2 People and organizations with an active concern about a community need or problem.

3 Grants that lead to organizations competing with each other for funding.

7 A grant that provides funding for assessing a community need or problem and planning a program to meet those needs.

10 A grant application also referred to as an RFA (abbreviation).

*Note: The crossword puzzles for Chapters 10 and 11 are identical.

Appendix 10A.1: Business Plan Feasibility Checklist

Sections and Feasibility Checks	Feasibility Check-Off*
1. Problem or need identification	
2. Product definition	
3. Market analysis	
4. Budget estimates	
5. Additional financial analysis	
6. Timeline	
7. Conclusion and feasibility statement	

*Briefly explain why each section does or does not support project feasibility.

Appendix 10A.2: Business Plan—To Initiate the Cleaning of Hospital Privacy Curtains to Reduce Nosocomial Infections at Bay General Hospital's 4B Progressive Care Unit

Corinne Allen, Whitney Bralye, Madeira Macedo, Alysia Porter, and Heather Rothhammer

EXECUTIVE SUMMARY

In 2002, The Joint Commission first created a set of national patient safety goals to identify problem areas within health care organizations and to set annual goals for achieving improvement. Preventing nosocomial infections has become a recurring goal over the years, which demonstrates how prevention remains to be a challenge and is a necessity for delivering care safely. Infection control ranges from practicing hand hygiene and wearing personal protective equipment to prescribing prophylactic antibiotic treatment. An often neglected component, however, is hospital cleaning of inanimate objects (Dancer, 1999). Properly disinfecting objects such as call lights and bedside tables helps decrease microorganism colonization and thereby decreases the possibility for infection in patients and hospital staff.

One potentially contaminated object that is easily overlooked and present in most patients' rooms is the privacy curtain. Various studies have shown just how contaminated privacy curtains can become due to reoccurring use and lack of disinfection. A study by Trillis, Eckstein, Budavich, Pultz, and Donskey (2008) swabbed hospital curtains and took handprint samples with sterile gloves to show how much bacteria could potentially be transferred to patients and staff. Almost 42% of the curtains were infected with Vancomycin-resistant *Enterococci* (VRE) and 22% with Methicillin-resistant *Staphylococcus aureus* (MRSA), while 20% of the gloves picked up the VRE, and 22% of the gloves picked up MRSA. Promoting hand hygiene is one way to help decrease transmission. However, disinfection of the actual curtains could lead to greater success in reducing the potential for nosocomial infections.

The proposed solution is to incorporate privacy curtain disinfection on a progressive care unit at Bay General Hospital. Cleaning would occur within housekeeping's routine of cleaning patient rooms. The easiest and most cost-effective way of doing this is to use a water-diluted 3% hydrogen peroxide spray on the curtains. We propose that disinfecting

Materials & Labor	First-Year Costs	Second-Year Costs
Lab technician wages	$35.50/hr x 8 hr day = $284	N/A
3% hydrogen peroxide	276 bottles/yr x $16.50 each = $4516	276 bottles/yr x $16.50 each = $4516
Paper	3 boxes X $22 each=$66	3 boxes X $22 each=$66
Hand held mister	2 per unit X $17 each=$34	N/A
Testing supplies	10 test kits X $10 each=$100	N/A
Printer/computer	$580	N/A

Notes: Total start-up expenses = $5970. Total second-year expenses = $4692.
Estimated costs over a 2-year span for materials and labor required for project implementation. Total start-up expenses are projected to be $5970. Materials such as hand-held misters, testing supplies, printer, and computer will not need to be purchased again in the second year, therefore estimated costs will decrease to around $4692.

Figure 10A.2.1 *Estimated Costs for Materials and Labor for the First and Second Years*

hospital curtains will decrease the incidence of infections so the hospital can meet Joint Commission patient safety goals and save money in regard to the expenses associated with nosocomial infections.

The budget expenses for implementing the project are estimated to be $5970 for the first year and $4692 for the second year. These are estimated costs for materials and labor, which include lab technician wages, 3% hydrogen peroxide, hand-held misters, testing supplies, a printer, paper, and a computer (Figure 10A.2.1).

The estimated cost for installing the program is $5970, while the projected savings for reducing 10 patients' length of stay by one day is $50,000. Therefore, roughly $45,308 would be saved each year once this program has been implemented. Because the second and consecutive years are expected to cost $4692, the hospital will save an average of $7.60 for every $1.00 that they put into installation of the program. The benefits of cleaning the curtains clearly outweighs the costs needed to support the business plan.

PRESENT SITUATION AT 4B PROGRESSIVE CARE UNIT

Bay General Hospital is the only public hospital in the city that serves an ethnically and socially diverse patient community by offering a humanistic, cost-effective, and culturally competent type of care despite the patient's ability to pay. Due to its Level I trauma status, it holds a continual high volume of patients. Unit 4B of the hospital houses patients suffering from traumatic brain injury as well as cardiac, respiratory, gastrointestinal, hematological, and congenital diseases and disorders. There are also patients diagnosed with cancer who are receiving treatments and are continually immunosuppressed. There are about twenty rooms that have two to four patient beds and are usually full a majority of the time. These inpatient beds each have three curtains to provide privacy between patients. Since this unit is a progressive step down, there are patients that are not stable enough to be in medical surgical floors. This entails patients who are acute, immunosuppressed, and require specialty care ranging from tracheostomy, dressing changes, PICC and CVC care, and epidural placements. These procedures may require sterile technique and there are many opportunities for a patient to become contaminated from a simple touch of the curtain to a patient's break in the skin.

Bay General Hospital (BGH) has had "an alarming increase in infections with *Clostridium difficile* and multidrug-resistant organisms," according to a BCH manager (personal communication). There is emphasis on health care personnel to wash hands before and after entering the patient rooms, but there has been a lack of cleaning important patient surroundings. In each patient room, there are a total of three curtains that separate the two beds. A majority of the time, the patients use these curtains to protect their privacy and allow for adequate rest during the day. Through research, these curtains have been shown to be infested with multiple microorganisms that nurses, doctors, therapists, and even patients continually touch or brush against while in the room.

Microorganisms such as *Clostridium difficile* (*C. difficile*) and MRSA are very hardy, can survive on inanimate surfaces for months, and do not require direct transmission. Just a simple touch of a contaminated object has the capacity to transfer one of these serious pathogens to a patient.

In a California Department of Public Health (CDPH) brief review of hospital-acquired nosocomial infection of *C. difficile*, BGH ranked among the highest rates of cases (100) associated with *C. difficile* infections (CDI) within these years. This exemplifies the increasing need to make changes to better patient care and reduce nosocomial infections. According to the CDPH, "Costs associated with CDI have been estimated at $3.2 billion per year in the United States." It is evident that BGH is a hospital that encounters a high amount of hospital-acquired diseases and would benefit from a program entailing more vigorous cleaning of patient rooms, especially the curtains between patient beds. Weeks states that, "better cleaning, less hospital crowding, and cutting back on antibiotic use are among measures needed to stop superbugs" (Weeks, 2011).

PROPOSED SOLUTION

The lack of privacy curtain disinfection increases a hospital's risk for nosocomial infections. The proposed solution is to incorporate privacy curtain disinfection within housekeeping's routine of cleaning patient rooms. Neely and Maley (1999) suggest the easiest and most cost-effective way of doing this is to use a water-diluted 3% hydrogen peroxide spray on the curtains. The cleaning staff should spray the curtains until visibly wet and then let dry for 2 hours to ensure all bacteria are killed. Hydrogen peroxide is the best cleaning agent because it is the cheapest alternative and is odorless, therefore nonirritating to patients or staff members. If housekeeping were to incorporate disinfecting hospital curtains into their cleaning routine and thereby decrease the incidence of infections, the hospital will then meet Joint Commission patient safety goals and save money in regard to the expenses associated with nosocomial infections. This would be especially important for BGH, where many of the patients are uninsured and cannot pay for their own medical care.

GOALS AND OBJECTIVES

The primary goal of this business plan is to decrease the spread of infection on BGH's Progressive Care Unit, or 4B. In order to obtain this goal, we propose the instillation of a new process that initiates the cleansing of privacy curtains in patient rooms. By using hydrogen peroxide spray to sanitize the curtains, one avenue of hospital-acquired infections will be greatly diminished. The business plan projects that staff will uphold the cleaning schedule and, therefore, infection rates on the unit will decrease. With infection rates declined, the length of stay for patients will also decrease and therefore save money for the unit. The plan projects an approximate $40,000 to $50,000 savings over the next year, based on an average of 10 patients' length of stay reducing by 1 day.

The focal objective of the business plan involves reducing the costs on 4B that are associated with hospital-acquired infections. Also, by decreasing the costs, there will be a concurrent increase in the benefits derived from cleaning the privacy curtains. Due to the potential need for antibiotics, wound care, and more frequent blood cultures, treatment of hospital-acquired infections can be very costly. In contrast, the implementation of the new process of cleaning the privacy curtains is very inexpensive. After the initial lab results prove the efficacy of the hydrogen peroxide spray, regular lab testing will no longer be required. The expenses included with purchasing the spray and misters are minimal, as shown in Figure 10A.2.1.

One of the primary aspects of quality improvement always includes reducing a patients' length of stay in the hospital. Another objective of the business plan is to reduce the length of stay for 4B patients. Reed and Kemmerly (2009) report that patient length of stay increases by 12 days for vascular catheter-associated infections with an estimated attributable cost of $36,441. Patient length of stay increases by 1 to 3.8 days for catheter-associated urinary tract infections with an estimated attributable cost of $1006. By decreasing the risk for infection for a patient, which can prolong a patient's need for treatment, there is a simultaneous decrease in length of stay as well as financial savings.

The business plan will also create awareness among the unit's staff regarding the importance of keeping the curtains clean in order to protect their patients. By introducing staff to the new process and educating them regarding the risks involved with not cleaning the curtains, there will be greater knowledge of how the plan will affect their patients' outcomes. Improving patient outcomes continues to be a constant goal for BGH, so this easy and simple way of doing so will be attractive to the BGH staff and administration.

OPTIONS TO CONSIDER

To decrease nosocomial infections at BGH, the staff has a few potential options to address this issue. Perhaps the easiest option is to simply do nothing. However, this will not help the problem at hand and nosocomial infections will continue to plague patients and staff. This means more hospital expenses and less open beds, so this is not the best solution.

Another option is to implement the proposed business plan of spraying hospital privacy curtains with a 3% hydrogen peroxide spray (Neely & Maley, 1999). This plan could potentially take as little as 2 months to implement on the unit and could be easily altered to meet the needs of the unit or even other units in the hospital. When comparing the cost of handling a nosocomial infection such as C. *difficile* or MRSA with the estimated costs of beginning a program to spray hospital curtains, the benefits greatly outweigh the costs. Later, the costs and benefits as well as an implementation timeline will be discussed in greater detail.

Like all business plans though, spraying the curtains may not actually work once implemented in the clinical setting and, for this reason, it is important to have a backup plan to address the nosocomial infection problem. One potential backup plan is to spray down hospital curtains with hydrogen peroxide during known outbreaks of nosocomial infections, rather than routinely after each patient discharge (Huang, Mehta, Weed, & Savor Price, 2006). This will not help with the prevention of outbreaks, but may help with the spread of outbreaks to or from the unit. This is not an ideal solution but could be better than doing nothing, and may save BGH some money.

MARKET ANALYSIS

BGH is a county hospital, and the only Level I trauma center and provider of emergency psychiatric services for Bay City. BGH provides over 20% of the city's inpatient services, and serves over 100,000 patients each year (Bay General Hospital, 2011). BGH is also a teaching hospital, and partners with Bay University School of Medicine. It has students from various disciplines that attend school across the Bay Area.

According to the BGH website, BGH has approximately 598 beds. The patient diversity at BGH mirrors that of the Bay City. BGH has a higher percentage of Hispanic patients (30%), and also has patients of white (25%), Asian (23%), African American (17%), Native American (1%), and other (4%) ethnicities (BGH, 2011). For the 2010 to 2011 fiscal year, 51% of patients were male, and 49% were female. The hospital serves a higher percentage of people between the ages of 18 and 64, compared to the Bay City population (BGH, 2011).

BGH is unique in that the majority of outpatient encounters (36%) involve uninsured payer sources. Uninsured patients also made up 31% of inpatient days for the 2010 to 2011 fiscal year. This is partly due to the high volume of homeless patients seen at BGH. Other payer sources and the associated percentages of inpatient days/outpatient encounters include commercial (3% and 1%); Medi-Cal (39% and 28%); Medicare (22% and 16%); and other sources such as Healthy Families, Workers. Comp, etc (6% and 19%) (BGH, 2011).

As a trauma center, BGH provides care to victims of various traumatic injuries. This includes thermal, penetrating, and blunt injuries. These injuries can be further broken down into falls, stab wounds, gun shot wounds, motor vehicle accidents, and pedestrian versus auto accidents.

Due to the high percentage of its homeless patients, BGH is at a higher risk for outbreaks of nosocomial infections. According to David Young of the American Medical Association (Young, 2004), "Certainly, injection drug use is a risk factor for soft tissue infections. Homelessness and inadequate access to health care for these patients are also risk factors." Until recently, California hospitals were not required to make their [nosocomial] infection rates public. Currently, there is a hospital infection rate law that mandates California hospitals to report on certain infections. From April 2010 to March 31, 2011, information was made available for California hospitals, including BGH. Results were made available for a variety of infections including MRSA and *C. difficile*. These results showed that for MRSA and *C. difficile* infections among acute care patients at BGH, there were a higher number of cases and a higher number of hospital onset incidents when compared to some other local hospitals. At BGH, hospital-acquired *C. difficile* infections led to 94,532 hospital days, had a hospital onset rate of 12.9%, and an overall 122 cases. Some other local hospitals had lower hospital onset rates. One hospital, for example, had a hospital onset rate of 5.3%, a second hospital had a rate of 11.5%, and a third hospital had a rate of 5.8% (Gore, 2012). Hospital-acquired MRSA infections at BGH lead to 98,479 hospital days, had a hospital incidence rate of 1.2, and an overall 12 cases.

Based on the above demographic data and statistical information, a simple, yet cost-effective solution is needed to reduce hospital-acquired infection rates at BGH. Before planning and budgeting for a new implementation, it is important to consider what options already exist in the current market.

Currently, BGH has an Integrated Soft Tissue Infection Service Clinic (ISIS). The clinic was established to provide quality care to patients with soft tissue infections in an outpatient setting (Young, 2004). The patients are either walk-ins or are referred from the ED. They do not offer services for inpatient units. Creation of this clinic ended up saving the hospital an estimated net of $8,765,200 (Young, 2004).This program was created under the premise that the clinic prevented more patients from becoming inpatients, taking up acute care beds, and potentially contracting a nosocomial infection. A similar intervention is needed to prevent infections on inpatient units. The use of hydrogen peroxide to clean hospital curtains would not only be a simple, inexpensive way to clean, but it would also help prevent patients from acquiring and spreading infections during their hospital stay. This would be a cost saving measure for BGH.

TWO-YEAR BUDGET PROJECTIONS

There are many elements to consider when creating a budget. This includes indirect and direct costs. Direct costs for this implementation include items such as salaries and spraying. Indirect costs include printing fees. The budget for the implementation is based on three stages. The first stage is gathering samples from the curtains to test for bacterial colonies. The second stage involves spraying the curtains, and the third stage involves distributing patient satisfaction surveys.

Implementing this change would merely involve purchasing supplies. The labor required to do the cleaning already exists at BGH. The housekeeping employees would add the task of cleaning the curtains to their current list of responsibilities. The cleaning supplies would be stored with the other supplies already in use. Figure 1 is an operating budget for the start-up year. It is based on the labor, supplies, and testing required for making this idea a reality.

This project is very feasible because it requires very little. The main requirements are the solution and the sprayers. The projected second-year expenses will be less due to the nonrecurring expenses from the start up year. The nonrecurring expenses are the lab tech salary, hand-held mister, testing supplies, printer, and computer. The difference between the first-year and second-year expenses is $1278. The revenue from this implementation is seen through decreased hospital infection rates and increased patient satisfaction surveys. This is further explained in the cost-benefit section.

COST-BENEFIT ANALYSIS

In order to determine whether cleaning privacy curtains is a cost-effective business plan for BGH, an analysis of the business plan costs and benefits must be analyzed. As a patient develops a hospital-acquired infection, there is a multifactorial medical and nursing care plan that comes along with that. The normal protocol for treating a hospital-acquired infection involves the administration of antibiotics, a complete blood count to monitor the effects on the patient's blood, and wound care. As mentioned earlier, when a patient has an infectious disease there is an increase in the length of stay. The economic benefit of a reduced hospital stay must be weighed against the cost of the treatment or processes necessary to achieve the reduced length of stay (Kozma et al., 2010). The primary economic benefit of this business plan is the savings that would ensue.

There would be ample savings derived from using the spray to clean privacy curtains. As a whole, the cost of cleaning the privacy curtains is much less than the cost of treating patients with hospital-acquired infections. Antibiotics are traditionally administered via intravenous access in the hospital. According to the 2011 Chargemaster for BGH, an IV Administration Adult Set costs $29. Depending on the exact drug, the actual IV antibiotic can cost anywhere from $50 to $5000. While a patient is treated for an infection, there are usually prescribed and administered forms of antibiotics. But if a patient doesn't acquire an infection while at the hospital, then antibiotics aren't necessary, which saves more money. The range of antibiotic costs varies greatly but is rarely inexpensive. While fighting an infection, a patient is at risk for developing sepsis, which can lead to shock and require the attention of a hospital's rapid response team. Again, by preventing infection, the chance for sepsis greatly reduces, which, in turn, reduces the potential need for the rapid response team.

A valuable benefit of the business plan includes greater patient satisfaction. Cleaning curtains will give the 4B patients reassurance that the hospital staff is taking additional measures to prevent hospital-acquired infections. In turn, patients will feel more comfortable and satisfied with the treatment that they are receiving on BGH's Progressive Care Unit.

It is projected that it will cost approximately $5970 to start the program during the first year. In addition, if there is an average of 10 patients a year whose length of stay is reduced by one day, it represents a $50,000 decrease in costs over a year. The second year of the business plan should cost roughly $4692, considering the expenses that will no longer apply after the first year. Therefore, if we spend $4692 in the second year and years to follow, yet save $50,000 a year because of shortened length of stay, that creates $45,308 that could potentially be saved each year with the implementation of this program. That $45,308 is a significant benefit to the hospital. The estimated benefits of $45,308 would allow the hospital to save about $7.60 for every $1.00 that is put into creating the program. The analysis between the costs and benefits makes the advantages of installing this program even more evident.

IMPLEMENTATION

In order for this business plan to be successful, keeping the key stakeholders informed and involved in the changes being made is crucial. Sometimes, if this is not done, ideas may be rejected or staff may be more resistant. It is important for the agent implementing the business plan to present the evidence behind cleaning the curtains because once staff acknowledges the benefits of the plan, they will most likely welcome it. The change agent should bring a presentation of research articles that include the type of pathogens that are harbored on curtains, what can be used to disinfect it, and how this will work in the clinical setting. It is also important to explain in detail what the plan means for everyone involved. For example, explaining that housecleaning will have one extra task to do and that nurses know that the privacy curtains may be wet upon a patient discharge. After getting all of the necessary approval from the unit and administration, the business plan can be put into action.

Next, the agent will need to gather the necessary resources, such as spray bottles and hydrogen peroxide. With the resources in hand, housekeeping can then be trained to spray the curtains. Written instructions for spraying the curtains and the resources behind the plan should be provided to housekeeping services as well as unit 4B so that these references can be on hand at any time. The cleaning will only be done after a patient is discharged, so the curtains can simply be added to the list of other things that housekeeping needs to clean in the patient's room at this time.

TIMELINE

Facilitating change is a vigorous and long journey that entails empowerment within oneself to make a difference and motivation to achieve better patient outcomes. Nurses must be successful change agents by creating a vision, using evidence-based research, and then finding the appropriate and successful ways of implementing change. In order to do this successfully, there are many objectives, rules or regulations, concepts, processes, decision styles, and obstacles that one may face in order to implement a change. It requires leaders, managers, and staff to collaborate and build upon others ideas in an effective way and create a timeline in which the change can be implemented successfully (Figure 10A.2.2).

The first step of the timeline is to gather statistics based on the patient population of the unit and then assess the setting in which the change will be applied. This involves understanding the patient demographics, analyzing the patient rooms, becoming aware of how the housekeeping staff cleans the rooms, and assessing the patient's medical conditions within the unit. This will provide for better understanding of where the change will be taking place.

The next step would be to analyze the big picture: The rate of nosocomial infection in this particular unit. This encompasses evidence-based research and statistics on infection rate and readmission. It is also important to research the cost of readmitting and treating the patient who has acquired this infection. This will provide a way to outweigh the cost and benefits of facilitating this change in the unit.

Once the evidence-based research points to the problem of high infection rates within this hospital, the problem can now be addressed. This involves pinpointing the problem and understanding the reasons for which this has become a concern. This can be achieved, over a few-week period, by watching patients' rooms and tallying up how many times the curtains were touched, who touches them, and who washes their hands after touching them. Culturing the bacteria from the unit's curtains can also be done now to compare for later evaluation.

This next stage in the timeline of curtain cleaning change would be to gather resources to come up with a solution to increased numbers of nosocomial infections from hospital curtains. This stage will likely take a couple of weeks to a month because gathering evidence is time consuming. Comparing statistics from other hospitals that regularly clean their privacy curtains to ones that do not give important information to facilitate this change. Researching articles about different ways of reducing bacterial colonization on curtains can aid in finding a way of cleaning, that works best for the unit. At this point it would be useful to consult with other staff members, such as housekeeping, unit managers, and staff nurses, to help decide the best way to reduce infection. Collaboration of the staff, with emphasis on actively listening and reorganizing the steps of implementing this change, will increase acceptance because everyone will feel included in the plan.

After much research, the solution of using 3% hydrogen peroxide for curtain cleaning will be chosen and a plan will be put into action. It is important to approve this change with the necessary administration offices in order for housekeeping to receive proper funding for the spray bottles and hydrogen peroxide. Next comes the actual training of housekeeping staff, including managers. This will include training them to dilute hydrogen peroxide with water, spray the entire curtain from the midway point down until it is visibly wet, and then keep the curtain spread to let it dry for 2 hours (Neely & Maley, 1999). It is important to train not only the people who actually clean the rooms on a day-to-day basis, but also the staff who are responsible for training new employees. It is crucial to provide a step-by-step instruction sheet of the cleaning process and a document that explains its importance so that those involved will have a source to refer to for information or if questions arise. The training of hospital staff, management, and housekeeping would take about 2 weeks.

After the change has been implemented in this unit, it is important to monitor progress and make any adjustments needed. This would include monitoring the times that patients are discharged and making sure the curtains are being cleaned. Observing housecleaning staff as they spray the curtains would be insightful as well because it will show if they are cleaning them according to the guidelines provided. If they are not, then retraining staff and possibly creating a set of instructions that are clearer or even in different languages could be useful. It would also include collaborating with the housekeeping staff to see if

Privacy Curtain Cleaning	Wk 1	Wk 2	Wk 3	Wk 4	Wk 5	Wk 6	Wk 7	Wk 8	Wk 9	Wk 10	—	Mon 6	—	Yr 1
Diagnosing Problem	░	░	░	░	░	░	░	░	░	░	░	░	░	░
Recognizing Problem														
Determine Cause			░	░	░	░	░	░	░	░	░	░	░	░
Researching Evidence														
Evaluating Resources	░	░	░			░	░	░	░	░	░	░	░	░
Implementing Change	░	░	░	░	░	░	░	░	░	░	░	░	░	░
Evidence to Admin.														
Train Housekeep Mngmt.		░	░	░	░		░	░	░	░	░	░	░	░
Train Housekeep Staff														
Evaluating Change														
Getting Unit Feedback	░	░	░	░	░	░	░	░						
Culturing Curtains														
Monitoring # Infections	░	░	░	░	░	░	░	░	░					░
Spread to Other Units														
Technique Maintenance	░	░	░	░	░	░	░	░	░	░	░		░	

Notes: Timeframe and action plan for CNL implementation of hospital privacy curtains with 3% hydrogen peroxide solution. Each phase, diagnosis, implementation, and evaluation is depicted here with expected lengths of each sub-phase. Wk = week; Mon = month; Yr = year; — = time between two columns.

Figure 10A.2.2 *Action Plan for Implementation of Hospital Privacy Curtain Cleaning*

this change is not too time consuming and getting feedback from their staff. Being open to suggestions allows for staff to accept and keep the suggested change.

The last step is to finalize and stabilize the change. At this stage, the change will have been in place for a couple of months and the unit staff has become accustomed to the curtains being cleaned regularly. This will include making sure the curtains are being cleaned at the appropriate times with the correct technique. Continuing to get feedback is also essential in making sure that the best technique for the unit is used. Assessing results of the change is also important for administrative purposes so that housekeeping can continue to receive funding for the hydrogen peroxide spray. After a year of this change, the rate of nosocomial infections can be calculated so that there can be a measurable outcome of the implemented process of cleaning hospital curtains.

REQUIRED RESOURCES AND KEY STAKEHOLDERS

There are several key stakeholders in this change to hospital privacy curtain cleaning, which include but are not limited to the housekeeping staff, the Clinical Nurse Leader (CNL), the unit nurses and patient care assistants, and, of course, the patients. The housekeeping staff will be most affected by this change because they will be facilitating the action of cleaning the curtains. They will be the ones that actually clean the curtains when the patient vacates the room. In addition, the housekeeping services will have to train their employees to add another cleaning procedure that will increase the amount of time it takes to clean a patient room. However, they will not have to actually take down the curtains and send them to a specific laundry service that would end up taking up more time and less cost-effective. The CNL will be responsible for gathering resources and training housekeeping services how to properly disinfect the curtains so that they will be able to train their own staff in the future. Nurses and NAs most likely will not be directly involved in the actual cleaning, but they will benefit from decreased infections due to contaminated curtains. Patients will also have a reduced chance of infection, which is very important on the 4B unit because an infection could be life threatening in someone who is immunosuppressed and unstable.

EVALUATION OF SOLUTION

Evaluating the outcomes resulting in the implementation of hospital curtain cleaning can determine its effectiveness on the unit. Measurements will be made in regards to the number of bacterial colonies present on curtains and the nosocomial infection rate before and after the project's implementation. The number of bacterial colonies can be determined by culturing a sterile cotton swab swept over the curtain and a sterile gloved hand that grabbed the curtain. This action can determine how many contaminants are present on the curtain and how many are transferred by touching the fabric (Neely & Maley, 1999). The colony number will be recorded before and after the hydrogen peroxide treatment. More importantly, the nosocomial infection rate will be determined before and after the treatment to see how effective its implementation is on improving patient outcomes. The nosocomial infection rate will be associated with the unit's budget, for it is more costly to care for a patient who has acquired other illnesses during their stay. Therefore, the unit's expenses related to patient care can be evaluated to determine whether the reduction of nosocomial infections helped decrease the costs for the unit. Patient satisfaction scores can also be assessed to see whether a cleaner room helped reassure patients they are being cared for safety.

CONCLUSION

By implementing the use of 3% hydrogen peroxide to clean hospital curtains, BGH can reduce its infection rates, improve patient safety, and deliver better patient care. This budget plan lays out the foundation and reasons why this intervention is needed on acute care units at BGH. This is a quality improvement measure that is inexpensive, yet effective.

REFERENCES

Bay General Hospital (BGH). (2011). *BGH & Trauma Center annual report fiscal year 2009–2010.* Bay City, CA: BGH.

Dancer, S. J. (1999). Mopping up hospital infection. *Journal of Hospital Infection, 43,* 85–100. doi:10.1053/jhin.1999.0616

Gore, A. (2012). *Healthcare-associated infections detailed in new reports* (12-001). California Department of Public Health. Retrieved from http://www.cdph.ca.gov/Pages/NR12–001.aspx

Huang, R., Mehta, S., Weed, D., & Savor Price, C. (2006). Methicillin-resistant *Staphylococcus aureus* survival on hospital fomites. *Infection Control and Hospital Epidemiology, 27,*1267–1269. doi:10.1086/507965

Kozma, C. M., Dickson, M., Raut, M. K., Mody, S., Fisher, A. C., Schein, J. R., & Mackowiak, J. I. (2010). Economic benefit of a 1-day reduction in hospital stay for community-acquired pneumonia (CAP). *Journal of Medical Economics, 13,* 719–727.

Neely, A. N., & Maley, M. P. (1999). 3% Hydrogen peroxide for the gram-positive disinfection of fabrics. *Journal of Burn Care & Rehabilitation, 20,* 471–478.

Reed, D. and Kemmerly, S. A. (Spring 2009). Infection control and prevention: A review of hospital-acquired infections and the economic implications. *The Ochsner Journal, 9*(1), 27–31.

Trillis, F., Eckstein, E. C., Budavich, R., Pultz, M. J., & Donskey, C. J. (2008). Contamination of hospital curtain with healthcare-associated pathogens. *Infection Control and Hospital Epidemiology, 29,* 1074–1076. doi:10.1086/591863u

Weeks, C. (July 12, 2011). Handwashing alone won't stop *C. difficile,* experts warn. *Globe and Mail.* Retrieved from http://www.theglobeandmail.com/life/health-and-fitness/handwashing-alone-wont-stop-c-difficile-experts-warn/article4257233

Young, D. (2004). An epidemic of methicillin-resistant *staphylococcus aureus* soft tissue infections among medically underserved patients. ARCH SURG 2004 *American MedicalAssociation, 139,* 947–953.

Appendix 10A.3: Respiratory Project Committee—Fairfield County Hospital

Samanthika De Alwis, Jasmine Erguiza, Candace Fleming, and Jennifer Ma

EXECUTIVE SUMMARY

In response to the frequent admission of pediatric patients with asthmatic exacerbations, the Respiratory Project Committee (RPC) proposes the development of an outpatient Asthma Prevention Teaching Clinic in Fairfield County Hospital. The clinic would enable patients and their families to gain a better understanding of their asthmatic condition, which provides individualized treatment plans and the tools and skills to minimize the risk for an Emergency Department (ED) admission.

Demographic analysis shows that children under the age of 18 make up almost a quarter of the Fairfield County population. The Port of Wayland and several highways that run through Fairfield County add to the high particulate matter from the emissions of commuting automobiles, exporting and importing cargo ships, and diesel trucks. Air pollution is just one factor that can induce asthma attacks and contributes to the high asthma prevalence in Fairfield County.

The RPC has estimated profit and loss statements (Tables 10A.3.1 and 10A.3.2). Table 10A.3.1 reports increasing ED admission volumes each year without the implementation of the Asthma Prevention Teaching Clinic. Table 10A.3.2 reports a decline in ED admissions 2 and 3 years after the start of the Asthma Prevention Teaching Clinic, with a reduction in profit loss (i.e., improved profitability) each year. The Asthma Prevention Teaching Clinic will be located adjacent to the Respiratory Services Unit and furnished with office equipment, teaching material, and medical supplies. The RPC believes that the outpatient Asthma Prevention Teaching Clinic will positively impact the ED by reducing cost and admissions of pediatric asthmatic exacerbations (Tables 10A.3.1 and 10A.3.2).

Table 10A.3.1 *Profit and Loss Statement for Fairfield County Hospital ER Asthma Services Prior to Opening of Asthma Prevention Teaching Clinic*

Emergency department asthma services without the asthma prevention teaching clinic		
	FY 2013	FY 2014
Volume	2219	2286
Charge per patient	36,830	38,303
Net revenue per patient	22,098	21,877
Cost per patient	28,569	28,846
Total charges	81,725,402	87,544,250
Net revenue	49,035,241	50,001,235.25
Total operating expenses	63,393,705	65,929,453
Performa P&L	($14,358,464)	($15,928,218)
Profit margin %	−29.3%	−31.9%

Assumptions

Volume	3% increase each year
Charges	4% increase each year
Net revenue	1% decrease each year, due to health care reform and exchange
Operating expenses	4% increase each year

Fairfield County Hospital is a public organization consisting of hospitals and health centers that have provided medical services to Fairfield County residents since 1864, and has an operating revenue of $556.9 million and operating (expense) budget of $491.4 million in fiscal year (FY) 2011 (Fairfield County Hospital, 2006a). The Fairfield County Hospital, with 236 beds, is equipped in providing Fairfield County's Level II Trauma Center and serves as a teaching hospital for medical students in a broad spectrum of practices, including emergency medicine, surgery, internal medicine, and primary care. This business plan is a proposal for an outpatient Asthma Prevention Teaching Clinic that would facilitate preventive care and reduce Fairfield County Hospital's ED visits due to pediatric asthma exacerbations.

PROBLEM OR NEED IDENTIFICATION

As of 2010, Fairfield County had 1.5 million residents, including 399,000 children under the age of 18. There are approximately 73,000 annual ED admissions, with an average quarterly ED admission of 3679 comprising of pediatric patients in 2011 and 3931 in 2010 (Office of Statewide Health Planning & Development [OSHPD], 2011). Of the ED admissions, total respiratory diagnoses (adult and pediatrics) account for average quarterly admissions of 4728 in 2011 and 4115 in 2010 (OSHPD, 2011). The implementation of the Asthma Prevention

Table 10A.3.2 *Profit and Loss Statement for Fairfield County Hospital ED Asthma Services With the Asthma Prevention Teaching Clinic*

Emergency department asthma services with the asthma prevention teaching clinic		
	FY 2013	FY 2014
Volume	1997	2057
Charge per patient	38,876	40,431
Net revenue per patient	23,326	23,092
Total charges	77,639,132	83,167,038
Net revenue	46,583,479	47,501,173
Total operating expenses	57,054,335	59,336,507.88
Performa P&L	($10,470,856)	($11,835,334)
Profit margin %	−22.5%	−24.9%
Projected profit & loss of prevention teaching center	($69,248)	($69,253)
Profit margin % after prevention center	−22.6%	−25.1%
Improvement in profit margin	$3,818,360	$4,023,631
Improvement in profit margin %	6.7%	6.8%

Assumptions

Volume	Prevention teaching would reduce ER volume by 10% in first 2 years and 15% and 20% thereafter
Net revenue	The reduction is 50% of the original net revenue per patient (Note: Most patients are uninsured)

Teaching Clinic would reduce the number of pediatric ED admissions from asthma attacks and decrease operating cost by at least 6% each following year, with a cost benefits ratio of $5 saved for every $1 invested in the program.

The American Academy of Allergy Asthma and Immunology (2012) reported 24.6 million people in the United States having asthma in 2009, with approximately 250,000 people dying prematurely every year. A total of 8.9% of children in 2005 had asthma, with approximately 4 million children experiencing an asthma attack in the previous year. Among the children who had asthma, 59% missed school due to an asthma attack in 2008 (American Academy of Allergy Asthma and Immunology, 2012). Of the total pediatric ED admissions at Fairfield County Hospital, 46% of the payer source came from nonfederal programs, 24.5% from Medicaid, 18.9% from the patient, and 1.1% from HMO (OSHPD, 2011). In 2010, Fairfield County was comprised of Whites (45%), White persons not Hispanic (34%), Asian (26%), and Blacks (12.6%; U.S. Census Bureau, 2012). Moreover, 1675 of 10,000 5–17-year-old children who were admitted to the ED in Fairfield County due to asthma were Blacks, followed by Latino (446), White (410), and Asian/Pacific Islander (135; Wayland Community Action to Fight Asthma, 2008).

The Respiratory Project Committee identifies African American children <5 years of age as a high-risk group, with Wayland as one of the high-risk communities for ED visits. Wayland has a large African American population surrounded by the Port of Wayland and three highways, an area vulnerable to environmental and health disparities. The Port of Wayland is a source of diesel emissions from ships and trains transporting goods for businesses, with the addition of diesel trucks traveling through Wayland. Hence, the average diesel emissions in Wayland are over 90 times higher per square mile than the average for the rest of California (Coalition for Wayland Revitalization, 2003). According to State of the Air 2011, published by the American Lung Association, the Fairfield County–Wayland area ranks in the top 25 U.S. Cities Most Polluted by Short-term Particle Pollution, another contributing factor for respiratory illnesses.

PRODUCT DEFINITION

The proposed Asthma Prevention Teaching Clinic would be located at the Fairfield County Hospital in a current vacant space adjacent to the Respiratory Services Unit. For the first year, the clinic will be staffed with one medical assistant and one registered nurse who will teach two classes per week in the evening to accommodate working parents and school dismissal hours. A 4-hour day will be dedicated to administration tasks, such as, scheduling, follow-up appointments, and outreach. Patient referrals will derive from the ED, Respiratory Services Unit, and Fairfield County community health clinics. The 1-hour class sessions will include an individualized asthma prevention action plan for each family and instruction on proper usage of peak flow meters, spacers, metered dose inhalers, and medication resources. The space will be furnished with two desks and approximately 10 chairs, educational material (pamphlets and brochures), and office supplies. One computer will allow staff to access patient information for outreach, follow-up calls, and for patient documentation on EPIC, Fairfield County Hospital's health software. To accommodate the pediatric population, toys and children's books will be available for use during the teaching session.

Table 10A.3.1 shows the profit and loss statement for Fairfield County Hospital ED asthma services before the Asthma Prevention Teaching Clinic, with an alternative scenario, Table 10A.3.2, depicting the profit and loss statement after clinic implementation. Ultimately, the Asthma Prevention Teaching Clinic will reduce the number of ED admissions due to asthma attacks in pediatric patients (<18 years of age) and minimize the annual ED operating expenses. At the end of the 2013 fiscal year, an analysis of the cost will be determined for the ED. A reduction of operating cost by 6% each year will constitute as an achievement by the Asthma Prevention Teaching Clinic.

MARKET ANALYSIS OR ENVIRONMENTAL SCAN

Fairfield County Hospital is a public hospital serving Fairfield County's population of 1.47 million with a pediatric population ages 0 to 19 years at 380,000 (U.S. Census Bureau, 2012). Nearly 17.7% of children ages 0 to 19 years in Fairfield County have been diagnosed with asthma (California Health Interview Survey [CHIS], 2009). The 10.7 million children statewide have a lower asthma prevalence rate of 14.6%, a variance of 2.5%. Fairfield County Hospital had an annual admission of 75,000 patients into the ED; 13,469 patients were admitted with a principal diagnosis of the respiratory system from 2009 to 2011 (OSHPD, 2011). The cumulative total of pediatric patients admitted into the ED from 2009 to 2011 was 11,828. The estimated percentage of pediatric patients having respiratory distress, specifically with asthma diagnosis, admitted into Fairfield County Hospital's ED is unknown. Fairfield County Hospital's ED had 7.5% market share of pediatric encounters in 2011.

Major hospital competitors having an on-site asthma-teaching clinic in Fairfield County include Wayland Medical Center and Children's Hospital (Fairfield County Hospital, 2011). Wayland Medical Center is located within a 5-mile radius from Fairfield County Hospital. A review of Wayland Medical Center's patient payer source revealed the top payer sources in 2011 ED encounters were 34% for Medicaid, followed by 20% for preferred provider organizations (PPOs). Based on the total number of pediatric patient encounters in the ED in 2011, Wayland Medical Center had a market share of 10 percent (OSHPD, 2011).

Wayland Medical Center established the Asthma Resource Center in 2000, providing asthma teaching and treatment supplies, such as a month-supply of medicine to asthmatic patients who previously visited the ED in either one of their campuses. The Asthma Resource Center targets the general asthmatic patient residing in Fairfield and has successfully reduced asthma-related ED visits from 847 in 2001 to 634 in 2004, a 25.0% reduction (Wayland Medical Center, 2011).

The Children's Hospital's asthma clinic is specifically tailored to the pediatric population, 0–19 years of age, which had 82.0% of the pediatric market share in 2011 ED encounter. Children's Hospital's top three payer sources included Medicaid (71.8%), PPO (9.0%), and self-pay (7.3%; OSHPD, 2011). With a well-established reputation in the local community for its pediatric medical services, Children's Hospital is Fairfield County Hospital's top competitor, located 4 miles from Fairfield County Hospital. Although Children's Hospital serves a large percentage of the pediatric population, this does not dispute the county's noteworthy statistics of asthma-related ED visits, which more than doubled in 2009, at 22.6% compared to 10.0% in 2005 (CHIS, 2005, 2009). Moreover, when comparing asthma prevalence in prior years, the percentage of children in Fairfield County having an asthma diagnosis fluctuated between 2005 and 2007, reporting 18.7% and 21.6%, respectively (CHIS, 2005, 2007).

In reviewing Fairfield County Hospital's 3-year average trend analysis (2009–2011), patient payer sources in the ED showed other nonfederal programs (45.2%), followed by Medicaid (22.2%), self-pay (21.1%), and Health Maintenance Organization (HMO; 1.0%). Pediatric patients admitted into the ED predominantly spoke English (77.0%) compared to Spanish (15.9%). The racial diversity consisted of 44.4% Black or African American, 32.8% identified as other race, 14.8% White, 7.7% Asian, and 0.5% American Indian or Alaska Native (OSHPD, 2011).

Grass root organizations, legislators, and policy makers have championed for reducing the burden of asthma among pediatric patients with effective therapeutic management through education and medication. The Strategic Plan for Asthma in California 2008–2012 (California Department of Public Health, 2008) advocates for closing the asthma disparities gap, promoting asthma awareness and education, improving systems and policies within organizations, and generating health-protective asthma policies. With progressive rates of ED admissions and asthma prevalence, there is a need for proactive measures that will contribute in reducing ED revisits and unnecessary exacerbations. Fairfield County Medical's mission, "to maintain and improve the health of all residents of Fairfield County regardless of ability to pay" should be upheld and put into practice with the establishment of an asthma teaching clinic (Fairfield County Hospital, 2006b). With strong patient-centered care and dedicated health professionals in the respiratory and asthmatic departments, we have reached a general consensus that the establishment of the Asthma Prevention Teaching Clinic will be of considerable benefit in improving the quality of life for the pediatric population in Fairfield County. It behooves a reputable public hospital such as Fairfield County Hospital to be competitively established with an outpatient asthma clinic for the next 5 years.

BUDGET ESTIMATES

The first budget estimate, Table 10A.3.1, shows includes the profit and loss (P&L) statements without the Asthma Prevention Teaching Clinic for 2013 and 2014. The second set, Table 10A.3.2, the operating expenses and budget projections for Fairfield County Hospital's ED with the Asthma Prevention Teaching Clinic for the 2013 and 2014. The numbers have been tabulated based on the estimates from the Fairfield County Charge Master Respiratory Services Department and OSHPD Emergency Respiratory Services statistics for pediatric patients.

Budget Estimates for the Asthma Prevention Teaching Clinic

The capital budget for FY 2013 and the operating budget projections for FY 2013–2014 for the Asthma Prevention Teaching Clinic are detailed in Tables 10A.3.4 and 10A.3.5. Assumptions are summarized in the notes of each budget table. The start-up costs are represented in the capital budget for the Asthma Prevention Teaching Clinic with an estimation of $5280, which includes office furniture (two desks and ten chairs); a computer for data collection and teaching; medical supplies, such as nebulizers, peak flow meters, pamphlets; and other teaching supplies. Utilizing current vacant space adjacent to the Respiratory Services Unit eliminates the need for building renovations, thus reducing start-up costs. In 2013 the proposal will be implemented with a total operating and capital start-up costs of $69,248, which includes $5280.

Most of the operating costs are allocated to staff salaries. The clinic requires one part-time nurse for 12 hours a week and one part-time medical assistant on an as needed basis. The salaries are estimated at $51,168 of the total operating budget of $69,248 for 2013. The referral volume is estimated at 10% of the ED volume in the first 2 years, and 15% and 20% thereafter, which will contribute to larger class sizes. The plan includes hiring another part-time medical assistant in 2014 to accommodate anticipated needs, which increases the operating budget to $69,253.

FINANCIAL ANALYSIS

Table 10A.3.1 shows the estimated costs and losses for the ED asthma services prior to the start of the Asthma Prevention Teaching Clinic for FY 2013 and FY 2014. The total loss from ED respiratory services for FY 2013 is 29.3% and FY 2014 is 31.9%.

Table 10A.3.2 illustrates the estimated costs, including the start-up costs and the reduction in loss after opening the Asthma Prevention Teaching Clinic. The total loss for FY 2013 and 2014 is 22.5% and 24.9%. The reduction in loss after opening the teaching center is 6.7% in FY 2013 and 6.8% in FY 2014. After opening the Asthma Prevention Teaching Clinic, pediatric patient ED visits are reduced by 222 and 229, and hospital admittance days reduced by 55 and 57 days in FY 2013 and FY 2014. Financial approximations were based on Fairfield County Charge Master Respiratory Services Department estimates and OSHPD Emergency Respiratory Services statistics for pediatric patients.

Table 10A.3.3a shows the cost-benefit analysis for the Asthma Prevention Teaching Clinic. For every dollar spent on the clinic there will be savings of $5 in reduced ED visits and hospital stays.

The Asthma Prevention Teaching Clinic provides not only financial benefits to the hospital but also for the community. It provides an additional health resource to community members and fulfills Fairfield County Hospital's vision as a leader in health promotion and prevention. By implementing the Asthma Prevention Teaching Clinic, it is our goal that pediatric patients with asthma and their families gain control of their condition, thus reducing missed days from school, improving self-confidence and efficacy, and an overall improvement of their quality of life. In an area stricken by social, environmental, and health injustice, the clinic serves as a common ground to empower community members to take action for their health. At a low cost to the hospital, the Asthma Prevention Teaching Clinic has immeasurable gains in improving community health.

Table 10A.3.3 *Fairfield County Hospital Profit and Loss Comparison Before and After the Asthma Prevention Teaching Clinic Prevention Center*

Year	ER volume before prevention center	ER volume after prevention center	Profit & loss before prevention center	Profit & loss after prevention center	Improvement in profit & loss
2013	2219	1997	−29.3%	−22.6%	6.7%
2014	2286	2057	−31.9%	−25.1%	6.8%

Table 10A.3.3a *Cost–Benefit Analysis*

Cost–benefit analysis	2013	2014
Reduction in volume in ER	222	229
Reduction in patient days (assumed 25% of patients will get admitted and stay 1 day)	55	57
Variable cost per day	6000	6000
Reduction of variable costs	332,850	342,836
Program cost per first year	$69,248	$69,253
CBA amount	$263,602	$273,582
CBA ratio*	$5	$5

* Every $1 spent on the program would save $5 of ED cost.

Table 10A.3.4 *Fairfield County Hospital Asthma Prevention Teaching Clinic—Projected Capital Budget/Start-Up Costs*

Office furniture	1250
Computer	–
Pamphlets & other teaching supplies	1650
Start-up medical supplies	1250
Other	650
Subtotal	4800
Sales tax @ 10%	480
Total estimated start-up costs	5280

Assumptions

Office furniture (two desks and 10 chairs)	$250 per desk and $75 per chair
Computer	$1500
Computer is depreciated over 5 years	$300 per year
Office furniture is depreciated over 5 years	$250 per year
Other expenses, including medical supplies	Expensed in the first year

Table 10A.3.5 *Fairfield County Hospital Asthma Prevention Teaching Clinic—Projected Profit and Loss Statement*

	FY 2013	FY 2014
Volume	222	229
Net revenue	–	–
Salaries	$51,168	$52,703
Medical supplies	6250	5000
Nonmedical supplies	1000	1000
Housekeeping	7800	7800
Depreciation	250	250
Teaching supplies	1650	1500
Other	1130	1000
Total operating expenses	$69,248	$69,253
Projected profit & loss	($69,248)	($69,253)

Assumptions

Volume		
First 2 years 10% of the ER volume and 15% and 20% thereafter	10%	10%
Operating expenses		
Salaries–3% annual inflation factor		
1 part-time registered nurse 12 hr per week	$70	$72
1 part-time medical assistant	$12	$12
1 part-time medical assistant		
Housekeeping–1hr per day, 3 days a week	$50	$50

TIMELINE

Table 10A.3.6 presents the timeline for the proposed Asthma Prevention Teaching Clinic. The timeline begins from the submission of the proposed business plan, May 4, 2012, through the inception of the clinic on February 15, 2013.

EXPLANATION OF BUDGET TABLES

Seven tables were prepared to compare budget estimates for the FY 2013 to FY 2014.

Table 10A.3.1 shows the budget pro forma P&L and margin profit without the Asthma Prevention Teaching Clinic. Respectively, projections for pro forma profit margins without preventive services decrease at a higher annual rate than implementation of the Asthma Prevention Teaching Clinic. Table 10A.3.2 shows projections after the start of the Asthma Prevention Teaching Clinic. Table 10A.3.2 illustrates improvement in profit margin from FY 2013 to 2014.

Table 10A.3.6 *Fairfield County Hospital, Asthma Prevention Teaching Clinic Proposed Timeline, FY 2012–2013*

Date	Activity	Authority/Responsibility
05-04-12	Proposal submission for the asthma prevention teaching clinic to CEO & CFO	Respiratory services project committee (RSPC)
09-15-12	Pending CEO & CFO approval, proposal revised & sent to Board of Directors	CEO, CFO, and RSPC
11-12-12	Proposal approval by board of directors	Board of directors
01-05-13	Purchase office supplies and order start-up medical supplies	RSPC
02-01-13	Hire RN and medical assistant	RSPC
02-15-13	Opening of the asthma prevention teaching center	RSPC

Table 10A.3.3 is a summarized, before and after comparison for 2013 and 2014. Table 10A.3.3a is a cost benefit analysis that shows a savings of 5 dollars for each dollar spent on the Asthma Prevention Teaching Clinic as a result of reduced ED visits and hospital admittance. Table 10A.3.4 is a capital budget and includes start-up cost of equipment for FY 2013. Table 10A.3.5 is a projected profit and loss statement identifying total operating expenses. Table 10A.3.6 is a timeline for the proposal. Assumptions are summarized at the bottom of each table.

CONCLUSION AND FEASIBILITY STATEMENT

The demographic market analysis and profit and loss statements indicate that the proposed outpatient Asthma Prevention Treatment Clinic is beneficial for the hospital by reducing ED admissions and overall operating cost. The clinic provides the Fairfield County residents with educational information about asthma and proper training with medication treatments, thus decreasing the potential for an ED visit from an asthma attack.

While Fairfield County Hospital has several competitors, this does not justify a significant reason to deny the proposal due to its benefits to the hospital and community. In fact, having another outpatient Asthma Prevention Teaching Clinic within Fairfield County offers another resource for the community; thus, reaching out to more community members and simultaneously bringing awareness to the significance that asthma has on the pediatric population.

From our projections, it is likely that ED admissions will continue to rise in the coming years without our proposal. Comparable to Wayland Medical Center and the Children's Hospital, an asthma clinic at Fairfield County Hospital will reduce overall expenses and ED visits.

We strongly suggest the approval of the Asthma Prevention Teaching Clinic to reduce operating cost, ED admissions, and closing asthma-related health disparities within the neighborhoods of Fairfield County.

REFERENCES

Fairfield County Hospital. (2006a). *Hospitals and health centers–Fairfield County hospital.* Wayland, CA: Fairfield County Hospital.

Fairfield County Hospital. (2006b). *Our mission, strategic vision, and history.* Wayland, CA: Fairfield County Hospital.

Fairfield County Hospital. (2011). *Report to our community 2011.* Wayland, CA: Fairfield County Hospital.

American Lung Association. (2011). State of the air. *American Lung Association.* Retrieved from http://www.stateoftheair.org/2011/states/california/alameda-06001.html

American Academy of Allergy Asthma and Immunology. (2012). Asthma statistics. Retrieved from http://www.aaaai.org/about-the-aaaai/newsroom/asthma-statistics.aspx

California Department of Public Health. (2008). Strategic plan for asthma in California. *California Breathing. 2008–2012.* Retrieved from http://californiabreathing.org/phocad-ownload/asthmastrategicplan.5–5-08.pdf

California Health Interview Survey. (2005). AskCHIS data query system. Retrieved from http://www.chils.ucla.edu/

California Health Interview Survey. (2007). AskCHIS data query system. Retrieved from http://www.chils.ucla.edu/

California Health Interview Survey. (2009). AskCHIS data query system. Retrieved from http://www.chils.ucla.edu/

Coalition for Wayland Revitalization. (2003). *Clearing the air: Reducing diesel pollution in Wayland.*

Office of Statewide Health Planning & Development. (OSHPD). (2011). Emergency department profile reports. Retrieved from http://www.oshpd.ca.gov/MIRCal/default.aspx

U.S. Census Bureau. (2012). State and county quickfacts, Fairfield County. *U.S. Census Bureau.*

Wayland Community Action to Fight Asthma. (2008). Report of asthma in the community. *Fairfield County Public Health Center.*

Wayland Medical Center. (2011). *Asthma resource center.* Wayland, CA: Wayland Medical Center.

Appendix 10A.4: Increasing Patient Volume at the Bay General Hospital Cardiac Clinic

Yonatan (Ty) Breiter, Seth Cloues, Caitlin Flanagan,
Alex Guevarra, and Hector Solano

EXECUTIVE SUMMARY

The purpose of this business plan is to increase the number of outpatient Left Heart Catheterizations (LHCs) in a preventative and diagnostic manner, thus decreasing the number of Emergency Department (ED) admissions; this plan will potentially increase savings and reduce expense costs at Bay General Hospital (BGH). Currently, not every outpatient LHC referral from the 1M clinic can be performed due to low staffing in the recovery unit. Therefore, hiring a new 1.5 FTE recovery nurse for post-LHCs will increase the number of outpatient procedures performed.

It has been proposed that a full-time recovery nurse at BGH with 1.5 FTE will cost a total of $120,000 annually, providing a total cost for LHCs at $741,648 per year from January 2012 to this date. The desirable outcome from diagnostic outpatient LHCs is to prevent serious cardiac complications, which will result in lower costs and improve quality patient care.

Savings were theoretically estimated by having two out of 10 patients not admitted to the ED due to receiving diagnostic LHCs and by following preventative measures. The total savings per benefit equaled $30,084, which represented a 20% cost reduction to BGH. In addition, a Quality-Adjusted Life Year (QALY) analysis indicated that the cost of funding this project results in an increased amount of healthy life for patients. The analysis proves the value to be at least three times greater than the initial investment.

A plan of action has been initiated through brief meetings with the 1M nurse case manager, the Chief Cardiologist for the Cath Lab, and the Billing Services staff. The results of this proposal will potentially benefit both the patients and the hospital. Patients will benefit from receiving an elective procedure that will decrease and potentially prevent the likelihood of future cardiac emergencies, and the hospital will save money by admitting fewer cardiac emergency patients through the ED.

THE PURPOSE AND THE PROBLEM

The purpose of this business project is to prevent further cardiac complications and decrease the amount of patients being admitted through the Emergency Department (ED). Performing more diagnostic outpatient Left Heart Catheterizations (LHCs) could potentially decrease cardiac complications such as myocardial infarctions, aortic stenosis, valve malfunctions, and others. These complications can be preventative, therefore by resolving them promptly could lower hospital costs and improve the patients' quality of life. Enabling the Cardiac Catheterization Lab (Cath Lab) to increase its daily caseload of scheduled procedures by hiring a new 1.5 FTE recovery nurse at 4C will reduce the proportion of costly emergency procedures, while focusing more on providing quality preventative care.

The necessity for a new 1.5 FTE is illustrated by the inflexibility of patient scheduling that delays efficacious diagnostic catheterization. The case manager nurse for the GMC Cardiac Clinic in 1M schedules LHCs ordered by cardiologists with the Cath Lab and Recovery Room. The case manager nurse shared a specific case of a patient in which the cardiologist referred a patient who *urgently* needed to be catheterized, but an ED admission was not indicated. Because of difficulty arranging for Recovery Room coverage, the patient had to wait until the next available catheterization appointment on a later day. This patient could have benefited from a catheterization to diagnose a potential coronary artery blockage.

Prompt diagnosis and treatment of coronary artery blockage can prevent a potential MI. However, as in the above example, many 1M outpatients must wait for LHC procedure because the Recovery Room is not available. This problem would be resolved hiring the new 1.5 FTE, which would allow for more 1M outpatients to be catheterized and prevent delays in catheterization.

Cath Labs can perform a number of procedures to help diagnose and provide therapeutic interventions to the patient. Typical procedures in a Cath lab include angiograms, right and left pulmonary artery catheterization and stent placement, trans-esophageal electrocardiography, loop recorder placement and removal, pace maker placement, and battery replacement. Many procedures in the Cath Lab are performed in emergency situations and require a relatively long length of stay (LOS). Procedures that are diagnostic and do not discover complications demand a relatively short LOS. The group of Cath Lab procedures that are outpatient, scheduled, preventative, and low LOS are the ones that are relevant to our proposal.

BENEFITS AND PREVENTION

The benefits of cardiac catheterization far outweigh the risks, of which it is very important for the patient to be aware, especially when scheduling a diagnostic procedure. The benefits include retrieving information about the heart's pumping function and the condition of the coronary arteries and heart valves, which may not be able to be found by any other means, unless through further invasive procedures. In addition, as compared to other diagnostic tests, cardiac catheterization provides more accurate and detailed information. This test provides the doctor with an image of the arteries of the heart and allows him to assess the presence, location, and degree of severity of blockages in the coronary arteries, or dysfunctions on ventricles and valves. This assessment tool will allow the doctor to make an accurate diagnosis and begin treatment before irreversible damage to the heart occurs.

Patients can be diagnosed at an early stage from any condition and be treated accordingly without having complications; thus preventing them from being admitted to the ED, and the medical surgical unit. It will be more beneficial if patients can come for routine LHC outpatient procedures, spend 6 to 8 hours in recovery, and then be discharged home.

QSEN Competencies

This project seeks to bring quality and safety improvements to the hospital by following the Institute of Medicine's 6 core QSEN competencies (Institute of Medicine, 2003). Increasing the number of preventative cardiac catheterization procedures relates to these competencies in the following ways:

1. Patient-centered care: Focusing on the needs of cardiac patients in the Bay City area, more scheduled preventative procedures at BGH will help these patients to avoid future emergency room visits and live longer, healthier, and more productive lives.
2. Teamwork and collaboration: Helping two different but interdependent units at BGH work together for the patients' cardiac health and the hospital's financial solvency, this project promotes teamwork and collaboration at a systems-level.
3. Evidence-based practice: When indicated and performed correctly, minimally invasive cardiac procedures using catheterization techniques are a safer, evidence-based way to deal with many common cardiac conditions. In many cases, the alternative is ED visits and open-heart surgeries.
4. Quality improvement: By reducing the overall number of future ED visits, due to untreated cardiac conditions, this project will bring significant quality improvement to BGH.
5. Safety: As mentioned, preventative cath procedures are minimally invasive, have fewer adverse effects, and require much less recovery time than emergency open-heart procedures.
6. Informatics: Cardiac catheterization techniques require an arsenal of high tech equipment to image and guide the passage of catheters through a patient's vessels, as well as to safely control repairs. Taking full advantage of these technologies helps us to rely less upon more invasive methods of repairing damaged hearts.

THE HOSPITAL

Bay General Hospital (BGH) is a large public hospital serving the Bay City. It is a licensed general acute care facility. The hospital's mission is "To provide quality health care and trauma services with compassion and respect." The Vision Statement at BGH is to "Advance community wellness by aligning care, discovery, & education." Being the only Level 1 Trauma Center serving 1.5 million people in Bay City and the surrounding area, the BGH Trauma Center is open 24/7/365 and provides comprehensive care to over 3900 severely injured patients per year in addition to the more than 50,000 annual admits to the hospital's Emergency Room (Bay General Hospital Foundation, 2011).

Drawing from the extreme racial and cultural diversity of the area, BGH serves a patient population that is approximately 31% Hispanic, 24% Caucasian, 21% Asian/Pacific Islander, 18% African American, and 8% homeless (Bay General Hospital, 2011). There are 10 operating rooms, upon which 6588 procedures were performed; approximately 45% of these operations were performed in emergency situations in 2009 and 2010 (Bay General Hospital Foundation, 2011). With an operating budget of approximately $640 million, BGH receives approximately 20% of its funding from the city government's general fund and around 80% from a combination of Medi-Cal, Medicare, other insurance plans, and direct payments from patients. Payments for services at BGH come from a variety of sources, as illustrated in Table 10A.4.1.

Stakeholders

In order for a plan to be successfully implemented in an organization as large and complex as BGH, it seems prudent to consider the perspectives of all potential stakeholders who will be

Table 10A.4.1 *Payer Mix at BGH*

	Inpatients (%)	Outpatients (%)
Medi-Cal	39	24
Medicare	19	16
Commercial insurance & other sources	9	20

affected by the plan. It stands to reason that if more stakeholders come into agreement about the overall value and specific details of a plan, there will be a greater chance of eventual success. In terms of the plan being proposed here, the most important stakeholders include the Cath Lab staff, the Recovery Room staff, the 1M outpatient clinic, the BGH administration, cardiac patients and their families, as well as the Bay City region as a whole.

The Cath Lab staff, including the chief cardiologist and the case manager nurse, seems to have a stake in this plan, which is motivated by a sincere belief that they are an underutilized resource at BGH and would be happy to increase patient traffic through their unit. According to the chief cardiologist of the Cath Lab, the Cath Lab already has the staffing capacity to perform more scheduled LHCs, yet they are unable to because there is not enough staffing in the Recovery Room (4C) for PreOp and PostOp care. In other words, additional daily procedures could be performed with only marginal additions in supply and labor costs, yet a simple bottleneck in the system is stopping this from happening.

On the other side of the coin, the Recovery Room nurse manager explains that she cannot reserve more daily bed space specifically for Cath Lab patients because of staffing limitations. The Recovery Room nurse manager believes that patient safety, nursing morale, and quality of care might be compromised if Recovery Room staff is given more work without any new FTEs to cover that work.

A third party involved in these discussions will be the appropriate BGH administration. We feel that if provided with the evidence and arguments in this business plan, these stakeholders will recognize that the hospital could benefit from the combination of additional revenues brought in by more elective Cath Lab procedures. Furthermore, the hospital could benefit from the preventative nature of this work by generating savings in a reduction of cardiac emergency procedures.

Patients are another group of stakeholders who will certainly benefit from this plan. When indicated and performed successfully, elective and minimally invasive LHC procedures have the potential to diagnose potentially serious diseases, reduce the likelihood of cardiac emergencies, increase quality of life, and prevent unnecessary death. Finally, the public health of Bay City and the metropolitan area should improve through the proposed increase in preventative health-care, lower per-unit procedure costs, shorter LOS, and fewer ED visits. And as any taxpayer knows, improvement in public health often brings savings in healthcare spending and less waste of scarce tax dollars.

BUDGET

The budget for this plan includes the cost of 1.5 FTEs of Recovery Room nursing support. This expense will help the Cardiac Cath Lab maximize revenues by filling their excess capacity with more LHC procedures. The wages and benefits for a full-time nurse are estimated at $80,000 per year, so 1.5 FTEs are estimated at $120,000 annually. Of course, when there is not a full load of Cath Lab recovery patients to care for, this nurse will be assigned to care for patients coming in from other areas of the hospital, but the nurse's primary responsibility will be to the Cath Lab.

The additional cost of this project is based on the number of additional LHCs the Cath Lab is expected to perform with the increased Recovery Room support. The procedure cost is estimated at $4074 and the Recovery Room costs are estimated at $1682 per case. The total annual cost for 108 more procedures are therefore estimated at $621,648. Although the Cath Lab generates revenues, the actual reimbursement is uncertain, as many BGH patients are covered by public programs or are unable to pay. A conservative estimate is that $100,000 of the procedure costs are not covered by a patient's insurance or self-pay over a year. The total cost of increasing the Cath Lab utilization is therefore estimated at $220,000 over the coming year.

Savings are estimated based on the assumption of 2 fewer ED visits per year and four fewer inpatient days a year related to preventable coronary artery blockage managed by increasing utilization of the Cath Lab. An ED visit is estimated to cost $3042, so the estimated ED savings per year is $6084. An inpatient day is estimated to cost $6000, so the estimated savings per year is $24,000. The total savings over the coming year is estimated at $30,084.

A cost-benefit analysis (CBA) shows a loss of $189,916 over the coming year as the estimated expenses of $220,000 exceed the estimated savings of $30,084. However, the setting is a public hospital where community health is valued. This leads to the Quality-Adjusted Life Year (QALY) analysis discussed in the next section.

QALY Analysis

In deciding whether or not the benefits of our project outweigh the costs, we feel that the most important benefits derived from more LHCs can be found using the concept of QALY. QALY is often used in the medical field to assess whether or not the benefit of a treatment is worth the cost (Lee, Chertow, & Zenios, 2009; Winkelmayer, Weinstein, Mittleman, Glynn, & Pliskin, 2002). One single QALY refers to an extension of exactly 1 life-year for one perfectly healthy person. From this perspective on health, a person who lives one additional year at only 50% health would be receiving only 0.5 QALY. Likewise, a perfectly healthy person whose life is extended by only half a year would also receive only 0.5 QALY.

Because BGH is a public facility dedicated to improving the health of the Bay City region, the hospital does not seek to make a profit per se, but rather seeks to improve and extend the lives of the people it serves. Therefore, we think it would be a mistake to only ask how profitable this project can be; on the contrary, using QALY in our cost/benefit analysis captures the true value of the work done at BGH. Although assigning an exact monetary value to a year of life for a human being is somewhat subjective and hotly debated in the field of health-care finance, the most commonly used estimates for a QALY range between $50,000 and $129,000 (Lee, Chertow, & Zenios, 2009; Winkelmayer et al., 2002).

Considering the fact that only patients with serious cardiac abnormalities are indicated for LHC, we will assume that getting this important diagnostic procedure done will add at least 0.5 QALYs to each of these patients' lives. This may in fact be a conservative estimate, knowing that an undiagnosed cardiac problem represents a sort of "ticking time-bomb" that a person carries around until it is too late. Note that we use a conservative estimate for the dollar value of 0.5 QALY ($25,000) in our savings calculation, derived from performing more elective LHCs at BGH. To be even more conservative with our estimates, we assume that only half of the patients receiving more timely LHCs will experience the 0.5 QALY benefit. We therefore estimate the total QALY savings for 54 procedures at $25,000 QALY benefit as $1,350,000 over the coming year. This is the savings expected in the community from implementing our project.

The CBA that includes the estimated QALY savings is estimated as $30,084 plus $1,350,000, or a total of $1,380,084 over the coming year. When compared to the total expenses of $220,000, the CBA shows savings of $1,160,084 over the coming year. The benefit/cost ratio is estimated at 6.27 ($1,160,084 ÷ $220,000). In other words, the project returns $6.27 in benefits to BGH and the Bay City community for every $1 spent.

Potential Cost-Shifting

An added benefit to performing more outpatient procedures in the Cath Lab will derive from changes in this unit's payer mix and an opportunity to perform cost-shifting. In general, hospitals will profit more from a Payer Mix that includes a higher percentage of bills paid through private insurance and a lower percentage paid through government insurance. Referring back to Table 10A.4.1, we see that outpatients at BGH carry a much higher percentage of private insurance (20%) than do inpatients (9%). Therefore, it is fair to assume that doing a higher proportion of emergency in-patient procedures in the Cath Lab (the current situation) tilts the payer mix more toward unprofitable government insurance.

In terms of cost-shifting, it is common knowledge in the health care industry that some health plans, such as Medicaid, reimburse at a rate that is lower than the hospital's costs. On the other hand, private health plans often reimburse at a rate that is higher than the hospital's costs. Attracting more patients who are covered by private health plans thus enables the hospital to cover more of the costs for patients whose costs are not fully reimbursed. Clearly, the change in Cath Lab payer mix described above provides a perfect opportunity for cost-shifting.

A final added benefit derived from higher patient volume in the Cath Lab will be a reduction in the per-unit cost of performing procedures. This will happen because performing more procedures in the same Cath Lab with the same staffing takes full advantage of the high fixed costs already put into the unit and adds only marginal inputs (i.e., costs for medical supplies) to the cost of each additional procedure. In other words, more Cath Lab volume reaps the benefits of economies of scale.

TIMELINE

This project could be implemented as soon as the unit leaders and necessary administrators agree that funds should be made available for additional nursing staff in the Recovery Room. This could happen in the next month or 2, with official plan implementation beginning this summer. If approved and implemented, we think that it would also be prudent to gather data and analyze the actual costs and benefits of this plan 12 months after implementation. After analysis is complete and data are compiled into a compact, manageable format (handout, PowerPoint), a follow-up meeting of unit leaders and administration will make the decision whether or not to continue the plan. The Gantt Chart (Table 10A.4.2) clearly lays out this timeline.

Table 10A.4.2 *Project Timeline (Gantt Chart)*

	Spring 2012	Summer 2012	Fall 2012	Winter 2012	Spring 2013	Summer 2013	Fall 2013
Phase 1	[ ]						
Phase 2		[ ]					
Phase 3					[ ]		
Phase 4						[ ]	
Phase 5						[ ]	

Notes:
Phase 1 = Meet with unit leaders & appropriate hospital administration.
Phase 2 = If budget approved, implement plan: hire Recovery Room RN & increase Cath Lab procedures.
Phase 3 = Evaluation stage: gather data & perform 12-month review of actual costs/benefits of plan.
Phase 4 = Meet with unit leaders & appropriate hospital administration to determine if plan continues.
Phase 5 = Continue or terminate plan from this point into the future.

CONCLUSION

In conclusion, the ability to have an additional recovery nurse available for the recovery Cath Lab at BGH could play a significant role in improving patient care by performing more outpatient procedures and reducing admissions through the ED. The addition of just one recovery bed per day that is reserved for patients from this unit could double the total amount of procedures performed on a weekly, monthly, and yearly basis. The addition and full-time use of a second recovery bed could decrease the length of stay for some patients, due to the fact that scheduled LHCs procedures are more preventative in nature and prevent catastrophic emergencies. This could potentially decrease the total number of cardiac patients admitted through the ED.

Performing more diagnostic outpatient LHCs will potentially prevent serious cardiac complications that have a lower cost and will provide BGH with an estimated 20% reduction cost in savings. With the proposed 1.5 FTE nurse at BGH, more preventative measures can be completed, thus few patients will come to the ED, which will save the hospital thousands of dollars. With the savings theoretically calculated, BGH can save up to $30,084 if only two ED visits and four inpatient days are prevented. BGH will then potentially attain these savings if more preventative diagnostic LHCs are performed.

Finally, it was decided that in order to provide a greater benefit to this proposal a QALY estimation will be elaborated; this estimation will assess whether or not the benefit of a treatment is worth the cost, and how effectively the treatment could be in preserving more years of healthy life to indicated patients. The QALY analysis indicates that the cost of funding this project results in an increased amount of healthy life for patients valued to be at least three times greater than the initial investment. Since BGH is a public facility dedicated to improving the health of the Bay City region, it is an excellent use of resources.

REFERENCES

Bay General Hospital (BGH). (2011). BGH & Trauma Center annual report fiscal year 2009–2010. Bay City, CA: BGH.

Bay General Hospital Foundation. (2011). *About bay general hospital and trauma center.* Bay City, CA: BGH

Institute of Medicine. (2003). *Health professions education: A bridge to quality.* Washington, DC: National Academies Press.

Lee, C. P., Chertow, G. M., & Zenios, S. A. (2009). An empiric estimate of the value of life: Updating the renal dialysis cost-effectiveness standard. *Value in Health, 12,* 80–87. Retrieved April 23, 2012 from http://www.scribd.com/doc/13230503/Empiric-Estimate-of-the-Value-of-Life-Stanford-Study

Winkelmayer, W. C., Weinstein, M. C., Mittleman, M. A., Glynn, R. J., & Pliskin, J. S. (2002). Health economic evaluations: The special case of end-stage renal disease treatment. *Medical Decision Making, 22,* 417–430.

Appendix 10A.5: Business Plan—Probiotic Use With Antibiotics

*Natalie Bower, Gehrig Ertle, Emily Finzen,
Lindsey Reardon, and Cassen Uphold*

EXECUTIVE SUMMARY

This business plan strongly supports the use of probiotics in combination with antibiotic treatment on Unit A. Probiotics given prophylactically with antibiotics reduce the rate of antibiotic-associated diarrhea (AAD) and *Clostridium difficile*-associated diarrhea (CDAD), two common hospital-acquired complications associated with antibiotic treatment that can lead to death (McFarland, 2008). In addition, a decrease in the length of patient stay and a lower cost of patient care will be realized.

Treating AAD and CDAD can cost up to $80,000 per patient and increase patient length of stay by 24 days. Multiple randomized studies have proven the efficacy and safety of probiotic administration with antibiotic therapy, reducing incidence rates of AAD and CDAD by 95% (Gao, Mubasher, Fang, Reifer, & Miller, 2010). In addition, there have been no reported adverse effects associated with probiotic therapy (Avandhani & Miley, 2011). The unit will realize substantial cost savings within the first year.

The cost for implementing the plan will be minimal, at only $65,929 the first year, and $25,929 annually after that, for a total of $91,858 over 2 years. With the major reduction in the incidence of both AAD and CDAD, and therefore the cost of its treatment, the hospital will see a $4,657,018 savings each year ($4,591,089 the first year). That is a total of $13,828,527 back into the hospital's budget over the 3-year period.

In addition to saving the hospital a substantial amount of money, this business plan improves patient outcomes and reduces the risk of prominent hospital-acquired infections. At the same time, patient satisfaction will increase while the average length of stay decreases, freeing up beds for new patients. Ultimately, this will allow the hospital staff to focus their time on other patients.

INTRODUCTION AND PROBLEM IDENTIFICATION

Diarrhea, a frequent side effect of antibiotic treatment, can lead to further complications, such as increased health care costs and increased length of stay in the hospital. Antibiotic-associated diarrhea (AAD) is the most recurrent complication of antibiotic use (McFarland, 2008). The bacteria C. *difficile* is highly implicated in AAD, as AAD caused by C. *difficile* is a complication in an estimated 5% to 25% of antibiotic treatments (Hickson et al., 2007). In some instances CDAD can be fatal, with mortality rates as high as 30% in elders and severely ill patients (Nelson et al., 2011).

Health care-associated outbreaks have the highest frequency of AAD, with incidence rates at times occurring in 34 out of 100 patients. According to McFarland (2008), while other nosocomial infections have declined from 2000 to 2009, The National Nosocomial Infections Surveillance reports that the number of CDAD infections among hospitalized patients each year has more than doubled from 139,000 to 336,600. According to the Center for Disease Control's Emerging Infections Program data in 2010, 94% of identified C. *difficile* infections were associated with health care treatment (Centers for Disease Control and Prevention [CDC], 2012). AAD typically lasts from 1 to 7 days and can increase a hospital stay by up to 24 days. The cost of caring for a single patient with AAD or CDAD can range from $3500 to $77,483 (McFarland, 2008). The annual cost for C. *difficile* infection in the United States is $3.2 billion. Up to 60% of patients with CDAD experience a recurrence, even after numerous antibiotic treatments. In some instances these recurrent episodes can occur for upto 4 years (McFarland, 2008). Overall, these complications validate the significance of implementing a plan to prevent AAD and CDAD.

PROPOSED SOLUTION

Probiotic administration during antibiotic therapy is a cost-effective intervention to prevent ÀAD. This business plan includes a review of current literature to confirm the efficacy of probiotic use for the prevention AAD and CDAD. As antibiotic use destroys the natural flora in the gut, it also increases the risk of diarrhea, promotes toxic metabolite production, and changes the immunity within the gut due to increased growth of pathogenic bacteria.

Many researchers have proven that probiotics can prevent AAD by interrupting the possible mechanisms; by preserving gut flora and ongoing carbohydrate fermentation; and/or by competitively preventing the growth of pathogens (Hickson, 2011). In a randomized trial study the incidence of AAD was reduced by 64% and CDAD by 95% with probiotic use (Gao et al., 2010). Avandhani and Miley (2011) conducted a meta-analysis of studies that tested the efficacy of probiotics used for preventing AAD and CDAD in adults in the acute care setting. The intervention on average lowered the risk of AAD by 44% and CDAD by 71% (Avandhani & Miley, 2011). The general consensus from the current literature is that probiotics can significantly reduce the occurrence of AAD and CDAD (Table 10A.5.1).

Therefore, based on current literature, this business plan is focused on reducing the incidence of AAD and CDAD in hospitalized patients requiring antibiotic therapy. In addition, the average length of patient stay and the cost for treating AAD and CDAD related to antibiotic therapy will be reduced. Probiotics will be given prophylactically while patients are undergoing antibiotic therapy. The hospital should benefit from a substantial reduction in the number of AAD and CDAD complications, with an average decrease between 55% and 85%, respectively.

PROGRAM GOALS AND OBJECTIVES

We will target a 20-bed medical surgical unit with a high incidence of AAD and CDAD. Patients are at a high risk for AAD and CDAD because the majority of patients are on continuous antibiotic infusions and the majority of the patient population is 65 or older, two significant risk factors in the development of both AAD and CDAD.

The goal of the program is as follows:

1. By the conclusion of the 1-year trial period, the program will have effectively prevented high-risk patients on antibiotic therapy from developing AAD and CDAD with the use of prophylactic probiotic treatment (PPT) as supported by a statistically significant reduction in the incidences of AAD and CDAD and by substantial financial savings for the hospital. Assuming success, this program can then be extended to appropriate patients on multiple units so that by the end of year two the program is hospital-wide in applicable units.

The objectives of the program are as follows:

1. Reduce the incidence of AAD by 55% and CDAD by 85% within 2 years.
2. Reduce patient length of stay related to AAD and CDAD by 75% within 2 years.
3. Reduce overall hospital costs related to AAD and CDAD by 65% within 2 years.

Table 10A.5.1 *Description of Randomized Control Trials Evaluating AAD and Probiotics*

Authors/year of citation	Type of study	Data collection methods	Sample characteristics	Key findings
Hickson et al. (2007)	Randomized, double-blind, placebo- controlled	Occurrence of AAD and presence of CDAD	135 inpatients on antibiotic therapy	Significant reduction, but fail to differentiate which bacteria species is most effective. Financial savings with the administration of probiotics.
Safdar, Barigala, Said, and McKinley (2008)	Randomized, double-blind, placebo-controlled	Daily assessments of inpatients and survey reporting from discharged patients	39 inpatients, age 47 to 72, placed on antibiotic therapy for a minimum of 72 hours	Some support of probiotics use, but possible response bias and underreporting.
Psaradellis and Sampalis (2010)	Randomized, double-blind, placebo-controlled	Duration of diarrhea, severity of diarrhea	216 adult patients on antibiotic therapy for a minimum of 2 to 3 days	Coadministration of the probiotic reduced the risk of AAD by 37.3% and decreased duration by one-half.
Gao et al. (2010)	Randomized, double-blind, placebo-controlled	Incidence of AAD and CDAD	255 adults, age 50 to 70 years, on antibiotic therapy for at least 3 days	Incidence of AAD and CDAD was significantly reduced with probiotic use and higher dosages that resulted in greater efficacy.

BUDGET

Based on the best estimates, it is calculated that the cost of this program will be $65,929 the first year and $25,929 annually after that (Table 10A.5.2). This cost is based on the potential cost of administering one of three proposed probiotics to 30 patients per month, for an entire year. The clinical nurse leader (CNL) will already be employed as salaried staff on the unit, however an additional cost of $40,000 will be needed for the first year to pay another part-time nurse to help the CNL in training the staff. The CNL will take on the administrative management of this project, and the training nurse will teach the justification for probiotics in patient care, and educate nurses and physicians on the possible probiotic prescriptions. Additionally, the physicians and nursing staff will not be required to spend any extra time outside their normal hours to facilitate this program, nor will they incur any additional costs.

COST-BENEFIT ANALYSIS

Although there is a rising problem with AAD and CDAD, one option is for the hospital to do nothing. If the hospital chooses not to take any action, AAD and CDAD will continue to be a substantial cost to the hospital (Table 10A.5.3). The cost of AAD/CDAD was conservatively calculated using the average cost of a 1-night hospital stay and the cost of personal protective equipment (PPE) needed by the staff to care for these patients. This number ($7402) was multiplied by the average increased length of stay for AAD/CDAD patients, 10.7 days (Pepin, Valiquette, & Cossette, 2005), and then by the average cases of AAD/CDAD per month (seven cases) on the unit. AAD and CDAD are causes of preventable readmissions; the current emphasis on reducing these readmissions supports the need for some sort of intervention rather than doing nothing. This calculation estimates that if the hospital chooses to do nothing to address the incidence of AAD and CDAD that related costs will continue to be $6,652,884 per year. Financially, this is not a good option.

Table 10A.5.2 *Two-Year Projections 2013 to 2015*

Annual cost of PPT prescriptions	$25,929 (at most, depending on which probiotic is prescribed) ($)
Training nurse (year 1)	40,000
Assumed annual savings[1]	4,657,018
Total savings in first year[2]	4,591,089
Total savings in second year[3]	4,618,719
Cost from 2013 to 2015 without PPT program[4]	19,958,652
Savings with implementation of PPT program from 2013 to 2015	13,828,527

Notes:

[1] Assumes decrease in incidence of AAD and CDAD of 70% (average of estimated decreased incidence of 55% for AAD, and 85% of CDAD).

[2] Based on assumed annual saving minus cost of PPT program for first year (includes cost for training nurse, first year only).

[3] Based on assumed annual saving minus cost of PPT program (not including training nurse).

[4] Based on estimated annual cost of one fiscal year of 84 cases, average cost of 11.7 day hospital stay ($6,605,256), plus average cost of PPE needed in AAD/CDAD cases per day ($47,628) with total cost $6,652,884.

Table 10A.5.3 Cost of AAD/CDAD

	One day of AAD/ CDAD ($)	AAD/CDAD increases pt. stay by average 10.7 days ($)	Average seven cases/month ($)	One fiscal year of 84 cases with each case with add 10.7 day stay ($)
Average cost of one night hospital stay	7349	78,634	550,438	6,605,256
Average cost of PPE needed in ADD/CDAD cases per day	53	567	3969	47,628
Total	7402	79,201	554,407	6,652,884

Table 10A.5.4 Probiotic Rx Costs

	Cost for one patient per day ($)	Cost for 30 patients per day ($)	Cost for 30 patients per day for a year ($)
VSL#3 (*Lactobacillus* bacteria) Dose: 2 capsules/day	2.37	71.04	25,929
Culturelle (*Lactobacillus* rhamnosus GG) Dose: 1 capsule/day	0.44	13.19	4814
Florastor (*Saccharomyces Boulardii Lyo*) Dose: 1 capsule/day	0.69	20.70	7555

If the hospital chooses to implement the prophylactic probiotic program it will be at a small cost with the potential for significant savings. The cost of administering probiotics varies from $0.44 to $2.37 (Table 10A.5.4) a day per patient depending on the probiotic prescribed by the physician. This equals as little as $4814 to $25,929 to medicate thirty patients a day for an entire year. If the program is successful and reduces the incidence of AAD and CDAD by 55% and 85% respectively, it could save the hospital upwards of $6 million in prolonged length of stay and equipment used. Additionally, the prophylactic treatment program has the potential to reduce preventable readmission rates related to AAD and CDAD. While it is hard to determine an exact number, preventing readmissions has the potential to save the hospital millions of dollars annually. The assumed annual savings with implementation of the PPT program is $4,657,018, and the projected 2-year savings are $9,314,036 (Table 10A.5.2).

If the hospital chooses not to implement the prophylactic probiotic program, but wants to do something about the increasing issue of AAD and CDAD, it could put every patient that presents with diarrhea on contact precautions until the cause of the diarrhea is determined. This will help reduce the spread of CDAD to other patients. Assuming that 55 patients a month, a conservative estimate, are put on contact precautions for a minimum of 2 days, the PPE and the laboratory tests to rule out CDAD will cost about $138,600 (Table 10A.5.5). It is hard to determine how effective and how cost-effective this plan would be. It would potentially help reduce the spread of CDAD, but not the development of AAD.

AAD and CDAD are complications in an estimated 5% to 25% of antibiotic treatments (Hickson, 2007) and *C. difficile* alone is estimated to cost $3.2 billion annually in the United States, lengthening hospital stays by an average of 3.6 days (Salkind, 2010). For the elderly

Table 10A.5.5 *Cost of CDAD*

	Minimum 2 days contact precautions before cause is determined	Average of 55 patients a month put on precautions for minimum 2 days	Total for a year of 55 patients a month put on precautions for minimum 2 days
Cost PPE per patient ($53/day)	$106	$5830	$69,960
Cost of lab test per patient	$104	$5720	$68,640
Total cost	$210	$11,550	$138,600

Table 10A.5.6 *Hidden Cost Savings*

Reduced expense areas	Influencing factors
Decreased patient care time (RN, CNA)	Fewer incidents of incontinence, fewer patient calls to use restroom/commode, fewer laboratory sample collections, lest time spent donning PPE
Fewer physician visits	Physicians will experience decreased calls for AAD and CDAD
Fewer laboratory tests	Few orders for *C. difficile* stool testing
Fewer diarrhea-associated adverse events	Decreased mortality, decreased falls
Decreased equipment usage	Less usage of sheets, bed pans, chux, gowns, gloves, masks, etc.

population, who experience incontinence more frequently, diarrhea can also be a very time-consuming issue to the nurses who must either help patients to the commode frequently or perform linen changes and bed baths when bed pans are not used. *C. difficile* is also highly contagious if the proper precautions are not used.

Upon successful implementation of the program, there will be several benefits that will influence cost savings beyond simply the cost of increased length of stay; these savings are difficult to quantify (Table 10A.5.6). Patients will require less incontinence care from CNAs and nurses, and will need to make fewer calls to use a restroom or commode. CNAs and nurses will experience improved productivity, as administration of the probiotics will be given with patients' other medications and will not take substantially more time. Doctors will benefit from fewer calls to visit patients who have developed AAD and CDAD, and all staff will save time because the need to implement contact precautions will be decreased. In addition, the patient will benefit from increased peace of mind, satisfaction, and comfort for the patient and family.

MARKET ANALYSIS

This treatment plan will be applied to a varied mix of clients on the unit. Clients will be hospitalized for an assortment of procedures, and will have varied nutritional and medical needs. Probiotics will not be prescribed to patients on total parental nutrition, but may be administered to patients with gastric or nasogastric tubing who are not NPO. The clients will share the commonality of concurrently being on oral or IV antibiotics, as these patients are at risk. The payer in this proposed plan will be the hospital. Insurance and Medicare policy is changing so that hospitals will not be reimbursed for nosocomial infections, therefore, the hospital will benefit financially from prophylactic treatment of AAD and CDAD.

As popularity of probiotic treatment has increased in recent years, it is expected that potential competitors will also use probiotic treatment in some form. It is also expected that patients will be amenable to this additional treatment because of its positive reputation. With the formalized treatment plan, a measurable decrease in AAD and CDAD is expected, which may improve statistics for the unit, influencing the program to be adopted hospital-wide. With improved statistics for nosocomial infections and with probiotic treatment free to patients, the hospital may attract more patients for elective in-patient procedures, therefore increasing market share.

The program currently includes the option of three possible probiotics that physicians may prescribe to patients. These options may change if supply or demand affects pricing, and as more probiotics are offered on the market. Physician autonomy in prescribing will potentially increase compliance to the program.

PROGRAM IMPLEMENTATION AND SCHEDULE

This program will be implemented over 2 years and will include several milestones (Table 10A.5.7). Initially, baseline data will be collected retroactively for the previous

Table 10A.5.7 *Timeline for Necessary Tasks (Preimplementation)*

Tasks to be completed to run test of change	Who	When	Tools or training needed	Measures
Collection of baseline data	Team	Weeks 1 to 3	Staff surveys, statistics of incidence and prevalence of CDAD and AAD, additional unit information	N/A
Solicit input and approval from staff (RNs, MDs, NMs, ANMs)	Team	Weeks 1 to 3	Initial communication via e-mail and posters, time in staff meeting (daily huddle, weekly meetings), availability	Staff provide input, feedback obtained
Finalize program and teaching materials	Team	Weeks 4 to 5	Baseline data and staff feedback, generate information brochures and documents	N/A
Collaboration and training with staff (RNs, MDs, pharmacy)	Team, pharmacy	Weeks 6 to 7	Provide final information for staff, ensure supply of probiotics with pharmacy	All staff on unit and pharmacy on board
Data and evaluation measures put in place	Team	Weeks 6 to 7	Surveys printed, patient contact information	All measures in place for go-live
Finalize start date with staff	Team	Week 7	N/A	Start date finalized
Final team meeting ("huddle")	Team	1 to 2 days prior to start date	Any final questions answered; generate enthusiasm for program implementation	Patients participate, program begins

6 months by the CNL, including AAD and CDAD rates, respective costs for AAD and CDAD, average length of stay, recurrence of diagnosed *C. difficile*, morality, and diarrhea associated adverse events. It is important to establish these numbers to accurately determine the success of probiotic administration.

While baseline data are being collected, the unit will concurrently gather the tools and training materials needed for both patients and staff. It will be important to educate both the nurses and physicians on the unit regarding this program, as their participation is crucial to its success, and appropriate funding is budgeted for this to be accomplished. The CNL and the training nurse will conduct the teaching and education for the staff prior to implementation. Nurses will also be informed via e-mail and postings in break rooms, as well as reminded during daily huddles and weekly meetings on the unit. Interns, residents, and attendings must be notified and become enthusiastic regarding this program, as they will be prescribing the probiotics. Their responses and feedback will be gauged at the multidisciplinary rounding sessions. Additionally, the unit will work closely with pharmacy to ensure that an adequate amount of appropriate probiotic supplies are on hand. Once everything is in place to begin the implementation phase of this program, available nurses, nurse managers, and physicians will go over the finalized protocol, after which point patients will then be started on the probiotic program.

The main limitation facing the success of this business plan will be determining the appropriate prescription based on the patient's data, current medications, and specific antibiotic therapy. To combat this barrier, proposed probiotics will be suggested. Proper dosing amounts and schedules will be determined in consultation with a committee comprised of selected physicians, nurses, and pharmacists. During the first 6 months of the business plan's implementation, doses and medications will be adjusted based on data collected from patients placed on the probiotic administration and the committee's feedback. After this time, appropriate dosing should be determined for selected patient profiles.

CNL AS PROGRAM LEADER AND SUMMARY OF REQUIRED RESOURCES

The CNL will be the program leader for the PPT program. The CNL's main role will be to oversee the management of the program and ensure adherence to the proposed timeline. Specifically, the CNL will be responsible for collecting the baseline data for the previous 6 months of AAD and CDAD rates, respective costs, and all other associated factors and events, as previously explained. Additionally, the CNL will prepare the educational material needed for staff teaching regarding the PPT program, and will follow up with staff for feedback regarding the program. The CNL will also be responsible for monitoring and tracking lab results of the patients who are given the PPT, as well as other associated data. The main resources necessary for program implementation will be staff participation, from both physicians and nurses, as well as from the pharmacy to ensure the probiotics will be available as needed.

The key stakeholders include the patients, the hospital and specific unit, physicians, and nurses. The role of the patient in implementation of the PPT will be related to participation. Patients always have the right to refuse medications and cannot be forced to comply with the proposed plan. The physician's role will be to prescribe probiotics prophylactically and concurrently with oral and IV antibiotic prescriptions. The nurse's role will be to administer the medications, and theoretically, assist in encouraging the patients to take the medications by educating them on the associated benefits. Additionally, the nurses will be responsible for collecting stool samples for cultures, when necessary.

EVALUATION OF PROGRAM

Following program implementation, program success will be evaluated based on its object-ives. The 2 metrics used to measure this will be the incidence of AAD and the number of negative stool cultures for *C. difficile*. Other metrics will also be collected, including length of hospital stay, mortality, adverse events, and recurrence of *C. difficile* infection. Additionally, the CNL will collect patient and staff surveys regarding satisfaction, to assess if the pro-biotic administration was a practical and positive experience.

As the program progresses, the CNL and hospital administrators will be able to more accurately assess its success, as data will be collected in real time. The unit will hold interim analysis conferences every 50 patients to determine how probiotic administration is affect-ing AAD and CDAD incidence. Assuming savings following year 2, the program will be expanded to other units in the hospital.

CONCLUSION

In summary, evidence strongly supports the use of probiotics in combination with anti-biotic treatment. This business plan demonstrates that implementing such a program on Unit A will improve patient outcomes and reduce the risk of prominent hospital-acquired infections, while drastically reducing costs to the hospital. Since the cost to implement the program will be minimal ($91,858 over 2 years) and the savings to the hospital are substan-tial ($9,248,107 over 2 years), there is no reason this plan should not be implemented.

REFERENCES

Avandhani, A., & Miley, H. (2011). Probiotics for prevention of antibiotic-associ-ated diarrhea and *Clostridium difficile*-associated disease in hospitalized adults-A meta-analysis. *Journal of the American Academy of Nurse Practitioners, 23,* 269–274. doi:10.1111/j.1745–7599.2011.00617.x

Centers for Disease Control and Prevention (CDC). (2012). EIP surveillance methodology for *Clostridium difficile* infections. Atlanta, GA: US Department of Health and Human Services.

Gao, X. W., Mubasher, M., Fang, C. Y., Reifer, C., & Miller, L. (2010). Dose-response efficacy of a proprietary probiotic formula of *Lactobacillus acidophilus* CL1285 and *Lactobacillus casei* LBC80R for antibiotic-associated diarrhea and *Clostridium difficile*-associated diarrhea prophylaxis in adult patients. *American Journal of Gastroenterology, 105,* 1636–1641.

Hickson, M. (2011). Probiotics in the prevention of antibiotic-associated diarrhea and *Clostridium difficile* infection. *Therapeutic Advances in Gastroenterology, 4,* 185–197.

Hickson, M., D'Souza, A., Muthu, N., Rogers, T., Want, S., Rajkumar, C., & Bulpitt, C. (2007). Use of probiotic *Lactobacillus* preparation to prevent diarrhoea associated with antibiot-ics: randomized double blind placebo controlled trial. *British Medical Journal.* doi:10.1136/bmj.39231.599815.55

McFarland, L. V. (2008). Antibiotic-associated diarrhea: Epidemiology, trends and treatment. *Future Microbiology, 3,* 563–578.

Nelson, R. L., Kelsy, P., Leeman, H., Meardon, N., Patel, H., Paul, K., & Malakun, R. (2011). Antibiotic treatment for *Clostridium difficile*-associated diarrhea in adults (Review). *The Cochrane Library,* 1–3.

Pepin, J., Valiquette, L., & Cossette, B. (2005). Mortality attributable to nosocomial *Clostridium difficile*-associated disease during an epidemic caused by a hypervirulent strain in Quebec. *Canadian Medical Association Journal, 173,* 2–6.

Psaradellis, E., & Sampalis, J. (2010). Efficacy of BIO K+ CL1285® in the reduction of anti-biotic-associated diarrhea – a placebo controlled double-blind randomized, multicenter study. *Archives of Medical Science, 6,* 56–64. doi :10.5114/aoms.2010.13508.

Safdar, N., Barigala, R., Said, A., & McKinley, L. (2008). Feasibility and tolerability of probiot-ics for prevention of antibiotic-associated diarrhoea in hospitalized US military veterans. *Journal of Clinical Pharmacy & Therapeutics, 33,* 663–668.

Salkind, A. R. (2010). *Clostridium difficile*: An update for the primary care clinician. *Southern Medical Journal, 103,* 896–900.

Chapter 11: Health Program Grant Writing

I have never been in a situation where having money made it worse—Clinton Jones

Learning Objectives

1. Compare at least two similarities and differences between business plans and health program grant proposals.
2. Select at least three sections of a health program grant proposal and explain why these sections should be included in a grant application.
3. Design a SMART program objective with at least one related activity and one evaluation method for the objective.
4. Apply budgeting skills in determining personnel and nonpersonnel expenses in developing at least two health program grant proposal budget estimates.

Key Terms

business grant proposal
capability statement
capital improvement grant
competitive grant
demonstration grant
extramural funding
fiduciary agency
health program grant proposal
in-kind contributions
intramural funding

logic model
memorandum of understanding (MOU)
needs assessment
ongoing activity grant
operational assistance grant
planning grant
request for applications (RFA)
request for proposals (RFP)
research proposal

seed money
soft money
sole source grant
solicited grant proposal
special project grant
stakeholders
technical assistance grant
technical grant proposal
training grant
unsolicited grant proposal

Nurses who are employed or who volunteer in the community may see the need for resources to support a health program. Nurses working in inpatient facilities may also need resources for projects that provide community outreach. Grantwriting is a way for nurses to obtain resources for health care programs. More and more, health care is moving to the community, a setting in which grant funding is frequently available. For example, programs focusing on health care screening, education, and prevention may be eligible for grant funding.

This chapter presents a comparison of business plans and grant proposals. After discussing definitions associated with grant writing, the chapter recommends important content sections to include in grant proposals. A worksheet to use as a guide in grant writing is in Appendix 11A.1. Sample grant proposals are available in Appendices 11A.2 through 11A.4 to use as examples for grant writing.

One category of grant proposals frequently seen in health care is the **research proposal**. Rather than developing a health program, research proposals present an investigator's topic and methodology for a scientific study. A research proposal's primary purpose is to obtain resources to increase knowledge in an academic discipline. It is important to recognize that research proposals are not the focus of this chapter. This chapter focuses on health program grant proposals that seek funding for health services. Sources such as Gitlin and Lyons (2008), the Agency for Healthcare Research and Quality (AHRQ) Funding Opportunities website (www.ahrq.gov), and nursing research textbooks provide information for nurses writing a research proposal.

The category of grant proposals covered in this chapter is the **health program grant proposal**. Health program grant proposals are developed as an application to request funding in order to provide a specific service or set of services to a target population. The overall purpose of the health program grant proposal is to obtain resources in order to improve the health and wellness of individuals and populations in a community.

BUSINESS PLANS AND GRANT PROPOSALS

Business plans and health program grant proposals are similar in several respects. Both documents are written in order to convince the reader of an important need or problem that must be addressed. Business plans and grant proposals both describe an intervention or program that addresses the need or problem. A review of available and needed resources and a budget are usually required for both documents. Both business plans and grant proposals present a convincing justification for obtaining resources and funding to accomplish the project's or program's objectives within a specified time period.

Business plans and health program grant proposals also differ. A business plan's focus is usually internal, directed to administrators within the organization (or in some cases, investors or bank officers) who are asked to fund the project. The purpose of a business plan is to increase profitability. In some cases, the business plan increases profitability by generating revenues. In other cases, the business plan increases profitability by generating savings. Business plans are generally proprietary and are usually not shared with the public, the community, or other organizations.

In contrast, health program grant proposals are often directed to external funders and funding sources, referred to as **extramural funding**. For example, a nurse at Bigtown Hospital might write a grant proposal directed to the Robert Wood Johnson Foundation. Some organizations might offer **intramural funding** opportunities for grant writing. For example, Bigtown Hospital sponsors the Bigtown Health Foundation as a community service. The Bigtown Health Foundation funds health program grants that are written by Bigtown Hospital employees and implemented in Bigtown Hospital.

The funding for health program grant proposals usually comes either from a private foundation or a government funding agency. Health program grant proposals are often developed to meet community needs and provide community outreach. Grant funders may expect or even require community coordination and collaboration for resources and services that are part of the grant proposal. Grant proposals therefore have much more of an external, community-based focus than business plans. The Kaiser Permanente Grantmaking Funding Priority website lists initiatives and partnerships to improve health care in communities (http://info.kaiserpermanente.org/communitybenefit/html/grantmaking/global/grantmaking_1.html).

An example of a health program grant proposal to improve community health is the sample proposal in Appendix 11A.2. The applicants propose funding to purchase, equip, and staff a mobile van to provide dental care to underserved residents in an urban area.

Types of Health Program Grant Proposals

There are several types of health program grant proposals, and each type has a purpose. Health program proposals may request funding to plan for services. This type of health program proposal is a **planning grant**, which provides funding for assessing a community need or problem and planning a health program to meet those needs. Planning grants also provide resources for networking **stakeholders**, or people and organizations with an active concern about the community need. Stakeholders may include community providers, advocates, agencies, clients, caregivers, and experts who are actively interested in the community need. The planning grant often helps stakeholders establish coordination, collaboration, and partnerships in addressing the community need. Planning grants are usually funded only for 1 to 2 years. For example, the Healthy Start Initiative provides up to $50,000 over 1 to 2 years for collaborative planning for the health of school children in eligible schools.

Other types of grant proposals include **training grants** that fund staff training and education, and **technical assistance grants** that fund developing, implementing, and managing the activities of a community organization. The Health Resources and Services Administration (HRSA) provides resources and funding opportunities for technical assistance at its Health Center Planning Grants Technical Assistance website (www.hrsa.gov).

One of the most frequently seen types of health program grant proposals is the **demonstration grant**, which funds evidence-based, state-of-the-art, or model programs and services. For example, the U.S. Department of Housing and Urban Development (HUD) provides demonstration grant funding to protect children from housing-related hazards at its Healthy Homes Demonstration Grant Program website (www.hud.gov).

Planning grants are frequently linked to technical assistance or demonstration grants. An agency or group of agencies may apply for planning grant funds to assess community need, design a program or service, and establish community collaboration. Once that stage is complete, application is made for health program funding to implement the plan.

Capital improvement grants, which provide funding to build or renovate buildings and to acquire capital equipment, are fairly rare in the health arena. One exception is the American Recovery and Reinvestment Act (ARRA) Capital Improvement Program funding for health centers. **Operational assistance grants** that fund overhead expenses and the day-to-day support for the organization implementing the program or service are also unusual. Funders typically expect applicants to fund their own operational and capital expenses from sources other than grants. Figure 11.1 summarizes the major types of grant proposals and their purposes.

Health Program Proposal Purposes

Health program grant proposals serve several purposes. The health program proposal is a written plan describing a health care program. The proposal also specifies available and

Type	Purpose
Planning	Requests funding a community needs assessment, program planning, and networking to develop and enhance community-level coordination, collaboration, and partnership in addressing the health problem.
Training	Asks for funding to provide staff training and education.
Technical assistance	Justifies funding for developing, implementing, and managing the activities of a community organization.
Demonstration	Requests funding for model programs, services, or methodologies.
Capital improvement	Applies for funding to build or renovate buildings or to acquire capital equipment.
Operational assistance	Requests funding to help fund overhead and maintain the organization's day-to-day activities.

Figure 11.1 *Types and Purposes of Health Program Grant Proposals*

needed resources, activities required to carry out the program, and budget requirements, all within a given time frame. Once funding is obtained, a well-written proposal serves as a guide for implementing, managing, and evaluating the program.

Health program grant proposals may also serve as contracts. The grant proposal makes a request for specific resources as well as a promise of performance within the budget that is funded. Government funders frequently use contracts. Although private foundations may not specify a formal contract, there is usually an expectation that funding will be used to develop and provide the program described in the proposal. Both government and private funders increasingly require periodic recording and evidence of accountability in managing the grant funding.

Primarily, however, the health program grant proposal provides a convincing justification for funding that improves health and wellness. By identifying and targeting one or more community needs that require the proposed program, the grant proposal convinces the funder that a serious problem or gap in services exists. Further, the grant proposal convinces the funder that the proposed program is the best way to address this problem or gap in services, and that the applicants submitting the proposal are the best qualified to provide the proposed program.

Terms Used in Grant Writing

Some additional terms and definitions are helpful for nurses to understand when writing health program grant proposals. **Special project grants** typically fund new, special, pilot, or demonstration projects. Funding for special project grants is often referred to as **seed money**, because the funds are used to start a program. The grant funder generally only funds the program for 1 to 2 years, and then expects the program to be funded from other sources. In contrast, **ongoing activity grants** may extend for 3 to 5 years, or even longer, to continuously fund the program.

Depending on the funder, grant proposals may be **solicited**, in other words, formally and periodically requested by the funding agency. Solicited requests are often referred to as **requests for proposals (RFPs)** or **requests for applications (RFAs)**. In an RFP or an RFA, application and funding criteria are specific and detailed. Applicants must clearly target and address these criteria in order to qualify for funding. There usually is a specific deadline for proposal submission that must be adhered to without exception for the grant proposal to qualify for review. Government funders typically use the RFP or RFA approach, with application forms, guidelines, and deadlines for submitting proposals.

Many grant proposals are **unsolicited**. Private foundations may establish some policies around funding, such as only funding programs in a particular geographic area or for a particular health problem. However, foundations often accept proposals without specifying the extent of formal criteria that are typically specified for solicited grant proposals. Foundations also frequently accept proposals submitted at any time of the year, rather than adhering to specific schedules and deadlines. Grant writers often contact private foundations to find out if the foundation might be interested in reviewing a proposal for a given program.

Technical grant proposals focus on the program's objectives, activities, methods, organization, and staffing. In contrast, **business grant proposals** describe the budget, pricing, and all other financial information. In most cases, these are two sections of the same grant proposal, rather than two separate proposals. Most grant funders require both technical and business information.

Funders frequently restrict funding to direct service provision as provided by the project or program described in the grant proposal. Funding is usually not provided for capital, indirect, or organization operating expenses. Some funders may allow equipment purchase or rental directly related to program operation, but rarely fund construction, renovation, or major capital equipment purchase expenses. Some funders, mostly government funders, allow a percentage of funds to the sponsoring organization for overhead or indirect expenses such as administrative costs. However, funders typically restrict operational assistance funding. In most cases, grant funders expect that applicants are able to make capital investments, cover indirect costs, and maintain the day-to-day operations of their organization independent of grant funding.

Grant funding also varies depending on the amount of competition. **Sole source grants** may be made available when one and only one organization in the community demonstrates a unique ability to carry out a program and is selected without competing with other organizations. Even in the case of sole source funding, a proposal is required. Grant funding is usually provided through **competitive grants**, with several or more agencies applying for the program funding available. Increasingly, funders are encouraged to require interagency planning, coordination, collaborative efforts, and partnerships as a criteria for grant funding in order to reduce unnecessary duplication of programs and services and to make better use of the scarce funding available for health care programs.

FUNDING SOURCES

There are many sources for grant funding. However, it may be difficult to find a satisfactory match between funding that is needed and funding that is available for specific health care programs. Funding sources are often classified as government funders and private or charitable foundations. Federal, state, and local agencies typically use an RFP or RFA process to notify the public. A good source for finding federally-funded health program grants is the Grants.gov website. State and local health departments might be sources of information for state and local health program grant opportunities. The California HealthCare Foundation website (www.chcf.org) presents an RFP for the implementation of electronic prescribing of controlled substances (EPCS) in outpatient settings. An example of an RFP issued by a government agency is shown in Text Box 11.1.

Charitable foundations, such as the Baxter International Foundation (http://www.baxter.com/about_baxter/sustainability/international_foundation/index.html), typically represent private funders. Foundations may solicit grant proposals via an RFP or RFA process. In many cases, private foundations use a less structured and formal approach so that the proposal need only meet the foundation's requirements for funding to be reviewed.

Text Box 11.1 *Example of a Request for Proposal (RFP), Government Funder*

TITLE: Alcohol Education Project Grants (NIH Guide Sept. 10, 1999, PAS-99–165)
AGENCY: National Institute on Alcohol Abuse and Alcoholism (NIAAA)
   SCOPE: Broad ranges of educational approaches are included within the context of this announcement. Examples of anticipated activities include: (1) Educational activities directed to patients, their families, and the general public, which impart knowledge gained through research on alcohol-related health issues, including those related to screening, treatment, and prevention; (2) Educational activities directed toward enhancing the knowledge of primary and secondary school educators and/or students on alcohol-related problems; and (3) Educational activities directed toward college students and college-age individuals, which apply knowledge gained through research in addressing the particular alcohol issues confronting this age group.
   DEADLINE: Ongoing.
   CONTACT: Application Kits: (301) 435–0714. Programmatic Information: [personal name and direct phone number excluded]
   Source: Rural Information Center Health Service. (September 15, 2002). Federal Grant Opportunities Relevant to Rural Health. Beltsville, MD: National Agricultural Library. http://www.nal.usda.gov/ric/richs/grants.htm

---

Nurses should know how to locate funders that can be appropriately targeted for grant proposals. Public libraries frequently have directories for government and private funding sources. Although traditionally hard copy government catalogs and directories such as *The Foundation Directory* served as the key ways to locate grant funders, this directory and most grant funders now provide websites.

One suggestion in locating as many potential funders as possible is to do an Internet search, using a search engine and combining the search terms "grant funding" with the key word for the program. For example, searching on the terms "grant funding and child health" locates the website for the Bill & Melinda Gates Foundation Funding for Maternal, Newborn, and Child Health website (www.gatesfoundation.org), as well as other private and government funders.

GRANT PROPOSAL SECTIONS

Although funders may vary in their specific requirements for the content, and the page length may also vary accordingly, this chapter presents all of the sections of health program grant proposals that the funder is most likely to require. These are sections that nurses learning to write grants will find helpful to consider and address.

Cover Letter

Even if not specifically required, it is customary to include a cover letter when sending the health program grant proposal to the funding agency. This letter is frequently the first part of the proposal the funding reviewer may see, so it sets the tone for the proposal. The cover letter introduces the applicants who are sending the proposal, as well as the participating agency or agencies requesting the funding. The cover letter should be brief, clear, and accurate, and printed on the official letterhead of the agency represented in the proposal. It is essential to not only send the grant proposal to the funding agency, but to be sure the proposal is addressed to the correct department within the funding agency, and to the correct contact person.

The cover letter should include the name, address, phone number, and e-mail address of the primary contact who is applying for the grant funding. In other words, the reviewer must know who to contact in the agency regarding any questions or further discussion of the proposal, and how this person is reached. A proposal summary should make up the body of the letter, including a brief explanation as to why this particular funder was selected for the funding request. The letter often concludes by reviewing the capability of the applicant and requesting agency. In many cases, one person in the funding agency may only review the cover letter, and others may review the entire proposal. It is therefore important for the cover letter to be brief, yet as complete and convincing as possible.

Organization

Organization is not a section of the grant proposal, but a consideration for the proposal as a whole. The proposal document should be clearly and logically organized so the reviewer locates all important information quickly. It is important to write clearly and to make sure that reviewers easily understand the information presented in the proposal.

Grant proposals should begin with a title page that includes not only the title and the date the proposal was submitted, but the name and address of the funding agency and of the agency or agencies submitting the proposal, along with any needed contact information. The proposal itself should be organized logically. Proposals should begin with an introduction and continue through the various sections as outlined in this chapter or as specified by the funding agency. Proposals longer than six to eight pages should use headings and subheadings that clearly indicate the location of important content. Proposals longer than 30 pages should include a table of contents so reviewers can quickly locate information. Keep in mind that the reason for using a title page, headings, and table of contents is to organize and clearly communicate the message in the proposal.

The program grant proposal requires careful proofreading and revision. If possible, an outside reader should be invited to review the proposal and make critical comments, particularly related to clarity. Jargon and slang should be avoided, and acronyms should be spelled out the first time they are used. Any items in the appendix should be clearly identified and discussed in the proposal, with the appendices numbered in the order in which they are mentioned in the proposal. The reviewer should not have to puzzle over the meaning of a term or search through the proposal trying to identify where items are located.

Note that the sample grant proposals in Appendices 11A.2 through 11A.4 are also academic papers submitted for course credit. As a result, the authors of these papers followed American Psychological Association (APA) guidelines for citing and referencing all outside sources. Grant proposals prepared for actual grant funders might not require citations and references. However, it is still essential to be able to locate one's sources of financial data and other supporting evidence if the application reviewers have questions. As a result, it is important to keep a file of all sources used in the grant proposal, if citations and references are not included.

Proposal Introduction

The introduction should establish the proposal's tone and theme, and reinforce the content in the cover letter. The introduction should begin with the title, name of the applicant organization, contact information for the applicant, and name of the funding source. It should be clear what RFP, RFA, or funder interest the proposal addresses. The beginning of the proposal may therefore repeat some of the information that is in the cover letter.

In addition, the introduction should briefly describe the program's geographic area, target population to be served, purpose and significance, and the basic approach and major activity of the program. The introduction should also capture the reviewer's attention and interest, increasing the likelihood that the proposal will be closely reviewed and funded.

Problem Definition

Following the introduction, it is important to justify why the applicant sees a need for the proposed program. The problem addressed by the proposed program requires a problem definition that describes the nature, extent, and seriousness of the problem in enough detail to convince the funder of the problem's importance. For example, if the problem is a communicable disease, the problem definition might include an overview of the disease process, the extent of the disease, mortality and harmful outcomes attributed to the disease, costs of the disease, and health risks if the disease is not addressed.

The program's purpose should then be discussed. The overall program goal or goals should be stated, based on the program's purpose. Program and activities are developed later in the program description section. In the problem definition section, the proposal should focus on a brief program description and the program's overall purpose, goals, and benefits rather than its mechanics. For example, the proposal in Appendix 11A.2 discusses the problem of poor access to dental care for many low-income and uninsured in the community, and presents the idea of a mobile van as a program to address this problem. The overall goal is to improve community dental health.

Needs Assessment

At this stage, the funder should have at least an introductory understanding of the problem the proposed program addresses, and the overall goals and approaches the program will utilize. It is important to clearly and convincingly present the extent and seriousness of need for the program in the target population by reporting a **needs assessment**. The needs assessment is an evidence-based review of the community health need or problem.

There are various ways to document need. One approach is to present quantitative data, such as statistical or epidemiological findings and or demographic information. These data must be accurate, relevant, and clear to the reader. Any data reported in a table should be explained in the text of the proposal. Care must be taken to ensure that these data are accurate and that data sources are clearly identified. Moreover, data should be included only when it is relevant to the needs assessment and the proposal. Avoid the temptation to include data tables that do not serve a clear purpose in describing the need.

The results of relevant surveys to assess community needs can be quite helpful. These surveys may have been funded from a related planning grant, in some cases. Quantitative data should report and reinforce evidence of the extent and seriousness of the need, such as the extent of demand, characteristics of the target group, and the extent of persons in need who are unserved or underserved by current programs. The needs assessment in Appendix 11A.2 reviews the literature on unmet needs for dental care. The needs assessment then uses local data to estimate the extent of dental care need in Bay City.

Qualitative data may include observations or stories indicating and supporting the existence of need. For example, the needs assessment in Appendix 11A.2 describes how people arrive at the Waterhouse Health Clinic before business hours to try to be seen as one of only six walk-in dental appointments that are available. Stories are often powerful and convincing in documenting need. For example, the nurse might include a story about a client who could not obtain dental care and who suffered considerable pain as a result. For privacy, client names can be changed, or a story can be developed based on several clients so that personal identity is concealed.

Documentation of need may include a discussion of existing program limitations, comparing differences between the proposed program and existing programs. The description of an existing dental clinic in Bay City (Appendix 11A.2) points out the limited appointments available, reinforcing the need for more dental services.

Resources for community needs assessment may include local health departments, often good sources for information on health risks in the community. San Francisco provides a Healthy Development Measurement Tool website (www.thehdmt.org) with information useful to community needs assessment such as asthma hospitalizations in San Francisco neighborhoods. The Association for Healthcare Philanthropy (AHP) provides a website of resources for community health needs assessment (www.ahp.org).

Program Theory or Model

It is important to discuss the theory or model that provides a conceptual framework for the proposed program. In many cases, this discussion is included as part of the program description. Nurses developing programs for health education, health promotion, and wellness should be familiar with the current theories in those fields. Health program grant proposals are often more convincing if the program is supported by evidence-based theory.

Although many programs are not based on a theoretical framework or model, there are reasons to use theory in program planning and development. One reason for using theory is that it improves the chances of developing an effective program. A program that applies theory that has been extensively tested and adopted by other similar programs is more likely to demonstrate desired outcomes. It is helpful to conduct a thorough literature search to find evidence about programs addressing the community need or problem of interest.

Another reason for using theory is that it enables the applicant to more clearly explain how and why the program is expected to succeed. For example, the program in Appendix 11A.2 might have been based on program activities on the Health Belief Model, with an emphasis on Self-Efficacy Theory. According to Self-Efficacy, people are more likely to attempt to do something they believe they can accomplish compared to something they believe they cannot (Hayden, 2009). This theory might be applied to the Smiles on Wheels preventive dental education, using strategies to improve a person's personal dental hygiene and prevent serious dental problems.

Program Description

A program description explains details about the program and its activities. The program's methods and operations should be clearly discussed. The program proposal should indicate how program activities will be performed. For example, the proposal in Appendix 11A.2 describes how the dental van will travel to local health clinics to provide care. The dental van proposal also briefly describes what types of dental care will and will not be provided, with a clear rationale.

One approach useful in describing the program is to develop a **logic model**. A logic model uses a table, flow chart, or other visual layout to summarize and describe what a program will do and achieve. Logic models frequently present the program's assumptions, inputs, activities, and outputs. In addition, logic models estimate the short-term impact as well as the anticipated long-term outcomes of the proposed program (Issel, 2009).

Figure 11.2 shows a logic model, with definitions of terms and examples from Smiles on Wheels, formatted as a table. Figure 11.3 shows a logic model as a visual representation that includes program inputs, outputs, activities, impact, and outcomes. Both of these figures are based on the Smiles on Wheels grant proposal in Appendix 11A.2. More information about logic models is available at the National Network of Libraries of Medicine (NNLM) Guide 5: Define How a Program Will Work – The Logic Model website (http://nnlm.gov/outreach/community/logicmodel.html).

Elements of Logic Model	Definition	Smiles on Wheels Example
Assumptions	Beliefs guiding the program's development.	Underserved populations need access to dental services.
Inputs	Resources including staff and funding to support program activities.	Van, dental equipment, staff, student volunteers.
Activities	Specific tasks that achieve program objectives.	Arrange schedules to visit clinics in Bay City to provide dental services on a regular basis.
Outputs	Program-generated products or services.	Number of clients who are enrolled and receive dental care.
Short-term impact	Short-term effect on program clients.	Improved dental health of clients seen in mobile dental clinic.
Long-term outcomes	Long-term effect on program clients and the community.	Improved self-esteem, self-efficacy in dental hygiene, and better nutrition. Less use of Emergency Room and hospital for dental-related symptoms and complications.

Figure 11.2 *Logic Model for Smiles on Wheels*

Source: Adapted from Issel, L.M. (2009). Health Program Planning and Evaluation: A Practical, Systematic Approach for Community Health, 2nd ed. Jones & Bartlett Publishers.

Inputs	Outputs	Activities	Impact and Outcomes
Grant funding Van Dental equipment Dentist Support staff Student volunteers	Number of clients Number of sites Dental procedures Education sessions Number of students	Purchase van Equip van Hire staff Recruit students Schedule clinics Provide education	Impact: Dental health Pain relief Outcomes: Self-image Self-efficacy Reduced ER visits

Figure 11.3 *Visual Representation of Smiles on Wheels Logic Model*

SMART Objectives

The proposal's program objectives must be developed and included, often as part of the program description. Text Box 11.2 gives an example of a **SMART objective** taken from the proposal in Appendix 11A.2. Program objectives provide clear steps that must be taken for the program to achieve its goals. Nurses should learn to develop SMART objectives that are specific, measurable, achievable, relevant, and time-bound.

SMART health program objectives should be *specific*. Purchasing and equipping the dental van is a specific step toward achieving the program's goal of improving the community's dental health (Appendix 11A.2). Program objectives must be *measurable*, so that achievement of the objective can be evaluated. The purchase and equipping of the van can be clearly determined, so this indicator serves as a measure of achievement.

SMART health program objectives must be *achievable* and *relevant*. SMART objectives should also contain a *time frame* so there is a clear deadline for achieving the objective. The Smiles on Wheels team should be reasonably confident that the purchase and equipping of the van can actually occur (is achievable) within the 2-month time frame proposed in Text

Text Box 11.2 *Example of a SMART Program Objective Linking Program Activities and Program Evaluation*

Objective I: By the end of the second month of grant funding, the dental van will be purchased and equipped for community outreach in providing dental care services.

Activities to achieve Objective I:
a. Smiles on Wheels staff are currently researching the purchase and delivery information for obtaining a van.
b. Smiles on Wheels staff are negotiating with the local dental school to obtain equipment donations for the van.

Evaluation of Objective I:
a. The van is equipped and available by the specified start-up date, to be determined once funding is available.

Box 11.2, when the team develops this objective. The purchase and equipping of the van are also relevant activities in meeting the overall goal of the dental care program.

In many situations, measures are set as percents. Setting the achievement level for an objective at 100% may be unrealistic. For example, vaccination programs are unlikely to reach 100% vaccination levels for populations. It is often more realistic to set an achievement level less than 100 percent. On the other hand, objectives should be set at a level that would reasonably satisfy funders that the program is worthwhile.

It is often helpful to review health objectives that have already been developed. Healthy People 2020 objectives provide examples of SMART objectives. Some of these might be included as program objectives in grant proposals. Healthy People 2020 objectives are also developed as State and Territorial Healthy People Plans, which are more specific to the needs of populations across the United States.

Program objectives should be reasonably limited in number. Many beginning grant writers try to accomplish too much in their proposals. Remember that for each program objective specified in the proposal, there must be associated program activities and measures to evaluate the achievement of the objective. In addition, the more objectives proposed for the program, the more difficult it may be to demonstrate success, as it might only be possible to achieve some of the objectives.

Students writing their first health program grant proposal are encouraged to develop no more than three to five SMART program objectives. It is often helpful to write down a number of possible objectives, then review the list and select only a few of those most important that the program should achieve. Be sure to keep the program's overall goal in mind, so that the selected objectives contribute to achieving the goal.

Linking Objectives, Activities, and Evaluation

The SMART program objectives should be linked to activities required to achieve the objectives. The objectives should also be linked to methods for evaluating whether the objectives are achieved. Linking the objectives to required activities and evaluation methods help in developing a logical program plan, as well as planning for program evaluation. One way to effectively link program objectives, program activities, and program evaluation is to utilize the following 3-step approach for writing program objectives in the proposal:

1. Develop three to five SMART objectives for the health program grant proposal.
2. Specify one to three activities that are required to achieve each objective.
3. Describe the evaluation methods to show how achieving each objective will be measured.

Some funding agencies may require reporting objectives in a different format than the 3-step approach. The 3-step approach may also become tedious if the proposal requires more than just a few program objectives. However, this approach is very helpful in clearly identifying and linking program objectives, activities, and evaluation methods. Particularly for a smaller program grant proposal, this approach reduces the amount of additional discussion needed for the sections on program activities and evaluation, since the program activities and evaluation plan are discussed in the discussion of the objectives. This is also a helpful approach for nurses who are learning to write grant proposals, as it helps ensure that there is a logical flow in program planning (objectives), implementation (activities), and evaluation. Text Box 11.2 presents an example of a program objective written with links to program activities and program evaluation.

Resources and Resource Needs

This section of the health program grant proposal first describes resources that are available for use by the proposed program, and then identifies resources that are needed. The resource needs can then be itemized and estimated in the program proposal budget. The program proposal should describe the organizational structure of the agency or agencies applying for the grant, including the number of employees, numbers of clients, annual budget, board of directors, and physical space. The organizational administration and persons responsible for decision-making, coordination, and accountability should be identified. An organizational chart, if relevant, may be included. If the proposed program is part of a larger operation, the proposal should explain how the new program will fit in the organization as a whole.

A description of available staffing, physical facilities, and equipment should be discussed in relation to the proposed program. Funders look favorably on organizations that show a strong willingness to contribute to the implementation of their proposed programs or services. Resources that are already available and that will be contributed by the applying organization are frequently referred to as **in-kind contributions**. Staffing should be described in terms of qualifications, responsibilities for program activities, and the amount of time they will contribute to the proposed program. Physical facilities typically include office, clinic, classroom, or other space needed by the proposed program, its clients, and its staff. Equipment may include vehicles, office equipment, or other equipment needed for program implementation.

Increasingly, funders want to encourage the development of community partnerships and collaborative efforts to help reduce unnecessary service duplication, make the best use of scarce funding resources, and ensure that communities work together, rather than in opposition, to resolve problems and meet needs. For this reason, many health program grant proposals are strengthened by including a description of agency partnerships, coalitions, and successful collaborative efforts. Letters of support, in which agencies and influential individuals in the community endorse the applicant's efforts, provide evidence of good inter-agency and community relationships. A sample letter of support is in the Smiles on Wheels grant proposal in Appendix 11A.2.

It is important to include copies of **memoranda of understanding (MOUs)** that document the contributions collaborating agencies will provide to the proposed program. Although MOUs are not absolute guarantees that these promises of contributions will be honored in full, they are strong indications of collaborative support. Many funders strongly approve of MOUs, and some funders, such as the Healthy Start Program, require MOUs.

The use of MOUs is increasingly important in grant proposals that focus on addressing community-level problems that require inter-agency collaboration and coordination. A sample MOU is in the Smiles on Wheels grant proposal in Appendix 11A.2. The MOU confirms that the Bay City Dental School will provide dental faculty volunteers and will donate equipment for the van. Letters of support and MOUs should be placed in the proposal's appendix.

Resource needs represent the staffing, physical space, equipment, supplies, and any other resources not provided via an in-kind or MOU contribution. This section must be linked to the objectives and program activities, and should logically relate to the budget.

Budget and Explanation

The health program proposal budget is a special purpose budget, discussed in more detail in Chapter 7. The budget presents and explains estimated expenses and revenues for the proposed program. It is often simpler and clearer to prepare a budget table with the line item details for expenses and, if applicable, revenues. Expenses are reported as categories of personnel and nonpersonnel budget items. Nonpersonnel items only include capital items such as equipment if allowed by the grant funder. Key items and highlights of the overall budget are discussed in the budget section of the proposal. For example, the Smiles on Wheels proposal in Appendix 11A.2 includes budgeting for the van, van maintenance, and supplies for the dental care program.

A 2-step process may be very useful in preparing a proposed program expense budget. In the first step, the grant writer identifies the resource needs and converts these needs to expense budget line items within categories of personnel, and the nonpersonnel categories of equipment and supplies. Associated dollar figures are linked to the line items and the expense budget is totaled.

In the second step, the grant writer critically reviews each line item with the intent of reducing the expense as much as possible, or even eliminating the expense. In this second step, the grant writer re-evaluates how to increase the amount of in-kind contributions available, and re-examines potential community contributions via MOUs. In the example of the dental van, a review of the budget might lead to exploring whether local service station would provide an MOU that it will donate or discount the cost of some of the fuel. This re-evaluation of the budget might therefore reduce the budget accordingly. The 2-step budgeting approach is an effective technique for realistically reducing an initial expense budget. A lower budget may increase the likelihood of grant funding compared with competing proposals. This approach also reinforces the importance of cultivating community partnerships.

Budget estimates should be as accurate as possible, so the budget is realistic and justifiable to the funder. Proposal reviewers frequently have considerable familiarity with programs and program budgets. Funders are likely to recognize when grant writers over-budget or under-budget in their proposals.

Over-budgeting may seem a good strategy for several reasons. The extra resources would cover unanticipated expenses or organizational needs such as a staff position. Funders may provide less funding than the proposed budget, so it may seem prudent to ask for more money than needed and to expect the budget to be cut. Program management appears efficient, as the manager is more easily able to remain within the budget if more funding than needed is provided. In addition, over-budgeting helps cover expenses not anticipated in the proposed budget. However, funders are likely to recognize over-budgeting, and may favor competing proposals that show more accurate budget estimates and demonstrate a more cost-effective approach.

Under-budgeting may also appear to be a good strategy, as it appears the proposed program is more cost-effective than competing programs. However, funders are likely to recognize under-budgeting and to question the capability of the agency or agencies submitting the proposal if the budget estimates are not realistic. It is advised to develop and present the most accurate and realistic budget estimates possible.

In some cases, despite the best efforts to present a realistic and accurate budget, the funding agency offers funding far below what is necessary to implement or maintain the proposed program. After reviewing budget figures, and repeating the process of determining whether line items might be further reduced by additional in-kind contributions and community support, the available funding might not be adequate to realistically implement or maintain the proposed program. At that stage, it is advisable to diplomatically refuse unrealistic expense budget cuts, with a careful re-explanation of the expense budget. In many cases, other funding sources are available and a search for these sources and proposal re-application to a new funding source may eventually provide support for the proposed program.

Resources for developing a grant proposal budget include the Nonprofit Works website (www.nonprofitworks.com). Chapter 7 provides information on preparing a special purpose budget for a grant proposal. The Foundation Center provides a free online tutorial, Proposal Budgeting Basics (www.foundationcenter.org).

Program Implementation Timeline

The funder needs to know the estimated timeline for program development and implementation once grant funding is provided. The health program grant proposal should provide a timeline that specifies the estimated completion dates for key activities. For example, the Smiles on Wheels program in Appendix 11A.2 estimates the dental van will be purchased and equipped within the first 2 months of funding.

Chapter 10 suggests the use of a **Gantt chart** in presenting a program's timeline. A resource for creating a Gantt chart in Excel is provided at http://office.microsoft.com/en-us/excel-help/create-a-gantt-chart-in-excel-HA001034605.aspx. A visual depiction of the program's timeline is helpful, as the reviewer can quickly see and understand when key implementation activities are planned to occur.

Evaluation Plan

Although an evaluation plan is not always mandatory, it is becoming increasingly important as funders focus on the achievement of objectives outlined in the proposal. If this section is not required for the proposal, it is still a good idea to draft an evaluation plan while preparing the proposal. If the program is funded, it is likely that an evaluation will be required, and an evaluation plan helps in preparing for the evaluation as the program becomes implemented. The 3-step approach discussed earlier in this chapter, that links SMART objectives to activities and evaluation, is an approach that incorporates program evaluation planning with the development of program objectives.

A timeline should be part of the evaluation plan. This timeline should include periodic monitoring of the proposed program, not just evaluation at the end of the funding year. Program evaluation for monitoring purposes should probably take place at least monthly, with quarterly reports and a final end-of-year evaluation report. Some funders will require periodic evaluation reports. Remember, this is not the timeline for program implementation, but for evaluating the program objectives and achievements.

It is important to identify data requirements and sources for the data needed to evaluate the program. Measurement instruments should be clearly described, such as questionnaires. If it will be necessary to develop a measurement instrument, such as a client satisfaction survey, a time frame and plan for development, pretesting, and instrument refinement should be discussed.

The evaluation plan should indicate the methods that will be used to collect data, including sampling methods, if applicable. Data reporting and analysis should be explained, with an overview of the content of the evaluation reports. Evaluation staffing and management should be described, so it is clear to the funder that staff and management are designated to be accountable for performing and reviewing the evaluation.

Remember that using the 3-step approach in developing objectives linked to activities and evaluation often addresses many of the areas of a program evaluation plan. If the 3-step approach is used, the program evaluation plan section might only need to refer to the objectives and summarize the evaluation methods that will be required. The CDC's publication, *A Framework for Program Evaluation in Public Health* (http://www.cdc.gov/eval/framework/index.htm), is a helpful resource in developing a health program evaluation plan.

Capability Statement

The **capability statement** section presents a convincing description of the qualifications of the agency or agencies and participating staff in implementing the proposed program. It is first necessary to remember that the quality of the proposal itself is essential. The proposal must be sent to the appropriate funder and contact in the funder's organization. Proposal guidelines must be adhered to throughout. The proposal must be carefully written, proofread, and revised for clarity, organization, grammar, and spelling. The tone should be convincing and the writing should stimulate interest in the proposed program.

The capability statement should summarize the abilities, competence, resources, personnel, experience, achievements, reputation, and philosophy of the persons and agency submitting the proposal. The grant writer should briefly discuss the applicant organization's origins and history, particularly as related to the proposed program. For example, the Waterhouse Health Center already operates a successful dental clinic, but lacks the capacity to expand the clinic and sees the dental van proposal as a way to serve more clients in need (Appendix 11A.2). Evidence of adherence to standards, community endorsements, and ongoing support such as partnerships should be provided. Any other relevant information regarding capability, such as previous success in programs with the same or similar populations, should be included.

Sustainability and Future Funding

Increasingly, funders want to see planning and development strategies for maintaining programs beyond the proposal's funding period. Frequently, the funder's mission is to only provide seed money to help grant applicants start up the proposed program. Many funders expect applicants to develop plans and strategies for ongoing program operation and sustainability once the grant funding has expired.

The section on program sustainability should describe ongoing program operation plans and strategies. For example, the applicant may describe efforts to develop ongoing community partnerships for future resources or fund-raising strategies. There may be plans to introduce fees for services, or to obtain approval for reimbursement by payers such as Medicaid or insurers. If the proposed program is based within a larger agency, such as a nonprofit organization or a health department, plans for increasing agency support beyond the proposed funding period may be discussed.

Figure 11.4 presents all of the sections recommended for health program grant proposals, and the purpose of each of these sections. Although specific proposal criteria may differ, a review of these sections helps a nurse learning to write health program grant proposals include all the necessary information to make a convincing request for funding.

AFTER THE APPLICATION IS SUBMITTED

Writing a grant proposal is challenging, and an accomplishment to complete. However, the time spent waiting for news of funding to arrive must be used productively, so that program start-up is not delayed once funding becomes available. Gitlin and Lyons (2008) advise using the time after the application is submitted, and before funding arrives, to prepare items

Program description	Describes the program that is designed to meet program objectives. Includes a logic model for visualizing the program.
Program objectives	Presents methods to achieve program goals that are limited in number, achievable, measurable, set within a time frame, and linked to program activities and the program evaluation plan.
Available resources	Identifies resources available within the applying organization (in-kind contributions) and from outside partnering organizations (MOUs).
Resource needs	Identifies resources beyond those available, which are linked to the proposal budget and funding request.
Budget	Itemizes personnel and non-personnel costs linked to program objectives and resource needs.
Timeline	Indicates when key activities for program implementation will occur.
Evaluation plan	Details a plan to evaluate the extent to which program objectives are met.
Capability statement	Explains how the applicants (both individual and organizational) are qualified to carry out the proposed program.
Plan for future funding	Explains how the program will be supported beyond the proposal's funding period to ensure sustainability of successful programs.
Conclusion	Sums up and ends the document to convince the reader that funding is justified.
Letters of support and memos of understanding (MOUs) in the appendix	Written evidence of inter-agency cooperation and support.

Figure 11.4 *Sections and Their Purpose in a Health Program Grant Proposal*

such as job descriptions in advance. Communicate with partnering agencies to negotiate MOUs and develop preliminary plans for program implementation. Think about any other preparations that can realistically be planned in advance of actual funding, and keep files and records so information can be accessed quickly.

How Funders Evaluate Proposals

All of the recommendations provided in this chapter on successful grant writing may be applied to the evaluation of health program proposals. Typically, funders evaluate health program proposals on the basis of clarity, completeness, responsiveness, internal consistency, external consistency, understanding of problem and services, capability and effectiveness, efficiency and accountability, and realism. Remember that it is essential to target the health program proposal to the right funder, the right contact in the funding agency, and to thoroughly adhere to the funder's proposal guidelines.

Managing the Grant

The applicants and applicant organization must assure effective program and financial management. Many financial management principles are covered in other chapters of this text, including budgeting and financial reporting. Although principles of program management are beyond the scope of this text, books and other resources are available for program management information. For example, the World Health Organization (WHO) provides resources on managing health programs.

In many settings, the applicant agency enlists the assistance of a **fiduciary agency**, which assumes the responsibility for financial management of the grant and handles activities such as writing reimbursement checks and paying bills, salaries, and wages. The fiduciary agency may be the sponsoring agency for the proposed program. For example, the Smiles on Wheels dental van program is sponsored by the Waterhouse Health Center, so the health center serves as the fiduciary agency (Appendix 11A.2). The fiduciary agency may require a specified percentage of the grant award for their services.

One simple way to revise the program budget for grant management is to add a column for actual expenses next to the column of budgeted figures. Use the skills discussed in Chapter 5 to monitor budget variances and ensure that all the grant funding is spent as planned by the end of the funding year. Be accurate and consistent, and do not make changes in how grant money is spent without authorization from the funder. Fiscal inconsistency or mismanagement can lead to a damaged reputation, denial of grant funds, and the loss of future funding opportunities.

Grant Renewals

Grant funding is sometimes referred to as **soft money**, or agency revenue that may or may not be available from year to year. Even if funding is approved for more than one year, the release of funds is on a yearly basis. It is therefore necessary to provide an annual report, any required mid-year reports, and to re-apply for continued funding. It is essential to carefully adhere to funder requirements, and to implement effective reporting mechanisms that provide evidence that funding requirements were met. It is also important to maintain positive relationships with the funding agency and to be in close communication regarding any changes or updates in guidelines.

It is important to prepare a successful reapplication for grant renewals. Careful record-keeping, evidence of outcomes and program success, and strategies for expanding or revising the program are elements to consider in a successful grant renewal.

CONCLUSION

This chapter describes various types of health program proposals and their purpose. The sections of a typical health program proposal are provided, with information on grant funding and evaluating proposals. On-line resources are made available and it is recommended to search the Internet for more information on grant writing for health care programs helpful to the nurse seeking funding opportunities. A worksheet for grant proposal preparation is in Appendix 11A.1.

Discussion and Exercises

1. Think about a new program that would benefit from grant funding in your work setting or a health care setting of interest. Identify at least three potential funders for this program. Narrow your selection to a single funder you believe would be most likely to fund your proposal, and explain your rationale for targeting this funder. Who is the best contact in this funding agency?

2. Identify what you believe would be the three easiest and the three most difficult elements to prepare if you were writing a health program proposal for the work or selected health care setting identified in Exercise 1. In other words, would the needs assessment, program description, and budget be easiest or most difficult; or the objectives, evaluation plan, or capability statement? Compare your assessment with that of other students and discuss.

3. Using the selected health care setting from Exercise 1, prepare a draft grant proposal and exchange it with other students (or show it to an outside reader) for feedback on clarity, formatting and capability. How does this help you revise and re-think your final proposal?

4. Search for grant writing resources on YouTube. Stage a contest to feature the "Best Grant Writing Video Ever" that sums up the most helpful information in the most interesting way that applies to health program grant writing.

REFERENCES

Gitlin, L. N., & Lyons, K. J. (2008). *Successful Grant Writing: Strategies for Health and Human Service Professionals*, 3rd edn. New York, NY: Springer Publishing Company.

Hayden, J. (2009). *Introduction to health behavior theory*. Boston, MA: Jones & Bartlett.

Issel, L. M. (2009). *Health Program Planning and Evaluation: A Practical, Systematic Approach for Community Health* (2nd ed.). Boston, MA: Jones & Bartlett.

CROSSWORD: *Chapters 10 and 11—Plans and Proposals**

Across

4 The name of a chart that helps the reader visualize a timeline.

5 A document that describes the contributions collaborating agencies will provide to the proposed program (abbreviation).

6 A type of money that represents funding for special project grants.

8 A type of money that represents grant funding that may or may not be available from year to year.

9 A grant application also referred to as an RFP (abbreviation).

11 An employee working within an organization to improve production and profitability.

Down

1 A person starting or managing his or her own business enterprise.

2 People and organizations with an active concern about a community need or problem.

3 Grants that lead to organizations competing with each other for funding.

7 A grant that provides funding for assessing a community need or problem and planning a program to meet those needs.

10 A grant application also referred to as an RFA (abbreviation).

*Note: The crossword puzzles for chapters 10 and 11 are identical.

Appendix 11A.1: Worksheet for Preparing a Health Program Grant Proposal

Section	Check-off	Notes
Cover letter		
Title page, headers, table of contents		
Introduction		
Problem definition		
Needs assessment		
Program theory or model		
Program description		
Program objectives		
Available resources		
Resource needs		
Budget		
Evaluation plan		
Capability statement		
Plan for future funding		
Conclusion		
Letters of support and MOUs		

Appendix 11A.2: Dental Care Van Grant Proposal

Angelica Holguin, Christina Nardi, Diane Trinh, Paige Weisbrod, and Sara Moschetto

May 11, 2012
Karen Johnson, Grant Coordinator, Goodwell Charities
[contact information]

RE: Smiles on Wheels Dental Van Project

Dear Ms. Johnson,
Smiles on Wheels is a nonprofit organization created in 2012 to meet the dental care needs of economically-disadvantaged individuals in Bay City. We look forward to starting a mobile dental van in order to increase access to dental services for the underserved Bay City population. The goal of this program is to increase access to care and reduce overall health care costs.

There are approximately 96,000 Bay City residents living below the poverty level and 60,000 adults are without dental care. This does not even account for the children who lack dental coverage. The Smiles on Wheels dental van will provide care to children, adults, the elderly, and the homeless of all ethnic backgrounds with low incomes.

In order to accomplish this, we are seeking a $186,000 grant to cover start-up costs and the first year of operations. We will operate throughout the community and work in conjunction with Bay City public health clinics, local dentists, and dental schools. Many of these clinics provide care, but do no have the resources to reach the number of people necessary. Furthermore, many services are for emergency care, which is more costly, and we hope to improve overall health by providing preventative care.

We believe that with funding and support from Goodwell Charities we can help improve the lives of the economically-disadvantaged population of Bay City. We appreciate your review of our grant proposal. Please contact us with any further questions.

Sincerely,
Development Director
Smiles on Wheels
Waterhouse Health Center
[contact information]

DENTAL CARE VAN GRANT PROPOSAL

Smiles on Wheels is a newly-formed organization in Bay City that began in 2012, with the mission to provide quality preventative and routine dental care and dental health education to low-income children, adults, senior citizens, and the homeless. We acknowledge the importance and need for the population that has limited access to dental care. Dentists, hygienists, and the average person cannot handle the complications of oral infections and conditions alone. It takes partnerships to solve public health problems. Our goal is to partner with social workers, dental students, and others to make progress with our community's oral health by promoting oral health and prevention of oral disease.

According to the U.S. Surgeon General, tooth decay is the single most common chronic childhood disease. More than 50% of children between the ages of 5 and 9 have at least one cavity or filling. Also, in our nation, 22% of adults have reported that they have felt oral pain within the past 6 months. Other oral complications common among adults are toothache and craniofacial disorders. The elderly face complications of oral and pharyngeal cancers. Annually, 30,000 Americans are diagnosed and 8000 people die from these diseases (U.S. Department of Health and Human Services, 2003).

Smiles on Wheels will provide a fully-equipped mobile van in accessible locations with a dental team that will expect to serve 280 patients who do not have easy access to dental care; low-income children, adults, senior citizens, and the homeless. The mobile van will have a licensed dentist and dental team to provide the patients with services such as comprehensive examinations, teeth cleaning, X-rays, fluoride, preventative and oral hygiene education, and instructions. The staff will also spend time with each patient to explain preventative methods that can improve their oral health, such as proper brushing and flossing, use of fluoride rinse or toothpaste, healthy eating, and limiting alcohol and tobacco use.

The lack of access to dental care among low-income children and adults is a critical concern, as the need for dental care is growing faster than the care that the community is able to provide. Additionally, fewer providers are willing to treat low-income individuals with Medicaid coverage because of the low provider payment rates and the associated paperwork. Increased funding is critical in order to treat these patients and give them a positive impact on their overall, long-term health. Therefore, it is important for our organization to also reach out to donors, partners, employees, and board members to relay the message of how tooth decay has become the silent epidemic that may be prevented through generous support and if we all work together to improve dental health in our community.

The dental van will have initial start-up costs that include personnel, supplies, and equipment. We estimated that the project's costs for the first year will be $186,000 and $133,579 in the second year (see "Budget Table for Smiles on Wheels" that follows for complete expense report, p. 285). Our organization believes that we are successful if we are able to educate and gain the support from the public and health professionals about the limited access low-income population has to dental care and the importance of oral health at every stage of life. We are successful if our organization is able to bring the community together to promote oral health, improve the quality of life, and eliminate oral health disparities.

This proposal benefits all those involved: both the population served and the dental care providers. The economically disadvantaged population does not have to worry about cost or transportation issues, and they receive dental care without having to locate a willing provider. The dental team benefits because they can provide a much-needed service to patients who are unable to obtain their own regular dental care. The mobile van will be operated by a licensed dentist, on board at all times, along with the rest of the dental team. Patients will receive a comprehensive examination, X-rays, fluoride, preventative and oral hygiene education, and instructions upon their visit. After the initial visit, patients can then be scheduled to receive further treatment, if necessary. Because we are providing general comprehensive care, the dental van will not use sedatives or nitrous oxides while treating patients (Dental Access Carolina, n.d.).

NEEDS ASSESSMENT

As of 2009, an estimated 130 million adults and children (42.6%) in the United States lacked dental coverage (National Association of Dental Plans, 2009). Also in 2009, 4.6 million children did not obtain dental care because their families stated that they could not afford it (Bloom, Cohen, & Freeman, 2009). Throughout the ongoing health care reform debate, concerns are not raised about dental care, an integral piece of overall health that is neglected all too often. While programs such as Medicare and Medicaid attempt to assist particular populations, such as those over 65 years of age, pregnant mothers, children of low-income families, and people with disabilities, among others, these programs provide very little if any dental services. According to the Henry J. Kaiser Family Foundation (2008), approximately 44 million, or 15%, of the United States population are enrolled in Medicare, all of which have no dental coverage or services provided under Medicare. Similarly, Medicaid provides care to nearly 60 million Americans, of which some dental care is provided to people under the age of 21, but not for persons 21 and older.

While dental care is not considered a part of medical care, the problems that can arise as a result of poor oral care result in medical problems that are beyond the dentistry field. Yoneyama, Yoshida, Matsui, and Sasaki (1999) found a correlation between poor oral care and an increased likelihood of developing pneumonia, especially in the elderly population. Pneumonia development in elderly people can be fatal due to compromised immune systems and impaired mobility. In addition, Lockhart et al. (2009) identified a connection between poor oral health and an increased risk for infective endocarditis, a bacterial infection of the heart. There has also been research conducted on the association between Type 2 Diabetes and periodontal disease. In addition, according to an Institute of Medicine report in July 2011, "strong evidence documents the clear linkages between oral health and respiratory disease, cardiovascular disease, and diabetes" (National Research Council, 2011). Many of these health problems that result from poor oral care become chronic diseases that require life-long treatment or are acute conditions requiring immediate medical attention. When taking into account the array of general health risks associated with poor dental care, the long-term benefits of the dental van can be appreciated.

The barriers to oral care are numerous and complex, which explains the great need for more dental services. Factors such as culture, economics, structure, and geography, among others, contribute to problems with health care access (National Research Council, 2011). In such a place as Bay City, where the population is large and diverse, access to health care and even more so, oral care, is hardly an option without insurance. While Bay City sponsors a health plan for low-income residents who are not eligible for Medicaid, dental care is not included in the benefits. The biggest obstacle to people without insurance is paying for required dental care treatment.

In 2010, the Bay City health plan had close to 53,400 people enrolled out of the 60,000 uninsured adults in Bay City. So there are 60,000 adults without dental coverage in Bay City, excluding the homeless and residents with Medicare and Medicaid coverage. There are currently 6455 homeless residents in Bay City (Sherbert, 2011). So the total continues to 66,455 people without dental coverage, still not including the number of people with Medicare and Medicaid. Current statistics for the number of people enrolled in these services cannot be located by city.

However, Bay City has a population of 805,235 people as of 2011, and 13.6% or over 109,000 are over the age of 65, which is the qualifying age to receive Medicare (U.S. Census Bureau, 2012). Furthermore, as of 2010, 11.9% of residents in Bay City were living below the poverty level, which is close to 96,000, people assuming that the population in 2010 is close to the population in 2011 (U.S. Census Bureau, 2012). As the numbers continue to grow in the running total of adults without dental coverage in Bay City, not including the number of children whose parents do not have dental coverage, we can see that there is a great need for access to dental services in Bay City for the uninsured.

At the Waterhouse Health Center in Bay City, dental services are provided once every 2 weeks. The Waterhouse Health Center is located in an area of downtown Bay City that is easily accessible by public transportation. However, simply being able to travel to the clinic does not improve access to care. The clinic can only accept 6 walk-in appointments, so people start lining up as early as the night before the clinic to 6:00 am in the morning in hopes of getting a chance to see the dentist. The small number of patients being seen by dental clinics is not enough to keep up with the ever-growing population.

PROGRAM OBJECTIVES

The program objectives in this section are important to the dental van program's success. Objectives are developed using a 3-step design that includes the measurable objective, activities to achieve the objective, and methods for evaluating the objective.

Objective I: By the end of the second month of grant funding, the dental van will be purchased and equipped for community outreach in providing dental care services.

Activities to achieve Objective I:

a Smiles on Wheels staff are currently researching the purchase and delivery information for obtaining a van.
b. Smiles on Wheels staff are negotiating with the local dental school to obtain equipment donations for the van.

Evaluation of Objective I:

a. The van is equipped and available by the specified start-up date, to be determined once funding is available.

Objective II: The Smiles on Wheels staff will serve at least 280 dental patients in community outreach during the first year of operation.

Activities to achieve Objective II:

a. Smiles on Wheels staff will establish agreements for the van to visit local clinics on a specified schedule to reach underserved children and adults who need dental care.
b. Smiles on Wheels staff will explore opportunities for the van to visit local public schools and community centers to further expand its community outreach.

Evaluation of Objective II:

a. Smiles on Wheels staff will keep monthly statistics to ensure that program enrollment will reach at least 280 clients by the end of the funding year.

Objective III: By the end of the funding year, Smiles on Wheels will sponsor at least 3 professional education sessions to increase awareness of the dental health needs of the underserved populations in Bay City.

Activities to achieve Objective III:

a. Smiles on Wheels staff will contact the local dental, nursing, and social work schools to offer free guest presentations to students and faculty.
b. Smiles on Wheels staff will work with a local health care faculty to arrange clinical rotations and internships for dental, nursing, and social work students in the Smiles on Wheels van.

Evaluation of Objective III:

a. Evaluations will be distributed to the audience following presentations by Smiles on Wheels staff to determine the effectiveness of the educational offerings.
b. Smiles on Wheels will evaluate the clinical rotation and internship experience, and will request the school's evaluation of the clinical rotation and internship experience to ensure the students contribute to the Smiles on Wheels program while gaining a meaningful learning experience.

As we implement the Smiles on Wheels program, more objectives and activities will be developed. However, the key objectives discussed in this section are among the most important in the start-up of this program.

BUDGET

The dental van will have initial start-up costs as well as personnel, supplies, and equipment costs. The personnel will include dental staff and coordinators, as well as a licensed bus driver. The supplies and equipment needed include items such as patient care supplies, dental equipment, and equipment maintenance, as well as fuel, licensing, parking fees, and permits. The start-up costs will be in the initial start of the program and then over time there will be day-to-day expenses as it progresses.

The personnel costs will be the bus driver. The dental staff such as the dentists and hygienists will be volunteers from partnering dental schools. The dental students will receive volunteer credit for their hours as an incentive for them to participate. The dental van managers will be nursing students who will be volunteering their time, as well, and receive credit as part of their senior thesis. The administrative staff will be interns that volunteer at the clinic.

Moreover, equipment costs include; dental chairs, dental lights, dental hygienist stool, sterilizer ultrasonic cleaner, a compressor, etc. Next, there is the cost of patient care supplies such as air and water syringe tips, antibacterial gel, bibs, gloves, mouth mirrors, hand soap, hand wipes, light-handle covers, etc. We plan to receive many of the supplies and equipment through donations from large distributors such as SF Dental Supply, LLC, and Patterson Dental Supply. Maintenance includes cleaning and repair costs for the vehicle from those associated with the dental equipment. Luckily, SF Dental Supply, LLC offers cost-effective dental equipment maintenance and we will look for volunteer mechanics for any vehicle maintenance issues.

Next, there are other nonpersonnel costs that must be considered, which include licensing, hook-up, dumping, permits, and fuel/fluid costs for the vehicle and generators. In projecting fuel cost, there is to be an expected increase over the coming 2 years and we will use our best estimate. Moreover, insurance is needed both for the vehicle and for the staff (the staff need both malpractice and liability insurance). There will also be telephone, fax, and Internet charges, as well as educational materials in the form of handouts as well as the cost of office supplies separately from office equipment.

Financial funding sources include internal funding, (e.g., from an organization's affiliated Foundation or Board/Trustee earmark/donation), local community fundraising, local community partners (for operating the intended mobile clinic), and grants (e.g., from national foundations or federal/state agencies). Moreover, the estimated savings amounts may not cover costs for the first year because of the start-up costs, but as the years progress the program will be more cost effective. The revenue will be nonpatient revenue, which includes $186,000 in the form of grants.

Expenses for the dental van are from equipment and supplies, quality control, staffing, and various other needs. We have used the 2009 average retail prices to estimate the costs of the supplies we will need to operate the van. The expense of purchasing durable equipment (e.g., mouth mirrors, explorers, cotton roll holders, trash cans, dishpans, extension cords, and tray tables) is approximately $5000. The annual infection control and supplies costs are approximately $17,746. The approximate cost of equipment needed to start a dental van is about $29,666. The salary for the bus driver for a 2-week period is $1200. Finally, the miscellaneous operations cost, which includes contracts, clinical supplies, office supplies, equipment maintenance, housekeeping, gasoline/oil, storage rent, staff training, lab fees, copying and postage, billing service fee, professional fees, audit/administration, communications, insurance, bad debt, equipment reserve fund, and depreciation, will amount to $132,299 (see "Budget Table for Smiles on Wheels" for complete expense report, p. 285).

FINANCIAL ANALYSIS

A 2-year variance analysis is utilized to demonstrate how the first year costs will exceed that of the second year. This is primarily due to the start-up tools and supplies needed for the dental van not needing to be re-purchased for the second year. In addition, the dental van project has a chance of receiving increased revenue, in terms of grants, in the second year because of the project's ability to demonstrate to donors the success of the initial year. The project will also have to expect a termination of cash flow from some start-up grants. Ultimately, after the first year, if revenue is not matching costs, it may be necessary to make adjustments to the project. The dental van can consider leasing the mobile unit to others in the community, increasing operating hours, adding an administrative charge to the agencies served or for uninsured patients, or establishing new expectations for the project.

Cost-benefit analysis is used to support the dental van project's feasibility. The project's budget will be around $186,000 in the form of grants. Understanding that the costs will most likely exceed revenue during the first year of the project due to increased expenses (i.e., start-up costs). Project savings will be expected in the second year when start-up costs are not applicable. The major costs come from funding supplies, hiring staff, and general start-up costs. The project will be functioning optimally during the second year because the costs will more closely match the budget and the van will have the potential to reach out to a greater number of clientele. We would expect the second-year cost to be about $133,579, which is calculated by subtracting the start-up costs from the first year total operating expense (see "Budget Table for Smiles on Wheels" that follows for details, p. 285).

The ultimate goal of the dental van project is to improve community oral health through offering cleanings, X-rays, fillings, and abscess treatments. When a greater proportion of the community has proper oral health care we would expect a decrease in the number of health defects associated with poor oral health. Therefore, a primary benefit of the dental van would be increased oral health of the population served, and a secondary benefit would be decreased health care costs of emergency room visits in the community related to oral health-associated diseases or infections. The dental van would expect to serve approximately 280 patients per year (considering operation days and number of clinicians available). Of those 280 patients it is estimated that 20% would have dental health complications that would result in emergency room visits, and possibly hospitalizations.

Based on Bay General Hospital's charge description master, a visit to the emergency department can cost on average from $500 to $2000, not including additional tests, procedures, surgery, treatment, or hospitalization that may occur and can drastically increase the price (Bay General Hospital Medical Center, 2011). If 56 (20%) of the dental van patients developed health complications and sought emergency care, it would cost approximately $56,000. Based on this estimate, the first year of the dental van program would expect to lose approximately $130,000. The financial loss in the program's second year is estimated at $77,579. However, the overall purpose of this program is not to save money, per se, but to provide accessible dental care to persons in need.

Other nonquantifiable, or nonmonetary, benefits of the program include improved self-esteem of care recipients, as well as an increased ability to enjoy food. With this increased ability to enjoy food comes a chance for better nutrition. Additionally, with the reduction in dental caries, or other dental diseases, there will be an overall decrease in the amount of oral pain or discomfort for the clientele.

The dental van project is not considered profitable, but will ultimately save the community's health system money by decreasing the number of oral health-related illnesses and infections, therefore decreasing the number of costly emergency room visits. Based on the Surgeon General's report on oral health care in the United States, studies have demonstrated an association between periodontal diseases and diabetes, cardiovascular disease, stroke, and adverse pregnancy outcomes (U.S. Department of Health and Human Services, 2000).

CONCLUSION

The dental care van will provide economically-disadvantaged populations with dental services that they would not otherwise be able to receive. Though Medicare and Medicaid provide health care to our target population, they provide little to no dental care coverage. This may be due to the perceived disconnect between dental health and overall health. However, evidence suggests that poor dental health contributes to the development of cardiovascular and respiratory diseases and also diabetes. Since disadvantaged populations have difficulty accessing health care in general, mobile dental services provide an opportunity to prevent more complicated and costly diseases that they may not be able to afford to treat either. If we demonstrate these benefits to insurance companies, including Medicare and Medicaid, we have the potential to expand the dental van services by getting them to cover some of our services with the money they save by not having to treat more complicated diseases.

The dental van has significant start-up costs, which is why we are seeking funding from Goodwell Charities. With your grant, Smiles on Wheels will have the opportunity to provide care to a community in need. Our partnerships with community clinics, nursing and social work schools, dentists, and dental schools will help make our van a sustainable project. Please see the letter of support in "Letter of Support" that follows (p. 286), and the "MOU" that follows (p. 286) for evidence of our community support and partnerships.

While continuing grant support will be needed, expenses will decrease in the coming years, possibly allowing us the resources to serve even more. The most important thing to consider is how a dental van can reduce overall health care cost while improving the health of a population in need. The bottom line is that support from Goodwell Charities gives Smiles on Wheels the opportunity to create a healthier life for the disadvantaged population of Bay City.

REFERENCES

Bay General Hospital Medical Center. (2011). *Charge master description.* Bay City, CA: Bay General Hospital Medical Center.

Bloom, B., Cohen, R. A., & Freeman, G. (2009). *Summary health statistics for U.S children: National Health Interview Survey, 2008.* Hyattsville, MD: National Center for Health Statistics.

Dental Access Carolina. (n.d.). Dental Access Carolina, LLC. Retrieved from http://www.dentalaccesscarolina.com/index.html

Henry J. Kaiser Family Foundation. (2008). Medicare now and in the future. *Medicare Policy Project.* Retrieved from http://www.kff.org/medicare/h08_7821.cfm

Lockhart, P., Brenner, D., Thornhill, H., Michalowica, B., Noll, J., & Sasser, H. (2009). Poor oral hygiene as a risk factor for infective endocarditis–related bacteremia. *Journal of American Dental Association, 140,* 1238–1244.

National Association of Dental Plans. (2009). *Dental benefits improve access to dental care.* http://www.nadp.org/Libraries/HCR_Documents/nadphcr-detnalbenefitsinfprove-accesstocare-3–28-09.sflb.ashx

National Research Council. (2011). *Improving access to oral health care for vulnerable and underserved populations.* Washington, DC: National Academies Press.

Sherbert, E. (May 19, 2011). Bay homeless people: how many are there really? *Bay City Weekly.* Retrieved from http://blogs.sfweekly.com/thesnitch/2011/05/sf_homeless_count_2011.php

U.S. Census Bureau. (2012). *The 2012 statistical abstract: Medicare, Medicaid.* Retrieved from http://www.census.gov/compendia/statab/cats/health_nutrition/medicare_medic-aid.html

U.S. Department of Health and Human Services. (2000). *Oral health in America: a report of the surgeon general.* Rockville, MD: U.S. Department of Health and Human Services, National Institute of Dental and Craniofacial Research, National Institutes of Health. Retrieved from http://www.surgeongeneral.gov/library/reports/oralhealth

U.S. Department of Health and Human Services. (Spring 2003). *National call to action to promote oral health.* Rockville, MD: U.S. Department of Health and Human Services, Public Health Service, National Institutes of Health, National Institute of Dental and Craniofacial Research. NIH Publication No. 03-5303. Retrieved from http://www.surgeongeneral.gov/library/calls/oralhealth/nationalcalltoaction.pdf

Yoneyama, T., Yoshida, M., Matsui, A., & Sasaki A. (1999). Oral care and pneumonia. *The Lancet, 354,* 515.

BUDGET TABLE FOR SMILES ON WHEELS

Expenses	
I. Start-up costs	
Large equipment	$29,666
Supplies, instruments, and small equipment	$22,746
Start-up costs total	$52,412
II. Operating expenses	
A. Personnel	
Bus driver salary	$1200
B. Miscellaneous operating expenses	
Contracts	$0
Clinical supplies	$9210
Office supplies	$200
Equipment maintenance	$8794
Housekeeping	$0
Gasoline/oil	$3600
Storage rent	$3413
Lab fees	$257
Copying and postage	$264
Billing service fee, professional fees	$20,000
Audit/administration	$9361
Communications	$1738
Insurance	$8879
Bad debt	$41,583
Equipment reserve fund	$25,000
Depreciation	$0
Miscellaneous operating expenses subtotal	$132,299
Total Annual Operating Expenses	$185,911

LETTER OF SUPPORT

Judith Rayburn, RN, MSN, DNP
Dean, Bay City School of Nursing
[contact information]

March 15, 2012

Development Director
Smiles on Wheels
[contact information]

Dear Ms. Holguin:
I am pleased to write a letter of support for your proposed Smiles on Wheels dental van program. The work you and your colleagues have done in the community has been impressive.

For the last decade, our nursing students have had excellent clinical rotation experiences at the Waterhouse Health Center. We are excited by the opportunity to place students in your proposed Smiles on Wheels dental van to obtain hands-on experience in health education and health promotion.

You have the strongest support possible from the Bay City School of Nursing. My best wishes to you on obtaining the funding for this program to improve community health.

Sincerely,
Dr. J. Rayburn

MOU

Roy Baldwin, DDS
Dean, Bay City Dental School
[contact information]

March 30, 2012

Development Director
Smiles on Wheels
[contact information]

Dear Ms. Holguin:
This is a memorandum of understanding (MOU) that specifies our agreement to provide volunteer dentistry services for your Smiles on Wheels program. Once you have obtained grant funding, please contact me to develop a schedule for dental school faculty to participate in this program.

As previously discussed, once your van is purchased we will also want to work with you to donate equipment for the van.

We strongly support the work you are doing through Waterhouse Health Center to improve the health of the Bay City community. We know there are many underserved, uninsured people who need dental services. We hope you obtain grant funding soon, and look forward to working with you.

Sincerely,
Dr. R. Baldwin

Appendix 11A.3: Grant Proposal—Decreasing High Utilizers of the Emergency Department

Alexandra Carr, Cara Perlas, Deb Rosenberg, and Asja Serdarevic

Bay General Hospital
[address]

April 27, 2012
Goodwell Charities
[address]

To Whom It May Concern:

We are requesting funding through Goodwell Charities in an effort to decrease high-utilizer emergency department use at Bay General Hospital (BGH) and to improve quality of life for 10 high utilizers by implementing individualized home nursing care. We chose Goodwell Charities because your organization promotes innovative ideas in health care. The home nursing care program is not a new concept yet it is not widely implemented. Current research indicates that such service can increase quality of patient care, increase patient access to primary provider care, and essentially decrease total cost of care. Patients who participate in our program will receive both health and financial benefits through the financial incentive program.

BGH is a full collaborating partner in this initiative, part of project planning and implementation. We are extremely enthusiastic about this program's potential and request your consideration for this application.

We are requesting funding in the amount of $261,800 for the 2-year period of June 1, 2012 to May 31, 2014.

If you need additional information please contact Deb Rosenberg. Thank you for your consideration.

Best regards,
Deb Rosenberg, applicant team leader

PROBLEM DEFINITION

In a hospital in Camden, New Jersey:

Nine-hundred people accounted for more than 4000 hospital visits and about $200 million in health care bills. One patient had 324 admissions in 5 years. The most expensive patient cost insurers $3.5 million.

If Dr. Jeffrey Brenner could find the people whose use of medical care was high, he could do something to help them. If he helped them, he would also be lowering their health care costs. His calculations revealed that just 1% of the 100,000 people who made use of Camden's medical facilities account for 30% of its costs.

The first person they found for him was a man in his mid-forties, Frank Hendricks. Hendricks had severe congestive heart failure, chronic asthma, uncontrolled diabetes, hypothyroidism, gout, and a history of smoking and alcohol abuse. He weighed 560 pounds. In the previous year, he had spent as much time in hospitals as out. (Gawande, 2011, p. 2)

According to the Agency for Healthcare Research and Quality (AHRQ; 2012), in 2009 U.S. health care expenses totaled $1.26 trillion, but generally, medical care expenses are incurred by a small number of individuals. In 1996, the top 1% of the U.S. population accounted for 28% of the total health care expenditures and the top 5% for more than half (AHRQ, 2012).

Emergency departments (EDs) are decreasing across the nation due to rising health care costs. Today, EDs are plagued with overcrowding and underfunding due to this decrease combined with an aging population with chronic co-morbidities who rely on federally-funded health programs such as Medicare. One significant source of ED misuse is the high utilizer, also known as the frequent flyer, frequent user, or other such terms. Definitions of high utilizer vary, but according to Locker, Baston, Mason, and Nicholl (2007; as cited in Althaus et al., 2011), frequency is defined as more than 4 visits to the ED in 1 year.

High-utilizer visits to the ED are often questioned. Was the ED visit necessary? Could a primary care provider have treated the patient? The majority of high utilizers use EDs as a source of primary care. These patients are often of low socio-economic status and lack a primary care physician, knowledge of other urgent care options, health insurance, or transportation. High utilizers experience acute episodes related to multiple chronic conditions such as diabetes mellitus, congestive heart failure, substance abuse, and/or mental health issues.

NEEDS ASSESSMENT

Bay General Hospital (BGH) and Trauma Center is a nonprofit, acute care hospital owned and operated by the Bay City Department of Public Health (BCDPH). BGH provides a variety of services to a diverse clientele. These services include inpatient, outpatient, emergency, rehabilitative, and mental health. BGH is the only Level I trauma center for Bay City and the surrounding area, and serves an estimated 1.5 million residents (Bay City Department of Public Health [BCDPH], 2012). As a Level I trauma service, BGH operates 24 hours a day, providing care to 98,000 patients annually (BCDPH, 2012).

One main objective is to ensure that these high-utilizer patients visit primary care providers (PCPs) instead of going to the BGH ED. According to 2008 statistics, the average cost of primary care is $199, as opposed to the ED, which is $900 (Machlin & Chowdhury, 2011). In 2010, BGH had 1180 high-utilizer visits (see "BGH ED Visits" that follows, p. 295). Only 4% of the patients who passed through the ED were high utilizers, but they made up 17% of the total ED visits for that year. Most visits to the ED are categorized as Level 3 visits, which include those patients that arrive on ambulances, those that come in for mental health treatment, and those that require intravenous medications. The average cost associated with each of these visits is $2024, which is the cost of a Level 3 visit (see "Facility Level Charge Form" that follows, p. 296). Therefore, the top 10 high-utilizer patients of the ED at BGH, with their combined 366 visits, cost approximately $740,784 over the course of a year.

Reducing the number of high-utilizer visits can potentially improve patient care in the ED. In 2009, the average time a patient spent in the ED was 4 hours and 7 minutes (Press Ganey Associates, Inc., 2010). Indeed, the highest-frequency users typically present with low-acuity complaints, and, if admitted, the high-utilizer often experiences shorter length of stay than the occasional ED user (LaCalle & Rabin, 2009). By reducing the number of high-utilizer visits, which are unnecessary if treated appropriately through primary care and preventive services, the hospital can reduce wait room times and move other patients in and out of the ED more efficiently. Additionally, there is an inverse correlation between patient satisfaction and time spent in the ED (Press Ganey Associates, Inc., 2010). Eighty-nine percent of patients who spent fewer than 2 hours in the ED reported satisfaction with their visit. Only 77% of patients who spent more than 6 hours in the ED were satisfied with their experience (Press Ganey Associates, Inc., 2010).

Improved coordination of care for high utilizers will also lead to lower ED costs. In a 2011 systematic review studying the effectiveness of interventions targeting frequent ED users, case management was determined to be more cost-effective because it improved clinical and social outcomes without additional costs (Althaus et al., 2011). To put this into perspective, in 2006, under a recent Medicare demonstration program, medical institutions were given an extra monthly payment to finance care coordination for their most chronically expensive patients (Gawande, 2011). If total costs fell more than 5%, the program allowed the institution to keep part of the savings. Massachusetts General Hospital had 2600 chronically high-cost patients, who together accounted for $60 million in annual Medicare spending. To improve coordination of care for these patients, the doctors saw the patients, and, in between, the nurses provided individualized, patient-centered care in the form of longer visits and phone calls to the patients, while consulting with doctors to preemptively recognize and address problems. Three years later, ED visits dropped 15% (Gawande, 2011).

PROGRAM GOALS AND OBJECTIVES

The overall program goal is to decrease high-utilizer ED use at BGH, thereby reducing hospital costs related to unnecessary, frequent ED use while also improving the quality and access to health care for 10 high utilizers. The program aims to achieve this goal by hiring a 1.0 FTE registered nurse (RN), titled "High Utilizer Program Nurse" (HUPN), who will have a 10-patient case load and implement intensive home nursing care for these patients.

The first program objective is to identify and select the 10 high utilizers at BGH ED. Patient data will be collected via BGH electronic health records, and the 10 patients will be selected if they meet the following criteria: patient has 10 or more ED visits per year; patient has multiple, chronic conditions; and, finally, the patient consents to participate in the program for a minimum of 3 months.

The second objective is to reduce each patient's ED visits to 3 visits or less by the end of the program year. Thus, this patient will no longer be considered a high-utilizer by definition. We will take into consideration visits to the ED that are necessary and not considered inappropriate use of services. The HUPN will monitor patient visits to the ED via electronic health records and through patient verification.

The third objective is improved patient outcomes by the end of the patient's participation in the program. Measures include improved compliance, well-controlled symptoms, and the patient's health is the same as or better than baseline.

PROGRAM DESCRIPTION AND ACTIVITIES

Dr. Brenner had figured out a few things he could do to help. Some of it was simple doctor stuff. He made sure that he followed Hendricks closely enough to recognize when serious problems were emerging. He double-checked that the plans and prescriptions the specialists had made for Hendricks's many problems actually fit together and, when they didn't, he got on the phone to sort them out. He teamed up with a nurse practitioner who could make home visits to check blood-sugar levels and blood pressure, teach Hendricks about what he could do to stay healthy, and make sure he was getting his medications.

A lot of what Brenner had to do, though, went beyond the usual doctor stuff. Brenner got a social worker to help Hendricks apply for disability insurance, so that he could leave the chaos of welfare motels and have access to a consistent set of physicians. The team also pushed him to find sources of stability and value in his life. They got him to return to Alcoholics Anonymous, and, when Brenner found out that he was a devout Christian, he urged him to return to church. He told Hendricks that he needed to cook his own food once in a while, so he could get back in the habit of doing it. The main thing he was up against was Hendricks's hopelessness. He'd given up (Gawande, 2011, p. 2).

Brenner worked closely with his patients, as will the HUPN. This individualized patient-centered home health care program will be a small test of change based on the success of Brenner's program. The program targets 10 individuals determined to be ED high utilizers at BGH. The HUPN will work with each patient to reduce ED visits, produce better outcomes, and improve quality of life. This nurse will visit patients at their residence and the nurse will have access to providers and resources from BGH to assist with patient care.

The HUPN will be a qualified BGH RN, preferably bilingual, with a minimum of 5 years experience. The supervisor will be in the Quality Improvement department. The HUPN will be available 5 days a week, 8 hours a day (selected hours), and will carry a pager. The HUPN will meet with the patient at home for the first 3 days following discharge to review health history and to assess medical, psychosocial, and economic needs in order to create a comprehensive, patient-centered plan of care. After the first 3 days the nurse will then visit twice a week for a month. After this initial period, the nurse will meet with the patient at least once per week, more if needed. The patient will determine the frequency of nurse visits; the patient and nurse visits will be coordinated together. Although the work schedule is flexible, the nurse is not a replacement for emergency services, and is thus not "on call" for emergencies that may occur outside the HUPN's work schedule.

The nurse will assist with coordinating PCP appointments if the patient, for any reason, prefers not to schedule the appointment(s). If the patient does not have a PCP, then the nurse will work with the patient to find an appropriate provider. In addition, the HUPN will accompany the patient to the initial PCP appointment. The health care providers and the patient will discuss and determine the plan of care together.

Furthermore, the HUPN will connect the patient to other health care providers as necessary and will help the patient navigate the health care system. For example, if the patient needs a nutritionist to assist with meal planning, the nurse will assist with arrangements for the patient to meet with a nutritionist at BGH. The nurse will follow up with the patient and nutritionist if the patient is not adhering to appointments. If a patient, due to a medical condition(s), needs the home assessed for safety, then the HUPN will assist the patient in coordinating an appointment with a BGH occupational therapist. In addition, if patients need social support services, the nurse will be involved with helping them to locate the appropriate groups or services for their needs. If the patient requires help accessing Medicare benefits, the nurse will provide information or will contact a Medicare representative.

Continual HUPN patient follow-up will be integral to the program. Throughout this process the nurse will identify and anticipate problems and modify the plan as needed during the course of each patient's care. The nurse will educate each patient regarding pertinent issues related to medication, disease process, and personal needs. Patient progress and status will be reported weekly to the case manager at BGH.

The goal of the program is to reduce ED visits using highly individualized, preventive care. Due to the unique nature of each patient's health condition and socio-economic situation, the HUPN must anticipate and adapt to each patient's needs and provide innovative solutions.

Patient Compensation

During recruitment of high-utilizer patients for this study, they will be informed that they can earn up to $1500 in gift cards (e.g., Safeway, Walgreens, etc.) over the course of the 9 months that the nurse will be working with them. This is not an incentive to comply with their health care regimens, but rather it is meant to encourage them to continue meeting with the HUPN at least weekly. The patient will receive compensation at the end of each month for agreeing to stay in the program. Compensation will be $100 per month for the first 3 months, $150 per month for the following 5 months, and $300 for the last (ninth) month. Patient compensation increases as the program progresses to encourage patients to stay for the duration of the program. This allows us to best measure HUPN effectiveness.

TIMETABLE

The 2-year timetable below represents the approximate timeline to complete our program goals and objectives. The HUPN will be hired with the task of providing home care for 10 patients for Year 1. Despite best efforts to maintain patients, attrition may occur, so the nurse may recruit new patients if needed to maintain workload. Program evaluation will be done quarterly and a full-year review will be done at end of Year 1. For Year 2, should the HUPN decide to continue, the HUPN will proceed to recruit 10 new patients, and the timeline for implementation, evaluation, and review will be similar to Year 1.

Year 1:

- June 1 to June 30, 2012—Identify and recruit high utilizers for program
- July 1 to July 31, 2012—HUPN recruitment/hiring
- August 1 to August 15, 2012—HUPN orientation
- August 15, 2012 to May 15, 2013—Program implementation
- August 15, 2012 to May 15, 2013—Program evaluation every 3 months
- May 16 to May 31, 2013—Program review

Year 2:

- June 1 to June 30, 2013—Identify and recruit high utilizers for program
- July 1 to July 31, 2013—HUPN recruitment/hiring*
- August 1 to August 15, 2013—HUPN orientation*
- August 15, 2013 to May 15, 2014—Program implementation
- August 15, 2013 to May 15, 2014—Program evaluation every 3 months
- May 16 to May 31, 2014—Program review

*If the HUPN decides to stay with the program a second year, there will be no recruitment, and the HUPN will have this time off (Table 11A.3.1).

Two-Year Budget Estimates

Table 11A.3.1 *Estimated Budget for High-Utilizer Project, Year 1 and Year 2*

Item	Year 1 cost ($)	Year 2 cost ($)	Program cost (Year 1+ Year 2) ($)
RN salary[1]	72,000	72,000	144,000
RN benefits[2]	25,000	25,000	50,000
Mileage[3]	4400	4400	8800
Parking[4]	2000	2000	4000
Medical supplies for home health care	5000	5000	10,000
Administrative and indirect costs	5000	5000	10,000
Compensation to patients[5]	15,000	15,000	30,000
Start-up costs	5000	0	5000
Total cost	133,400	128,400	261,800

Notes:

[1] This figure pays the RN at a rate of $45/hour. The RN will have the week of Christmas to New Year's Day off, since most medical offices will be closed. Year 1 dates: August 1, 2012 to May 15, 2013. Year 2 dates: August 1, 2013 to May 15, 2014.
[2] RN benefits at BGH are approximately 35% of the nurse's salary (S. Penner, personal communication, April 21, 2012).
[3] This allows for 200 miles per week at the standard rate of $0.55/mile.
[4] $10 per day toward parking.
[5] Each patient qualifies for $1500 compensation for his or her participation. This will be given out in increasing increments to ensure they stay throughout the duration of the program.

Budget

In this section we discuss available and needed resources. A budget is then presented and explained.

Available Resources

The HUPN will work from home, thus, no office space is needed. Since travel throughout Bay City is a requirement for the position, the nurse must have a reliable car that is registered and insured. The HUPN will be reimbursed for use of this car. The HUPN will also have access to many of the services and supplies at BGH, including interpreter services, taxi vouchers for patients, and medical supplies.

Resources Needed

The primary need is to hire an RN at 40 hours a week (1.0 FTE) to work as the HUPN. The HUPN will receive compensation for traveling throughout the city, which includes mileage and parking. To perform in the HUPN role, the hired RN needs a phone, office equipment and supplies, and nursing equipment (e.g., a stethoscope), which will be considered start-up costs. There may also be administrative and indirect costs. Finally, as an incentive for patients to participate in the program, gift cards and vouchers for patient compensation are needed.

Highlights of the Budget

The start-up costs are minimal for this program, and they will only be needed for the first year. Also, the HUPN will be hired as a per diem RN. The RN will be employed during the 9 months each year that the patients are actively participating in the program. Finally, since the HUPN will be working from home, there is low overhead expense.

COST-BENEFIT ANALYSIS

Based on the expected costs of the resources, the program cost for 2 years is $261,800. Since the average cost per BGH ED visit is $2024, and the program will recruit 10 patients who have had at least 10 ED visits in the past year, the anticipated program benefit over 2 years is $404,800. Therefore, over the course of the program's 2-year implementation, we anticipate a net savings of $143,000 for the ED. The cost-benefit analysis shows that for every dollar spent in this program the ED can expect to save $1.50.

Additionally, the program has nonmonetary benefits. For instance, reducing the number of overall visits to the ED will reduce wait times for other patients. The program also offers social benefits by improving the overall quality of life for a few individuals. Patients will feel empowered to manage their own care, wellness, and prevention.

EVALUATION AND MEASURABLE OUTCOMES

Atul Gawande spoke to Hendricks recently. He has gone without alcohol for a year, cocaine for 2 years, and smoking for 3 years. He lives with his girlfriend in a safer neighborhood, goes to church, and weathers family crises. He cooks his own meals now. His diabetes and congestive heart failure are under much better control. He's lost 220 pounds, which means, among other things, that if he falls he can pick himself up, rather than having to call for an ambulance (Gawande, 2011, p. 2).

Our program's success is based on the reduction in number of high-utilizer ED visits to 3 or less per year so these patients are no longer considered "high utilizers." Achieving this goal will lead to decreased hospital costs while increasing both quality and access to health care for these high-utilizers. It is critical to collect both quantitative and qualitative data to measure outcomes and to evaluate the overall program success. The HUPN will keep track of services and costs that the patient incurs during the program. The HUPN will also keep track of the activities, hours, and expenses related to providing the patient intensive home nursing care.

Specifically, the HUPN will collect the following quantitative data: the number of patients the program served, noting patient's disease(s) or illness(es); the number of patient ED visits, noting visits both before and after program implementation; cost of each ED visit, if any; the number of patient visits to PCPs and to other health care services; the number of phone calls made and received by the HUPN; and finally, the nurse's number of patient home visits.

The HUPN will collect qualitative data for the identification and analysis of barriers to access encountered during the course of the program (Penner, 2004). In addition, qualitative data related to each patient's overall physical and psychological improvement and improved quality of life will be collected. Data from a patient satisfaction survey will be collected, as well.

The HUPN will analyze cost-effectiveness and write quarterly progress reports for each patient detailing activities and costs. The HUPN will do a full utilization review and summarize the results in a report at the end of the program.

FUTURE FUNDING

If proven to be cost-effective through the benefit of the 2-year Pioneer Portfolio grant, we hope BGH will continue the program to ensure maximum benefit to both patients and the hospital. If the program expands, we will endeavor to hire and train more HUPNs and to service additional BGH units that experience high-utilizer patients. We will prepare a report on the program success, and we will also present a business plan to increase support and to ensure the continuity of the program.

CAPABILITY STATEMENT

The HUPN will be affiliated with BGH, which is a Level I trauma center for the Bay City area. BGH has been serving the vulnerable population since 1872. Based on similar programs, such as the medical home model, that have been implemented across the country and that have been successful, we predict that we can reduce costs, improve patient care and outcomes, enhance patient quality of life, and increase access to primary care and social services for these patients.

REFERENCES

Agency for Healthcare Research and Quality (AHRQ), Medical Expenditure Panel Survey. (2012). *The Concentration of Health Care Expenditures and Related Expenses for Costly Medical Conditions, 2009 (Statistical Brief #359)*. Retrieved from meps.ahrq.gov/mepsweb/data_files/publications/st359/stat359.pdf

Althaus, F., Paroz, S., Hugli, O., Ghali, W. A., Daeppen, J. P., Peytremann-Bridevaux, I., & Bodenmann, P. (2011). Effectiveness of interventions targeting frequent users of emergency departments: A systematic review. *Annals of Emergency Medicine, 58,* 41–52. doi:10.1016/j.annemergmed.2011.03.007

Bay City Department of Public Health. (2012). *Bay general hospital trauma center: The level I trauma program.* Bay City, CA: Bay City Department of Public Health.

Gawande, A. (2011). *The hot spotters. The New Yorker.* Retrieved from http://www.newyorker.com/reporting/2011/01/24/110124fa_fact_gawande

LaCalle, E., & Rabin, E. (2009). Frequent users of emergency departments: The myths, the data, and the policy implications. *Annals of Emergency Medicine, 56,* 42–48. doi:10.1016/j.annemergmed.2010.01.032

Locker, T. E., Baston, S., Mason, S. M., & Nicholl, J. (2007). Defining frequent use of an urban emergency department. *Emergency Medicine Journal, 24,* 398–401. doi:10.1136/emj.2006.043844

Machlin, S., & Chowdhury, S. (2011). Expenses and characteristics of physician visits in different ambulatory care settings, 2008. *Medical Expenditure Panel Survey, Statistical Brief #318.* Retrieved from http://meps.ahrq.gov/mepsweb/data_files/publications/st318/stat318.pdf

Penner, S. J. (2004). *Introduction to health care economics & financial management.* Philadelphia, PA: Lippincott Williams & Wilkins.

Press Ganey Associates, Inc. (2010). Emergency department pulse report 2010: Patient perspectives on American health care. Retrieved from http://www.pressganey.com/Documents_secure/Pulse%20Reports/2010_ED_Pulse_Report.pdf?viewFile

BGH ED VISITS

Number of ED visits under a single medical record number in 2010	Count of patients
1	25,949
2	4183
3	1216
4	460
5	244
6	127
7	82
8	59
9	47
10	33
11	16
12	14
13	13
14	15
15	11
16	6
17	7
18	8
19	2
20	5
21	6
22	3
23	4
24	2
25	1
26	1
27	2
29	1
30	1
31	1
32	1
35	3
37	1
39	1
50	1
69	1
73	1

FACILITY LEVEL CHARGE FORM

FACILITY LEVEL CHARGE FORM - ENCIRCLE APPLICABLE LEVEL

LWBS N/C 55188080	LEVEL 1 316	LEVEL 2 946	LEVEL 3 2024	LEVEL 4 3334	LEVEL 5 6730	CRITICAL CARE (ED NON-TRAUMA ONLY) 5324	ADDITIONAL CRITICAL CARE TIME (ED NON-TRAUMA ONLY) 7331
55086009	55186023 / 99281	55186031 / 99282	55186049 / 99283	55186056 / 99284	55186064 / 99285	55103204 / 99291	55103220 / 99292

FACILITY LEVEL ASSIGNMENT: The Level assigned is justified by and based on the interventions on the part of the nursing and ancillary staff in the ED. Interventions include discharge instructions. The Level assigned is always the highest level at which a minimum of one intervention is found.

Level 1 - Possible Interventions

- Initial Assessment
- Rx refill only; asymptomatic
- Note for work or school
- Wound recheck
- Suture removal
- Dressing change (Uncomplicated)
- D/C Instructions * "STRAIGHTFORWARD

Level 2 - Possible Interventions

Any from previous level plus:
- POCT (Point of Care Testing)
- Obtain clean catch urine
- Visual acuity (Snellen)
- Apply ace wrap or sling
- Prep or assist with minor lac repair
- I&D simple abscess
- D/C Instructions * "SIMPLE

Level 3 - Possible Interventions

Any from previous level plus:
- Receipt of ambulance patient
- Saline lock
- Plain X-Ray - 1 area
- 1 Nebulizer treatment
- Foley catheter / Straight cath
- Cervical-spine precautions
- Incontinence care
- Routine psych med clearance
- Mental health - Pt anxious, simple Tx
- Post mortem care
- D/C Instructions * "MODERATE COMPLEXITY

Level 4 - Possible Interventions

Any from previous level plus:
- Plain X-Rays - multiple areas
- Prep for CT, MRI
- Cardiac monitoring
- 2 Nebulizer treatments
- Pelvic exam
- Administration of parenteral meds (IV, IM, IO, SC)
- Nasogastric tube placement
- Psychotic pt, not suicidal
- D/C Instructions * COMPLEX

Level 5 - Possible Interventions

- Critical care LESS THAN 30 minutes

Any from previous level plus:
- Patient admit
- RN monitoring during in-hospital transport
- More than 3 Nebulizer treatments
- O2 via face mask or Nonrebreather mask.
- Moderate sedation
- Central line insertion
- Lumbar Puncture, Paracentesis, or Thoracentesis
- Gastric lavage
- Cooling or heating blanket
- Extended Social Worker intervention
- Physical or chemical restraints

Critical Care - Possible Interventions

(ED NON-TRAUMA ONLY)

- Includes the FIRST 30-74 minutes of critical care

Any from previous level plus:
- Multiple parenteral meds requiring constant monitoring
- Major trauma care
- Chest tube insertion
- Major burn care
- Treatment of active chest pain in ACS
- Admin of IV vasoactive meds
- CPR
- Defibrillation / cardioversion
- Intubation
- Ventilator management
- Arterial line placement
- Delivery of a baby

Additional Critical Care Time

(ED NON-TRAUMA ONLY)

- BEYOND the FIRST 74 minutes
- Additional Critical care time of AT LEAST 30 minutes
- Record the TOTAL critical care time: _____ minutes

ED_2of2 / CDM ER HIM MM / 090111

* DISCHARGE INSTRUCTION DEFINITION

STRAIGHTFORWARD: Self-limited condition with no meds or home treatment required. Signs/symptoms of infection explained; return to ED if problems develop

SIMPLE: OTC meds or treatment; simple dressing changes; patient demonstrates understanding quickly and easily

MODERATE: Head injury instructions; crutch training; bending, lifting, weight-bearing limitations; Rx med with review of side effects and potential adverse reactions; pt demonstrates adequate understanding of instructions

COMPLEX: Multiple meds and/or home therapies with review of side effects and potential reactions; diabetic, seizure or asthma teaching in compromised, non-compliant pts; may require additional directions to support compliance with prescribed tx

Appendix 11A.4: Incorporating Massage and Healing Touch Therapies on a Specialized Nursing Unit at Seaview Hospital—A Grant Application

Janet Giachello and Jennifer Schmid

Jennifer Schmid and Janet Giachello
[address]

> Ms. Sharon Smith
> Grants Coordinator
> Healing Therapies Foundation, Inc.
> [address]

May 1, 2012

Dear Ms. Smith,

Seaview is a leader in caring for patients with ear, nose, throat and head disorders. Seaview's Department of Head and Neck Surgery has a mission to provide the highest possible care to patients. The Healing Hands program will help accomplish the overall objectives of this department.

Our proposal is to incorporate massage and healing touch therapies as post-operative pain management interventions to head and neck oncology patients while they are hospitalized. Project goals include the following: (1) to improve patient outcomes via both physiologically measurable means (heart rate, blood pressure, and respiratory rate) as well as more subjective means (0-10 pain scale and customer satisfaction surveys); (2) to improve nursing satisfaction through decreased patient reliance on opioid medication; and (3) to decrease costs to the facility by improving patient satisfaction and reducing length of stay.

We are requesting a grant in the amount of $12,000 to initiate our one-year project on a specialized nursing unit at Seaview Hospital. Healing Hands will be led on-site by Jennifer Schmid with the assistance of Janet Giachello. We will train three oncology massage therapists as well as three certified healing touch therapists. Survey data will be collected to evaluate the effectiveness of the program. We appreciate your consideration and humbly ask for your support.

> Sincerely,
> Jennifer Schmid
> Janet Giachello

The staff of Healing Hands respectfully requests a $12,000 grant to initiate a program to examine the possible advantages of integrating massage and healing touch as adjunct pain management interventions on a specialized nursing unit at Seaview Hospital. This unit houses ear-nose-throat (ENT), plastics, hands, urology, and trauma. Seaview Hospital and its clinics have a close relationship with Seaview University School of Medicine. As a teaching hospital, Seaview provides an ideal environment to present new knowledge to the rest of the medical community. We at Healing Hands hope that these impressive credentials provide credence to our program and impetus for the Healing Therapies Foundation, also striving to affect a global community, to help us launch our innovative program. Please contact Jennifer Schmid if there are any questions concerning this application.

PROBLEM DEFINITION

Pain is a shared human experience that in basic terms needs little definition; we have all experienced it at some point in our lives. However, pain is a complex, remarkably individualized phenomenon. Considered a subjective experience, pain is often misinterpreted in the clinical setting for a variety of reasons. Unfortunately, patients continue to report negative experiences with post-operative pain relief, the majority of which focuses, not surprisingly, on pharmacological treatment (Gunningberg & Idvall, 2007; Sindhu, 1996). In fact, in January 2001, The Joint Commission (JC) established new standards for pain management for all patients at JC-accredited health care institutions (Joint Commission, 2001). These were the result World Health Organization (WHO) reports indicating that pain was underassessed, underreported, and undertreated (Gureje, Von Korff, Simon & Gater, 1998). As a result, many health care institutions adopted protocols and practices to better assess and treat patients' pain, going so far as to identify pain the as "fifth vital sign" (Bertagnolli & Kaplan, 2004). Clearly pain management, or the lack thereof, is at the forefront of modern day health concerns and a prevailing nursing concern.

Presently, no formal clinical practice guidelines on the use of nonpharmacological pain management strategies exist, though preliminary guidelines were proposed by Williams, Davies, and Griffiths (2009). However, even with the plethora of medical community knowledge regarding adverse and potentially serious complications of pain medications (Odera et al., 2007), there seems to be a disproportionate reliance on opioids and their derivatives as the main alternative to alleviate pain. Sometimes patients' pain is resolved by these medications, but if not, they must wait 2 to 4 hours to be remedicated, and physicians are not always available to respond to pages regarding ineffective pain management. As patient advocates, we would like to bridge the research-practice gap by providing not only important nonpharmacologic pain interventions to patients, but also by providing education to both patients and health care providers. Desirable outcomes include decreased pain and anxiety, improved heart and respiratory rates, improved mobility, decreased opioid use, improved patient satisfaction, improved staff satisfaction, decreased length of stay (LOS), and decreased cost.

NEEDS ASSESSMENT

As mentioned, Seaview serves a worldwide population; however, our research will focus on ENT oncology patients within that populace. Undertreated pain goes beyond physical discomfort. When a person is uncomfortable, it prevents them from accomplishing many of the tasks needed for them to recover, ambulate, and ultimately become independent enough to leave the hospital. Particularly problematic is limited mobility, especially following any type of surgery or procedure, which can have far reaching consequences on an individual's health. Immobility can affect important postoperative objectives such as: deep breathing, preventing atelectasis and pneumonia; decreased venous stasis, triggering blood clots and thromboembolisms; pressure ulcer prevention; reduction in the need for catheters, thereby deterring urinary tract infections; and overall improvements in general healing, by improving circulation and motivation to improve. Postoperative complications not only cause additional pain, suffering, and emotional stress to the patient, but they also place undue pressure on the lives of their families and loved ones. Likewise, the additional hospital resources consumption, including the requisite nursing care, can dramatically increase costs to the hospital.

Some patients may not want to take pain medications because they wish to avoid potential side effects, such as constipation, nausea, and vomiting, as well as adverse reactions such as respiratory depression (Pellino et al., 2005). They may also fear dependency on these medications or simply do not want to "bother" the nurses. There can also be a problem with inexperienced or biased clinicians or nurses, who may hold personal prejudices toward specific groups of people, causing ineffective medication administration (Mitchinson et al., 2007). In general, when it comes to meeting unique needs and complex pain assessment and relief, it can be extremely challenging to meet basic requirements for comfort, decreased anxiety, and increased mobility, as well as helping the patient to feel empowered.

Healing Hands proposes incorporating massage and healing touch therapies as adjunct treatments to pharmacologic pain relief. A substantial body of research have proven these therapies to improve patient outcomes and nursing satisfaction, while decreasing costs by primarily by reducing the length of stay in the hospital. For instance, MacIntrye et al. (2008) found in a randomized trial that providing healing touch therapy to patients recovering from coronary bypass surgery significantly reduced the length of hospital stay and would save their hospital approximately $500,000 per year, or $2000 per patient. This would more than pay for qualified staff to provide for these services. In addition, according to Odera et al. (2007), approximately 2% of all patients suffer from adverse drug events (ADE) related to opioid medications, increasing length of stay by 10.3%, and cost of hospitalization by 7.4%.

Personnel costs make up the primary percentage of any hospital budget. Seaview Hospital no longer provides massage to patients as a part of their care but rather charges patients $30 for 30 minutes of massage. However, knowing that disparities in health care have far-reaching consequences (Marmot, Friel, Bell, Houweling & Taylor, 2008), the funding obtained for this project in order to pay for certified massage and healing touch therapists would allow for all eligible patients to participate in the program without regard to the patient's financial status.

Nurses formerly provided massage therapy during daily nursing care, but the increased reliance on technology combined with greater patient acuity has made it extremely difficult for nurses to take the time to implement massage as a standard of practice. These interventions are considered independent actions within a nurse's scope of practice (Tracy et al., 2006). Even though the demand for complementary techniques has increased substantially in the last ten years or more (Barnes, Bloom & Nahin, 2008), and despite myriad empirical studies substantiating alternative therapies and their positive effects on pain, especially when provided concurrently with pharmacological analgesics, only a small percentage of nurses describe incorporating nonpharmacologic methods adjunctive to relief with drugs such as morphine, Fentanyl, and hydrocodone (Wessman & McDonald, 1999). Furthermore, younger nurses are even less likely to recommend nonpharmacologic pain intervention (He et al., 2011), and nurses of all backgrounds have indicated a need to know more about different pain relief methods (Holley, McMillan, Hagan, Palacios & Rosenberg, 2005).

PROGRAM GOALS, OBJECTIVES, ACTIVITIES, AND EVALUATION

The program goals and objectives, activities, and evaluation are summarized below. Plan evaluation will be an ongoing process. Input from all parties involved will be promoted so that adjustments can be made to continuously improve on the process. The practice will be revised as necessary data and research become available.

Objective I: To improve patient response to pain as measured both subjectively (0-10 pain scale) and physiologically (improved vital signs).

Activities to achieve Objective I:

1. Provide daily 20-minute massage or healing touch therapy sessions during hospitalization. Patients can elect to have one 20-minute massage or healing touch session per day, starting on the day of surgery. Massage therapy will consist of a standardized 20-minute session in collaboration with MDs and therapists, not to include massage above the clavicle per MD orders, but may include muscles below clavicle, low back, hands, and/or feet. Healing touch therapy will consist of a standardized 20-minute session in collaboration with patient physicians and therapists.

Evaluation of Objective I:

1. Have nurses document patients' pain levels at least every four hours throughout the shift as well as before and after nonpharmacologic interventions.
2. Require nurses to document patients' vital signs every four hours throughout the shift as well as before and after nonpharmacologic interventions.

Objective II: Improve nursing satisfaction through decreased patient reliance on pharmacologic pain management.

Activities to achieve Objective II:

1. Provide nurses with educational materials regarding massage and healing touch therapies before the program begins and throughout the program.

Evaluation of Objective II:

1. Assess nurses' knowledge and awareness of massage and healing touch therapies as nonpharmacologic pain interventions before and after the program via an anonymous survey.
2. Assess nurses' satisfaction with patient pain management before and after the program via an anonymous quantitative survey.

Objective III: To increase awareness and knowledge to all parties involved in patient care, including the patient, as to nonpharmacologic pain interventions available.

Activities to achieve Objective III:

1. Provide patients with both preoperative and postoperative educational materials on massage and healing touch therapies. Materials will be provided both visually and verbally.
2. Provide the above materials to family members and patients on the unit.

Evaluation of Objective III:

1. Assess patients' knowledge and awareness of massage and healing touch therapies as nonpharmacologic pain interventions before and after care via an anonymous survey.

Objective IV: To improve patient outcomes and decrease anxiety associated with uncontrolled pain.

Activities to achieve Objective IV:

   Provide daily 20-minute standardized massage or healing touch therapy sessions during hospitalization.

Evaluation of Objective IV:

1. Assess patient satisfaction with pain management after care via an anonymous quantitative survey (adapted from Tracy's Nondrug Complementary Pain Index [NDCPI; 2011]). See "Non-drug Complementary Pain Interventions" (p. 306) for the survey we intend to use.

Objective V: To decrease costs to the facility by decreasing length of stay (LOS) and improving overall patient satisfaction.

Activities to achieve Objective V:

1. Compare LOS for similar patients who received non-pharmacologic pain interventions during their stay with those who did not.
2. Compare overall patient satisfaction for similar patients who received non-pharmacologic pain interventions during their stay with those who did not.
3. Formulate an internal report by key staff involved and overseeing the program at Seaview, including recommendations for improvement and possible interest in continuing past the funding year.

TIMETABLE

The timetable for development and implementation of this plan will be projected for the first year of its existence, and will assume financial support is received by the beginning of the fiscal year, July 2012. Each stage of the program will be allotted the following intervals:

- July 1 to July 31—Stakeholders meet to decide on details of protocol
- August 1 to August 31—Orientation for therapists
- September 1 to September 30—Program implementation
- Quarterly reports submitted October 1, 2012; January 1, 2013; April 1, 2013; July 1, 2013
- Final annual report submitted October 1, 2013

RESOURCES, RESOURCE NEEDS, AND BUDGET

Necessary resources include but are not limited to funding to pay for the massage and healing touch therapists, pre-op patient education, and educating the nursing staff. Because of the specific nature of our patients' diagnoses and procedures, Healing Hands has proposed to

Seaview Hospital the use of their C2 medical-surgical unit as the location for our program. We will have limited use of in-house resources such as computers, telephones, staff, and pagers.

The main financial needs for implementation of massage and healing touch therapies will be for the therapist themselves. Healing Hands has recruited several potential therapists, all with training and experience to manage this special population of ENT oncology patients. The majority of the budget will be allocated for the patients' massage therapy. The supplies for each session will be minimal. Patient beds will be used in place of special massage tables, because hospital beds are adjustable and easily adapted for massage. The budget is presented in Table 11A.4.1.

FINANCIAL ANALYSIS

Because of the high hospitalization costs, even the smallest reduction in length of stay (LOS) can create major savings to a health care organization. The approximate average LOS for ENT oncology patients on this unit is 4.5 days. Based on our projections, using data obtained from the unit, decreasing the LOS by 0.4 days for patients receiving massage and healing touch therapy would result in a savings of $18,198 for the fiscal year in which the Healing Hands program is implemented. Likewise, using data from Odera et al. (2007), we estimate that five patients in one year will experience an ADE, costing the hospital approximately $1110 per patient in increased costs and LOS. Therefore, anticipating that decreased reliance on opioid medications could eliminate the risk of ADE in our patients, we conservatively estimate an additional savings of $1000 to the hospital during our program. See Table 11A.4.2 for a 3-year financial analysis and budget variance.

FUTURE FUNDING

Healing Hands is optimistic that our program will demonstrate the far-reaching benefits of massage and healing touch, and hope that if approved and funded by the Healing Therapies Foundation, they may also expand their support for a second year. We anticipate that even if Seaview does not see a direct cost to benefit ratio, they will realize these modalities are affecting their client population in many beneficial ways, and also assisting staff on the unit, as well as promoting global health objectives of reducing health care costs in general and improving patient-centered care. Patients' tendency for decreased anxiety, muscle tension, and fatigue allows them to rest and sleep better/faster. Relaxation achieved can potentially help them dissociate from

Table 11A.4.1 *Healing Hands Nonpharmacologic Pain Intervention Budget, FY 2012-2013*

	Cost/unit	Quantity	Amount
20-minute healing touch sessions	$20	273	$5460
20-minute massage sessions	$20	273	$5460
Therapist training	$40	6	$240
Patient brochures	$1	150	$150
Nurse brochures	$1	40	$40
Consultant fee (Dr. Suzanne Tracy)	$100	1	$100
Massage oils	$18	30	$540
Total cost			$11,990

Table 11A.4.2 *Financial Analysis and 3-Year Budget Variance*

Expenses	Year 1	Year 2	Year 3	Total
20-minute healing touch sessions	5460	5460	5460	
20-minute massage sessions	5460	5460	5460	
Therapist training	240	120	120	
Patient brochures	150	150	150	
Nurse brochures	40	20	10	
Consultant fee (Dr. Suzanne Tracy)	$100.00	$0.00	$0.00	
Massage oils	$540.00	$540.00	$540.00	
Total expenses	$11,990.00	$11,750.00	$11,740.00	$35,480
Savings	**Year 1**	**Year 2**	**Year 3**	
Total decreased LOS (0.4) savings related to nonpharmaceutical therapies	$18,198.18	$18,198.18	$18,198.18	
Potential savings r/t reduced opioid ADE	$1000.00	$1000.00	$1000.00	
Total savings	$19,198.18	$19,198.18	$19,198.18	$57,594.54
Total profit	$7208.18	$7448.18	$7458.18	$22,114.54
Patient days	1092			
Massage sessions	273			
Healing touch sessions	273			
Number of patients receiving massage	68.25			
Number of patients receiving healing touch	68.25			
Number of patients receiving therapy after surgery	136.5			
Number of patients not receiving therapy	136.5			
Number of patients with opioid ADE	5.46			
Cost of hospitalization/patient	$15,000.00			
Cost of hospitalization/patient/day	$3333.00	based on average LOS 4.5 days		
Cost of ADE/patient	$1110.00			
Decreased LOS (0.4) savings r/t nonpharmaceutical therapies per patient	$133.32			
Total LOS savings r/t above	$18,198.18			

the pain and increase the overall effectiveness of pain medications. Healing Hands foresees a future where there is less reliance on pharmaceuticals and more on complementary means of pain management, such as massage and healing touch. Even though there is some evidence as mentioned above, demonstrating these therapies can reduce length of stay in a hospital, we believe both the benefit to the patient and the potential cost savings to be the primary impetus behind the research. The program is enthusiastic from past studies that this will be very successful, while operating on a modest budget. The goal is that Seaview will eventually see the cost savings in implementation, and ultimately hire staff to provide massage and healing touch. As the funding draws to a close, we will formulate a business plan to present to Seaview, utilizing our evaluation findings to support the cost-effectiveness of sustaining this program.

CAPABILITY STATEMENT

Seaview Hospital has the mission to provide the highest possible quality of care to its patients. Likewise, Seaview's Department of Head and Neck Surgery (ENT) is a leader in the treatment of patients with ear, nose, throat, and head disorders, and prides itself on carrying out active research as well as the finest educational experience to trainees (Seaview School of Medicine, Department of Medicine, 2012). We believe this training ground and the vast population it serves will be an ideal environment for conducting our program. ENT oncology patients often have significant pain, and many are facing uncertain futures, which can increase their stress and anxiety levels.

Applicant Backgrounds

Jennifer Schmid, a full-time RN/MSN/CNL graduate student, is an active proponent of non-pharmacologic nursing interventions as well as complementary and alternative medicine (CAM). Having received her doctorate in Naturopathy in 2008, Jennifer has published, presented, and taught extensively about CAM throughout the United States. A member of the American Holistic Nurses Association and a certified Reiki II practitioner, Jennifer strives to incorporate holistic nursing interventions into her patients' daily care. In addition, Jennifer desires to work with ENT patients because, as a former professional classical singer, she understands what it means to lose one's ability to communicate with the voice and how it can be so discouraging that one stops advocating for oneself—in this case, advocating for adequate pain management postoperatively. Jennifer will graduate with a Masters of Science in Nursing in December 2012, at the same time receiving her certification as a Clinical Nurse Leader (CNL).

Janet Giachello received her bachelor's in Biomedical Engineering 1985. A change of careers led to 13 years with the Wayland Fire Department, where Janet sustained many injuries, including one severe neck trauma and one final back injury that ended her career in 2001. Massage therapy was the main source of pain relief for her discomfort and rehabilitation, so much so that she entered massage school after a disability retirement. Janet has a degree and is certified in holistic healing massage. After beginning a practice out of her home, Janet decided to start nursing school to expand her healing learning and incorporate the holistic practices from both fields.

CONCLUSION

We submit this grant application to support our proposed project that would provide massage therapy for post-surgical oncology patients at Seaview Hospital. We believe this will contribute to the quality of care for these patients. Once fully implemented, we also believe that Seaview Hospital will review the evaluation results and agree to support this program after the funding period ends.

REFERENCES

Barnes, P., Bloom, B. and Nahin, R. L. (2008). Complementary and alternative medicine use among adults and children: United States, 2007. *National Health Statistics Reports. No. 12.* U.S. Department of Health & Human Services publication no. (PHS) 2009–1250. Hyattsville, MD: U.S. Dept. of Health and Human Services, Centers for Disease Control and Prevention, National Center for Health Statistics.

Bertagnolli, A. and Kaplan, D. (2004). Pain: The 5th vital sign. *Patient Care, 38*(9), 66.

Gunningberg, L. and Idvall, E. (2007). The quality of postoperative pain management from the perspectives of patients, nurses and patient records. *Journal of Nursing Management, 15*(7), 756-766.

Gureje, O., Von Korff, M., Simon, G. E., and Gater, R. (1998). Persistent pain and well-being. *The Journal of the American Medical Association, 280*(2), 147-151. doi:10.1001/jama.280.2.147

He, H., Lee, T., Jahja, R., Sinnappan, R., Vehviläinen-Julkunen, K., Pölkki, T., and Ang, E. (2011). The use of nonpharmacological methods for children's postoperative pain relief: Singapore nurses' perspectives. *Journal for Specialists in Pediatric Nursing, 16*(1), 27-38. doi:10.1111/j.1744-6155.2010.00268.x

Holley, S., McMillan, S. C., Hagan, S. J., Palacios, P., and Rosenberg, D. (2005). Pain resource nurses: Believing the patients, believing in themselves. *Oncology Nursing Forum, 32*(4), 843-848.

Joint Commission. (19 January 2011). Facts about pain management. Retrieved from http://www.jointcommission.org/pain_management/

MacIntyre, B., Hamilton, J., Fricke, T., Ma, W., Mehle, S., and Michel, M. (2008). The efficacy of healing touch in coronary artery bypass surgery recovery: A randomized clinical trial. *Alternative Therapies in Health & Medicine, 14*(4), 24-32.

Marmot, M., Friel, S., Bell, R., Houweling, T. A., and Taylor, S. (2008). Closing the gap in a generation: Health equity through action on the social determinants of health. *Lancet, 372*(9650), 1661-1669.

Mitchenson, A. R., Hyungjin, M. K., Rosenberg, J. M., Geisser, M., Kirsh, M., Cikrit, D., and Hinshaw, D. B. (2007). Acute postoperative pain management using massage as an adjuvant therapy. *Archives of Surgery, 142*(12), 1158.

Odera, G.M., Said, Q., Evans, R.S., Stoddard, G.J., Lloyd, J., Jackson, K., and Samore, M.H. (2007). Opioid-related adverse drug events in surgical hospitalizations: Impact on costs and length of stay. *Annals of Pharmacotherapy, 41*, 400-407.

Pellino, T. A., Gordon, D. B., Engelke, Z. K., Busse, K. L., Collins, M. A., Silver, C. E., and Norcross, N. J. (2005). Use of nonpharmacologic interventions for pain and anxiety after total hip and total knee arthroplasty. *Orthopaedic Nursing, 24*(3), 182-192.

Sindhu, F. (1996). Are non-pharmacological nursing interventions for the management of pain effective? – a meta-analysis. *Journal of Advanced Nursing, 24*(6), 1152-1159.

Seaview School of Medicine, Department of Medicine. (2012). *Head and Neck Surgery (Ear, Nose and Throat).* Seaview, CA: Seaview Hospital.

Tracy, S. M., Dufault, M., Kogut, S., Martin, V., Rossi, S., and Willey-Temkin, C. (2006). Translating best practices in nondrug postoperative pain management. *Nursing Research, 55*(2S), S57-S66.

Wessman, A. C. and McDonald, D. D. (1999). Nurses' personal pain experiences and their pain management knowledge. *The Journal of Continuing Education in Nursing, 30*(4), 152-157.

Williams, A. M., Davies, A. and Griffiths, G. (2009). Facilitating comfort for hospitalized patients using non-pharmacological measures: Preliminary development of clinical practice guidelines. *International Journal of Nursing Practice, 15*, 145-155. doi: 10.1111/j.1440-172X.2009.01739.x

NON-DRUG COMPLEMENTARY PAIN INTERVENTIONS

This survey has been designed to require you to provide an answer to each question before you are allowed to proceed to the next question. This means you will not be allowed to skip any questions nor proceed until you have answered all questions. The survey purposely refrains from giving you the option to remain neutral (that is, there is no option for "do not agree nor disagree"), thereby requiring you to make a decision about your response to each question.

Please put a number from 1 to 4 after each statement to indicate your level of agreement with each of these statements. When responding, please evaluate each question separately and choose your response independent of responses to other items. The survey should take an average of 15 to 25 minutes to complete. Thank you for your input.

4 = strongly agree, 3 = agree, 2 = disagree and 1 = strongly disagree

1. The main reason for getting healing touch is to help a person relax so pain medicines can work better.
2. Massage helps people relax the most when the pain level is severe.
3. Massage and healing touch are supposed to increase the desired effects of pain medicine.
4. The main purpose of massage is to help people stop thinking so much about their pain.
5. The most common reason massage and healing touch are used infrequently for pain relief is that people know little about its benefits.
6. The main benefit of massage is to decrease pain by helping people rest better.
7. The best time for people to get a massage is shortly after taking a pain medicine.
8. People get the most help from non-drug methods when their pain is mild to moderate.
9. The use of healing touch can help pain medicines work better.
10. Massage is most helpful in easing the tension that often accompanies pain.
11. Nursing care should include using non-drug methods shown to be best for managing pain.
12. Massage and healing touch may be an important way to decrease pain.
13. Doctors and nurses would benefit from increased knowledge about non-drug methods to help their patients in pain.
14. The medical pain treatment might be improved if non-drug methods such as music, imagery, and massage are offered to patients in pain.
15. I believe massage can reduce people's stress.
16. I believe healing touch does not offer any real help in pain treatment.
17. Nurses should be able to tell patients how massage and healing touch can help manage their pain.
18. Massage and healing touch may help reduce pain after surgery.
19. I plan to use massage as part of my pain management plan.
20. Knowing about non-drug methods for pain management is important to me as a patient.
21. Teaching booklets given to patients before surgery should explain how to use non-drug methods to help decrease pain.
22. Knowing how massage helps manage pain improves a person's sense of control over their own health.
23. Patients' perspectives about drug and non-drug methods used to treat pain are important.
24. Doctors and nurses should invite patients to contribute to the plan for pain management. (S. Tracy, personal communication, November 28, 2011)

Chapter 12: Financial Statements and the Nurse Entrepreneur

It's not how much you earn that counts, it's how much you spend—Archie Penner

Learning Objectives

1. Compare cash and accrual accounting approaches applied to health care settings.
2. Critically review a hospital's annual report to identify whether the organization is profitable over the fiscal year.
3. Explain at least two reasons why it is important for health care organizations to monitor and report cash flow.
4. Explain and interpret at least one profitability ratio and one liquidity ratio reported for a health care organization.

Key Terms

accounts payable	assets	current ratio
accrual basis of accounting	balance sheet	days in accounts receivable
accrued expenses	book value	debt management ratios
accumulated depreciation	capital structure ratios	debt ratio
activity ratios	cash basis of accounting	debt-to-assets ratio
adjusted occupied bed	cash flow	disclosure
adjusted patient day	cash flow statement	efficiency ratios
aged trial balance	collectibles	equity
annual report	common size analysis	equity ratio
asset management ratios	current liabilities	equity to total assets ratio

fair market value

financial accounting

financial costs

fiscal conservatism

fixed assets

functional classification

Generally Accepted Accounting Principles (GAAP)

goodwill

gross patient revenue

horizontal analysis

illiquid assets

income statement

interest

inventory

leverage ratios

liabilities

limited use assets

liquid assets

liquidation

liquidity ratios

long-term debt to equity ratio

long-term debt to net PPE ratio

managerial accounting

marketable securities

matching principle

materiality

natural classification

net assets

net collection rate

net deficit

net income

net income margin

net long-term debt

net patient revenue

net PPE per licensed bed

net return on total assets (NROA)

net surplus

net working capital

net worth

noncurrent assets

noncurrent liability

nonoperating revenue

notes payable

operating margin

other operating revenue

owners equity

patient revenue margin

payout ratio

percentage change analysis

performance ratios

profitability ratios

ratio analysis

real assets

retention ratio

revenue and expense summary

revenue cycle management

statement of activities

statement of cash flows

statement of financial operations

statement of financial position

statement of operations

statement of revenue and expenses

total margin

trade credit

turnover ratios

vertical analysis

This chapter presents information useful to nurses, nurse executives, and nurse entrepreneurs. Some hospital-wide indicators are described as overall organizational performance measures. An introduction to some relevant accounting concepts is provided to give nurses a working knowledge necessary for reviewing financial statements. Basic principles for reviewing financial statements are explained in the context of inpatient health care institutions. Some commonly used financial ratios and other indicators are presented to help nurses assess the financial health of a hospital or other business. The chapter ends with a discussion of outpatient practice management issues and advice for nurse entrepreneurs.

Chapter 8 explains that, for many years, hospital charge master descriptions (CDMs) have not been publicly available. The same is true for hospital budgets and other financial and performance reports. It is ideal for nurses to review budgets and financial reports generated by their own work settings. However, this information is not always shared with nurses.

This chapter refers to hospital data available since 2005, reported in the California Office of Statewide Health Planning and Development (OSHPD) Hospital Annual Financial Data Pivot Profiles (http://www.oshpd.ca.gov/HID/Products/Hospitals/AnnFinanData/PivotProfiles/default.asp). Case mix index (CMI) data are available at the OSHPD Healthcare Information Division–Case Mix Index website (www.oshpd.ca.gov). Another source of publicly available hospital data is from the Washington State Department of Health Community Hospital and Financial Data website (www.doh.wa.gov).

Both the OSHPD and the Washington State Department of Health websites provide data as downloadable spreadsheet files that can be used to review financial performance. Another source of hospital financial data is the American Hospital Directory AHD.com Free Hospital Profiles website. Increasing demands for transparency will likely lead to greater availability of hospital financial data.

HOSPITAL-WIDE INDICATORS

As mentioned in Chapter 4, hospitals employ the majority of U.S. nurses, and nursing labor typically represents one of the highest costs for hospitals. In most situations, nurses will be more involved and more interested in reviewing indicators specific to the inpatient nursing units where most of these nurses work. However, this chapter focuses on indicators and reports that evaluate the performance of a health care institution or organization as a whole. These indicators enable nurses to assess the overall financial health of the facility in which they provide care.

Figure 12.1 presents indicators used in reporting hospital-wide operations. The indicators are grouped according to the categories of capacity, utilization, performance, and financial measures, as presented in Chapter 4 in analyzing smaller nursing work units. Most of these indicators are the same as presented in Chapter 4. Indicators such as staffed beds, patient days, average daily census (ADC), and average length of stay (ALOS) are measured and reported across the entire hospital, rather than a nursing unit. A few of the measures in Figure 12.1 are discussed in more detail in this section, as they typically are only used as hospital-wide indicators.

Adjusted patient day. Although hospitals are providers of inpatient care, increasingly hospitals provide outpatient care, as well. The trend of hospital outpatient services is expected to accelerate with health reform, as discussed in the online article, Ambulatory Care Stands Out Under Reform (www.hfma.org). Calculation of the **adjusted patient day** allows for meaningful comparison of hospital utilization among hospitals that vary in the amount of outpatient services they provide compared to inpatient services.

The adjusted patient day is calculated by multiplying the patient days for a specified time period by the proportion of gross patient revenues to gross inpatient revenues for the same time period (Figure12.1). When the 116,711 patient days for 2010 are adjusted for outpatient services, the public hospital reports 160,318 adjusted patient days.

Indicator	Calculation	Value
Capacity		
Licensed beds	Licensed for hospital occupancy	439
Available or staffed beds	Equipped and staffed for occupancy	415
Potential patient days	Available beds × days in time period	151,475
Utilization		
Patient days	Sum of census count for time period	116,711
Adjusted patient day	Inpatient days × (gross patient revenue ÷ gross inpatient revenue)	160,318
Case mix index (CMI)	Sum of DRG relative weights ÷ medicare patients	1.2
Average daily census (ADC)	Patient days ÷ days in time period	319.8
Average occupancy rate	Patient days ÷ potential patient days	77.0%
Adjusted occupied bed	(Occupancy rate × beds) × (total gross patient revenue ÷ gross inpatient revenue)	439.2
Performance		
Discharges	Designated transfers off the unit including deaths	21,194
Average length of stay (ALOS)	Total patient days ÷ discharges	5.5
Financial		
Gross patient revenue	Total charges for patient care before deductions	$1,406,995,183
Gross inpatient revenue	Total charges for inpatient care before deductions	$1,024,288,056
Net patient revenue	Total charges for patient care less deductions to revenue	$324,049,206
Other operating revenue	Revenue from operations other than patient care	$7,788,268
Nonoperating revenue	Revenue from sources other than hospital operations	$46,358,561
Operating expenses	Expenses generated from hospital operations	$386,137,115
Nonoperating expenses	Expenses generated from activities other than hospital operations	$9475
Net income	Net patient revenue + other operating revenue + nonoperating revenue − operating expenses − nonoperating expenses	($7,950,555)

Figure 12.1 *Hospital-Wide Indicators for Public Hospital, 2010*

Source: Adapted from OSHPD Hospital Annual Financial Data Pivot Profiles and Glossary, 2010 (http://www.oshpd.ca.gov/HID/Products/Hospitals/AnnFinanData/PivotProfiles/default.asp).

Adjusted occupied bed. The calculation of the **adjusted occupied bed** adjusts the ADC based on the proportion of outpatient utilization in the facility. The adjusted occupied bed is calculated by first multiplying the average occupancy rate by the number of available beds, then multiplying that value by the proportion of gross patient revenues to gross inpatient revenues (Figure 12.1). This indicator allows for comparing bed occupancy across hospitals that may vary in their extent of outpatient services. When the 415 staffed beds are adjusted for outpatient services in 2010, there are 439.2 adjusted occupied beds for the public hospital.

Revenue sources. As mentioned in Chapter 5, inpatient nursing units typically report gross revenue, which represents gross inpatient revenue. A hospital-wide measure shown in Figure 12.1 is total **gross patient revenue**, which includes all inpatient and outpatient charges before deductions are applied. **Net patient revenue** is calculated as gross patient revenue less any deductions to revenue. Deductions to gross patient revenue include deductions negotiated by insurance payers, as well as reimbursement less than full charges paid by government programs such as Medicare and Medicaid. Bad debt (unpaid bills) and charity care (deductions from payment for clients who cannot pay) also represent deductions to gross patient revenue.

Other operating revenue from activities other than patient care, such as revenue from the hospital's gift shop, is added to net patient revenue to report total operating revenue. **Nonoperating revenue** includes revenue sources not related to business activities, such as tax revenues received by public hospitals.

Expense sources. As reviewed in Chapter 5, operating expenses represent all costs generated from the hospital's business activities, mostly from patient care services. **Nonoperating expenses** are costs not related to business activities, such as sponsoring a medical conference (Figure 12.1). Operating revenue, other operating revenue, and nonoperating revenue are added together. Operating and nonoperating expenses are subtracted from the total revenue. The resulting value is **net income,** or the amount of profit or loss generated by the hospital over the reporting time period. The net income for the public hospital is a negative $7,950,555, showing a loss in 2010. After a review of some fundamental accounting concepts, net income is discussed further in the section on financial statements.

ACCOUNTING CONCEPTS

Financial accounting and reporting progressed through the course of history, from using piles of stones as measures of value to spreadsheet software to develop complex financial models. However, the age-old difficulty of translating resources, economic activities, and intangibles into financial units persists. For example, what is the best way to place a value on a community hospital? Its price on the market? The cost of its physical plant and inventories? The qualifications of its medical, nursing, and other staff? What about the value of the hospital's reputation? Indicators and financial reports attempt to accurately measure and describe the value of hospitals and health care enterprises.

Financial regulations in the United States were prompted by the economic upheaval and disorder brought about by the Great Depression in the late 1920s and early 1930s. Health care organizations are generally required to implement accepted financial practices and periodic audits to ensure financial accountability. A few examples of regulatory bodies and organizations that establish financial standards relevant to health care organizations are presented in Figure 12.2.

Financial accounting includes activities involved in collecting, reporting, and analyzing data presented in financial statements. Financial accounting usually occurs across an entire organization, such as Bigtown Hospital, rather than for a smaller department or work unit. By contrast, **managerial accounting** involves activities often focused at the department or work unit level, such as budgeting and planning. Chapters 5, 6, and 7 focus on managerial accounting related to budgeting and budget reports. This chapter focuses on financial accounting and the interpretation of financial statements.

Time Periods

As in budgeting and budget analysis, it is important to consider the time period for recording financial activities. The time periods are usually reported as months, quarters, or the

Acronym	Name	Purpose
SEC	Securities & Exchange Commission	U.S. government regulatory agency that specifies and enforces the form and content of financial statements—noncompliant businesses are prohibited from selling securities to the public.
FASB	Financial Accounting Standards Board	A private organization to which the SEC delegates to establish standards.
GASB	Government Accounting Standards Board	Similar to FASB, but established for public businesses.
GAAP	Generally Accepted Accounting Principles	A set of objectives, conventions, and principles established as guidelines issued from the FASB and other regulatory organizations that continue to develop over time.
AICPA	American Institute of Certified Public Accountants	Professional association of public financial accountants, with similar authority as the AMA exerts over physicians.
HFMA	Healthcare Financial Management Association	An organization that participates in setting specific standards around health care finance.

Figure 12.2 *Regulatory Bodies and Organizations Establishing Financial Standards for Health Care Settings*

fiscal year (FY). One fiscal year may also be compared to another to report and analyze financial performance over the longer term. When financial reports alert the nurse to concerns, it is advisable to drill down and obtain reports in more detail and over shorter time periods to better identify the source of possible financial problems.

Cash and Accrual Basis of Accounting

The way in which revenues and payments are perceived and recorded differ depending on the purpose of the financial report. There are two approaches to recording financial activities relevant to health care organizations. The main difference between these two approaches is the timing of the reporting of financial events.

The first approach is the **cash basis of accounting**, in which revenue is recorded at the time of payment, and expenses are recorded at the time expenditures are made. The following example illustrates cash accounting:

> Mr. Jones visits a nurse practitioner (NP) at the Millway University Nurse-Managed Health Center (MNC) for treatment of a wound. The NP cleans and dresses the wound, and gives Mr. Jones a tetanus booster. Mr. Jones pays the nurse practitioner $50 in cash, so the revenue and payment are recorded within the same accounting time period as the service is provided.

In cash accounting the financial event is recorded and reported at the time cash is exchanged. Cash accounting is the system most of us use to "balance the checkbook" in managing our personal finances. Most people acknowledge revenues (income) when they receive a paycheck or fee, and acknowledge their expenses when they pay bills or make cash disbursements for goods or services. This is a simple and intuitive approach to recording financial activities.

Cash accounting is useful in health care organizations for managing their cash flow. The cash flow budget discussed in Chapter 7 reflects cash accounting. It is important to be able to cover day-to-day expenses and to meet financial obligations on time. Therefore, cash accounting is used for an organization's cash management.

However, in most health care organizations there is often a considerable lag between the time goods or services are provided and the time that payment is received. In these situations, it makes more sense to use the **accrual basis of accounting**, in which revenues are recorded when earned, representing an obligation for payment. Expenses are recorded when financial obligations are created, at the time the business consumes resources. The following example illustrates accrual accounting:

> On March 5, during the first quarter of the fiscal year, the NP at MNC treats Mr. Jones' wound and gives him a tetanus booster. Mr. Jones pays the $5 copay in cash, and the nurse practitioner bills Mr. Jones' insurance company for the remaining $45 for Mr. Jones' care. The entire $50 is recorded as revenue at the time of service, although the insurance company does not actually pay the $45 to the MNC until May 21, the second quarter of the fiscal year.

In accrual accounting, revenue is reported in the same accounting time period as when the goods or services are provided, generating an obligation to pay that may not be fulfilled until a future accounting time period. In other words, revenue recording does not represent the receipt of payment, but the implied promise of payment. Frequently, services are provided under the provisions of an existing contract for payment.

In accrual accounting, expenses represent the utilization of personnel, supplies, or equipment, such as the hours of direct nursing care scheduled or the amount of supplies used over a given time period, not the financial expenditures or cash disbursements made over another time period to pay for these inputs. Frequently, disbursements for accrued expenses are made in compliance with contract terms and conditions. For example, employees are typically paid semi-monthly or monthly, not at the end of each work day. Although somewhat more complicated and less intuitive than cash accounting, accrual accounting is a standard accounting method that is applicable to health care financial activities and payment systems.

The operating revenue and expense budgets are prepared using an accrual accounting approach. For example, for Bigtown Hospital's East Wing medical-surgical nursing unit, the per diem bed revenues are recorded according to the monthly census (in other words, as services are provided), not when the payment is received. Expenses, such as for hourly staff, are recorded within the time periods in which they are used. Capital and operating budgets both forecast and record financial activity over specified time periods. Other financial reports based on accrual accounting also record these financial activities when services are provided or when resources are used.

One advantage of using accrual accounting is that it more realistically and accurately portrays the financial activities of most health care organizations. The operating revenue and expense budgets reflect the application of accrual accounting. For example, the Director of Central Supply at Bigtown Hospital approves the purchase of 300,000 pairs of sterile latex gloves for patient care that are prepaid in February 2011, received in March 2011, and used within the second quarter (April through June) 2012. The director budgets and records this expense for the second quarter 2012, not February 2012, as that is the time period within which these inputs are used.

Accrual Accounting and the Matching Principle

Another advantage of using accrual accounting is that it helps guard against financial manipulation. Cash accounting reports results only when money is exchanged, not when goods and services are actually provided or utilized. A manager could therefore make costs appear lower by delaying payment on bills due at the end of the fiscal year. Accrual accounting reflects the **matching principle** of accounting, in which revenue is matched to the time revenue is earned, and, to the greatest extent possible, revenue is matched with the expenses used to generate that revenue.

Principles of Consistency and Conservatism

Consistency is an important factor in measuring and recording financial activities. Financial accountants not only use accepted accounting rules and practices to maintain consistency, but apply the same rules from year to year to allow meaningful comparisons of financial status and performance. Regulatory and industry bodies such as the FASB determine standards as new accounting issues evolve, such as capitation financing. These regulatory and industry bodies have developed **Generally Accepted Accounting Principles (GAAP)**. GAAP consists of standards, procedures, and principles for preparing financial statements so that accounting information is reported consistently.

Another accounting practice employed in measuring and recording financial activities is **fiscal conservatism**, in which probable losses to a business are recorded if they may be reasonably predicted, while gains are not recorded until they are actually realized. For example, if Bigtown's financial officers believe that some of the hospital's diagnostic equipment is obsolete, they may write the equipment off as a loss, even though it still generates revenue. By contrast, even after Bigtown Hospital administrators negotiate a profitable contract, the revenues are not reported until they are actually generated.

Another example of fiscal conservatism is that many physician group and nurse-managed practices distribute their income on a cash basis rather than on an accrual basis. In other words, the income from the practice is based on actual cash receipts rather than revenue that has not yet been collected. This is the more conservative approach, ensuring that the practice does not attempt to distribute money it does not possess.

Materiality Principle

Another factor in measuring and recording financial activities is the principle of **materiality**, in which separate categories of financial entries are recorded only if they are relevant to the financial condition of the enterprise or organization, or to understand the financial statements. In addition, figures are frequently rounded rather than exact, as long as the reviewer obtains a fairly stated view of the entity's financial condition. Financial statements for large institutions often report figures rounded to the nearest thousand. If more detail is required, the nurse manager or nurse executive can drill down by requesting that the report include more specific information.

Disclosure Principle

Disclosure is closely related to the principle of materiality. It is important to accurately report on all of the aspects of financial transactions, including how much, what, and when. Accountants may use footnotes, notes, attachments, and explanations of assumptions to provide a fair view of financial activities, condition, and performance. Disclosure is important because, in many cases, information could be omitted from financial statements, which would make the financial situation appear better or worse than it actually is.

Periodic (frequently annual) financial audits performed by qualified, objective, and independent accounting firms require full disclosure and review of the financial accounting practices of health care organizations. The use of financial audits increases confidence in the organization's financial reporting. An example of a financial audit report is presented in the Audited Consolidated Financial Statements for Cleveland Clinic. Text Box 12.1 presents and summarizes the factors in measuring and recording financial activities discussed in this section.

Text Box 12.1 *Factors in Measuring and Recording Financial Activities*

- Time period: months, quarters, or the fiscal year (FY)
- Basis of accounting:
  - Cash accounting (report revenue when payment is received) vs.
  - Accrual accounting (report revenue when goods or services are provided, generating an obligation to pay)
- Matching principle:
  - Match revenue with the accounting period in which it is generated
  - Match expenses with related revenues, if possible
- Consistency principle:
  - Use accepted accounting rules and practices
  - Apply the same rules from year to year to allow meaningful comparison
- Fiscal conservatism principle:
  - Record probable losses if they may be reasonably estimated
  - Do not record gains until they are actually realized
- Materiality principle:
  - Only create categories for entries related to financial performance
  - Figures reported may be rounded or estimated, not exact, as long as they provide a fair view of financial activities, condition and performance
- Disclosure principle:
  - Related to the principle of materiality
  - Report how much, what, and when for financial transactions
  - Utilize footnotes, notes, attachments, and explanations of assumptions to provide a fair view of financial activities, condition, and performance

FINANCIAL STATEMENTS

The following sections present and explain several financial statements commonly encountered in hospital institutions. These statements might also be prepared and reviewed for smaller organizations such as a nurse-managed clinic. Related financial concepts are discussed in the context of these statements. Financial statements and their analysis enable nurses to assess the financial health of the program or organization. Nurses typically do not prepare financial statements, but may have opportunities to review the financial statements in their settings.

The first of the four financial statements discussed is the **annual report**, which is an overall summary of an organization's financial performance prepared largely for the review of persons outside the organization. The second document discussed is the **income statement**, which discloses the profitability of an organization and the use of any profits. The section of the chapter presenting the income statement explains concepts of for-profit compared to nonprofit status. The third statement discussed is the **balance sheet**, which provides information about the organization's resources and how those resources are acquired. The **statement of cash flows**, which provides details about the sources of cash and how cash is used, is the fourth and final financial report discussed in this section.

Annual Report

The annual report is the financial statement with which most people, including health care professionals, are familiar. Serving as an overall summary of an organization's financial position, the annual report is generally the most important financial statement released to the general public and others outside the organization. The annual report is the financial statement that is also typically more widely available and widely distributed within health care organizations. Many hospitals now publish their annual reports on the Internet. An example of a hospital report is The University of Kansas Hospital 2011 Annual Report (http://www.kumed.com/annualreport/2011/grow.aspx).

The annual report consists of three major parts. First is the text, usually in the form of a letter from the chief executive officer (CEO) or head of the organization. This section presents the current status of the organization and goals and plans for the future. The CEO's letter also reports any accomplishments, awards, or other items that enhance the institution's reputation.

The next section presents an overall summarized income statement, balance sheet, and statement of cash flows, often comparing the current year of the annual report to the prior year. Financial statements prepared for the annual report provide less detail than standard financial statements. Many annual reports simply summarize revenues and expenses over the fiscal year.

The final section of the annual report consists of footnotes, or brief notes providing information not covered in the financial statements. The annual report also may include accountant's or auditor's opinion letter in the footnotes. Some state laws and the Patient Protection and Affordable Care Act of 2010 (Patient Protection and Affordable Care Act, 2010) require increased hospital reporting of charity care. Hospital annual reports therefore often include a summary report of charity care in the annual report.

The annual report should be able to provide a nurse with at least some basic financial information about the health care organization. The net income that is reported in a summary income statement enables the nurse to determine whether the organization generated a profit or loss over the fiscal year. A positive net income indicates a profit, and a negative net income indicates a loss. A comparison of current assets to current liabilities enables the nurse to determine the amount of assets that are readily available to the organization (explained in more detail in the discussion of working capital). The summary statement of cash flows enables the nurse to determine if cash flow is positive (favorable) or negative (unfavorable). This basic information provides an overall indication of the financial health of the organization.

Income Statement

Probably the simplest yet most meaningful financial question is, "Is the business making money?" For this reason, the income statement, also referred to as the **statement of financial operations**, is an important financial report to review because it focuses on revenues, expenses, and profitability. Income statements differ among organizations, and the name of this report may differ, such as **statement of operations, statement of activities, revenue, and expense summary**, or **statement of revenue and expenses**. The income statement reports the difference between revenues and expenses to show net income (profit) or net loss, thus measuring the organization's profitability. The time frame for the income statement is often monthly, quarterly, or annually.

Table 12.1 presents a public hospital income statement adapted from the California Office of Statewide Health Planning and Development (OSHPD) Hospital Annual Financial Data Pivot Profiles (http://www.oshpd.ca.gov/HID/Products/Hospitals/AnnFinanData/PivotProfiles/default.asp). The pivot profiles display the hospital income statement as part of a spreadsheet file.

The income statement begins by reporting gross patient revenue, which consists of all charges made for inpatient and outpatient care. Net patient revenue is calculated as gross patient revenue less any deductions to revenue. Other operating revenue is added to net patient revenue to report total operating revenue (Table 12.1).

Operating expenses are subtracted from total operating revenue to report net from operations (Table 12.1). Nonoperating revenues are added to the net from operations, and nonoperating expenses are subtracted from the net from operations. As this hospital is a public institution, there are no taxes deducted from the net from operations. The remaining negative $7,950,555 is the net income (net loss) reported by the public hospital for 2010.

Table 12.1 *Public Hospital Income Statement, FY 2010*

Item	FY 2010	Per Adjusted Day*
Gross patient revenue	$1,406,995,183	$8776.28
- Deductions from revenue	($1,082,945,977)	($6754.99)
Net patient revenue	$324,049,206	$2021.29
+ Other operating revenue	$7,788,268	$48.58
Total operating revenue	$331,837,474	$2069.87
- Operating expenses	($386,137,115)	($2408.57)
Net from operations	($54,299,641)	($338.70)
+ Nonoperating revenue	$46,358,561	$289.17
- Nonoperating expense	($9475)	($0.06)
- Income taxes	$0	$0.00
Net income	($7,950,555)	($49.59)

Notes: *160,318 adjusted patient days. Values in parentheses refer to loss.

Source: Adapted from OSHPD Hospital Annual Financial Data Pivot Profiles, 2010. (http://www.oshpd.ca.gov/HID/Products/Hospitals/AnnFinanData/PivotProfiles/default.asp).

Balance Sheet

The balance sheet, also referred to as the **statement of financial position**, provides information about the financial condition of an organization at a given date, not over a specified time period. The balance sheet can therefore offer a "snapshot" view of an organization's financial status, useful because factors such as seasonal demand or rapid growth may cause large changes in financial activities within the course of a fiscal year.

For example, a surge in respiratory disorders typically increases the census of Bigtown Hospital from early November through mid-February, related to a rise in influenza and pneumonia infections. This rise in the census increases revenues as well as expenses beyond the usual patterns seen at Bigtown Hospital, strengthening the financial status over that time period. Increases occur in both cash received and money owed to Bigtown Hospital, as well as in expenses for items such as medical supplies and nursing care required for these additional patients.

Assets are resources held by the organization that possess or create economic benefit. Most assets are **tangibles,** or measurable resources, such as property or cash. Some assets are **intangibles,** or unmeasurable resources, such as reputation. The balance sheet is a report about assets (the organization's resources) and the financing required to acquire those assets, which include **liabilities** (claims on assets established by contract) and **equity** (ownership claim on assets). In other words, the balance sheet reports an organization's resources and claims against those resources, or what an organization owns, owes, and its owners have invested.

The layout of a balance sheet is as follows:

$$\text{Assets} = \text{Liabilities} + \text{Equity}$$

Note that the balance sheet "balances" assets compared to liabilities and equity. For example, if Company A has $1,500,000 in assets and $1,250,000 in liabilities, it must have $250,000 in equity. In other words, Company A owns $1,500,000 in assets, for which it owes (or is liable to pay for) $1,250,000 with $250,000 contributed by its owners. Figure 12.3

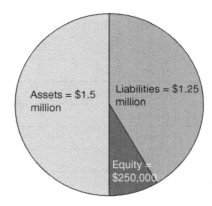

Figure 12.3 *Company A, Illustration of Accounting Equation (A = L + E) in Balance Sheet*

illustrates the accounting equation for Company A as a pie chart. The following sections discuss the parts of the balance sheet and related concepts in more detail.

Current Assets

Table 12.2 shows a balance sheet adapted from the California Office of Statewide Health Planning and Development (OSHPD) Hospital Annual Financial Data Pivot Profiles (http:// www.oshpd.ca.gov/HID/Products/Hospitals/AnnFinanData/PivotProfles/default.asp). This is a balance sheet for the same public hospital reporting the income statement in Table 12.1.

Current assets represent **liquid assets**, or resources that represent cash or that can read-ily be exchanged for or converted into cash. Assets such as **receivables** (payments due for goods or services provided), **inventory** (supplies kept on hand), and current prepayments are examples of current assets.

Noncurrent Assets

Noncurrent assets include long-term investments, **fixed assets** (also referred to as **real assets,** or property, plant, and equipment), which are relatively permanent resources, and other assets (assets that are intangible or fixed assets that do not generate revenue). Long-term investments and fixed assets represent **illiquid assets**, or resources that cannot readily be exchanged for or readily converted into cash. The fundamental rule is that current assets are expected to be converted to cash within a fiscal year; noncurrent assets are not expected to be converted to cash within a fiscal year.

Limited use assets are assets that carry restrictions imposed by the hospital board, donors, or other third parties. For example, a donor may specify that the money given to a hospital be used only to build a new pediatric wing.

Property, Plant and Equipment, and Construction-in-Progress

Property, plant, and capital equipment (PPE) are fixed assets that are held over the long term and unlikely to be readily or quickly converted into cash. The extent of these fixed assets is typically set to handle peak demand. For example, a hospital with 110 staffed beds might report an ADC of 80 and an average occupancy rate of 73% for 2012. The hospital can accom-modate 110 acute care patients at full capacity, as during an influenza outbreak.

Net PPE represents the value of PPE less **accumulated depreciation**. For fixed assets such as buildings, land, and major capital equipment, accountants spread the original purchasing cost over the asset's useful lifetime using various methods for depreciation.

Table 12.2 *Public Hospital Balance Sheet and Common Size Analysis, December 31, FY 2010*

Assets		% of Total	Liabilities and Equity		% of Total
Current assets	$159,314,968	44.07%	Current liabilities	$64,197,616	17.76%
Limited use assets	$19,948,126	5.52%	Net long-term debt	$217,447,110	60.16%
Net PPE	$147,025,433	40.67%	Total liabilities	$281,644,726	77.92%
Construction-in-progress	$31,821,474	8.80%			
Intangible assets	$3,357,861	0.93%	Equity	$79,823,136	22.08%
Total assets	$361,467,862	100.00%	Total liabilities & equity	$361,467,862	100.00%

Source: Adapted from OSHPD Hospital Annual Financial Data Pivot Profiles, 2010. (http://www.oshpd. ca.gov/HID/Products/Hospitals/AnnFinanData/PivotProfles/default.asp).

Accumulated depreciation is the total dollars of depreciation expensed over time. Table 12.2 shows the net PPE for the public hospital.

Construction-in-progress is the accumulated cost of construction that will be used for hospital operations. California hospitals must demonstrate compliance with seismic retrofitting laws and regulations. Many California hospitals, including the public hospital in Table 12.2, therefore report construction-in-progress in their balance sheets.

Intangible Assets

A frequently listed intangible asset is **goodwill,** which represents the difference between the **fair market value** (the price paid to the owners) and the **book value** (balance sheet value of owners equity) of an asset, often obtained via merger or acquisition. No monetary value is entered for intangible assets in the balance sheet for the public hospital in Table 12.2. This may reflect the accounting principle of fiscal conservatism, so that the valuation of intangible assets does not inflate the balance sheet. Total assets for the public hospital add to $361,467,862 for 2010.

Liabilities and Equity

Liabilities and equity are the categories of items that are recorded on the right side or bottom half of the balance sheet. The liabilities and equity categories represent the capital raised (in other words, money borrowed or contributed) to acquire the assets recorded on the left side or top half of the balance sheet. Liabilities may be estimated as follows:

Total Liabilities = Total Assets – Equity

Liabilities are claims against the assets of an organization that are fixed by contract. Bankruptcy is a likely result of default (failure to pay interest or principal or maintain financial covenants) on such claims, which may result in **liquidation** (dissolving the business and distributing its assets). By law, if liquidation occurs, assets must first be used to fulfill claims on liabilities, then distributed to shareholders (if a for-profit enterprise) or contributed to charity (if a nonprofit enterprise). In recording liabilities, short-term debts or other financial obligations are listed first, then long-term debt or other financial obligations.

Current Liabilities

Current liabilities include debts or other financial obligations that must be paid within the short term or fiscal year. One current liability entry is **accounts payable**, or **trade credit,**

which is the amount due to vendors for supplies. Another current liability entry is **accrued expenses**, which is comprised of expenses that are generated daily, with periodic payment. Employee wages and benefits, interest due on loans, and taxes are examples of accrued expenses. Short-term debt, or debt expected to be repaid within the year, is another current liability. **Net working capital** is the difference between current assets and current liabilities. The public hospital reporting the balance sheet in Table 12.2 has $23,333,000 net working capital. The hospital therefore has more than enough current assets to pay off its current liabilities. Working capital is discussed further in the section about practice management.

Long-Term Debt

Long-term debt represents debt financing (loans) with remaining maturities greater than one year, including debts to banks, bondholders, and some lease arrangements. The borrower must pay a specified portion of the **principal** (amount borrowed) each year, as well as **interest** (a percentage rate representing the price for borrowing). Long-term debt is a **noncurrent liability**, or liability entry not due within a fiscal year. **Net long-term debt** represents long-term debt less the amount of debt expected to be paid off in the next fiscal year. In Table 12.2, current liabilities and net long-term debt add to total liabilities of $281,644,726 for 2010.

Equity

Equity, also referred to as **owners equity**, represents the ownership claim on an organization's assets, or the amount of total assets financed by nonliability capital. Public and non-profit organizations owned by the community often use the terms **net assets** or **net worth** instead of equity. Equity may be estimated as follows:

$$\text{Equity} = \text{Total Assets} - \text{Total Liabilities}$$

The equity for the public hospital is $79,823,136. Note that equity plus liabilities equal $361,467,862, which balances with the hospital's total assets.

Statement of Cash Flows

Over the short term, an organization's financial condition (and survival) depends more on cash flow than on profits. Bankruptcy can occur with positive income, in other words, profitable enterprises can go bankrupt if they run short of cash. It is therefore essential to forecast cash flow, prepare cash flow budgets (Chapter 7), and report cash flow in and out of the organization.

When the accrual basis of accounting is used in financial reporting, neither revenue nor net income may equal cash inflow. In addition, expenses likely do not equal cash outflow. Therefore, it is important to review the statement of cash flows (also referred to as the **cash flow statement**), that focuses on financial condition based on cash flow rather than revenues, expenses, or net income. The statement of cash flows is often reported monthly, quarterly, or annually.

The statement of cash flows provides information about the sources and uses of cash and cash resources. It is a useful management tool that helps prevent liquidity problems, thus protecting the enterprise from cash flow difficulties and the threat of bankruptcy. The following section explains how the statement of cash flows is linked to the balance sheet and the income statement.

The statement of cash flows is a report of the cash sources and cash requirements for three categories of financial management: operating activities, investing activities (also referred to as capital investing), and financing activities. **Cash flow** is calculated as the change or net increase or decrease in cash. Cash flow is reported for each of the three categories, which appear as sections of the statement of cash flows.

The amounts reported in the statement of cash flows represent changes in cash, requiring prior-year financial statements to calculate the amount of change. The statement of cash flows uses information from the balance sheet to adjust information from the income statement. These adjustments essentially transform the reporting from accrual to cash accounting (Wayman, 2010).

The nurse should evaluate whether if the business is generating enough cash to cover operating, capital investing, and financial investing expenses. A positive cash balance is desirable, indicating that more cash is coming into the organization than is going out. Enough cash needs to be on hand to pay bills and purchase assets. Surplus cash should be invested.

Cash flows from operating activities. The OSHPD pivot tables do not report a statement of cash flows for hospitals. Table 12.3 presents a statement of cash flows for a sample hospital adapted from the online article, What Is A Cash Flow Statement? by Heakal (2010). This statement of cash flows is not a financial report for the public hospital reporting the income statement in Table 12.1 and the balance sheet in Table 12.2. However, Table 12.3 provides an example of a statement of cash flows that illustrates the relevant concepts for this financial report.

The first section of the statement of cash flows reports cash increases or decreases that are directly related to operations (patient care). The most important entry is net income, which for 2010 is $3,000,000. The amount of net income is taken from the income statement for FY 2010. However, as net income does not equal cash flow, this amount must be adjusted.

Table 12.3 *Sample Hospital Statement of Cash Flows, FY Ended December 31, 2010*

Cash Flows from Operating Activities	
Net income	$3,000,000
Additions to cash	
Depreciation	$15,000
Decrease in accounts receivable	$20,000
Increase in accounts payable	$25,000
Increase in taxes payable	$0
Subtractions from cash	
Increase in inventory	($20,000)
Net cash from operating activities	$3,040,000
Cash flow from investing	
Equipment	($600,000)
Cash flow from financing	
Notes payable	$20,000
Cash Flow for FY Ended 31 Dec 2012	$2,460,000

Source: Adapted from Heakal (2010).

Although depreciation is recorded as an expense, it does not represent actual cash flow. The cash outflow for the fixed assets that are depreciated occurred when the payment for the fixed assets was made. Depreciation is an estimate of the reduction in the value of fixed assets, and does not represent a cash expenditure. The amount of depreciation is therefore added back to the net income.

Accounts receivable (also frequently referred to as receivables or **collectibles**) are the cash payments the hospital expects to collect. Accounts receivable represent the largest and most important source of cash in most health care organizations. The change in cash flows from accounts receivable is calculated by subtracting the prior year (FY 2009) amount of accounts receivable from the current year (FY 2010) amount of accounts receivable. The amount of accounts receivable is obtained from the December 31 balance sheets for FY 2009 and FY 2010.

The decrease in cash flows from accounts receivable means that more cash is flowing into the hospital from payers making reimbursement. If there was a reported increase in accounts receivable, it would be deducted from net income, and would be reported as a negative value (Heakal, 2010).

An increase in cash flows from accounts payable is added to net income, because it represents purchase made on credit that increases the amount of cash available (Table 12.3). The change in cash flows from accounts payable is calculated by subtracting the prior year (FY 2009) amount of accounts payable from the current year (FY 2010) amount of accounts payable. The amount of accounts payable is obtained from the December 31 balance sheets for FY 2009 and FY 2010.

If a decrease in cash flows from accounts payable were reported, the amount would be a negative value, as it would represent a decrease in cash. Although this hospital does not pay taxes (assume it is a public or nonprofit institution), a change in cash flows from taxes payable are also added to the net income, if applicable. Cash payment for purchases or taxes would be subtracted from net income as they reduce the amount of available cash, so they would be reported as negative values (Heakal, 2010).

Cash outlays to increase inventory and any other prepaid goods and services are subtracted from net income (Table 12.3), as these expenditures decrease available cash. The change in cash flows from inventory is calculated in the same way as the change in cash flows from accounts receivable, using the inventory amounts reported in the December 31 balance sheets for FY 2009 and FY 2010. The increase in cash flows from inventory for the sample hospital in 2010 is reported as a negative value. If the cash flows from inventory decrease, the amount of decrease is added to net income (Heakal, 2010).

A key part of the cash flow statement is the reported net cash from operating activities, amounting to $3,040,000. The adjustments made based on cash flows from accounts receivable, accounts payable, and inventory reflect changes in working capital. Net cash from operating activities is calculated by summing all of the operating activities in the 2010 statement of cash flows. The net cash from operating activities informs the nurse about how well the hospital is generating cash. The net cash from operating activities reported in Table 12.3 shows a positive inflow of cash.

Cash flows from investing activities. The second section of the statement of cash flows represents cash flow from investing, also referred to as capital investing. Capital investing represents investment in fixed or noncurrent assets, not financial investing. Depreciation is already adjusted in the noncash section of the operating cash flows, so is not included in this section. Table 12.3 reports a $600,000 decrease in cash from the purchase of equipment. The change in cash flows from investing is calculated using information from the December 31 balance sheet for FY 2009 and FY 2010, in the same way as for calculating the change in accounts receivable.

Cash flows from financing activities. The third section of the statement of cash flows records the flow of cash related to financing, or financial investments rather than the capital investments recorded in the second section of the statement of cash flows. As shown in

Table 12.3, a $20,000 increase in financing cash flow is reported for the change in **notes payable,** or written promises of future payment made by the hospital. An increase in notes payable (a type of loan) increases the cash amount. The change in cash flows from investing is calculated using information from the December 31 balance sheet for FY 2009 and FY 2010, in the same way as for calculating the change in cash flows from accounts receivable.

Other sources of financing cash flow are not reported but may appear in other cash flow statements the nurse reviews. An increase in financial investments such as **marketable securities** (liquid, low interest-bearing investments) decreases the cash amount. An increase in long-term debt increases the cash amount.

This statement of cash flows shows a positive cash flow largely generated by the hospital's operations, which is a sign of financial health. There is enough cash available to purchase more inventory and to invest in new equipment. The cash flow also appears to be healthy enough to pay off the notes payable when due. More information about the statement of cash flows is available at the Accounting Coach website (www.accountingcoach.com). A slideshow introductory review of the income statement, balance sheet, and statement of cash flows is available at the Wisc-Online Financial Statements website (www.wisc-online.com).

Classification of Expenses

Expenses represent the cost of doing business. As presented in Chapter 5, operating expenses or costs include salaries and wages, supplies, equipment, and other costs related to providing goods or services. Chapter 7 defines capital expenses, or costs associated with the purchase of major equipment, renovation, building, or other large, long-term purchases. **Financial costs** are expenses incurred in obtaining funds to purchase the organization's assets, such as interest on debt.

Expenses may be classified in financial statements in two ways. The **natural classification** method classifies by the type of input accruing the expense. For example, a natural classification of expenses might include entries for inputs such as salaries and benefits, medical supplies, or property lease. Line item budgets as presented in Chapter 5 are examples of natural classification.

The **functional classification** method classifies by the type of output accruing the expense. For example, a functional classification of expenses might include entries for inpatient services, outpatient services, and administration cost centers. An operating expense budget summarizing the total costs for each department or cost center of an organization would be an example of functional classification. Both natural and functional expense classifications are reported in the California Office of Statewide Health Planning and Development (OSHPD) Hospital Annual Financial Data Pivot Profiles. (http://www.oshpd. ca.gov/HID/Products/Hospitals/AnnFinanData/PivotProfiles/default.asp).

The number and nature of expenses may vary widely on the income statement, depending on what is relevant and of most interest from organization to organization. Smaller organizations typically report fewer categories of expenses, and larger organizations typically have a more detailed expense report on the income statement. Most users of financial statements desire more detail rather than less, because more insights are obtained if the organization reports revenues and expenses both by type or as a natural classification (for example, salaries vs. supplies) and by a service breakdown, or as a functional classification (for example, inpatient vs. outpatient services).

Nonprofit Versus For-Profit Financial Status and Reporting

Nurses should understand that the type of ownership, in other words, for-profit or nonprofit status, is important in financial reporting. In the United States, hospitals proliferated as nonprofit institutions, and nonprofit hospitals and hospital chains continue to dominate the industry, although for-profit hospitals and hospital chains are increasing. According to economic theory, nonprofits are able to address market failures in supplying greatly needed yet unprofitable services such as burn units and emergency departments (which generate high costs not covered by revenues). Because providing these services that address market failures is perceived as beneficial to the community, nonprofit hospitals receive favorable tax treatment.

The favorable tax treatment extended to nonprofits because they provide services to the community is a key concept in differentiating these enterprises from for-profits. However, a frequent misunderstanding is that nonprofit enterprises do not, and need not, make a profit. This view of nonprofit status is not accurate. In order to survive and grow, it is as important for a nonprofit as a for-profit organization to be profitable. The difference lies in the requirement for nonprofits, in order to retain favorable tax treatment, to reinvest all net income (profit) back into the business. Even if the organization or enterprise is nonprofit, the financial report must include a performance indicator, which represents net income, also reported by nonprofits as **net surplus** or **net deficit**.

By contrast, for-profit (investor-owned) enterprises are permitted to pay out some or all of their net income (profit) as dividend payments to shareholders, after, of course, paying taxes. The proportion of after-tax net income paid out to shareholders is the **payout ratio**. The proportion of net income reinvested in the business is the **retention ratio**. For example, Goodman General Hospital, one of Bigtown Hospital's competitors, is a for-profit with a net income in FY 2011 of $7,000,000. If $2,000,000 are paid out to shareholders in FY 2012, then $5,000,000 remain to be reinvested in Goodman General Hospital's operations. The 2012 payout ratio is 28.6% ($2,000,000 ÷ $7,000,000). The 2012 retention ratio is therefore 71.4%. Note that the dividends plus reinvestment amount must equal the net income, and the payout ratio plus the retention ratio must equal 100%, to account for all of the net income.

For nonprofit enterprises, all net income must be reinvested, so in many nonprofit reports an entry after the net income entry reconciles net income with the net assets reported in the balance sheet. In other words, for nonprofits, net income equals reinvestment, and is reported on the balance sheet accordingly. For example, Bigtown Hospital, a nonprofit, earned $3,253,000 net income in FY 2011, all of which represents funds that will eventually be reinvested into the business.

ANALYZING FINANCIAL STATEMENTS

Unlike budgets, the preparation of credible financial statements requires an understanding of accounting and compliance with accepted accounting principles. Nurses therefore are unlikely to prepare an income statement, balance sheet, or statement of cash flows. However, nurses should be prepared to review and interpret these statements, and to obtain at least a general idea of the organization's financial health.

Percentage Change Analysis

One way to assess a health care organization's financial condition is to compare its own performance over time. **Percentage change analysis,** or calculating the percent of change for each item on a financial statement from year to year, is very similar to the method explained for percent budget variance analysis in Chapter 5. The financial statements analyzed usually include the income statement and the balance sheet. Percentage change analysis is also referred to as **horizontal analysis** because the calculations are worked across the rows of the financial report, from one time period to another.

Percentage change analysis is calculated by subtracting the earlier year's value from the later year's value in the financial statement to obtain the amount of change over time. This value is then divided by the earlier year's value. Note that if the earlier value is zero or negative, the percentage change is not reported as it is not a meaningful value.

Table 12.4 shows a percentage change analysis for the 2009 to 2010 income statements in the public hospital. The gross patient revenue for 2009 is subtracted from the gross patient revenue for 2010 to obtain $60,609,188, or the amount of change from 2009 to 2010 ($1,406,995,183 – $1,346,385,995). This difference is then divided by the 2009 value to report a 4.5% increase in gross patient revenues from 2009 to 2010 ($60,609,188 ÷ $1,346,385,995). The remaining items in the income statement for FY 2009 to 2010 are calculated in the same way. The net income for this hospital fell nearly 1.5 times from 2009 to 2010. The drops in operating and nonoperating revenue and the increase in operating expenses help explain reasons for the reported loss in FY 2010.

Common Size Analysis

Another method for converting data in the income statement and balance sheet to percentages for comparison over time, among similar organizations or to industry standards, is **common size analysis.** For common size analysis of the income statement, each item is displayed as a percent of total revenues (operating and nonoperating); for common size analysis of the balance sheet, each item is displayed as a percent of total assets. Common size analysis is also referred to as **vertical analysis** because the calculations use data from the columns of financial statement values, over the same time period. It is possible to compare this hospital's performance to other hospitals, or to industry benchmarks by using common size analysis.

Table 12.2 shows the common size analysis for the December 31, 2010 balance sheet for the public hospital. The common size analysis shows that about 44% of the hospital's assets are current assets. Nearly 50% of the hospital's assets are fixed assets (PPE) or construction-in-progress. A little over 60% of the hospital's liabilities and equity are net long-term debt. The high proportion of long-term debt may be related to construction required by California regulations mandating seismic retrofitting.

Table 12.4 *Public Hospital Income Statement, Percentage Change Analysis, FY 2009–2010*

Item	FY 2009	FY 2010	Percentage Change 2009–2010
Gross patient revenue	$1,346,385,995	$1,406,995,183	4.50%
- Deductions from revenue	($1,020,051,172)	($1,082,945,977)	6.17%
Net patient revenue	$326,334,823	$324,049,206	(0.70%)
+ Other operating revenue	$7,353,536	$7,788,268	5.91%
Total operating revenue	$333,688,359	$331,837,474	(0.55%)
- Operating expenses	($375,520,911)	($386,137,115)	2.83%
Net from operations	($41,832,552)	($54,299,641)	29.80%
+ Nonoperating revenue	$59,007,402	$46,358,561	(21.44%)
- Nonoperating expense	($4551)	($9475)	108.20%
- Income taxes	$0	$0	0.00%
Net income	$17,170,299	($7,950,555)	(146.30%)

Note: Values in parentheses refer to loss.
Source: Adapted from OSHPD Hospital Annual Financial Data Pivot Profiles, 2009–2010.
(http://www.oshpd.ca.gov/HID/Products/Hospitals/AnnFinanData/PivotProfles/default.asp).

Financial Ratios

The primary purpose of financial statement analysis is to evaluate the fiscal performance of an enterprise. In other words, the reviewer's questions include "is this enterprise's financial performance good, poor, improving, or worsening?" In order to have a basis for evaluation, one more question is required: "Compared to what?" As explained in Chapter 5 regarding the evaluation of budget variances, it is necessary to be able to compare data from financial statements with past and projected data, and with data from other organizations or industry benchmarks to understand what the level of financial performance represents.

In reviewing financial statements, a method often employed is **ratio analysis**, or converting values from financial statements into proportions that allow for interpretation. Ratio analysis enables comparison to past performance as well as comparison to other similar organizations and benchmarking. Ratio analysis is another method for nurses to assess the financial health of the organization using values reported in financial statements.

There are a number of categories and purposes for ratios used in ratio analysis. **Profitability** (also referred to as **performance**) **ratios** help reviewers understand how well the enterprise generates profits, related to its assets and revenues. **Liquidity ratios** describe an enterprise's capability to turn assets into cash or to cover current debt with cash and other assets available. **Debt management** (also referred to as **capital structure** or **leverage**) **ratios** show the extent of an enterprise's debt burden, the extent to which investors are financing the enterprise, whether debt payments are covered by current earnings, and the likelihood of the enterprise paying its debts. **Asset management** (also referred to as **activity, efficiency,** or **turnover**) **ratios** help reviewers determine how effectively the enterprise is using its assets, and how liabilities are affecting the enterprise.

Some caution should be exercised in using ratio analysis, especially when comparing one institution to another. It is important to consider whether one institution resembles another across many criteria, such as size, patient mix, and the extent of inpatient to outpatient services. There are also differences, allowable under financial accounting standards and regulations, in the ways financial statements are reported that may cause ratios to differ.

Many ratios exist in each of these categories for use in financial statement analysis. This section presents ratios reported in the California Office of Statewide Health Planning and Development (OSHPD) Hospital Annual Financial Data Pivot Profiles (http://www.oshpd.ca.gov/HID/Products/Hospitals/AnnFinanData/PivotProfiles/default.asp). Figure 12.4 presents FY 2010 hospital financial ratios for the public hospital reported in Tables 12.1 through 12.3.

Median and quartile values are typically used to report financial ratio benchmarks, as they are less influenced by extremes than average values. A limited number of benchmarks for the public hospital's financial ratios are available from an annual publication (The Risk Management Association [RMA], 2010). The upper quartile value for these financial ratios are used as benchmarks in this section.

Profitability Ratios

Profitability is an important sign of financial health. Recall that revenues generated by the provision of goods and services represent cash payments or the obligation to make payments over time. Revenues less expenses represent profit (or loss), so expenses (costs of inputs) reduce profitability. Revenues are typically based on volume, and are reported at the time goods or services are provided. Capitation contract revenues are reported when contractual coverage begins.

Net return on total assets. Net income divided by total assets results in the financial ratio **net return on total assets (NROA)**. This profitability ratio indicates the profit generated by the assets of a business. The net income for the public hospital was negative in 2010, so

Financial Ratio	Calculation	Value	General Medical & Surgical Hospitals	General Medical & Surgical Hospitals (Nonprofit)
Profitability				
Net return on total assets	Net income ÷ total assets	(2.20%)	7.2%	4.7%
Patient revenue margin	(Net revenue − operating expenses) ÷ net revenue	(19.16%)		
Operating margin	Net income from operations ÷ (net patient revenue + other operating revenue)	(16.36%)		
Total margin	Pretax net income ÷ (net patient revenue + other operating revenue)	(2.40%)		
Net income margin	Net income ÷ (net patient revenue + other operating revenue + nonoperating revenue)	(2.10%)		
Cost-to-charge ratio	(Total operating expenses − other operating revenue) ÷ total gross patient revenue	26.89%		
Liquidity				
Current ratio	Current assets ÷ current liabilities	2.48	2.7	2.5
Debt management				
Long-term debt to net PPE	Net long-term debt ÷ (net property, plant & equipment + construction-in-progress)	121.58%		
Long-term debt to equity	Net long-term debt ÷ equity	272.41%		
Equity to total assets	Equity ÷ total assets	22.08%		
Asset management				
Days in accounts receivable	Net accounts receivable ÷ (net patient revenue ÷ days in the reporting period)	70.75	38.0	38.0
Net PPE per licensed bed	(Net property, plant, and equipment + construction in progress) ÷ licensed beds	$407,396		

Figure 12.4 *Hospital Financial Ratios, Sample Hospital, 2010*

Note: Benchmarks from (The Risk Management Association [RMA], 2010).
Source: Adapted from OSHPD Hospital Annual Financial Data Pivot Profiles and Glossary, 2010. (http://www.oshpd.ca.gov/HID/Products/Hospitals/AnnFinanData/PivotProfiles/default.asp)

the NROA is a negative 2.2%. Each $1 of assets results in a loss of $0.022 (Figure 12.4). The higher the NROA, the more productive the assets. Because this hospital does not pay taxes, it is assumed that net income equals profit before taxes. The public hospital's financial ratio is therefore compared to the RMA (2010) benchmark ratio of profit before taxes divided by total assets. The benchmark for nonprofit hospitals is 4.7%.

Patient revenue margin. Net revenue less operating expenses divided by net revenue is the profitability ratio **patient revenue margin**. This ratio only includes information from patient care revenues and operating expenses, to show the profit generated solely from patient care operations. As patient care is the key business activity for hospitals, this is a measure of the hospital's core business operations profitability. The public hospital's patient revenue margin of −19.16% in Figure 12.4 is a negative value, indicating that net revenue is not covering operating expenses. This public hospital likely experiences low reimbursement from government and self-pay sources, and must rely on donations and tax revenues for fiscal support.

Operating margin. Net income from operations divided by net patient revenue and other operating revenue results in the **operating margin** (Figure 12.4). The operating margin is a profitability ratio that shows how much patient care revenue contributes to profits from patient care. The public hospital operating margin of negative 16.36% indicates that every $1 of revenue results in a loss of $0.1636 from patient care services. This ratio reinforces the observation that inadequate revenues affect profitability for this public hospital over FY 2010.

Total margin. The pretax net income divided by the net patient revenue and other operating revenue is the **total margin**. The total margin is a profitability ratio indicating the profitability generated by total operating revenues. For the public hospital in Figure 12.4, the negative 2.4% total margin shows that every $1 of total revenue results in a $0.024 loss. Notice that the total margin is higher than the operating margin, suggesting that sources of income other than patient care revenue help contribute to this hospital's financial support.

Net income margin. The **net income margin** is calculated by dividing net income by the sum of net patient revenue, other operating revenue, and nonoperating revenue (Figure 12.4). This profitability ratio indicates the profits generated by total revenues. In the public hospital example reporting a net income margin of negative 2.1%, every $1 of total revenue results in a $0.021 loss.

Cost-to-charge ratio. The **cost-to-charge ratio (CCR)** is discussed in Chapter 8 as a method for nurses to understand the relationship of costs to charges in their work units. However, for Medicare reporting, the CCR is more frequently calculated at the hospital level. The CCR is calculated as a hospital-wide indicator by subtracting other operating revenue from total operating expenses, and dividing that value by total gross patient revenue (Figure 12.4). Remember that gross patient revenue represents the hospital's full charges, hence the term "cost-to-charge ratio." This profitability ratio measures the costs of generating patient revenue.

A low CCR indicates relatively high hospital charges. A higher CCR indicates that a hospital's charges more closely reflect the hospital's costs. The public hospital's CCR of 26.89% may indicate cost-shifting. If reimbursement is available, the higher charges collected from payers help cover costs and reduce overall financial losses.

Liquidity Ratios

Liquidity is important to financial health because liquid assets make cash available when needed on short notice. Cash flow problems can lead to bankruptcy, even if the business is profitable overall, so ratios that measure liquidity are important in assessing financial performance. One commonly used liquidity ratio is reported for California hospitals.

Current ratio. The **current ratio** is a liquidity ratio calculated by dividing current assets by current liabilities. The public hospital's current ratio reported in Figure 12.4 is 2.48. In other words, the hospital has nearly two-and-a-half times more in current assets than in current liabilities. A standard rule-of-thumb benchmark is that it is desirable to report a current ratio of 2.0 or greater. The public hospital's current ratio compares well with the nonprofit hospital benchmark of 2.5 (RMA, 2010).

Debt Management Ratios

Debt management ratios show the ability of a health care organization to manage and pay its debts. Note that owners (or in the case of nonprofit organizations, the community) take out the loan, so that debt management is closely related to equity. It is important to measure and analyze debt management because debt increases the organization's financial risk, cost of capital, and claims on assets in the event of bankruptcy and liquidation.

Debt increases the organization's financial risk because, regardless of profits or losses, debts are obligations requiring repayment or claims on assets. In addition, debt increases the cost of capital because interest as well as the principal must be paid to the creditor. An organization using debt financing must carefully forecast its revenues to be reasonably sure that the future earnings are adequate to cover the debt expense as well as all other expenses, or it risks default.

On the other hand, equity financing typically does not result in claims on assets, because in the event of bankruptcy and liquidation, creditor claims are paid out before the claims of owners or investors. Equity financing also typically does not require repayment. However, it may be difficult for health care organizations to raise capital via equity financing. In the first place, many health care organizations are nonprofits, so they cannot sell stock or allow private investors or owners to invest in the business. For-profit health care organizations may have poor returns on their stock given limited profits, so may use debt financing as the capital needed may not be available via equity financing.

If earnings from investments financed with debt are greater than the interest paid on the loan, the return on equity increases (or is "leveraged up"). In many cases, health care organizations use long-term debt to finance fixed assets. These fixed assets, whether a new structure, major renovation, or state-of-the-art equipment are typically expected to maintain and increase earnings, or "pay for themselves" by attracting volume and generating revenue. However, it may be difficult to match the costs of debt with the revenues from investments such as fixed assets financed by the debt.

For financial security reasons, creditors prefer low debt ratios, and pay attention to the amount of equity capital provided to the enterprise. If the owners (or community) provide only a small amount of total financing, there is greater risk on default of loans should bankruptcy and liquidation occur. However, owners of for-profit enterprises may seek higher debt in order to increase their return on equity, or because they do not want to give up control by selling stock. Managers of nonprofit organizations may seek higher debt to provide more services to the community. Therefore, debt management should help maintain a reasonable balance between financing by creditors and owners.

Long-term debt to net PPE. Dividing net long-term debt by net PPE plus construction-in-progress results in the financial ratio **long-term debt to net PPE**. This debt management ratio is an indicator of fixed asset financing. The public hospital long-term debt to net PPE ratio of 121.58% indicates that every $1 of net PPE is financed by $1.2158 of long-term debt (Figure 12.4). A lower ratio indicates better performance. In this example, the higher long-term debt to net PPE ratio is likely related to construction that puts the hospital in compliance with the California seismic retrofitting mandate.

Long-term debt to equity. Dividing net long-term debt by equity results in the financial ratio **long-term debt to equity**. This debt management ratio shows the proportion of long-term debt to net worth. A lower ratio indicates a hospital's greater ability to meet its long-term debt obligations. The public hospital ratio of 272.41% (Figure 12.4) is likely related to long-term debt incurred as a result of construction required for compliance with California seismic retrofitting regulations. The public hospital, as a government institution, can rely on public government support and on tax revenue to help finance the long-term debt.

Equity to total assets. Dividing equity by total assets results in the financial ratio **equity to total assets**, also referred to as the **equity ratio.** The equity ratio indicates the proportion of total assets that are financed by the owners of the hospital (in this case the local county) compared to debt financing. The equity ratio of 22.08% in Figure 12.4 indicates that each $1 of assets is financed by $0.2208 of equity.

The equity ratio is also the inverse of the **debt-to-assets ratio,** or **debt ratio**. The debt ratio is calculated by dividing total debt (including current liabilities, leases, and long-term debt) by total assets. Although not reported for the public hospital in Figure 12.4, the debt ratio is 77.92%, or the inverse of the equity ratio (100%–22.08%). Every $1 of the public hospital's assets is financed by $0.7792 of total debt.

Asset Management Ratios

Asset management ratios tell the nurse how efficiently the business is using its assets to generate revenue. Both current assets such as receivables and noncurrent fixed assets such as PPE can be evaluated for their performance.

Days in accounts receivable. Dividing the accounts receivable by the average daily patient revenue (net patient revenue divided by the days in the time period) calculates the **days in accounts receivable**. Days in patient accounts receivable is an asset management ratio that is also sometimes reported as a liquidity ratio. This ratio is of interest because it is important to collect receivables as soon as possible in order to maintain adequate cash flow and reduce the amount of uncollectibles. Figure 12.4 reports 70.75 days in accounts receivable for the public hospital. The benchmark for nonprofit hospitals is 38 days in accounts receivable (RMA, 2010). The public hospital's ratio is likely related to the higher proportion of poor, uninsured patients and lower collection rates compared to most private hospitals.

Net PPE per licensed bed. Dividing the value of net PPE plus construction-in-progress by the number of licensed beds results in the ratio **net PPE per licensed bed**. This asset management ratio indicates the financial value of net fixed assets per licensed bed. When comparing hospitals, it is important to consider the age of the hospital, as net PPE is reduced by accumulated depreciation. The public hospital net PPE per licensed bed of $407,396 must therefore be compared to hospitals at a similar stage of construction.

This is a brief review of some commonly used financial ratios to evaluate hospital performance. An overview and checklist for using additional financial ratios is available at the QFinance Using and Understanding Financial Ratios for Analysis website (www. qfinance.com). More discussion of assessing the financial health of public hospitals that serve as a safety net for vulnerable patients is available at the assessing the Financial Health of Hospitals website (http://archive.ahrq.gov/data/safetynet/needleman.htm). Financial statistics and financial ratios for nonprofit hospitals in 2011 are available at the Becker's Hospital Review website (www.beckerhospitalreview.com).

PRINCIPLES FOR PRACTICE MANAGEMENT

The previous sections of this chapter focus on reporting and evaluating financial health and performance for larger institutions such as hospitals. Many of the concepts presented in these previous sections can be applied to assessing the financial health of smaller health care facilities such as medical practices and nurse-managed health centers. A few principles more specific to practice management are discussed in this section.

Working Capital and Cash Flow

One of the most important considerations for a small practice is adequate working capital. If current assets do not exceed current liabilities, it may be difficult to pay employees and vendors, and the practice is at risk of bankruptcy. Larger institutions are more likely to hold cash reserves that can be used to cover cash shortfalls. Small practices such as nurse-managed clinics frequently lack large cash reserves and must carefully manage working capital. Cash flow is important to working capital, as cash and accounts receivable are current assets. Preparing and monitoring the cash flow budget, reviewed in Chapter 7, is therefore essential as an ongoing management activity, in addition to monitoring working capital. Cash flow budgeting enables nurses to plan for cash shortfalls in their practice.

Revenue Cycle Management

Related to working capital and cash flow budgeting is **revenue cycle management**, the process of billing, collecting, and negotiating reimbursement contracts. Monitoring the days in accounts receivable and the amount of bad debt is important to understand the impact of uncollectibles on revenue.

Net collection rate. Chapter 4 explains that the contractual allowance is the difference between gross charges and actual reimbursement. Deducting contractual allowances from gross charges results in the net charges. Dividing actual collections by net charges calculates the **net collection rate**. The net collection rate is an indicator of the practice's ability to collect reimbursement (Satinsky, 2007).

Aged trial balance. Another way to evaluate collections is to review the amount and percent of account receivables that are 30, 60, 90, and over 120 days old, known as an **aged trial balance** (Satinsky, 2007). The longer collectibles are outstanding, the more difficult they are to collect. It is helpful to compare the aged trial balance to the net collection rate, as delays in collection may be impacting unfavorably on the collection rate. One practice management expert recommends the benchmark of no more than 11% collectibles over 120 days outstanding, as presented in the Getting Paid Video Update—Key Performance Indicators in Medical Billing: Tip #2 website (www.kareo.com).

Policies and procedures. Establishing and following systematic policies and procedures is an important step in revenue cycle management. Obtaining insurance and other patient information when the patient schedules the visit is more efficient than waiting to collect this information when the patient arrives for the appointment. It is also helpful to provide patients with written policies for issues such as charges for missed appointments, when out-of-pocket payments are due and payment plans (Satinsky, 2007).

The practice should keep updated on accurate coding so that potential revenue is not lost in billing. Policies should be in place to appropriately control free care provided to family members or practice employees. The practice should also protect itself from fraud by requiring that all staff members are bonded (Satinsky, 2007).

This section discusses a few steps to consider in monitoring and safeguarding the capital and cash flow of small practices. An example of financial statements for an outpatient clinic is available at the Cleveland Clinic website (www.myclevelandclinic.org). Vonderheid et al. (2004) present a study and review of performance and financial indicators for academic nurse-managed health centers. The America's Health Insurance Plans (AHIP) website (www.aahp.org) has a Self-Assessment Tool for Physicians/Providers useful in evaluating the management of claims and payments for a small practice.

More discussion on financial ratios and benchmarking relevant to small practices is available in the online article, Financial Benchmarking and Ratio Analysis in the Health Care Industry (Cimasi, 2004). RMA (2010) also reports benchmarks for physician offices and some other types of medical practices. Another source of medical practice benchmarks is the Getting Paid online article Benchmarks for Your Medical Practice (Satiani, 2011).

STARTING YOUR OWN BUSINESS OR AGENCY

Many nurses think about starting their own business or nonprofit agency. Nurses can use their knowledge and experience to create an enterprise that meets needs in the community.

Some examples of a nurse-run business are providing private case management services for elderly or seriously disabled clients and presenting educational offerings on nutrition and obesity control. Nurses might start a nonprofit agency to provide services such as health care for homeless clients or therapeutic art programs for children who are at risk. An online presentation on nurses entrepreneurship, Nursing Workforce—New Roles, encourages and inspires nurses to think about starting their own businesses (www.icn.ch).

As mentioned in Chapter 10, this textbook is more focused on nurses as "intrapreneurs" employed in a health care setting. However, many of the concepts and skills presented are useful to nurse entrepreneurs, as well. A few additional recommendations and resources are provided in this section for nurses to review if they consider starting their own business or nonprofit agency.

Mission, vision, and values. Review Chapter 7 to recall the relationships of an enterprise's **mission, vision,** and **values** to **strategic planning**. It is important to clearly define the purpose of your business or agency, the vision of this enterprise over the next three to five years, and associated values. A private nursing case management business will likely focus on identifying and serving isolated and vulnerable elderly clients by coordinating medical care and other support services. A nonprofit health center for homeless clients will identify and serve these indigent patients at a location accessible to this population.

Financing. Whether this is a for-profit or nonprofit enterprise, it is essential to consider how income will be generated. Elderly clients or their families might be willing to pay out-of-pocket for nurse case manager services. Health care for the homeless might be financed through grant funding or by contracting with a local hospital or ACO.

Nurses often overlook their personal income needs when starting a business or agency, assuming that they will "live off the profits" or "donate their time." However, profits must often be reinvested in the business, particularly for new enterprises. Donating one's time may not be feasible for one's personal financial health over the long term. Remember that labor costs are an operating expense, and should be budgeted as such. Think carefully about the personal impact on your time and personal finances, and budget your salary as a personnel expense. Be aware that the salary from your own business or agency will likely be substantially less than what a hospital or other health care employer might pay.

Budget estimates and P&L statement. Review Chapters 6 and 7, and estimate a statistics or volume budget, an operating revenue and expense budget, a capital or start-up budget, and a cash flow budget. Create these budgets on a monthly basis for at least two or three years to obtain insights on the flow of volume, revenues, expenses, and cash over time. The statistics budget is the basis for other budgeting. How many elderly clients can realistically be expected to utilize nurse case management services over the next three years? How many homeless clients are likely to visit the nurse-managed health center?

What reimbursement, revenues, or other income do you expect to receive? What grant funding or donations might be available for a nonprofit agency? This information should be entered into the revenue budget. What personnel and nonpersonnel expenses will the enterprise generate? Are there indirect costs such as rent or clerical services that need to be budgeted? What start-up costs, such as office furnishings, should be considered?

Estimate a **P&L statement** by subtracting all the start-up and operating expenses for the first year of the enterprise's operations from the anticipated revenues for the first year. Use estimates for the second and third years of operations to prepare P&L statements for future years. Will revenues be sufficient to cover costs? If not, are there strategies to increase revenues or decrease costs?

Information. There is information available on the Internet that is useful to entrepreneurs. One example is the Women's Health Free Clinic Toolkit, which explains how to start a free clinic. The U.S. Small Business Administration has resources on starting a new business. The National Council of Nonprofits has information at the How to Start a Nonprofit website (www.councilofnonprofits.org). The Nursing Entrepreneur website shares information and provides networking opportunities (www.nursingentrepreneurs. com). Another resource is the Nurse Practitioners in Business blog (http://www.blog-catalog.com/blog/nurse-practitioners-in-business). These are only a few examples of resources on entrepreneurship; a few minutes searching the Internet can yield an abundance of helpful information.

Expert consultation. Before launching a new business or nonprofit agency, it is important to obtain expert advice and consultation from an accountant, and possibly from a lawyer, as well. Compliance with tax and other laws is essential, as is compliance with any relevant health care laws or regulations. Nurses must be sure they operate within their clinical scope of practice. Nurse entrepreneurs must also maintain appropriate records, file necessary forms, and follow other legal and regulatory provisions that are required.

Get started. Review Chapters 10 and 11 to develop a business plan or grant proposal that creates the business or nonprofit agency. The eHow Money web page, How to Write a Marketing Plan for a Home Health Care Agency has helpful tips on promoting a nurse-run business. Kawasaki (2004) offers advice on writing a business plan, raising capital, branding, and other points helpful to new entrepreneurs. Kawasaki emphasizes that throughout the steps of starting a project or business, an essential activity is to *get started* by creating or delivering the product or service that fulfills your enterprise's mission. Good luck!

CONCLUSION

This chapter reviews financial indicators with an emphasis on financial statements and financial ratios. Nurses should be able to assess the financial health of their work setting, whether providing inpatient or outpatient care. More nurses are becoming interested in starting their own business, and can apply the concepts in this chapter to entrepreneurial enterprises.

Discussion and Exercises

1. Obtain a recent annual report for your work setting or clinical assignment. If not available, obtain a recent annual report for a local hospital. What information is included in the annual report? If included, review the summary income statement, balance sheet, and statement of cash flows. What is your assessment of the financial health of this organization?
2. If available, obtain a recent income statement and balance sheet for your work setting or clinical assignment. If not available, download hospital financial data from the California Office of Statewide Health Planning and Development (OSHPD) Hospital Annual Financial Data Pivot Profiles (www.oshpd.ca.gov) or from the Washington State Department of Health Community Hospital and Financial Data website (www.doh.wa.gov). Note whether the net income is positive (profit) or negative (loss) and whether current liabilities exceed current assets (positive net working capital). Calculate and interpret at least one profitability, liquidity, debt management, and asset management ratio. What is your assessment of the financial health of this organization?
3. Think of a business or nonprofit agency that you or another nurse would consider starting. Discuss the mission, vision, and values for this business or agency. Describe the consumers or target population for the business or agency, and brainstorm at least two ways you might obtain financing. Estimate an overall annual budget, and if the business generates revenues, estimate whether the first year of operations will generate a profit or loss. Compare your findings with other students, and discuss sources of additional information and expert consultation that would be helpful.

REFERENCES

Cimasi, R. J. (2004). *Financial benchmarking and ratio analysis in the health care industry*. Retrieved from http://www.cpareport.com/newsletterarticles/2004articles/financialbenchmarking_oct_2004.htm

Heakal, R. (2010). *What is a cash flow statement? Investopedia website*. Retrieved from http://www.investopedia.com/articles/04/033104.asp#axzz1wrOMolho

Kawasaki, G. (2004). *The art of the start: The time-tested, battle-hardened guide for anyone starting anything*. New York, NY: Penguin Group

Patient Protection and Affordable Care Act. (2010). Pub. L. No. 111–148, §2702, 124 Stat. 119, 318–319. Retrieved from http://housedocs.house.gov/energycommerce/ppacacon.pdf

Satiani, B. (2011). *Benchmarks for your medical practice: A vital part of critical practice analysis*. Retrieved from http://www.kareo.com/gettingpaid/2011/06/benchmarks-for-your-medical-practice-a-vital-part-of-critical-practice-analysis

Satinsky, M. A. (2007). *Medical practice management in the 21st century: The handbook*. London, UK: Radcliffe Publishing.

The Risk Management Association (RMA). (2010). *The annual statement studies: Financial ratio benchmarks, 2010–2011*. Philadelphia, PA: The Risk Management Association.

Vonderheid, S., Pohl, J., Schafer, P., Forrest, K., Poole, M., Barkauskas, V., & Mackey, T. (2004). Using FTE and RVU performance measures to assess financial viability of academic nurse-managed centers… full-time equivalencies and advanced practice nurses. *Nursing Economics, 22,* 124–134.

Wayman, R. (2010). *Operating cash flow: Better than net income? Investopedia website*. Retrieved from http://www.investopedia.com/articles/analyst/03/122203.asp#axzz1x1dGfmBE

CROSSWORD: *Chapter 12—Financial Statements*

Across

5 Dissolving a business and distributing its assets.

6 Net income divided by total assets, indicating the profit generated by the assets of a business (abbreviation).

9 Supplies a business keeps on hand.

10 Assets that cannot readily be exchanged for or readily converted into cash, such as fixed assets.

11 Reporting on all of the aspects of financial transactions so the financial condition of the business is accurately represented.

15 Claims on assets established by contract, reported in the balance sheet.

16 A percentage rate representing the price for borrowing when transacting a loan.

18 Resources held by the organization that possess or create economic benefit, reported in the balance sheet.

19 A debt management ratio calculated by dividing total debt by total assets, that is the inverse of the equity ratio.

20 A liquidity ratio calculated by dividing current assets by current liabilities.

Down

1 Assets representing cash or that can readily be exchanged for or converted into cash, reported as current assets.

2 A common set of standards, procedures, and principles for preparing financial statements consistently (abbreviation).

3 Another term for accounts receivable or receivables.

4 The difference between the fair market value and the book value of an asset.

7 Assets representing property, plant, and equipment (PPE).

8 An accounting principle that records separate categories of financial entries only if they are relevant for reporting or understanding the financial condition of the business.

12 A ratio that reports the proportion of net income reinvested in the business, and the inverse of the payout ratio.

13 Ownership claim on assets, reported in the balance sheet.

14 Expenses that are generated daily, with periodic payment, such as employee wages.

17 A ratio that reports the proportion of after-tax net income paid out to shareholders, and the inverse of the retention ratio.

Chapter 13: Ethical Issues and International Health Care Systems

Don't tell me where your priorities are. Show me where you spend your money and I'll tell you what they are—James W. Frick

Learning Objectives

1. Analyze a current health care concern using the ethical principles of autonomy, justice, beneficence, and nonmaleficence.
2. Explain how nurses can avoid the risk of at least two types of health care fraud.
3. Compare the health care financing of one other country to the U.S. health care system.
4. Summarize at least three concerns shared by many countries related to health care quality, access, and costs.

Key Terms

autonomy	justice	nonmaleficence
beneficence	kickbacks	patient engagement
brain-drain	medical tourism	pluralistic health system
explicit rationing	national health	socialized health
fraud	insurance	service
implicit rationing	national health service	upcoding

Nurses do not work in isolation. Nurses provide care in the context of their community, within the values and belief systems prevalent in society. Nurses provide care around the world, in a variety of health care systems within countries that may be developing or industrialized. This chapter begins by reviewing some basic ethical principles that may be applied in making economic decisions about health care services. A discussion of unethical practices in health care finance is then presented.

An overview of international health care financing systems is provided in this chapter. Comparisons between the United States and other countries illustrate how different cultural values may impact on the delivery of health care throughout the world. A review of health system problems shared between the United States and other countries reinforces that health financing is a worldwide concern.

BIOETHICS AND HEALTH ECONOMICS

Four basic bioethics principles, often applied to health care overall, are **autonomy, justice, beneficence,** and **nonmaleficence**. The principle of autonomy refers to the right of individuals to make their own decisions about their care. The principle of justice supports the equal or fair distribution of health care benefits and risks across society. Beneficence requires that the fundamental goal of health providers is to do good and to provide the most benefit possible. Nonmaleficence requires health providers to avoid or at least minimize harm when providing care. An on-line interactive tutorial reviewing these principles is available at the PHG Foundation website (www.phgfoundation.org).

Autonomy. An example of current health care financing policy that supports autonomy include provisions of the Patient Protection and Affordable Care Act ([PPACA], 2010) that apply to accountable care organizations (ACOs). ACOs are required to promote **patient engagement,** or active patient and family participation in making informed health care decisions. Patient engagement includes shared decision-making about treatment alternatives as well as health services provided within the context of the patient's values and beliefs. Improving health literacy is another responsibility for health care providers in promoting patient engagement and autonomy (Cady, 2011).

Justice. An example of a current concern about the principle of justice is the U.S. controversy surrounding health care rationing. Although **implicit rationing** based on a person's inability to pay for care worsens outcomes for the 49.1 million uninsured Americans, it is tolerated as policy makers cannot easily assign responsibility or blame for the situation. On the other hand, **explicit rationing** that directly denies scarce health care resources to some Americans is a highly controversial and politically charged issue. For example, some might argue that providing expensive health care that benefits only a few individuals thereby deprives many individuals of less costly but equally necessary care. Others might respond that all people have equal worth and that care should be given without concerns for financial cost. As health care costs continue to increase, the debate about rationing policies and decisions will likely intensify (Gruenewald, 2012).

Beneficence. A current issue of beneficence is the conflict of interest that occurs when health professionals attempt to advocate with their employers on behalf of patients. For example, a hospital might improve its profitability by establishing nurse-patient ratios at levels that nurses and nurse managers consider to be undesirable and potentially unsafe. One approach is for nurses and nurse managers to take a collaborative, evidence-based approach in addressing this type of concern. By gathering and sharing data, engaging with administrators and the health care team, and suggesting possible solutions to resolve concerns, nurses may be able to promote initiatives that benefit nurses, patients, and the health care organization (Manthous, 2012).

Nonmaleficence. A current example of the nonmaleficence principle is the situation of kidney transplant recipients who require ongoing immunosuppressive drug therapy, but whose insurance does not cover or only provides a few years of coverage for the treatment. The lack of coverage not only puts these lives at risk, but increases health care costs in the long run. Although Medicare limits benefits for some persons with kidney transplants, other countries such as Australia, the United Kingdom, and Canada provide lifetime benefits with better outcomes than the United States. A bill proposed to the U.S. Congress, H.R. 296, the Comprehensive Immunosuppressive Drug Coverage for Kidney Transplant Patients Act of 2011, would amend the Social Security Act to provide lifetime benefits to these individuals. Proponents argue that over the long run, the added costs of providing coverage for immunosuppressive therapy will reduce total expenditures (Gill & Tonelli, 2012).

This review of ethical principles puts concerns about health ethics in the context of current health care issues. Nurses must weigh the benefits and risks of economic decisions that affect the health care of patients and populations. Thinking about decisions related to autonomy, justice, beneficence, and nonmaleficence can be helpful in balancing demands and resources for health care.

Appendix 13A features a worksheet based on the ethical principles discussed in this section. Nurses can use the worksheet to evaluate the extent to which health care policies or problems fulfill each ethical principle. Actual or potential concerns can be noted on the worksheet, and an overall evaluation of the health care policy or problem can then be recorded related to each ethical principle. This is one way that nurses can explore the ethical implications of health care policies and problems they may encounter.

Health Care Fraud

Unfortunately, unethical practices may occur in health care provision. The example discussed in this section is health care **fraud**. Fraud may be defined as intentional deception or misrepresentation in order to obtain something of value that is owned by another party. Fraud encompasses a broad range of conduct that burdens both public and private payers as well as health care providers. Health care fraud includes unethical practices such as billing for goods or services never provided, or billing at a higher reimbursement rate than allowable. Deliberate deception such as medical identity theft is another example of health care fraud.

Improper practices also include inadequate documentation for services that were actually provided, and other inadvertent errors such as incorrect billing or coding of procedures. Nurses need to be aware that their documentation may be important in audits or other reviews to determine fraud.

Fraud is a burden on the U.S. health care system. Estimates are that fraud could account for up to 10% of the approximately $2.5 trillion annual spending on U.S. health care (Krause, 2010). Medicare is a frequent target for fraudulent schemes such as double billing, kickbacks, and billing for unnecessary or unperformed laboratory tests. The U.S. Government Accountability Office (2011) estimates that of the $509 billion that Medicare spent in FY 2010, about $48 billion was improper payments.

In some cases, patient quality of care is directly affected by fraudulent activities, so that not only financial losses are incurred, but threats to patient safety. For example, a nursing home might neglect its patients' health and safety needs, but continue to bill Medicaid and other payers for services. Not only are the payers defrauded, but the patients are placed at risk.

The False Claims Act Resource Center website (www.falseclaimsact.com) describes various types of health care fraud. Improper billing or billing for services not rendered is one of the most common fraudulent practices. Another type of health care fraud is **upcoding,** or misrepresenting the patient's diagnosis in order to justify a higher payment for services rendered than should be authorized. **Kickbacks** involve requesting, offering, or receiving favors or payments that influence purchases. For example, a provider might receive a bonus for referring patients to a laboratory.

The Health Care Fraud and Abuse Control Program (HCFAC) was established from the Health Insurance Portability and Accountability Act of 1996 (HIPAA). This program prevents, identifies, and investigates health care fraud in both the public and private sectors. For the 2010 fiscal year, defendants paid back over $78 million in criminal settlements (Parver & Goren, 2011). Nurses and consumers should be prepared to report suspicious practices. A Fraud Prevention Toolkit for patients and providers is available at the Centers for Medicare & Medicaid Services (CMS) website (www.cms.gov), with information and links on preventing and reporting suspected fraud.

Some implications for nurses in preventing fraud include the following recommendations:

- Thorough and accurate documentation of services and procedures to verify that medically necessary care was provided and appropriately billed.
- Clear understanding of appropriate coding and billing practices relevant to the services provided in the nurse's work setting.
- Verifying patient identity to help ensure against medical identity theft and abuse.
- Keeping updated on changes in coding and other billing policies by government and other payers.
- Monitoring vulnerable patient populations such as the elderly, who are often the targets of financial fraud and abuse.
- Ongoing vigilance and reporting the occurrence of suspected fraud.

Counterfeit Drugs

Another example of health care fraud is the production and sale of counterfeit drugs. Counterfeit drugs not only defraud consumers financially, but pose serious health risks, as they fail to treat the disease for which they are prescribed and they may cause allergies or other serious reactions from the substances they contain. One example is the recent identification of fake Avastin for cancer treatment. A slideshow presenting more details about the Avastin incident, the background of counterfeit drug trafficking, and ways of preventing the spread of counterfeit drugs is available from The Partnership for Safe Medicines (http://www.slideshare.net/SafeMedicines/beyond-avastin-the-ongoing-dangers-of-counterfeit-drugs-to-american-patients).

Health care fraud is an increasingly important source of waste and consumer risk in health care. Fraudulent practices such as the sale of counterfeit drugs not only increase health costs, but may endanger consumer safety. Nurses play a role in understanding, preventing, and combating the ethical and financial problems presented by health care fraud.

INTERNATIONAL HEALTH ECONOMICS ISSUES

Why consider the economics of health care in countries other than our own? One reason for discussing international health care economics is to understand how other countries finance the delivery of health care services. Another reason for examining international health care economics is to make comparisons between the United States and other countries across measures such as per capita expenditures and health status indicators. An additional reason to think about health care economics from an international perspective is that globalization and the current global economic downturn are factors influencing health care economics and financing worldwide.

Learning about international health care economics also provides insights regarding concerns that many nations share in common. Three expectations for health care are quality, access, and cost control. Payers, providers, and consumers around the world share these same expectations. This section provides an overview of international health care systems, economic comparisons in health care, and common health care economics concerns shared by the United States and other countries.

Health Care Systems

Figure 13.1 shows three major types of health care systems prevalent in the major industrialized nations. The United States has a different health coverage history and tradition than most other industrialized nations, as reviewed in Chapter 1. These differences have influenced health systems development around the world.

Pluralistic health system. The first type of health care system, represented in the United States, is known as the **pluralistic health system**. The pluralistic system relies on a combination of government and nongovernment providers and payers (Rodwin, 1999). However, the pluralistic system does not provide universal health care coverage for its citizens. The pluralistic "system" is actually an incredibly complex and fragmented set of insurers and providers, which evolved over time from an earlier, almost entirely private approach to health care in the United States. This system reflects the American culture's resistance to government intervention in business or individual affairs.

Medicare and Medicaid programs, established in the 1960s as part of the Johnson Administration's War on Poverty efforts, provide funding to cover the health care of persons age 65 and older and some poor and uninsured persons and families. Many employed persons are able to purchase health insurance for themselves and their families through group plans offered by their employers. Other persons do not meet government or nongovernment insurance criteria, and are uninsured unless they are able and willing to pay for private health insurance.

The PPACA (2010) expands preventive care, private insurance coverage, and mandates the purchase of insurance to move the United States closer to universal health care coverage by 2015. Chapter 1 reviews some historical attempts to provide universal health care in the United States. Chapter 2 provides details around the financial and medical problems of America's growing uninsured population. Political debate continues as health costs and the numbers of elderly and uninsured Americans continue to rise.

National health insurance. Many industrialized countries in Europe, as well as Canada and Japan, represent the system of **national health insurance**, where the national government provides health coverage for all its citizens, but does not own or employ the health care providers, as shown in Figure 13.1 (Rodwin, 1999). For example, Canadians are covered by national health insurance mandated by the Canadian government, but private sector physicians and other health professionals are not directly employed by the Canadian government. Hospital operating costs are funded through the Canadian national health insurance system. Provincial governments must approve hospital budgets, allowing for some regional government control

Type of System	Pluralistic	National Health Insurance	National Health Service
Principal features	Some uninsured citizens and foreign residents; government and nongovernment providers; multiple government and non-government funding streams	Universal coverage; government and nongovernment providers; often national and provincial budgets	Universal coverage; largely government providers; largely government-funded with some self-pay
Typical problems	Uninsured populations	Health care rationing	Health care rationing
Examples of countries	United States	Canada, Japan, many European nations	Great Britain

Figure 13.1 *National Health Systems*

Source: Adapted from V.G. Rodwin, in Kovner and Jonas, 1999.

over the size and scope of health services. More about the Canadian health system, its background, and its services is available at the Health Canada website (www.hc-sc.gc.ca).

Many of the European nations with national health insurance systems have similar control over hospital capacity and costs. One problem with national health insurance systems is limited capacity. Capacity limits may lead to waiting lists for elective or nonemergency health care services.

National health service. Great Britain is an example of the **national health service** system (Rodwin, 1999), not only covering health care for all its citizens but also owning and employing many of the health care providers (Figure 13.1). The number of private providers available in Great Britain is growing as the number of persons willing to pay out-of-pocket for health care grows. However, most health care is provided through publicly owned and operated hospitals, clinics, and other settings. Waiting lists for some health care services is a problem under national health service systems, which is one reason for the growing popularity of private providers. Consumers must pay more for private sector care, but can be treated more quickly than when placed on a waiting list for care. More information about the National Health Service in Great Britain is available at the U.K. Department of Health website (www.dh.gov.uk).

Socialized health service. One other health system should be mentioned, the **socialized health service** system established in the former U.S.S.R. and its satellite countries, and in a few other countries such as Cuba. The socialized health system allows for little or no privately owned or employed providers, and requires its citizens, who have universal health coverage, to seek services solely through government providers.

Many people believe that if a government mandates universal health care coverage, health care must become socialized, but this is not the case. The predominant system among the industrialized nations is for the government to mandate universal health care coverage, but allow private entrepreneurship in the provision of health care services. The Public Broadcasting Service (PBS) makes its Frontline documentary Sick Around the World available for viewing online (http://video.pbs.org/video/1050712790/). This documentary reviews the health systems in five industrialized nations, compares their systems to the U.S. health care system, and discusses problems and issues each health system faces.

Comparison of Industrialized Nations

U.S. health spending and health status. Table 13.1 shows per capita health expenditures and infant mortality rates for 34 industrialized nations that are part of the Organization for Economic Co-operation and Development (OECD). The United States has the highest per capita health expenditures, at $7720 in 2008. However, the U.S. infant mortality rate, an indicator of overall population health, is 6.5 deaths per 1000 live births, among the highest rates of all the OECD countries (Organisation for Economic Co-Operation and Development [OECD], 2011). The higher amount of money spent on health care in the United States does not necessarily improve the American population's health status. KaiserEDU.org provides more information about health system comparisons among the United States and other countries in the International Health Systems portion of their website.

Issues Among Developing Nations

Developing nations face difficulties that compound problems of limited capacity and inadequate health care access. The typical developing nation has a very small health care budget, possibly supplemented by financial donations, resulting in chronic serious resource shortages. A relatively high proportion of this budget is often spent on personnel and other operating costs, with little investment in the construction or maintenance of health care facilities. There are significant gaps in the availability and use of technology, even for interventions such as antibiotics that are commonplace in industrialized nations.

Table 13.1 *International Comparison of Per Capita Health Expenditure in US$ and Infant Mortality Rate, 2008*

OECD Country	Per Capita Expenditure	Per Capita Expenditure Rank	Infant Mortality Rate	Infant Mortality Rate Rank
Australia	$3445	15	4.1	23
Austria	$4128	6	3.7	15
Belgium	$3714	12	3.7	16
Canada	$4024	8	n/a	n/a
Chile	$1092	31	7.8	31
Czech Republic	$1839	26	2.8	9
Denmark	$4052	7	4.0	22
Estonia	$1331	29	5.0	26
Finland	$3158	17	2.6	5
France	$3809	10	3.8	18
Germany	$3963	9	3.5	13
Greece	n/a	n/a	2.7	8
Hungary	$1495	28	5.6	27
Iceland	$3571	14	2.5	4
Ireland	$3784	11	3.8	19
Israel	$2142	24	3.8	20
Italy	$3059	18	3.3	10
Japan	$2878	20	2.6	6
Korea	$1736	27	3.5	14
Luxembourg	$4451	4	1.8	1
Mexico	$892	33	15.2	33
The Netherlands	$4241	5	3.8	17
New Zealand	$2784	21	5.0	25
Norway	$5230	2	2.7	7
Poland	$1265	30	5.6	28
Portugal	$2508	22	3.3	12
Slovak Republic	$1859	25	5.9	29
Slovenia	$2451	23	2.4	2
Spain	$2971	19	3.3	11
Sweden	$3644	13	2.5	3
Switzerland	$4930	3	4.0	21
Turkey	$902	32	14.9	32
United Kingdom	$3281	16	4.7	24
United States	$7720	1	6.5	30

Source: Adapted from OECD Health Data 2011. Infant mortality: deaths per 1000 live births.

http://www.oecd.org/document/60/0,3746,en_2649_33929_2085200_1_1_1_1,00.html

Low-income countries bear a large portion of the total disease burden in the world. In addition, noncommunicable diseases such as chronic diseases and accidents now account for nearly half of the disease burden in developing countries. However, these countries only contribute 2% of health care spending worldwide, about $7 billion annually. Most of the contributions from donor nations are directed to communicable diseases, overlooking the large and growing burden of noncommunicable disease in developing nations (Committee on the U.S. Commitment to Global Health, Institute of Medicine [IOM], 2009).

Health Care Rationing

As mentioned earlier, many countries with national health insurance or a national health service system must place consumers on waiting lists for care. Waiting lists are a form of explicit health care rationing. Policies limiting health care expenditures are a way for countries to control their health care costs.

As health care costs continue to increase worldwide, some industrialized nations as well as many developing nations employ some form of rationing. As mentioned earlier, the United States implicitly rations health care, but the state of Oregon is one of the few examples in the United States of attempts at explicit health care rationing. Figure 13.2 summarizes two of the most commonly used approaches to health care rationing among industrialized and developing nations.

The first approach, which is the most commonly used, is to limit the national budget for health care to what is considered an affordable level, without targeting specific diseases (such as HIV/AIDS) or interventions (such as cardiac catheterizations) for budget priorities or budget cuts. One problem with this approach is that the parties in power often control the resource allocation decisions, so that these decisions favor the relatively wealthier and more powerful citizens at the expense of those who are poorer and less powerful.

The second approach is to base the national (or state, in the case of Oregon) health care budget on specific priorities targeting diseases or interventions, using established criteria. For example, a country may establish priorities for the vaccination of all children at the expense of the purchase of life-support or dialysis equipment largely used by the elderly. One advantage of this approach is its potential to incorporate "rationality" into rationing, by utilizing social and cost-effectiveness criteria in addition to political criteria.

Attempting to establish a budget with rationally based priorities also poses potential problems. When consumers demand services not included in the approved set of benefits, providers face ethical and financial incentives to provide these services regardless of the

Approach	Strict Controls Limiting the Health Care Budget to an Affordable Level	Establish Controls Based on specific Priorities Determined by Preset Criteria
Target	Does not target specific diseases or interventions	Often provides an affordable "basic" or "essential" package of interventions
Principal features	Most common approach; most frequently used in countries with national health budgets	Social, political and cost-effectiveness criteria used to determine priorities
Typical problems	Resources managed according to politics, often favoring the higher income citizens at the expense of the poor	Providers respond to demand for services outside the approved package; limitations to cost-effectiveness criteria
Examples of countries	Pre 1990 National Health System in the U.K., some European Union countries, some developing nations	The Netherlands, New Zealand, Norway, Sweden, Oregon (U.S.), Mexico, Bangladesh, Columbia, Zambia

Figure 13.2 *Approaches to Health Care Rationing*

Source: Adapted from WHO, World Health Report (2000).

policy mandate. For example, if government policy does not fund dialysis for the elderly, providers may charge out-of-pocket fees for consumers who can pay and provide dialysis on a private basis, or find other ways of subsidizing this service. Another problem is that the cost-effectiveness criteria used to develop priorities for rationing have limitations (Chapter 9). Politics may influence cost-effectiveness decisions, favoring more powerful populations and interests.

In short, there is no care rationing method that meets everyone's expectations of high quality and access while controlling costs. However, in a time when health care resources cannot increase to sufficiently meet all demand, rationing is an attempt to control and, if possible, improve the delivery of services.

Globally Common Concerns

Although the U.S. health care financing and delivery system differs from many other countries, there are a number of common concerns facing health systems around the world. These concerns influence decisions about access to services and resources available for health care.

Nursing shortages and migration. Nursing shortages are a common concern for many industrialized and developing countries around the world. The World Health Organization (WHO) estimates there is a worldwide shortage of 4.3 million health professionals for delivering essential health care services (Taylor, Hwenda, Larsen, & Daulaire, 2011). Factors such as increasingly complex technologies and aging populations are likely to intensify the demand and worsen the shortages of nurses and other health professionals.

The term **brain-drain** is often used to refer to the migration of professionals to other locations or countries in order to benefit from higher wages and better living conditions. In 2010 an estimated 5.4% of the U.S. nursing workforce consisted of international nurses (Slote, 2011). The WHO has established a Global Code of Practice with objectives including the development of sustainable health care systems in low- and middle-income countries (Taylor et al., 2011). The recruitment of international nurses needed in their home countries to work in the United States presents ethical concerns for consideration. More information about the WHO Global Code of Practice is available at the WHO Health Workforce Migration and Retention website (http://www.who.int/hrh/migration/code/practice/en/).

Aging populations. Longer life spans contribute to the growth in the numbers of persons over age 60 worldwide. In addition, the impact of the "baby booms" in the 1940s and 1950s among industrialized nations, and in the 1960s and 1970s in developing nations contributes further to the growth in elderly populations. Although the global population of children under age 5 is expected to fall by 49 million as of 2050, the number of people over age 60 is predicted to increase by 1.2 billion. A recent study found that over 40% of Americans age 50 to 64 have difficulties in performing activities of daily life, such as climbing 10 steps without resting (Longman, 2010). Increases in chronic conditions such as Alzheimer's disease pose global concerns, as well as concerns about poverty and social isolation among the elderly.

Currently, the United States is debating about how to address concerns about financing the Medicare program for American elderly. Japan introduced a national old-age nursing care insurance plan financed by the government and by contributions from persons over age 40 in 2000. As of 2004, 19 countries in the OECD have adopted patient classification systems similar to the Medicare DRGs as part of their health care reimbursement systems (Forgione, Vermeer, Surysekar, Wrieden, & Plante, 2004). The 2012 World Health Day topic focused on aging and health concerns. More information about global aging is available at the WHO Aging website (http://www.who.int/topics/ageing/en/). Multimedia presentations about global aging are available at the Center for Strategic & International Studies (CSIS) Global Aging Initiative website (www.csis.org).

Health care quality and patient satisfaction. A survey of 1200 patients in the United States, Brazil, China, Germany, India, Japan, and Russia compared overall satisfaction with health care systems. Respondents in the United States were among the most satisfied overall with their health care system. However, American respondents were among the least optimistic that their country's health care system will improve over the next 5 to 10 years. American respondents are also the most concerned about medication and treatment costs (HawkPartners/ICARE, 2012).

Another survey of 18,000 recently hospitalized adults in Australia, Canada, France, Germany, The Netherlands, New Zealand, Norway, Sweden, Switzerland, the United Kingdom, and the United States found that Americans have greater concerns than patients in other countries about health care affordability and medical debt. American adults under age 65 who lacked Medicare coverage were particularly concerned about health care costs and were more likely to report not getting needed care because of costs. Adults with more complex care needs reported better quality and coordination of care, including fewer medical errors, if they obtained their care from a medical home. Sicker adults in the United Kingdom and Switzerland were the most likely to receive care in a medical home setting (Schoen et al., 2011). Compared to the citizens of other industrialized countries, Americans pay and know they pay high costs, but they are not necessarily more satisfied with the U.S. health system or U.S. health care delivery.

Global economic downturn. Health care expenditures continue to increase at a rate greater than economic growth in most OECD member countries. On average, OECD health spending reached 9.5% in 2009, an increase from 8.8% in 2008 (OECD, 2011). At the same time, a global economic crisis not only increases health risks but is leading to austerity measures that result in health care spending cuts (Benatar, Gill, & Bakker, 2011; Davis, 2009).

The global recession presents even greater challenges for low- and middle-income countries in obtaining and allocating resources to support health care. The situation is more challenging for low- and middle-income countries because many higher income nations are also facing continued economic downturns (IOM, 2009). International aid is therefore increasingly limited as the higher income nations face budget reductions.

Medical tourism. A small but increasing trend among Americans is **medical tourism**, or travel to other countries to receive health care that is not affordable in the United States. For many years, international patients from low-income countries travelled to the United States for health care and better access to advanced health care technology. More recently, American patients are travelling to low-income countries to obtain care from providers that have established health centers for medical tourists.

A 2008 study identified 63 companies that offer medical tourism services. The top destination countries were reported as India, Costa Rica, Thailand, Mexico, and Singapore. Examples of popular medical procedures include knee arthroplasty, cosmetic surgery, and dental procedures. The study also concludes that the actual medical tourism cost savings may be less than anticipated (Alleman et al., 2011). More information about medical tourism is available at the Centers for Disease Control and Prevention (CDC) Medical Tourism website (www.cdc.gov).

CONCLUSION

This chapter opens with a review of ethical principles related to health policies and health care financing. An overview of unethical practices, including fraud and counterfeit drug trafficking, is presented, with advice and resources for nurses to help address these problems. International health systems are described and compared to the pluralistic system represented in the United States. Although the United States spends more on health care than any other nation, quality and access as measured by consumer surveys and health indicators is often worse than in other countries. Concerns such as global aging and the impact of the current global recession are shared by countries around the world.

Discussion and Exercises

1. Think of a health care problem and evaluate it using the Appendix 13A worksheet. What steps might a nurse advocate take to address ethical issues related to this health problem? Point out ways in which knowledge of health care financing, budgeting, and making a business case might be applicable in resolving the ethical issues.
2. Prepare a 15-minute presentation comparing at least one other country's health care system to the United States. What are advantages and disadvantages of the other health care system or systems? What might Americans learn from another country about organizing health care? What might Americans teach another country about organizing health care?
3. Based on your own experience as a provider and consumer of health care goods and services in the United States, discuss how you would rate the United States in terms of health care quality, access, and cost. How would you rank the United States in health care performance, compared to other countries?

REFERENCES

Alleman, B. W., Luger, T., Reisinger, H., Martin, R., Horowitz, M. D., & Cram, P. (2011). Medical Tourism Services Available to Residents of the United States. *Journal of General Internal Medicine, 26*, 492–497.

Benatar, S. R., Gill, S., & Bakker, I. (2011). Global Health and the Global Economic Crisis. *American Journal of Public Health, 101*, 646–653.

Cady, R. F. (April/June 2011). Accountable care organizations: What the nurse executive needs to know. *JONA's Healthcare Law, Ethics, & Regulation, 13*, 55–60.

Committee on the U.S. Commitment to Global Health, Institute of Medicine. (2009). *The U.S. commitment to global health: Recommendations for the public and private sectors.* Washington, DC: The National Academies Press. Retrieved from http://www.nap.edu.

Davis, C. (2009). Life support. *World Today, 65*(6), 13–15.

Forgione, D. A., Vermeer, T. E., Surysekar, K., Wrieden, J. A., & Plante, C. A. (2004). The impact of DRG-based payment systems on quality of health care in OECD countries. *Journal Of Health Care Finance, 31*, 41–54.

Gill, J., & Tonelli, M. (2012). Penny wise, pound foolish? Coverage limits on immunosuppression after kidney transplantation. *New England Journal of Medicine, 366*, 586–589.

Gruenewald, D. (2012). Can health care rationing ever be rational? *Journal of Law, Medicine & Ethics, 40*, 17–25.

HawkPartners/ICARE. (2012). *Global patient pulse: Executive summary.* New York, NY: HawkPartners LLC. Retrieved from http://www.hawkpartners.com/perspectives/2012-patient-pulse-executive-summary

Krause, J. H. (2010). Following the money in health care fraud: Reflections on a modern-day yellow brick road. *American Journal of Law & Medicine, 36*, 343–369.

Longman, P. (November 2010). Think again: Global aging. *Foreign Policy, 182*, 52–58.

Manthous, C. A. (2012). Current controversies in critical care. Hippocrates as hospital employee: Balancing beneficence and contractual duty. *American Journal of Critical Care, 21*, 60–66.

Organisation for Economic Co-Operation and Development. (2011). *OECD health data 2011,* November 2011. Paris, France: Author. http://www.oecd.org/document/60/0,3746,en_26 49_33929_2085200_1_1_1_1,00.html

Parver, C., & Goren, A. (2011). Significant details from the 2010 health care fraud and abuse control program report. *Journal of Health Care Compliance, 13*, 9–22.

Patient Protection and Affordable Care Act. (2010). Pub. L. No. 111–148, §2702, 124 Stat. 119, 318–319. Retrieved from http://housedocs.house.gov/energycommerce/ppacacon.pdf

Rodwin, V. G. (1999). Comparative analysis of health systems: An international perspective. In A. R. Kovner & S. Jonas (Eds.). *Health care delivery in the united states* (6th ed., pp. 116–151). New York, NY: Springer Publishing Company.

Schoen, C., Osborn R., Squires, D., Doty, M. M., Pierson, R., & Applebaum, S. (2011). New 2011 survey of patients with complex care needs in 11 countries finds that care is often poorly coordinated. *Health Affairs Web First*. Retrieved from http://content.healthaffairs.org/content/30/12/2437.abstract

Slote, R. J. (2011). Pulling the plug on brain-drain: Understanding international migration of nurses. *MEDSURG Nursing, 20*, 179–186.

Taylor, A., Hwenda, L., Larsen, B., & Daulaire, N. (2011). Stemming the brain drain--a WHO global code of practice on international recruitment of health personnel. *New England Journal of Medicine, 365*, 2348–2351.

U.S. Government Accountability Office. (2011). *Medicare program remains at high risk because of continuing management challenges*. Testimony before the Subcommittee on Oversight and Investigations, Committee on Energy and Commerce, House of Representatives. Statement of Kathleen King Director, Health Care. GAO-11–430T www.gao.gov

CROSSWORD: *Chapters 13 and 14—Ethical Issues, International Systems, Policy and Trends**

Across

4   Principle of bioethics requiring that health providers avoid or at least minimize harm when providing care.

6   Applications of telecommunications technologies to health education and patient care.

8   Requesting, offering, or receiving favors or payments that influence purchases.

9   Distributing the burden of cost fairly based on the ability to pay.

10   The provision of relatively equal access for all persons.

12   The relative equality of resource allocation to various disease entities, populations, or interventions.

13   Misrepresenting a diagnosis in order to justify a higher payment for services rendered than should be authorized.

Down

1   Travel to other countries to receive health care that is not affordable or available in one's own country.

2   Principle of bioethics requiring that health providers do good and provide the most benefit possible.

3   Principle of bioethics that supports the equal or fair distribution of health care benefits and risks across society.

5   Intentional deception or misrepresentation in order to obtain something of value that is owned by another party.

7   Computer technology and software that replaces paper-based health record systems (abbreviation).

11   Principle of bioethics that refers to the right of individuals to make their own decisions.

*Note: The crossword puzzles for Chapters 13 and 14 are identical.

APPENDIX 13A: ETHICS WORKSHEET FOR EVALUATING A HEALTH POLICY OR PROBLEM

Principle	Autonomy	Justice	Beneficence	Nonmaleficence
Definition	The right of individuals to make their own decisions about their care	Equal or fair distribution of health care benefits and risks	Health providers must do good and provide the most benefit possible	Health providers must avoid or minimize harm
Fulfills ethical principle				
Actual ethical concerns				
Potential ethical concerns				
Overall ethical evaluation				

Chapter 14: Health Policy and Future Trends

*Many people take no care of their money till they come
nearly to the end of it, and others do just the same
with their time*—Johann Wolfgang von Goethe

Learning Objectives

1. Summarize at least three key policy questions for a current development in health policy, economics, or financing.
2. Point out the impact of a current trend that affects health care policy, economics, or financing in the United States or worldwide.
3. Analyze how a provision of the PPACA or another current health policy influences health care costs.
4. Justify the nursing and nurse leadership roles in meeting the future needs and demands for health care quality, access, and cost control.

Key Terms

electronic health record (EHR)   majority-minority populations   telehealth
equity   parity   universality

In the previous chapters, this text introduced concepts of health care economics, managed care, budgeting, financial reporting and analysis, steps in writing business plans and grant proposals, and international health care issues. A further question is "where are we headed from here?" Developments in health care policy, economics, and financing quickly become outdated, particularly in this time of rapidly changing policies to address rising costs and demand.

This chapter discusses possible future directions and trends in health care related to economics and financing, and suggests methods for health care professionals to keep up-to-date on relevant economic and financial issues. The chapter first discusses policy questions that might be applied in following future trends, followed by a brief review of possible trends in the immediate future, concluding with suggestions for keeping abreast of health care economics and financing over time. This chapter focuses on policies relevant to health care professionals in the United States, although the concepts may be applied to other industrialized and developing nations' policies around the world.

HEALTH POLICY QUESTIONS

As shown in Figure 14.1, Roberts and Clyde (1993) pose seven policy questions that may be used as a framework for tracking future trends in health care, and relating these trends to health economics and financing. Figure 14.1 also includes possible trends for the immediate future, discussed later in this chapter. A copy of Figure 14.1 is adapted as a worksheet for nurses to use as Appendix 14A.

Roberts and Clyde's (1993) policy questions include health care consumers' and providers' three expectations of cost, quality, and access. The policy questions are listed in Figure 14.1 with cost as the first question, as it is seen to be the most relevant to future trends in health economics and financing, as well as related to any health care trend or policy. For example, one may anticipate ongoing requirements for measuring and reducing costs, as costs continue to rise. It is essential to think about the impact policies, plans, and decisions have on cost and change in cost for health care goods and services. Cost control is also a fundamental expectation of health care consumers and providers. One implication is that budgeting skills will become increasingly important for nurses and other professionals working in health care settings.

Policy Question	Future Trends
Cost	Ongoing need for improved cost measures; rising costs; cost concerns influence all policy questions
Quality	Increased application of quality management concepts and techniques; improved outcomes measures; increased emphasis on outcomes research and tracking
Access	Parity vs. disparity; design of entitlement programs; demise of charity care
Universality	Debates about expanding coverage or national health coverage
Equity	Controversy about health care rationing and priority setting
Efficiency	Increased emphasis on productivity; increased application of other industry models; computerization
Choice	Willingness to pay for choice; demand for choice vs. limited resources
Prevention	Increased concerns about bio-terrorism; better methods of disease detection; CBA, CEA, and outcomes research

Figure 14.1 *Policy Questions for Tracking Future Trends in Health Care*

Source: Adapted from Roberts and Clyde (1993).

Quality and access are the next policy questions posed by Roberts and Clyde (1993), which are also fundamental expectations of health care consumers and providers (Figure 14.1). Problems in analyzing these issues include difficulties in measuring both quality and access. However, resource allocation decisions based on health economics and financing are likely to affect both the quality of care available, and access to health care. It is likely to see increased application of quality management concepts and techniques in health care, with improved clinical outcomes measures linked to costs of care, as the result of increased emphasis on outcomes research and tracking. Issues likely to arise related to access include debates about **parity,** or the relative equality of resource allocation to various disease entities, populations, or interventions.

Universality, or the provision of relatively equal access for all persons, and **equity,** or distributing fairly the burden of cost based on the ability to pay, are related policy questions (Roberts & Clyde, 1993), shown in Figure 14.1. Health economics and financing policies would substantially influence both universality and equity. For example, debates about implementing the Patient Protection and Affordable Care Act (PPACA) to expand health care coverage for most Americans is a current policy question linked to universality. Equity issues include controversy about health care rationing and priority setting, related to concerns about the sustainability of the Medicare program.

Roberts and Clyde (1993) pose the policy question of choice (Figure 14.1). Choice is an important incentive both for health care consumers and providers. Chapters 2 and 3 both discuss consumer and provider behavior and choice as important in health care decisions that affect costs. Strategies such as managed care mechanisms reduce both consumer and provider choice. It is anticipated that consumers will continue to demand choice in health care and will demonstrate willingness to pay for choice, but that the consumer and provider demand for choice will be countered by the impact of limited resources.

Prevention is another policy question posed by Roberts and Clyde (1993) in Figure 14.1. As reinforced by the World Health Organization (WHO) Chronic Diseases website (www. who.int), the world's population now faces more risk from death due to chronic diseases than from communicable disease. Prevention and management of disorders such as cancer, diabetes, and cardiovascular disease will become more important for health systems in the United States and worldwide. Increased concerns about bio-terrorism and disaster preparedness will also influence prevention strategies in the future.

One may also predict continued improvement in disease detection, in part related to advances in genetic and genomic research. The increased use of **cost-benefit analysis (CBA), cost-effectiveness analysis (CEA),** and **comparative effectiveness research (CER)** discussed in Chapter 8 will likely influence policies related to prevention efforts and the evaluation of prevention programs.

FUTURE TRENDS

A lot is happening in health care today. There are many events occurring that will influence health care policy, financing, and economics over the years to come. Nurses must be aware of these trends and prepared for changes over the short- and long-term. This section discusses some future health care and social trends and implications for nurses.

Continued Economic Downturn

The recovery from the economic downturn that began in December 2007 continues to be slow. Overall U.S. unemployment in May 2012 was reported at 8.2% (Bureau of Labor Statistics, 2012). The economic problems affect national, state, and local government, and put pressure on high-cost government-funded health programs such as Medicaid and Medicare. The stagnant economies and debt crises in other industrialized and developing nations increase the risk of a worsening economic situation in the United States. As mentioned in Chapter 13, the economic concerns in other countries affect health care funding worldwide.

Increasing Environmental Concerns

There is scientific consensus about global climate change. Climate change will likely lead to droughts and flooding that impact the health and food supply of people around the world. Changes in disease spread and population displacement are other events anticipated with climate change (Frumkin, Hess, Luber, Malilay, & McGeehin, 2008). Examples of the impact of climate change in the United States include Hurricane Katrina, Hurricane Sandy, and wildfires in the West and Southwest. Health care demands related to factors such as natural disasters, air pollution, and food shortages will pose increasing concerns as weather patterns continue to change (Walker, 2008).

A related concern is the increased likelihood of water shortages and scarcity. About 1.2 billion people around the world, for the most part in developing countries, lack access to safe drinking water. By 2025, the number of people facing water scarcity is expected to reach 2.7 to 3.5 billion, roughly one-third of the world's population (Mukheibir, 2010). Concerns about the water supply also can affect Americans, for example, people in the state of Georgia (Walker, 2008). Nurses realize that safe water is an essential resource for public health. The burden of disease and health care costs will be impacted by problems with the world's water supply.

Changing U.S. Demographics

The U.S. population is changing. One change is the aging of our population, accelerated by the aging of the Baby Boomers. By 2030, about 78 million Baby Boomers will be over age 65. This increase in the elderly will increase utilization of physician office visits, pharmaceuticals, long-term care, and other medical services. In addition, the U.S. health workforce is aging. For example, approximately 40% of the nation's physicians are over age 55, as well as about a third of nurses (Carnevale, Smith, Gulish, & Beach, 2012). The increase in the elderly and the retirement of health care workers will likely result in physician and nurse shortages over the coming years.

One example of health care concerns and costs for aging populations is the increase of Alzheimer's disease and other dementias. The Obama Administration released a national plan for prevention, treatment and support for Alzheimer's disease on May 15, 2012. More information is available at the National Plan to Address Alzheimer's Disease website (www.aspe.hhs.gov).

The racial and ethnic demographics in the United States are also changing. More than half of the growth in the U.S. population from 2000 to 2010 is attributed to growth in the Hispanic population. The Asian population grew faster from 2000 to 2010 than any other major race group. Nearly half of the Western region's population was reported as minority in the 2010 census. California, the District of Columbia, Hawaii, New Mexico, and Texas reported **majority-minority populations,** or a population comprised of more than 50% minority races in the 2010 census. About 10% of all counties across the United States reported majority-minority populations in the 2010 census (Humes, Jones, & Ramirez, 2011). These demographic changes will likely put increased demands on health care providers for more cultural awareness and services such as improved translation and health literacy, as well as concerns about health disparities.

Health Care System Developments

Many developments are occurring in the U.S. health care system. One of these developments is the continued unfolding of Patient Protection and Affordable Care Act provisions through

2015. For example, as of January 1, 2014 health insurance exchanges must be established for Americans who do not have employer health insurance. Most Americans who can afford to pay will be required to purchase health insurance or pay a fee by January 1, 2014 (Patient Protection and Affordable Care Act [PPACA], 2010). A timeline for the PPACA and its development is available at the HealthCare.gov What's Changing and When website.

As has been mentioned earlier in this chapter, the health reform initiatives in the PPACA enacted in 2010 are under debate regarding provisions that affect policy areas such as universality, equity, and cost. In June 2012 the Supreme Court supported most of the provisions of the PPACA. Chapter 2 points out that the June 2012 U.S. Supreme Court ruling upheld the PPACA provisions, but allows states to opt out of the Medicaid expansion to Americans with incomes under 133% of the federal poverty level (Galewitz & Serafini, 2012). This and other developments may support or hinder PPACA implementation and efforts to expand health insurance coverage for Americans.

A number of health care experts, as discussed in Kaiser Health News (http://www.kaiserhealthnews.org/stories/2012/june/19/health-system-changes-supreme-court.aspx?referrer=search), predict that health reform efforts will continue whether the PPACA is fully implemented or not. The pressures of increasing costs and demands of our aging population push providers and health care systems to find better ways of financing health care. A Public Broadcasting System (PBS) documentary, *U.S. Health Care: The Good News*, is available as a free video (www.pbs.org). This documentary presents innovative ideas for improving health care quality, access, and cost controls that are developing in areas across the nation. Nurses will have increased opportunities to contribute to innovations in health care reform.

Another development is the requirement for health providers to come into compliance with the transition to ICD-10 coding, used for diagnostic and inpatient procedures. Full compliance is mandated by October 1, 2014. It is anticipated that the more specific coding required by ICD-10 will improve documentation. Improved documentation will result in more accurate coding, and is expected to lead to more accurate payment for health care services (Zenner, 2010). More information about ICD-10 implementation in Medicare is available at the Centers for Medicare & Medicaid Services (CMS) ICD-10 website (www.cms.gov).

More health care providers are adopting the **electronic health record (EHR)**, which replaces paper-based health records. Related computer technologies that are increasingly popular in health care include clinical decision support systems and computerized provider order entry (CPOE) systems. Point-of-care nursing systems allow nurses to retrieve and share patient data, make charges, and document care without leaving the patient's bedside. Bar coding and other devices aid in patient identification and tracking items such as medications. **Telehealth** technologies that utilize telecommunications are increasingly used in areas such as patient diagnosis and monitoring, professional consultation, and decision support and education (Hebda & Czar, 2009).

These computer technologies have tremendous potential to reduce medical errors, increase productivity, and improve the capture of charges in health care settings. Telehealth is a cost-effective approach to improve specialty care for patients in remote or underserved areas. Other benefits to computer technologies in health care include better fraud control and reduction, and providers' capability to share patient data within settings such as an accountable care organization (ACO) or medical home (Hebda & Czar, 2009).

There are some challenges for health care providers implementing computer technologies. The implementation costs can be high. Data sharing can be difficult if computer systems vary among providers. Risks of compromising patient privacy must be addressed. Staff training and resistance to computerization may pose implementation problems. In addition, there are concerns about computer malfunctions and information back-up processes. However, despite the challenges, the potential for quality improvement and cost savings results in increased reliance on computer technologies in health care.

Health care technologies may reduce health care costs in some cases, and contribute to health care costs in other cases. For example, a greater understanding of genomics is improving the treatment of cancer and other diseases. On the other hand, Americans are experiencing more drug shortages, including cancer drugs and some surgical anesthetics. More information about drug shortages is available at the U.S. Food and Drug Administration Frequently Asked Questions about Drug Shortages website (www.fda.gov). As mentioned in Chapter 9, comparative effectiveness research (CER) will increasingly influence screening and treatment decisions, as well as the use of new technologies.

Another trend in the United States is linking health care reimbursement to quality initiatives. Medicare's Hospital-Acquired Conditions initiative withholds additional payment for selected conditions such as Stage III pressure ulcers that were not present upon a patient's admission to the hospital. The Patient Protection and Affordable Care Act has not yet implemented financial penalties for selected preventable hospital readmissions (PPACA, 2010). However, the 30-day readmission rates for Medicare patients with heart attack, heart failure, and pneumonia are included in the CMS HospitalCompare website for public review (www.hospitalcompare.hhs.gov). The Partnership for Patients (http://www.healthcare.gov /compare/partnership-for-patients/) initiative has the goal of reducing hospital-acquired conditions by 40% and preventable hospital readmissions by 20% from 2010 to 2013. These quality improvements should also help to better control Medicare costs.

Implications for Nursing

As mentioned in Chapter 1, the continued economic downturn pushes nurses to work full time instead of part time, and delay retirement from the nursing workforce (Staiger, Auerbach, & Buerhaus, 2012). However, as older nurses retire, as the economy improves, and as the aging population demands more health care, nursing shortages are predicted (Carnevale et al., 2012).

Another factor in the future demand for nurses is the anticipated shortage of primary care physicians (PCPs), which will require more services from nurse practitioners (NPs) and physician assistants (PAs). NPs and PAs are cost-effective alternatives to supplement PCPs, and their employment could not only fill primary care gaps but result in considerable cost savings (Dower & O'Neil, 2011). A map of health professional shortage areas is available at the National Conference of State Legislatures (NCSL) Primary Care Workforce website (www.ncsl.org).

In April 2012, the Obama Administration changed CMS hospital participation conditions to allow advance practice RNs and other health professionals to be included as eligible candidates for the medical staff with hospital privileges in accordance with state law (Centers for Medicare & Medicaid Services, 2012). This regulatory change expands opportunities for advance practice RNs to work at the full extent of their scope of practice, and could lead to cost savings for inpatient care.

The Institute of Medicine (IOM) released a report on the future of nursing that stresses how nurses are needed to make health care system improvements, including managing chronic conditions, primary care, disease prevention, and reducing medical errors. Other needs such as palliative care and transitional care are also areas in which nursing services are required. There are an estimated 250 nurse-managed health centers across America, and potential for nurses to manage patient-centered medical homes. Allowing nurses to perform at their full scope of practice is seen not only as a way to improve patient care quality, but to better control health care costs throughout the United States (Institute of Medicine, 2011).

Nurses are expected to increasingly shift their services from inpatient to community-based care. From 2008 to 2018, the job growth rate for RNs is predicted to be 48% in physician offices, 33% in home health, and 25% in long-term care settings. The job growth rate for nurses is anticipated to only reach 17% in hospital facilities from 2008 to 2018, because lower patient length of stay and more outpatient care will reduce the increase in the inpatient population (Domrose, 2010).

The Patient Protection and Affordable Care Act and other Federal initiatives support community-based health care (PPACA, 2010). Nurses are key players in this shift to community-based care. More information about nurse-managed health centers and nurse-managed medical homes is available at the National Nursing Centers Consortium (NNCC) website (www.nncc.us).

It should be clear that nurses of today and on into the future will benefit from expanding their understanding of the economics and financing of health care. Nurses are needed not only as caregivers and clinicians. Nurses must also serve as leaders in developing and managing high-quality and cost-effective programs and services for inpatient and community-based care. Nurses increasingly must know how to review a budget, write a business plan or grant proposal, or review the financial performance of their work setting, in addition to providing quality patient care.

KEEPING UP TO DATE

Health policies, financing initiatives, and economic concerns are constantly developing and changing, both in the United States and around the world. Nurses cannot learn everything they need to know from a single course or textbook. Keeping updated on changes and new developments is an important skill that supports lifelong learning and the development of expertise.

Many good sources of health care economics and finance information are available freely on the Internet. One recommended source is the Henry J. Kaiser Family Foundation (KFF) website (www.kff.org), which provides current information on health programs such as Medicare and Medicaid, global health issues, and topics such as minority health and HIV/AIDS. The KFF website also offers links to websites such as KaiserEDU.org that provide evidence-based learning modules on health topics related to health care costs and spending.

Other sources of information include The Commonwealth Fund, offering current resources on health reform and health services delivery. The academic journal Health Affairs is another valuable source for updates on health care economics and financing. Many professional organizations, including the American Nurses Association (ANA) website (www.nursingworld.org), offer updated policy and advocacy information. The websites recommended in this section typically allow subscription for news or other updates so nurses are alerted to changes and developments.

Additional sources of information are referenced throughout this textbook, including government sources such as HealthCare.gov. Nurses are encouraged to search for evidence-based information about economics and financing in their topics of interest, such as maternal-child care, long-term care, and community health care. An ongoing commitment to lifelong learning will help nurses better understand changes in health care. Nurses become better patient advocates and patient educators by keeping up with new developments in health care policies, economics, and financing. Nurse leaders are more effective in directing and educating their staff if they anticipate policy and financing changes.

CONCLUSION

This chapter presents concepts about reviewing health policy, and an overview of trends in the United States and international health systems. Implications for nursing reinforce that nurses need to understand the basics of health care economics and finance. Nurses have increasing opportunities for leadership, expanded roles in health services, and health care programs management. Sources and recommendations for keeping updated about changes in health policies, economics, and financing are provided.

Discussion and Exercises

1. Using the worksheet in Appendix 14A, analyze a policy question that you anticipate will present health care economics or financing concerns in the near future. How is this policy question related to the elements of cost, quality, access, universality, equity, efficiency, choice, and prevention?
2. Discuss how new technologies and changes in the health system such as the adoption of ICD-10 coding, the EHR, and new methods of health financing are affecting your work setting or clinical assignment. Compare your experience with that of other students. What opportunities do these new technologies and changes create for making a business case to improve care?
3. Explore the suggested sources for keeping updated, or find other reliable sources for updating information on health care services and financing. Prepare a 15-minute presentation updating health policy information from this textbook. Explain how you plan to keep updated in the years to come.

REFERENCES

Bureau of Labor Statistics. (2012). Latest numbers. Home page. Retrieved June 25, 2012 at http://www.bls.gov

Carnevale, A. P., Smith, N., Gulish, A., & Beach, B. H. (2012). *Healthcare.* Georgetown University Center on Education and the Workforce. Retrieved from http://www9.georgetown.edu/grad/gppi/hpi/cew/pdfs/Healthcare.FullReport4.pdf

Centers for Medicare & Medicaid Services. (2012). *Medicare and Medicaid Programs; Reform of Hospital and Critical Access Hospital Conditions of Participation. Final Rule. 42 CFR Parts 482 and 485 [CMS-3244-F] RIN 0938-AQ89 Department of Health and Human Services (HHS).* Retrieved from http://www.ofr.gov/inspection.aspx?AspxAutoDetectCookieSupport=1

Domrose, C. (2010). *A new era in nursing: Community health and aging population shift RN employment. Nurse.com. Gannett Healthcare Group.* Retrieved from http://news.nurse.com/article/20100912/NATIONAL01/109130045/-1/frontpage

Dower, C., & O'Neil, E. (2011). *Primary care health workforce in the United States. The Synthesis Project, Issue 22.* Princeton, NJ: Robert Wood Johnson Foundation. Retrieved from http://www.rwjf.org/files/research/070811.policysynthesis.workforce.rpt.pdf

Frumkin, H., Hess, J., Luber, G., Malilay, J., & McGeehin, M. (2008). Climate Change: The Public Health Response. *American Journal of Public Health, 98,* 435–445.

Galewitz, P., & Serafini, M. W. (2012). *Ruling puts pressure on states to act. KHN Kaiser Health News Judging The Health Law. Henry J. Kaiser Family Foundation.* Retrieved from http://www.kaiserhealthnews.org/Stories/2012/June/28/pressure-on-states-to-act-after-supreme-court-ruling.aspx

Hebda, T. L., & Czar, P. (2009). Handbook of informatics for nurses and healthcare professionals (4th ed.). Upper Saddle River, NJ: Prentice Hall.

Humes, K. R., Jones, N. A., & Ramirez, R. R. (2011). *Overview of race and Hispanic origin: 2010. 2010 Census Briefs. U.S. Department of Commerce Economics and Statistics Administration U.S. Census Bureau.* C2010BR-02. Retrieved from http://www.census.gov/prod/cen2010/briefs/c2010br-02.pdf. CensusOverviewRace-11.pdf

Institute of Medicine. (2011). *The future of nursing: Leading change, advancing health*. Committee on the Robert Wood Johnson Foundation Initiative on the Future of Nursing, at the Institute of Medicine. Washington, DC: The National Academies Press. Retrieved from http://www.nap.edu/catalog/12956.html

Mukheibir, P. (2010). Water access, water scarcity, and climate change. *Environmental Management, 45*, 1027–1039.

Patient Protection and Affordable Care Act. (2010). Pub. L. No. 111–148, §2702, 124 Stat. 119, 318–319 (2010). http://housedocs.house.gov/energycommerce/ppacacon.pdf

Roberts, M. J., & Clyde, A. T. (1993). *Your money or your life: The health care crisis explained*. New York: NY: Doubleday.

Staiger, D. O., Auerbach, D. I., & Buerhaus, P. I. (2012). Registered nurse labor supply and the recession—Are we in a bubble? *The New England Journal of Medicine*. Online First (DOI: 10.1056/NEJMp1200641). Retrieved from http://www.NEJM.org

Walker, D. (2008). Time to embrace public health approaches to national and global challenges. *American Journal Of Public Health, 98*, 1934–1936.

Zenner, P. (2010). ICD-10 impact on provider reimbursement. Milliman White Paper. Indianapolis, IN: Milliman. Retrieved from http://www.milliman.com

CROSSWORD: *Chapters 13 and 14—Ethical Issues, International Systems, Policy and Trends**

Across

4   Principle of bioethics requiring that health providers avoid or at least minimize harm when providing care.

6   Applications of telecommunications technologies to health education and patient care.

8   Requesting, offering, or receiving favors or payments that influence purchases.

9   Distributing the burden of cost fairly based on the ability to pay.

10 The provision of relatively equal access for all persons.

12 The relative equality of resource allocation to various disease entities, populations, or interventions.

13 Misrepresenting a diagnosis in order to justify a higher payment for services rendered than should be authorized.

Down

1   Travel to other countries to receive health care that is not affordable or available in one's own country.

2   Principle of bioethics requiring that health providers do good and provide the most benefit possible.

3   Principle of bioethics that supports the equal or fair distribution of health care benefits and risks across society.

5   Intentional deception or misrepresentation in order to obtain something of value that is owned by another party.

7   Computer technology and software that replaces paper-based health record systems (abbreviation).

11 Principle of bioethics that refers to the right of individuals to make their own decisions.

*Note: The crossword puzzles for Chapters 13 and 14 are identical.

APPENDIX 14A: POLICY QUESTION WORKSHEET FOR TRACKING FUTURE TRENDS IN HEALTH CARE

Policy Question	Future Trends
Cost	
Quality	
Access	
Universality	
Equity	
Efficiency	
Choice	
Prevention	

Source: Adapted from Roberts and Clyde (1993).

Glossary

Absenteeism Excessive use of employee sick leave.

Accountability Extent of responsibility for managing a situation.

Accountable care organization (ACO) New model of health care financing and delivery featuring shared savings strategies for all providers for an episode of patient care.

Accounts payable The amount due to vendors for supplies, also called trade credit.

Accrual basis of accounting Accounting that records revenues when earned, representing an obligation for payment, and records expenses when financial obligations are created, at the time the business consumes resources.

Accrued expenses Expenses that are generated daily, with periodic payment, such as employee wages.

Accumulated depreciation The total dollars of depreciation expensed over time.

Activity-based costing (ABC) A cost allocation method that focuses on the indirect and direct costs of specific activities performed within cost centers.

Activity ratios Another term for asset management ratios.

Actuarial Having to do with insurance risks.

Acuity Level of patient illness or case complexity.

Adjusted FTE An FTE calculation that accounts for all paid time and for 7-day per week coverage.

Adjusted occupied bed Inpatient average daily census adjusted based on the proportion of outpatient services provided by a hospital.

Adjusted patient day Inpatient days adjusted based on the proportion of outpatient services provided by a hospital.

Adjustment authority Allowing a manager to revise the budget over remaining fiscal year to adjust for the excessive unfavorable variance.

Administrative loss ratio (ALR) The portion of a health plan's expenses allocated to administrative costs and profit compared to total revenue.

Admission Patients transferring from home or another facility to an inpatient facility, used as a measure of inpatient utilization.

Admission rate The number of admissions divided by member months for the same time period, times 1000 used to measure hospital utilization.

Adverse selection Over-selection of a health plan based on its coverage of persons likely to have high health care costs.

Advertising Mass media communication purchased by a sponsor to persuade an audience.

Aged trial balance A method for evaluating collections by analyzing the amount and percent of account receivables that are 30, 60, 90, and over 120 days old.

Agency nurse Temporary nurse staffing from outside firms, also known as per diem nurse.

Agent A party in authority acting on behalf of a principal.

Align incentives Strategic application of incentives to improve consumer, provider, and payer behavior.

Allocative efficiency Minimizing the amount or cost of inputs while maximizing the value or benefit of outputs, or producing outputs of maximum value or benefit for a given amount or cost of inputs.

Allowable costs Costs directly related to providing an acceptable standard of health services, used by Medicare before prospective payment.

Annual report A financial statement that presents an overall summary of an organization's financial performance, and is often shared with the public.

Annual spend down A budgeting approach that requires that unspent budget funds are cut from the next year's budget so managers have incentives to spend the entire budget each year.

Annualizing A method of budget adjustment by calculating an average monthly budget value based on changes in actual performance, and multiplying the value by 12 to estimate the budget for a year.

Area wage index (AWI) Adjustment factor for differences in wage rates across geographic areas of the United States.

Asset management ratios Financial ratios that show how effectively the enterprise is using its assets, and how liabilities are affecting the enterprise.

Assets Resources held by the organization that possess or create economic benefit, reported in the balance sheet.

Assumptions Expectations or beliefs about the internal or external environment that influence administrative and financial decision-making.

Asymmetric information Unequal information among parties in a transaction.

Autonomy Principle of bioethics that refers to individuals' rights to make their own decisions.

Available beds Inpatient beds staffed and equipped for patient care, also known as staffed beds.

Average daily census (ADC) Average number of patients in a nursing unit calculated as the patient days divided by the number of days in a time period.

Average length of stay (ALOS) Total inpatient days by the number of admissions.

Bad debt Uncollected payments from payers (usually self-pay consumers) considered to be able to pay.

Balance sheet A financial statement that provides information about the organization's resources and how those resources are acquired, also called the statement of financial position.

Balance the budget Strategies to adjust actual expenditures to budgeted expenditures.

Barriers to entry Restrictions on entering markets.

Bed turnaround time Measure of the time from discharge until an inpatient bed is ready for an admission.

Bed turns The number of times an inpatient bed is used for an admission or observation, calculated by dividing admissions and observations by the number of staffed beds.

Benchmark A value that represents performance targeted to an internal or industry standard.

Beneficence Principle of bioethics requiring that health providers do good and provide the most benefit possible.

Benefit-cost ratio (B/C ratio) Dividing total benefits by total costs to determine the dollar amount of benefits per dollar spent on the objective function.

Benefits The outputs or contributions produced by the objective function, including cost savings achieved by the intervention.

Benefits management Case management focused on monitoring and conserving health insurance benefits for long-term and often high-cost cases.

Book value The balance sheet value of owner's equity of an asset.

Brain-drain The migration of professionals to other locations or countries in order to benefit from higher wages and better living conditions.

Brand-name medication Patented medications associated with a pharmaceutical company, usually higher in cost than equivalent generic medications.

Break-even analysis Determining the UOS required to cover the costs of business and make a profit, related to costs and revenue associated with the UOS.

Budget cycle An organization's schedule for budget preparation, negotiation, approval, and implementation.

Budget justification Presenting a rationale or a business case for an unusual or excessive budget variance, often with a plan for improved performance.

Bundled Reimbursement system that includes payment for all care provided from disease onset to recovery.

Business case A business plan or other presentation that convinces the reviewer to provide resources for a program or project.

Business grant proposal A proposal that describes the budget, pricing, and all other financial information.

Capability statement A section of the health program grant proposal that describes the qualifications of the agency and staff.

Capacity The extent to which a health care setting can meet consumer demand.

Capital Long-term expenditures such as construction and equipment purchases.

Capital budget A budget for long-term investments with a useful life of more than a year, and that are often high cost.

Capital improvement grant A grant that funds construction, renovation, or the purchase of capital equipment.

Capital structure ratios Another term for debt management ratios.

Capitation Reimbursement by prepaying for the care of a specified population over a specified time period, used in managed care contracts.

Capitation revenue The amount of authorized capitation reimbursement.

Carve-in When a specialist MCO operates within a medical MCO, addressing problems of under-care related to gatekeeping.

Carve-out When a specialist MCO contracts with a medical MCO, addressing problems of under-care related to gatekeeping.

Case mix index (CMI) Measure of overall acuity among Medicare patients in hospitals (abbreviation).

Cash basis of accounting Accounting that records revenue at the time of receipt of payment, and records expenses at the time expenditures are made.

Cash flow The change or net increase or decrease in cash.

Cash flow budget A budget that estimates the flow of money in and out of the business.

Cash flow statement A financial statement that provides details about the sources of cash and how cash is used, also called a statement of cash flows.

Cash flows from operating activities Revenues, cash received by the business, also called cash inflows and reported in the cash flow budget.

Cash inflows Revenues, cash received by the business, also called cash flows from operating activities and reported in the cash flow budget.

Cash outflows from operating activities Operating expenses as reported in a cash flow budget.

Census The number of inpatients on a nursing unit at any point in time, often measured at midnight.

Charge The full price assigned to a good or service, before discounts or other reductions.

Charge description master (CDM) A hospital's comprehensive list of the prices of all goods and services for which a separate charge exists, also called a chargemaster.

Charge-based reimbursement Allowing the provider to bill the payer for the full charges of the good or service.

Chargemaster A hospital's comprehensive list of the prices of all goods and services for which a separate charge exists, also called a charge description master.

Claims review Retrospective review that occurs after health care is provided and the claim for reimbursement is filed.

Coinsurance A percentage of a given health care cost that is required by the insurer to be paid by the plan member.

Collectibles Another term for accounts receivable or receivables.

Common size analysis Reporting each item of an income statement as a percent of total revenues or each item of a balance sheet as a percent of total assets, also called vertical analysis.

Community rating A specified dollar amount of a given health care cost required of the plan member.

Comparative effectiveness research (CER) A method for guiding health care decisions based on new and existing research comparing treatments, tests, procedures, or services.

Competitive grant Grant applications with several or more agencies applying for the program funding available, which is the usual situation in grant funding.

Competitive market Free or open markets supporting competition that is reflected in the U.S. economy and many economies world-wide.

Compounded The interest earned in each time period earns interest in future time periods.

Concurrent review Utilization review that occurs during hospitalization to determine whether continued hospitalization is necessary.

Conflict of interest An ethical discord between two or more desired but opposing circumstances.

Consumer-driven health plans (CDHPS) Health plans with high deductibles thought to encourage consumer wellness (abbreviation).

Contractual allowance The difference between the amount the insurer pays compared to the charges.

Contribution margin (CM) The dollar amount available from revenues to first cover fixed costs (including overhead), then contribute to profits, calculated as TR less TVC.

Control Putting management strategies in place to address and prevent unfavorable budget variances.

Copayment A dollar amount of a health care cost paid by a beneficiary.

Cost Resource or expense required as input to produce goods or services.

Cost allocation Determining the total direct and indirect costs attributed to cost centers.

Cost centers Work units that generate and report operating expenses.

Cost driver A measure or specification for allocation of costs from a cost pool, such as pounds of laundry for laundry services.

Cost per unit of effectiveness (CE) The total program cost for each program compared in a CEA is divided by the appropriate unit of effectiveness.

Cost pool Costs grouped or selected for allocation to other cost centers.

Cost pool method A direct distribution costing method using cost drivers that reflect the estimated resource use of revenue cost centers.

Cost-based reimbursement Reimbursement based on allowable costs used by Medicare until DRGs were developed.

Cost-benefit analysis (CBA) A method of evaluating the benefits relative to the costs of a program or service.

Cost-effectiveness analysis (CEA) A method of evaluating and comparing the benefits and costs among two or more alternative programs or services.

Cost-finding Identifying all the sources and amounts of costs involved in producing a UOS.

Cost-plus pricing A profit-focused pricing method that sets the price at the cost of production cost plus a profit margin.

Cost-sharing Strategies such as coinsurance and copayments that require consumers to contribute to health care costs.

Cost-shifting Passing the costs of one party to another party.

Cost-to-charge ratio (CCR) Dividing hospital costs by hospital charges (gross revenues) to determine the relationship of costs to charges.

Cost-utility analysis (CUA) A method of evaluating the benefits to quality of life relative to the costs of a program or service.

Cost-volume-profit (CVP) analysis Another term for break-even analysis.

Current liabilities Debts or other financial obligations that must be paid within the short term or fiscal year.

Current ratio A liquidity ratio calculated by dividing current assets by current liabilities.

Customer-focused pricing Setting the price based on the value the customer attributes to the product or service, also called value-based pricing.

Cyclical When values rise or fall in a repeating pattern, such as more respiratory disease occurring in the winter, also known as seasonal.

Dark-green dollars Savings or benefits that can actually be tracked in budgets and other financial reports, compared to light-green dollars.

Days in accounts receivable Dividing the accounts receivable by the average daily patient revenue, an asset management ratio that is also sometimes reported as a liquidity ratio.

Debt management ratios Financial ratios that show the extent of an enterprise's debt burden, the extent to which investors are financing the enterprise, whether debt payments are covered by current earnings, and the likelihood of the enterprise paying its debts.

Debt ratio Dividing total debt by total assets, a debt management ratio that is the inverse of the equity ratio, also called the debt-to-assets ratio.

Debt-to-assets ratio Dividing total debt by total assets, a debt management ratio that is the inverse of the equity ratio, also called the debt ratio.

Deductible A required payment made by a consumer before the health plan begins to cover costs.

Default Failure to repay a loan.

Defensive medicine Provider gives excessive care in order to prevent possible malpractice suits.

Demand The quantity of a product for which consumers are able and willing to pay at a given price over a specified time period.

Demonstration grant A grant that funds evidence-based, state-of-the-art, or model programs and services.

Depreciation Estimating and allocating the cost of a capital asset over its useful life.

Derived demand The quantity of products demanded for the sake of an ultimate output.

Direct care hours Productive hours of inpatient staff nurses providing patient care, also referred to as nursing hours per patient day (NHPPD) or productive nursing hours per patient day (PNHPPD).

Direct costs Expenses required and budgeted for direct goods and services such as direct patient care.

Direct distribution A costing method that allocates indirect costs from support services to profit centers.

Direct staffing FTEs based on volume, also called variable staffing or flexible FTEs.

Discharge The release of a patient to home or another facility, usually includes deaths.

Disclosure Reporting on all of the aspects of financial transactions so the financial condition of the business is accurately represented.

Discount rate The rate of interest used in discounting.

Discounted charge Payer reimburses a non-negotiable specified payment amount.

Discounting Converting the future value of a monetary unit to its present value.

Disproportionate share hospitals (DSHS) Hospitals caring for a higher proportion of low-income patients than other hospitals.

Drilling down Obtaining more detail from summary or aggregate data to better determine the source of a problem.

Dual eligibles Persons who are enrolled both in Medicare and Medicaid, often with high-cost, complex health problems.

Economies of scale When the fixed costs of production can be spread across a large number of products, and the variable costs decrease.

Economies of scope When the costs of production decline if two or more goods or services are produced together.

Effectiveness per unit of cost (EC) The appropriate unit of effectiveness is divided by the cost for each program compared in a CEA.

Efficiency Maximizing the production or value of goods or services while minimizing the resources or costs required for production.

Efficiency ratios Another term for asset management ratios.

Electronic health record (EHR) Computer technology and software that replaces paper-based health record systems.

Ending cash balance Total cash inflows less total cash outflows, reported in the cash flow budget.

Entitlement A government benefit that people have a right to receive as long as they are eligible.

Entrepreneur A person starting or managing their own business enterprise.

Equity Ownership claim on assets, reported in the balance sheet; in health policy, distributing the burden of cost fairly based on the ability to pay.

Equity ratio Dividing equity by total assets, a debt management ratio indicating the proportion of total assets that are financed by the owners compared to debt financing, also called the equity to total assets ratio.

Equity to total assets ratio Dividing equity by total assets, a debt management ratio indicating the proportion of total assets that are financed by the owners compared to debt financing, also called the equity ratio.

Evidence-based practice (EBP) The application of research evidence to improve health care interventions.

Evidence-informed case rate (ECR) A budget based on an episode of care, often used in ACOs to develop bundled payments for all providers involved in the episode of care.

Experience rating Basing premiums the history of the group, rather than on the characteristics of the community's population as a whole.

Explicit rationing Policies that directly deny health care to conserve scarce health care resources.

Exporting risk A risk-sharing strategy requiring the provider to share some of the financial risk of care in order to better control costs.

Externalities Costs of production not borne by the producer, or costs of consumption not paid for by the consumer.

Extramural funding External funders and funding sources, such as government agencies or private foundations.

Fair market value The price paid to the owners when purchasing a business.

Favorable budget variance A desirable difference between budgeted and actual amounts, for example, when actual expenses are less than budgeted.

Fee-for-service (FFS) Retrospective payment of all allowable costs meeting accepted standards of care.

Fiduciary agency An entity that assumes the responsibility for financial management of the grant, including activities such as paying wages and bills.

Financial accounting Activities involved in collecting, reporting, and analyzing data presented in financial statements.

Financial costs Expenses incurred in obtaining funds to purchase the organization's assets, such as interest on debt.

Financial indicator Measure of a monetary value, or incorporated with other indicators to measure the associated monetary values.

Financial threshold A dollar value specified as a limit, for example, a policy that any expenditure on equipment over $1000 must be included in the capital budget.

Fiscal conservatism An accounting principle that records probable losses to a business if they may be reasonably predicted, while gains are not recorded until they are actually realized.

Fiscal year The annual reporting period that may follow the calendar or other designated 12-month period, such as July 1 to June 30.

Fixed assets Property, plant, and equipment (PPE), also called real assets.

Fixed capacity Capacity that does not change with volume.

Fixed costs Costs that do not change if production volume changes.

Fixed costs per unit (FCU) The fixed costs associated with each UOS, calculated by dividing TFC by the volume.

Fixed FTEs FTEs that do not change based on volume, also referred to as permanent staffing or indirect staffing.

Flexible FTEs FTEs based on volume, also called direct staffing or variable staffing.

Flexible spending account (FSA) A pretax account used for expenses not covered by health insurance (abbreviation).

Formulary Approved prescribing list for pharmaceuticals.

Fraud Intentional deception or misrepresentation in order to obtain something of value that is owned by another party.

Free-rider problem When shortages of a product occur because consumers have access to the product but are not required to pay for the product.

FTE coverage factor An adjustment for inpatient staff FTEs to include 24-hour and 7-day per week staffing needs.

Full-time equivalent (FTE) A standard measure for hourly employment, indicating a full-time employee working eight hours a day, five days a week, for 52 weeks a year, for a total of 2080 hours per year.

Functional classification Financial reporting that classifies expenses by the type of output accruing the expense, such as inpatient services.

Gainsharing ACO incentive in which a negotiated portion of the savings is returned to the providers as an incentive, also called shared risk or shared savings.

Gantt chart A type of bar chart that enables the visualization of a project's schedule.

Gatekeeping Managed care requirement that access to specialists or other specified services must be authorized by a PCP or other designated provider.

Generally accepted accounting principles (GAAP) A common set of standards, procedures, and principles for preparing financial statements so that accounting information is reported consistently.

Generic medication Pharmaceuticals equivalent to brand-name drugs, but not associated with a particular pharmaceutical company and usually lower in cost.

Global budgeting A financing strategy such as capitation that prepays total revenues as a fixed payment.

Goal A broad statement regarding what the organization or program intends to accomplish.

Goodwill The difference between the fair market value and the book value of an asset.

Gross patient revenue All inpatient and outpatient hospital charges before deductions are applied.

Gross revenue The full charges for a good or service.

Group model When an HMO contracts with a physician group practice.

Group purchasing organization (GPO) An organization that negotiates prices with vendors on behalf of member hospitals so that purchasing contracts are more favorable for medical supplies and capital equipment.

Health maintenance organization (HMO) A managed care organization or plan that provides health care to persons enrolled in a pre-paid plan.

Health program grant proposal A proposal developed as an application to request funding in order to provide a specific service or set of services to a target population.

Health reimbursement arrangement (HRA) A pretax or tax-deductible health care account to which only the employer may contribute.

Health savings account (HSA) A pretax or tax-deductible health care account in which an employer or employee can make contributions.

Healthcare common procedure coding system (HCPCS) A coding system developed by CMS to classify services and products not included in the CPT® codes.

High-deductible health plans (HDHPS) Health plans that require a minimum $1000 deductible for single coverage or $2000 deductible for family coverage.

Horizontal analysis Calculating the percent of change for each item on a financial statement from year to year, also called percentage change analysis.

Horizontal integration Increasing the market share of enterprises across the same level of services, such as a health care system acquiring more hospitals.

Hospital insurance (HI) Medicare Part A.

Hospital-acquired conditions (HACS) Preventable conditions as specified by Medicare for which hospitals may not be reimbursed.

Hospitalization rate The number of inpatient days divided by member months for the same period times 1000, used to measure hospital utilization.

Hours per patient day (HPPD) The amount of time an inpatient requires of direct nursing care per day.

Hours per unit of service (HPUOS) A measure of direct care hours for settings that do not provide inpatient care, such as settings that perform procedures.

Human capital A method of valuing human life using the present value of a person's future earnings.

Illiquid assets Resources that cannot readily be exchanged for or readily converted into cash, such as fixed assets reported in the balance sheet.

Implicit rationing Indirect denial of health care resources, often based on a person's inability to pay for care.

Incentive A reward or encouragement, often financial, that influences behavior.

Income redistribution Transferring income from one group to another based on established criteria.

Income statement A financial statement that discloses the profitability of an organization.

Incremental budgeting A budgeting approach in which the current year's budget is used as the base for the next year's budget.

Incurred but not reported (IBNR) Expenses that are not yet reported for a specific time period, but that the MCO or other organization will be responsible to pay.

Independent practice association (IPA) A physician group practice model where the physicians own the practice but contract with an MCO for members and reimbursement.

Indicators Measures that signify a specific condition or a specified level or value, also called metrics.

Indirect costs Expenses required and budgeted for indirect goods and services such as administration, also called overhead.

Indirect hours Productive hours such as staff education, orientation, and meetings that do not involve direct patient care.

Indirect staffing FTEs that do not change based on volume, also referred to as permanent staffing or fixed FTEs.

Influence Impact from the input a person provides in a situation.

Information problem When consumers, providers, or insurers do not possess enough information to make a rational economic choice.

In-kind contributions Resources that will be contributed by the organization applying for grant funding.

Inputs Resources and raw materials needed for production.

Intangibles Measures or resources that cannot be converted to dollar amounts.

Interest A percentage rate representing the price for borrowing when transacting a loan.

Intramural funding Funders or funding sources within one's organization, such as a hospital's nonprofit foundation.

Intrapreneur An employee working within an organization to improve production and profitability.

Inventory Supplies a business keeps on hand.

Investigation Identifying the source or sources of a budget variance, and determining whether the variance can be controlled.

Job position A defined occupation within the employing organization, often the staffing model for outpatient and community-based nurses' work settings.

Justice Principle of bioethics that supports the equal or fair distribution of health care benefits and risks across society.

Kickbacks Requesting, offering, or receiving favors or payments that influence purchases.

Lag time A delay in reporting actual financial figures related to the time required for collecting and tabulating the data.

Lagged value Budget or other financial figure that reflects prior financial activities for specified periods of time.

Leverage ratios Another term for debt management ratios.

Liabilities Claims on assets established by contract, reported in the balance sheet.

Licensed beds A specified number of inpatient beds approved by regulatory agencies that represent fixed capacity but may or may not be staffed and equipped for patient care.

Light-green dollars Theoretical or potential savings or benefits, compared to dark-green dollars.

Limited use assets Assets that carry restrictions imposed by the hospital board, donors, or other third parties.

Line item The specific types of items in each row (line) of the budget.

Line item flexibility Management authority to transfer funds in one line item to another line item.

Liquid assets Resources that represent cash or that can readily be exchanged for or converted into cash, reported as current assets in the balance sheet.

Liquidation Dissolving a business and distributing its assets.

Liquidity ratios Financial ratios showing an enterprise's capability to turn assets into cash or to cover current debt with cash and other assets available.

Logic model A visual layout using a table, flow chart, or other depiction to summarize and describe what a program will do and achieve.

Long-term debt to equity ratio Dividing net long-term debt by equity, a debt management ratio that shows the proportion of long-term debt to net worth.

Long-term debt to net PPE ratio Dividing net long-term debt by net PPE plus construction-in-progress, a debt management ratio that is an indicator of fixed asset financing.

Majority-minority populations Demographics of greater than 50% of the population comprised of minority races.

Managed care organization (MCO) A managed care plan that provides health care to persons enrolled in a prepaid plan.

Managerial accounting Financial activities often focused at the level of departments or work units, such as budgeting and planning.

Market A group of buyers and sellers of products such as goods and services.

Market disequilibrium When a product's price, quantity demanded, and quantity supplied are out of balance.

Market equilibrium The price of a product reaches a level satisfactory to both the buyer and the seller, and the quantity supplied equals the quantity demanded.

Market failure When markets are unable to allocate resources efficiently.

Market power When one party has control over price compared to other parties.

Market share The estimated percentage of the entire market for a product or service that is managed by a provider or organization.

Market share pricing A pricing approach in which prices are lowered to make the product more competitive, also called penetration pricing.

Marketable securities Liquid, low-interest-bearing investments.

Master budget A budget report that combines the organization's strategic plan and all of the organization's budgets and budget proposals into one document.

Matching principle An accounting principle that matches revenue the time revenue is earned, and tries to match revenue with the expenses used to generate that revenue.

Materiality An accounting principle that records separate categories of financial entries only if they are relevant for reporting or understanding the financial condition of the business.

Medical home A collaboration of patients with their primary care and other health care providers in offering culturally sensitive, comprehensive health care.

Medical loss ratio (MLR) The portion of a health plan's expenses allocated to clinical services compared to total revenue.

Medical tourism Travel to other countries to receive health care that is not affordable or available in one's own country.

Medicare advantage (MA) Medicare Part C.

Medicare Advantage prescription drug plans (MA-PDPs) Medicare Part D for Medicare Advantage enrollees.

Medicare Part A Hospital insurance paid from beneficiary earnings contributions.

Medicare Part B Supplementary Medical Insurance program for physician, outpatient, and other services, financed by premiums.

Medicare Part C Medicare Advantage enrollment in private plan to cover Part A, Part B, and Part D.

Medicare Part D Prescription drug plan financed by premiums and cost-sharing.

Medicare severity diagnosis-related groups (MS-DRGs) A classification used by Medicare to establish prospective payment rates for hospitals, incorporating quality initiatives.

Medigap insurance Insurance offered by private health plans to cover services not covered by Medicare Part A or Part B.

Member months The total of all months of coverage for each health plan enrollee over the plan year.

Memorandum of understanding (MOU) A document that describes the contributions collaborating agencies will provide to the proposed program.

Metrics Measures that signify a specific condition or a specified level or value, also called indicators.

Microsystem A specified work unit, such as an inpatient nursing unit or an Emergency Department.

Mid-level provider (MLP) Health professionals who enable expansion of primary care services, including nurse practitioners, nurse midwives, and physician assistants.

Mission statement A brief statement that communicates the overall purpose of an organization.

Monitoring Ongoing critical review of the budget focused on identifying performance problems that require investigation.

Monopoly When one party has control over production, thus controlling price.

Monopsony When one party has control over consumption of a product, thus controlling price.

Moral hazard Over-utilization of health services because of insensitivity to costs rather than medical necessity.

National health insurance A health system in which the national government provides health coverage for all citizens, but does not own or employ the health care providers.

National health service A health system that covers health care for all its citizens, and that owns and employs many of the health care providers.

Natural classification Financial reporting that classifies expenses by the type of input accruing the expense, such as supplies or salaries.

Natural monopoly When one producer can supply a product more efficiently or at a lower cost than if two or more producers enter the market.

Needs assessment An evidence-based review of the community health need or problem.

Negative externalities Risks and problems borne by third parties from production or consumption.

Negotiated charges Reimbursement strategy when the payer negotiates a reduced rate that is less than the charge.

Net assets Owner's equity as reported by public and nonprofit organizations that are owned by the community, also called net worth.

Net benefits The dollar value of all the benefits less the dollar value of all the costs associated with an objective function, also called net contribution.

Net collection rate Dividing actual collections by net charges, an indicator of a practice's ability to collect reimbursement.

Net contribution The dollar value of all the benefits less the dollar value of all the costs associated with an objective function, also called net benefits.

Net deficit Negative net income.

Net income The amount of profit or loss generated by a business over the reporting time period.

Net income margin The net income divided by the sum of net patient revenue, other operating revenue, and nonoperating revenue, a profitability ratio indicating the profits generated by total revenues.

Net increase or decrease in cash The ending cash balance plus the beginning cash balance, reported in the cash flow budget.

Net long-term debt Long-term debt less the amount of debt expected to be paid off in the next fiscal year.

Net patient revenue Gross patient revenue less any deductions to revenue.

Net PPE per licensed bed Dividing the value of net PPE plus construction-in-progress by the number of licensed beds, an asset management ratio indicating a hospital's financial value of net fixed assets per licensed bed.

Net return on total assets (NROA) Net income divided by total assets, indicating the profit generated by the assets of a business.

Net revenue Gross revenue less any deductions or discounts.

Net surplus Positive net income.

Net working capital The difference between current assets and current liabilities, also called working capital.

Net worth Owner's equity as reported by public and nonprofit organizations that are owned by the community, also called net assets.

Noncurrent assets Long-term investments, fixed assets, and other relatively permanent assets, reported in the balance sheet.

Noncurrent liability Liability entry not due within a fiscal year.

Nonmaleficence Principle of bioethics requiring that health providers avoid or at least minimize harm when providing care.

Nonoperating expense Expenses for goods or services not related to the organization's primary purpose in providing health care services.

Nonoperating revenue Revenue sources not related to business activities.

Nonpersonnel expenses Operating expenses such as medical supplies and equipment maintenance that are not labor costs.

Nonproductive hours Paid hours such as sick leave, holidays, and vacations that do not represent productive hours.

Nonproductive percent The proportion of all paid hours that are nonproductive hours.

Nonrevenue cost center A cost center that generates expenses but not revenues, and typically provides indirect services.

Nonservice revenue Revenue received for goods or services other than direct care, such as revenue from a hospital's gift shop.

Notes payable Written promises of future payment made by a business.

Nurse to patient (N/P) ratio The maximum number of patients assigned per nurse per shift.

Nursing hours per patient day (NHPPD) Productive hours of inpatient staff nurses providing patient care, also referred to as direct care hours or productive nursing hours per patient day (PNHPPD).

Objective A specified task that must be accomplished over the long- or short-term to achieve a goal, ideally developed as a SMART objective.

Objective function What the program or service is intended to achieve.

Observation Patients who require close monitoring but who usually occupy an inpatient bed for less than 48 hours.

Occupancy rate Measures how closely the utilization of a 24-hour nursing unit approaches its full capacity, calculated by dividing the census by the number of staffed beds, reported as a percent.

Omaha system A coding system used by nurses and other health professionals in settings across the continuum of care.

Ongoing activity grant A grant that funds the continued operation of a program for three to five years or longer.

Operating budget A budget used in the day-to-day management of a work unit or facility.

Operating expense Expenses that enable the setting to achieve its primary purpose in providing health care services, whether fixed or variable.

Operating leverage Financial risk related to volume and reimbursement, particularly in settings with high fixed costs compared to variable costs.

Operating margin Net income from operations divided by net patient revenue and other operating revenue, a profitability ratio that for hospitals shows how much patient care revenue contributes to profits from patient care.

Operational assistance grant A grant that funds overhead expenses and the day-to-day support of an organization implementing a program.

Opportunity cost The value of a trade-off.

Other operating revenue Revenue from activities other than patient care, such as revenue from the hospital's gift shop.

Outcome and Assessment Information Set (OASIS) A coding system CMS developed as a set of data items for the assessment and outcomes evaluation of adult home health clients.

Outlier Unusually costly and frequently long-term cases, usually in acute care settings.

Out-of-pocket Payment a health care consumer makes directly, also called self-pay.

Outputs Goods, services, or other outcomes produced from inputs and throughputs.

Over-care Providing more health care services than medically necessary.

Overhead Indirect, administrative, and support expenses such as rent and clerical services.

Overhead rate A direct distribution costing method in which the indirect cost per UOS is calculated and applied to allocate indirect costs.

Overtime Work hours exceeding eight hours per day (without prior agreement to work 10-hour or 12-hour shifts at regular pay) or more than 40 hours per week.

Owners' equity The ownership claim on an organization's assets, or the amount of total assets financed by nonliability capital.

Paid charges The charges authorized by the capitation plan and used as a measure of costs.

Parity The relative equality of resource allocation to various disease entities, populations, or interventions.

Patient day The count of 24-hour days that patients occupy an inpatient setting.

Patient engagement Patient and family active participation in making informed health care decisions.

Patient flow The efficient and timely transfer of patients to the appropriate level of care.

Patient revenue margin Net revenue less operating expenses divided by net revenue, indicating the hospital's profit generated solely from patient care operations.

Payer mix Sources of reimbursement, usually insurance plans, which contribute to a health setting's revenue.

Payout ratio The proportion of after-tax net income paid out to shareholders, and the inverse of the retention ratio.

Penetration pricing A pricing approach in which prices are lowered to make the product more competitive, also called market share pricing.

Pent-up demand Increased demand because consumers have deferred consumption, such as waiting for insurance coverage to utilize health care.

Per diem A set amount of reimbursement per patient day.

Per diem nurse Temporary nurse staffing from outside firms, also known as agency nurse.

Percent variance The proportional difference between budgeted and actual values, calculated as the variance divided by the budgeted value.

Percentage change analysis Calculating the percent of change for each item on a financial statement from year to year, also called horizontal analysis.

Performance How efficiently a setting's capacity operates in managing production or utilization.

Performance ratios Financial ratios that help reviewers understand how well the enterprise generates profits, related to its assets and revenues, also called profitability ratios.

Performance target An indicator that specifies whether a performance standard is reached in actual practice.

Permanent staffing FTEs that do not change based on volume, also referred to as indirect staffing or fixed FTEs.

Personnel expenses Operating expenses that represent labor costs such as employee salaries, wages, and overtime.

Physicians' current procedural terminology (CPT®) A coding system the AMA developed to classify outpatient services and costs.

Planning grant A grant that provides funding for assessing a community need or problem and planning a program to meet those needs.

Pluralistic health system The U.S. health care system that relies on a complex and fragmented set of payers and providers, leaving millions of Americans uninsured.

PMPM A managed care indicator in which the revenue, cost, or utilization measure is divided by the number of plan enrollees for a monthly time period.

PMPY A managed care indicator in which the revenue, cost, or utilization measure is divided by the number of plan enrollees over a year.

Point-of-service (POS) A managed care plan that covers services from providers within the plan more generously than services from providers outside the plan.

Positive externalities Benefits for third parties, from production or consumption.

Potential patient days The maximum possible utilization over a specific time period given the bed capacity, calculated by multiplying the number of staffed beds by the number of days in the time period.

Preauthorization Reviewing a provider's plan for care prior to the intervention to determine whether or not the plan will pay the costs, also called prospective review.

Preexisting condition clause Requires new enrollees to disclose medical condition to the health plan, and may lead to exclusion from the health plan.

Preferred provider organization (PPO) A managed care plan contracting with independent providers at a discounted rate, and offering more generous coverage if members select these preferred providers rather than providers outside the plan.

Prescription drug plan (PDP) Medicare Part D.

Present value The monetary value of an investment and its discount (interest) rate for a specified number of years into the future.

Primary benefits Benefits that result directly from the objective function.

Primary care Diagnosis, treatment, maintenance, and prevention services provided by PCPs or MLPs.

Primary care physicians (PCPs) Physicians in general or pediatric practice who are often the first point of patient contact for diagnosis, treatment, and prevention.

Principal A party lacking knowledge who delegates authority to an agent; the amount of money borrowed when transacting a loan.

Principal proponent A person who directly benefits, or whose work setting and staff directly benefit from writing a business plan.

Priorities Organizational activities or issues that are believed to be of the most importance for profitability or survival.

Priority matrix A tool, usually in the form of a grid, that helps identify a project's priority level or capital expenditure.

Product line budget A budget focusing on a clinical specialty or on selected groups of patients with the same or very similar diagnoses, also called a service line budget.

Production efficiency Minimizing the costs of producing outputs, or maximizing the production of outputs at a given cost.

Productive hours The time that employees are paid to carry out their work assignments.

Productive nursing hours per patient day (PNHPPD) Productive hours of inpatient staff nurses providing patient care, also referred to as direct care hours or nursing hours per patient day (NHPPD).

Profit & loss statement (P&L) Total revenues less total expenses, calculated to estimate the amount of profit or loss over a specified time period.

Profit center A cost center that generates both expenses and revenues, and typically provides direct services, also called a revenue cost center.

Profit-focused pricing Pricing methods using the desired level of profit as a basis for setting prices.

Profit margin Profit ÷ Total Revenue expressed as a percent, measuring the amount of profit generated per dollar of revenue.

Profitability ratios Financial ratios that help reviewers understand how well the enterprise generates profits, related to its assets and revenues, also called performance ratios.

Program evaluation The application of analytic methods to determine whether a program is needed, utilizes its resources effectively, operates as planned, and meets its objectives.

Prospective forecasting Using current information to predict future events.

Prospective payment Reimbursing a predetermined fixed amount for the care of a patient case.

Prospective review Reviewing a provider's plan for care prior to the intervention to determine whether or not the plan will pay the costs, also called preauthorization.

Prudent layperson's standard A prudent layperson with average knowledge of health and medicine would seek medical attention, used as a standard for emergency care requirements.

Public goods Goods that are collectively consumed and relatively inexhaustible and nonexclusive.

Qualitative Using or relying on non-numerical data.

Quality-adjusted life year (QALY) A method that assigns dollar values to human life by weighting each remaining year of life by the expected quality of life measure for that year.

Quantitative Using or relying on numerical data.

Ratio analysis Converting values from financial statements into proportions that allow for interpretation.

Real assets Property, plant, and equipment (PPE), also called fixed assets.

Receivables Revenue sources for organizations such as hospitals that bill and await payment for most of their services.

Reciprocal distribution A costing method that allocates costs for support services to all cost centers, not just to revenue cost centers.

Referral An individual directed to a health care setting for health care services.

Referral percentage The number of patient visits with specialists referred by the PCP divided by all of the PCP's visits times 100; could apply to other providers and referrals in other settings.

Referral rate The number of patient visits with specialists referred by PCPs divided by all PCP visits and converted to a rate; could apply to other providers and referrals in other settings.

Reimbursement The actual payment for health care services that may be less than the charges.

Relative value unit (RVU) Cost assignment under the RBRVS coding system that includes the three components of physician work value, practice expense, and malpractice liability insurance expense.

Request for applications (RFA) A grant application that is formally and periodically requested by a funding agency, also referred to as an RFP or a solicited proposal.

Request for proposals (RFP) A grant application that is formally and periodically requested by a funding agency, also referred to as an RFA or a solicited proposal.

Research proposal A proposal that presents an investigator's topic and methodology for a scientific study.

Resource-based relative value scale (RBRVS) A coding system that quantifies physician services for reimbursement purposes.

Retention ratio The proportion of net income reinvested in the business, and the inverse of the payout ratio.

Retrospective forecasting Using past performance as a guide for predicting future performance.

Retrospective payment Historical practice of reimbursing a provider at the end of the care of the patient case, typically based on the provider's bill.

Retrospective review Review that occurs after health care is provided and the claim for reimbursement is filed.

Revenue Income from reimbursement or payment provided for goods and services.

Revenue and expense summary Another term for income statement.

Revenue cost center A cost center that generates both expenses and revenues, and typically provides direct services, also called a profit center.

Revenue cycle management The process of billing, collecting, and negotiating reimbursement contracts.

Revenue per unit (RU) The reimbursement amount for each UOS, also called the price.

Risk Probability of an adverse event

Risk pooling Spreading the risk and costs of a catastrophic event across a specified population.

Risk sharing A reimbursement strategy requiring the provider to share some of the financial risk of care in order to better control costs.

Rule of Seventy An investment earning 7.2% compounded annually is estimated to double every 10 years.

Salary Employee compensation that does not change regardless of the number of hours worked over the year.

Seasonal When values rise or fall in a repeating pattern, such as more respiratory disease occurring in the winter, also known as cyclical.

Secondary benefits Indirect contributions that result from the objective function.

Seed money Funding for special project grants.

Self-pay Payment a health care consumer makes directly, also called out-of-pocket.

Self-referral Patient selection of a provider.

Service line budget A budget focusing on a clinical specialty or on selected groups of patients with the same or very similar diagnoses, also called a product line budget.

Service revenue Operating revenue generated from providing direct care services, such as revenue received when a hospital provides patient care.

Shared risk ACO incentive in which a negotiated portion of the savings is returned to the providers as an incentive, also called gainsharing or shared savings.

Shared savings ACO incentive in which a negotiated portion of the savings is returned to the providers as an incentive, also called shared risk or gainsharing.

Shortage Excess demand resulting from the market price for a product falling to a level lower than the equilibrium price.

Skill mix The proportion of RNs compared to other nursing staff, such as licensed practical nurses (LPNs) nurse assistants.

Skimming Setting an excessively high price for health care goods and services when the demand is inelastic.

Small test of change Small health care quality improvement projects that often use measures or indicators to provide evidence of successful outcomes.

SMART objective Program or organizational objectives that are specific, measurable, achievable, relevant, and have a time frame for achievement.

Socialized health service A health system that does not allow privately owned or employed providers, only allowing health services from government providers.

Socialized medicine Linking ideas for universal health coverage to communism.

Soft money Grant funding representing revenue that may or may not be available from year to year.

Sole source grant A noncompetitive grant application made available when only one organization in the community is capable of managing a program.

Solicited grant proposal A grant application that is formally and periodically requested by a funding agency, also referred to as an RFP or RFA.

Solvent An individual or business that is able to pay its bills and meet its liabilities.

Special project grant A grant that funds new, special, pilot, or demonstration projects.

Special purpose budget A budget prepared for any purpose that has not been otherwise budgeted, such as a business plan or grant proposal.

Specialty care Physician practices such as dermatology and psychiatry that may be referred from PCPs or MLPs, particularly when gatekeeping is required.

Staff model HMO in which physicians are employees and are paid a salary.

Staffed beds Inpatient beds staffed and equipped for patient care, also known as available beds.

Staffing capacity The maximum number of patients health care providers can manage at any point in time.

Staffing indicators Measures of the workload and labor needed for providing health care services.

Stakeholders People and organizations with an active concern about a community need or problem.

Starting cash balance The amount of cash on hand at the beginning of the cash flow budget time period.

Start-up costs One-time expenses for items such as equipment that enable a project to be implemented.

Statement of activities Another term for income statement.

Statement of cash flows A financial statement that provides details about the sources of cash and how cash is used, also called a cash flow statement.

Statement of financial operations Another term for income statement.

Statement of financial position A financial statement that provides information about the organization's resources and how those resources are acquired, also called the balance sheet.

Statement of operations Another term for income statement.

Statement of revenue and expenses Another term for income statement.

Statistics budget A budget that presents an estimate or forecast of the UOS or volume over a specified time period.

Step-down distribution Costing method mandated by Medicare that enters cost centers into cost allocation in sequence, and removes the cost center from calculations once all its costs are allocated.

Step-fixed Budgets or budget items that remain fixed until changes in volume require a change in capacity.

Stop-loss insurance Coverage that protects providers or MCOs from unusually costly cases or from overall financial losses related to managed care contracts.

Strategic plan A report that presents a plan for organizational financial management and performance for several fiscal years into the future.

Strategic planning A process for determining the organization's long-term goals.

Structural capacity The capability for providing services allowed by the facility's layout.

Substitute A product that is similar to and reduces demand for another product.

Supplementary medical insurance (SMI) Medicare Part B.

Supplier-induced demand When agents use their knowledge and authority over the principal to increase demand.

Supply The quantity of a product that producers are able and willing to produce and sell at a given price over a specific time period.

Supply chain management Managing and supervising the policies and procedures for ordering and purchasing products used in patient care.

Support services Nonrevenue cost centers or cost pools that contribute costs to profit centers.

Surplus Excess supply resulting from the market price for a product rising to a level higher than the equilibrium price.

SWOT matrix A tool that helps in identifying and analyzing the strengths, weaknesses, opportunities, and threats related to a decision, project, or capital expenditure.

Tangibles Measures or resources that either are or can be converted to dollar amounts.

Target return pricing A profit-focused pricing method that sets the price to achieve a targeted return on investment.

Technical assistance grant A grant that funds developing, implementing, and managing the activities of a community organization.

Technical efficiency Producing the maximum amount of outputs (goods or services) compared to the inputs (resources) required for production.

Technical grant proposal A proposal focusing on the program's objectives, activities, methods, organization, and staffing without reporting a budget.

Telehealth Applications of telecommunications technologies to health education and patient care.

Third-party payers Entities that pay on behalf of another party, such as a health plan paying a member's health care costs.

Throughputs Activities, processes, or work applied to inputs in order to achieve outputs.

Total cash inflows An organization's service and nonservice revenues, added together and reported in the cash flow budget.

Total cash on hand A cash flow budget's beginning cash balance plus the total cash inflows.

Total cash outflows All sources of cash outflows, including personnel, nonpersonnel, and capital expenses added together and reported in the cash flow budget.

Total costs (TC) Total fixed costs plus total variable costs, thus reflecting all costs associated with a given level of volume.

Total costs per unit (TCU) The total costs associated with each UOS, calculated by dividing TC by the volume.

Total fixed costs (TFC) All direct fixed costs plus all indirect fixed costs associated with a given level of volume.

Total margin The pretax net income divided by the net patient revenue and other operating revenue, a profitability ratio indicating a hospital's profitability generated by total operating revenues.

Total revenue (TR) The revenue associated with a given level of volume at a given price or amount of reimbursement.

Total variable costs (TVC) All costs associated with a given level of volume that change based on changes in volume, usually consisting of direct costs.

Trade credit The amount due to vendors for supplies, also called accounts payable.

Trade-off When in order to increase or acquire a benefit or value, one must give up all or part of another benefit or value.

Training grant A grant that funds staff training and education.

Transparency Making information available, such as health care pricing.

Travel nurse Agency nurse filling a position for weeks or months.

Trend A performance pattern, such as a budget expense item increasing month after month.

Trend line A visual representation of a trend.

Trusts Business agreements or practices that restrict free trade and are often illegal.

Turnover ratios Another term for asset management ratios.

Uncollectibles Bills not paid in full, or not paid at all.

Under-care Providing less health care services than medically necessary.

Unfavorable budget variance An undesirable difference between budgeted and actual amounts, for example, when actual expenses are greater than budgeted.

Union A group of workers attempting to influence power in a labor market by bargaining with the employers.

Unit contribution margin (UCM) The CM per UOS, which may reflect overhead, handling fees, mark-ups, or surcharges, calculated as price less VCU.

Unit of service (UOS) The extent of consumer demand for services in a health care setting, measured by indicators such as patient days, patient visits, or procedures, also called volume or utilization.

Universality The provision of relatively equal access for all persons.

Unsolicited grant proposal A grant application that often lacks formal criteria and is often available for application any time over the funding year.

Upcoding Misrepresenting a diagnosis in order to justify a higher payment for services rendered than should be authorized.

Utilization The extent of consumer demand for services in a health care setting, measured by indicators such as patient days, patient visits or procedures, also called volume or UOS.

Utilization review Concurrent review that occurs during hospitalization to determine whether continued hospitalization is necessary.

Value-based pricing Setting the price based on the value the customer attributes to the product or service, also called customer-focused pricing.

Value-based purchasing An ACO reimbursement provision that directly links payment to quality of care.

Values A brief statement that incorporates the ethics and beliefs reflected in the organization and the individuals who work in the organization.

Variable capacity Capacity that changes with changes in volume.

Variable costs Costs that vary based on production volume.

Variable costs per unit (VCU) The variable cost associated with each UOS.

Variable staffing FTEs based on volume, also called direct staffing or flexible FTEs.

Variance The difference between the budgeted target and actual performance.

Vertical analysis Reporting each item of an income statement as a percent of total revenues, or each item of a balance sheet as a percent of total assets, also called common size analysis.

Vertical integration Combining and coordinating various levels of services, such as hospitals acquiring and operating home health services.

Vision A brief description of where an organization wants to be or what the organization plans to accomplish.

Visit An outpatient contact with a physician, MLP, or other health care professional that meets criteria for billing and reimbursement.

Volume The extent of consumer demand for services in a health care setting, measured by indicators such as patient days, patient visits, or procedures, also called utilization or UOS.

Volume-based Based on utilization such as the number of patients, patient days, patient visits, or procedures.

Wage Employee compensation based on the number of hours worked.

What-if scenario Analyzing the possible impact of changes in revenues, expenses, or other outcomes, often by using spreadsheet software.

Willingness to pay A method of valuing human life using the amount that the consumer or employer would pay for prevention or offsetting the risk.

Working capital Cash and other liquid assets such as savings accounts that enable a business to remain solvent, also reported as net working capital.

Year to date (YTD) A total of financial performance measures from the beginning of the budget year to the current time period.

Zero-base budgeting (ZBB) A budgeting approach that requires a detailed analysis of every line item as it is added to the budget, thus improving budget accuracy and reducing waste.

Crossword Puzzle Answer Key

CHAPTER 1—ECONOMICS

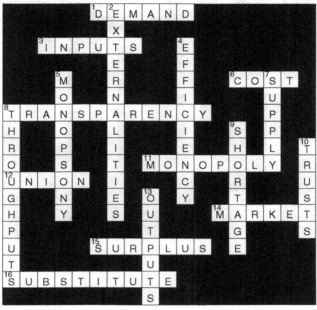

Across

1 The quantity of a product for which consumers are able and willing to pay at a given price over a specified time period.

3 Resources and raw materials needed for production.

6 Resource or expense required as input to produce goods or services.

8 Making information available, such as health care pricing.

11 When one party has control over production, thus controlling price.

12 A group of workers attempting to influence market power in a labor market by bargaining with the employers.

14 A group of buyers and sellers of products such as goods and services.

15 Excess supply resulting from the market price for a product rising to a level higher than the equilibrium price.

16 A product that is similar to and reduces demand for another product.

Down

2 Costs of production not borne by the producer, or costs of consumption not paid for by the consumer.

4 Maximizing the production or value of goods or services while minimizing the resources or costs required for production.

5 When one party has control over consumption of a product, thus controlling price.

7 The quantity of a product that producers are able and willing to produce and sell at a given price over a specific time period.

8 Activities, processes, or work applied to inputs in order to achieve outputs.

9 Excess demand resulting from the market price for a product falling to a level lower than the equilibrium price.

10 Business agreements or practices that restrict free trade and are often illegal.

13 Goods, services, or other outcomes produced from inputs and throughputs.

CHAPTER 2—INSURANCE

The crossword solution grid contains the following answers:

- 1 Across: COINSURANCE
- 3 Across: ADVERTISING
- 6 Across: HDHP
- 9 Across: CDHP
- 14 Across: FFS
- 15 Across: CMI
- 16 Across: ENTITLEMENT
- 17 Across: INCENTIVE
- 18 Across: AWI
- 20 Across: HRA
- 21 Across: FSA
- 2 Down: REIMBURSEMENT
- 4 Down: DSH
- 5 Down: RISK
- 7 Down: DEDUCTIBLE
- 8 Down: OUTLIER
- 10 Down: PRINCIPAL
- 11 Down: CAPITAL
- 12 Down: AGENT
- 13 Down: ACTUARIAL
- 19 Down: HSA
- 20 Down: HAC

Across

1 A percentage of a given health care cost that the insurer requires the plan member to pay.

3 Mass media communication purchased by a sponsor to persuade an audience.

6 Health plan that requires a minimum $1000 deductible for single coverage or $2000 deductible for family coverage (abbreviation).

9 Health plan with high deductibles thought to encourage consumer wellness (abbreviation).

14 Retrospective payment of all allowable costs meeting accepted standards of care (abbreviation).

15 Measure of overall acuity among Medicare patients in hospitals (abbreviation).

16 A government benefit that people have a right to receive as long as they are eligible.

17 A reward or encouragement, often financial, that influences behavior.

18 Adjustment factor for differences in wage rates across geographic areas of the United States (abbreviation).

20 A pre-tax or tax-deductible health care account to which only the employer may contribute (abbreviation).

21 A pre-tax account used for expenses not covered by health insurance (abbreviation).

Down

2 The actual payment for health care services that may be less than the charges.

4 Hospital caring for a higher proportion of low-income patients than other hospitals (abbreviation).

5 Probability of an adverse event.

7 A required payment made by a consumer before the health plan begins to cover costs.

8 Unusually costly and frequently long-term case, usually in acute care settings.

10 A party lacking knowledge who delegates authority to an agent.

11 Long-term expenditures, such as construction and equipment purchases.

12 A party in authority acting on behalf of a principal.

13 Having to do with insurance risks.

19 A pre-tax or tax-deductible health care account in which an employer or employee can make contributions (abbreviation).

20 Preventable conditions as specified by Medicare for which hospitals may not be reimbursed (abbreviation).

CHAPTER 3—MANAGED CARE

Across

4 Reimbursement by pre-paying for the care of a specified population over a specified time period, used in managed care contracts.

6 Health professional who enables the expansion of primary care services, such as a nurse practitioner (abbreviation).

8 A managed care organization or plan that provides health care to persons enrolled in a pre-paid plan (abbreviation).

9 The portion of a health plan's expenses allocated to clinical services compared to total revenue (abbreviation).

10 New model of health care financing and delivery featuring shared savings strategies for all providers for an episode of patient care (abbreviation).

12 A managed care indicator in which the revenue, cost, or utilization measure is divided by the number of plan enrollees for a monthly time period (abbreviation).

13 An outpatient contact with a physician, MLP, or other health care professional that meets criteria for billing and reimbursement.

15 ACO incentive in which a negotiated portion of the savings is returned to the providers as an incentive, also called shared risk or shared savings.

18 Reimbursement system that includes payment for all care provided from disease onset to recovery.

Down

1 Physician in general or pediatric practice who is often the first point of patient contact for diagnosis, treatment, and prevention (abbreviation).

2 Managed care requirement that access to specialists or other specified services must be authorized by a PCP or other designated provider.

3 Approved prescribing list for pharmaceuticals.

5 Expenses that are not yet reported for a specific time period, but that the MCO or other organization will be responsible to pay (abbreviation).

6 A managed care plan that provides health care to persons enrolled in a pre-paid plan (abbreviation).

7 A managed care plan that covers services from providers within the plan more generously than services from providers outside the plan (abbreviation).

10 Total inpatient days divided by the number of admissions to determine, on average, how long patients are hospitalized (abbreviation).

11 Indirect, administrative and support expenses such as rent and clerical services.

12 A managed care indicator in which the revenue, cost, or utilization measure is divided by the number of plan enrollees over a year (abbreviation).

14 A managed care plan offering more generous coverage if members select the preferred providers rather than providers outside the plan (abbreviation).

16 A physician group practice model where the physicians own the practice but contract with an MCO for members and reimbursement (abbreviation).

17 The portion of a health plan's expenses allocated to administrative costs and profit compared to total revenue (abbreviation).

CHAPTER 4—MEASURING NURSING CARE

Across

5 The amount of time an inpatient requires of direct nursing care per day (abbreviation).
6 A value that represents performance targeted to an internal or industry standard.
8 Another term for utilization (abbreviation).
10 Patients who require close monitoring but who usually occupy an inpatient bed for less than 48 hours.
12 Income from reimbursement or payment provided for goods and services.
14 Employee compensation that does not change regardless of the number of hours worked over the year.
16 A standard measure for hourly employment, indicating a full-time employee working 2080 hours per year (abbreviation).
17 A specified work unit, such as an inpatient nursing unit or an Emergency Department.
22 The extent of consumer demand for services in a health care setting, measured by indicators such as patient days.
23 Productive hours of inpatient staff nurses providing patient care (abbreviation).
25 Measures that signify a specific condition or a specified level or value, also called indicators.

Down

1 A measure of direct care hours for settings that perform procedures (abbreviation).
2 Excessive use of employee sick leave.
3 Level of patient illness or case complexity.
4 Another term for utilization.
7 An individual directed to a health care setting for health care services.
9 The extent to which a health care setting can meet consumer demand.
10 Work hours exceeding 40 hours per week.
11 Measures that signify a specific condition or a specified level or value, also called metrics.
13 Employee compensation based on the number of hours worked.
15 How efficiently a setting's capacity operates in managing production or utilization.
18 The number of inpatients on a nursing unit at any point in time, often measured at midnight.
19 Patients transferring from home or another facility to an inpatient facility, used as a measure of inpatient utilization.
20 The release of a patient to home or another facility, usually includes death.
21 Another term for NHPPD.
24 Average number of patients in a nursing unit, calculated as the patient days divided by the number of days in a time period (abbreviation).

CHAPTER 5—BUDGET MANAGMENT

Across

3   The difference between the budgeted target and actual performance.
5   Estimating and allocating the cost of a capital asset over its useful life.
6   When values rise or fall in a repeating pattern, such as more respiratory disease occurring in the winter, also known as seasonal.
8   When values rise or fall in a repeating pattern, such as more respiratory disease occurring in the winter, also known as cyclical.
9   A performance pattern, such as a budget expense item increasing month after month.

Down

1   Identifying the source or sources of a budget variance, and determining whether the variance can be controlled.
2   Ongoing critical review of the budget focused on identifying performance problems that require investigation.
4   Putting management strategies in place to address and prevent unfavorable budget variances.
7   A total of financial performance measures from the beginning of the budget year to the current time period (abbreviation).

CHAPTER 6—BUDGET PLANNING

Across

2 Impact from the input a person provides in a situation.
3 An organization that negotiates prices with vendors on behalf of member hospitals (abbreviation).
4 A method of budget adjustment by calculating an average monthly budget value and multiplying the value by 12 to estimate the budget for a year.
6 Using or relying on numerical data.
7 Using or relying on non-numerical data.

Down

1 Extent of responsibility for managing a situation.
5 A budgeting approach that requires a detailed analysis of every line item as it is added to the budget (abbreviation).

CHAPTER 7—CAPITAL AND OTHER BUDGETS

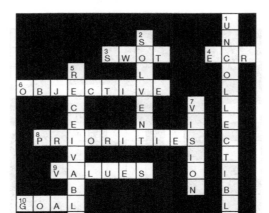

Across

3 Strengths, weaknesses, opportunities, and threats (abbreviation).

4 A budget based on an episode of care, often used in ACOs to develop bundled payments (abbreviation).

6 A specified task that must be accomplished to achieve a goal, and preferably SMART.

8 Organizational activities or issues that are believed to be of the most importance for profitability or survival.

9 A brief statement that incorporates the ethics and beliefs reflected in the organization.

10 A broad statement regarding what the organization or program intends to accomplish.

11 Expectations or beliefs about the internal or external environment that influence administrative and financial decision-making.

Down

1 Bills not paid in full, or not paid at all.

2 An individual or business that is able to pay its bills and meet its liabilities.

5 Revenue sources for organizations such as hospitals that bill and await payment for most of their services.

7 A brief description of where an organization wants to be or what the organization plans to accomplish.

CHAPTER 8—COST-FINDING, BREAK-EVEN, AND CHARGES

Across

2 All direct fixed costs plus all indirect fixed costs associated with a given level of volume (abbreviation).

4 The fixed costs associated with each UOS, calculated by dividing TFC by the volume (abbreviation).

6 A cost allocation method that focuses on the indirect and direct costs of specific activities (abbreviation).

8 The dollar amount available from revenues to first cover fixed costs (including overhead), then contribute to profits (abbreviation).

9 All costs associated with a given level of volume that change based on changes in volume (abbreviation).

10 Setting an excessively high price for health care goods and services when the demand is inelastic.

11 The CM per UOS, which may reflect overhead, handling fees, mark-ups, or surcharges, calculated as price less VCU (abbreviation).

13 A coding system that quantifies physician services for reimbursement purposes (abbreviation).

14 The full price assigned to a good or service, before discounts or other reductions.

16 The amount of reimbursement for each UOS, also called the price (abbreviation).

Down

1 The variable cost associated with each UOS (abbreviation).

2 The total costs associated with each UOS, calculated by dividing TC by the volume (abbreviation).

3 A coding system CMS developed to classify services and products not included in the CPT® codes (abbreviation).

5 A hospital's comprehensive list of the prices of all goods and services for which a separate charge exists.

7 A coding system CMS developed to assess and evaluate outcomes for adult home health clients (abbreviation).

8 A hospital's comprehensive list of the prices of all goods and services for which a separate charge exists (abbreviation).

9 Total fixed costs plus total variable costs (abbreviation).

12 The revenue associated with a given level of volume at a given price or amount of reimbursement (abbreviation).

14 Dividing hospital costs by hospital charges (gross revenues) to determine the relationship of costs to charges (abbreviation).

15 Cost assignment that includes the three components of physician work value, practice expense, and malpractice liability insurance expense (abbreviation).

CHAPTER 9—CBA, CEA, CUA, AND CER

```
              1C  E   R
              O                   2D
              M              3C   E   A
       4E  B  P                   F
       C            5C   U   A    6D
       U    7T               A    I
       8I  N  T   A   N  G  I  B   L   E   S
       D    N                T    C
       E    G                     O
       D    I                     U
            B                     N
       9Q  A   L   Y              T
  10C      11C         E          I
  12B  E   N   E   F   I   T  S    N
   A       R                      G
```

Across

1 The total program cost for each program compared in a CEA is divided by the appropriate unit of effectiveness (abbreviation).
3 A method of evaluating and comparing the benefits and costs among two or more alternative programs or services (abbreviation).
4 The application of research evidence to improve health care interventions (abbreviation).
5 A method of evaluating the benefits to quality of life relative to the costs of a program or service (abbreviation).
8 Measures that cannot be converted to dollar amounts.
9 A method that assigns dollar values to human life by weighting each remaining year of life by the expected quality of life measure for that year (abbreviation).
12 The outputs or contributions produced by the objective function, including cost savings achieved by the intervention.

Down

1 The interest earned in each time period earns interest in future time periods.
2 Failure to repay a loan.
4 The appropriate unit of effectiveness is divided by the cost for each program compared in a CEA (abbreviation).
6 Converting the future value of a monetary unit to its present value.
7 Measures that either are or can be converted to dollar amounts.
10 A method of evaluating the benefits relative to the costs of a program or service (abbreviation).
11 A method for guiding health care decisions based on new and existing research comparing treatments or procedures (abbreviation).

CHAPTERS 10 AND 11—PLANS AND PROPOSALS*

```
                              ¹E
              ²S        ³C     N
     ⁴G A N T  T        ⁵M O U  T
              A         M       R
              K         P       E
           ⁶S E E D     E       P
     ⁷P     H           T       R
      L    ⁸S O F T     I       E
   ⁹R F A   L           T       N
      N     D      ¹⁰R  I       E
      N     E       F   V       U
     ¹¹I N T R A P R E N E U R
      N     S
      G
```

Across

4   The name of a chart that helps the reader visualize a timeline.

5   A document that describes the contributions collaborating agencies will provide to the proposed program (abbreviation).

6   A type of money that represents funding for special project grants.

8   A type of money that represents grant funding that may or may not be available from year to year.

9   A grant application also referred to as an RFP (abbreviation).

11 An employee working within an organization to improve production and profitability.

Down

1   A person starting or managing their own business enterprise.

2   People and organizations with an active concern about a community need or problem.

3   Grants that lead to organizations competing with each other for funding.

7   A grant that provides funding for assessing a community need or problem and planning a program to meet those needs.

10 A grant application also referred to as an RFA (abbreviation).

*Note: The crossword puzzles for Chapters 10 and 11 are identical.

CHAPTER 12—FINANCIAL STATEMENTS

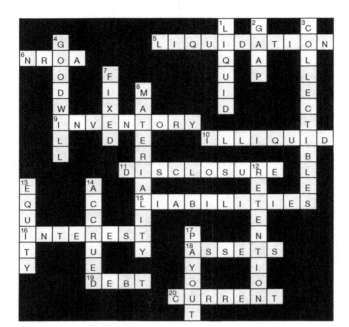

Across

5   Dissolving a business and distributing its assets.

6   Net income divided by total assets, indicating the profit generated by the assets of a business (abbreviation).

9   Supplies a business keeps on hand.

10 Assets that cannot readily be exchanged for or readily converted into cash, such as fixed assets.

11 Reporting on all of the aspects of financial transactions so the financial condition of the business is accurately represented.

15 Claims on assets established by contract, reported in the balance sheet.

16 A percentage rate representing the price for borrowing when transacting a loan.

18 Resources held by the organization that possess or create economic benefit, reported in the balance sheet.

19 A debt management ratio calculated by dividing total debt by total assets, that is the inverse of the equity ratio.

20 A liquidity ratio calculated by dividing current assets by current liabilities.

Down

1   Assets representing cash or that can readily be exchanged for or converted into cash, reported as current assets.

2   A common set of standards, procedures, and principles for preparing financial statements consistently (abbreviation).

3   Another term for accounts receivable or receivables.

4   The difference between the fair market value and the book value of an asset.

7   Assets representing property, plant, and equipment (PPE).

8   An accounting principle that records separate categories of financial entries only if they are relevant for reporting or understanding the financial condition of the business.

12 A ratio that reports the proportion of net income reinvested in the business, and the inverse of the payout ratio.

13 Ownership claim on assets, reported in the balance sheet.

14 Expenses that are generated daily, with periodic payment, such as employee wages.

17 A ratio that reports the proportion of after-tax net income paid out to shareholders, and the inverse of the retention ratio.

CHAPTERS 13 AND 14—ETHICAL ISSUES, INTERNATIONAL SYSTEMS, POLICY AND TRENDS*

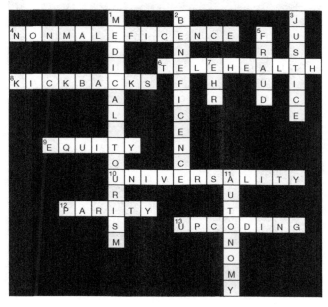

Across

4 Principle of bioethics requiring that health providers avoid or at least minimize harm when providing care.

6 Applications of telecommunications technologies to health education and patient care.

8 Requesting, offering, or receiving favors or payments that influence purchases.

9 Distributing the burden of cost fairly based on the ability to pay.

10 The provision of relatively equal access for all persons.

12 The relative equality of resource allocation to various disease entities, populations, or interventions.

13 Misrepresenting a diagnosis in order to justify a higher payment for services rendered than should be authorized.

Down

1 Travel to other countries to receive health care that is not affordable or available in one's own country.

2 Principle of bioethics requiring that health providers do good and provide the most benefit possible.

3 Principle of bioethics that supports the equal or fair distribution of health care benefits and risks across society.

5 Intentional deception or misrepresentation in order to obtain something of value that is owned by another party.

7 Computer technology and software that replaces paper-based health record systems (abbreviation).

11 Principle of bioethics that refers to the right of individuals to make their own decisions.

*Note: The crossword puzzles for Chapters 13 and 14 are identical.

Index